Contemporary Islam and the Challenge of History

worship
86
108
195
Islam
way of life
(w/ mos.
say)

Contemporary Islam and the Challenge of History

Yvonne Yazbeck Haddad
ASSOCIATE PROFESSOR OF ISLAMIC STUDIES
HARTFORD SEMINARY

State University of New York Press · Albany

Chapter III and portions of Chapter II appeared as "The Arab Israeli Wars, Nasserism, and the Affirmation of Islamic Identity" in John L. Esposito, ed., *Islam and Development*, Syracuse: Syracuse University Press, 1980.

Chapter V appeared as "Traditional Affirmations Concerning the Role of Women as Found in Contemporary Arab Islamic Literature" in Jane I. Smith, ed., *Women in Contemporary Muslim Societies*, Lewisburg: Bucknell University Press, 1980.

Published by State University of New York Press, Albany

Printed in the United States of America

For information, address State University of New York Press, State University Plaza, Albany, N.Y., 12246

Library of Congress Cataloging in Publication Data

Haddad, Yvonne Y., 1935–

Contemporary Islam and the challenge of history.

Bibliography: p.

1. Islam—20th century. I. Title.

BP163.H22 1982 297'.09'04 81-8732

ISBN 0-87395-543-9 AACR2

ISBN 0-87395-544-7 (pbk.)

To Wadi Haddad, Susan Haddad, and Ramsey Haddad, who have given me unwavering support and encouragement throughout this endeavor.

Contents

Acknowledgments

Thanks are due to the several persons who have guided and encouraged me in the pursuit of this study. Interest in the idea of history in Islam was first generated in a seminar at the Hartford Seminary Foundation under the guidance of Professor Willem A. Bijlefeld. Professors George Hourani of the University of New York at Buffalo and Issa J. Boullata of McGill University provided valuable insights and constructive criticism of the text. Research facilities at McGill were made available from 1976 to 1978 by Professors Donald Little and Charles Adams, who also discussed with me the significant aspects of the methodology of history. To all of them I am extremely grateful.

Prologue

THE CONTEMPORARY ARAB Muslim's concern for the study of history is a part of his total search for dignity,[1] identity, and purpose. The impact of the power of the West has challenged to the core his concept of who he is and where his destiny lies. It has questioned his perception of the world and the totality of life; his faith in the adequacy of his norms and ideals has been eroded.

The importance of developing a concept of history as a means of preserving Islam appears to be a nineteenth and twentieth-century phenomenon. Utilized in the last century as a rallying cry against the erosion of confidence in Islam as a viable way of life in the modern world, the concept of history has served as a basis for political unity for nationalists and supranationalists alike, as a focus of pride in the heritage of the elders and as a common memory of a great achievement that endows the individual with pride and dignity.[2]

The Muslim Empire was built on the promise of support from God for the community's efforts in establishing Islam throughout the world. ⦃God has promised those of you who believe and do works of righteousness that He will make you His viceregents on earth as He made others before you. And He will surely establish for them their religion which He has favored for them, and He will exchange for them their fear for security. They worship Me; they do not worship others beside Me.⦄[3]

Ever since the Muslim community first responded with obedience and commitment to the message of the Qur'ān as revealed to Muhammad, it has functioned within the scope of the divine promise that those who believe and are faithful will be rewarded with victory and assurance of divine approval. The experience of the community in its formative period fulfilled that promise since Islam was able to establish its hegemony over large areas of the world, not only supplanting the former rulers of the areas but also establishing the religion of

Islam more firmly as increasing numbers of their subjects became Muslim. From early on, the whole world was divided into the House of Islam, *dār al-Islām,* where the Muslim *sharī'a* (religious law) was practiced and the worship of the one God was established, and the House of War, *dār al-ḥarb,* which encompassed the rest of the world where Islam was not paramount and where many people lived who ignored the worship of the one God. It was incumbent upon Muslims to strive to change this situation so that the whole world would be part of *dār al-Islām.*

There are several ways of looking at Islam as an historical religion. One is to see it as established in a certain place at a certain time, its faith having been preserved in the experience and life of the "historical" community which is in constant awareness of the special role it has as the community of faith practicing the religion that God revealed to His Prophet Muḥammad. Related to that conception, but subtly different from it, is the idea of Islam as the religion of God which He has revealed to pious men from the earliest historical times; in this understanding Muḥammad is not the initiator of the faith but is rather the restorer, correcting and confirming previous experience and bringing the final revelation in the series of revelations that have constituted the religion of God. In a third sense Islam is historical insofar as it has had a certain number of years of specific continuity of existence and of experience as a community of faith.

To understand the significance of the concept of history for modern Muslims is an immense task, involving a comprehensive study of what Muslims in various areas have thought as well as a knowledge of the forces of history that are operative in defining or illuminating that concept. This work is therefore limited to a study of writings in Arabic on the subject, with specific consideration of the contingent and relevant economic, social, political, military, and intellectual factors that impinge on the Muslim understanding of the world and of history. The author is aware that the scope of such a study is extensive and needs documentation through further study. What is presented here is the general structure of what appears to be operative for Muslims themselves as they perceive their reality.

The first part of this study is an attempt to analyze the forces and events of the twentieth century both within and without the Islamic community that have made it necessary for Muslims to redefine and articulate their understanding of Islam. These developments have presented the Islamic world with challenges in a variety of realms.

The early part of this century saw the repeated military defeat of Islamic nations by the militant forces of Europe, accompanied by a decline of Muslim economic and political power. This resulted in a reversion of major portions of the *dār al-islām* to *dār al-ḥarb.* In the middle of the century came the establishment by Western powers of the state of Israel in the heart of the Muslim world, with the resulting series of repeated military defeats. As will be seen in the writings of many of these authors, the existence of Israel, supported by the West, continued to have serious ramifications for Muslim theological thought.

A significant social challenge has been posed by those who adhere to the ideals of the Western feminist movement and its attempt to raise the social standards in the Muslim countries according to its own conceptions of justice and freedom. This challenge has engendered a continuing response from conservative Muslims who see in it a conspiracy to undermine Islamic society from within. Through its efforts to sanction Marxism, Islamic socialism has provided a serious ideological challenge. By advocating a Marxist reordering of society as Islamic, it has attempted to justify socialism by according it a divine mantle and the validation of tradition. And in the intellectual arena, Islamic teaching has been struggling against the importation of both Western ideas and Western methodologies. This is especially evident in some of the controversies around issues of scriptural exegesis, in which Western principles of interpretation have been perceived as antithetical to the ultimate authority of the Qur'ān.

Crucial to the analysis of this part of the study is a consideration of the responses of the Muslim community and of individual thinkers to such challenges, including the ways in which they have rejected or appropriated various elements, have sought guidance and answers to the perplexing problems faced by Islam today, and have as a result of these efforts set in motion new ideas and generated new forms of religious response. In the process of this kind of redefinition, Islam has come to be seen as by necessity providing relevant answers to the problems of this century not only for Muslims but for the whole world.

The second part of the book deals with seven contemporary Arab authors whose works have not yet been translated or evaluated in Western sources. They are distinguished from those discussed in the first part by the fact that they have specifically addressed themselves to an Islamic understanding of history, several attempting to delineate the nature and scope of this discipline. In this section I look specifically at the ways in which these individual authors have used passages of the Qu'rān both for purposes of legitimating their own perspectives and in a genuine attempt to search for a Qur'anic answer. An attempt is made to analyze the degree to which the authors are aware of, make use of, and/or appropriate Western ideologies. Appended to the study as a whole is a translation of relevant passages from the works of these writers.

In undertaking this study, I have been very much aware of the Muslim contention that to understand the true meaning of Islam is in fact to be addressed by God's truth. Consequently for many Muslims, any non-Muslim scholar can grasp only a partial understanding, for to truly understand is to know and bear witness to the truth, i.e., to speak from a position of commitment. Despite efforts on the part of many Western scholars of Islam to do justice to the material they are studying, many Muslims maintain a deep distrust of the motives of non-Muslims and feel with certainty that only those who have accepted and committed themselves to the faith of Islam can fully understand its significance and import.

Another dimension of this issue is the question raised by many Muslims as to whether or not a non-Muslim can adequately present and expound on the teachings of Islam. For Muslims, to teach is to inculcate, and to teach Islam properly is to preach God's eternal and final message to humanity. Islam therefore can only be articulated by a committed Muslim. All other efforts are marginal because they do not address humanity with the complete truth, with the challenge to renounce commitment to material pleasures and to appropriate the moral imperative of living life in accordance with the wishes of God and attuned to His laws and purposes in the world.

This problem relates with particular force to the question of the appropriateness of a non-Muslim attempting to see the world and the flow of history as the Muslim sees it. The perpetual fear of criticism, that Islam somehow may be judged inadequate or obsolete, still pertains. In fairness, it must be said that such a fear is understandable in the light of many centuries of insidious commentary made by Western observers about Muslims and their ways and traditions. It is also true, however, that enormous strides have been made in the past several decades away from the Orientalist perspective in which value judgments totally unacceptable to Muslims were frequently implicit and sometimes explicit. Even the next stage of the Western approach to the study of religion, however, the phenomenological suspension of judgment in favor of dispassionate and objective judgment, often falls short of the sensitive understanding necessary to see that each phenomenon of religious life must be dealt with in the context of the whole. For the Muslim, of course, anyone having been addressed by the truth of God who continues as a scholar, observer, or student of Islam to exercise this kind of *epoche* or suspension of judgment, is a rejectionist by definition because he chooses to operate outside the community of faith that is committed to the propagation of God's way for humankind.

On another level it is also true that to study Islam is to change it. No matter how one tries to ask questions that Muslims would and do ask in the ways that they ask them, the very raising of certain questions may in some cases elicit responses that might not otherwise have been specified. Thus there is a sense in which something new is added to the corpus of Islam when these responses are made, and in a rapidly changing world in which Muslims are reacting to a multitude of different situations, it becomes increasingly difficult to pose questions that have for them anything resembling universal applicability. When we say that Islam is what Muslims say it is, we must constantly ask, Which Muslims?

Despite these very real problems, it may also be the case that the non-Muslim willing to approach his material with sensitivity and appreciation is in a good position to balance attempts at sympathetic interpretation with the objectivity that sometimes only distance can afford. With an awareness that one can never completely escape his own prejudices and preconceived categories, I am attempting in this study to present as descriptively as possible the ways in which (at least some) contemporary Muslims have outlined their understanding of history. Analysis and critical evaluation of the material, insofar as it is offered, is given not according to Western theories or a priori frames of reference but from the perspective of the individual writers and in light of the criteria Islam holds up for itself. The various works analyzed have been approached with the following kinds of questions in mind:

—How does the author perceive Islam and Islamic teachings?

—How does he utilize or exegete the Qur'anic message?

—What are the questions he perceives that the Islamic community is facing, and from what vantage point is he attempting to answer them?

—Does the author set up any criteria of judgment that are unacceptable to other Muslims? How does he use/defend his criteria? Is he consistent with the standards he establishes?

—What is the purpose of the work? Why does the author feel that it is needed?

This study does not attempt to provide an historical review of the developments that led to these writings, but rather seeks to highlight the key challenges as perceived by Muslims. The Western market provides a healthy collection of books on the topic written by Western social scientists. Summary or evaluation of this material is offered only insofar as it appears to have influenced the Muslim Arab community or individual writers in a significant and self-conscious way. Western writings are not, of course, considered as standards by which Muslims and their ideas are to be judged, nor is there any attempt to determine areas in which there are lacunae in Islamic articulation of history as compared with that of the West. Challenges posited by Western writers are assessed only in the analysis of the responses they have elicited in the different schools of thought within the Islamic community. The limitations of this approach are obvious but unavoidable, as I am dependent on the writings of those who have felt disposed to address the subject. This naturally means that we have access primarily to the thoughts of the educated literate which may or may not reflect the responses of the masses whose knowledge of current events through radio and televison is greater than ever before.

The very attempt to ask questions from the inside as Muslims are asking them also has, as we have noted, some real limitations. The questions Muslims raise are conditioned to some degree from the outside, because of the felt necessity to respond to persons, such as missionaries and Orientalists, who have attempted to measure the contribution of Islam and to assess its adequacy. Despite these outside influences, however, it still must be maintained that to the extent to which those Muslims, having been challenged by these or other Western criteria, have framed their questions and responses from within the Muslim context, they are in fact truly Islamic.

The aim of this study, then, is to determine whether or not amid the various kinds of responses there is any one answer to the questions posed by the confrontation with the modern world and the discipline of the study of history that can be called "the Muslim answer." Or must we say that there are areas of agreement and areas of disagreement and that no one response can be considered as universal? In the analysis of this material there has been a consistent attempt to discover that which for Muulims is the ultimate given, the irreducible factor, that which cannot be altered, compromised, or ignored. This is done not to show dissension or division, but in the hope of assessing the ways in which intellectual ferment and religious sensitivity are working together to help provide meaning and direction to a society that has become fractured, and purpose to a religious community that has been deeply and seriously challenged.

Part One
The Significance of History: Social, Political, Economic, Military, and Intellectual Considerations

Introduction

> Where is Islam now in the life of the Arabs and the Muslims? Where is its important hoped-for role? Where are its movements and its men, or those who claim they are its men?
>
> Where is the daring Islamic statement? Where are the noble Islamic positions? Where is the effective true existence, if there is for those who work for Islam a true effective role?
>
> Where is the impact of this existence on the official level?
>
> Where is the impact of this existence on the popular level? Where is the impact of this existence on the local and international level?
>
> Where, where is the impact of this existence?
>
> It is the astonishing absence . . .
>
> Is it written for the Muslims to live in their land and their world marginal lives? Is it written for them to live outside the scope of time and the important events and outside the scope of effective influence on time and its important events?
>
> Government in our countries is not for Islam. The opposition in our countries is not from Islam. Our rulers talk as Americans or Russians, as Westerners or Easterners or something else, this or that, but it does not proceed from Islam.
>
> The opposition to the rulers talk in a similar language as that of the rulers, they are as the rulers warring against Islam, distant from it or ignoring it.
>
> Where, where is Islam in our lives?[1]

Written on January 11, 1977, this statement articulates the question that has challenged and haunted Muslims in a very direct way during this century.

With the rise of the West as a colonial power the Muslim universe contracted, and the *dār al-Islām* as the area in which Muslim will was manifest was severely restricted from its former broad expanse. Under the rule of the European imperialist powers, the "Islamic world" changed to "Islam in the world." The impotence of Muslims was illustrated daily in their apparent inability to plan and organize their own lives, or determine the content and scope of their intellectual civilization. Others dictated for them what was to be acceptable and established norms of civilized behavior and ways of living. Thus Muslims perceived their choice as limited to two options—either to participate in the modern world or to be disparaged as insignificant people.

While some Muslims found themselves entranced by the rising potency of the West, many continued to insist that Western civilization by definition is alien and to imitate it is apostasy. Muslims to be truly Muslim must be faithful to their own heritage, their own civilization, and their own norms. The strength and effectiveness of this voice of conservatism has varied at different times in the last two centuries, depending on the fortunes of the Islamic community and what was perceived as victory or defeat.

Recent writings coming out of the Muslim world continue to reflect the crises of the modern period, responding particularly to challenges to the authority of Islam in the lives of the believers. These new works appear to follow similar attempts of the earlier generation in trying to elicit an emotional response as a drive to action, to involve the Muslims in shouldering the responsibility for their lives as Muslims rather than copying certain Western ideologies. Even more than the earlier writings, however, they focus on the Qur'anic, which is by definition the Islamic, understanding of history. This rewriting of history is perceived as providing a base for the survival of the community more crucial than mere political unity can offer. Its scope is universal and cosmic since it is through living in accordance with the laws and governance of history that useful benefit can be gleaned from any political or social aggregates. Only when Muslims live and think as Muslims can they reappropriate their leadership role in the world.

Like earlier modern writings on reform, revival, or modernism, these words seek not only to move emotions but to engender deep zeal and commitment to action. Basking in the glorious memory of the past has ceased to be sufficient as a dam on the erosion of confidence. The Qur'ān has revealed that without zeal there cannot be victory; deep emotional commitment is thus both necessary and truly Islamic. The progress and development of a nation are corollary to and contingent on its resolution to serve the purposes of God. Thus history is to be used to move Muslims to a dynamic participation in the destiny of the world through reappropriation of their God-given responsibility to guide the world in Islam.

The increased Muslim concern for history and the methodology of history can be seen clearly in the number of publications on historical figures, events, and theories that have flooded the market. The stream of polemical writings on history, which reached the peak of fashion a few years ago, continues unabated. Much of this polemic appears to be the result of the challenge presented to Islam since the middle 1960s by Marxism. Islam was seen to be in jeopardy not so much by the Marxist interpretation of history per se, which was not new at this time in the Arab world, but through the attempts at methodological rewriting of Islamic history according to Marxist interpretation. It was to this challenge that committed Muslims responded by more concerted efforts at an Islamic understanding of history and the historical process. Although the crisis appears to have peaked a few years ago, the current freedom of publication in Egypt provides the opportunity for a new outcropping of material in which the same issues are treated, often with little fresh insight.

The spread of literacy has given rise to a class of educated and semi-educated people with whose aspirations the concerns of the Westernized elite do not always coincide. Thus we find that much of the new outpouring of historical interpretation comes from persons who are not part of that intellectual class. Historical writings are available by everyone from trained historians, lawyers, engineers, and religious leaders to persons with no specialized training whatsoever. The question of Islamic history, its meaning and significance for Arabs and for Muslims, is debated everywhere at the present time. This debate involves Arab Muslims, non-Muslim Arabs, Orientalists, historians, and social scientists. It is argued on the pages of journals and periodicals, on television and radio, in textbooks, in the speeches of political leaders, and the sermons of preachers. When permitted it has engaged people in public debate; where deviation from the official governmental position is considered seditious, it is discussed in small cells, and books and articles on the topic are spread underground.

The study of history is, of course, not a new phenomenon for Muslims. Arabs boast that Ibn Khaldūn was the world's first true social scientist, articulating a philosophy of history that attempted to discern the patterns and general laws that govern history and lead to the rise and fall of nations. More recently, however, Islam has witnessed its history as written and interpreted by Orientalists and historians using Western analytical methods. This history has served various purposes for Muslims, but in general has been used as support for the nationalistic hopes of Arabs endeavoring to find a new identity based on old and deep roots.

For the committed Muslim, neither the flow of history itself nor the study and interpretation of it can be considered apart from the realm of the sacred and the workings of the divine. God as creator is also the maker of history; His hand controls every moment in time, every historical event. History is the arena in which His will is made manifest, His dominion is expressed, and His commitment to the fulfillment of its divinely ordained rules is evidenced. And yet in the Islamic understanding it is not God alone who is responsible for the historical process. Every individual shares in that responsibility insofar as he has assumed through his heritage and according to the verification of the Qur'ān a part of the God-given legacy to be a vicegerent, to represent the divine will on earth. That role which the Jews and Christians relinquished by veering away from the true worship of the one God is assumed by Muslims as their full and final responsibility. There will be no further revelation. Islam thus bears the full obligation to make known to the world the reality of the historical revelation of the Qur'ān, that which provides for the proper understanding of God's continuing action in history.

For the Muslim, then, history means a recognition of the plan and the significance of what has already happened and the role that the past plays in helping us understand God's purposes for the present, as well as an active and creative involvement in shaping the present moment so that it can most clearly reflect God's divine purposes and plan for humanity. To be part of the historical process is to be aware and to be active, bearing fully the responsibility placed on God by His creation: man. Nicholas Berdyaev in *The Meaning of History* offers a description of the function of history which captures well, though it was not his intention, the significance of the relationship of past and present for the Muslim:

> History invites two elements, the creative and the conservative. The historical process would not be possible without their union. By the conservative element, I mean a tie with the spiritual past, an inner tradition, and an acceptance of the sacred heritage of the past. But history also demands a dynamic-creative element, a creative sequence and purpose, an urge towards self-fulfillment.

> Thus the free audacity and the creative principle coexist with an inner tie and a profound communion with the past. The absence of either of these elements invalidates the postulates of history.[2]

This dual recognition in which past and present, recognition and action, combine into a creative whole is part of both the individual and the communal understanding. Thus for modern Muslims the past, the tradition, is crucial to the working out of the present.

One of the tasks of this study is to attempt to present the ways in which the particular political and social events of the twentieth century have been radically determined by the understanding of the Islamic heritage from its beginning. In order to sense the full import of the formulations summarized in Part Two one must see them from the perspective of a community challenged with, and fully assuming, the responsibility of bearing the message of God as revealed in the Qur'ān. It is in this light that the full tragedy of the defeat represented by the continuing existence of Israel must be seen; Muslims have had to take with utmost seriousness the apparent judgment of God at this historical moment that the *Umma* has been tried and found wanting. The victory is to God and to His people; defeat and failure cannot but mean that the community has failed not only itself but God and the true way of Islam.

To assert that Islam is historical is in a sense to have to grapple with an essential part of history—change. That the fortunes of the Muslim world have changed is admitted by all contemporary Muslims. However, their analysis of what has led to the historical reverses, their prescription for remedial action, and their vision of the route to ascendancy vary substantially. These different perspectives can be generally subsumed under two rather broad descriptive categories, two ways of viewing the relation of Islam to the world. It is possible, perhaps, to trace them to the time of the earliest formulations of the doctrines of Islam; for our purposes here it is important to understand that they are clearly relevant to an understanding of the way in which modern Muslims view Islam and history. Two perspectives are referred to throughout this study as normative Islam and acculturating Islam.

The terms normative and acculturating suggest a useful distinction, although the context in which they are applied needs careful explanation. Various attempts have been made to classify different manifestations of Islam, a common one being a distinction between its classical and popular forms. This recognizes that there is an ideal that can be referred to as Islam, as distinguished from local, regional, or ethnic manifestations of Islamic life.[3] Such a distinction implies an identification of ideal Islam with that articulated by the classical Muslim writers, as well as an understanding of popular Islam as acculturating by mixing with elements of local culture. That, however, is not the sense in which the terms ideal and acculturating are used here.

Normativist is applied to those who believe that Islam in its full articulation in history achieved its zenith somewhere in the past, whether that point was in the Medinan society under the guidance of the Prophet Muhammad or includes the time of the four rightly guided caliphs, and whether or not it also encompasses the laws of the faith as developed during the early centuries of Islam when the "door of *ijtihād*" was open. Thus Islam is conceived as a closed cultural system that allows for no change.

In their attempts to make Islam relevant to modern society, those Muslims referred to here as acculturating are of course articulating what to them is normative. Here, however, the term acculturationist is used to designate those who deliberately attempt to provide a contemporary Western ethos to Islam. They reinterpret its fundamental teachings in such a way that it provides a sanctioning forum for the introduction of new ideas borrowed from European thinkers and authenticates the adoption of Western legal, social, and economic institutions. Acculturationist refers to those writers who perceive that the closing of the door of *ijtihād* was an error and that Islam is always to be seen as open to reinterpretation. It can interact with "alien" cultures and appropriate what is beneficial for the *Umma*. This maintains its ability to sustain life, to grow, and to participate in the modern world. Although the proponents of normative and acculturating Islam share a pride in the glory of the past, are unhappy with the situation of Muslims in the present, and have confidence in the prospects of a better future, their views of past, present, and future vary greatly. The tension between normativist and acculturating historians stems from the fact that both deal with the same basic facts concerning the life of the community. They are both concerned with specific ideas, dates, and events, but from different vantage points. Acculturationists use the past and endow it with a significance that reflects their present stance and belief and provides justification and precedent for their position. The normativists, on the other hand, find no justification for the existence of anything new. Newness bears the indelible mark of deviation; all that is new is inherently to be mistrusted.

For acculturationists, the past is crucially important because of the element of pride it gives the individual. Dignity is appropriated from a glorious past where the community has provided the world with leadership in the intellectual, technological, artistic, and ethical fields among others. Thus Islam, which has provided the world with excellence, endows the Muslim with the ability to function in the modern world.

As to the question of identity, there are various interpretations within the acculturating group, although they all emphasize the ability to be respected in terms and norms that are set by the West. They seek acceptance by the Western world as effective individuals and collectivities. They vary in whether they seek their total present identity from within the Islamic tradition, from the West, or from some kind of compromise between the two. All acculturationists seek to be relevant to the modern world and are therefore open to appropriating Western technology. This they may either justify as being outside the realm of religion and therefore permissible, or else they may say that it is Islamic in origin and that all they are doing is reappropriating technology which has been refined by the West.

The normativists, on the other hand, find the authority of the past valid for the present and the future. They refuse any compromise on technology or identity. The past is ideal, and if Islam were to reappropriate it, it would regain its ascendancy in the world.

For the normativist, religion is not only the central part of life, it is the totality of life, that from which all of reality proceeds and has its meaning. What Muslims have to do is to approximate this eternal reality that God has revealed, and implement the teachings of the Qur'ān. Classical Islam is seen as exemplary because it received its validation from God, a validation that has been manifestly vindicated in history.

Among the acculturationists, on the other hand, are some who seek a thoroughgoing Westernization. They are willing to ascribe to religion a personal status that has bearing only on the individual life divorced from the social and cultural context. For while the normativists tend to see culture as a product of Islam, acculturationists, or at least the secularists among them, accept the theories of social scientists who see religion as one of the several factors that make up the fabric of culture. The secularists are ready to surrender to Western influences and compromise with Western ideology. They see themselves as vanguards of a modern revival in the Arab world. To save the Arab world from its degenerate state, they advocate secularization.

In the process of secularizing the society, they have abandoned the principles on which it is structured and in seeking a method of revitalization they have acquired a new world view from which Islam is essentially left out. Furthermore, in seeking to emulate Western methodology, by separating religious institutions from political institutions, they have undermined the Islamic political system and disparaged the *ʿulamāʾ* who were the guardians of its functioning.

The *ʿulamāʾ*, meanwhile, have found themselves increasingly under attack as old-fashioned, irrelevant, and unable to cope with the modern world. They have been relegated to a lesser status, their hard-earned knowledge rendered obsolete by newly established institutions and new knowledge. Not only has their expertise been ignored, but they have been dismissed as erring as well as obstacles to progress and impediments to the march of the Muslim *Umma.* Stripped of their authority and status, they have become objects of ridicule and contempt.

Both the normativists and the acculturationists feel that the condition of the Muslims needs reform. To the former reform means renovation, since Islam is perceived as a living organism to which alien bodies have attached themselves, draining the life out of the faith. The only way to save Islam is to eliminate, "surgically" if necessary, all these foreign bodies. The acculturationists, on the other hand, perceive reform as creative innovation; to them Islam as a living organism is suffocating because it has not adjusted to changing realities. It has not kept up with the march of history and has been arrested in its growth and development. To progress in health, it needs new sustenance and changes in its stultifying habits.

Among the acculturationists are reformers whose major concern is modernity. For them being "modern" is the essential normative value. The difference between them and the secularists is one of focus. For while secularists are concerned with the influence of religion on the political structure, ascribing to religion preservative functions that maintain obsolete, decadent, or oppressive institutions, the modernists' primary concern is appearance. They do not hesitate to relinquish the "old" in favor of what is new or fashionable. They appropriate Western methodolgy and technology for its own sake, rather than for its proven efficacy in the Arab environment.

Because some of the acculturationists have sought validity in foreign approval, the normativists have dismissed them as irrelevant since the norms they sought came from outside Islam. This explains why many of the acculturating Muslims, though borrowing freely from the West, have been anxious to show immediate corporate benefit. They have nationalized or Arabized foreign ideologies and in some cases validated them in a new hermeneutics of the heritage of the past in order to ascribe *aṣāla,* authenticity, to them.

The romantics come from among the ranks of the modernists. They believe that Western solutions for local problems will render the Arab world strong, modern, and potent in a very short while. Western social customs, as well as political, economic, and cultural institutions are recommended as the means of salvation from retardation. Not only are these solutions perceived as remedies for local malaise, they are recommended for their intrinsic and extrinsic worth regardless of their adaptability to the local milieu.

Those persons who are referred to in other studies as modernists, secularists, and Westernizers are treated here as acculturationists. It is clear that within the general categories suggested by the terms normative and acculturating there is a variety of subgroups whose precise interpretations and opinions differ to some extent from each other, although not to as great a degree as from representatives of the other major division. One of these subgroups actually emerged with sufficient self-identity to be given its own designation.

The discussion between normativists and acculturationists appears to have spawned a vibrant and militant modern interpretation of Islam. Mostly expounded by members of the Muslim Brotherhood, this literature can be called neo-normativist. Such a designation is not proposed to give the impression that this approach is singularly identifiable; within its various stances there are affirmations that seem to appeal to a majority of those who are disenchanted with the West and are seeking an authentic Muslim answer to questions raised by Muslims about life. The affirmation of the efficacy of Western norms for local problems left its impact on the normativists. While it led some into a rigid stance affirming the totality of the past, others, the neo-normativists, responded with new zeal, interpreting Islam for modern man. The literature they have produced evidences assimilation and integration of some new tools of hermeneutics and explication, but the content of what is affirmed is the eternal message of Islam, the same message given to man at creation, valid for today and forever. What is being advocated is a new articulation of the faith, relevant for modern challenges, but not a new Islam.

This study is restricted to the modern period. It deals with the contemporary understanding of history, but leaves the task of providing historical detail to other studies. Here issues raised by modern Muslim writers are presented and studied in terms of the ways in which they are utilized, accentuated, and manipulated to serve modern purposes.

Chapter One The Challenge of Ascendancy and Decline

"THE CONDITION OF MUSLIMS is unacceptable both from a religious standpoint as well as from the standpoint of the world, in both the material and the spiritual realm."[1]

Inherent in all the writings concerning the question of the decline or retardation of Muslims is an awareness of impotence before the power of the challenge of the West. There has also been a great deal of speculation over the causes of the apparent decline of the Arab Muslim world, which has taken the form neither of resignation to the situation nor of an ascription of causes solely to the forces of destiny. The authors struggle to isolate the reasons for ascendancy and decline in order to appropriate the first and avoid the latter; this raises the Muslim community to the dignity it deserves as the sole possessor of the Truth and as the only faithful people of God. There is also a fear on the part of normative Muslims that seeking answers outside those revealed by God might lead to a further degeneration and separation from the true path. Is it possible, they ask, to seek ascendancy on Western models without in some manner detracting from the inherent authority of Islam or undermining its claim to be the complete and fully adequate way of life in the world?

The awareness of decline is not new to the Islamic community. Muslims in the nineteenth century, faced with the impotence of the Ottoman Empire and the power and influence of the European nations, realized that all was far from well in *dār al-Islām.* The early contacts with Europeans were primarily with missionaries and with diplomatic and military personnel; through these contacts Muslims became increasingly aware of the low esteem in which they were held by the Western world in general.

In the latter part of the century Jamāl al-Dīn al-Afghānī and Muḥammad ʿAbdu, concerned about the situation of the Muslim world, called for an Islamic convention to meet during the pilgrimage in Mecca in order to delineate the causes of the decline and initiate a design for revival.[2] This idea has never been implemented in a practical way, but the concern with the state of retardation has produced numerous efforts to understand its causes so as to be better able to rectify the situation and bring the Islamic countries back to their proper place in the world. In 1907, for example, the Russian Muslim Dr. Gasprinski called for a Cairo conference; insisting that Muslims should avoid being embroiled in politics, he outlined for the occasion the causes of decline as he saw them and proposed a general campaign to educate all Muslims.[3] This conference, too, failed to materialize and attempts to organize for collective action to deal with the situation were never realized. This particular meeting was opposed by Sulṭān ʿAbd al-Ḥamīd II and by the British who ruled vast areas of Muslim land and feared Pan-Islamism as a potential source of trouble for their rule. Also militating against it were internal reasons such as the lack of agreement as to what were the real causes and what solutions would be most viable.[4]

Missionaries and Orientalists in writing about Islam in the late nineteenth and early twentieth centuries ascribed the cause of the retardation of Arab countries vis-à-vis Europe to its religion Islam.[5] Islam as practiced at the time was often a mixture of folk Sufism and what can be called superstition, making it especially susceptible to the charge of being the major cause of decline. This kind of criticism and negative evaluation sparked a special kind of literature in response, generally known as modern apologetic, which constituted what we can call "the defense of Islam." This genre of writing has continued to be the dominant form of Muslim writing in this century, and is characterized by the grave concern that Islam is in particular danger because of the divisive attempts of foreigners who in their attacks on the faith aim to put a deeper wedge between Islam and Muslims.

Orientalist investigation of Muslim religious literature has been viewed with particular suspicion because it does not take seriously Islamic claims to the faith. Not only have the Orientalists delved into the study of *ḥadīth,* finding that a substantial amount of it is fabricated, but they have claimed that the *sharīʿa* was influenced by other religions and/or Roman law. They have written about the influence of Western (Greek) philosophy on Islamic philosophy. They have affirmed that the Qur'ān was written by Muḥammad and that the spread of Islam was motivated by the desire for material and territorial gain. Furthermore, they have theorized that early converts to Islam, whether Jews or Christians, were motivated by the desire to avoid the *jizya* and the *kharāj* taxes rather than being attracted by its truth and validity.[6]

Thus the defense of Islam has centered on several areas. On the one hand, it has sought to preserve Islam as the valid religion, attempting to answer all accusations and purify Islam from all error or human contamination. In the area of Qur'anic exegesis this has led to the ignoring of a great wealth of textual and linguistic studies of the Qur'ān; instead all efforts have concentrated on the understanding of the unique perfection of the Qur'ān and its validity for all time.

The defense of Islam has also sought to find out what the causes of decline are. All writers agree that it is not Islam that is the cause of the retardation, but the Muslims themselves and what they have practiced in place of pure Islam.[7] Secularists, while willing to grant that Islam in its pristine purity may not be an impediment to progress, are anxious to relegate it to the realm of the personal in order to proceed with the necessary task of development. They perceive that too much effort is wasted on delving into the past and dwelling on it. Salāma Mūsā (a Copt) advised severance from the past and concentration on the future; since the past was filled with ignorance and fantasy, he saw no benefit in the process of dredging it up. He advised concentration on economic planning and sound economic policies as the foundation of shaping the present and building for the future. He advocated building an industrial society to replace the agrarian economy and cottage industries. Dwelling on the past, he said, has led to retardation in the field of ethics, the role and status of women, and the condition of workers.[8]

For Sāṭiʿ al-Ḥuṣrī, the idea of severing oneself from one's past was more than treasonable, it was near to suicidal. For he saw that one of the major causes of retardation of the Muslim people is ignorance of their history. The past itself is the crucial remedy for the ills of the nation, for in the past lies the Muslim soul without which they cannot survive effectively:

> The nation that preserves its language and forgets its history is similar to an individual who has lost consciousness, or a man in deep sleep, or a sick man without feeling. He is still alive, but his life has no value unless he awakens and regains the consciousness he has lost.[9]

Al-Ḥuṣrī does admit that there are many causes for the weakness of the Arabs: "The most important among them in my opinion is the erroneous way in which we consider the history of the Arab nation and the lack of study of the history of the different civilizations."[10]

Ḥusayn Mū'nis's concern is not that the past is insignificant but that the whole Arab ethos is enveloped by it. He says that Arab governments are enchanted by their own rhetoric and that this enchantment will be an impediment to progress. It keeps them from concentrating on the real problems of the *Umma,* the problems of the future. This he considers a shortcoming of the Eastern man who is "busied by the simplest of his daily needs rather than the great needs of the morrow. He is concerned about the food of the hour rather than the supplies for the one that follows."[11]

Mū'nis sees the problem as intrinsic to the nature of the Arab and his language. Arabic grammar divides time into past and present, but its mechanism for designating the future is vague. "As for the future, it is the present with an added *sīn* or *sawfa* which in the consciousness of the Easterner implies doubt and uncertainty."[12] Al-Ḥuṣrī rejects Mū'nis's theories not because they are necessarily erroneous, but because they are not useful for his own purposes. Whether or not a particular theory is true is not of crucial importance for al-Ḥuṣrī; what is important is that it can be beneficial in raising the Arab civilization from its slumber. Thus truth per se is seen of less significance in this respect than utility. Al-Ḥuṣrī says, "If we accept [Mū'nis's] theory, we would surrender to the determinism of nature and history and would cease from awakening the Arabs and calling them to think about the matter of the morrow."[13]

Other nationalists found the causes of retardation in the military conquests of the Arabs by Mongols and Ottomans.[14] These armies destroyed Arab civilization and left it in darkness for four hundred years; the seat of government was moved to Istanbul and the Arab world was subjected to oppressive military rule which led to ignorance and decay. This theory was very popular in the middle part of the century and was propagated in textbooks and other writings. Normativists, however, do not agree with it primarily because it places blame on fellow Muslims. The normativists view the Ottomans as defenders of Islam for four centuries. They may not have championed Arab nationalism, but then Arab nationalism is not Islam. In fact, they see nationalism as against the universal nature of Islam that transcends all ethnic identity. Nationalism is an enemy of Islam since it leads to division and disunity among Muslims. To blame the Ottomans for the decline of Islam is unacceptable to normativists because it seeks causation outside the laws of history as revealed in the Qur'ān. The decline of Islam is due to the Muslim's distance from true Islam.[15] If the Arabs tolerated Islamic oppressive rule, that was a cause of retardation since the Qur'ān holds Muslims responsible for their own destiny.

This, however, has not kept normativists from blaming outsiders and outside influences for the decline. The relentless enmity of the West is cited as a major cause, especially the Crusades and missionaries whose only aim was to destroy Islam by leading Muslims astray. It continued with the Orientalists who persistently worked at destroying Islamic foundations by shaking the Muslims' faith in their religion, by "taking our learning and spreading falsehood in its place,"[16] by deliberately hiding the truth from the Muslims. It proceeded through colonial conquests that carved up the Muslim world into separate national entities and fostered sectarianism, enmity, and regional and national consciousness. Muḥammad Quṭb sums up this view when he says:

> The future belongs to Islam . . . yes . . . the imperialist Crusaders have spent all they can to destroy it. . . . They crumbled the Muslim world into small nations. . . . They took hold of each nation separately and kept it from its brother and raised enmity and tension between them. . . . In all, religion was separated from society, and religious law from life . . . They fought every movement that attempted to revitalize religion and bring it into active reality. They established an educational policy that put a distance between budding youth and the source of the religion; they kept only the questions [about religion]. They were anxious to raise an "intellectual" generation in each Islamic country, one that rejects religion and avoids it, perceiving it as stagnation, retardation, retreat, ossification, and degeneration. They were anxious to destroy every movement, especially among the educated, which calls for the return to Islam, for that would have impeded the efforts of the imperialist Crusaders in the last two centuries. They succeeded in their efforts. . . . They were successful in separating Muslims from their faith. They were successful in delaying any religious movement in the Arab East for one, or several, generations . . .[17]

Modern authors have also found Sufism to be one of the dominant influences on Muslims in the early part of the twentieth century. Consequently, a great amount of literature has been produced attacking it as one of the major culprits leading to the decline of the power of the Muslim people in the world. It was attacked primarily because it was perceived as giving undue attention to personal and individual attainments over those of the *Umma*. It was also accused of emphasizing the joys of the hereafter at the expense of life in this world. Thus it was portrayed as the champion of apathy and personal indulgence and thus one of the causes of the lack of Muslim concern for social and economic development, for scientific research, and for military preparedness.[18]

These authors in singling out Sufism for blame completely ignored the militant zeal that Sufis appeared to have engendered in social and political reform in West Africa, in the Sudan, and in India. They accused the Sufis, for example, of advocating

> docility, passivity, and contentment. Even worship of God in Sufism degenerates into a search for aesthetic pleasures. Such qualities as vigour, courage, patriotism, pursuit of lofty ends, and active interest in the material and moral welfare of one's fellow-beings are repugnant to the spirit of Sufism.[19]

Efforts to rehabilitate Sufism in more recent times have succeeded in Egypt under the government of Anwar al-Sadat. Sixty-six orders have been allowed to resume their public activities after years of functioning underground. The late ʿAbd al-Ḥalīm Maḥmūd, Rector of al-Azhar, was the head of the Shādhilīyya order. The present editor of *al-Azhar* magazine, ʿAbd al-Wadūd Shalabī, is also a Sufi. In his writings Maḥmūd distinguished two kinds of worlds (*dunyā*). The world Sufism rejects is the world that distracts and enslaves, leading to an indulgence of whims and desires that precipitates the Muslim's forgetfulness of God. As for worldly possessions, such as money, property, and riches, Maḥmūd affirmed that the Sufis are not against these unless they are harmful.[20]

Some contemporary Arabs see the cause of the retardation in inadequate preparation due to emotional and ideological commitments that do not take the basic needs of the society into consideration. They have advocated a total commitment to science and technology—"We have had a call for independence *al-daʿwa al-istiqlāliyya,* and a call to nationalism *al-daʿwa al-qawmiyya,* and a call to socialism *al-daʿwa al-ishtirākiyya*"—but all have been of no avail. What the society needs is scientific preparedness, "modern science, technology, industrialization, planning, production, savings, and rational thought."[21] Thus the "call which must supersede all others, is to modern science and abundant production. This is the surest way to liberation."[22]

The normativists, on the other hand, believe that technology, science, and civilization are the by-products of faith and must therefore not be sought for their own sake, for that would lead to apostasy and inevitable failure. The superiority of military technology is irrelevant in the process of victory and defeat in wars. What is tested is one's commitment to the truth of God:

> Those who claim that military defeats are the cause of the degeneration of the Islamic nation must look for other causes for this degeneration. The reason is our great deviation from the spiritual message of Islam. We forgot our spirit and looked after our bodies. We discarded our ideals and marched with our desires. . . . We hid Islam, and all the benefits of civilization were hidden from us. The crisis that the East suffers from at present, and the crises that have repeatedly befallen us during many centuries are spiritual and our defeats are spiritual. These prepared the way for our military defeats.[23]

The causes of the decline have been expounded in many books and articles. They continue to vary according to ideological commitments. There are those who maintain that Islam as a religion and as a way of life has explored all possible avenues and has selected only that which is in accordance with God's will and therefore cannot seek to achieve a future different from that which was in the glorious past. For them, the decline set in when Muslims slackened in their efforts to maintain pristine Islam, when they allowed alien accretions to alter the basic tenets of the faith, when they lost their zeal and became apathetic, allowing others to take over the leadership of the world.

The secularists, on the other hand, separate religion from technology; they find the dependence on religion and the commitment to blind faith impediments in the way of progress. This has led them to simple reiteration of verbal slogans. They see the decline of Muslims in the historical causation, in the inefficiency of the Islamic political system, in the inability of the Islamic rulers to maintain economic progress due to developments outside of *dār al-Islām,* developments which eroded its strength such as capitalism, industrialization, and the rise of colonialism. They also include the military factor which came as a result of the Mongol and Turkish invasions, the development of gunpowder which gave military supremacy to the Europeans, and the general decline of learning.[24]

The neo-normativists delineate an area between these two groups. They admit the superiority of Islam as a comprehensive and universal system, yet they appear convinced by the efficacy of some European ideas. These they have either appropriated and Islamized by stating that all scientific learning is Islamic or that Islam is science. The cause of decline was that Muslims failed to maintain their scientific knowledge through research, allowing the West to outpace them. Thus it is not only legitimate to study scientific knowledge from the West, it is necessary to do so in order to return science to its true home. Science is Islamic in origin and is therefore acceptable in the process. Others, maintaining that the Qur'ān has urged Muslims to learn and search and study, see this as legitimating the search for Western technology as one sanctioned by Islam since it would lead to the new revitalization of Islam.

One of the causes of the decline of the Arab Muslim world was the general neglect by the Ottoman Empire of its constituent areas and peoples. In contrast to the image of the Empire waning at the end of the nineteenth century, Arabs saw with increasing clarity the Western model of nationalist identity. The hope for a revival based on nationalism sparked the spirit and zeal necessary to remove the Arab Muslims from the doldrums in which they found themselves. Initiated at the turn of the century, the nationalist enthusiasm peaked in the 1930s and was realized finally in the next several decades as individual countries attained their independence from what had then become European rather than Ottoman hegemony.

The victory of nationalism is the result of many factors, including the parceling of the Arab areas of the Ottoman Empire into separate entities and the creation of several national identities among them under the direct colonial rule of Britain and France. Not only was inter-Arab cooperation frowned upon, but the division of the land into areas of British and French influence left any collective action of the indigenous people with their neighbors susceptible to the accusation of cooperating with a foreign nation or even of espionage. Each created nation now struggled alone to free itself from the stranglehold of colonialism. Although Syrians sympathized with Algerians, for example, they were unable to do anything to help. Thus the focus was centered on regional concerns and problems.

Arab nationalism did take hold. It became a major force in the identity of several Arab generations, aided by the Turkification program of Turkey and the abolition of the Caliphate. It was also nourished by the spread of literacy and a press that provided material supporting its aims. To be an Arab nationalist was not seen as anti-Islamic, since the Arab nation got its identity, its glorious history, its language, and its culture from Islam. Thus nationalism in the eyes of those who advocated it was not contrary to the good of Muslim unity. The Muslim Brotherhood and other normativist Muslim groups such as the Ḥizb al-Taḥrīr as well as Pan-Islamists, however, denounced regionalism and nationalism as alien ideologies since they established norms for the formation of a collectivity that are foreign to Islamic revelation. The criteria for inclusion were linguistic as well as primary identification with a collective past and heritage and a commitment to work for a common future. The *"Umma,"* the distinctive name of the Islamic community or people of God, is supplanted by an Arab community whose primary goals and modes of operation, its hopes, and its criteria of judgment, are not only man-made and therefore possibly competitive with the purpose of God, but also in direct opposition to the precepts of Islam. A national identity supplanted a religious one seen as defined, ordained, granted, and sanctioned by God.

Besides the challenge of nationalism, other "isms" imported from the West began to be nurtured locally. The Arab world absorbed its ideology from whatever Western sources were available. Salvation for the decadent present was sought from Western models and prescribed for what was perceived to be the local ailments. The acculturationists felt that once the secret magic of Western dominance was isolated, it could be harnessed for a revival. Thus various remedies were advocated by various enthusiasts.

One of the earliest and most persistent theories was that if democracy were translated into the Arab milieu, it would help ameliorate the decadent conditions. The Arab people would once again feel responsible for government and for collective participation. Through parliaments and constitutions the rights of the individual would be preserved. Arabs would be challenged to respond to their duties; active, they could rise again as a great civilization as their forebears had done. The magic once ascribed to parliamentary and constitutional government faded quickly as the rule of colonial powers proved no less autocratic than that of the Ottomans whom they replaced. The treatment of Arab subjects as less than human was a travesty of the liberalism and humanism they had ascribed to Europeans.

Another magic cure sought by the early reformers was education. Contemporary Arabs rightly fault the colonial powers for failing to establish sufficient educational institutions where they ruled. Any schools opened were aimed not at educating the populace but at providing civil servants for the governmental bureaucracies who pushed, stamped, and filed papers all day. The proponents of education felt that the prosperity of the West rests with its educated elite who have learned how to harness the forces and powers of the natural order for their use. Furthermore, education, they thought, would provide an enlightened populace whose achievements would be on a par with those of Europe. Education by its more sincere advocates was perceived as a means of salvation from retardation and decadence.

Closely allied to education was the belief that the use of Western technology would help bring the Arabs to the level of their Western rulers. The technology of earlier Islamic civilization had not kept up with the new developments. Successive reverses in the military field due to the superior armaments of the enemy, however, raised the possibility and the hope that if such knowledge were appropriated it might help the Muslims to be equal to their opponents. Although of Western origin, technology was accepted with interest at first since it made work easier and allowed for more rapid and efficient means of production. Very few Arabs believed that the appropriation of this technology would necessitate a change in ideological commitment, although Westerners have continued to insist that unless the Arabs can shed their own ideologies and appropriate Western technological commitments they would not be able to prosper.[25] Much of Western opinion has continued to insist that a technological orientation is by definition a secular one since it seeks an ever-increasing rational control of human activity which, once initiated, is very hard to contain since it is a catalyst of change in the political, social, and economic as well as the religious area.

Western norms have thus been accepted as superior by a sizable portion of the Arab population.[26] These people were encouraged by the governments of occupation and have provided articles extolling Western norms.[27]

Other reformers isolated the secret of Western dominance in the secular nature of European society. The renaissance was seen as a result of the separation of church and state. Secularists felt that, should influence of religion on society in the Middle East be decreased, there was a chance for a great revival. Religion, they felt, was restrictive because of the censoring power that the *ʿulamāʾ* appear to have ascribed to themselves, condemning every step of progress as a further obeisance to the enemy and as a step away from Islam. The romantics felt that appropriation of the secrets of the West would provide the impetus by which Arab society could be raised to the level of that of Europe and would suffice to move the Arabs to new levels. They would thus be able to reappropriate their position of leadership and shed the complexes of a conquered and despised nation. Thus the romantics believed that if the Arabs were to modernize, Westernize, secularize, industrialize, or acquire Western education and Western know-how they would cease to be pushed around and bullied by Western nations.

Chapter Two
The Nationalist and Socialist Challenge

THE SOCIALIST CHALLENGE to Islam in the last two decades acquired menacing proportions when perceived by normativist Muslims as an ideology seeking to eradicate Islamic principles and guidelines. This challenge was not supported by occupying armies as the Western colonial powers had done; rather, it had taken hold of the minds and hearts of young Muslims who saw in it an alternate means of participating in the modern world.[1] Its appeal to the young lay in its being interpreted as a short route to industrialization and modernity. It offered a hope for the end of exploitation by the feudal authorities and the capitalists and a prototype of efficacy in providing equality and social justice.

Its acceptability was enhanced through its antipathy to the colonial West and its affirmation of innate human dignity and worth unrelated to Christian principles. Like nationalism, it provided an extra-religious structure for cooperative effort in striving for new goals.

By the late 1940s, after the establishment of the state of Israel, the heyday of Arab enchantment with Western technological advancement and Western political systems had clearly passed. Supported by the strongly anti-Western sentiments fostered by the Muslim Brotherhood in Egypt, Arabs were keenly aware of the failure of democratic elected governments in the light of continued European, especially British, interference. Disillusionment turned to strong agitation, and the result was the military revolt of 1952 under Gamal Abdel Nasser. With the full blessing of the general populace of Egypt, the revolt was a move to rid the country of the corruption of the monarchy and the power of the ruling landed gentry.

When the Free Officers came to power in 1952 they had very little knowledge of government, as well as little clear understanding of where they wanted to take Egypt. Their concern had been mainly to rid the nation of the so-called treacherous leaders who were puppets of the imperialist forces. The officers also believed that they were executing the will of the Egyptian people who would then show where the revolution was to go. Nasser was later to write:

> I had imagined that the whole nation was ready and prepared, waiting for nothing but a vanguard to lead the charge against the battlements, whereupon it would fall in behind in serried ranks, ready for the sacred advance towards the great objective.[2]

After the success of the revolution, the reality that faced the officers was different from the one they had imagined. They became aware that they had to shoulder the responsibility of leadership in Egypt because there was no consensus of where the nation was to go or how it was to get there. Nasser wrote:

> We needed order, but we found nothing behind us but chaos. We needed unity, but we found nothing behind us but dissension. We needed work, but we found behind us only indolence and sloth. It was from these facts, and no others, that the revolution coined its slogans.[3]

The forces that supported the revolution were anticolonial, antimonarchy, and anticorruption, representing persons from all walks of life. Included also was the organization of the Muslim Brotherhood, *al-Ikhwān al-Muslimūn,* who had a very effective organization that could be mobilized with great efficiency. Their anti-imperialist feelings were fed by their perception of Westernization as not only alien to true Islam, but actually the enemy of Islam. Thus they were opposed to the old regime because of its association with ungodly forces and its compromise with unbelievers. They, with the disenchanted nationalists and some Westernizers, had been disappointed with the previous experiments in secular education, parliamentary government, and other institutions left as vestiges of Western occupation.[4]

The central ideology under which Nasser operated at the beginning was that of Egyptian nationalism. It was later to move into Arab nationalism, to socialism, and to Arab or Islamic socialism. In his *Philosophy of the Revolution* he outlined the inner circle from which he operated as an Arab. In this he found Islam to be important as the moving force and strong motivation behind Arab civilization (p. 62). As a focus of identity, however, religion was secondary to geographical and national considerations.[5] In a speech in June of 1956, in fact, he clearly delineated his primary objectives as the preservation of independence, the maintenance of border security, and the development of the homeland.[6]

The relegation of religion to what was in effect a secondary role in the state was one of the immediate causes of a falling-out between the new revolutionary government and the Muslim Brotherhood. Free Officers and members of the *Ikhwān* had cooperated in bringing about the overthrow of the old regime, and the latter were invited to participate in the new ministries. They preferred to maintain themselves as an agency outside of the government, however, keeping watch on the new administration and urging it to implement the doctrines of the organization of which the fundamental one was the adoption of Islam as the basis of the state. The Brotherhood was strong, had a well-trained militia, and exercised control over a large segment of the population. Confrontation between the new regime and the *Ikhwān* was inevitable when attempts of the Revolutionary Council to emphasize the Islamic nature of their efforts[7] failed to satisfy the Brotherhood. Fearing the strength of their old allies, the military regime, in order to centralize power in its own hands, moved to get rid of the Brotherhood. The first clash came in 1954 when the party was officially dissolved. Four hundred and fifty of its leaders were arrested, while two thousand of its local branches all over Egypt were closed. When, ten months later, there was an attempt by one of its members to assassinate Nasser, six of the *Ikhwān* were hanged in reprisal while its chief leader was sentenced to life imprisonment.

The involvement of the Free Officers with the religious institution was not restricted to suppression of the Muslim Brotherhood. In their efforts to centralize the power of the government and curb the influence of the *ʿulamāʾ* and the religious establishment over a population that was itself essentially "religious," the officers incorporated the staff of the *sharīʿa* and communal courts into the ministry of justice.[8] In 1954 they appointed as rector of al-Azhar the Sorbonne-educated and supposedly Westernized ʿAbd al-Raḥmān Tāj. Tāj's traditional conservative Islamic perspective dominated his administration, however, and along with insisting that the students and faculty of al-Azhar wear the traditional garb of that institution, he was active in opposing such government policies as the curbing of polygamy.

When Tāj died in 1958 he was replaced by Maḥmūd Shaltūt, a reformist whose ideas coincided with many of those of the Revolutionary Council. In 1961 some major changes were instituted at al-Azhar because of a reform that Shaltūt had planned and helped to institute.[9] This reform was expounded in Law 103, a law that reorganized that venerable institution.[10] A ministry of al-Azhar was begun, making religion one of the areas supervised and maintained by the government. Official academic recognition was extended to graduates of al-Azhar, placing them on a par with graduates of secular institutions of learning. Furthermore, the title Rector was changed to the more religious one of "The Grand Imam and Shaykh al-Azhar." It was also determined that the Vice-Rector and all the college deans were to be appointed by presidential decree.

Through the action of this reform, the Azhar was divided into five institutions. These included:

(1) Al-Azhar Higher Council, which was to function as the general administration of the complex, and was constituted of a score of scholars and civil servants appointed by the government.

(2) The Islamic Researches Academy, whose members were not to exceed fifty in number, all to be directly appointed by the government. Not more than twenty of the members of the Academy could be non-Egyptian. It was perceived as the highest body for Islamic research and was "to work to revitalize Islamic culture, purify it from unwelcome foreign accretions and traces of political and sectarian fanaticism, and restore it to its pristine condition." The Academy was also charged with formulating Islamic opinion concerning juridical and social problems.

(3) The Institute of Islamic Missions designed to provide trained religious leaders to help spread Islam abroad.

(4) Al-Azhar University, which was to consist of several colleges concerned with Islamic Studies. It was also to include colleges for Arabic studies, business administration, engineering, agriculture, medicine, and industry (Art. 34). These colleges were empowered to grant academic degrees commensurate with those of other institutions of higher learning including the equivalent of a B.A., an M.A., and a Ph.D. (Art. 75). The law provided for free education and an equal opportunity to all Muslims.

(5) Al-Azhar Institutes, including the al-Azhar Institute for Women, providing primary and high school education for women in preparation for university training.

Several *ʿulamāʾ* resigned in protest against the meddling of the state in the "internal" affairs of al-Azhar. They were replaced by Shaykhs who were more cooperative with the government and more willing to comply with and carry out its policies.[11] The reforms at al-Azhar came during the same year that Nasser implemented stronger government control of financial and business institutions. These came on the heels of the dissolution of the union with Syria,[12] and were interpreted as socialist reforms because they were aimed at curbing the powers of financial institutions.

Also in 1961 the government nationalized the press and the news media. All writers and authors, even literary artists, as well as any person involved in the dissemination of news, became employees of the government. With this kind of tight control the government was able to censor anything not in line with its own propaganda. In 1962 further consolidation of governmental authority was attempted. A charter entitled *al-Mīthāq* was published outlining the guidelines of the revolution and presented to the National Conference of Popular Forces for deliberation. Whereas the Constitution of 1956 declared Islam as the state religion,[13] the draft of the Charter of 1962 advocated religious freedom and gave equal status to all religious faiths:

> In their essence all divine messages constituted human revolutions which aimed at the re-instatement of man's dignity and his happiness. It is the prime duty of religious thinkers, then, to preserve for each religion the essence of its divine message. . . . The essence of the religious message does not conflict with the facts of our life; the conflict arises only in certain situations as a result of attempts made by reactionary elements to explain religion—against its nature and spirit—with a view of impeding progress. These elements fabricate false interpretations of religion in flagrant contradiction with its noble and divine wisdom. All religions contain a message of progress . . .[14]

Besides elevating other faiths to the status of Islam, the *Mīthāq* emphasized national consciousness. The true expression of Arab national consciousness was "unity, liberty, and socialism";[15] Islam was merely a component of Arab nationalism.[16] It was recognized as an element in the achievements of the revolution in the past ten years, but ranking only fifth in importance.[17] The *Mīthāq* also proposed socialism as the direction of the state; Nasser, in a speech on May 21, 1962 to the National Conference of Popular Forces, said that the Charter was to guarantee that 50 percent of the seats were to be occupied by workers and peasants.[18]

With the al-Azhar reforms of 1961, the government relegated the religious institution to an arm of its own operation. A great number of *ʿulamāʾ* became government functionaries, and a substantial amount of their literary output was a religious justification or apologetic of the regime. An article in *Majallat al-Azhar* explained that "the task of al-

Azhar in its new era is to inculcate the new, revolutionary thought and understanding in the people's mind."[19] A book was published on *Religion and the Charter*[20] which provided a Qur'anic justification for the idea of the Charter.[21] The book also makes note of the number of times the words faith (*īmān*) and religion (*dīn*) appear in the text. In general, however, the tone of the book is in accord with the ideological concerns of the government and is sprinkled with words such as "struggle," "reactionism," "imperialism," and "revolutionary vanguard." Furthermore, it exhorts the readers "to beware of monopolies, exploitation, and reactionary thought"[22] and affirms that "Arab Socialism is guided by the *sharīʿa* of justice and the *sharīʿa* of God."[23]

Political, economic, and military considerations led to a refinement in the ideas of Arab socialism as expressed in the *Mīthāq*. These in turn were followed by an attempt to indoctrinate the *ʿulamāʾ* and inculcate in them the principles of Islam that they were supposed to propagate. These shifts in policy were a response to the realization that the suppression of the Muslim Brotherhood in 1954 did not eliminate its support among the masses. The uncovering of a "conspiracy" in 1965 to overthrow the government led to the execution of three leaders of the Muslim Brotherhood.[24]

Meanwhile, the Nasser government was becoming increasingly anti-Western and fearful of Western attempts to topple it. Nasser became involved in the war in Yemen, which set him against Saudi Arabia and its ally, America.[25] The emphasis on "Islamic socialism" gave Nasser the freedom to attack Saudi Arabian Islam as reactionary and stifling. He did not need to say that socialism was against the religion of Islam, but rather that true Islam was that which would lead to the modern victory of the Arab people and not to retardation and decline. It was through appealing to the religious sentiments of the populace and maintaining that socialism is Islam that Nasser was able to attack the Saudi efforts to convene an Islamic summit.

This summit meeting was sponsored by King Fayṣal and the Shah of Iran. Nasser attacked this "Islamic Pact"[26] in a speech on February 22, 1966 and condemned it as an imperialist conspiracy "using religion as a tool with which it can restore its influence."[27] The "Islamic Pact" was portrayed as a move away from Arab unity. "The imperialist reactionary alliance aimed at spreading the idea of Islamic unity to counter Arab unity. It agreed that the Islamic countries of the Baghdad Pact should work for Islamic unity. . . ."[28] Nasser saw this stress on Islamic unity as a threat because it would of necessity include non-Arabs, thus diffusing the efforts that were needed in addressing the immediate problems of the Arab world. It would place the Arab nations in the center of East-West confrontation without solving their own needs:

> The Arab countries would thus emerge from the limited scope of Arab nationalism in which there is no room for understanding, to the wide scope of the Islamic creed, which embraces the Arabs, Turks, Iranians and Pakistanis in a wide area where their nationalities are forgotten and they think only in terms of Islam. In this way the Arab countries can reach an agreement with the West and Israel.[29]

The slogan "Religion is for God and the homeland is for everyone" (*al-dīn li'llāh wa'l-waṭan li'l-jamīʿ*) popular at this time in the Nasser regime suggested the relegation of faith to the private sphere as a personal affair between the individual and God. The efforts of the nation were to harness the capabilities of all its citizens to strive to fulfill the hopes of the nation and to establish its role in the world. It was felt that the goal should be cooperation between nations for the service of God and Islam, rather than the use of Islam to serve the interests of Western imperialism in the area.[30] Referring to his call for an Islamic conference to be held annually during the Hajj in *The Philosophy of the Revolution* (p. 77), Nasser explained that his concern in this was to help establish social justice, to eradicate imperialism, and to serve the interests of Islam and not the interests of the enemies of the Arabs.[31]

Meanwhile, Saudi Arabia's efforts to form an Islamic organization continued. In the spring of 1965 the Muslim World League, Rābiṭat al-ʿĀlam al-Islāmī, held its second conference in Mecca,[32] agreeing to espouse Islam over and against nationalistic considerations. This was, of course, contrary to the Egyptian ideology of Arab nationalism. Nasser perceived in the League's goal an imperialist conspiracy to eradicate the gains of the revolution. Fayṣal concentrated his efforts on gaining support for the Rabiṭat. From December of 1965 to September of 1966 he visited Iran,[33] Jordan, Sudan, Pakistan, Turkey, Guinea, Mali, and Tunisia.[34]

Relations between Egypt and Saudi Arabia worsened. While Egypt supported the Yemeni Republicans, Saudi Arabia gave aid to the Royalists. Both nations worked to undermine each other's ideologies. It is as a result of the sharpening of this controversy between the Islamic and the Nationalist ideologies that we find the most intense debate about the present and future of Islam. And it is in the context of this debate, particularly on questions of allegiance and destiny, that one finds the focus of the ideological concerns of the seventies. The debate, of course, was in effect the continuation of the 1952 revolution. Manning the agencies of the Muslim World League and editing its publications were many of the members of the Egyptian Muslim Brotherhood who sought asylum in Saudi Arabia when their society was banned.

Egyptian attacks on Saudi efforts continued. Saudis were accused of championing imperialistic causes and of impeding the liberation of the struggling Islamic nations.[35] Besides attacking the reactionary forces (*al-rajʿiyya*), the Egyptian government sought to insure that its employees supported its ideology.[36] Thus it embarked on a thorough program of indoctrination that included the *ʿulamāʾ*[37] to prepare them for their revolutionary role in society.[38] The program appears to have included study of the *Mīthāq*[39] as well as lectures on religion, socialism, science, and the Islamic theory.[40]

The fear of subversion or the teaching of unauthorized interpretations of Islam led to a censorship of the Friday sermon and insistence on focusing on pertinent topics.[41] Among the themes expounded in the literature was the affirmation that the revolution was based on faith, *thawra muʾmina.* It did not draw its ideas from posited theories or rational philosophies, but rather was inspired by the *sharīʿa,* "one that is whole, eternal, and valid for every time and place."[42]

The ideology of the revolution was presented as the heart of the Islamic *daʿwa.* Islam was seen as identical with socialism,[43] and deviation from socialism in Islam as one of the causes of retardation. Had Islamic civilization avoided the class structure, it would have been modern and revolutionary since "Islamic civilization was established on the basis of interaction between religious knowledge and life. . . . Islam is the religion of socialism. If we mention socialists, Muḥammad is their leader (*imāmuhum*)."[44]

Other expressions of the intricate relations between socialism and Islam led to interpretations such as that which said Muḥammad's message was a socialist response to a capitalist society in Mecca which had a class structure. "Muḥammad forbade usury because it is an expression of the capitalist system,"[45] thus suggesting that the Qurʾān may be of human rather than divine origin. Even Sufism was seen as socialist in origin by the head of the Sufi orders.[46]

Besides being socialist, Islam was presented as revolutionary. It was seen first and foremost as a revolution against corruption,[47] and the revolution of July 23, 1952 was said to have "materialized the heart and content of Islamic revolutionism in a practical manner."[48] It came into being "for spiritual values and the revivification of the religious heritage of the Arab person."[49] In fact, not only was Islam presented as revolutionary and as a driving force, but Nasser even said that "Islam *is* revolution."[50]

The literature in Islamic socialism is extensive. Various efforts were made to reinterpret the life of the Prophet and his Companions so that one finds titles describing the socialism of the Prophet (*Ishtirākiyyat Muḥammad*),[51] of his wife (*Umm Ishtirākiyya: Khadīja Bint Khuwaylid*),[52] of ʿUmar (*Ishtirākiyyat ʿUmar*),[53] and of Abū Bakr (*Ishtirākiyyat Abū Bakr*).[54] Typical are works such as that by Aḥmad Farrāj entitled simply *Islam, the Religion of Socialism*.[55] Other books examined the Islamic content of the *Mīthāq* and endeavored to justify it on Islamic grounds.[56]

Thus it is not surprising that the effort to systematically "Balshefy Islam" has led to the strengthening of normativist Islam. The menace of socialism was not a threat from attacking armies, but became a persistent dilution of the faith through reinterpretation according to alien norms and standards.

Also operative in the heightened normativist response is the absence of alternate avenues of political resistence to the government. Thus religious commitment to Islam, as it had repeatedly done throughout history, provided a haven for protest for the disenchanted and disenfranchised.

Chapter Three
The Zionist Challenge

A VISITOR TO the Arab world cannot but note the intensification of Islamic identity that has taken place in the past several years. The Islamic nature of the area is apparent in the flood of conservative religious literature in the bookstores of Egypt, the availability of Muslim Brotherhood publications in Baʿthist Damascus, the rise in the number of veiled educated "liberated" women, and the general tenor of the society. The militant actions of Jamʿiyyat al-Takfīr wa-al-Hijra, the attempt to enforce Islamic laws of reform in Egypt and Kuwait, the permission for Maʿrūf al-Dawālībī to visit Syria, the rising academic respectability of writing texts from the Islamic vantage point—these and many other phenomena can be cited as illustrations of the increased measure of Islamic identity.

The writing of texts from a specifically Muslim perspective, of course, is in part due to the competition among faculty at Egyptian universities for the highly remunerative teaching positions at the many new institutions of higher learning in the Arabian peninsula. Also influential are the academic conferences on Islamic subjects sponsored by these Arabian universities and by the Muslim World League. By focusing on Islamic topics, they have directed historical and social science research into specific channels, and have fostered a network of authors and professors committed to the pursuit of such research.

The rise of Islamic consciousness is in no small part the result of the Arab-Israeli wars of 1967 and 1973. It is also the result of political and military realities, realignments and perceptions of these confrontations as well as the end of the Nasser regime and its policies. The existence of Israel in the heart of the Arab world has had a dramatic effect on the growth and development of modernity, reform, and Westernization in the area.

Western historians and social scientists will never be able to understand fully the Arab/Islamic interpretation of the current state of affairs in the Arab world as well as the Muslim view of historical process without coming to terms with the meaning of the existence of Israel for Arabs. Although Israel and its supporters may perceive its existence in the heart of the Arab world as a purveyor of modernity and technology for the area, for Arabs both Muslim and non-Muslim it serves as a constant reminder of their impotence and failure. It is crucial to the understanding of the Islamic view of history to see that for Muslims the existence of Israel is a condemnation and a sign that the forces of darkness and immorality, of wickedness and apostasy, have for reasons yet unexplained, taken the ascendancy in the world.[1]

After thirty years of pain and struggle, of sacrifice and suffering, the Arab cannot fathom why Israel continues to prosper and become stronger while his people are weaker and more helpless. Israel is seen as part of the confrontation and effort at domination of the Arab world by the Western colonial powers. Many publications refer to Zionism as a modern version of the Crusades,[2] an insidious conspiracy of the Western Christian world in its continued hatred and enmity towards Islam. Recent publications about the role of the city of Jerusalem and its central place in Muslim piety echo the concerns of medieval writers who saw in the Crusades an infidel incursion against Islam. Jerusalem must be under Muslim domination in order to guarantee the worship of the true God. Both the Christians and the Jews have deviated from the true way; control of this sacred city must therefore be in the hands of Muslims whom God has appointed to be the guardians of His truth.[3] "Oh ye Muslims . . . ," exhorts Isḥāq al-Ḥusaynī, "Will you forsake the Aqṣā Mosque, the Dome of the Rock, in the darkness of oppressive Israeli imperialism? How will you face God on the Day of Resurrection? Do you allow the Holy Kaʿba and the grave of the Prophet to be a prey to conquest and destruction?"[4]

The religious significance of the Arab-Israeli conflict was enhanced by the loss of the holy city of Jerusalem (al-Quds). This loss was aggravated by Israel's attempts to Judaize the city through systematic eradication of its Arab influence.[5] This was carried out by the policy of expropriation of Arab land and the demolition of Arab housing, the expulsion of eminent intellectuals and leaders of the Arab community, and the imposition of the Israeli curriculum on Arab schools which distorted the historical claims Arabs have to Palestine. Israeli policies also encouraged Jewish settlement of the area by providing subsidies for settlers as well as the construction of high-rise apartments, "the

Cement Jungle," around the Arab sector of Jerusalem aimed at truncating it from other Arab communities and rendering it into a ghetto.

The activities and speeches of Rabbi Shlomo Goren of the Israeli armed forces alerted many Muslims to the possibility of the destruction or expropriation of the Muslim holy places. Besides holding services in the Aqṣā Mosque, Rabbi Goren affirmed his intent to rebuild Solomon's Temple on the grounds where the Mosque now stands.[6] These fears were also fanned by the archeological excavations around the mosque which precipitated the weakening of the existent structures and necessitated the installation of supportive beams. The several Zionist conferences calling for the restoration of Jewish places of worship and the high-handed manner in which the Judaizing policy was and continues to be implemented did little to allay the fears in Arab minds that the Israeli government would seek the eradication of Muslim holy places, especially the Aqṣā Mosque because of its historical significance. Thus, burning of the Mosque on August 21, 1969, by an Australian Christian fanatic escalated the fear of what was perceived as part of the Zionist conspiracy.

The religious significance of the Israeli occupation of the Holy Land and the burning of the Aqṣā Mosque in 1969 was reflected in a letter written by Nasser to the armed forces:

> I have waited and thought a great deal about the terrible crime inflicted against the holy of holies of our religion, our history, and our civilization. At the end, I did not find anything but the new affirmation of the meanings that were evident to all of us from the first day of our terrible experience. There is no alternative, no hope, and no way except through Arab force, using all we are able to muster, to allocate, and to pressure with, until the true victory of God is achieved.
>
> We have opened every door to peace, but the enemy of God and our enemy closed every door in the way of peace. We left no means untried, but the enemy of God and our enemy obstructed the means, blocked the roads, and made evident to the world what was hidden about his nature and intent.
>
> We are before an enemy who was not satisfied by challenging man, but through his arrogance and insanity transgressed by challenging the sacred places that God blessed and willed as houses for Himself.
>
> I want our men, officers and soldiers to understand the feelings of the last two days and be aware of their meaning, to appropri-

> ate in their conscience the conscience of their nation and to know in their depths that they shoulder the responsibility not carried by any army since the descent of revelations from heaven as guidance and mercy for the world.
>
> They, in their next battle are not the soldiers of their nation only, but the army of God, the protectors of His religions, His houses, and His Holy Books.
>
> Their next battle is not a battle of liberation only, it has become necessary for it to be one of purification.
>
> Our vision is focused on the Aqṣā Mosque in Jerusalem as it suffers from the forces of evil and darkness.
>
> Whatever our feelings at this moment may be, we pray to God as believers, in awe, that He may grant us patience, knowledge, courage, and capacity to remove evil and darkness.
>
> Our soldiers shall return to the courtyards of the Aqṣā Mosque. Jerusalem will be returned to what it was prior to the age of imperialism which strove to spread its hegemony on it for centuries until it (Imperialism) gave it to those who play with fire.
>
> We shall return to Jerusalem and Jerusalem will be returned to us. We shall fight for that. We shall not lay down our arms until God grants His soldiers the victory and until His right is dominant, His house respected and true peace is restored to the city of peace.[7]

A flood of literature appeared as an essential response affirming the centrality of Jerusalem for Islam.[8] The Fifth Conference of the Academy of Islamic Research of Al-Azhar in 1970 devoted a substantial part of its proceedings to the topic of the Islamic nature of Jerusalem and Palestine. In his opening speech, Muḥammad Faḥḥām, Rector of al-Azhar, affirmed that historically, the Arabs were the first to inhabit Jerusalem (3000 B.C.). Jewish settlement in the area came later (1200 B.C.). Consequently, if historical precedence is used as an argument for right of possession the Arabs were the original inhabitants.[9]

Moreover, the religious arguments that Palestine is the promised land for the Jews is rejected as obsolete since God's promise had been fulfilled in history and the Jews had forfeited their right to the land having broken the covenant and committed evil.[10]

Crucial to an understanding of the wars with Israel is the perception of victory and defeat within the Qur'anic context. The Qur'ān is very explicit that victory will be given to those who are with God.

Israel's victories then stand as a condemnation of the Muslim *Umma*. The Arabs apparently have lost because God has forsaken them. This gives rise to a series of related questions: Has God given the victory to Israel because Israel has been more zealous in commitment to His purposes? Has God forsaken the Muslim nation? What are the reasons for the apparent victory? Have the Muslims been tested and found wanting? Is it possible that Judaism is the more correct way of life? Each war with Israel has elicited different justifications and reasons, depending on the particular perceptions Muslims have had of themselves.

It has been relatively easy to justify the debacle of 1948. The loss of Palestine can be blamed on the colonial powers, especially Britain, that nursed the Jewish immigrants into a sizable community in Palestine and provided them with training and armaments, while decimating the Arab resistance and bleeding its human and material resources during the disturbances of 1936–1939. The Jordanian army in the meantime was led by British officers who deliberately disobeyed the orders of King Abdullah in favor of England's command to cease fighting once the demarcation lines were reached. Jerusalem, which had already surrendered to the Transjordan army, was granted as a gift to the Israelis by Glubb Pasha.

The defeat of the Syrian forces, meanwhile, was clearly due to their disorganized condition, lack of leadership, and the treasonable behavior of some government officials. During the French occupation, which had ceased only three years earlier, the Syrian army was led by Christians, Alawis, and other minorities due to France's policy of ruling the majority (Sunni Muslims) by the use of minorities. Upon gaining independence the Syrian government had removed the core of officers, who had been pawns of the French regime, rendering the army ill equipped with no trained officers and in no way ready to fight the Israeli forces. The Egyptian army was in no better condition. Egypt itself was occupied by British forces, and the king and government were puppets administering the policies of the resident British High Commissioner.

Thus, although the 1948 war ended in defeat of the Arab armies by 1949, genuine reasons and excuses were found to cope with its disastrous impact. Given the condition of the Arab forces, it has been easy for Arab historians to understand the ease of the Israeli victory, especially given the duplicity of the colonial powers in providing Israel with arms while denying the Arab troops any such assistance during the armistice. The defeat was not only proof of the present military impotence of the Arab nations; it also provided a dramatic end to the romantic period in which the West was perceived by many modernizers as primary representative of a system worthy of emulation in the search for full participation in the modern world.

Events had been leading in that direction for decades. The occupation of the Arab world by Western forces, the failure of Britain to live up to its agreement after the First World War, the mockery made of parliaments by occupying forces, the travesty of the human rights of indigenous citizens, and the steady and insistent support of Western nations for the creation of the state of Israel put an end to the dreams of the romantics. Any student of the careers of literary and reformist figures such as Ṭāhā Ḥusayn, ʿAbbās Maḥmūd al-ʿAqqād, Sayyid Quṭb, and Aḥmad Amīn can find in thir writings the shock of realization that the West they loved and championed had spurned them again as unfit partners. These and other authors turned back to their roots in an attempt to find a more authentic existence and a reliable raison d'être. For each one the creation of the state of Israel was incomprehensible. The West that had promised so much had in the end jilted them, not because they did not measure up to its requirements but for the specific reason that they were Arabs. By treating them as nonpersons the West not only violated Arab faith, but in effect invalidated their very existence.[11]

The revolt of 1952 in Egypt was welcomed by the masses and the army because it eliminated the discredited leadership under King Farouk who were puppets of the British and who had proved impotent in Palestine. Also backing the revolt was the Muslim Brotherhood organization, then in its heyday of power. They rejected the West not because it had failed to live up to its promise as did the romantics; rather they rejected it because of what it was, alien, and therefore potentially leading Arabs astray from the true path of Islam. The Brotherhood, along with the conservative Muslims, maintained that the Muslims were weak because they had abandoned Islam. If the Muslims were in a defeated and backward condition, it was because they had ceased to strive for God's purposes and consequently God had abandoned them. For the Arabs to regain their position of leadership, of ascendancy, and of power, they must cease to champion alien ideologies, put away the worship of the gods of materialism and technology, and return to the true faith and a life committed to the way of God in obedience and humility. Only then will God give victory over the enemies of Islam. The Muslim Brotherhood was not opposed to technology. It established factories in different areas of

Egypt to provide sources of employment, and was progressive to the point of organizing unions for workers and championing their rights. Its main creed was that to be modern is not to be Western, but to be truly Muslim, recognizing the traditions of Islam and its authority over all aspects of life, seeking answers to today's problems from within the Qur'anic revelation which is eternally sufficient and valid.

Others reacted to the creation of Israel by calling for a rearmament program that could match Israeli power and be able to replace the foreign rule that was established on Arab land. What was most galling to them was the fact that while most colonies were winning their freedom from colonial rule, the British with the might of the Americans planted an alien people in the heart of the Arab world. The Israelis were seen as the tools by which the colonial powers would suppress the hopes and wills of the burgeoning Arab nations.

Rejection of the West, of course, was not the only response to the 1948 war. Some actually called for a renunciation of all Arab culture and the total appropriation of Western technology, on the grounds that Israel's victory is the proof that to be modern one has to be Western. In this understanding traditional moral and ethical considerations must be renounced and the "new morality" of might over right adopted. Israel has provided the perfect example of this kind of modern morality in which people count only insofar as they can successfully fight for their rights. The United Nations, on which was pinned all hope for the ushering in of an era of brotherhood, human rights, and equality, turned out to be a tool in the hands of the imperialist Western forces. True justice was ignored in favor of force and the might of arms as thousands of Palestinians were thrown from their homes in order to make room for the European Jews that Europe and the United States did not want.

The second major confrontation between the Arabs and Israel occurred in 1956. It confirmed for the Arabs Israel's role in the area as an agent of imperialism and colonialism. The confrontation came as a result of collusion between the governments of Britain, France, and Israel as a response to Nasser's nationalization of the Suez Canal. Rebuffed by John Foster Dulles because he had purchased arms from Czechoslovakia, Nasser saw no alternative but to seek Russian help in building the Aswan Dam. Once again the Arab world became a victim of the Cold War which was then at its peak.

Although Britain, France, and Israel occupied the Sinai and the Canal areas in a very short time, the outcome of the war was perceived as a victory for Nasser. For centuries the Western powers had pressured the Middle Eastern nations to follow policies that were beneficial to the West. They removed rulers who refused to do their bidding, formulating legal and economic policies favoring Westerners over the native peoples. They used their armies and navies to eradicate all resistance. Thus Nasser's ability to stand up to the dictates of the West and insist on making decisions that benefitted the interests of the Egyptian people was hailed as a great achievement. Whether he won or not in practical terms was insignificant. The important thing was that he was able to withstand pressure and to tell the aggressors that the Arabs would not be pushed around any longer. Despite the fact that the tripartite aggression resulted in extensive devastation of Egyptian land, and that the army was routed and the economic loss was huge, Nasser came out of the war with the image of a hero who saved the world of Islam from another humiliation. He had led Muslims, therefore, to what was perceived as a moral victory.

Political events following the 1956 war led to the further growth of Nasser's prestige and power. These included union with Syria and the insistence on a policy of nonalignment with either the East or the West. Nasser was also successful in obtaining Russian aid in building the Aswan Dam and in training and supplying the armed forces. The union with Syria encouraged socialist planning for the United Arab Republic. When Syria broke away, Nasser set in motion socialist reforms that were meant to fashion a new Egypt, a program that was to remove it from its backwardness and bring it into the twentieth century. The landowner class was legislated out of existence through the Land Reform Act that limited the acreage any person could possess. The land was distributed to the farmers and cooperative agricultural societies were initiated.

Western occupation of Egypt provided Nasser with the opportunity to rid Egypt of its resident entrepreneurs. As agents of Western influence on the economy, they were perceived as a threat to Egyptian interests. Thus Nasser nationalized both Western companies and large indigenous businesses. The effort was concentrated on the development of a new Egypt and its citizens as persons who can proudly raise their heads among other men.

In this brave new world of the revolution that was to lead Egypt to its longed-for goals, there was no room for critics or dissidents. The Muslim Brotherhood was silenced through the execution of a few of its leaders and the imprisonment of a substantial number of its members. Al-Azhar and Islam were reformed by several decrees, leading to virtual nationalization of the religious institution. Thus the religious leaders and most religious literature became an effective agency legitimizing the government and its policies. Whereas orthodox Muslims have always believed that the Islamic state "would protect and propagate Islam, would strive for the realization of Islamic ideas, and would apply Islamic laws,"[12] under the Nasser regime its function became one of providing Islamic apologetics and interpretations for the policies of the government in order to propagate socialism and implement its goals.

In retrospect it is clear that Nasser maintained power through the support of the military who were given a more central role in running the affairs of the nation. The officers, provided with suitable housing and economic remuneration, replaced the Western entrepreneur class in running factories, banks, and businesses. Nasser was also supported by the masses because he nourished the ideas of victory and well-being. Not that the regime lacked critics. The jails were filled with those who believed that the course chosen by the Egyptian government was leading to deviation from the true heritage and the right goals for the Arab nations, or felt that Nasser was leading the country too far into the Soviet orbit. It was able, however, to maintain through its carefully orchestrated propaganda machine (which included the religious leaders and institutions) a feeling of developing power, of potency, of belonging to the modern world. A sense of pride was growing, an identity as a people who could no longer be described as "the mat over which powerful nations wipe their shoes." Suddenly, the Arab as well as the Egyptian felt that he was emancipated from the decadence and defeat of the past, that he was freed to participate in the world and in the formulation of policies that weighed upon his life and controlled his destiny.

The third Arab-Israeli war in 1967 came at a time of the recapturing of Arab pride, of great hope, and of a feeling of maturity. The internal and external causes of the war for both Israel and Egypt are not crucial for an understanding of Arab Muslim response. What is important here is that the defeat was total and catastrophic. While the Israelis felt bolstered in confidence and powerful in their strengthened position and holdings, the Arab world, defeated, stood once again naked, vulnerable, the laughingstock of all the world. Less agonizing than the humiliation of the present defeat was the collapse of faith in the future and despair over any means of survival.

For the conservative Muslims, the war of 1967 proved a vindication of what they had been saying all along. The ways of "Islamic socialism" are not the ways of God. The defeat came as a punishment from

God because the Muslims once again had placed their faith in alien systems and devoted their energies to the posited purposes of these systems rather than zealously working for the purposes of God. They had marshaled their efforts for the pursuit of materialism, not only ignoring God, but manipulating His revelation to serve their own purposes. The only way to recapture ascendancy and victory is by a total renunciation of man-made ideologies and a reorientation toward an unwavering commitment to the realization of Islam in the world. Israel did not get the victory because it represented a better system or a truer religion or a more perfect response to God's revelation; rather God used Israel to punish His errant nation and allowed the forces of evil to conquer the Muslims because they had strayed from the Straight Path. The defeat was thorough because they had deviated so greatly.[13]

Other Muslims, less conservative yet just as painfully feeling the defeat, ascribed it to lack of preparation and planning. The causes of the defeat, they felt, were in the inability to mobilize the masses and bring them into the twentieth century. Still others felt that the defeat was a failure of the Arabs to modernize. Ascendancy in the modern world comes only through creative inventiveness and technological know-how. Unless the Arabs were willing to discard their worn-out heritage, irrelevant to the modern world, they would never be able to join the ranks of the civilized nations.

Many of the more radical socialists felt that this defeat may have brought an end to the socialist experiment in the Arab world. What they regretted was that socialism had been neither radical enough nor sufficiently influential to bring about its purposes. It had compromised itself by allowing the revolution to be colored with an Islamic aura which rendered it vulnerable in several areas. By maintaining the influence of religion over people's lives, it thus restricted the liberating forces of revolutionism from implementing drastic changes to produce the new Arab person.

Thus after the initial shock of defeat, self-criticism and condemnation became common responses. No one, of course, was satisfied with the state of affairs, but while all advocated some kind of definitive action, there was no unanimity concerning what that course of action should be nor what role the Islamic heritage ought to play. There was again division, in other words, over the constitution of the ideal society for which they were striving as well as what means were to be used to arrive at that goal.

The Arab world descended into a kind of psychological morass while struggling with these questions, from which it did not emerge until the 1973 war with Israel, referred to as the October or Ramaḍān war. As if the pendulum had again made its swing, Arabs viewed this conflict as a clear victory over Israel. That is, had not the United States intervened so decisively and replaced Israeli armaments, the Arabs would surely have defeated their opponents.

The portrayal of the "Crossing" (*al-ʿubūr*) has acquired Exodus dimensions in the recounting of the war. In the religious literature that is produced by the Sādāt propaganda organization there is a definite indication of an Islamic victory.[14] This is supported in the first place by the Sadat maneuver of ridding himself of the socialists in 1971, referred to as the Rectification (*al-taṣḥīḥ*). Seen from the perspective of political science as a move to the right, this action had a strong religious connotation; President Sadat in announcing the Rectification program made it clear that the nation would henceforward be built in *īmān* (faith) and *ʿilm* (knowledge, science). *ʿIlm,* being validly open to interpretation as religious knowledge, has been seen as a clear support of the role of religion in the state. Even Sufi orders that had gone underground during the Nasser regime now operate in the open and hold their Mawlid services in season.

The symbolism of the 1973 conflict as the Ramaḍān war is obvious, this being the holy month of Islam. The code name for the war was Badr, a reminder of the first Islamic victory under Muḥammad in A.D. 623 over the forces of apostasy which, like its twentieth-century counterpart, was fought against seemingly overwhelming odds. In the 1967 war the battle cry of the Arabs was "Land, Sea, Sky," implying faith in equipment and the tactics of military engagement. In 1973 the cry was more explicitly Muslim, the call of "God is great (*Allāhu Akbar*)," with which Islam has spread the message of God through major portions of the world.

It is not unusual to find Muslim writers who specifically ascribe the 1973 victory to God and His forces. One even wrote that "white beings" were seen aiding in the fighting on the side of the Egyptian army, an obvious reference to the angelic assistance rendered according to the Qur'ān to the early Muslims in their battles against apostasy. The 1973 war is also seen as an Islamic victory because it was the result of the oil boycott by Saudi Arabia. God thus has favored Saudi Arabia because it is the only nation among Arab/Muslim countries that declares itself to be truly Muslim in that it is the only place where religious law and the tenets of the Qur'ān are literally implemented.

Saudi Arabia is also looked on as a concrete example of God's favor precisely because of its rise in power and prestige. Wealth and progress, as we have seen, are regarded in Islam as signs of God's approval and potency as a gift of His mercy. Thus Saudi success has provided an impetus to a reemerging sense of Islamic identity for all Muslims at the same time as its financial support of other Arab states tends to temper their socialist zeal. Saudi Arabia did not come into this role suddenly. As explained earlier, Fayṣal's efforts at combating the influence of Nasserism date to the early sixties. The formation of the Muslim World League and its efforts at propagating the Islamic way of life through sponsorship of conferences and lectures on Islamic subjects maintain the Islamic alternative in clear focus.

In a sense the Muslim World League has inherited the vacuum left by the retreat of Islamic socialism. In its efforts to compromise Islam through socialist ideology, Nasserism compromised itself. Under Nasser Islam continued to provide the aura of divine legitimation and validity for proposed social, political, and economic reforms. Even though the programs failed, Islam survived precisely because of the Nasserite emphasis on the Islamic aspect of this brand of socialism which kept radical groups from introducing extreme proposals for change. When Muslim conservatism regained ascendancy, it denounced the perversions of the former regime as deviation and innovation. Its role as the true interpreter of Islam has been enhanced because it had suffered under the previous regime. Islam is now presented as free to function again because the few persevered in maintaining its purity, some even to the death.

Enhancing the newly emerging image of Islamic identity is the evident failure of the Western experiment as perceived not only in the Arab world but also in the West itself. The West that the last century Arabs idealized as ethical, honest, and enthusiastic is flawed by racism, by corruption, by a degenerate "pornographic" society in which every person seems to strive for his own interests rather than for the collective good. The disenchantment with the West is due not only to its treatment of Arab hopes and goals vis-à-vis Israel, but also to the apparent inconsistency of Western ideals and what is perceived as the imminent collapse of the West. Such an image frees Islam, purified and committed, to resume its sacred role of spreading the faith to all corners of the world.

The events of Lebanon during the last few years, which have pitted Christian against Muslim and revealed a collusion between the Maronites of Lebanon and the Israelis, have led to the disenchantment of some of those who believed in Arab nationalism as a unity that transcends religious identities. These events, especially recently in Syria and Jordan, have led many to place an increasing stress on religious identity as the identity par excellence, over and against regionalism, nationalism, or socialism.

In February of 1970 the Supreme Islamic Research Council in its Fifth Conference addressed itself to the question of Palestine and the occupied territories. In its published findings it says, "The Palestine Question is not a national issue nor is it a political issue. It is first and foremost an Islamic question."[15] It is clear that the military fortunes of the Arab people in relation to Israel are directly involved in the ways in which Muslims perceive themselves, the world, and history, and that that perception is intricately involved in the question of how they marshal their efforts in order to formulate the goals they seek and the methods they use to achieve these goals.

Chapter Four
The Case of a Qur'anic Exegete

THE TENSION BETWEEN the acculturationists and the normativists in Egypt was not restricted to areas dealing with social, political, and economic issues; it also impinged on intellectual concerns including the perception of the faith. Several controversies dealt with the new articulations of doctrine. Anwar al-Jundī in his *al-Musājalāt wa-al-Maʿārik al-Adabiyya fī Majāl al-Fikr wa-al-Tārīkh wa-al-Ḥaḍāra* (Cairo, 1972) lists fifty-seven issues over which major controversy has taken place among Arab Muslims since the First World War. These range over a variety of topics, including the adequacy and flexibility of the Arabic language for the modern world, the scope and purpose of Arabic literature, the interpretation of Islamic history, the preservation and reform of thought and civilization including the polarity of religion and learning, materialistic philosophy, Orientalism, Western culture, Islam and society, Westernization and conservatism, the role and status of women, Sharīʿah and civil law, and many others.

Among these controversies was one concerning the historical authenticity of the Qur'anic narratives. The problem arose when Muḥammad Aḥmad Khalaf Allāh presented his thesis on the narratives of the Qur'ān at Kulliyat al-Ādāb at Cairo University in 1947.[1] Using the inductive method, *istiqrā'*,[2] Khalaf Allāh studied the narratives as literature, judging them by modern historical and literary standards. The controversy began when the press reported that his thesis was passed by his advisor Dr. Amīn al-Khawlī,[3] who later wrote an introduction to the work when it was published, pronouncing it a worthwhile achievement and one that should be defended in the interest of freedom of speech. He saw in it an interpretation that would help preclude a split personality in intellectual Muslims who take their faith seriously.

Using the inductive method, Khalaf Allāh attempted to cull out the truth of the teachings of the Qur'ān in the context in which they were revealed. Guided by the principle that one is not to deduce from the Qur'anic text anything not specifically intended, he came to the conclusion that "the intent of the Qur'ān in the narratives was nothing but admonition (*ʿibra*) and exhortation (*ʿiẓa*) and never was instruction in history or explication of its truth."[4]

Khalaf Allāh felt that the exegetes and the Orientalists have misunderstood the purpose of the Qur'anic narratives since they studied them as historical reports and tended to judge the Qur'ān as an historical text rather than a literary or religious document. His efforts were therefore aimed at silencing the critics of the Qur'ān for good by emphasizing the artistic purposes of the narratives, thus putting an end to what he perceived to be unjustified attacks on a vulnerable position of the Qur'anic text.

Khalaf Allāh notes that except in very rare cases the Qur'ān does not intend to report history; rather it deliberately ignores the factors of time and place that are central in an historical text. The narrative is aimed at enhancing the *daʿwa* through the means of attraction (*targhīb*), intimidation (*tarhīb*), exhortation (*mawʿiẓa*), admonition (*ʿibra*), guidance (*hidāya*), and direction (*irshād*). The Orientalists have failed completely in understanding the method and style of the Qur'ān, which led them to the erroneous thesis that there is a development in the characters of the narratives. They erred in their understanding of the purpose of the Qur'ān, asking irrelevant questions such as whether or not an event took place, and if it did, when and where it happened and what its cause was.[5]

To Khalaf Allāh, the Qur'ān is neither antihistorical nor nonhistorical. He is aware that the revelation came to the Prophet Muhammad at a certain time and under certain circumstances in Mecca and Medina. Thus although the revelation was received in historical context and the narratives may refer to historical events, their purpose in the Qur'ān is not to present a record of the history of the people of God. They are not meticulous historical documentations of events, but rather a means of instruction and admonition to all who hear to heed the call to the worship of God. They are thus ahistorical in the sense that they are not interested in history for history's sake.

The Qur'anic disregard for historical detail, Khalaf Allāh feels, was either because the contemporaries of the Prophet already knew what the references in the narratives implied, or a deliberate effort on the part of the Qur'ān to shift the attention of the listeners to the purpose of each narrative. Thus by focusing on the historical details the exegetes missed the essential meaning of Islam, expending their efforts in explaining the problem of repetition in the narratives and in dealing with the question of the obscure (*mutashābih*) parts of the Qur'ān. Had the exegetes understood the true meaning of the narratives, they would have known that there is no repetition and no obscurity since each narrative is independent of the other. Had they understood the literary method used in the Qur'ān, they would not have dwelled on the narratives and the question of reality.[6] By using the literary method of interpretation, he feels, and refraining from justifying the narratives as history, Muslims can free themselves of the *isrā'īliyyāt* and be able to guide the human mind to the social and religious meaning of the narratives.[7]

According to Khalaf Allāh, the ahistorical nature of the narratives is evident from the following observations: (1) The Qur'anic narratives tend to ignore time and place. There is not a single narrative in the Qur'ān whose chief purpose is to determine the time or place of an occurrence. Some narratives even ignore the characters. (2) The Qur'ān appears to be selective in the events it chooses to refer to, at no time attempting to present a comprehensive account of one person.[8] (3) The narratives tend to refrain from taking into account the time factor, or the element of progression.[9] (4) Some events are attributed to different characters in different places.[10] (5) The character in the narrative sometimes says a different thing in a different account of the same event.[11] (6) Some narratives report on future events while talking about past events.[12]

Khalaf Allāh suggests three categories into which the narratives fall: history, parable, and allegory:

The historical narratives deal with prophets and messengers and those references that are considered by some to be specifically historical:

> This type of Qur'anic narrative is historical-literary (*adabī-tārīkhī).* The Qur'ān takes the material of the narratives from the events and occurrences of history, relating them in a literary and emotional manner which explains the meaning and supports the purpose in such a way as to elicit a response from the listener whose emotions and conscience are affected.[13]

To Khalaf Allāh, the literary character of the historical narratives is evident from the following characteristics: (1) Their purpose is to instill the fear of punishment. The choice of references to be included in these narratives is dictated by the literary method which selects what is capable of eliciting an emotional rather than an intellectual response. (2) The narratives deal with the guidance God provides for nations through the prophets, the rejection of these prophets, and the punishment meted out to the rejectors.[14] (3) The purpose of the narrative is that which dictates its style and method. Thus differences in the accounts can be explained in terms of the different emotional responses they are meant to elicit. (4) The Qur'anic narratives appear in several places to hold the contemporaries of the Prophet responsible, as though they had participated in the rejection of the forebears.[15] (5) Some narratives are presented in different versions in accord with the emotional responses they are supposed to evoke, which explains what some have seen as inconsistency.[16] (6) The Qur'ān at times talks about reality as perceived by the listeners rather than as absolute truth. This has led exegetes like al-Rāzī to insist that allegorical interpretation (*ta'wīl*) is necessary in these cases.[17] (7) Other evidences of the literary rather than historical nature of the narratives are found when the Qur'ān talks about events as contemporary with each other when they were in fact separated by generations, places words in people's mouths which they could not have said, ascribes events in one place to one person and to another person in another place.

The second type of Qur'anic narrative is the parable (*tamthīliyya*). It is graphic in its use of imagery and is given as an example to illustrate a didactic point.[18] We have no historical or real knowledge of these events but are able to perceive them as hypothetical. Khalaf Allāh's discussion of this category is very brief.

The third type is what is called myth or allegory (*al-usṭūriyya*). The literary material of the historical narrative is composed of actual events that the Qur'ān used in such a way as to fulfill the purpose of the Qur'anic narrative. However, the narrative material of the *usṭūra* is totally a story; all of these are Meccan.[19] The important thing, according to Khalaf Allāh, is that the Qur'ān does not deny that these narratives are *asāṭīr*. All it denies is that their source is Muḥammad and not God. Thus if the Orientalists say that some of the narratives of the Qur'ān, such as that of the *ahl al-kahf*, are mythological, we can answer that that does not detract from the Qur'ān. It is one of the characteristics of world literature as well as of the texts of the great religions. Muslims are proud that the Qur'ān has pioneered in setting the standards and measures by which the material can be appreciated.[20]

The reaction to Khalaf Allāh's theories was swift and uncompromisingly negative. The *Risāla* magazine carried scores of attacks on him and his advisor as well as his responses to these attacks.[21] They ranged from calling him a novice who was tackling with unfamiliar tools a job for which he was not prepared, to labeling him a *kāfir* and a liar. The *ʿUlamā'* of al-Azhar sent a letter to the king and the government which read:

> This leads us to believe that the matter is grave and must be remedied forthwith because it is a new plague more destructive and more effective than cholera in these days. It destroys the spirits and not the ghosts and undermines the *umma* in its religion which is more important to it than its life.[22]

And *al-Ikhwān al-Muslimūn* magazine gave these commentaries on the thesis:

> It is not sufficient for the author to burn it with his own hands or someone else's hands in view of and within hearing distance of teachers and students; it is necessary for him to announce his return to Islam and to renew his marriage vows if he is married. . . .
>
> Burning the thesis is insufficient; first you must burn the *shayṭān* who has filled your soul with his drivel and dictated it to you. If you burn the devil, retire from the College of Arts and its doctrate and go to the seclusion of your own room where you can weep about Satan's deceit until God may accept your penitence.[23]

Khalaf Allāh's lack of scholarly precision in dealing with several passages was noted by some of his critics, who saw it as evidence of his questionable motivation. They were correct in accusing him of selective quoting, especially from passages of al-Rāzī and ʿAbdu in which he uses only those sections of their discussions with which he agrees and ignores the context in which they appear.[24] In some instances he quotes only questions raised by some exegetes, refraining from citing their answers.[25] In other places he uses a partial quote (*batr*) which misrepresents the author he is quoting. Thus he was seen as a falsifier and dismissed by some as ignorant (*jāhil*), a liar (*kādhib*), and a traitor (*khā'in*).[26]

His contention that the Jews were considered the final arbiters in the question of whether the narratives were revealed by God or fabricated by the Prophet Muḥammad is contrary to the teachings of the Qur'ān. Furthermore, if carried to its logical conclusion, his thesis would jeopardize the Muslim belief that the Qur'ān is the final revelation from God and is a correction of the corrupted scriptures of the People of the Book. To claim that the Qur'ān revealed what the Jews already knew regardless of reality is to question the veracity and authenticity of the Revelation. The critics were not concerned with Khalaf Allāh's insistence that the narratives were literary and artistic. That they would happily grant him. What they emphatically denied is that the material of the Qur'ān is woven from anything save the pure, unadulterated truth not altered by any considerations of imagination and supposition.

Khalaf Allāh's attempt to defend the narratives as ahistorical for the purpose of protecting the Prophet and the Qur'ān from the attacks of the Orientalists was not seen as justifiable. In fact, rather than a defense of the Qur'ān, it was perceived as initiating a process that would lead to the destruction of the faith.[27] He is ridiculed by ʿAbd Rabbih, for example, who affirms that had the missionaries and Orientalists convened a conference and struggled through collective effort to find a statement to degrade and discredit the Prophet and the Qur'ān, they could not have come up with a worse one than the ridiculous lie perpetrated by Khalaf Allāh, who is known in any case to have been guided by their books since he agrees with their accusation that there are historical errors in the Qur'an.[28] Others noted that Khalaf Allāh appears to have copied some of his ideas from the missionary St. Claire, whose book *Sources of Islam* [sic] had been translated into Arabic,[29] or that in certain of his affirmations he appears to agree with Rodwell and Margoliouth.[30] Thus he was accused of masquerading under the guise of Islam, a *mutamaslim*.

Khalaf Allāh erred in the eyes of his critics by setting an alternate standard of truth, the discipline of "history." To judge the Qur'ān by historical criteria is to admit that it is inferior. This no committed Muslim could allow. As the final arbiter of truth, the Qur'ān cannot be judged by an inferior man-made system. "It does not deduce the laws of history, it judges them," says ʿAbd Rabbih. "The Qur'ān is truthful even if it contradicts history. History is the liar because its sources are varied and contradictory."[31]

The Qur'ān is unchanging while history continues to revise its theories and rearrange its facts. If we wait but for a while, history will find new evidence which will corroborate the arrangements of events as revealed in the Qur'ān.[32] God alone knows the truth and is the source of what is ultimately real. To argue otherwise not only discredits the Prophet but imputes lies to God. Even science,[33] considered for several generations to be the final test of validity and authenticity, tends to say different things at different times. Its adherents have produced contradictory theories using the same facts. Only the Qur'ān provides certitude since its author is the Lord of creation and the source of all truth and knowledge. The contention that the Qur'ān revealed that which the contemporaries of the Prophet believed and could understand without regard to truth and reality was also rejected by the critics since it cast aspersions on the validity of the Qur'ān for all times, to all peoples in all places. For to imply that it compromised truth and reality to reach a specific audience at a specific time would render the Qur'ān today an obsolete document.

Khalaf Allāh's affirmation that the Qur'ān does not deny that some of its contents are *asāṭīr* was refuted through a careful analysis of the *asāṭīr* verses in the Qur'ān by ʿAbd al-Karīm al-Khaṭīb.[34] He found that when the verses were studied in the context of the Qur'ān they could not be interpreted to agree with Khalaf Allāh's theory. Had Khalaf Allāh said that it was his own *ijtihād* that led him to such a surmise, one would judge him in that light. But for him to claim that the Qur'ān itself advocated this kind of understanding contradicts the Qur'ān's concept of itself as a book of guidance to the righteous in which there is and can be no falsehood.[35]

In the refutation of the work of Khalaf Allāh his opponents reaffirmed the traditional understanding of the narratives of the Qur'ān. Thus, they said, the real purpose of these narratives is to affirm and make evident that:

(1) The message and revelation received by Muḥammad and contained in the narratives had a divine origin, since he was illiterate and had not studied the scriptures of the *ahl al-kitāb.*[36]

(2) All religion is from God, all believers are one nation from the time of Noah to the time of Muḥammad, God is the one Lord of all, and the narratives are therefore a sign for all men to end their divisions.

(3) The common source of all religion and faith and the common experience of all Prophets and their *Umma* is *tawḥīd,* through which comes liberation from slavery to false gods and commitment to the only God.[37]

(4) The methods of the prophets in the *daʿwa* are similar and the reception of the prophets by their followers is similar.[38]

(5) The *daʿwa* expressed in the Qur'ān is illustrated by the use of parable (*ʿibra*).[39]

(6) God gives the victory to His prophets and destroys those who belie them by revealing how the enemies of former prophets were destroyed. In this the Qur'ān confirms Muḥammad's prophethood

and urges the faithful to steadfastness to the message. In this sense God is faithful; He has been faithful, and He will surely be faithful in punishing those who belie His prophet.[40]

(7) The preaching of Muḥammad and the prophets is authenticated by the examples of what happened in previous eras.[41]

(8) God's grace is abundant for His prophets and those who are committed to Him.

(9) The sons of Adam are warned about Satan's treacherous ways and the enmity between Satan and Adam's progeny is eternal.

(10) God is omnipotent and His power transcends all nature.

(11) Good and evil are inevitably recompensed.

(12) Man's inadequate knowledge is as nothing compared with God's all-encompassing wisdom which penetrates beyond the unknown.

It is apparent from the discussion above that conservative Muslims have responded vehemently, not only to those who sought Western solutions to indigenous problems, but also in a special way to those who attempted to indigenize Western methodology in the study of scripture. The charge of anathema to the literary, historical, or critical study of religious texts, however, does not extend to exegesis of the Hebrew and Christian scriptures. In fact, many Muslim scholars delight in quoting extensively from Western sources on Biblical criticism. These quotations are used to affirm the Muslim contention that the Biblical texts are not authentic. They have been tampered with and are therefore useless, since they are not a direct verbal revelation from God to one prophet. This proves for Muslims their contention that Christians and Jews have distorted their own scriptures to validate their own evil ways.

The paradox of the validity of one methodology for the study of the scriptures of one faith and the sanctity of the traditional method for the study of the Qur'ān is not noted by a single author. It might be argued that the reason for this protectiveness about the "valid" method of studying the Qur'ān is out of fear that other methods may raise grave doubts about the authenticity of the divine origin of the Qur'ān or its validity for all time, especially if it is proved to have been revealed piecemeal according to the needs of certain occasions. In fact, however, Muslim writers do not talk about it in this context, but rather reject categorically any methods of study that do not proceed from the premise of the divine origin of the Qu'rān. In this way they remain committed to the affirmation of its superior authenticity and its unique position as the measure by which all preceding scriptures are judged.

Chapter Five
The Case of the Feminist Movement

ANOTHER ISSUE that has been of major concern to Arab Muslims is that of the role and status of women. Western writers have disparaged Islam as inferior because the perception of the division of roles in the family varied from the Western ideal. Particular criticism has been leveled against such patterns as polygamy, arranged marriages, seclusion, and what has been perceived as an inferior status ascribed to women.

The social norms were also challenged within the Islamic community in the nineteenth and early twentieth centuries by reformers who were anxious to "elevate" the status of women. Efforts at providing education were started as early as 1831 when Muḥammad ʿAlī opened a school for midwives. The first government-sponsored school for girls in Egypt was opened in 1874, one year after Rifāʿat Rāfiʿ al-Ṭahtāwī wrote *al-Murshid al-Amīn li-al-Banāt wa-al-Banīn* (The Faithful Guide for Girls and Boys) in which he advocated education for girls in order that they might be better wives for the educated young men.

Women's involvement in politics in the Arab world was evident in their anticolonial demonstrations as early as 1879 in Egypt when they helped distribute leaflets, and in the march against the British in 1919. When Mme. Hudā Shaʿrāwī formed the Feminist Union and dramatically removed her veil in 1923, it was with the intent of raising the status of women in Egypt to that of women in Europe. Thus efforts on behalf of the liberation of women were justified as maximizing the value for the local culture, the males being the ones benefiting most by acquiring parity with "civilized" culture.

The efforts to liberate and educate women were most successful among the educated urban elite. However, they were rejected by the recently urbanized since they exposed their women to the company of strange men. While acculturating Muslims in control of government policies continued to pay lip service to liberation policies, they were nonetheless very mindful of the strong resistance to such efforts by the normativists and the growing influence of the organization of Muslim Brotherhood.

As the pressures of the normativists and the neo-normativists increased in the early 1950s, so did those of the feminists. In 1951 they demanded political rights and marched on parliament, to little avail. In 1952 they organized a boycott of British goods and marched on Barclay's Bank. The coming of the revolution was welcomed by them, but when little attention was paid to their cause Durriyya Shafīq went on a hunger strike in 1954. Later she was to write,

> We had organized marches, held conferences, distributed pamphlets, trained scouts, occupied the parliament. There was nothing left but for women to fight with the men in a civil war, a thought we never contemplated, naturally. For our fathers, brothers, husbands, and sons are not our enemies no matter what they do and no matter how fast they hold to obsolete tradition.[1]

The conflict between the normativists and the neo-normativists on the one hand, and the acculturationists on the other, came to the fore during the preparation of the National Charter in Egypt. Both groups lobbied for their cause, the former insisting that women were to be restored to their traditional roles while the latter affirmed that not enough was being done to advance the cause of women.

In May 1962, the National Charter was published, reflecting the modernizing influence under the socialist reforms of Nasser. According to the Charter, "Woman must be regarded as equal to man and must therefore shed the remaining shackles that impede her free movement so that she might take a constructive and profound part in shaping life."[2]

The uproar with which this was received by the normativist Muslims is documented below. The fact that they had made their point by 1971 and have come into ascendancy under Sādāt is reflected in Article 11 of the constitution of the Arab Republic of Egypt: "The state shall guarantee the proper coordination between the duties of woman towards the family and her work in the society, considering her equal with man in the fields of political, social, cultural, and economic life without violation of the rules of Islamic jurisprudence."[3]

The material surveyed for this study of traditional affirmations concerning the role of women in Islam is taken from neo-normativist writings of the decade immediately following the formulation of the National Charter. Mainly apologetic in nature,[4] it was primarily aimed at women in an effort to stem the tide of imitating Western standards that were eroding the religious and legal foundations of Islamic society. In this context Islam is presented as the culmination of the historical development of the liberation of women. Surveys of the condition of women in different civilizations—Greek, Roman, Jewish, Persian, Chinese, Indian, Arab (pre-Islamic), and Christian—reveal that women were oppressed, for they were treated with disdain, as nonentities, nonpersons, or as delinquent. Men were allowed an indefinite number of women. Meanwhile Islam, the religion of God, has liberated women and restored them to their role, to which they were preordained. Thus Islam did not only free women from slavery, it elevated their status to that of human beings and gave them the right to live, the right to inherit, the right to learn, the right to keep their own names, and the right to have possessions.[5] One gets the feeling that most of these authors

> have packed their writings with the glories of the Arab woman in all the ages. However, no matter how extensive their collection of material may be, one is incapable of discerning a correct general opinion about woman in Islam. How did Islam save her? How did Islam elevate her to new heights? Rather, one finds in most of it general rhetorical words that need verification, documentation, and evidence.[6]

For most authors, what appears to be at stake is not the role of women per se, but rather the validity of Islam as the final revelation of God for mankind. Their works appear to be the echo of conservatism reaffirming the belief that Islam is *The Way of Life* and that all life is Islam. There is no differentiation between the secular and the sacred, between custom and the law. All life in Islam is to follow the teachings of the Qur'ān and the way of the Prophet—*sunnat al-nabī.*

Thus the writings of these authors in the defense of Islam are also aimed at the secularists, men like Qāsim Amīn and Khālid Muḥammad Khālid who ascribe the role of women to customs, which are subject to change and reform. Qāsim Amīn wrote: "Yes, I come with an innovation, however, it is not of the essence of Islam, rather it is of customs and methods of interaction in which it is good to seek perfection."[7] Thus by relegating the role of women to customs rather than the tenets of religion, Amīn could call for change and progress.

This approach is conceived by the conservative leaders as contrary not only to the teachings of the Prophet, but to the revelation of God. The role of women as prescribed by the Qur'ān is part of God's blueprint for man's happiness in this world and the next. It cannot be changed or altered. Muḥammad established the perfect society in Medina. Any change that would be tolerated in Islam would be to remove vestiges of pagan customs or innovations from the West, thus purifying society from corrupt practices and returning to the Way of God as decreed in the Holy Book.

Furthermore, these works are not only aimed at secularists and the women who are led astray by them, they are also addressed to those religious leaders who tend to ignore some verses in the Qur'ān that may not sound progressive, preferring rather to emphasize some positive aspects that agree with the movement to grant women social and political equality under the law. They are probably aimed at the writings and decrees of Maḥmūd Shaltūt, Rector of al-Azhar (d. 1963),[18] who reformed that institution and allowed women to be accepted as students. He also insisted that Islam gave women political rights since the Prophet accepted the *bay'a* from the women of Medina, meanwhile affirming that the Qur'ān treats male and female as equal in the sight of God. Woman thus is a partner in the initial formation of humanity and has the right to education and religious responsibility before God.[9]

At the heart of the debate is the attempt to limit the role of the woman to that ascribed to her by the traditions and to which traditional society had restricted her—that of wife and mother. This is not only her role, it is to be her sole identity. For in Islam marriage is a central institution; it is seen as an important social duty incumbent on each individual.[10] It is prescribed by the Qur'ān: ﴾And of everything we have created pairs: that ye may receive instruction﴿,[11] and by the Prophet who reportedly said, "If a person marries, he has fulfilled half the religion."[12] Consequently, "the individual has no right to do as he pleases. . . . If one does not marry, he deprives another from getting married, thus making him susceptible to temptation and evil."[13] In this context, marriage is seen as providing physical fulfillment for natural desires and a healthy channel for sexual and psychological needs, as well as the maintenance of society through progeny. Celibacy is reduced to a deviation, "contrary to the order of the universe as created by God,"[14] for it renders the goals of life inoperative.[15] Thus a Muslim girl should be brought up and educated in preparation for these roles. Any other education is at best superfluous, if not actually harmful.[16]

Contemporary discussion concerning the education of women is centered around the content, purpose, and utility of that education.

That women are to be educated seems to be taken for granted.[17] What is questioned is the policy of some departments of education to provide the same academic preparation for both boys and girls,[18] thus undermining the Islamic definition of the female role:

> If a woman is to be educated, what is suitable would be to learn the principles of religion, homemaking, child rearing and what is necessary concerning health, worship and human relations. For she who helps her husband in his life, cleaning his house, straightening his bed, and arranging his furniture is better than she who reads newspapers, writes articles, demands voting rights, and equal participation with men in Congress. By God she is not fit for that.[19]

A different education for women is necessitated not only by the roles they have to assume, but also by the fact of basic differences between the sexes. These differences are not culturally conditioned;[20] rather they are of the essence of creation, part of God's wisdom as he provided for balance and harmony in life. Male and female complement each other, each to fulfill the role for which they were preordained, each to uphold the other in their areas of weakness. It then becomes incumbent on Muslim society not only to refrain from tampering with God's order by introducing innovations, but also to maintain the differences:

> We must guide boys to roles that affirm their capabilities, and likewise the girls. Thus every sex should be placed in a fitting role. The Muslim administration of the home should be centered on the principle that the man is chief and is responsible for the administration of the external matters of the home, whereas the woman is responsible for raising the children, social services, and other necessities of society.[21]

Other authors elaborated on these differences, extolling the virtues of males and the weakness of females. The authority is given to man because he is the natural leader and reality thus necessitates his being in control.[22]

> The differences between males and females are due to (a) [a woman's] menstruation, conception, giving birth, breast feeding, staying up nights, and hard work during the day. [These] lead a woman to symptoms of depression and weakness of constitution. The man is free from all this. (b) Her work at home is limited in

> scope and experience; it is almost routine. As for the work of the man, it is wide in scope, extensive in experience and varied in relationships, full of scheming and artfulness. This leads to a marked difference in their intellectual capacity. (c) The woman in singing lullabies to her child does not need a powerful brain, or perfect genius; rather, she needs a kind nature and a gentle disposition. Nothing gives her more joy than to descend to the level of her child and to live with him in the scope of his world, thinking with his brain, talking in his language, playing with whatever pleases him. As for the male, he does not need affection to deal with people outside, rather he needs perseverance and strength of character, incisive intellect and initiative.[23]

The childishness of women is also seen by al-ʿAqqād:

> A woman is obsessed with the forbidden because she is silly, she has bad faith, she contradicts, she is ignorant, has a weak will and is incapable of patience in adversity. All this is because of a natural weakness in character. . . . She is similar to a developing child in her instinctive ignorance and curiosity. Ignorance and curiosity are concerned with destruction before they are trained to lead to constructive purposes.[24]

Thus Islam gives precedence to man because of the way he is created for he has been endowed with characteristics and capabilities, both physical and intellectual—which have not been given to women—that enable him to earn a living. Furthermore, scientific research has found that there are biological, physiological, and psychological differences which account for the "higher percentage of geniuses among men and the higher incidence of imbeciles among women."[25]

These elaborations on the shortcomings of women must not be seen as an indictment of the female sex, nor are they an attempt to subjugate women because of an innate male chauvinistic outlook. They must be viewed within the context of the faith and the defense of Islam. They are a response to condemnations from the outside, from missionaries and Orientalists, and to revolt from the inside, from secularists and women liberationists, who accused Islam of relegating women to an inferior status. The imitation of the West is seen as social imperialism. It is not imposed by the outside, but rather is generated from a feeling of inferiority and psychic servitude on the part of the women in the Arab world who appear to have no confidence in the validity and the adequacy of the Arab civilization. Thus where the missionary and the Orientalist have failed in undermining the culture, the women and their supporters are carrying the banner of insubordination. They are responding to acquired values, and flirting with alien and un-Islamic standards. Hence, the appeal is to women to preserve the Islamic society and protect it from Western influences and fluctuating institutions. It is a plea to stand united in defending Islam against innovation and change, a desperate appeal against participation in self-destruction.

Thus to contemporary writers, Islam does not say that women are inferior, rather that they are different. They have been created for a specific function in which they can excel.[26] Liberation should not mean acquiring male characteristics or performing masculine functions, which is reprehensible.[27] Rather, liberation for the woman is being herself and fulfilling the destiny to which God has created her. Liberation is not freedom from obedience to men, or freedom from the restrictions of the faith; rather, liberation must be freedom from the corruption and alienation that have been brought about by Western impingement on the East. It must be a liberation from measuring up to Western standards that erode the basic foundations of the community of God, a liberation from colonial status and imperialistic politics, a liberation to be oneself as God has willed for the welfare of humanity within the *Umma* of Islam.

At the heart of the argument is the traditional interpretation of S. 4:34 of the Qur'ān:

> ﴾Men are in charge of women, because God has endowed the one with more, and because they spend of their property for their support. Therefore the righteous women are the obedient, guarding in secret that which God has guarded. As for those from whom you fear rebellion, admonish them and banish them to separate beds, and scourge them. Then if they obey you, seek not a way against them. For God is High, ever Exalted, Great.﴿

This verse has led contemporary authors not only to emphasize the traditions that medieval Islam ascribed to the Prophet, but also to quote selective material that may substantiate an interpretation to the effect that man is in charge of the woman, that the wife must obey her husband, and that the husband has the right to discipline his wife.

Thus the emphasis on differences between the sexes upholds the necessity of man being responsible for women and defends the relevance and validity of the teachings of the Qur'ān for today. Islam is the natural religion and as such it affirms the goodness of human instincts and needs.

There seems to be a consensus of opinion that man is in charge of women; however, there are differences about what that involves. For some, a literal interpretation of the verse in the Qur'ān would imply superiority for the male as he is the provider of financial support.[28] Others see a potential threat in that interpretation.[29] For if superiority is contingent on capability to provide, the whole structure would be undermined if a woman acquired independent means and was able to support herself or her husband. Consequently, they ascribed superiority to physical and other differences.

Meanwhile, those who refuse to interpret the verse as an indicator of superiority of the husband over the wife interpret "in charge" to mean "having responsibility for."[30] Every social institution, no matter how small, needs a leader, for where there is no leadership, chaos and disintegration take over. In the case of the family, the role of leadership belongs to the husband, not because of extra merit, but as a responsibility assigned to him by God to safeguard society. This does not deny that the financial support of the family is the husband's responsibility; it just affirms that it is expected of him.

The insistence of most authors on the necessity of confining the woman to the house and not allowing her outside employment may stem from the contemporary situation in some Arab countries. One can see, for example, in socialist Syria, how the power of the husband over his wife and his absolute authority over the administration of the house and its finances is seen as being undermined. As more women seek employment and supplementary means of support, they are not only breaking the restrictions of seclusion by coming in contact with other people, both male and female, but they are also flirting with independence. The fact that the government guarantees the jobs of all who are employed provides more security than the marital status which is threatened by divorce. Furthermore, social security benefits liberate the employed female from being dependent on her children for support. It is reported that many women refuse to resign their jobs despite the insistence of their husbands. Thus independence breeds disobedience.

As mentioned above, that the wife should obey her husband is seen as the second teaching of S. 4:34 of the Qur'ān. This is usually bolstered by traditions ascribed to the Prophet that stipulate obedience as the means by which a wife attains heaven.[31] Asked who the best woman is, the Prophet is reported to have said, "She is the one whose sight gives you pleasure and the one who obeys your order without contradiction."[32] At another occasion it is reported that he said, "If it were permissible to have a human being worship another, I would order the woman to prostrate herself before her husband."[33]

Thus constant obedience is seen as sanctioned by the Qur'ān and the *ḥadīth.* It is part of the innate nature of things and the way a wife finds fulfillment and meaning in her life.

> The happiest hour for a woman is the hour of her surrender and obedience to the man. Her greatest desire is to have a husband whose power she can feel. . . . Being subservient is painful to a living being generally; however, for the woman, subservience fulfills the purpose of her femininity. She is grateful in her pain and victorious in her obedience.[34]

Furthermore, obedience to the husband does not demean the woman or detract from her self-respect, for that is the order of things.[35] She should not be in a position of authority because she is not qualified for that role. She lacks experience as well as ability, for she has not been capable of maintaining a position of responsibility despite opportunities to do so over the years. Thus:

> The best wife is she who is lively but obedient, affectionate and bears children, deferent, obedient to the reins, faithful when he is absent, modest when in company, reverent in her appearance, self-effacing when standing, sincere in her service of her husband, increasing his little into abundance, and removing his sorrow with her good conduct and gentle conversation.[36]

The authority of the husband is not limited to the administration of the house and the finances. The wife is required to be totally obedient concerning who visits her and where she can go. Her obedience is especially imperative in matters of sex, for the Prophet is reported to have said, "If a man calls his wife to his bed and she does not come and he sleeps in anger, the angels shall curse her until the morning."[37]

Al-Bayḥānī notes that Islam does not require of women more than was required of the Prophet's wives. Thus:

> The greatest thing in which obedience is imperative is intercourse, which is the goal of marriage. It is the most important thing the man asks of his wife. It is not permissible for her to

> refuse it except for a legal purpose such as menstruation, sickness, and childbirth. For if she does, she commits sin, and her right of clothing, housing, and upkeep from her husband becomes invalidated and God's curse will be upon her.[38]

Meanwhile, not all wives live up to the ideal. In fact, some authors note that women are incapable of doing so because of their innate nature, for the female tends to be obsessed with what is forbidden: "The story of the fall is the eternal symbol of the nature of women which never changes: i.e., she does whatever she is told not to do."[39] Consequently, women are prone to depravity if left to their natural instincts:

> Men are the sole source of every accepted definition of good conduct whether for men or for women. Woman has never been a true source of anything to do with ethics or good character even though she brings up the children. The guidelines are provided by the male.[40]

Therefore, the woman should be disciplined by her husband. His right to discipline is derived from his superior knowledge of what is good and beneficial. This right has been recognized and sanctioned by the Qur'ān and the Prophet and upheld by centuries of Islamic law.[41] Thus if she disobeys and is hard to manage, he should talk to her. If she "fails to respond to her husband's kind reproach, he should admonish her, for that is a sign that she has lost her human sensitivity and probably considers kindness as weakness in the man's character."[42] If she does not respond to admonition, he is to boycott her bed, for

> that is a treatment that restrains women from persisting in being contrary. [It is] humiliating to her pride for the thing she values most is her femininity and the strongest thing for attack she uses against man is this weapon. Thus by withholding sex from her and showing her that he is above her, that he does not care for her, he disarms her and cheapens her wares. That is the worst defeat she could suffer.[43]

If these methods do not work, physical punishment must be used for it is now clear that she has become like an animal. Most of the sources do insist that the husband must beat her gently.[44] If these methods do not work, he should seek arbitration. His final weapon, of course, is divorce.

A review of the contemporary literature on the role of women in Islam presupposes the husband-wife relationship as one threatened by antagonism, or at best a struggle for self-assertion and dominance. This is generally based on the idea of the polarity of the sexes, each sex representing different instincts and needs. Islam has provided the legislation that eradicates contention and leads to harmony and peace.

Parallel to the discussion of the role of the wife, the sources attempt to answer questions raised about polygamy. Generally, there is a consensus of opinion in defense of the custom. Several authors justify it as a means of safeguarding the family, since it does not necessitate divorce of the first wife as a prerequisite of marrying another as is the custom in the West. For, whereas Western man practices polygamy through multiple marriages contracted successively, in Islam, the possibility of having four wives concurrently protects these innocent women from the pain of separation and the shame of divorce.

The modernists' interpretation of S. 4:34 ⟨And if you fear that you will not deal fairly by the orphans, marry of the women, who seem good to you, two or three or four; and if you fear that you will not deal justly, then one or what your right hands possess. Thus it is more likely that ye will not do injustice⟩ puts the emphasis on one woman since the marriage of multiple wives is contingent on justice and the verse says that "ye will not do injustice." Thus modernists like Muḥammad ʿAbdu and his students have emphasized the necessity of limiting the number of wives to one. This interpretation is surprisingly contested by Shaltūt, who attacks the Egyptian Ministry of Social Affairs for its attempt in 1945 to introduce legislation that would restrict the number of wives to one. This legislation gives the judge the right to grant permission for marrying more wives after examination and verification that the man's character and financial means would support a second wife.[45]

> Any one who interprets the verse about plurality of wives and restricting their number to one is falsifying the revelation. . . . Polygamy is Islamic and the Sharīʿa has sanctioned it. As for the question of justice, that is left for the individual.[46]

Shaltūt's objection to restrictive polygamy or conditional monogamy is based on his sense of social justice. If the law stipulates that the man has to have the means to support more than one wife before he is allowed to marry another, only the rich can benefit. Consequently he suggests that "the leaders of the nation should seek legislation not to limit or restrict polygamy, but rather to put a limit on celibacy and to produce legislation to aid (financially) those who marry more than one to encourage others to follow suit and to help them pay for their wives and progeny."[47]

Others see S. 4:34 as restricting polygamy to four wives. Thus the Qur'ān did not initiate polygamy, they say, nor did it give license to multiple marriages; rather Islam limited, restricted, and regularized polygamy which is the law of nature. Furthermore, the virtues of polygamy allow justice for the husband in cases where the wife is barren, when she is sick, or is sexually frigid. It also has social benefits as it helps restore population in underpopulated areas, especially when there is an abundance of women after a war.[48]

Polygamy also helps solve social problems, such as when the wife is sick or suffering from a contagious or debilitating disease:

> What should a man do in this condition? Should he abstain for the rest of his life, and abstinence after marriage—as they say—is harder on the soul than before marriage? Should he divorce his sick wife and abandon her or expel her from the house in order to marry another? How could he send her out when she is in this condition? Where would she go, and where would she find shelter? What religion, what human conscience accepts that he would do this contemptible act, what could be more unjust than this? Should he bother the sick woman on her bed when she is in her weakest and least capable condition? What should the husband do . . . ?[49]

Another interpretation of the verse that is offered is that God made marrying more than one wife contingent on solving the problem of orphans, especially after a war.[50] The verse was revealed because these Muslims had obeyed God and refrained from burying their daughters when young; this legislation was intended to solve the problem of the abundance of women. Multiple wives insure that orphan girls are not left unmarried. This is consistent with the Islamic injunction against celibacy. Hence we note that current writings on the role of women tend to insist on polygamy as Islamic, as right, and as necessary.

One of the reasons given in defense of polygamy is the problem of the barren wife. A wife should be capable of bearing children. The Prophet is reported to have said, "A black woman who can bear children is better than a beautiful woman who is barren."[51] Children fulfill man's instinct for procreation and for the preservation of the species. They also provide support for the parents in their old age.[52]

The role of the mother in Islam is highly respected. It is attained by those who have persevered and fulfilled their duties as wives. The Qur'ān prescribes that parents should be respected and honored. Some *ḥadīths* suggest that the role of the mother is superior to that of the father:

> A man came to the Prophet and asked him "Who should I respect and obey?" The Prophet answered, "Your mother." Then he asked, "Who then?" The Prophet answered, "Your mother." Then he asked, "Who then?" The answer came, "Your mother." Then he asked, "Who then?" He answered, "Your father. Thus obedience comes three times to the mother before the father."[53]

The relationship between a mother and her son is considered a very deep and special one, a spiritual endowment that makes her the sole "source of life."[54] It is a relationship that does not involve the father. Whereas the husband-wife relationship is seen as a polarity of two elements often in tension, that of mother and son is one of serene harmony. The son not only obeys his mother, but he provides for her needs and protects her from whatever disturbs her:

> For the mother has suffered a great deal for her son. Long has she stayed up so he can sleep, and labored and became tired that he may rest, and suffered so he can be happy, was hungry so he can eat, she put him above herself. Her happiest moment is when she sees him happy, smiling, healthy, intelligent. She is always ready to ransom him with whatever she possesses—no matter what the price is. Can the son forget her good deeds?[55]

Thus the patience of the wife pays off in great dividends. She is recompensed by the devotion and obedience of her children. As a mother, her life is fulfilled and her identity is established, for a careful observation of Arab society reveals that the dual and complementary role of wife and mother presents a generally accurate picture of the way a woman is perceived and of the way she perceives herself.

The special role of the mother may be attributed to the fact that in most cases the son is the only man in her life with whom she has a loving relationship. This may be caused by the general attitudes and sanctions of society concerning male-female relationships. These include the tendency to segregate the sexes, the emphasis that any association between male and female can only be or lead to a sexual relationship,[56] the restrictions against women openly expressing emotions towards men, the predominance of arranged marriages, the frequent discrepancy in the age of the couples, and the woman's fear of divorce and its contingent stigma.

Thus the only free and loving relationship is that between a mother and her son. It is free because it is the only one sanctioned by society. By the time the son is in his late teens or early twenties, he assumes the role of the provider. Thus the older the son becomes, the greater the increase in the status of the mother as she tends to centralize power and assume the running of the household. Where there is a great discrepancy in age between husband and wife, the old and tired husband retires while the wife comes into her own.

When the son marries, the daughter-in-law is initiated into the role of the wife who labors patiently and obeys silently, waiting for the day of her liberation through her son. Meanwhile, the mother, having survived the test of being a wife, can now become a member of the elite—those who supervise and regulate the mores, customs, and sanctions of society.

The traditional role of the mother includes the supervision of her son's wife and making sure that her daughter-in-law adheres to her role as defined by society and sanctioned by Islam. It will be interesting to observe how this role of the mother changes as the incidence of nuclear families increases and that of extended families declines.

One wonders whether the shift in emphasis in contemporary literature from the superiority of the male per se to an analysis of differences and an affirmation of religious models for the roles of women is an attempt to maintain a status quo in a society that is changing rapidly, or whether it is a traditional Islamic attempt at recapturing an "idealized reality" in a situation of flux.

The latter alternative would explain the current discussion and debate concerning social and political rights of women. That women have been given these rights in Egypt is a matter of fact. Futhermore, there are professional women working as secretaries, engineers, lawyers, hostesses, congresswomen, doctors (even taking care of male patients), etc. What is surprising is the amount of literature published during the last ten years that condemns these achievements, affirming that such innovations undermine society and lead to its disintegration.

These authors tend to view the demands for social and political rights as at best misguided:

> Women have misunderstood the Islamic principle. The decrease in the woman's responsibility does not mean a decrease in her

> worth. Justice means that each should do what is best for him and this is what Islam has decreed.[57]

That the witness of a woman in Islamic law is equated to half that of a man is cited by several authors as the proof of the inability of a woman to be rational, detached, and fair. As a female she is overcome by emotion, which is the single governing factor in her life. Consequently al-Ghazzālī asks, "How can half a witness be a judge?"[58] And al-ʿAqqād repeats that being a judge is not within the realm of her role, nor are social and political rights:

> Women have rights other than those of voting—these are the rights of a mother, the rights of a wife, of a fiancée, of a friend, who inspires the mind, the emotion and the imagination. If these rights are paralyzed in her hands, that would be the bankruptcy of femininity which cannot be replaced by law or by voting rights.[59]

The fairness of the discrepancy between the rights of husbands and wives is justified, for

> Justice is well served in this system, for a woman always knows that the child she is bearing is definitely hers, whereas the man never has that certainty concerning those that are called his children.[60]

In this manner, we note that the contemporary conservative arguments are necessarily repetitious inasmuch as they are an affirmation of an inalienable truth. Male and female they were created by God; they may be equal in His sight, but He did create them as male and female, distinct—each for a specific purpose and function to fulfill His will in creation. The roles have been defined and delineated by Islamic law to uphold the community of God, the community of the faithful.

Hence Westerners attempting to understand the contemporary liberation of women in the Arab world must seek to comprehend the objections and restrictions that these movements face. The "liberated" Arab woman must seek to find her identity within the community, for Islam exists as the integration of the individual and the communal. What this means in practical terms is that one cannot be a Muslim outside of the context of the community; consequently the emphasis is on cooperation versus competition. God's word, the Qur'ān, was not made manifest to redeem the individual as an individual and set him free; its primary goal was the establishment of a community living under the law and guidance of God, a community committed in prayer and obedience to His will.

In this context liberation is not seen as freedom from the "oppression" of men; rather, it is seen in cosmic dimensions as rebellion against God and His order for the world and mankind.

This is not to disregard the fact that several reformers have called for equality and the emancipation of women. Naẓīra Zayn al-Dīn, in *Al-Sufūr wa-al-Ḥijāb* in 1928, talked about the necessity of the freedom of each individual in order to build a progressive society. Her appeal was directed towards men in Egypt because they were in control.

In a similar manner, Qāsim Amīn, one of the pioneers of women's liberation through education in Egypt, wrote:

> Ask the married people if they are loved by their wives. Their answer is "yes." However, the truth is other than what they think. I have searched extensively in families where it is said that there is total harmony, but I have not yet found a man who loves his wife, nor a woman who loves her husband. As for the apparent harmony between the pair, it is due either to the fact that the man is tired and has left, or that the wife has permitted her husband to treat her as though she were his private property, or that both of them are ignorant and not aware of the value of life. This latter is the condition of most Egyptians. . . .
>
> As for the first two kinds, harmony has been bought at a high price—the disintegration of one of the partners for the sake of the other. All that I will admit is that it is possible at times to see what appears like affection between married couples. This is the exception that proves the rule, which is lack of love. It is lack of love on the part of the husband because his wife is below him in mentality and education—so that there is almost no communication that would lead to an instant of mutual happiness. There is almost nothing on which they agree. That is because she is so distant from his emotions, understandings, and matters that appeal to him, while she indulges in things in which he has no interest.[61]

In this commentary, Qāsim Amīn isolated one of the factors that plagued Egyptian society at his time. The education of women, he argued, would lead to mutual respect, understanding, and compatibility. He had to appeal to men and convince them of the utility of the education of women, for it would lead to a happier home life—for the man.

The present resurgence of Muslim garb for women is dismissed by cynics as a means for receiving a scholarship from funds allocated specifically for that purpose by conservative forces in the Arab world. While it might be true, this does not take away from the fact that young people appear to be responding favorably to the invitation to return to the roots of their heritage. This is done not only as a defense against what they see as the immorality and decadence of Western cultural patterns, but to appropriate anew God's guidance for family life in order to build a strong united nation committed to the ideology of Islam as the only road of salvation for the world.

Conclusion
Towards an Islamic Response to the Challenge of History

It is clear from the discussion presented above that Muslim thought has undergone some change in emphasis as a result of its generally defensive posture throughout the twentieth century. Questions raised and challenges perceived have elicited responses and proposed solutions offered by their advocates as representative of the true essence of Islam, an essence that has been hidden through years of accumulated acculturation. Islam is accepted by all Muslims, save atheistic Marxists, as the religion of God.

The discussion among acculturationist and normativist Muslims has focused not on the adequacy and validity of Islam for modern life, but on the definition of what constitutes true Islam. Both groups agree that Islam must continue to provide the purpose of the *Umma* for the future, although they disagree on the scope and content of this Islam. To some acculturationists religion is perceived as something that deals with the spiritual aspects of life, and as such must not be intricately involved in the shaping of the social order. The normativists, on the other hand, have insisted that Islam is a total system that is constantly molding and shaping all aspects of life to conform to divine guidance.

All of the literature affirms the validity, eternality, and inerrancy of the Qur'ān concerning all matters of life. The power of Islam comes in the affirmation that the Qur'ān is truly the word of God, and as such contains guidance for everyday living, as well as in the interpretation of the community of this guidance as it has been both manifested and preserved in history. Islam is thus a nation with a divine mission. That is to say that God has revealed His will in the Qur'ān, preserved in pristine condition, and the mission of the Muslim community is to live in dedication to carrying out that will and making it manifest to all mankind.

The Qur'ān can only be truly understood through the historical events and circumstances of the Islamic community. Without this kind of direct experience by the *Umma* it becomes only a document, rather than the potent record of God's word for His community as the locus for and record of the fulfillment of His guidance and promise. The community thus not only bears witness to this truth, but also becomes the living witness of the viability of God's way of life. By failing to live up to the promise of the Qur'ān, therefore, the Muslims have failed in their mission to the world. The *Sīra* of the Prophet and the continuing history of the community preserve the context of the revelation and imbue it with its particular divine significance. Thus the revivification of true Islam is necessary for the salvation of the world from itself, from self-centeredness, and from overindulgence in materialism.

Neo-normativist literature perceives Islam as intimately involved in history, both as an historical community and as a nation anxious to appropriate its role as shaper and maker of world history. The acculturationists tend to see reality in terms of the flow of history exclusively; the metaphysical is set aside, removed from view, lest it hinder Muslims from effectively participating in the movement of history and thus from having an impact on the human condition. For the neo-normativist, the Islamic world view and the human relationship to the word is integrally involved in history, not only as a record of this relationship but as its guidance and sustenance. To operate outside the Islamic sphere is to opt for the world of *Jāhiliyya,* outside the sphere of the mercy of God, and to live in evil and decadence.

Neo-normativist Islam affirms the unity of God and rejects the materialistic involvement of both the capitalist and communist West. This, however, does not lead to the kind of world-denying attitude that characterized much of Sufism. Rather, there is a constant affirmation of Islamic involvement in the world, not only as necessary but as an inherent part of God's will. Islam is seen as the religion of *dīn wa-dunyā,* the affirmation of this world and the hereafter, and of the direct link between the two.

According to this perspective, man assumes his true role as vicegerent of God on earth, functioning as His agent, guarding the interests and purposes of God for the welfare of humanity. This is not a return to the Muʿtazilite understanding, but rather a rejection of any tendency towards divine predestination. It does not assume that man's destiny is in any sense solely in his own hands, but challenges him with responsibility not only for his own actions but for the behavior of the

Umma. It urges him to respond with commitment both as a defensive posture, protecting the faith from outside assaults, and as the positive affirmation and acceptance of his commission to invite the world to participate in the true faith of God, in the community of Islam.

Part Two
The Significance of History: The Perspective of Neo-Normative Arab Muslims

Introduction

THE CONTEMPORARY ARAB'S search for dignity, purpose, and identity has led to an intense concern for the understanding of his own history and for the role of Islam in shaping this history. This concern, which has become almost an obsession, is manifested in the flow of new books on history inundating the Arab market. These writings differ in quality and in area of concentration; some are localized studies and others attempt a more comprehensive overview of the history of Arab Islam. Scarcely any works have been written, however, dealing with the philosophy of history, although there are a few translations of Western historians with discussion of their concepts of history.[1]

A small number of Arab writers have turned their attention to developing what might be called a philosophy, or perhaps more accurately, a theology of history. Part Two deals with seven such contemporary Arab authors whose works have not as yet been translated or evaluated in Western sources. They are distinguished from those discussed in the first section by the fact that they have addressed themselves to an Islamic understanding of history, several of them attempting to delineate the nature and scope of this methodology. The works, as might be expected, are written for different audiences. Some of the authors are academicians while others are so-called popular writers. Three common elements justify the inclusion of their writings in this study: they are recent (since the 1960s); they address themselves to the question of an Islamic methodology for historical study and an Islamic view of history; and they have yet to be analyzed by Western scholars. The recent emphasis on an Islamic consciousness discussed earlier in this study suggests the growing importance of these writers' concern for the understanding of history.

Most of these works are apologetic in nature. They perceive the Western world as a threat to Islam and Western scholarship as an undermining element, a potential tool for the destruction of Islamic identity. It is interesting to note that several of the authors are graduates of Western universities and appear to have reacted against the "intellectual imperialism" of the West. The writers considered in this study (with the possible exception of Jaʿfar) raise serious questions about the methodology of the secular historians.[2] To some extent they use it and in the process adapt and revise it so that it becomes de facto Islamic rather than Western. They also tend to look upon and therefore portray the West as the perennial enemy of Islam that has tried by different means to undermine and destroy the faith and has finally succeeded in making inroads into the Muslim community through the secularization of the educational system. In so doing, they say, the West in effect has usurped the role of guide and interpreter for the life of the Muslim community; several generations of educated people have arisen who have a vested interest in the perpetuation of this system.

In the opinion of these writers, the secularization of education has led to the writing of books on Islamic and Arab history from a secularized perspective. Thus events are judged by alien standards and an alien comprehension which threaten to undermine the cohesiveness of the Islamic community. Not only do secularizied Arab historians emulate Western methodology and understanding, they have even perpetuated the Orientalist misunderstandings concerning the dynamics of Islamic history in which Western achievements are glorified. Thus they have put the emphasis on sects, schisms, and civil strife in Islam rather than paying attention to the role of spiritual factors, motives, and forces at play in the understanding of the community.

In their exercise of *epoche,* contend these writers, the secularized historians are portraying at best partial truths, failing to see that the most dynamic force in history is the spiritual dimension. In their efforts they are portraying falsehood. By generally giving greater attention to Western achievements than to Islamic ones, they may well be fostering an inferiority complex in Muslim young people vis-à-vis the West. By emphasizing battles, they perpetuate the idea that the Islamic civilization is full of petty and perverse leaders, while those of the West are dynamic and forceful.

Consequently, several of the authors insist that there is a need to rewrite history from the Islamic perspective. Authors of such texts must be Muslims committed to the faith and must write the history from the perspective of their commitment, providing the world with an Islamic understanding of knowledge, the world, and reality. In this way history is perceived as a tool for preparing individuals to assume the role of committed Muslims. It is therefore utilitarian—didactic and even homiletic—guiding the community toward the way of God. History must show the areas of weakness in the community and indicate how these can be rectified. It must identify the strengths and powers of the Islamic way and help show the necessity of assuming this way for the welfare of all. Thus it can provide the incentive for and the prototype of what is to be recaptured from history of the true Islamic community. It must be written from a holistic point of view so that there will be no bifurcation of life into secular and sacred. Finally it must provide the correct appreciation of each achievement, separating that which is ephemeral and vacuous from that which is of eternal value.

All the authors discussing an Islamic interpretation of history emphasize the importance of unicity (*tawḥīd*) as the central Islamic concept through which everything is to be perceived. Although there are differences in emphasis on what this *tawḥīd* means, it is perceived as the integrating factor of all life. It is the means by which man assumes his vicegerency on earth and is able to function as an agent of God's will working for His purpose in this world. It denotes the freedom from submission to any being, ideology, or power other than God, as well as the liberation from servitude to the self and to others. It is the emancipation from the fear of the powers of evil. *Tawḥīd* makes possible the integration of the whole personality in both thought and conduct.

Tawḥīd is not only the primary factor in the integrating of individuals, it also operates in the community's affirmation of its commitment to the way of God. Thus the unity of God endows the faithful community with a unity of identity, of function, of destiny, and of purpose. Together the community commands the good and forbids the reprehensible, aiding in the eradication of falsehood and ungodliness from the earth.

Thus a community operating within the framework of unity strives to bring about an order which is in accordance with God's will for mankind. It endows the community with an apprehension of reality that allows no division between sacred and secular. The totality of life in all its aspects, whether social, political, or economic, is assumed by unicity. Thus all aspects of history are integrated into a whole. In this kind of holistic view there is no past, present, and future as distinct chronological divisions. From the divine perspective time is a single unit; all proceeds from God the creator and all returns to Him through whom every creature has its being and its fulfillment.

As indicated in Part One, the authors discussed here share in the general awareness that something has gone awry in the process of Islamic history and that the Arabs have lost their ascendancy and are in a state of retardation. This condition, they believe, was precipitated by the faithlessness of the Muslims and not from Islam itself as the missionaries, the Orientalists, the Westernizers, the secularists, and the Marxists have tended to emphasize. Islam is eternal and perfect and as such is separate from Muslims. They can only appropriate it by commitment, zeal, and fervor and not through acquisition of alien, hence ungodly, methods. In fact, the ascendancy of the materialistic West (both capitalist and Marxist) makes the challenge even greater as it demands extra sacrifices from the believers to reject the glitter of materialism and false ideology and seek perfection in the way of God through personal and corporate growth and constant awareness of God's dominion and majesty over all.

Only through this personal endeavor can Islam become dominant in the world, for God has promised victory to the believers if they are steadfast and constant in faithfulness. Only through consistent rejection of the West and its allures can the community restore its potency and effectiveness as an agency for the spread of God's word. Compromises with the forces of evil and the ungodly will lead to loss and the deterioration of mankind. Thus Muslims have a grave burden to carry. Entrusted with a precious message for the salvation of the world, they must either be responsible for the spread of that message or share the destiny of other unfaithful civilizations that preceded Islam which were reduced to ruins.[3] Implicit in the concern of the authors for an Islamic way of life is the fear that if Muslims fail in their mission God may raise others to carry the torch of "civilization" and "progress." Meanwhile, they are quite explicit about the fact that the present condition of Muslim states does not mean that the torch has been passed to the West. The West may be experiencing a period of strength, but its present ascendancy is the product of Muslim laxity. If the Muslims are willing to sacrifice and to assume the burden of leadership, they can recapture the glory of the past and establish God's order, thus gaining ascendancy, power, and potency in the world.

The authors arrive at their conclusions through different methods.

All, however, are constantly aware of the Qur'anic view of the rise and fall of nations and the flourishing and deterioration of civilizations. They seem to use the terms Islamic and Qur'anic interchangeably, and whenever an Islamic philosophy of history is advocated, it is seen from the perspective of the Qur'ān. In fact, the Qur'ān acts as the final arbiter of the authenticity or falsehood of the philosophies of Toynbee, Durant, Hegel, Spengler, and Marx. Several authors discuss these philosophers to reveal their inadequacies because of the popularity of their translated works among students of history. When their ideas are not explicitly repudiated, their similarity to the Qur'anic view of life (e.g., that nations flourish, mature, and die) is usually referred to as their partial truth, while that of the Qur'ān is complete and perfect and has preceded Western philosophies by many centuries.

This does not keep al-Jundī, for example, from providing a discussion of Islamic history by using Toynbee's framework. The emphasis on religious zeal as a factor in the rise of nations is appropriated and the role of the *mujaddid* (reformer of the age) in Islam is presented as the hero (*baṭal*) who faces all odds and restores civilization to truth and the rightful way.[4] His role becomes especially important since Muḥammad was the seal of the Prophets and no prophetic additions are allowed to God's word for humanity. The *mujaddid* is therefore limited to assisting in the purification of society from the accretion of alien matter and guiding it again to its determined fulfillment.

In the view of these writers, all the efforts of Western philosophers of history are paltry compared to the breadth and depth of the comprehensive view of the Qur'ān. While faithful to the Qur'anic understanding of life, the authors discussed below approach their material from several perspectives. Some expound the process, movement, and flow of history while others attempt to interpret the Qur'anic passages. Only Jaʿfar talks about history from the understanding of history of religions, comparing it to the Christian and Jewish ideas of God and His relation to the world.

For all the authors there is an awareness that there are some who denigrate their commitment to the faith of the fathers and accuse them of being backward and irrelevant. This, however, does not decrease their zeal. They welcome their position as a remnant of the faithful and believe they are courageous to voice what others may consider to be outmoded views. They expect to be attacked from without and within, but their assurance of the perfection of the revelation gives them the courage to face their critics. This assurance comes with the proof of the validity of the Islamic concept, because it has persisted despite incessant assault by its enemies since the beginning and because it offers the best understanding of the perfect and valid laws of history as revealed by God.

Chapter Six
The Apologetic Response

THE APOLOGETIC RESPONSE proceeds from the awareness of the decline of Muslim civilization vis-à-vis the West. It attempts to provide a justification for faithfulness to Islam despite its "apparent" inadequacy in the arena of nations. The defense rests on the unwavering belief in its eternal validity for all time and its relevance for the modern world.

Maḥmūd al-Sharqāwī's understanding of history is contingent on the significance of *tawḥīd* which he sees as the essential teaching of Islam.[1] He also perceives Islam as a total way of life, a complete system that speaks to all of life's questions, whether they deal with religion or worldly affairs. His *al-Tafsīr al-Dīnī li-al-Tārīkh* (*Religious Interpretation of History*),[2] however, suggests that this concept of unity may not be essentially or necessarily unique to Islam. It appears to him, in fact, to have been the secret behind the success of all great civilizations. Thus he assumes that it is what he calls the religious character in general which encompasses all life and which when diligently implemented assures progress of the nation. This religious character he equates with *tawḥīd*.[3]

Although the subtitle of *Religious Interpretation of History* specifies that "History Is Humanity's Way to God," the content of the book concentrates on God's laws and the necessity of individual attendance to them. Thus it is clear that for al-Sharqāwī history is in fact a record of man's efforts to live life according to divine commandments. The way to God is not through mere human endeavor or unguided exploration of various possible avenues, but in adherence to God's laws which have been preordained and are eternal and unchanging. These laws have a predetermined consequence from which there is no escape. Any deviation from God's way leads to destruction, annihilation, or at best degeneration in civilization. The factor that insures victory and success in matters of the world is what he calls "the spiritual breath" (*nafḥa rūḥiyya*), a kind of religious zeal that permeates the nation or community and leads to its victory.

Al-Sharqāwī's efforts to be consistent lead him to ascribe this religious zeal to every conquering nation. The very fact of victory is a positive proof that the nation was in accord with the requirements of the spiritual breath that permeated its society; moreover, its victory was part of divine design. God gives victory, hence it must be assumed that any nation that succeeds must by definition have been righteous and have followed the religion of God. Al-Sharqāwī reduces all history to God's constant victory over people who are unrighteous, living in error, or ignoring His presence. The consistency of this law as perceived by al-Sharqāwī is apparent in the history of all nations and all victorious societies. To their leaders, if not the common people, is ascribed, again by definition, a commitment to unicity.

Thus Alexander, Zoroaster, the Assyrians, and many other successful peoples are seen as actors in the drama of humanity in which righteousness invariably wins, not only in specific instances but in the wider scope of the dominance of its civilization and the ability to impose its will on others. To have a powerful, potent, and well-functioning civilization is to have God's approval because of a commitment to His religion, to unicity, and to an appropriation of the religious spirit, or spiritual breath. This spiritual breath is also a necessary component of progress and advancement. For although the rise and fall of nations is repetitive and bound by unchanging laws, it is the zeal with which the spiritual breath is appropriated that makes the difference between defeat and victory, between failure and success, between following and leading.

Although al-Sharqāwī states that progress and advancement are an essential part of life,[4] he does not articulate the specific ways in which one civilization is more progressive than the others. The implications are left for the reader to deduce. For him it appears that history is repetitive rather than cyclical, reduced to the rise and fall of empires as conditioned by their appropriation of or dissociation from the religion of unicity. Thus God is in control of all nations, deciding their destiny according to the choices they make and based on their steadfastness to His truth.

Al-Sharqāwī agrees with Sayyid Quṭb that Muslims are in a retarded condition.[5] This condition has been precipitated because they have ignored the truth as revealed in the Qur'ān. In the same manner as Sayyid Quṭb, al-Sharqāwī asserts that it is not Islam that is the cause of the Muslim's retardation, but rather the Muslims themselves as well as the imperialist states who have exploited them. (This opinion, as we shall see, is also shared by Anwar al-Jundī.)

Al-Jundī also supports the idea of borrowing from other civilizations caught in an eternal drama whose plot never changes. Not only are the laws of history constant, but the beliefs of men are the same, the questions are the same, the answers are the same—only the characters change. Those who ascend to a position of leadership are there because they have been judged more zealous than their contemporaries in adherence to the changeless truths. The competition between nations is not determined by political or military power or by cultural achievements and new breakthroughs. These are but the by-products of the real competition, which he sees to be the degree of zeal exhibited by nations in serving God's cause, or in al-Sharqāwī's phrase, in exhibiting and exemplifying the spiritual breath.

In his attempt to isolate the normative nature of the Qur'anic paradigms of history, he reduces Islam to a manifestation of the universal law rather than a unique paradigm that has succeeded in guarding the perfect and pure nature of the revelation. The a priori acceptance of a divine law that controls all history provides a uniformity of interpretation as we see in al-Sharqāwī's work. Anwar al-Jundī, on the other hand, attempting to give more credit to the idea of change, progress, and forward movement, is able to see a kind of integrative law, realizing that in fact some Islamic nations have functioned in a leadership position while others have faltered and lagged seriously behind.[6]

Al-Jundī views Islam as having appeared in the fullness of time when humanity was in dire need of its message. Islam, therefore, is "history's movement towards freedom."[7] Other societies, cultures, and religions have been partial, their experience and achievements limited by their lack of access to the truth in its entirety. Differing from al-Sharqāwī in this view of history, al-Jundī agrees with him in seeing religion as an active factor in the development of civilization:

> For humanity in its long progress and its continuous stages of growth meets in the realm of history with cultures and religions, with prophets, messengers, and guidance by stages, for religions are the source of civilization, while the messages of heaven and the call of reformers give guidance to humanity to the [right] way. However, it is all regional, appearing in one nation or culture.[8]

While other religions have been regional, national, or ethnic, Islam came as a new message that reformulated human thought and civilization according to the understanding of unicity. It is, therefore, both comprehensive and inherently perfect.

Based on unicity, the unity of the universe and the integration of the forces of nationhood, Islam is the only system that provides for the coming together of body and spirit in man, of worship and works in life, of the world and the hereafter in religion, and of heaven and earth in the universe.[9]

Whereas al-Sharqāwī sees all human history as Islamic history, the drama of commitment to God's cause followed by recompense or deviation followed by punishment, al-Jundī understands Islamic history as part of human history, and as such competing with other alien civilizations which are considered in a very real sense to be enemies of Islam. Al-Jundī also tends to see the rise and fall of the fortunes of the Islamic community as part of the natural process of history itself, just as an organism matures and dies, giving way to younger, more vibrant, and more potent forces. He is satisfied that Islam or the Islamic *Umma* has always provided the young leadership to take hold of the destiny of the community. He appears also satisfied that having done so before, the Islamic community will continue to provide the necessary leadership. The crisis in which Islam finds itself is not due to its having erred in any way, but is rather because Islam happens to be in the ebb phase of its natural growth and development.

Islamic history, according to al-Jundī, falls naturally into six divisions. The first he calls the age of building the Muslim community, which lasted 23 years and was supervised by the Prophet in Mecca and Medina. The second is one of expansion which lasted about 114 years. The third is the development of Islamic thought in an effort to stem the tide of growing diversity, accompanied by the building of an Islamic civilization. The fourth is the age of crisis and invasion by foreigners such as the Crusaders and Tartars from without and the Assassins from within. The fifth is the appearance of the Ottoman, Safavid, and Moghul Empires. This lasted until 1830 when France conquered Algeria and the East. The sixth and last stage is the Arab-Muslim awakening which began with the call to unity in the Arab world and the occupation of Muslim countries by Western powers.[10]

While al-Jundī admits that "Islam in history is a greater movement than the Arab nation, the Muslim nation or Islamic civilization, and deeper in scope than what ties it to politics, civilization or culture,"[11] he still sees a special role for the Arab people by virtue of their having been a chosen people and because the Prophet was an Arab and the Qur'ān was revealed in the Arabic language. He also sees a special role for Arab Muslims in the renewal of Islam in the contemporary period and underlines the necessity for Arabs to carry forward the message and understanding of Islam.[12] While he, of course, views

Islam as greater than the Arabs alone (Islam, he says, has always attacked and will continue to attack regionalism in favor of the totality of Islamic history and identity), he considers that there must now be a modern Arab renaissance. In this way Arabs will act as the vanguard for the resurgence of a dynamic Islam.

Modern civilization for al-Jundī is a development of Muslim civilization and is therefore not alien to it. It needs, however, to be more fully Islamized.[13] He has no hesitation in urging reappropriation of anything from the West, because it was all taken from Islam in the first place. When Muslims appropriate Western civilization, he says, they are not deviating from Islam but actually taking back that which was inherently part of their own system. Even scientific method itself is Islamic. Furthermore, Islam is not restricted to one cultural input but is the composite effort of all humanity with all of its experience and heritage amalgamated within the framework of an Islamic ideology and world view. The perversion of Western civilization has come through its addition of materialistic elements to what was originally Islamic, thus separating it from things of the spirit. In separating science and religion, the West has developed a system which is actually at variance with matters of religion, esotericism, and ultimately of unicity.

Al-Jundī also supports the idea of borrowing from other civilizations because he sees Islamic civilization as constantly being reformulated due to the process of challenge and response. Part of the dynamism of Islam, he says, comes from its ability to move forward progressively in response to every challenge from outside. Even decline, or what would appear to be decline, he understands as part of the process through which Islamic civilization is constantly being reformulated. Islam is resilient, strong, and fully capable of meeting all challenges. It absorbs the achievements of other cultures, Islamizes them, and, in the case of Western culture, restores them to their Islamic source.[14]

Because Islam has the potential to correct itself from deviation, it does not need guidance from the outside. The corrective forces are within it ready to redirect it whenever there is an error. Though the leaders may be different and the means varied, the goal is the same—to move forward and upward toward the unity of humanity in justice, equality, and freedom. Thus what Islam appropriates from other cultures (or reappropriates, as the case may be), it assimilates according to its own original Islamic concepts of unicity, prophecy, equality, and justice. While al-Sharqāwī sees a repetitious form in which all civilizations are built on unicity, which he understands as proof of their survival, al-Jundī sees non-Muslim cultures as coexisting but alien. Elements from these cultures can be appropriated and recast according to Islamic principles and norms, i.e., Islamized, assuring that this appropriation is not simply borrowing or copying.[15]

Al-Jundī borrows from Sidney Hook, the American philosopher, the concept of the hero (*baṭal*), which he interprets in the framework of the traditional Islamic *mujaddid* or reformer. In this process he is employing the methodology of appropriation and reintegration which he so strongly advocates. He considers the hero to be central in leading the community in four areas—as reformer, as the one invested with the responsibility to command the good and forbid the evil, as scientist, and as statesman. The hero is he who responds to the needs of society, who appropriates the necessary power, and leads the community forward. This leadership is essential for the progress of Islam and because of it "it is possible to say that the waves of Islamic history represent successive forward motions of effective leadership on the road to the realization of the inevitability of Islam."[16]

These concepts of motion and progress suggest that for al-Jundī the perfect Islamic society has yet to be realized. It was not fully achieved in the past and it is not existent today. It exists as a future ideal, however, and as efforts continue to be directed toward its implementation Islam continues to move toward that goal of a fully just and a fully integrated universal community.

Chapter Seven
The Traditional Response

THE TRADITIONAL RESPONSE can be distinguished from the apologetic response in method and content. While al-Sharqāwī and al-Jundī have integrated Islamic and Western methodology, streamlining their findings to appropriate for Islam all normative assertions, both Quṭb and al-Ḥajjī reject the ascription of validity to alien considerations. The content of their work is homiletic in nature, with a persistent warning that the West is to be rejected totally because only Islam can define the content and method of what is Islamic.

Sayyid Quṭb's *Fī al-Tārīkh: Fikra wa-Minhāj* is concerned with the defense of Islam and its history against its detractors.[1] Admitting that Islam is presently in a state of weakness and exhaustion due to the unrelenting assaults of the imperialists and the many centuries of carrying the burden of civilization for the world, he insists that this condition does not suggest that Islam suffers from an incurable disease that could lead to its demise. The very fact that Islam has survived long centuries of inactivity and persecution is actually an affirmation of its divine origin and approval and proves that it is God's will that Islam is to persist.[2] Thus its survival is a test of its validity, says Quṭb, the intimation of its divine origin and destiny, and the hope for its revival and victory. The preservation of the Islamic community or *Umma* is due to the persistence of the doctrine (*ʿaqīda*).[3] Imbued with the spirit of God, the *ʿaqīda* assures survival of the *Umma* precisely because God Himself does not die. His eternality endows the community with perseverance and continuity and assures its eventual supremacy. Thus it behooves Muslims to hold fast to this doctrine around which the Islamic civilization is to be rebuilt.

The *Umma* in its involvement with progress and social change does not act as an observer registering human frailty or achievement, but as an agent of progress urging humanity to develop, to grow, and to withstand pressures. "The mission of Islam is always to propel life to renewal, development, and progress and to press human potentialities to build, to go forth, and to elevate."[4] This progress cannot be achieved through imitation of the West, for though strong at present the West is destined to eventual failure because it is based on shaky foundations and because it worships the false gods of production, wealth, and pleasure. Quṭb records his own observations about American life in a striking passage:

> I do know how people live in America, the country of the great production, extreme wealth, and indulgent pleasure. . . . I saw them there as nervous tension devoured their lives despite all the evidence of wealth, plenty, and gadgets that they have. Their enjoyment is nervous excitement, animal merriment. One gets the image that they are constantly running from ghosts that are pursuing them. They are as machines that move with madness, speed, and convulsion that does not cease. Many times I thought it was as though the people were in a grinding machine that does not stop day or night, morning or evening. It grinds them and they are devoured without a moment's rest. They have no faith in themselves or in life around them. . . .[5]

Sayyid Quṭb's characterization of the West is not inspired merely by an inability to adjust to its fast pace; rather, it must be seen as a condemnation of the West's total concern with the material side of life and its lack of concern for humanity. His description is aimed at those who look at the West as charting the way of the future and emulate its methods in order to catch up with the march of civilization. He sees Western civilization as an alien and anti-Godly influence that has temporarily captured the leadership of the world through the glitter of the material inducements it provides. Viewing the West as inherently empty and doomed to failure, he stresses the importance of Islam's taking over the leadership of the world.

It is quite clear, however, that Quṭb's condemnation of the West does not imply a preference for communism as an alternative. He does admit that he does not know as much about the communist system as he does about the West,[6] yet he sees it as a contender with Islam for the leadership of the world. It too, however, has gone astray, taking economic materialism and Karl Marx as gods. Both capitalism and communism are doomed to failure, he says, because in their emphasis on materialism they are spiritually bankrupt and fail to offer effective answers to the real needs of people. Should the economy of the West falter, its working class, which is now content because of the high standard of living, would seek refuge in communism just as its intellectuals have done. This does not mean that communism offers a better alternative, for it is as vacuous and as devoid of values as is capitalism.[7] Both systems are bankrupt because they emphasize materialism and do not understand humanity's need for spiritual values.

Once the struggle between capitalism and communism is spent, when both systems have devoured themselves, then the humanistic view represented by God's revelation in Islam will emerge as victor over the forces of materialism. These materialistic forces Quṭb sees as having been represented by the Roman Empire, by Europe and the United States, and now by communism in its last stages. There is no doubt that victory for Islam is assured because of its self-evident superiority and because Islam occupies what he calls the all-important middle position. Islam offers the world a balance that is

> not to be found in idealistic Christianity nor in dogmatic communism but in a middle position about life. [Islam] as an ideology balances pure spirituality and moderate practical materialism and forms from them a system for the conscience and a way of life, an everlasting vision for humanity.[8]

Quṭb decries all extreme positions and draws a central stance of commitment to moderation. This position represents a careful balance between the rationality of the secularists and the spirituality of the Muslim Sufis. It moderates between two groups of Muslims: those who hold fast to tradition, looking back to the "Medinan ideal" as a society not only to be emulated but one that is constantly sought after to be re-created in every detail, and those who claim that the ideals of humanity have changed and that society has to catch up with the march of modernity through the discarding of all tradition. Quṭb also outlines a position that appears to be the moderate one between those who believe that Islamic law must be revised to accommodate modernity and those, like the Wahhābīs, who believe that the law must be executed down to its minutest detail.

Thus Islam as the *dīn al-wasaṭ,* the middle religion, encompasses all the fields of life. In economics it lies between communism and capitalism by emphasizing social justice, in politics it lies between overcommitment to either the individual or the community, and in the religious sphere it lies between the formalized law and nihilism.[9] Islam for Quṭb is unique. It is not a repetition of civilizations or ways of life which preceded it, nor has it been duplicated by what has followed.[10] Its realization is in the future as well as the past. Thus there is hope for those who are willing to struggle to establish it on earth:

> The divine plan, which is represented by Islam in its final form as it was revealed to Muḥammad, is not fulfilled in this world, in the world of man, by its mere revelation from God. It does not come into being with the divine word "be" at the time it is revealed. It is not realized merely through being known by people. Nor is it realized by divine fiat [in the same manner] as His laws are made manifest in the heavens and the motion of the stars. It is realized when a group of people appropriate it, believe in it totally, and live to every possible extent according to its principles, endeavouring to instill it in the hearts and lives of others and striving for this purpose with all their possessions.[11]

This, however, does not mean that human endeavor is all that counts. For though man is to bring about God's order in the world, he is not completely independent in this matter. God will aid those who struggle in his cause. God's will is decisive in the end, and without it man by himself can achieve nothing.

Meanwhile, says Quṭb, "there is a unique period in the history of this system—and in the history of all humanity—which continues to be perceived in the history of all humanity as it persists in its elevated place."[12] This period in which the community of Medina lived under God's guidance as related to the Prophet is not the totality of the Islamic age, but is the acme of that age, providing guidance and a model for others to follow. Quṭb differs here from traditionalists who see this period in Islamic history as having been a once-and-for-all, never-to-be-repeated time. For him the significance of this period lies precisely in the fact that it remains an ideal to be strived for and, because of human potentiality, this ideal is a realizable goal. "Truly this period is not the product of an unrepeated miracle; it was the product of the human effort exerted by early Muslims. It is attainable again when a similar effort is put forth."[13]

Thus the community at Medina is not only a unique experience in the history of humanity; it is also the prototype of the design for all life and can be re-created in time if enough effort is expended in obedience to God and faith in His unicity. For this order to come into being, however, Islam must gain political power:

> If Islam is to be effective, it is inevitable that it must rule. This religion did not come only to remain in the corners of places of

> worship, not merely to find a place in the hearts and consciences of men. It has come that it may govern life and administer it and mold society according to its total image of life, not by preaching or guidance alone but also by the setting of laws and regulations. It has come to translate its doctrines and theories into a system and [a way of] life, and to make by that which it commands and forbids a living society and a people of flesh and blood who move on this earth and demonstrate by their life and social interactions and ways of government . . . the principles and ideas, the laws and regulations of this religion.[14]

To be effective, Islam must be able to supervise the lives of the believers and assure that they obey the laws of God. This they are ordered to do by the Qur'ān. It involves not an infringement on the rights of people, but a guidance to them in articulating what God has ordered to be made known of His commandments and His prohibitions. In the final analysis, "There is no Islam without government, and no Muslims without Islam."[15] Islam as the creative movement is actualized by appropriation, not only by positive feelings. It is not an unrealistic vision but a view of life that can be realized in this world both because God has promised support in such an endeavor and *because it has been realized before.*[16] It is inevitable that Islam will be established on this earth again, says Quṭb, for it is only by the reappropriation of this ideal ordering of human life that mankind can be saved from annihilation.[17]

Sayyid Quṭb's understanding of history, then, sees Islam as the perfect social order for mankind, realized in its perfection for a brief period of time. Impurities and evils have seeped into it from within and without, and it has succumbed in some areas to the relentless pressures of the evil forces of worldly materialism. Islam is thus now in a weakened state, but it is inevitable that it will recapture its place in history, guiding and leading people in the way of God. This order will come about if there are enough people who are committed to the cause and who are able to acquire political power of government somewhere in the world where they can establish the perfect Muslim society for all to see. Then will mankind understand the truth as revealed by God and made manifest by his vicegerents here on earth, as they struggle and are ready to sacrifice all in His cause. This day, says Sayyid Quṭb, is imminent.

Given this orientation, one is not surprised to find that Quṭb spends a part of the *Tārīkh* discussing his belief that Islamic history has to be rewritten. It is imperative that it be interpreted in a truly

Islamic manner. This task needs committed people, those that are Arab and Muslim, who can understand the dynamics of the faith and are able to interpret events in their true meaning. As a living entity Islam cannot be described by an outside observer. It must be appropriated and experienced by the narrator,[18] and the author must understand that the Muslims whose history he is recording are a group of people living at a certain time and in a certain place but that they are not identical with Islam. Islam is a cosmic message which cannot be limited by time and place,[19] and all that the historian of Islam can describe is the experience of Muslims in this world. Quṭb stresses that Islamic history must be seen as part of human history, and advocates that the historian should have a detailed knowledge of world history in order to be able to place the Islamic story in its proper place. Furthermore, he says, Islamic history needs to be rewritten because Arab historians have exhibited a dependency on Orientalists and other Western writers of history who tend to come with preconceived ideas of man-made systems and therefore to judge Islam by their own rather than by Islamic norms.

Quṭb calls attention to what he describes as a tendency for Muslims to view themselves in the light of Western standards, ignoring the fact that many Westerners seek the destruction of Islam. School textbooks, he says, are often apt to glorify Western achievements and distort Islamic history. It is incumbent upon Muslims to correct this error that is being perpetrated by the enemies of Islam, so that the future generations of Muslims may be apprised of the truth of their heritage, the role of religion, and the progressive ideals it espouses. It is therefore in the interest of Muslims to understand their role in history and their worth in the world in order to fully apprehend their present purpose and to assume their responsibilities in the effort to reestablish the potency of an Islamic order in the world.

The specific aim of the study of history is not to provide a chronological and detailed narrative, but rather to suggest the general outlines of such a narrative. In other words, the purpose of such a study is to attempt to bring about "a special historical mentality," in order to benefit those who do not devote themselves to an elaboration of the details of history.[20] Quṭb sees this study as divided into several parts. The first would deal with Islam at the time of the Prophet, discussing such things as how the Prophet was chosen and the purpose of his mission. It would further treat the system initiated by Islam, its values and principles, describing the first Muslims who responded to its mission and the social, political, economic, and geographical ramifications of their willingness to heed the call of God. This would be followed by a treatise on Islamic expansion, the outpouring of zeal for the cause not only through military might but with spiritual, social, and ideological fervor. It would also deal with the interaction of the Muslim community with other peoples, their ideologies, and responses to the call of Islam. After this would come a section on the arrest of expansion, its apparent and its hidden causes, and its effects on humanity and human relations. Finally, this history would deal with the Muslim world today.[21]

In reflecting on circumstances of Islam in the world today, Quṭb condemns the borrowing that has taken place from the West. Islam is progressive and creative, he says, and does not entail surrendering Islamic principles and adopting methods from alien sources. The renewal of the Arab world must come from an Islamic understanding and an intimate knowledge of Islamic principles. All efforts at borrowing ideas and ideals are doomed to failure, for Islam has no need of foreign imports. There is not a single ideology that humanity has devised, whether concerning man, the world, or reality, for which Islam has not provided a superior formulation. With these Islamic principles lie the tools for regeneration and renewal.[22]

Important as the reinterpretation of history is for Sayyid Quṭb, however, it is only half of the process. The other half, as we have seen, comes not in looking back but in looking forward, in acquiring the strength and the political power to reestablish the Islamic state. This state will, of course, be different because of the very fact that history means progression. For Quṭb a means for renewal of Islam and a crucial element in the reestablishing of political power is the understanding of the distinction between the *sharīʿa* and *fiqh.* The *sharīʿa,* or divine law of Islam, as created by God and with the Qurʾān as its primary source, is complete, perfect, and changeless. "Islamic society did not make the *sharīʿa,*" says Quṭb, "but rather the *sharīʿa* made Islamic society."[23] The *sharīʿa* defines the perimeter within which Islam operates. In this manner it preserves the Islamic society from following the footsteps of the West, from deviation and falsehood, and guarantees as well that the future will be integrally tied to the past. *Fiqh* or the science of jurisprudence, on the other hand, is open to change precisely because it deals with local applications in a changing world.[24] In this understanding Quṭb sharply criticizes those who hang on to the literal interpretation of *fiqh* and seem therefore to render it as eternal and changeless as the *sharīʿa.*

The task of Muslims today, then, in the perspective of Sayyid Quṭb, is to reappropriate the understanding of true Islam so as to be able to apply it to the contemporary circumstance, for which task a rewriting of Islamic history is crucial, *and* to reappropriate the political power which was historically theirs so that the true *dīn al-wasaṭ* can be actualized as God's divinely ordained and guided community on earth. This middle position between the past and the future is indicated from another perspective in the emphasis Quṭb gives to Islam as the fullest expression of the totality of all of life. This all-inclusiveness, he says, is unique to Islam, a divinely originated and revealed unity to which no other nation or people has had access.[25] And in this understanding of unity is the reflection of the *tawḥīd* of God, the oneness of divine being through the reality of which man's communal life is both ordained and actualized.

When we turn to the work of ʿAbd al-Raḥmān ʿAlī al-Ḥajjī we find an understanding of history written from a very similar perspective.[26] For al-Ḥajjī, Islamic history is more than "thoughts, events, social patterns, political conditions or ruling nations"; it is the history of a comprehensive ideology. To him, commitment to this ideology is a test of one's commitment to God. In fact, he displays such a passionate defense of this ideology that he seems to value commitment to it over commitment to God. "We believe in Islam, in all the institutions that were established by it and through it, with all our capacity and ability. To it alone is our devotion."[27]

Al-Ḥajjī is convinced that Islam is threatened by hostile enemies that are organized with only one purpose in mind—the destruction of Islam. He outlines the drama of this conflict in the following way:

> *Enemies:* both local and foreign. *Goals:* to destroy Islam either through eradication or disorganization.
>
> *Motives:* hatred and greed (and misunderstanding that leads to errors).
>
> *Means:* varied, in the form of arrows aimed at the fortress of Islam.
>
> *Defenders:* its men and nations, doctrines, history, culture.
>
> *Other:* variety of movements and currents aimed against Islam throughout its history.[28]

Thus Islam is the beleaguered faith that is surrounded by enemies from without and enemies from within. History is one of the defenders of the faith and must be utilized and protected from being usurped by the enemy. The struggle of Islam to persist in the contemporary period is not unique since Islam has had to defend itself against detractors and enemies throughout its history, in its struggle to maintain truth in the face of falsehood.[29] Those who have sought to falsify Islamic history "are not only the Orientalists (*mustashriqūn*), Jews and Crusaders, but all those who follow in their footsteps repeating what they say and write." They use distortion, stultification, skepticism, fragmentation, and neglect as their tools.[30]

Al-Ḥajjī is cognizant of the efforts to reinterpret Islamic history from the Marxist point of view being carried out in different parts of the Arab world. He attacks this materialistic interpretation as partial and therefore a distortion of truth since it denies the spiritual dimension of man. Furthermore, it was not economic factors that led to the appearance or the spread of Islam. Any materialistic interpretation would deny the divine quality which is its driving force.[31] It was through religious devotion that the early Muslims, though inferior "in number, equipment, organization, capability, and training," were able to achieve victory.[32]

Other internal enemies of Islam are those who attempt to rewrite history from a nationalistic perspective. Al-Ḥajjī considers this a false endeavor and impugns their motives as possible attempts at rendering Islam ineffective. Islam transcends ethnicities; otherwise, people of different nationalities would not have joined the faith with such vigor and commitment, ready to amalgamate their identity into the Islamic one. To emphasize Arab nationalism is to misunderstand Islam. He concedes that most of the Islamic heritage has been written in Arabic, but says that that has nothing to do with race or nationality but was simply because God chose to reveal the Qur'ān in Arabic. This is the reason why the enemies of Islam chose also to attack the Arabic language, some seeking to sanction the use of colloquial Arabic, rendering the language of the Qur'ān obsolete, and others attempting to Latinize the script.[33] Arabic was used in the revelation because Muḥammad was an Arab. Thus although the language of the Qur'ān, the religion, and the heritage is Arabic, it does not make Islam Arabic. To emphasize the Arabhood of the first Muslims is to be in error, since they perceived themselves as Muslims. Furthermore, by stressing their Arabhood one runs the risk of suggesting that the early expansion was a kind of race war and that the first Muslims were empire builders and savage conquerors like the Tartars.[34]

Having pointed to the errors of some historians, the Marxists and the nationalists, al-Ḥajjī proceeds to explain the cause of the current weakness of Islam. He perceives the source of weakness in secularized education that was perpetrated by the foreigners and those who were educated by them. This has led to a neglect of religion and history and has overemphasized the achievements of the conquerors in the areas of political power and material production. Furthermore, efforts have been extended in revivifying non-Islamic cultures that flourished in the past in countries which are now Muslim. Funds have been allocated for research in the pre-Islamic civilizations of these countries and the restoration of their ruins. Institutes and museums specializing in such studies are maintained. These, says al-Ḥajjī, tend to glorify false civilizations. His protest is not that they are studied, but that the methodology and approach to these civilizations is not from the Islamic context. Thus Muslims will be unable to discern the truth about reality, for these efforts have resulted in excesses such as restoring statues of gods that are condemned by the Qur'ān. These images appear also on decorations of buildings, on names of places, and on postage stamps. His great fear is that some of the young people will begin to perceive Islam as imperialism from which one should seek to be liberated.[35]

Recent efforts to undermine Islam from within appear in the works of Muslim contemporaries who perceive Islam as a revolution or ascribe revolutionary zeal to some of the early Muslims. This is done in accordance with what he sees as the policy in Egypt to rewrite history from a revolutionary un-Islamic standpoint, accusing the companions of the Prophet of socialism.

Furthermore, the efforts supported by the Egyptian government for a rewriting of history have adopted the Western secularist understanding of history. They point to the fact that the West did not progress and achieve domination until it separated church from politics. The implication is that Muslims today should emulate them in order to achieve dominance. This al-Ḥajjī finds as erroneous because of the role of the religious leaders in Islam who have always been guiding all life and resisting oppression without fear. Islamic history must be written by committed Muslims who ignore the writings of the modern Arab historians and of the Orientalists, and avoid the use of the historical methods employed in American universities.[36]

The interpretation of history from an Islamic standpoint is necessary because those who developed Islamic civilization, science, and knowledge were devout believers (except in the case of those who studied polytheistic Greek philosophy such as al-Fārābī). Many of them used to pray before they attempted to solve problems. Furthermore, we must remember that Islam does not need to justify itself by scientific theories that are contradictory to the revelation of the

Qur'ān. Scientists will have to continue their research until they arrive at the truth, whereas Islam possesses the revealed truth and thus cannot be in error.

Al-Ḥajjī's further comments on how Islamic history must be written reveal his concern that modern historical works basing their reporting on the classical texts and Western methodology have presented Islamic history as embroiled in schism, conflict, and controversy. He advocates a more comprehensive history that attempts to understand the meaning and content of civilization, including its ethical values. He is willing to sacrifice the details, ignoring events and accuracy for the sake of preserving in youth the faith of their fathers. As for pre-Islamic history, it must be taught from an Islamic vantage point which contributes to the integration of the personality of the Muslim.

He is thus not interested in disseminating historical information to provide an objective source of knowledge of the past, its shortcomings, and the patterns that should be watched in order to avoid disaster in the future; rather, he is anxious that history serve in the structuring of values and attitudes that can lead to an Islamic identity. This he would not consider as distortion of the truth but as a service for the development of the proper order where God is worshipped as Lord of all. He would therefore marshal the facts in order to provide the motivation and conviction that the glory of the past can continue to be the lot of those who are steadfast and who labor diligently for the Islamic cause.

Chapter Eight
The Intellectualist Response

Thus far we have discussed the apologetic and the traditional neo-normativist articulation of the idea of history in Islam. In this chapter we will discuss three authors who attempt an intellectualist approach. Although the foundational principles of their work proceed from the same premise as those discussed earlier, these authors evidence an intellectual rigor absent from the writings of the previous authors.

Muḥammad Kamāl Ibrāhīm Ja'far addresses himself to the question of God's involvement in history.[1] This question is not dealt with by the other authors who tend to see historical laws functioning in fulfillment of predetermined cycles. Ja'far, in approaching history from the perspective of world religions, attempts to clarify the Islamic position vis-à-vis that of Christianity and Judaism. This position denies that God's *tawḥīd* can be perceived as a "unity of being." God is not identical with history nor is He a part of it, i.e., partaking or indwelling in any way or form in creation. The Islamic view denies the incarnation doctrine of Christians and the "in-dwelling" beliefs of extreme Sufis and Gnostics.[2]

Islam emphasizes the principle of the unity of history. This includes both the material and the spiritual aspects of life, the sacred and the secular. However, this unity is not one of being, for God, man, and the world cannot be one. Nor is it a sacred history of the chosen people. Islam as the final revelation is a correction of all the errors that crept into the messages of the previous prophets from Noah to Jesus. In this it is a reform movement and not a new religion. The Islamic community in Medina was a perfected reality, the culmination of human experience under the will of God. It was unique only in that its perfection has been carefully recorded in the Qur'ān and the *ḥadīth*. Other prophets have brought the message of unicity from God to other nations at other times and in other places in history. However, it is unique in Islam because it has not been corrupted. Its tenets have been preserved pure and perfect. Muslims may have deviated from them, but their validity and authenticity have been proved by their vindication through history.[3] Thus Islam is a link in the long chain of divine revelation.

The immutable laws of God as revealed in the Qur'ān maintain that the fall of civilizations is due to their wickedness, corruption, and oppression. God punishes them by destruction. This destiny does not await nations only but is valid for individuals who participate in the making of history. Nations may come and go, but God's law is permanent. It provides history with its unity and the student of history with the key to the understanding and interpretation of historical events. This law is necessary for the understanding of the flourishing and decline of both the material and spiritual aspects of culture. It is a comprehensive law that covers all aspects of life and governs the factors behind all events.[4]

The narratives of the Qur'ān are provided as examples of the application of the laws of God in history. From them we learn about God's relation to history in the past and the future. S. 14:5 and 45:14 talk about the "days of God." They refer men to God's action in history in the past and ask them to expect His action in the future. The past and the future are two dimensions of life. The present is fleeting and is seen as the moment that connects the two. For it is assured that just as God fulfilled His promise in the past, He will surely bring man to judgment in the future. "As for the present, it is the moment of consideration in which men are asked to look back and to look forward until the present is reformed." Thus the present finds its meaning in understanding God's ways and laws as they functioned in the past and the fulfillment of the promise of the judgment day in the future.[5]

The "days of God" provide us with an understanding of the times when God intercepts history to make His will known and to fulfill His promise, says Jaʿfar. The Sufis who explored the meaning of this term have helped us understand that just as God has days, He also has nights when He absents Himself from the running of the world and allows the eternal laws to function fulfilling themselves. Thus the days of God are "a consistent and necessary law which is fulfilled in a decisive way at special times."[6]

Unlike al-Sharqāwī, Jaʿfar admits that there have been civilizations that have progressed and prospered despite the primitiveness of their religion, such as the worship of idols or of deities to which human qualities were ascribed. However, he does insist that

> the excellent and abiding beliefs that the major religions have taught have been and continue to be the single proof of the divine origin of the ideal religion, and what contradicts that in religions is due to the forgetting of these ideas or their distortion or rejection while continuing in material progress.[7]

Thus the exceptions do not belie the laws of God in history nor their comprehensive nature.[8] What appears as varied and contradictory is in fact a framework in which unity is expressed through diversity.[9]

Jaʿfar sees authenticity (*aṣāla*) in interpreting Islam for today in the perfection and applicability of the Qur'anic truths at all times and in all places. Despite efforts to revivify the faith, we must never lose sight of the necessity of this authenticity.[10] Meanwhile, it must be made evident that the Qur'ān sees the integration of the totality of life—of knowledge and its scientific products. It integrates knowledge and work, and insists that growth and development come only through the interaction of the two.[11] Thus progress in Islam has a deeper dimension than in any other thought system. For it transcends this life and functions in the hereafter where growth and development continue. This refutes the ideas of the ossified traditionalists who attack every reformer as an innovator.[12]

Here, as in his discussion of God's action in history, Jaʿfar clearly makes use of Sufi interpretation in an effort to integrate progress and activity into the Islamic system. The Muslim can participate in the newness of life and respond to change because his experience is guaranteed its authenticity by his commitment to his faith and by the comprehensive ideas of the Qur'ān.

Turning to Rāshid al-Barrāwī, we find a consistent attempt to integrate Qur'anic teachings concerning the rise and fall of nations to economic factors and moral responsibility.[13] He cautions against viewing Islam as an alternative system to that of capitalism and Marxism. Islam is a religion with a divine origin, whereas social and economic systems are made by human beings. These are sometimes correct and at other times they may fall into error. Furthermore, whereas the social systems change from one age to another, Islam is constant and unchanging and is good for every time and place. Attempting to compare systems, he says, may lead to false understandings.[14]

According to al-Barrāwī, the Qur'ān shows that human societies develop due to human needs, then are replaced by others that are more capable of survival and development. Each social order is a progressive step forward in relation to that which preceded it.[15] The succession of nations implies that each civilization is established in order to realize social goals at a particular time under certain circumstances. With the passage of time, new needs arise which this civilization cannot meet; thus it loses its raison d'être and a new and more progressive civilization takes its place. There is no man-made civilization that can be considered eternal or good for all ages and all societies. The very fact of its being humanly constructed implies a weakness in its being.[16] For every society is responsible for the destiny that befalls it.

Any change and movement for progress must come from within the people.[17] Thus change is initiated by human will, with God providing the capacity and the responsibility for that change, having endowed man with a mind to guide thought, discernment, and judgment.[18]

The inevitable destiny of the oppressive nation is destruction, which is preceded by a period of deterioration in which the final causes for destruction are brought together.[19] Every civilization that has come into being has been created by design and effort. There is no element of chance in the progress and development of a nation.[20] Evil in a society will inevitably lead to destruction, although it may be a long process.[21] History is a witness to this truth. Most civilizations have passed through a period of economic, social, and political decline before their final end.[22]

There are several reasons for the collapse of nations. These include both the economic factor, which is necessary to maintain progress, and the social factor in which the class structure appears to play a role, as the first zealous adherents of every faith have been the lower classes and the oppressed among the nations. Excessive wealth is another factor, since wealthy people tend to usurp political power and make it serve their own interests.[23] Another reason is the corruption of government, as the wealthy appear to get better treatment which leads to inequality before the law.[24]

Al-Barrāwī notes that it may appear that the Qur'anic verses place the blame for the collapse of the social systems on the leaders who are oppressive. However, they are not solely responsible for the fate of their societies. The Qur'ān does categorically specify that all people are responsible, not only the leaders. If they shirk their duty in calling attention to the miscarriage of justice or fail to command the good and prohibit the evil, they are accountable for the decline and fall of their civilization.[25] Thus the community must bear the responsibility for following those who lead them to evil.[26]

Therefore, although he does not specifically say so, al-Barrāwī appears to be holding Muslims responsible for the cause of the decline of the Islamic countries. They are not only responsible for the state of deterioration but also must shoulder the responsibility for seeking change and establishing a viable system within the Islamic framework that is both responsive to the demands of the age and is also able to grow and develop.

The ascription of responsibility to human endeavor in the process of destiny and history prescribes the assumption of this responsibility by Muslims. It is aimed to shake loose the process of human liberation from determinism and total resignation to the forces of destiny and the vagaries of life. This does not mean that al-Barrāwī has reduced God to a silent observer as the Deists have done; rather, he has attempted to incite Muslims to activity within the framework of God's laws, His revelation, and His continuing guidance. Man's vicegerency on earth becomes a responsible commitment to the purposes of God in developing and managing all natural and human resources.

ʿImād al-Dīn Khalīl attempts to provide the contemporary Muslim student with an Islamic understanding of history.[27] He is keenly aware of the lack of an adequate Islamic philosophical interpretation that takes seriously God's action in history, as well as the paucity of Islamic literature[28] and the flooding of the Arab bookstores with works written from a human perspective.[29] He therefore attempts to provide the reader with a comprehensive analysis of the Qur'anic perception of the world, of history, of man, and of the crucial role of the moral life in determining the fortune and destiny of nations and peoples both in this world and at the time when men will stand before God for an accounting of their deeds.

The Qur'ān presents a comprehensive method of dealing with human history, he says, one whose final goal is the dynamic activity of the believer who responds to God's action. This method moves from an exposition of events to a discernment of laws and principles that govern social and historical matters and provide access to the positive values of the universe. Society is thus moved towards a harmonization of its energies with the goals of the universe fashioned by God, providing a plan for present and future action.[30] The superiority of the Islamic methodology is evident because of its divine origin. "Manmade" theories are the brainchildren of historians, who, conditioned by their milieu, their knowledge, and their limited vision, posit systems that are prejudiced by their preconceived ideas and ideologies which lead them to select and tailor their facts to fit into their own already formulated patterns. The Islamic understanding of history, on the other hand, is realistic and practical. It proceeds from the vantage point of God which "transcends time, place, and the relative concerns of the age."[31]

Historians treat the past selectively, choosing that which buttresses their theories and ignoring what may contradict their perceptions. The Qur'anic method is comprehensive. It views reality in the totality of its past, present, and future:

> History in the Qur'ān becomes unified time . . . the walls that separate the past, the present, and the future collapse and the three times commingle in a common destiny. Even the earth and the heaven, temporal time and divine time, the story of creation and the Day of Judgment . . . always meet in the present moment in the Qur'ān. . . . This fast movement between past and future, between present and past, between future and present clarifies the effort of the Qur'ān to remove the boundaries which separate time and show it as a contiguous living unity. This movement of history which encompasses creation becomes one movement beginning with the day of God's creation of the heaven and the earth and moving towards the Day of Judgment.[32]

Through the use of narrative the Qur'ān provides humanity with samples of objective history through which we can perceive God's wisdom (*ḥikma*) and the laws (*sunan*) which govern the dynamics of the historical process.[33] These laws are comprehensive and universal in nature, coordinated with human nature and human potentialities transcending geographical and economic considerations.[34] They are also constant, for any change in their fulfillment would disrupt the movement of history and render truth and justice inoperative in the world. Their constancy is assured in the Qur'ān, as they exist in the essence of creation and at the heart of the world.[35] They are part of the guidance God has promised Adam at creation since they provide humanity with an ability to perceive reality and function in accordance with God's will.

Thus the laws of history endow any community that contemplates them and appropriates them with the power to manipulate the dynamics of history. Control is gained as the community learns to avoid the pitfalls of those who preceded and to live in harmony with the powers of nature and the universe. The dynamics of history serve the present moment, and *now,* and provide assurance about the promise of the future.[36] Thus all time becomes encapsulated in the "moment," for it is only in the now that the volitional act of man, aware of the past and cognizant of the potentialities of the future, becomes an ethical choice which impinges on the whole dynamics of history in the world. For Khalīl, the judgment of history is not only inevitable, but it is also necessary in order to uphold the laws of justice with which God endows the universe. When man evidences the will to live in accordance with God's plan, a thriving civilization results which can avoid deterioration and destruction.

The national character (*nafsiyyat al-umma*) has a direct relation to the effectiveness of the process of building a civilization. This character is evident in the manner in which the members, individually and collectively, respond to God and to the world in their total way of life.[37] The size of the community is irrelevant; the historical record testifies that great nations have been humbled by God, who held them accountable for their choices and punished them for their apostasy.[38] From the human perspective, power and might of nations may appear as the secret to effective leadership; some may even find in it a proof of the capacity for development and progress regardless of any imbalance in the civilization between the forces of war and peace, of creativity and destruction. For God, as the Qur'ān reveals, the power of a nation is not the guarantor of its progress, because any discord or imbalance leads to lack of creativity, rendering the nation incapable of providing answers to new questions and challenges.[39]

Khalīl believes that the Qur'ān informs us that historical events occur as an expression of God's will which is implemented either through the framework of man's will or through a direct initiation (*mubāshara*). This initiation may be synchronized with the laws of nature, or it may take a form that supersedes the normal functioning of these laws, usually referred to as a miracle. In both cases, the purpose is to remind people of their creaturehood and of God's effective, unrestricted omnipotence.[40] God's will is thus made evident through natural events such as storms and floods or through the armies of angels he may use to alter the course of events.

> The Islamic interpretation of history is different from other interpretations because it gives great leeway to the unknown (*ghayb*) factor [functioning in the] past, present, and future, and makes it one of the fundamental principles of the faith.[41]

Theories of history that are bound by materialistic considerations and do not take the spiritual factors in life seriously are nothing but falsifications of reality and fragmentary hypotheses that do not deal adequately with human history and experience.[42]

Man is created to live in constant tension and eternal striving to overcome the perpetual challenges that arise to test his mettle.[43] This fate was initiated in the temptation of the first man, Adam, as he sought to taste the Tree of Eternity which was not to be his lot until he had completed a period of testing and decision-making in this world. Man does not participate in eternity until he is held accountable for the choices he has made.[44] Human volition and exercise of ethical principles determine the flow of history. Thus human responsibility and human accountability are intimately bound to historical judgment.

God's indirect action in history is made manifest through man's exercise of his freedom which is intricately bound to God's will. Khalīl admits that although it is extremely difficult to distinguish between the will of man and the will of God (for in the final analysis they are all within the scope of the omnipotent divine will which encompasses all), still the Qur'ān affirms that man possesses total freedom in the area of decision-making, planning, and execution.[45] It is this freedom that renders man accountable while God's constancy distinguishes every judgment of history as just and appropriate. Furthermore, it is this freedom that imparts meaning to the human condition which otherwise would be at the mercy of irrational forces.[46] Meanwhile, man must be aware that even this discussion of his freedom is an exaggeration because of his inflated feeling of worth. In truth, his creaturehood is an affirmation of his infinitesimal role in God's creation, for all his capabilities, powers, and knowledge are insignificant before God's creative omnipotence.[47]

The action of the individual is not the sole factor that impinges on the dynamics of history; human activity in the collective is equally responsible. Each nation will account for its actions as a collectivity on the Day of Judgment. The group's accountability is preceded by a call to the praxis of righteousness and the cessation of oppression which is addressed to the nation through revelation by a prophet from God. Awareness of the choices the nation faces is crucial in assessing justice which, in its Qur'anic context, is never arbitrary or sudden.[48]

Human freedom leads by necessity to an intimate interaction between human activity and the historical act. Man has been placed by God as a vicegerent in the world to care for creation and to develop the earth that has been entrusted to his care.[49] Man is the Lord of the World. "He subdues and is not subdued, forms and is not formed, plans and executes and is not a mere tool for the execution of the natural laws."[50] Historical events are the result of the interaction of man and matter.[51] However, this is not the limit of the significance or meaning of the historical act. It is here that the material interpretation of history fails, since it is incapable of explaining and interpreting the complexity of the human personality as an amalgam of the various elements of intellect, spirit, emotion, conscience, and the like.[52]

Mindful of his limitations, man is aware that there are certain stages in his life that are preordained. He is born to grow, to age, to die, to be raised from the dead, and to give an accounting of his life. The tribe, the nation, the race into which he is born are all outside the scope of his choice.[53] These and other factors give man a sense of his finitude and an insight into his primary role, which is the worship of God. This worship is not a periodic occurrence, but encompasses the totality of life. It is this individual and corporate commitment to a life of worship that gives a civilization its distinctive stamp. It provides it with a justification and a cause for creativity and progress. Thus worship is not restricted to ritual acts or liturgical forms, but is the intention behind every creative act.[54]

Furthermore, man's vicegerency is an affirmation of God's gifts that have been granted to man through the provision of opportunities for their exercise. Man's role in the world is thus one of "effective power, thoughtful, willful, executive, independent, and discerning."[55] These gifts are not to be enjoyed in laziness or mere contemplation; rather they are to be utilized in purposeful activity and moral choices. For "the central axis for the existence of a person—individual or corporate—on earth is to work, which is considered as the just measure in deciding destiny in this world and the next."[56]

The achievements of civilization are the by-products of a life lived in harmony with the laws of history and the will of God for the world. These achievements are not restricted to the material field, but include intellectual and spiritual factors that provide for the predominance of God's will on earth.[57] The maintenance of civilizational ascendance is dependent on two factors—reform and the cessation of corruption. The believing community fulfills its vicegerency through a continuous effort to face the challenges by maintaining unity and uprooting unrighteousness, as well as by a perpetual commitment to regeneration. Thus civilization continues its progress through the human will to perseverance, and commitment to utilize God's gifts of creativity in planning, design, and execution of development.[58]

Dynamic activity is perceived by Khalīl as the basic quality of creativity and production since it is the irreducible essence of all matter in the universe. Dynamic activity is enjoined in the Qur'ān. It leads humanity on the road to progress in accord with the laws of God in order to achieve prosperity and civilization. It necessitates a holistic approach where there is no bifurcation either of sacred and secular or between this world and the next, for all is completely consumed in the present moment. The Qur'ān calls for a civilization that progresses in all areas, spiritual, ethical, and natural. It stipulates that for a civilization to flourish it must be governed by religious values and ideals and purposes set by God for the world.[59]

For Khalīl, religion is not confined to the spiritual realm. It has not been revealed to divert humanity from actively participating in the material world, nor does it seek to reject this world, or isolate the community from it, perpetrating the false impression that this life is a mere phase that has to be tolerated.[60] Religion is a dynamic, active involvement in the material world, an involvement that seeks to reform and transform the world into that which God intended it to be. Thus he sees Islam and the Qur'ān as opposed to any theory that propagates a static view of religion or projects it as an impediment to progress and development. Religion is involvement in the civilizational process, and as such initiates inventiveness and inspires creativity.

Khalīl perceives in the Qur'ān an underlying principle which he calls "the dynamic equilibrium" (*al-tawāzun al-ḥarakī*) which abhors both deviation and rest. This principle guarantees a wholesome growth for any civilization which is able to maintain a balance between the experience of the spirit and that of matter. This creative equilibrium between the two dimensions of life maintains the true path, with neither constituent element superseding the other.[61] Furthermore, the Qur'ān provides us with an understanding of total harmony (*al-tanāghum al-kāmil*) between man, nature, and what is beyond. It is a harmony that incorporates both material forces and the worship of God. "It balances man's power and active will with his relative weakness and constant need of God." There is no separation between man and the world, nor is there a discontinuity between this world and the next.[62]

The balance of the creative equilibrium is maintained by the Qur'ān. Besides providing the philosophical framework for understanding the world, it reveals the laws that help harness the available creative powers. It also functions in a scientific capacity, for it urges the Muslims to study and research the laws of nature and the world on the theoretical as well as the practical level. It urges humanity to use knowledge to create a better and more progressive world in all spheres of life.[63] Despite his perception of the Qur'anic reality as dynamism and activity, Khalīl maintains that this ceaseless participation in the civilizational process, which is equivalent to persistence in the middle position, is truly peaceful since it provides equanimity. This he sees as the quality that distinguishes Muslims from other nations who are anxiety-ridden because they are nourished by relative truths and operate from tenuous positions.[64]

Thus Khalīl perceives a dynamic creative equilibrium as the essential characteristic for the maintenance of harmony with the purpose of creation of which civilization is an integral part. Man was created and placed in this world in order to exercise his vicegerency which manifests itself in civilizational achievements. This, however, is only a partial apprehension of reality. Khalīl also posits the necessity of maintaining a holistic perception, a total integration of all reality, past, present, and future, and the sustenance of an equilibrium between the spiritual and the material realms. This becomes necessary lest we give undue importance to the achievements of this world. Man must act with the realization that this life will inevitably come to an end. All our struggles and achievements are transitory. All we fashion and create comes to an end. The importance of this life despite its transient nature is in its being a preparation for the next. It is only when we perceive this truth that we are able to discern the significance and crucial nature of this life and the choices we made in actualizing it.[65]

The choices must be made constantly, for life is perpetual tension and struggle. The arena of struggle that the Qur'ān presents is very extensive; its central locus is the perennial conflict between man and Satan, the scope of which is so great as to include the universe and nature, which has inherent in it the complementarity of the positive and the negative. The dialectic between the dualities (*azwāj*) is the source of reproduction, of positive motion, and expansion. For movement is purposive and progressive, following an ascending line towards that which is better. That is the basic nature of things as created by God; the struggle inevitably leads to the survival of the fittest.[66]

Struggle is also evident among nations. This stems from the nature of creation, since not all men and nations are the same. Differences provide an incentive for competition which is an integral part of the drama of civilization. In the struggle is assurance of progress; zeal in the cause of supremacy leads to the discarding of useless accretions and the preservation of that which is best. Thus in the struggle between nations is the secret of rejuvenation and the revitalization of civilization. Khalīl equates corruption with inertness and stagnation; it is produced by lack of movement. Competition provides challenges which demand choices; this drama is similar to the shifting movement of a sieve. Survival hinges on the ability to maintain an intricate balance in the middle position for only the good maintain the role of leadership. Those who falter are discarded.[67]

The struggle is perennial and has been since creation. The believing community, whether it responded to the message of Noah, of Moses, of Jesus, or of Muḥammad, has faced identical situations; with Islam, however, revelation has ceased. The total responsibility is now assumed by the Islamic community. Individually and corporately Muslims are enjoined to struggle. The individual striving for excellence the Prophet called the "greater struggle" (*al-jihād al-akbar*). It is internal and personal as the individual strives to rid himself of negative impediments to his total integration into and acceptance of the message of Islam. The struggle is necessary to overcome the forces of evil. Without this perennial personal conquest, which the Prophet says continues until the Day of Resurrection, the world is not affected. The perpetuity of the struggle distinguishes it from posited utopias that dream of a world when all struggle has ceased; that would be contrary to the dynamic quality of human nature and to the basic criteria of human relations.[68]

Jihād is also an essential duty of the Muslim community. It guarantees its effectiveness as a repository of truth and as an agent of witness to God's will as manifest in the straight path, the middle position. It assumes the responsibility of fighting the forces of evil in the world, commanding the good and forbidding that which is reprehensible. Its ceaseless war through words and armaments on the forces of evil guarantees its victory over the powers of Satan.[69]

> *Jihād* . . . is Islam's continuous activity in the world to bring down the errant "*jāhilī*" leadership and to make freedom of belief possible for every person wherever he may be, regardless of time, space, race, color, tongue, education or allegiance. It is, in fact, the justification of the existence of the Islamic community in

> every time and in every place, the key to its role in the world and its ideological goal. . . . Without this *"jihād"* movement, the justification is eliminated and the key is lost. The Muslim community loses its capacity for unity, cooperation, and eternality.[70]

The Qur'ān reveals that God rotates the days among the nations. This destiny is inevitable since it is of the essence of human action. This rotation is a dynamic force in history since it guarantees the maintenance of competition among the various groups. It creates constant challenges to theories. This rotation is purposive as it is an agent of hope and becomes an incentive for perseverance since dynamism assures those on the bottom that if they commit themselves diligently to the struggle, they will rise to the position of leadership.[71]

The rotation of leadership among nations is evident in the historical process; at times, however, those who have labored long may weary awaiting its fulfillment. The believers may question the justification for the apparent prosperity of the unrighteous and ungodly. What may appear as delay in the meting out of justice is God's will to allow the unrighteous sufficient time that they may be ungrateful and oppressive. No community is spared its appointed destiny with God's inevitable judgment.[72]

Khalīl points out that both the leaders and the followers are held responsible in the dynamics of history. When a civilization is ripe for a fall, its leaders indulge in wealth and political power, which leads to oppression and a dysfunction of the social system. The more oppressive the political leadership, the more the administrative structure is apt to disintegrate. Power leads to the acquisition of wealth and vice versa.[73] Khalīl sees the wealthy as the reactionary forces in a society; they seek to uphold the status quo, aided by a priestly class that has throughout history exercised its treacherous activity by providing false guidance. Together they have stood in opposition to progress and the march of history.[74] Affluence and wealth are dangerous elements in the structure of society. They can destroy those who attempt to ignore them as well as those who seek after them, and may lead to defeatist attitudes on the part of the have-nots while blinding the wealthy to all ethical consideration.[75]

This is not to say that either wealth or the material world are inherently evil. What Islam condemns is the concentration of effort on the amassing of wealth and power at the expense of the spiritual life and the ethical existence. The spiritual realm is not merely a factor in human life; it is an integral part of the essence of the world and an essential element of being. To ignore it is not only to do a disservice to humanity but to deviate from the expressed way of God. Islam, however, does not posit a duality or polarity between the realm of the spirit and the realm of matter. They are both seen as integral parts of God's creation and must be approached from the position of the middle nation in which the material and the spiritual are in balance.

Khalīl is concerned to outline the ways in which the Islamic state as a whole can fulfill its role as this middle nation. The apparent prosperity of the West is transitory, he says, partial and merely apparent. If Muslims but look to their past and see its totality before they begin to emulate others they will realize the great potential awaiting rebirth that is the essence of Islamic life.[76] It is in the dynamics of change that Islam can provide for the recapture of ascendancy and the realization of its capacity for "renewal, progress, and creativity."[77] This cannot happen, however, unless

> the total civilizational leadership is assumed by men of faith in God and in the Day of Judgment (who do not seek glory in this world or evil) and until Muslims assume their position (the middle one) in the heart of the world that they may be (a witness to humanity and that the Prophet may be a witness for them).
>
> What distinguishes the Islamic position and separates it [from the others] is that it sets next to the question of the fall of nations, experiences, and civilizations what could be called "optimistic determinism" (*al-ḥatmiyya al-tafā'uliyya*). . . . It establishes the inevitability of deterioration and fall; however, at the same time, it asserts the ability of any nation or group to return repeatedly to reestablish another nation, or try a new experience, or to assume the leadership in civilizations and doctrine, as long as it fulfills the necessary conditions.[78]

The failures of earlier communities are direct or indirect divine punishments which groups bring on themselves when they shirk responsibility and decline in their ethical commitments to excellence and the way of God. If Muslims do not hasten to reassume their struggle and their leadership role they may end up with the same destiny as those past deviating communities.[79] The ebb and flow of the fortunes of nations must be seen from the perspective of the Qur'ān, in which all existence is a unity, and in which the material and the spiritual as well as past, present, and future are seen as a dynamic and creative whole.

Chapter Nine
The Qur'anic Foundation

THE ARAB MUSLIM WRITERS whose works are considered in Part Two have responded to the Western methodology of historical interpretation in a clear and decisive manner, rejecting its claim to validity and authenticity and reaffirming the Islamic interpretation of the laws and dynamics of history as the only interpretation endowed with veracity due to its divine origin. For them, any attempt to decipher the rise and fall of civilizations must be rooted in the sacred revelation of the Qur'ān.

For all these authors, the Qur'anic view of the rise and fall of nations is crucial to the understanding and articulation of the Muslim view of history. The various authors, however, use the material of the Qur'ān in differing ways to support their respective formulations of the structure and purpose of history. Quṭb, al-Jundī, and al-Sharqāwī, on the one hand, provide no quotations from the Qur'ān in their texts, although in each case the exposition is clearly within the framework of the Qur'anic revelation. At the other extreme are al-Barrāwī and al-Khalīl, both of whom quote the Qur'ān extensively. Jaʿfar and al-Ḥajjī offer occasional passages from the Qur'ān in support of specific points.

Al-Khalīl's exposition of the Qur'anic world view is more consistent and coherent than that of al-Barrāwī, although al-Khalīl admits dependence on al-Barrāwī as one of his immediate sources. Al-Barrāwī provides a great many quotations that first appear to be inappropriate as a basis of discussion of the Qur'anic view of history. His work shows the influence of some modern exegetes who attempt to prove that the Qur'ān is relevant for the technological society of today by freely applying its verses to the specific findings of various branches of the physical and social sciences.

Thus al-Barrāwī, influenced by his training as an economist, perceives man as a vicegerent of God on earth, responsible for the management of its resources.[1] This places man in a competitive situation where he has to struggle for survival, a struggle that may lead to bloodshed.[2] The creation of the world preceded that of man in order to provide for human needs, he says, and to allow man to use his intellectual capacity of discernment, of intellect and will in the discharging of his responsibility over his own life and destiny.[3] The animal kingdom was created to provide opportunities for hunting, trapping, fishing, cattle raising,[4] and other means for the provision of food for man. Man has used members of the animal kingdom for transport,[5] and for the production of products such as eggs, honey,[6] and silk,[7] and has sought to provide for his needs through use of vegetation in the growing of food and the manufacture of wood products.[8] In exercising his responsibility for the management of the world, man has also extracted pearls from the ocean and metals from the earth that have helped him initiate an industrial growth.[9] The industries mentioned in the Qur'ān include shipbuilding,[10] metallurgy,[11] pottery and glassmaking,[12] weaving,[13] and the manufacture of silk,[14] jewelry,[15] leather products,[16] furniture,[17] and toys.[18]

This shows, says al-Barrāwī, that Islam is concerned with the material as well as the spiritual aspects of life. The Qur'ān makes it clear that even the prophets by their own examples showed humanity that it is necessary to have a profession—Noah was a shipbuilder, while Abraham and Ishmael were engaged in construction, Solomon in iron works, Joseph in business management, Dhū al-Qarnayn and the people of Sabā' in the building of dams, and Muḥammad himself was both a shepherd and a businessman engaged in commerce.[19]

Al-Barrāwī also cites verses to support his thesis that the Qur'ān encourages work[20] and endeavor in earning one's livelihood,[21] as well as urging people to engage their economic resources in commerce, industry, and other forms of lawful employment.[22] It teaches that people should be self-sufficient and not depend on others unnecessarily. The injunction to work is not directly aimed at advocating development and industrialization as much as proposing that industry is Islamic and must therefore be encouraged in order to fulfill the purposes of God for humanity and for the Islamic *Umma* in particular. Verses that talk about nature are presented as enjoining production.[23] The Qur'ān is perceived as praising those who work the lands in ways such as planting and building dams and canals, for land is a gift of God whose value increases when it is tilled and irrigated.[24] To develop the land is to tap one of the prime sources of power that nations possess. The ability to develop the land in various ways is what distinguishes the advanced from the backward nations.[25]

Al-Barrāwī also cites the Qur'ān concerning the varieties of yield in farm lands.[26] Each land gives according to the needs of its inhabitants. Thus those working on agricultural development need to study the land and its capabilities in order to maximize productivity;[27] a Qur'anic justification is provided for the employment of modern methods of farming and production. Verses are quoted to justify the use of other economic terms in order to advocate development, as well as to show that it is Islamic to talk about products as marked either for consumption or investment.[28]

The importance of labor is emphasized as Qur'anic and is supported by such quotations from the Prophet as, "It is preferable for you to carry a load of wood than to beg," and "No one eats better food than that which is of the labor of his hands. Even David, the Prophet of God, used to eat of the product of his hands." Al-Barrāwī exhorts people to work, insisting that work is honorable since it preserves man's dignity and that even the prophets engaged in it. It is interesting to observe, however, that the Qur'anic passages he quotes as advocating labor actually refer to specific acts.[29] Thus he derives a kind of socio-economic theory from an analysis of deeds (*a'māl*) cited in the Qur'ān as those for which men will be held personally responsible and accountable.

Islam is seen as advocating labor as a "duty incumbent on the capable," making it the responsibility of the nation to provide work opportunities for all its citizens. It is in accordance with God's will that unemployment be eradicated and total employment be provided for all citizens whether male or female. Al-Barrāwī thus provides a Qur'anic sanction for female participation in the labor force which grants them equality with males, each to work according to ability and to receive equal pay for equal work.[30]

The Qur'anic injunction to do good deeds is therefore presented as a correct labor policy. Islam is perceived as advocating cooperative efforts since cooperation leads to better efficiency and production; this has been proved in the field of agriculture, which provides for the division of labor and specialization.[31] Al-Barrāwī cites China as an example of a country that provides for human investment and cooperation, with its population working collectively on the construction of roads, schools, and hospitals. Communes so organized on a cooperative basis are in accordance with the basic Islamic teaching of mutual cooperation. The Qur'ān also forbids the exploitation of labor, demanding that each work according to his ability.[32] Child labor is forbidden, as is heavy labor for women such as that in mines or quarries; women should be granted a rest period during pregnancy; labor hours of workers should be limited; sick leaves and annual leaves must be instituted. Furthermore, safety must be guaranteed in factories, while health and social services must be provided for workers during working hours. This same passage in the Qur'ān advocates excellence in work. It is thus Islamic that there be adequate compensation for work performed. This provides workers with the proper incentive for more fruitful production.[33]

Al-Barrāwī also manages to find Qur'anic references to support his ideas that management and planning are important. Thus it is necessary to be creative, he says, and provide for the future through planning as well as execution. This necessitates the proper assessment of all resources, the utilization of potentialities, and the maximizing of productivity.[34] As for the area of agriculture, the Qur'ān is quoted to support a sane policy that develops new irrigation projects, dams, and canals; searches for new water sources; and plans for efficient distribution of water and the reclamation of the desert and unproductive land.[35]

Al-Barrāwī also quotes the Qur'ān extensively in support of trade and commerce as necessary exponents of man's vicegerency on earth and his responsibility for the maintenance of the *Umma* in a position of strength.[36] The Qur'ān has designed a general outline of policy that nations have to follow for internal and international commerce. These include the banning of cheating to insure security, guarantee of legal transactions, as well as competition in order to have prices determined by the law of supply and demand, government intervention in cases of exploitation[37] and hoarding,[38] maintaining means of communication and transportation, and punishing of criminal elements. Thus al-Barrāwī can say, "When we study the policies followed in our age, we can determine that to a great extent they proceed from the noble principles instituted in the Qur'ān and the way of the Prophet fourteen centuries ago."[39]

Al-Barrāwī also sees other modern economic policies as justified by the Qur'ān. These include saving, lack of excessive spending, lending, and interest (a distinction being made between interest and usury, for the latter is specifically forbidden by the Qur'ān).[40] The Qur'ān also envisions the proper order for mankind as one where the right to private property is guaranteed, he says; in the interests of the public good, however, wealth should not be restricted to the privileged few.[41]

Islam as the religion of God, the guide to humanity on how to live responsibly in harmony with God's purposes for creation, rejects racism and discrimination whether based on color, sex, or national origin.[42] The Qur'ān does say that there are various degrees of difference (*darajāt*) among people. These, however, are not based on a class structure but are contingent on such things as faith, knowledge, wisdom, and good deeds.[43]

In the final pages of his book, al-Barrāwī turns his attention to the Qur'anic understanding of the laws of history. Like all the other authors in the study, he cites the Qur'anic verses ascribing the rise and fall of nations to God's laws and man's unwillingness to harmonize his life, his government, and the world to these purposes.[44] The destruction of nations occurs because they belie the Prophets who proclaim the words of God and call on people to live a moral life. Al-Barrāwī sees in this a natural development in societies whereby they meet certain needs; when these needs are not met for a period of time new societies take over. These, he feels, follow an ascending order from the lower to the higher to concretize general social progress. Thus he ascribes a progressive development in society to the Qur'ān. There is not one single "man-made" social order that is good for all times and all places, i.e., that is universal and comprehensive, for societies by their very nature reflect human deficiencies and weaknesses.[45]

By emphasizing man's responsibility for his own destiny, the Qur'ān has also stressed the fact that change occurs through human effort.[46] Thus when annihilation comes to a people, they have clearly deserved it. In the creation narrative, Adam provides an illustration of human responsibility in that he was initially warned by God against Satan's deception. Adam, al-Barrāwī claims, was deceived by Eve and thus deserved to leave the Garden[47] (although the Qur'anic creation narrative specifies that it was Adam who was tempted and deceived, and that an obedient Eve shared her husband's fate).

Al-Barrāwī's use of Qur'anic quotations in espousing a modern economic theory is not unique, but is the method that has been used by several generations of Muslim scholars attempting to bring about a modern Islamic understanding of the world, one that addresses itself to modern challenges and provides answers. If the answers that are advocated can be proved to be Qur'anic and therefore of the essence of Islam, then the community can appropriate them without feeling that it is abandoning the true faith.

One gets the clear impression that al-Barrāwī labored a bit to marshal full Qur'anic evidence to support his interpretations.[48] Al-Ḥajjī expresses some reservations about this method of substantiating modern economic or political theories by the use of Qur'anic verses. He perceives the Qur'anic references to the universe not as specialized or specific injunctions but rather as intended to be proofs or examples of the didactic message of the Qur'ān. This does not mean, he says, that what the Qur'ān says is not consistent with fact; on the contrary, a substantial number of verses do deal with universal, scientific, historical, and other topics. Thus the Qur'ān, he affirms, is consistent with reality. It is because of its miraculous nature that humanity has not as yet discovered all the truths that it is able to reveal.

Having affirmed the veracity and eternality of the Qur'ān, al-Ḥajjī warns against seizing every opportunity to find Qur'anic explanations and justifications for all things, although he affirms that the Qur'ān is a book of guidance for the totality of life.[49] He uses Qur'anic verses as aphorisms or maxims to illustrate some of the points he is making,[50] giving specific quotations very sparingly. Throughout the text, the term "Qur'anic" is used as synonymous with "Islamic."

Al-Ḥajjī sees Islam today as a continuation of the same movement that initiated the struggle between righteousness and evil in the world. What is of note is that for him, this initiation came through the prophetic work of Muḥammad (and not Abraham or Adam as other Muslims tend to interpret the Qur'ān). This initiation had its beginning in the specific history of the community. Thus he tends to identify Islam as coexistent with the historic community.[51] Several verses are quoted to prove his affirmation that the Qur'ān enjoins Muslims to seek and pursue knowledge at whatever cost in hardship, and that it equates the discovery of the universe with a form of worship.[52] Furthermore, al-Ḥajjī sees the true interpretation of human history in the two Qur'anic verses that affirm that those who belie the truth that has been revealed through the prophets are doomed to the same destruction as those who have preceded in such a folly.[53]

Jaʿfar's use of the Qur'ān is limited to a very few verses which provide the framework for his interpretation of the meaning of history in Islam. Thus for him, the purpose of creation is the worship of God[54] as well as the development of full human potentialities for a life of commitment and accountability.[55] Human history is governed by eternal laws, and oppression invariably precipitates God's punishment.[56] These laws are manifested through God's action in history, referred to in the Qur'ān as the Days of God (*ayyām Allāh*).[57] These actions are indirect since man fashions history by using his God-given potentialities and capabilities. These days vary in quality; they are either days of power where God's omnipotence is made manifest, or days of mercy, for God rotates the days among people. Ja'far sees these verses as saying that mercy and compassion are given to the pious while anger and destruction are meted out to the deviates and evil ones. We have already noted above that the other authors interpret the Qur'anic verse dealing with the rotation of days to be a description of the varying fortunes of nations and civilizations as they rise and attain great heights and are then destroyed, only to be replaced by others.

Thus we see that for all authors being considered in this study, whether implicitly or explicitly, the Qur'ān is the normative criterion by which all reality has to be measured and judged. Its perception of the world is valid because of its divine origin. Al-Khalīl is no exception. In fact, his work is an attempt at a comprehensive interpretation of the Qur'anic view of history. For him, the divine origin of the Qur'ān guarantees the infallibility of his method since it proceeds from God's all-knowing vantage point as contrasted with posited or "man-made" theories. Thus the Qur'anic interpretation is universal and comprehensive. It transcends and penetrates all time and space and is able to outline the meaning and significance of events in the lives of individuals and nations.

Al-Khalīl quotes extensively from the Qur'ān when he expounds the Qur'anic view of history. Although he attempts a systematic and coherent presentation, many of the verses he cites are only tangential to his theme and add nothing to the potency of his argument. It seems doubtful that any given point can be much strengthened if the case is made more on the basis of the number of verses an author can ferret out and present as relevant than on the content and immediate context of those verses.

Like other authors, al-Khalīl also tends to view every Qur'anic verse as an independent revelation and therefore liable to interpretation on its own merit and meaning rather than in a given context or in the light of specific causes or conditions of revelation (*asbāb al-nuzūl*). Thus every verse in the Qur'ān is seen as an eternal truth for all times and all places.

Al-Khalīl proceeds by providing a list of references to the prophets and their communities as mentioned in the Qur'ān, beginning with the second Surah which offers one of the several narratives of creation in the Qur'ān. The Qur'ān proceeds from the initial history of creation and the world through the story of Adam, his temptation and descent to earth, and God's promise of guidance. In this al-Khalīl sees the key to the whole purpose of the creation of man on earth and the understanding of history. Man was created to be in perpetual struggle, and must always be receptive to the guidance from God which makes evident the way to truth and righteousness. If this guidance is followed precisely it will lead man to a return to the Garden. God continued to provide this guidance through the prophets until he gave complete and perfect guidance to the Prophet Muḥammad through the Qur'ān, which can now be preserved for eternity.[58]

The Qur'ān does not restrict its references to guidance to those delivered to the different prophets; rather, it discusses the communities to whom guidance is addressed, their responses to the truth of the messenger and the message, whether positive or negative, and their destinies in history as contingent on the nature and quality of their responses. Revelation in the Qur'ān is not restricted to the past and the present. It also deals with the future and as such it is prophecy.[59]

The narratives of the Qur'ān, by providing a summary of the experience of humanity, are a means of provoking human thinking into a constant search for truth. They provide examples calling humanity to action and the renunciation of sloth, indolence, and inactivity. These narratives prove God's constancy and omniscience as they provide the proof that the messages with which the various prophets were entrusted were the same since they were revealed by the only God, the source of all truth.[60] This truth is made self-evident by the Qur'ān's attestation and witness to it.[61]

The narratives provide a persistent reminder of God's norms (*sunan*) and laws (*nawāmīs*) which order the flow of history in a consistent direction, apart from which no one can operate. They present objective history insofar as they provide a sampling of the operation of God's laws. These laws are coordinated with the essential nature of man, transcending geographical, economic, tribal, or any other differences. The judgment of these laws is the recompense or punishment that is meted out to those who heed them or those who ignore or violate them. These laws are eternal; they do not change. The judgment rendered in their name is inevitable. Their truth and constancy have been made evident since creation, but many continue to ignore them.[62] Once apprehended, these laws become the dynamic force of history. They unlock knowledge about the past. In this sense they are not theories, or literary or academic research. They are *real* history as they serve contemporaneity and the movement towards the future.[63] Thus the purpose of researching human history according to the

Qur'ān is the active search for guidance for the present and the future. Such an effort has significance only for those who are receptive to its meaning afforded by this understanding of history.[64]

Thus the Qur'anic revelation to the Prophet and the Meccans has universal applicability. What the Qur'ān revealed in order to comfort the few Meccans who courageously accepted the faith is valid for the weakened *Umma* of Islam as it now lies between contending and strong powers. God's laws do not alter. The apparent wealth and power of the Eastern and Western blocs cannot last because it is based on falsehood. The character of these nations is not fashioned according to the will of God. They consequently are doomed to failure. The examples of former nations once powerful and mighty and then lying in ruins at the time of the Prophet continue to be effective for the believing community today.[65]

It may be worthwhile to note here several interesting uses of Qur'anic material. Consistent with current "revolutionary" terminology, al-Khalīl accuses the wealthy of being the *rajʿiyya,* those who hold to the past. They seek positions in order to protect their wealth. Thus they are called "rightists." In order to support his allegation by a Qur'anic verse, however, he has to resort to quoting verses from the Qur'ān that use the term *aṣḥāb al-shimāl,* the people of the left, to describe the wealthy who seek to maintain power.[66]

Also reflecting contemporary Islamic revolutionary idioms is the call to Muslims to *hijra,* to leave the land of oppression in order to resist and reject the oppression of the current rulers in Muslim countries. Only then will the Muslims gain perspective in order to be able to return and reform the situation.[67]

It is incumbent upon Muslims to strive to change their world until it is in harmony with God's purposes. The condition of people here on earth portrays the judgment of God. Since all reality is unified, judgments here are a corollary of what awaits humanity in the hereafter.[68] Those who believe will be recompensed and will find happiness in this world. This, as the Qur'ān makes abundantly clear, is the will of God.[69]

We see, then, that while the four authors who do to a greater or lesser extent make specific use of Qur'ān quotations come at the material from somewhat differing perspectives, there is a certain common element in the themes they try to develop. Both al-Barrāwī and al-Khalīl cite the Qur'ān so extensively that the effectiveness of their presentations seems curtailed rather than enhanced. Al-Ḥajjī more moderately warns against what he sees as the excessive attempt to find Qur'anic support for details, and the other writers are clearly more selective—one might say judicious—in their offering of direct scriptural justification for particular points and issues.

On the whole, however, one can point to several themes that are generally common to the writers in question. While al-Barrāwī is particularly insistent that the Qur'ān fully supports modern economic theory and industrial growth, the idea that the Book is clearly relevant for today's technological society is one generally accepted and espoused. Implicit in this is the theme often repeated that man as God's vicegerent has the legitimate right and responsibility to develop the animal, vegetable, and mineral resources of the earth, and that this development has a direct relationship to such things as modern agricultural methods, the advancement of trade and commerce, careful use of natural resources, and thoughtful attempts at management and planning of both resources and personnel.

Another recurrent theme is the absolute importance of social responsibility and seeing the significance of God's message in a communal context. Although al-Barrāwī espouses the idea of social progress and progressive development as having a Qur'anic basis and justification, it is clear that for all the authors the laws of history as outlined in the scripture are recognized not only as descriptive of the past but as the basis and guide for present and future individual and communal decisions. The rise and fall of nations is seen as inevitably linked to the degree to which they heeded the commandments of God. Man has the capability, in fact the responsibility, to fashion history actively, but reward and requital are ultimately and always in the hands of God.

The Qur'ān, then, is looked to as providing the ultimate summary of human experience, the guide for all human activity. The Qur'anic interpretation of history is both comprehensible and comprehensive, and through the study and analysis of it man can better understand both the ethical and the technological factors relevant to the establishment of a socially and morally advanced Islamic society today.

Implicit in all these works is the affirmation that the Qur'ān is the final revelation of truth and reality. Western claims that a scientific grounding must be the arbiter of truth are dismissed as posited or "man-made" efforts which are bound to change and alter as man advances in his knowledge of the world and the laws which govern nature and history. The ascription of independent authority to science would provide an alternate source of prescription challenging the authority of God's Word and His *Tawḥid*. Islam does not allow two absolutes to operate simultaneously since that would lead to a confrontation between them and to the inevitable decline of one in favor of the other. Thus the Qur'ān judges and validates science. This does not mean that science has no authority; rather, that it is simply man's effort to unravel the mystery of the functioning of the universe, a mystery whose general laws God has made evident in His revelation.

Chapter Ten
The Use of Western Sources

SINCE THE ARAB WORLD was opened for Western intellectual penetration, Arab authors have borrowed content and method from the West, at times selecting their material rather uncritically. All the authors studied here deal with the meaning and significance of Islamic history and of the idea of history in Islam. They all portray an awareness of Western historical theories and methodologies, and their discussions of the Muslim idea of history in general are aimed at a public that is aware of Western ideas. The purpose in all of their writings, however, is to defend an ideological commitment. For all of them Islam has the definitive answers, and they attempt to expound their ideas from within the Islamic perspective.

The use of Western sources varies among these writers, as does the degree of their understanding of them. Al-Sharqāwī is an example of an uncritical recorder of Western theories of history. He quotes Will Durant, A. C. Morrison, Albert Schweitzer, George McCauley Trevelyan, Henry Smith Williams, Descartes, Carlyle, John Stuart Mill, Max Weber, Vico, and Toynbee. For him, the history of the world is nothing but the history of religions, since religion and the zeal and commitment to the spiritual aspects of life is what endows civilization with progress and power. Like the other authors, he does not distinguish between civilization and culture, nor is he concerned with the exact historical facts that would vindicate his stance. He is in agreement with the other authors in saying that the period in which the Prophet was alive is the example of the highest zeal and commitment, yet like the others he offers no explanation of why the glory of Islam as a civilization came under the ʿAbbāsids, several centuries after the death of the early Muslims.

Al-Jundī's work affords another example of the uncritical use of Western sources. He quotes such writers as Thomas Arnold, Tritton, and W. C. Smith among others, taking from them any commentary on Islam that he finds particularly favorable. Because of the eclectic nature of his sources, his work lacks coordination and integration, affirming a variety of approaches as Muslim in nature regardless of potential or inherent conflict in what the several authors have said. Al-Barrāwī, on the other hand, does not make any references to Western scholars, although the type of world order he advocates and interprets as Islamic has certainly been developed in the technological and scientific Western world.

Both al-Ḥajjī and Quṭb attack the West and the Western methodology of studying Islamic history, the latter insisting that Western scholars are incapable of understanding Islam.[1] Both perceive Western scholars as motivated by malicious intent, seeking to destroy Islam by belittling the Islamic heritage and achievements. The basic failure of Western scholarship in this area, they feel, is due to its inability to penetrate the dynamism and true meaning of Islam. Only a committed Muslim would be able to see things Islamic in true perspective. For both al-Ḥajjī and Quṭb, the purpose of the study of history is not to provide chronological details of events, but rather to propagate Islamic ideology. It aims therefore at guidance and the provision of a specific historical orientation which maintains that Islam is a universal human message, not limited by time, place, or a historical community.

Al-Ḥajjī criticizes the Western Arab secular interpretation of history, especially the works of Philip Hitti and Jurjī Zaydān. He finds fault with the writings of Ṭāha Ḥusayn and Aḥmad Amīn, and attacks the nationalist interpretations of ʿAlī Ḥusnī al-Kharbuṭlī and al-Ḥuṣrī. They have all been influenced by Western interpretations, he says, and are therefore misleading since they provide historical analyses from a different and inappropriate stance. He dismisses Orientalists and their followers as insincere and relegates their writings to the category of erroneous ideas based on personal whims rather than on facts.[2] In this he shows the influence of Muḥammad Asad and of al-Nadawī, both of whom he quotes.[3] He does admit, however, that some Orientalists may have been fair in their treatment of Islam, and these he feels must be thanked by Muslims because they have been able to present Islam in its glorious image. Those Orientalists who have maligned Islam may actually have done it a service, since they have spurred Muslims to search for the truth to combat their falsehoods.[4]

Al-Ḥajjī's dissatisfaction with Western and Westernized writers is due to the fact that they tend to perceive Islam as a regional or local manifestation and thus talk about "American Islam" or "Russian Islam." They also tend to emphasize *jihād* as an endless war and Islamic history as the history of battles rather than of obedience to God's commandments and a means of witnessing to God in the world.[5] Thus these writings on Islamic history are also unacceptable because they have ignored the lesson (*ʿibra*) that the occurrence or the event may teach about the reality and truth of Islam.[6]

Al-Ḥajjī attacks both the content and the methodology of the Western and Westernized historians because he believes that they emphasize the negative aspects, giving only inane reasons or even impugning evil intent as causes of events rather than accepting the sincerity of Islam and the call and message of the Prophet.[7] Furthermore, they portray Islamic expansion as motivated by the desire for booty as well as the delight in the use of the sword, thus dismissing the divine message as a relevant factor.[8]

Attacking the materialistic interpretation of history as a limited and narrow comprehension of reality, al-Hajjī says that it is in total error, as is the Freudian interpretation which claims that all things are motivated by sexual desires. In this he agrees totally with Sayyid Quṭb.[9] Such a perception, they both assert, suggests a distorted image of humanity as well as reality. Al-Ḥajjī further attacks the materialists because they deny other aspects of human behavior, including the psychological and intellectual as well as the spiritual. He accuses them of using violent methods to spread their ideology in contrast to the tolerant methods of Islam where people are given the freedom to choose.[10] The key to Islamic success in the spread of its hegemony over major parts of the world, he says, is the devotion and zeal of its adherents and not violence or materialistic considerations.[11]

M. K. Jaʿfar agrees that Orientalists seek to destroy Islam,[12] although this does not prevent him from extensive discussion and quotation from the works of Western historians of religion and theologians concerning the nature of religion. He evidences awareness of both English and German sources on the subject, discussing in some detail the works of such persons as Nicholas Berdyaev, W. G. DeBurgh, R. L. Shinn, William James, Rudolf Otto, F. Heiler, H. Gordon, A. G. Widgery, A. C. Bouquet, H. Dumoulin, E. Conze, C. E. Jung, and St. Augustine.

Jaʿfar condemns the Marxist interpretation of history as one that restricts life to this earth and assumes that humanity cannot be influenced by any forces beyond the material and sensual. In his criticism, he includes among the materialists all those who deny revelation and divinity.[13] He sees that the greatest weakness of the materialist interpretation is that its exponents consider themselves the only authoritative interpreters of history, claiming that materialism is most comprehensive despite the fact that it ignores or denies a major part of reality.[14] The materialist interpretation is rejected by most religions since it fails to take revelation, creation, and destiny seriously.

Of all the authors studied here, only Jaʿfar shows an awareness of the Christian literature dealing with history, revelation, and creation. He refers to the problems faced by Christianity in trying to cope with the reality of the spiritual world as well as that of the material world. This problem was highlighted, he says, in the controversy concerning a definition of the Incarnation. He notes that a similar problem was faced by Islam when it considered the question of the creation of the Qur'ān and decided that there is a total separation between man and God.[15] Ja'far is also the only one in this group of writers to note that certain Jewish and Christian works have highlighted aspects of history that all religions can benefit from. These include, among others, the following observation that Islam finds acceptable: "God's care for His creatures, the existence of a clear purpose for creation, the unity of history in an attempt to realize this purpose, and God's guardianship over His sincere creatures."[16]

Al-Khalīl, meanwhile, says that he considers Arnold Toynbee's *A Study of History* to be "a new triumph" in the field of interpretation. As a Christian, Toynbee has come to an understanding of the moral basis of the seeming vicissitudes of history which has much in common with the Islamic perspective. Al-Khalīl is well aware that Toynbee's book has been attacked by Western scholars as a work of theology, which actually raises it in his own esteem. He does recognize some real shortcomings in the work, however, which along with Spengler's *Decline of the West* suffers from a lack of balance in certain areas while still achieving some real insights into the laws that govern the rise and fall of nations. Both books, al-Khalīl feels, have a tendency to separate intellectual and spiritual values, making them particularly vulnerable to attack. Most historical methodologies avoid the question of the relation of God, nature, and man, and have centered on one of these elements to the exclusion of the others. This in some cases has led to a metahistory, or a special emphasis on the role of the hero or the natural forces in determining history, which in turn leads to the materialist interpretation that al-Khalīl so wishes to avoid.[17]

Historians such as Spengler, Toynbee, Kesserling, and Collingwood, says al-Khalīl, have rightly noted the errors to which such partial interpretations can lead, and have attempted to rectify them by proposing an interpretation of civilization. Their efforts, however, have lacked a comprehensive vision since they view civilization primarily from the secular vantage point. This suggests a duality between the visible and the invisible, God and man, matter and spirit, the natural and the supernatural. To achieve a true understanding of human history we need to avoid the fragmentation of reality. This cannot be achieved outside of the Islamic context which is coordinated "with the heart of the world, the dynamics of history, and the reality of human life and social existence."[18]

Al-Khalīl goes on to present a critical study of some historical theories based on studies or translation of these historians into Arabic. His refutation of Hegel is totally dependent on a translation by Siddiqi; he sees Hegel as presenting a philosophy based on contradictions (thesis, antithesis, synthesis). For Hegel the essence of progress is the struggle between these contradictions. Each phenomenon has its contradiction inherent in its being which urges it to strive forward to resolution.[19] Furthermore, al-Khalīl believes that Hegel failed to distinguish between the antithetical and the evident. He sees that Hegel, Spengler, and Marx all have used excessive imagination and theory in trying to determine the course of future events. Surprisingly, says al-Khalīl, they term their attempts at future prophecy scientific. This he feels is contradictory to the scientific method which refutes all suppositions, theories, and attempts to move beyond the events of everyday life to a prediction of what lies ahead.[20]

Al-Khalīl views Western thought as fluctuating between the extreme right and the extreme left. It tends to oversimplify reality, he says, by proceeding from a vision that is one-sided, crediting an individual or a collectivity with having an impact on history whether functioning as part of a class as Marx theorized or as a nation as perceived by Hegel. He sees an immense gap between the ideas propounded by Sidney Hook in *The Hero in History* and the historical materialism of someone like Stalin, a gap which cannot, in his opinion, be spanned. For, practically speaking, events do not occur except as a result of the interaction of the two.[21]

The Qur'ān clearly illustrates the importance of both the individual and the collectivity. The role of the Prophet as a messenger calling humanity to the truth, and the response of the community whether by following in obedience or rejecting the message, is crucial in delineating the key to the operation of history. In other words, there must be a balance between individual and corporate action.[22] The materialistic theory of history discounts the efficacy of individual initiative. The group becomes the entity that moves the world of matter. On the other hand, the idealistic interpretation places undue emphasis on the role of the hero; he becomes the tool of the intellect to materialize the goal. In this interpretation, too, the individual loses his importance. It is this inadequacy that Toynbee attempts to rectify, by injecting it with Christian theology which ascribes to the individual and to the group what al-Khalīl sees as an irresponsible assurance of salvation which leads to the separation of the individual from total responsibility for historical events.[23]

In al-Khalīl's view, the Qur'ān transcends all of this by placing total responsibility for the fashioning of events on the individual and the group together.[24] In the theories of Marx and Hegel man becomes a mechanical automaton interacting with nature. In the case of Marx, his theory is dismissed by al-Khalīl as oversimplistic in that it takes away from man his initiative and renders him predetermined. Historical movements, if studied carefully, will show categorically that beyond the purely physical in each of us there is an intricate and complicated mixture of "intellect, spirit, emotion, conscience, instincts, nerves, urges and desires" that are hard to fathom or predict.[25]

Meanwhile, Hegel's idealism led to the establishment of a fascist government that provided various justifications for aggressive behavior and oppression against humanity. Marx's dialectical materialism, on the other hand, led to the dictatorship of the working class as a goal of history, allowing for the justification of inhuman acts of cruelty against those who oppose such a goal. As an alternative to these, however, al-Khalīl sees Toynbee's pale Christianity as a nonrational approach providing Western civilization with hope rather than absolute assurance. It is a "patch-up operation," a combination of the religious values of Christianity with some of the teachings of Judaism, Buddhism, and Islam. As such it is contrary to the experience of the members of a faith who accept revelation from one source and thereby proceed towards a purpose and a specified destiny.[26]

The rational dialectic proposed by Hegel and the dialectical materialism advocated by Marx and Engels, says al-Khalīl, render man in each case a follower rather than a leader. Man becomes an element of civilization rather than its "active willing master," which is the position accorded to him through the message revealed in Islam.[27] Al-Khalīl also criticizes Hegel's theory that the forces of good are always in ascendancy, progressing towards the ideal society. He finds Toynbee closest to the truth because his theory of challenge and response allows for human wills to be effective in directing the destiny of history.[28] He dismisses all of them as unoriginal, however, and says that the Qur'ān has made it quite evident that the struggle between man and Satan began at the moment of the creation of man. Thus man and society are in a perpetual struggle as part of the nature of being.[29]

A further weakness of the "interpretive" theories of Hegel and Marx, as al-Khalīl views them, is the fact that they propose a goal for society wherein struggle will cease, a time of peace and love. The truth as revealed in the Qur'ān and the teachings of Islam, however, points to a perpetual struggle in the world. The perfect society is not a utopia on earth, but one that is achieved and maintained by perpetual personal and collective struggle.

The Christian interpretation of history which influenced Toynbee's theories accepts sin and redemption on both the individual and the corporate levels. This ascribes de facto to Christian nations an upward progressive movement leading toward the ideal, despite the evil these nations may have committed. In Islam the destiny of the society is not determined by its religious affiliation per se, but by its ethical and moral behavior. A society's progress is not inevitable, but rather fluctuates up and down in relation to the degree of commitment exhibited by the individual and the group to living a responsible life.[30] In the Christian apprehension of the world, al-Khalīl believes, God's judgment appears to fall on those who do not believe in original sin and in justification. In Islam it falls on every individual or group that veers from the straight path and ceases to practice self-regeneration, which alone leads to commanding the good, forbidding the evil, and bearing witness to the world.[31]

Toynbee's theory of challenge and response tends to portray the world and nature as things to be subdued, says al-Khalīl, as recently evidenced by the conquest of space. Islam, on the other hand, sees the struggle not with the world but with Satan and evil. For the world and man are in a relation of complementarity, integration, cohesion, and coherence between "spirit and matter, mind and heart, earth and sky, free will and predestination, action and contemplation, instinct and conscience, presence and absence, physics and metaphysics." Since man is both spirit and matter, any struggle between these two elements would lead to division and dysfunction. Unity and integration provide the incentive for creative development.[32]

Thus we can see that the impact of Western ideas and interpretations continues to be a major factor in the consciousness of modern Arab Muslims, even though it acts for some only as a challenge to provide a fresh interpretation of eternal truths. The motive behind the writing of all the works we have considered here is to bear witness to that unalterable reality as revealed to the Prophet Muḥammad from the source of all truth, God. Although Western philosophers may raise questions and propound theories, they can only apprehend partial truth. Truth, in other words, can be experienced and realized only within the Islamic context.

All authors evidence a conscious awareness that Islam is being judged. Their efforts are to provide a defense of the truth against what they see to be unrelenting threats buffeting Islam. The motivation for these threats is not necessarily belligerency, although missionaries and Orientalists get their full share of blame and criticism. These writers also see a threat in the works of philosophers simply because of their existence. Nothing from their perspective should or could be more eloquent or relevant than the message of Islam. Their defense, therefore, is against the erosion of faith on the part of members of the Muslim community, or against the shaking of the pride of Muslims in Islam itself.

Where it is possible to see corollaries between what Western authors are saying and what Islam teaches, then the response is clear: "This answer has been with us from the start." Where no direct correlation exists, efforts are put forth to accommodate the Western teaching whenever possible. If, however, it cannot be supported either by a Qur'anic revelation or by the examples of the Prophet, then it is generally attacked as error. Therefore, although efforts on behalf of Islam and in defense of its conception of the laws pertaining to the rise and fall of nations are articulated from within the faith, they continue to be a response to challenges perceived as coming from without.

The acculturationists are perceived as outside the pale of the faith because they have sought validation in authorities alien to Islam. They have perfected hermeneutical devices in order to provide a valid justification for change not on Islamic terms, but to imitate the West. In this they have opted for appearance rather than essence. By seeking to sound relevant and modern they have shortchanged Islam at its core by allowing its enemies and detractors to dictate the paths it is to seek and the ideas it is to hold.

For normativists and neo-normativists, on the other hand, the methodology is more authentically Muslim because it is grounded in the Word of God. It too seeks change and ascendancy for the community but not at the expense of authenticity. For Muslims to be truly faithful they must seek the restitution of the ideal which formed them as a nation and launched them as a beacon for humanity guiding the wayward to God.

Conclusion
Towards an Islamic Understanding of History

THE AUTHORS SURVEYED above agree on the general principle that only an Islamic answer can maintain the authenticity and integration of the community. Although they may differ in their understanding of where the perimeter of the domain of Islam has to be drawn in relation to the domain of the ungodly, they agree that for an idea to be valid, it has to be Islamic. Meanwhile, whereas al-Barrāwī, al-Jundī, and Jaʿfar appear to leave a wider avenue for incorporation of new ideas within the corpus of what is considered Islamic, they are aware that nothing can have a validity of its own outside the Qur'anic revelation. Their creative interpretations are finally validated by their apprehension of the Qur'ān and its teachings.

Several images of the drama of the history of nations can be seen in their work. In al-Sharqāwī, for instance, the line of history is constant from creation to judgment. Nations who appropriate God's way become dominant until they lose their zeal and are replaced by others. The following diagram suggests the structure of his thought:

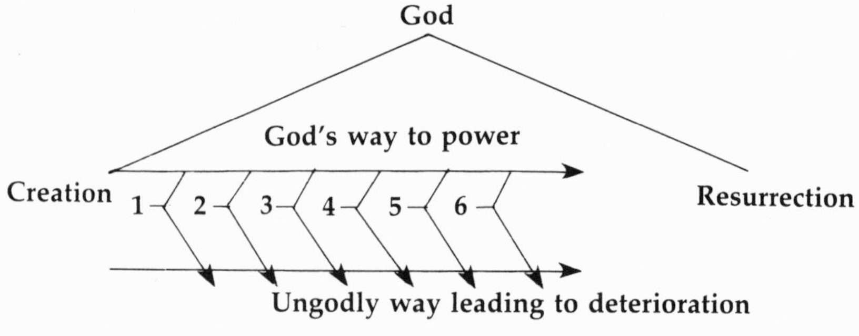

1-Egyptians
2-Assyrians
3-Jews
4-Christians
5-Muslims
6-West

For Ja'far the arena of history is not repetitive, but rather receptive to God's action. Past, present, and future are integrated in the perception of divine time:

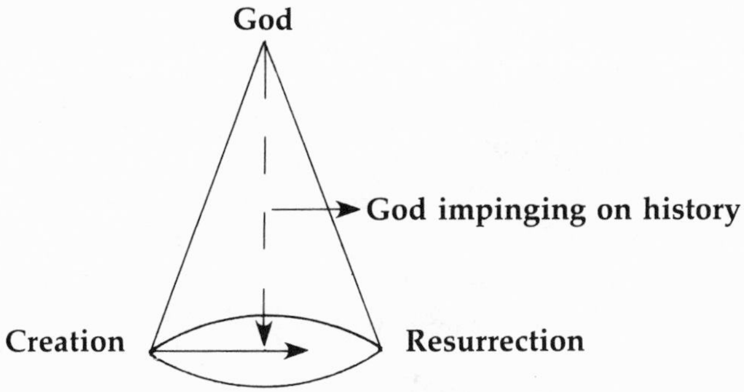

Al-Jundī perceives history as linear and cyclical. It starts with creation and comes to fulfillment with the resurrection. To march in the way of God, the community moves forward and upward in a spiral in order to continue to find its bearing. For it is only in looking back that it is able to attempt to re-create the perfect community in the world:

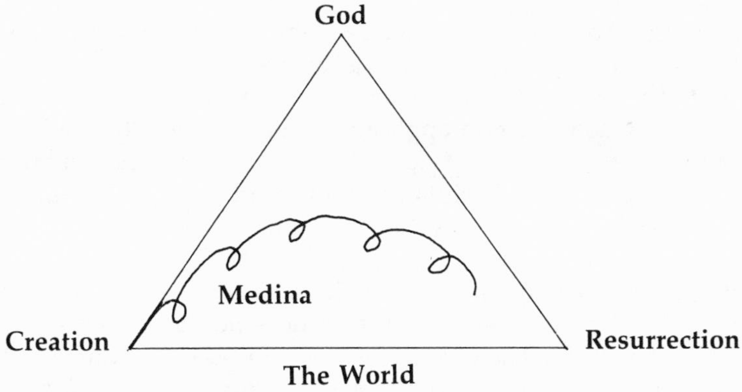

The Qur'anic view of history as perceived by Khalīl is a unity where past, present, and future meet in the present moment in the Qur'ān. For the Islamic community to continue to live under God, it must constantly strive to maintain a holistic balance between the spiritual and material parts of life, the middle position. Besides assuring the persistence of grace, a life thus lived will guarantee harmony with the forces of the world that provide progress and development and assure victory in this world and on the Day of Resurrection:

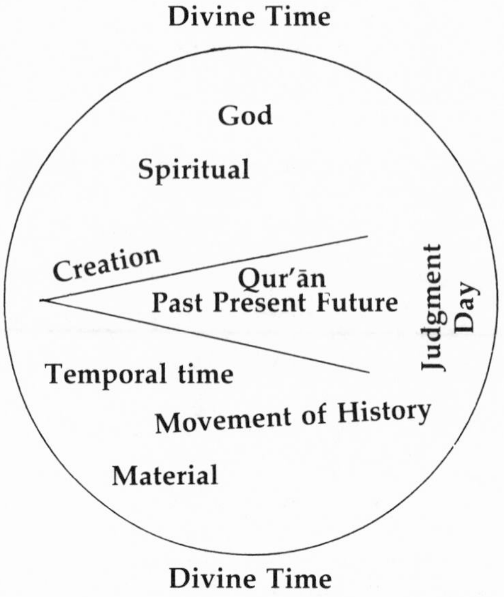

In general, we have seen that the contemporary Muslim views on history and its process are in agreement that the fluctuation in the condition of nations is ruled by God's laws which are regular, eternal, and valid. The fate of previous nations confirms the existence of these laws which are consistent in application and are eternally valid under all circumstances, a proof of God's constancy and dependability. For Muslims to regain their ascendancy in the world, they must function within the scope of these laws that are contingent on corporate steadfastness and commitment.

All the authors agree that the cohesion and unity of the *Umma* are an essential factor in its revival, for God does not favor a community divided against itself. The essence of God's message for humanity today, the only means for regeneration and restoration to power and effectiveness, is the same as it has been for all time. It has been preserved in pristine condition in the Qur'ān. Only when its true meaning is apprehended and its comprehensive nature is appropriated as a way of life will the *Umma* be able to break through its petrified and confused present and gain ascendancy in the future.

Islam is not simply an affirmation of creeds or an articulation of commitment to an accumulated and ossified tradition; rather, it is an appropriation of ultimate reality and participation in its daily fulfillment in everyday life, a total awareness of this reality in every act of eating, sleeping, working, praying, dreaming, in recreation and in interpersonal relations. To apprehend this religious reality, the Muslim must participate in the religious act and fulfill the prescriptions of the *sharīʿa*. *Jihād* on the part of the individual is the essential element in re-creating the Muslim person and hence the Muslim society, for every decision and every action undertaken in the present by or for the *Umma* has an impact on its future.

The insistence of the authors on the necessity of appropriation of the faith as a commitment to a way of life is a response to the modernizers and compromisers among Muslims who, aware of the present dominance of the West, are seeking answers from Western methods and experience in the hope of duplicating their success in the Arab world. The need for authenticity also sends them searching for parallel ideas in their own heritage. These they abstract from the special Islamic experience and universalize as the underlying forces of the system. The contextual framework of these ideas is not their concern. The past serves the utilitarian function of providing an authentic alternative to the vacuum in the identity of the new generation. Not only is it perceived as authentic, but as endowing the community with legitimacy and honor. For many, their heritage becomes an emotional attachment to the past, a focus of pride, and the hope of confidence for the future. This, however, leads to the abandonment of the central contextual framework of the glory of Islamic heritage, the commitment to Islam as a way of life.

In the eyes of these writers all efforts of the modernists, Westernizers, and compromisers are an indulgence in apostasy, a veering from the right path, a degeneration into *jāhilīyya*,[1] the ignorance of materialism, the establishing of other norms besides God, seeking other achievements besides His glory, and creating new orders to compete with His will for mankind. Thus those who advocate an Islamic response to the crisis of the present want not only to recapture the potency of the past, but to affirm that that potency cannot be recaptured outside of the prototype of the Medinan state as established during the life of the Prophet. It is not only a spirit of the age that needs to be recaptured, but a whole social and ethical order that needs to be re-created and reestablished. It is not an ideal or idealistic plan, but the only means to the salvation of the world and the ascendancy of God's way in the world.

The present authors emphasize the necessity of appropriating not only a sense of identity, glory, and achievement from the past as the compromisers had to do, but they are also anxious that the essential methods of the past that were attuned to correlate with the eternal laws of God be reappropriated due to their relevance to the present as well as to the future. And although the ideas and formulas they reiterate as necessary are identical with those discussed at the dawn of Islam, their content has changed. This comes about mainly as a result of the contemporary challenges and pressures the authors face. For while the answers are the same, they are attempting to respond to contemporary questions. In the process, traditional answers appear to acquire additional meaning, a more comprehensive applicability, and at times a specific dismissal of any alternate claims to universality as ungodly.

The reaffirmation of the old becomes new in a world that has ignored it and rejected it in some way or another for different periods of time. The new element is progressive precisely because it gives answers to perennial as well as to new questions. It newness comes from its tried and true efficacy in the past as well as its guaranteed success in the present, due to its divine origin. For although the answer may be "old," it is eternally applicable to every situation that may seem novel, to every generation that has to make its choices daily between the way of God and the way of ignorance. For the world changes and the "progressive" nature comes from the constancy of the efficacy of the answers for all new situations. The progressive nature is therefore inherent in the answer, and as it has responded to all challenges in the past, it continues to be effective in the present and is guaranteed to work in all possible situations in the future. Thus it is progressive not because it changes but because it is equipped to cope with all change. Progress is seen as motion and a change in sequence rather than a basic change in essence or being.

Islam can be understood as both transcendent and historical. In one sense it is not a "founded" religion, brought into being by the Prophet Muḥammad at a particular time in history. Rather it is God's one revelation to mankind, perpetually made known through the messages of the prophets. From this perspective Islam is a continual reformation and redirecting of humanity to the way of God, a cleansing from error and from the accretions of human motivations that have led humanity from the true path. As the agency of reform Islam stands as pure and unchanging, true believers sharing with each other throughout history a common commitment to God's purpose. In this sense there are no special local manifestations of Islam, no regional, cultural, or historical differences. One cannot in this light distinguish between Arab, Turkish, Indian, or American Islam any more than between medieval and modern manifestations of it. Islam is one as revealed in the Qur'ān, and the ideal and perfect Islamic community is that of Medina where the *Umma* lived under divine guidance through the mediation of the Angel Gabriel and the Prophet Muḥammad.

There is another way in which Islam can be viewed, however, and that is as the community that can trace its historical beginning to the reformation of existing beliefs and practices initiated through the actions of the Prophet. In this sense Islam *is* a "founded" religion, historical because its roots are in history. Without continuous reflection on the truths of transcendent Islam, the historical religion can be, and has been, occasionally led astray by the vagaries of any given moment. Thus Islam is participation in the experience of all Muslims through all time, a corporate body tracing itself back to an historical fact, documents, researched and maintained by the awareness of historical consciousness.

It is this historical consciousness that guarantees the authenticity and provides the validation of the experience of both individual and group in the present moment. The daily choosing to follow the way of God now and the pledge to follow it in the future is an expression of trust in God's faithfulness to His promise. As He has acted in the past, He continues to act in the present and will continue to so act until the Day of Resurrection. For the committed Muslim history provides authentication of God's constancy. History is that which has given the community its identity and each individual his own point of departure.

The history of Islam is the history of the salvation of humanity from corruption and materialism. After the Jews and Christians failed and after the great nations of Persia and Byzantium exhausted one another, God broke in and chose Muḥammad to bring the Qur'ān for the salvation of mankind. This was His fulfillment of His promise to Adam to provide guidance for humanity that it may not go astray. And yet in another way it can be said that God does not actually enter into history. That is, the Creator does not become tinged with the creation, but rather impinges through revelation to the Prophets and faithful believers. Through this guidance He reveals His purposes for the world and through the laws of nature and history He directs His creation to the realization of these purposes. History and nature are thus intimately related as the divine agents of revelation.

History is not perceived as a cyclical flow in which nations rise and fall. It is rather the direct process whereby God's purposes are made known, His constancy proved. It is not a continual return but comes to a consummation when men and their actions will stand accountable before the Lord. The apparent vicissitudes of history and the fortunes of nations provide a lucid illustration of the functioning of God's laws. History is thus seen not so much as having meaning per se as having direction. It is, in a sense, the vehicle for the unfolding of God's divine purpose. What happens is not chance but is of ultimate significance, saying something to humanity about humanity and about God.

It is for the *Umma* to be the agent of this divine purpose, that body responsible for making His will known to humanity, namely that all creatures should worship God and Him alone. Every effort of the *Umma* is to be synchronized towards the fulfillment of that good, both on the individual and the communal levels. Thus history is the arena in which is enacted the battle of the forces of good over evil, the struggle of the faithful community to maintain a truly Muslim order wherein God alone is worshipped and His divine laws respected.

Ashʿarite theology, whose interpretation dominated the orientation of Muslim thought until the last century, placed little significance on the individual or collective carrying out of responsibility as affecting or impinging on the teleological movement of history. To allow otherwise, in their conception, would be to detract from the full majesty and omnipotence of God Who does not need mankind and for Whom mankind's lack of faithfulness will not affect the scheme of the process of history. Their atomistic perception of reality deleted any effective influence of human action on the flow of history. Only by entering the fold of the *Umma* and meshing his efforts with those of the righteous community could the individual effectively participate in human history.

This Ashʿarite conception was, of course, a reaction to the Muʿtazilite emphasis on the importance of human responsibility. In all of modern Muslim understanding at the present time one finds again the stress on individual responsibility and thus individual participation in the historical process. Human history has been placed under man's vicegerency and man must assume full responsibility for it. Man is not innately sinful and therefore in inevitable need of redemption; he is rather susceptible to being faithless to the commitment to responsible choice. When one lives a life of *kufr* ignoring God the creator, he forfeits his happiness in both this life and the next. The interplay of responsibility and judgment form the drama of history. Recompense is meted out in this world as well as the next; what befalls individuals and nations now is but a foretaste of what awaits them in the life to come. A modern theology of history therefore centers on the story of the march of humanity from creation to resurrection, of the lives of the *Umma* of God, Muslims committed to the furthering of His order in the world.

Thus while medieval theology concentrated its concern for man's rule on a discussion of free will and predestination, one finds a clear change in the content of contemporary thinking. Man has become central; he matters. History in a sense is a record of human deeds as well as of God's actions. Particularly for the modernist, man has come into his own. With the emphasis on man's rational capacity and freedom, nature and history are now not only the arena for divine action. Man can participate in fashioning and changing the world, and in a more extreme interpretation can even be said to be the master of his own destiny. The consequences of this are serious. Modernity has placed on man a heavy burden, that of alienation, despair, and fractured hope. The result of this kind of assumed responsibility is the loss of the supportive function of the *Umma* and sometimes a schizophrenic confusion about individual goals and purposes. Man can no longer blame unforeseen forces or relegate responsibility to the winds of fate or the flow of God's unseen plan. He himself carries the burden for his life, for the life of the community, and for the destiny of Islam as an *Umma.*

Modernists by their emphasis on historical thought have necessitated a reinterpretation of Islam in historical terms. Historical consciousness is not only necessary, it is the purpose of life. That history has been important from the beginning of Islam in Medina is obvious. But the modern concern, which can almost be called an obsession, appears to agree with the Hegelian-Marxist emphasis on success in history as an obligation for all peoples. It becomes, in effect, an end in itself. Therefore there is an overriding concern for interpreting what has gone amiss, with the need to recapture history and make it subservient to the human will.

For the normativist Muslim, the efficacy of the *Umma* in history is guaranteed by coordinating its effort in the cause of God. Because He is ultimately the Lord, judge, and victor, man can only participate in the bringing about of that victory in history. The mission of the *Umma* is to strive that all may come to the worship of God through knowledge of the Qur'ān, and to live life as a witness to His providence and care. It is to remind men of their equal accountability before God and to summon them to strive for social justice.

For normativist Islam there can be no philosophy of history, for there is no development of civilization which is outside the perimeter of God's action and care; thus Islam and the history of the *Umma* cannot be a factor in that development. All historical considerations for the normativists necessarily form rather a theology of history, for they deal with the life of the *Umma* in its *jihād* to maintain the word and law of God operative in the world.

The influence of acculturationists on the normativist interpretation of Islam has been to demystify it. Islam as the natural religion is also the rational religion. It can be grasped by reason, because, unlike Christianity, it does not demand faith and the suspension of that which is of the rational order. Since there is no redemptive act of history, no incarnation, there is no need to justify Islamic reality. Islamic reality and objective reality are one and the same.

Normativists accuse the modernists and acculturationists of attempting to modify, change, and add to Islam in such a way that Islamic ideas are "patched" (*tarqīʿ*) over with Western ideas. They fear that in this kind of patchwork the tenets of the faith have lost their content and have become mere abstractions perceived as obsolete by the threat of Marxism and secularism. The modernist emphasis on the individual is seen as another example of *tarqīʿ* by many normativists, those for whom Islam is a community, a corporate body of committed people. If one individual deviates, the whole community suffers the consequences. The group is intimately bound both by common commitment to the goals revealed by God and by a sense of responsibility and guardianship for one another. Each is accountable both to and for the other; the mutuality of commitment and responsibility is seen as an agent binding the *Umma* to the purposes of God.

One of the primary concerns for the normativists is the danger of misinterpreting the Qur'ān, of taking sections out of context to prove specific points and of seeing it in ways not consistent with the understanding of traditional Islam. The Qur'ān is a given, an irreducible category, and to deny its eternal and divine nature is to deny Islam. The examination of any of the passages of the Qur'ān, as of any of the tenets of belief, according to norms and methods that are alien or novel threatens the very foundations of the faith. From the beginning the Qur'ān was questioned by Jews and Christians, the People of the Book; thus one of the elements of *īmān* is faith in the books of the prophets in their original and uncorrupted form. Norms coming from outside Islam have been suspect from the earliest days of the *Umma*, and are particularly so now as Orientalists and other Westerners come with their tools of scholarly criticism. Since the Qur'ān is of divine origin everything in it has its God-given authority simply by virtue of its inclusion.

For all modern Muslims, acculturationists and those who advocate normative Islam, the problem of the moment is to explain, understand, and rectify the situation of Islam in the modern world. That things are amiss, politically, socially, and culturally, is obvious. However one interprets the meaning of historical events, the warning to the Muslims of today seems clear: unless they cease from following the ways of the world and renew their effective participation in the fulfillment of God's order, they will continue to be backward; unless they appropriate the moral and ethical principles exemplified by the Prophet and revealed in the Qur'ān, they will certainly be punished by forfeiting forever any chance to recapture their God-given mission of leadership in the world.

These are not necessarily new ideas for those who seek to engage the allegiance of the members of the Islamic community. They are, however, being expressed by new and current voices supported by new energies and endowed with a new sense of urgency and expectancy. These new leaders understand that the teaching of the Qur'ān about God's judgment in history has clear implications for Islam today. Twentieth-century Muslims in seeking ascendancy of leadership on their own have floundered in giving allegiance to one ideology after another, and to one idolatry after another, forgetting or ignoring the vital force and key to the reappropriation of their destiny.

Skeptics who dismiss this use of history as gimmickry, saying that it will have no lasting effect on the community since it appeals to emotions and is unable to tackle the practical problems of the Arab world, forget that those who propound these theories seek to elicit emotion for its own sake. They seek to eradicate apathy and foster zeal and commitment. Zeal becomes an object in itself, a goal to strive for as a criterion by which to measure success. Any failure in achieving goals or realizing plans can be ascribed to unacceptable levels of zeal and commitment rather than to errors in the assessment of situations, unproductive plans, or technical failures.

For today's Muslim the goal is the manifestation of Islam in society as a reaffirmation of God's guidance in history and a guarantee of the success He gives to those who live lives of commitment. In so living, Muslims become vehicles of God's mercy to mankind, and the *Umma* participates in the original community of those who dared to take God at His word. As He has given victory repeatedly to the faithful in the course of history, so will He do now. The life of the Prophet and the experience of the early Muslims stand as the authority that challenges the modern faithful to commitment. The *Umma* today as it has done throughout its history is being called upon to reappropriate the guidelines of the revelation of God in the Qur'ān as guideposts for the future. In this the freedom of the individual and of the community are maintained, and God's continuing guidance and mercy insured. Only by a willful affirmation and appropriation of this heritage is Islam alive in its essential nature, and only by active participation in that heritage can God's purposes for mankind, as revealed throughout the course of history, be realized.

Appendix A
History Is Humanity's Way to God
by Maḥmūd al-Sharqāwī

ISLAM IS THE RELIGION of simplicity and unicity, a religion for all people. It seeks to lift man and prosper life. Religious character is the strongest effective factor in the life and progress of nations. It provides the strongest ties which bring together individuals from different nationalities and races. Religious events are the greatest events of history. The noblest deeds of nations are those that occur during its age of belief. There is no factor more potent over people than religion because in it is ideal happiness towards which human souls aspire and in which human nature finds rest, that [nature that] seeks eternity and fears annihilation, that is willing to sacrifice accidents in search of the essence.

It is the most effective factor through which a nation finds its unity, its interest, and its ideology. Religion shall remain alive and will not become extinct.

Religious character may weaken or become strong, die or live. These phases affect the progress of the nation which is established on religion. Nations in which religious character prevails are stronger, more powerful and capable of being patient in trouble, and more willing to sacrifice. History has not mentioned a single nation where the religious character is dominant which was conquered, except in the case where the conquerer was more noble in doctrine and stronger in faith.

Nations that are permeated by religious character follow their social program either to the highest places or to the lowest civil degeneration according to the implications of their religion, meanwhile preserving its structure and life.

In the history of the Arabs in the *Jāhiliyya* and in early Islam and the period that followed are the best examples of the development of the religious character.

In the history of the Arabs in the *Jāhiliyya* the Arabs were not deficient in character. They were very generous, dignified, strong, chivalrous, helpful, and faithful; however, they were not a nation with a social entity. Rather, they were tribes and clans without a notable or lasting civilization. None of their neighbors took cognizance of them, the reason being the lack of a bond to hold them together or a common character to unite them. When the message of Islam came and provided them with fellowship through its wisdom and ascribed to them a character in which they were amalgamated, their feelings were attracted by its power. They poured forth as a mighty torrent from the extremities of the desert to the greatest part of the civilized world. They washed away the thrones of the Persian kings (*akāsira*) and brought down the crowns of the Caesars. They endowed the thirsty earth with justice and generosity which brought forth the most perfect and complete civilization. Then there was a change. People rebelled against the authority of the faith. Emotions overpowered religion. It [religion] became a created being not the creator, a relative rather than the primary reference, a [body of] knowledge and not praxis. The world changed and the Arabs changed. Neither the temper of the *Jāhiliyya* was able to unite them, nor the character of Islam to raise them up. One rightfully can say of them: ⟨Nor would your Lord unjustly destroy the communities while their people were righteous.⟩ S. 11:117.

But for Islam, the Arabs would not have been a noteworthy community, likewise the Arabic language without the Qur'ān would not have been capable of spreading in other Islamic nations of different languages. Furthermore, but for the Book that Islam kept as a protective shield on their chests, they would have assimilated with other dominant nations a long time ago, and Arabic would have been nothing but undecipherable cryptic characters as was the destiny of previous nations and dominant languages.

As for the factors which led the Arabs to the utmost level of weakness, there are several, the most important of which is the weakness of true religious character in their souls.

If the Arabs desire to regain their glory, they must hold fast to their true religion.

Some people (Jamīl Jabr) claim that European culture alone is capable of being the source of light for our thought. They are like those who claim that the breaking of the dawn is tied up with a star that is a sun in some other galaxy. The star can help us by giving us rays, but it cannot bring forth the day. It can guide us on an expedition of exploration, but it cannot reveal to us the horizons of truth. Thus a foreign language with its binding connections to the history of its regions is a detriment to the development of culture. It destroys personal judgment and eliminates independent expression because it is copied from a foreign country that has its own history and its own development.

It is not my intent to reject contemporary knowledge that comes to us from the West, rather we must adopt it with gratitude, in fear of running behind it in the future and not being able to catch up. What I rebel against is the artificial system which promotes Western culture, wiping out our national thought and keeping it from creating new avenues by coordinating current truths. We must strengthen all the factors of our culture. We should not resist Western culture, rather we should take it, absorb it, and make it a useful nutrient rather than a heavy burden.

If we look at history from the time of Adam we find that the great civilizations were formed by spiritual breaths (*nafaḥāt rūḥiyya*) which elevated man above physical needs, instinctual necessities, and the desires of the self and restored to them [civilizations] their dignity and greatness and raised them to the highest levels.

God created Adam as vicegerent on earth. He lived with God, through God, and in God. He taught his children all he knew and built the first human society on wholesome principles. He taught his progeny that each deed will be weighed on its own merit and on its relation to the world and to humanity, for each person will be asked about his deeds on the Day of Resurrection.

The sons of Adam learned that sovereignty belongs to God, that wealth is His, that He made humanity His vicegerent over wealth and planted in the human conscience moral principles that are higher than the reality of the world.

Historical progress continued. People were on their own for a long time. The distance between them and heaven became greater, thus their hearts hardened and they thought of God as their equal. God therefore sent the prophets and the messengers calling men to worship God alone.

God sent Idrīs to Egypt prior to the period of the dynasties to call them to the worship of the one God and to tell the Egyptians that they were created for a Great Day. The Egyptians believed in God and the Last Day and built their civilization on spiritual values that purified their conscience and made them work for religion and the world. They erected the pyramids which are the largest graves civilization has known as a preparation for the Day of Resurrection. Idrīs was the first to teach the Egyptians how to write with the pen. He also taught them agriculture, how to use the waters of the Nile and to wear sewn clothes since they used to cover their bodies with feathers.

Idrīs built the Kaʿba—as the Ṣābi'a report—that it may be a guiding light for unicity. God revealed to him the book which is known among the Ṣaba'ians as "the Treasure" (*Kanz*). People lived according to the guidance of the book of God progressing diligently.

After time passed and the people's hearts were hardened, they fabricated myths about Idrīs and made him into Osiris, the judge of the dead and the one who places the weights in the balance on the Day of Resurrection.

In Iraq people worshipped gods they fashioned. God therefore sent them Noah to call them to the worship of the one God. However, they placed their fingers in their ears in order not to hear and were proud and boastful. God drowned them. In their oppression they sought to drown the march of civilization towards progress and development.

There arose in Babel a civilization based on religion and the efforts of the believers. It flourished and built a great civilization. They flourished for a long time, the true religion was corrupted and nothing but the trivialities remained. Myths were fabricated concerning that. Each person seeking sovereignty took a god and began to call for him, preferring him to other gods, and claiming that he is the Lord of Lords.

For the first time people in Babel heard about the convention of the gods and about the wars that take place among them in Heaven. They forgot the Day of Resurrection and said, "If man dies, he goes to the earth from which there is no return."

They began to worship the stars and the constellations. These were not worshipped for themselves but were a symbol of the gods and the holy family.

God sent Abraham as "a messenger" to his people to save humanity from apostasy and polytheism, and to bring them out of darkness into the light.

Abraham proceeded to call people to God in Iraq, in Syria, and in Egypt. Then he established the foundations of the House with Ishmael in Mecca that it may be a beacon of light for unicity on the earth. Abraham went to God after breathing a spiritual breath in humanity that pushed it on its way into historical development.

There arose around the well of Zamzam due to the influence of Abraham, Hagar, and Ishmael a new society devoid of [alien] customs and myths. That is why it survived more than a thousand years with no other god save God the lord of the worlds.

The Children of Israel arose calling men to Islam. That was prior to their being filled with conceit that they alone are the [chosen] people. They established their religion around them, then they went to Egypt because of what God had done for Joseph who had become the prime minister.

The spiritual message of Joseph and his brothers had an effect on the inhabitants of the Nile Delta. It permeated into the righteous group of Egyptians who had not submitted to the Hyksos. It left its impact on the religion of the pharaohs. They unified their gods into one—Amon.

Then Moses came calling men to Islam and taking the Children of Israel out of bondage. Moses marched out of Egypt with the Children of Israel and headed for a meeting with his Lord on Mount Ṭūr. When he returned to his people he found them worshipping the calf. He was angry and sought forgiveness from God. However, God punished them to roam in Sinai for forty years.

Moses was gone, but the *Tawrāt* remained to be a guide and a light for the believers. However, despite the existence of the *Tawrāt,* the Children of Israel worshipped heathen gods. They worshipped Baal and other gods. God sent them His Prophets to call them back to the faith. There arose in Iraq the Assyrian Kingdom, a nation that believed in its god, Āshūr. Its kings used to fight the enemies of Āshūr and to stack up the skulls of the enemies in piles and burn them. They also used to skin them alive, in order to please their god, Āshūr. God gave them power over the Children of Israel because they had apostasized after they had received the Book of Light, and over the sons of Ishmael who had abandoned the House of Holiness and spread into the world and worshipped Allāt and al-ʿUzza. Then the role of the Assyrians in history came to an end, their only role being the punishment of those who had returned to darkness after God had brought them out into the light.

There arose in Babel the New Babel Nation due to the spiritual revival that spread among those who worshipped Murdoch and they were able to destroy Assyria. They also destroyed the nation that claimed to be the chosen People of God. Thus Nebuchadnezzar attacked Jerusalem and killed the Jews, then he took the men, women, and children to Babel. In Exile, the leaders of the Jews rewrote the *Tawrāt* with their own hands.

Thus came to an end the Jewish role in spiritual history after their leaders became impotent even though their evil political role has continued.

The light of the spirit shone in Iran where Zoroaster arose calling people to the worship of the one God. He legislated five prayers a day and preached about the expected Arab Prophet that God would send to Arabia and he said to them, "Hold fast to what I have brought you until the coming of him with the red camel."

The spiritual fire ignited by Zoroaster began to disappear from the heart of the Persians; corruption appeared. The Persians began to disintegrate from inside as though God was about to replace them by others who would carry the spiritual fire for a time and promote civilization for a few steps on the way. ﴾If We desire to destroy a community, we command the people who live in luxury therein to commit evil. Then the word is true about them and we destroy them completely﴿ S. 17:16.

There arose in Greece philosophers that called for the one God and to ethical behavior and the building of virtuous cities. Alexander was the first believer who was in power in Plato's Republic. He arose and began to conquer the world to fulfill the dream of a world government.

Alexander crossed the Dardanelles without any opposition. The Persian army attempted to make a stand at Granicus River. However, the effort ended in the defeat of the army which was permeated by corruption. Alexander then headed South and East conquering some countries. His army later met the army of Darius the Third at Issus. The army whose members were full of faith won. Alexander won a noble victory over Darius.

Alexander's conquests spread East, West, North, and South and it appeared that the world government he dreamed of was about to be fulfilled; however, he died on his way from India to Babel and with his death, the philosophers' dreams about establishing the victorious city died.

In Rome there arose a Roman nation. It was built on religion. It spread in the world overcoming Greeks, Jews, Nabateans, Egyptians, and Persians. With the passage of days, oppression prevailed on earth and men began to enslave one another. Evil was spread by the Romans in the areas they ruled and civilization drowned in the darkness of materialism.

Through this awful dark night the light of the Lord Jesus shone.

Materialism was rampant, thus Jesus' message was pure spirituality in order to bring about a balance between materialism and spiritualism. Jesus went around calling men to the worship of the one God and to repentance.

The Romans accepted the religion that Paul called them to. It was a mixture of religion and philosophy. The followers of this religion split into many groups and sects, and the great unicity that Jesus called for—as Will Durant said in *The Story of Civilization*—became polytheism of the common man. And people's hearts became hardened after a while and they began to worship what their parents used to worship before they were guided to the true religion.

Mecca at the time was the guiding light of *tawḥīd*. It continued to adhere to the religion of Abraham. But the Meccans took the idols of the people they traded with and placed them inside the Kaʿba and claimed that they were daughters of God who would intercede with Him. Thus *Jāhiliyya* spread in the earth and God sent Muḥammad calling men to Islam. He revealed to him the Qur'ān to be a light to people until the Day of Judgment.

Islam became victorious over the Romans and the Persians because of the spiritual breath which filled the hearts of the believers.

History continued on its march, nations arising with the movement of the spirit and nations dying, drowning in materialism, luxury, depravity, and licentiousness. That is the law of God and you will find no alternative to the law of God.

The events of history do not contradict the laws of the world or the nature of things.

The first Islamic nation was established on the foundations of the teachings and the principles of religion. The world was awestruck by both its spiritual as well as its material achievements. The body of the believer is from the earth, his nature is of light. He is a servant who acquires the characteristics of His creator; his heart is in no need of the world.

The Western nations attacked Islam with the intent of destroying it. Muslims were satisfied by humility and luxury. The material civilization of the West had captured their imagination by its glitter. Thus they became weak and immobile. Islam had to face the challenge directed towards it from outside the Muslim world from the time of the Crusades until Israel was planted in the heart of the Arab world. Despite these awesome attacks, Islam stood alone facing the challenges. It is incumbent upon Muslims that they hold fast to their true faith and take the Qur'ān as a guide for life, for the Qur'ān guides to that which is best.

He who contemplates history becomes aware of the truth of these words. The Roman Empire disappeared with its civilization when it ignored God's teaching. . . .

The Pope who had no arms was able to conquer the emperor who had armies and a cavalry. Then this system disintegrated when the men of religion abandoned its spirit and sought material power and utilized it for suppression. This was demonstrated in the conflict between Pope Gregory the Seventh and Emperor Frederick the Second.

At the beginning of the seventeenth century the West underwent a great revolution that sought to rectify conditions which had led to the destruction of the Roman Empire and religious institutions. This revolution sought to place religion and the political system each in its own place. Civilization flourished again. Freedom increased when the West cooperated in the cause of God. . . . This situation persisted until the beginning of the Second World War when the Western nations became divided among themselves. The strength of the West was dissipated. It descended from the noble position it occupied until the First World War. It began to face a power which it could not destroy. Its only avenue for conquest is through conviction. However, it is unable to do so because its deeds are not coordinated with its ideals.

Every civilization that has led to the elevation of humanity was established on religion. There is no regression except when there is a deviation from this religion. It is of God's wisdom that when humanity is degraded, God permits His religion to be reborn that it may function again in guiding humanity to truth and the right way.

From: *Al-Tafsīr al-Dīnī li-al-Tārīkh,* vol. I (Cairo, 1975) Selections

Appendix B
The Philosophy of Islamic History
by Anwar al-Jundī

THE FUNDAMENTAL PRINCIPLE of Islamic history is a "community" which has a method it derives from "Islam." . . . This community formed "the Islamic society" and built the "Islamic civilization" on the foundation of basic ideas. The essence of its thought is a humanitarian message to the world calling for freedom, justice, truth, and equality.

In pursuing its goal, this movement has faced strong opposition attempting to hinder it from achieving its designated goal. This movement is susceptible from time to time to obstacles that hinder its course, and this is a law of life, strength after weakness, and weakness after strength.

The program of this community is its starting point; when it abandons it, it reaches the stage of weakness and retardation while those in opposition to it gain victory. If it returns to the principles of its source and holds fast to them, it becomes victorious after having been defeated. It is strengthened after being weak. The pages of Islamic history during the last fourteen centuries run accordingly. They follow a process of "program-events-leaders" in the light of a clear law that does not change.

The basic values of Islam were the source of strength and awakening. When society veered away from them, a period of weakness and degeneration ensued, and if a leader or a thinker restored the community to these values, a renaissance followed.

Islam in its true understanding is a "way of life" and a large frame for a comprehensive and complete ideology that links man with God, the universe, and life. Islam in the movement of history is not the Muslim state nor is it Islamic civilization or the Arab nation, except insofar as it is related to that Islam itself. Islam appears through its history as a "living being" which has two wings—thought and civilization, which renews its cells and passes through periods of strength and weakness. Its constant movement is ever forward, as is the nature of a living being. Whenever a limb contracts, the other limbs provide its strength, and whenever one of its parts is afflicted by defeat it is provided with growth through another part. Its [Islam's] most notable feature is the phenomena of renewal, change, and the rectification of the concepts in its comprehensive framework.

This is connected to both its wings; the wing of thought which is renewed by the appearance of thinkers and opinion makers, and the wing of civilization which is regenerated by builders of the nation and the makers of events. The thinkers renew the intellectual milieu, reformulate the program and destroy the evils of deviation, while the leaders build the inner structures and withstand the outside forces. The movement of Islamic history always combines the straight line and the circle. For it is through the linear process that it progresses forward, while the cyclical one provides it with ceaseless motions. At times the movement of history appears forward-backward; this is its temporary retreat in order to resume its forward motion.

Its [Islam's] appearance in the Arab milieu has a clear meaning. It is the choice of this nation to carry its message. [This was shown] in the sending of the Prophet from among its people and the Qur'ān in its language. Thus one cannot separate the history of the Arabs from the history of Islam from its beginning till now. Since Islam appeared it has been closely tied to Arab history . . . the Arab nation carried it to all parts of the world while the Arabic language was the instrument of its ideas, culture, and civilization. The thought that the Arab nation formed through the essence of Islam was the cooperative product of Muslims and Arabs. One cannot describe it as being either Arabic thought or Islamic thought. In a similar fashion one has to treat civilization. It [has to be seen] as an Arab-Islamic thought and an Arab-Islamic civilization in which all participated and into which different human cultures were integrated: Persian, Egyptian, Greek, Roman, and Indian. All of them were recast in a Muslim frame according to its understanding and content. Both Arabs and non-Arabs participated in this phase. Islam designed its understanding of the unity of its believers and those attached to it on thought and not ethnicity. It expanded the circle of human brotherhood and denounced sectarianism and racial discrimination. It made the foundation of excellence and superiority based on work and not race, on the person and not his heredity.

The study of the history of Islam at this juncture in our life is a necessity that cannot be ignored. [It is to enable us] to understand events and the development of society and to comprehend our place in the Muslim world and the Arab nation in the context of modern civilization. If we look at events they cannot be believed unless they are placed in the scope of a comprehensive understanding and in the confines of the history of Islam itself. Furthermore, our contacts with the West today must be based on the understanding of a phase which is a reaction to another phase that preceded it which views the contemporary Western civilization not as separate from the world of Islam, rather that its foundations were erected on the Islamic experimental system and on the structures erected earlier by Arab and Muslim scholars. Today, when we contact it we are not strangers from its sources. It is the property of all humanity which formulated it and participated in establishing its different sides. The Arab-Islamic thought has given this civilization its knowledge, its philosophy, its factories, and its universities. It also built its wide base in Spain. Today, when we appropriate it, we are integrated in it and not different from it.

History in reality is the movement of time through the medium of society. Islamic history has been connected with the primary channels of human history influencing it and being influenced by it. Its confrontations were always with sectarianism, alien forces, and deviation from truth [of the Qur'ān]. Islamic history is built around an idea, a message and a culture. It is an idea with its distinguishing characteristics where all factors of civilization meet and where society perceives "unicity" as a general idea which permeates all aspects of Islamic thought.

If the movement of history is evident in three ways, "program-events-heroes," the hero is always the primary mover of events and the one capable of designating the program if society deviates from the true understanding. The Muslim community has been able to provide the leaders, renovators, and reformers. It provided living examples in a continuing fashion without ceasing, in different phases and in different areas and groups. These leaders, thinkers, and reformers seek guidance from the example of the hero of heroes, "Muḥammad the messenger of God" and from the Qur'ān." [The community] has also provided a reserve of strength which produces the heroes and reformers at the time of need.

Heroism has manifested itself in reformers who rectify ideas, those who command the good and forbid evil, the mathematicians and the astronomers and the statesmen.

The hero is always the leader of the renaissance whether he be a statesman, a thinker, or a reformer. They all take their strength from the society. They are a response to the need which seeks a new young strength. Then the hero becomes evident fulfilling the goals and taking his strength from the hopes and needs of the society. Then he takes a bigger step leading the group to a new, stronger, and more positive phase.

The biggest internal challenges Islam faced were the efforts to interpolate the revelation or the efforts to eliminate one of the foundations of Islam. The reformers and renovators were always capable of eradicating these deviations, highlighting the new meaning of Islam, uncovering its essence and bringing it to its rightful place away from division, deviation, and ossification, into comprehensiveness, perfection, and unicity.

The movement of Islamic history from its dawn until today is a progressive comprehensive movement. In it is personified the ability of motion, resistance, continuation, and depth and the defense against every effort to stop or delay it. In its history is exemplified the capacity for constant awareness and responsiveness to civilizations and cultures. When it is restricted politically by foreign attack on the world of Islam, it opens a way in the barren land adding new nations that appropriate it and believe in it. For it is a persistent movement towards progress, construction, and the spread of the humanist spirit. From the appearance of Islam until today, every world event has been connected to it in some way or another.

The goal of Islamic history is the program of the future for humanity. For Islam is a positive humanistic message capable of life and of influencing the flow of time, events, and civilizations in an exalted vision whose horizons are integrated and which is at all times capable of providing humanity with positive solutions for problems and conflicts. The purpose of Islam in its historical flow is to arrive at the universal [dissemination] of the message since it is the only force capable of implementing human unity, justice, equality, and freedom.

The main features of Islamic history include:

(a) resistance which is its most prominent quality which was made evident as Islam struggled [against efforts] to eliminate it and battered the attempts of conspiracy and contradiction by winning the victory over the attacking forces or absorbing them into itself.

The resistance movement in the history of Islam is an important part of its fundamental being and nature. From it we get the understanding of *jihād* as vigilance and constant preparedness for confrontation with the enemy. The highest ideal of *jihād* is not to fear death as it is the source of life and to be prepared and strong to frighten the enemy and not to fight him. Islam has lived all its history a life of constant resistance that never ceased, always in touch with events, with crises, and with human problems.

Islam has been established in its various periods on "challenge and response" striving for the realization of human unity on the basis of justice, faith, and freedom, capable of banishing forces that prevent unity or proper understanding. Each foreign incursion was [followed] by a period of vigilance, strength, concentration, and an impetus for resistance.

(b) Another feature of the movement of Islamic history is its capacity for continuous interaction; for in its long march, it did not separate from the march of humanity. It has moved in a positive way with effective interaction.

(c) Also among the features of the movement of Islamic history is its capacity to correct its course if it deviates. Its life is an interconnected chain of movements of renewal, reform, and correction of understandings. Islamic thought has been and continues to be capable of correcting society and leading it to the right way. Each time a movement faltered or ossified, another took over pushing forward towards the same goal in a different fashion.

(d) Of the strong features of Islamic history is "continuity." What has attracted attention is not only the emergence of this great society and civilization in such a short time, but the lesson from its capacity to persist, continue, expand, and to have deep roots. For, but for these strengths and capabilities it would not have been able to withstand the foreign incursions that continued against the Muslim world and attempted to rupture the community. The firmness of the content of Islam preserved for it its ability to persist.

(e) Continuity. The events of Islamic history were not independent of one another; rather, they were always connected. There was no separation between the continuous waves. Each wave was a response to a previous challenge, or a challenge to a period of weakness.

(f) Unity of thought. One thought and one culture have informed the different facets, phases, and waves of Islamic history. It is the great common bond among all, whatever the region, the nation, or the system. This thought is the spirit of the group, the primary mover and the mold through which are formed all its concepts, ideas, and developments whether political, social, or economic. The primary feature of this thought is its "originality" for it has developed according to new principles that have no connection with Syriac, Persian, or Greek civilization. It is based on unicity, prophecy, equality, and justice.

(g) Integration. Islamic history is characterized by comprehensiveness, integration, balance, movement, and unity. If a sectarian movement appears, an integrated one would confront it. If a movement for laxity becomes prominent, it is opposed by a movement of vigilance. The interaction between division and integration, laxity and vigilance in society are two constant factors that do not cease.

Thus the movements of strength and weakness, laxity and vigilance are natural. The true cause of the crisis has always been exemplified by invasion by outsiders. It has always followed the loss of unity, strength, wakefulness, deterrence, movement with the time, and progress with civilization. All sections that have fallen have done so through an "outside force" as a result of neglect of military strength. The decline in social and moral values of society [has also resulted] in the inability to resist and the impotence of defense.

Islamic history—like Islam itself—cannot be understood except by the principle of integration and comprehensiveness. For it is a unity of interconnected links no matter how numerous the facets. It is an "integrated whole" which does not disintegrate despite the appearance of division.

For political, military, economic, social, and cultural history are an integrated whole that does not ever separate even though they may appear as different. Each facet is connected to the other and totally dependent on it. Together they form the perimeter of general civilization.

The most obvious characteristic of integration is that the whole of Islamic history has been replete with strength and movement and with leaders and reformers. The greatness of Islam has not been limited to its early stages; rather, it continued throughout its history in all its phases. Islamic ideology continued to be capable of motion throughout history and was not restricted to the early period or the first leaders. Nor are the early people the only ones who represented the concepts of Islam in society and government. Rather, throughout the ages, there have been persons with the notable Muslim personality in all aspects of life, such as statesmen, missionaries, and civil leaders.

The basic principles have remained constant despite the ability of motion in Islamic thought. These principles continue to be the sure [way] for the building of renaissance. If Muslims veer away from them, they fall back and enter a period of crisis [by becoming victims] of foreign conquest. These principles are unicity, unity, prophecy, strength, endeavor, faith, *jihād,* justice, and freedom. Thus Islam is basically religion, thought, civilization, and society. Its program is ideology, mutual relations, and ethics. Islamic society was perceived as a basis while religion is part of it. In it are the values of mutuality of the intellect and the heart, the world and the hereafter, the spiritual and the material, the community and the individual. If any of these foundations is weakened, a period of retardation ensues. If these concepts are sought after, a period of vigilance is initiated.

Islamic society has consistently moved with history and not against it, for it has not realized the highest ideal which Islam envisioned, and it continues to move towards its realization.

Islamic society has moved within the perimeter of Islam but it has not realized the concept of Islam. For Islam in itself is comprehensive basic principles that are pliant. It is not prescribed, determined, or static lines. In other words, it is a determined perimeter whose content and ideals are progressive, capable of producing numerous images that rotate in its orbit—at times close to it, at other times distant. If it is in contact with it and is able to approximate it, it [Islamic society] will be destined to live. If it falters, gets distant, or disintegrates, its weakness and anxiety become apparent.

The states and societies varied in their approximation of it and [in their] movement within its perimeter. This is the secret of the continuity of Islam while the states have changed.

It is possible to say that Islamic history has two tendencies, the tendency to spread and expand and the tendency to be implemented. The history of Islam has until now represented self-perpetuation after the initial period of expansion. As for the tendency of implementation it continues to be in its early stages.

Islamic society has not been able to exemplify the total concepts of Islam in its context.

From: *Al-Islām wa-Ḥarakat al-Tārīkh* (Cairo, 1968) Selections

Appendix C
History as the Interpretation of Events
by Sayyid Quṭb

IF IT WERE ORDAINED for the Muslim world to die, it would have died during the long centuries it had passed through, while chained and in a state of exhaustion and inaction after it had carried the burden of the civilizing of humanity for a long time. [It would have died] after it had lost its zeal and slept—giving Western imperialism, then young, the opportunity to get most of the world to follow its leadership, while a heavy burden rested on the chest of the Muslim world.

If it were destined for the Muslim world to die, it would have died during the period of softening and exhaustion while imperialism was young and strong. . . . However, it did not die . . . rather, it arose alive like a powerful giant breaking its chains and putting aside its weight and challenging the aging imperialism.

What was it that preserved for this nation its latent vitality after long centuries of sleep and inaction, of abatement and weakness, of pressure and subjugation, of hateful occupation which spent every effort to sunder its limbs and smother its breath?

It is its strong and deep doctrine, this doctrine which imperialism was unable to kill despite intellectual, spiritual, social, and political efforts on the part of imperialism . . . , this doctrine which calls upon its believers to be superior because supremacy belongs to God, the Prophet, and the believers. It also calls upon them to struggle and resist in order to materialize this superiority and not to succumb to the oppressors whatever their material power may be. Material power does not scare those who believe in God, the Mighty of the heavens and the earth, and the One exalted above all His creatures.

The Muslim world from one end to the other is in harmony in one cry against imperialism. It stretches its hand [of support] to all struggles and battles of liberation in all corners of the world. For the question of freedom is one that cannot be divided. The Islamic doctrine adopts all struggles of liberation in the world and supports them in every place.

The day of salvation is near. The dawn shall break through and the light shall shine in the horizon. This Muslim world will not sleep after its awakening, nor will it die after its resurrection. If it were ordained for it to die, it would have died. The living doctrine which led [Islam] in its struggle will not die because it is of the spirit of God. God is alive, He does not die.

Islam has come for the development and progress of life, not to accept its prevalent condition at a certain time in a certain place, nor to merely register what it has of impetus or restraints, of tendencies or fetters, whether at a special period or in the long run.

The mission of Islam is always to propel life to renewal, development, and progress and to press human potentialities to build, to go forth, and to elevate.

Islam does not deny that humanity has weaknesses; however, it also knows that its mission is to provide victory for strength over weakness, and to try to elevate humanity, to evolve it and have it progress, not to justify its weakness nor to beautify it.

Islam is a continuous movement for the progress of life; it does not accept the prevalent condition at a time or of a generation, nor does it justify it or beautify it because it is existent. Its primary mission is to change that condition and make it better, to continuously suggest the creative creating movement for the newer forms of life.

Islam does not establish its progressive movement on class hatred; rather, [it is based] on the desire to honor man and elevate him from subservience to need and necessity, and to set his humanity free from the obsession with food, drink, and the hungers of the body.

Islam is a creative movement that seeks to create a human life unknown before Islam and not known in other systems which preceded or followed Islam. . . . This creative movement is produced through a special vision of life with all its values and relationships, a vision which Islam brought in the beginning. It is a movement which starts in the depth of the conscience and actualizes itself in the realm of reality. It is not fulfilled until it is actualized in the realm of reality.

This is one of the major differences between the idealistic visions known in the West and the nature of Islam. For idealism is dreams and will continue to be dreams because it looks at a world that is not seen and whose realization is not sought after, because it cannot be realized on this earth. As for Islam, it is a creative force for the actualization of a particular vision of life which is capable of being brought into being, when one is influenced by it in a positive way which is not satisfied with emotions and feelings.

The old system which was built in the *Jāhiliyya* after a certain perception of life cannot remain or persist nor can it be patched up by the Islamic vision. Rather, a total shaking and destruction of the old system is necessary that it may be rebuilt according to the new plan and the new design.

It is possible that the way for creativity for the new life is to make it progressive but it cannot be mere repairs. There is a difference between having a certain design for a building you want to erect little by little and the repair of an existent building which is built according to a different plan. Repairs will not in the end give you a new building.

Islam provides a specific design for human life. It is a comprehensive image in which it delineates the human prototype it seeks to form, the economic and social relations that hold society together, and the government and international systems that regulate public life.

This specific vision which Islam designs for life cannot be actualized through mere reading of the Qur'ān whether through *tajwīd* or *tartīl*, nor by praising God day and night; rather, it is realized by translating praise into a concrete movement which becomes a perceived movement in the real world, and by translating the emotions into expressions whose aim is not mere expressiveness but what it transcends of movement and progress.

Islam came to humanity with a new idea of the totality of life. This idea did not develop from previous prevailing ideologies. It was totally new. It sprang from a source that is not human. It was the revelation of God for the formation of a new nation whose form was unique and which the Qur'ān describes: ﴾You were the best nation brought forth to mankind﴿ S. 3:110.

This new idea about the totality of life had its impact on all human concepts of life and in all their interactions and relationships. In it is social mutuality (*al-takāful al-ijtimāʿī*) which includes among its components the idea of social security.

In Islam, each individual has an ordained right to obtain what is sufficient for life in material and ideal matters.

Each individual has the right of food, drink, clothing, transportation, and housing. He also has the right of marriage which is one of the necessities as it is related to the preservation of life and the response to primary needs. [He also has] the right to medical treatment and medicine, education—which is a religious duty—and to work as long as he is capable of doing it, including the right to be trained for the work.

History is not events; rather, it is the interpretation of these events. It is also the discernment of the apparent and hidden connections that brings the separate parts together and makes of them a unified whole where parts are integrated. It is related to time and environment as the living being is related to time and place.

Islamic history must be rewritten according to new principles and a new methodology.

This history exists today in two forms: the form of the ancient Arabic texts and in this case it is a hyperbole to call it history. In fact, it is unfitting that it should be called that. For, it is fragments of events, occurrences, anecdotes, sayings, remnants, myths, fables, contradictory reports, and contradicting statements . . . even though it is a wealthy source of primary material of history which aids those who desire to study and patiently sift for the primary facts necessary for the structuring of an historical model.

The other place it is available is in the European sources, especially the works of the Orientalists, an idea that we have discussed earlier and shed light on before. [This European version of Islamic history] generally depends on the old Arabic sources. It does not, despite its organization and ordering, serve to assure those who are aware of it. In its best form, it is a study of the apparent [aspects] of Islamic life—if it is possible to coin this expression. The best that is in it is its attempt to gather, edit, and coordinate all sources, and balance the reports that are contradictory. This it does from an outsider's viewpoint not that of internal apprehension. This is due to the lack of feeling of Westerners towards Islamic life and their [questionable] intention, which in many cases disrupts the impartial coordination. Also lacking is the element of total integration of all factors.

There is a third form of writings on Islamic history which we did not mention in the earlier paragraphs. Besides its being incomplete, it is but a pale shadow or a total copy of European studies, despite the fact that at times it discusses or disputes these studies. For in the first place, it follows the Western method in its essence, with no additions. In the second place, it gets its components mostly from Western sources. In the third place, it is influenced by Western education, [and thus is unable] to understand Islam with a sound mind and in a sensible light. The mind that will judge Islamic life must be in its essence Islamic, saturated with the Islamic spirit to be able to understand the essential components of this life, to measure it, to integrate it, and thus bring together all the ingredients of explanation and appreciation.

The new study of Islamic history must have the Arabic sources as a primary source, while the Western sources can be used as secondary sources. The latter can be beneficial in editing and coordinating these sources, also in evaluating the different reports. Nothing more. The rest of the work must be totally personal, not affected by anything save the logic of the events themselves after the researcher lives with his mind, spirit, and feeling in the Islamic atmosphere as a doctrine, an idea, and a system. [He must experience] the Islamic atmosphere as a part of realistic human life. Life in this atmosphere is necessary in order that he may become aware in his understanding, not only to apprehend the quality of [Islamic] life, but to experience it as a living being and to comprehend the places of the events and their function in this living being.

It is difficult to conceive of the possibility of studying the total Islamic life without a complete understanding of the spirit of the Islamic doctrine, the Islamic ideology of the world, of life, and of man, also the nature with which the Muslim responds to this doctrine and the way he responds to life in general. These characteristics cannot be sought in a researcher who is not an Arab in general and specifically a Muslim. These characteristics are necessary when Islamic history is rewritten.

It is essential to understand the true motives behind the actions of people being studied in the context of Islamic history and the relation of these motives to events, developments, and changes. It is inevitable that these should be tied to the Islamic ideology and its content of upheaval and revolution—not in its apparent form as practical movement only, but in its interpretation of cosmic, human, and social relations. An understanding of the Islamic form of government, of economics, of legislative and executive methods is also necessary. All these are components of life, hence components of the history of this life.

All battles, political treaties, and international interaction . . . and other matters to which history usually pays special heed [to the expense of] other matters . . . all of these are governed by other factors which should be made apparent when history is being written. . . . These factors are what researchers differ about in apprehension and evaluation. Each one of them is under the influence of the philosophy which dominates his comprehension and judgment in his understanding of life in general. The Muslim researcher has a special characteristic in studying Islamic life because his concept of life is related to the essence of the factors that affect the march of history. Thus he is better equipped to apprehend it, internalize it, and respond to it in a true and total manner.

In the light of his apprehension of the nature of the Islamic doctrine and the Muslim response to it, he is able to weigh the forces of Islamic life in that period of history, the latent human values in it, and the causes of victory and defeat at each step. He is able to envision the apparent and the hidden life of this group of early Muslims and in the areas of expansion. He is able to add to the apparent reasons, which are the only ones Westerners generally understand, all the spiritual factors that Islam perceives as reality, and take note of it in the march of time, and in the formation of life in every time and place.

Islamic life is a period of human life and Muslims are a group of humanity in a period of time and at a certain place. Islam is a cosmic human message not limited by time and space.

We cannot separate Islamic history from world history. Undoubtedly, that period [Islamic history] has been affected by the experience of the humanity that preceded it, especially those events that occurred at the birth of Islam. Likewise, [Islam] has left its impact on the human experience that followed it, especially in the areas of expansion or in neighboring countries.

Thus when Islamic history is being written, it is necessary to have knowledge of the situation of human societies in the world, especially in the area of religious doctrines and all that is related to it [in the way] of ideas, philosophies, and theories. [Knowledge is also essential concerning] social situations and their relationship to political, economic, and social systems, ethical relations and customs and ideas that can be discerned through the light of the truth and the role and nature of Islam. It is possible to explain the response of the world to this new system as acceptance or rejection and to perceive the causes of struggle and the components of victory or of total defeat as the elements of interaction, struggle, and cooperation in the days that followed.

From: *Fī al-Tārīkh: Fikra wa-Minhāj* (Beirut, 1974) Selections

Appendix D
Basic Principles of Islamic History
by ʿAbd al-Raḥmān al-Ḥajjī

I PERCEIVE ISLAM as a tree that God revealed. He chose for it someone to plant it who was qualified to protect it and sacrifice in its cause. He is Muḥammad who expressed his utmost devotion for this trust at the Peace of Ḥudaybiyya when the Quraysh did not allow the Muslims to enter Mecca and visit the Holy House, when he said, "By God, I shall continue to struggle for that which God entrusted me with until it is victorious over all or until death."

The care for this tree increased as did the number of its protectors who inherited it as a trust and preserved it as a doctrine, as received from those who preceded. The branches of this tree increased and gave forth leaves, blossoms, and fruits. It received support and its many branches increased.

The roots of the tree represent the doctrines of Islam. Its trunk stands for its principles, its foundations, its goals, its way, and the total view of the world, man, and life. Each branch in it represents a side of Islam: history, jurisprudence, thought, ethics, systems for all aspects of life and its perimeters for the individual, the family, the society, and the nation, its internal and external relations and the quality of these relations and other details.

What runs in the veins of this tree, its branches, and fruits is the spirit of the Islamic doctrine and the relation to God and the work according to His will.

Each part or cell of this tree through which this spirit does not run is not of the tree and is alien to its body and nature. ﴾Do you not see how God has set as a parable the good word as a good tree whose roots are stable and its branches are in the heaven. Its fruit can be eaten at all times by the permission of its Lord. God sets parables to men that they may remember. The parable of the evil word is an evil tree which has been uprooted from the earth and which is unstable﴿ S. 14:24–26.

This tree which has a noble origin and a pure fountain is blessed, is bright and gives forth light. It is solely for Islam.

As long as the guardians of this tree are vigilant and alert to all that is related to it, it will give its fruits to humanity, all humanity, Muslims and non-Muslims who seek shelter under its branches. The day they neglect it, the envious, the enemies, the hateful, and the greedy will attempt to destroy it, in a collective manner using an evil coalition which is unholy and unrighteous. They agree concerning it and distribute their duties systematically and coordinately, thus collectively [seeking to destroy] the total parts of this tree and its good products, or it may be attacked by a single enemy who has specific goals.

These enemies have spent great efforts to sow mines and diseases in its land as well as injecting its branches with poison. Prior to that they attacked whoever had remained vigilant of its defenders after they had busied them in purifying it of what they injected in it.

Thus the war against Islam was [fought] on the principal doctrines of God, the Qur'ān, and prophethood, in jurisprudence, law, and heritage, and concerning the Islamic view of man, the world, and life. [It is] also [fought] in its history, in the onslaught against its nations, its leadership and its armies in every field, attacking them and raising doubts about their actions and motives.

Islamic history received a major part of these oppressive and poisonous arrows. The arrows were distributed in a just manner. The differences may have been according to the effectiveness of the target or its importance, or a combination of both.

Since Islamic history is one of the areas of the implementation of the practical side of Islam it was burdened with arrows. Islamic history in many ways is the history of practical Islamic law as long as it is practiced. History is the form in which Islam was realized. Each deviation from the straight path that took place in this history is a deviation from that study of those who were faithful to it and those who maligned it either from within or from without. [It is a means] of unveiling their methods.

By Islamic history I do not mean here the political side of it only, rather all that Islam produced and all guidance it provided to society whether in thought, deed or way of life, inside Islamic society or [in relation] to other societies, in war or in peace.

Thus, it must be said that it is impossible to understand Islamic history in a pure and practical manner without having some knowledge of the Islamic doctrine and its law.

Islamic society is connected to the doctrine in its drive and base, in its motivation and unchanging character. The effect of the doctrine is evident in efficacy and results, and whether one is constant to it or deviates from it. This history is a living being with a continuous life that persists in being effective and perpetual despite all that has befallen it.

All our concerns and criteria should be based on an Islamic foundation. This necessitates not only that Islamic history be taught from an Islamic point of view, but that all studies of the history of the period that preceded and that followed Islam of other nations be analyzed from that viewpoint, which must be precise and original.

With it we can measure and judge the deeds, social action, and the various forms of human life (without being misled by claims). In that, great care and faithful presentation must be maintained.

I go even beyond that and say that all studies of all knowledge and that different subjects on all levels must be made on an Islamic basis and from an Islamic point of view. Otherwise we may provide the possibility of contradiction in the personality of the young, which is something that may already exist—a struggle between the knowledge he has of Islamic concepts, some of it shallow or distorted, and that which he receives in the way of knowledge. For we do not instruct him in Islam and demand [knowledge] of religion, doctrine, and Islamic history, nor do we teach him the greatness of Islam and that it is a revelation from God. He studies the histories of other nations which precipitates concern in himself or uncertainty in his thought or an exaltation of their [other nations] history and contempt for his own. Or he may study in science and biology some theories that are contradictory to Islam—despite the fact that they have not been scientifically verified as yet, or that those who proposed them have made no such claims for them. How could we, for example, teach him that in religion usury is forbidden while the mathematics book is filled with usury problems?

All branches of knowledge and syllabi must cooperate in the building of the Islamic personality among the students. It is possible that the subjects from which doubts are raised, if studied in a more wholesome manner, may become a road to faith in God.

Biological science and others, if truthful, are a road to faith in God and a guide to Him and a proof [of his existence] and not the contrary. It is inevitable that these sciences and others must be taught from an Islamic point of view and from an Islamic starting point which is correct, safe, and right. ﴾And on earth are signs for those of assured faith. And in your selves, do you not see?﴿ S. 51:20–21.

I may also go beyond that and say that every scientific idea or truth that is valid cannot contradict Islam. For it is not possible that God who created the universe and all that is within it—for all that scientists do is discern and discover His truth and benefit from it, they do not create it—will reveal what contradicts those truths. For both are from one source. Our learned people say that valid knowledge does not contradict clear revelation.

In the third place, I may go beyond that and say that any scientific theory, whatever its source may be, if we find it contradictory to the Islamic doctrine, then the theory is wrong. It does not raise questions about Islam nor place it under accusation, for that would be because of the weakness of faith. It is proper that the one who proposes the theory seek further evidence and proof and not the contrary.

Our study of Islamic history must be comprehensive and not restricted to certain areas only, e.g., the battles. It must be an historical study, for history contains some—or all—the areas of human endeavor, the heritage of civilization in all its meanings, that is, civilization and its products in the intellectual, functional, social, and ethical aspects. These include the values which bring forth such results.

It is not necessary to have this study follow [closely] the stages [of Islamic history] in a narrative form without ignoring any event. Nor is it necessary for the student to learn—except in a [small] measure—about the political and intellectual conflicts of the early period of Islamic history that have led to consequences we wish had not happened. The study of these matters are not necessarily successful areas of instruction about this period. It is of no benefit to [the student] and he may fail to comprehend it, thus causing him harm.

Ancient history should be taught, like other subjects, not by glorifying it. At present, most of these studies are the product of idolatry. It must be taught on the basis of the Qur'anic world view and its events must be viewed from that vantage point. For, "The Qur'anic method takes humanity to the horizon and provides an interpretation of the events of human history. This method is not a way of thought and knowledge, rather, it alone possesses the correct interpretation of human history." (Sayyid Quṭb, *Fī Ẓilāl al-Qur'ān,* Vol. 7, p. 142.) ⟨Say, go forth in the earth and behold the end of those who belie the truth.⟩ S. 6:11. ⟨Did they not go through the earth and witness what the end of those who preceded them was. They were mightier in strength and had tilled the earth and built it more than they had. Their apostles brought them the clear signs. God did not wrong them; they wronged themselves.⟩ S. 30:9.

Our teaching of Islamic history must realize great goals besides those that are usually realized through the study of history in general. We must realize the good example, intellectual education, and Islamic personality which gives the individual dignity and makes the Muslim of noble character. [The study of Islamic history] cares for the nurturing of the Islamic character and offers the individual values, thus raising a generation that believes in its Islam. This cannot be achieved unless our history is written from an Islamic viewpoint.

From: *Naẓarāt fī Dirāsat al-Tārīkh al-Islāmī* (Damascus, 1975) Selections

Appendix E
Islam Looks at History
by Muhammad Kamāl Ibrāhīm Ja'far

WE HAVE EXPLAINED previously that there are truths concerning history that are contained in Judaism and Christianity which are relevant to those ascertained by Islam. As is well known, Islam does not claim that it initiated what did not exist before. For the Qur'ān informs us that God has instituted for us what he had previously given to Noah and Abraham and whoever followed them of the prophets. The Prophet, God's blessing and peace be upon him, sums up the content of his great mission as the fulfillment of the "noblest of virtues."

Therefore, it is acceptable to consider Islam as the last divine decree to purify what may have been misrepresented or misinterpreted of divine teachings that had been previously revealed; Islam itself being a link in the chain of revelations that have recurred throughout this life, is an indication to the unity of history insofar as it is a *composite of progress and regress in the material and spiritual realm.*

Any discussion of the concept of history in Islam has to begin with the explanation of the relation of *God to man and to the world as viewed in Islam.*

This relation cannot be explained in the light of the unity of being (that is that God, the world, and man are one thing), nor can it be explained in the light of God's indwelling (*ḥulūl*) in creation or in man, nor can it be explained in the light of the unity of origin which necessitates the existence of one truth and negates the personal or individual or partial existence of phenomena.

It is not true as some Orientalists claim, that Islam through Sufism has deprived itself of a higher principle with which it could have explained the relation of God to man and the world [sic]. This great principle to which this Orientalist refers is the Christian principle of unity, or what he calls deification.

The relation of God to His creatures is consummated effectively through His attributes, not by way of union with or connection to His essence. We shall see this in the discussion of the divinity in the section for comparative study.

However, we do want here to explain concisely the nature of the relation between God and creation (including man) as it is seen by Islam, by stating that it is a relation of a *creature to a creator who is omnipotent and omniscient power*; and every *talent*, every *capacity* and every *member* of humanity, in the opinion of Islam, is a *vocal witness* for this subservience. This subservience does not mean man's loss of all his individual capabilities which are a gift from God and whose activities and effectiveness function within the limits made available to him.

Thus man is not able to get out of his humanity to become divine and the divine cannot get out of his divinity to become man, or to incarnate himself in a man. If a man should show some special distinctiveness that suggests his connection to God, that happens by way of effusion (*inbithāth*) of divine attributes through its infinite effects without diminishing the holiness of (His) essence or infinitude.

As for the manner of the working of these attributes, it is impossible for the intellect to either imagine or define in a logical, intelligible manner. Otherwise they would not have been divine attributes. One can briefly describe this relation by saying that it is one of regulating (*taṣrīf*), management (*tadbīr*), supervision (*haymana*), and dominion (*sayṭara*) through the knowledge, the will*, the power and other most beautiful attributes [of God]. It behooves us now to discuss the major factors in the way Islam views history.

Some of the distinctive elements of the Muslim view of history

1. There is a purpose in creating, and a purpose for the creation. As for the purpose in creating, it is the knowledge of God, His worship, and the manifestation of His will and ideals. As for the purpose for the creation, it is the elucidation of the potentialities of the attributes, and the expression of the hidden powers and talents and the attainment in the end, of that which is in harmony with these powers and attributes. This purpose has a dual aspect. It can be viewed individually or collectively. The basis, however, is the individual, as He said, ❴To them the Day of Resurrection is coming individually❵ S. 19:95.
2. There is a solid foundation for a number of laws which govern

*The Arabic reads *idāra*; however, *irāda* would be more appropriate.

history. By these laws it is possible at the same time to explain [history] and to relate its events as cause and effect. The Qur'ān may refer to this when it reports the news of the conditions of previous peoples, commenting on their destiny, that it is [due] to the law of God.

The destruction of nations and the fall of states have their objective justification in the Qur'ān. For example, injustice is one of the reasons of divine vengeance, through destruction of nations in their totality or states in their entirety. S. 11:102; 11:17; 17:16

Here we find the attainment of the results of human endeavor which contributes to the making of history under the supervision of divine authority without indwelling or contact (*tamāss*). If this be true on the level of the village or city, it is no different in relation to the individual in any way: for Qārūn, Hāmān, Firʿawn and others are human types displayed by the Qur'ān, revealing their deeds and verifying the end they reaped in fulfillment of the same divine law.

Steadfastness then is of the divine law, which gives history its unity, and which at the same time enables the researcher of history to study it, understand it, and analyze the causes of its events.

The reasons of economic recession or material destruction can be studied historically according to Islam, and it can be analyzed rationally in the light of our ordinary human expressions, but behind all that, there remains divine law. For law is not chaotic that it cannot be understood, and history has a meaning without the need for the idea of incarnation or union.

This same law is applicable to spiritual and material revival which provides us with objective principles which can be analyzed and understood. Beyond this comes the broad practical application of the wisdom of God and His universal law.

This is the lesson the Qur'ān taught to the Muslims concerning some of the narratives relating to the conditions of the ancients. The Qur'ān is not an historical book that attempts to give data about previous peoples or persons, it desires that we should learn from their experience and understand these firm unchanging laws, and that for the purpose of benefit and admonition in our present life.

Here we find no deterrent in considering the previous personalities and past nations whose mention appears in the Qur'ān as examples of persons and nations in the present and the future.

If man makes his history by the positive role which he undertakes, he uses all his capabilities and talents which are of the creation of God, and through this he comprehends the indirect aspects of the divine. However, there is another aspect which is direct, which cannot be perceived but by those who possess spiritual insight or keen sensitivities.

And if people and nations have days and nights, likewise does God have days and nights through which He unveils the victory of His principles and laws, as a fulfillment of His promises or threats, whatever the discrepancy of the results of these days and nights might appear in relation to people.

The term "the days of God" (*ayyām allāh*) appears in the Qur'ān in two ways. The first aspect refers to the past while the second points to the future. These are the two dimensions of life. This expression has a corollary in Arabic usage, where the term "days" when used as a construct with the term "the Arabs" points to the periods of struggle, heroism, and battles among the Arabs. It doubtless includes happiness and well-being to the victor and misery and suffering to the losers. What is important is that it points to the period of vitality, positiveness, and effectiveness.

However, the Qur'anic usage has been explained by the linguists as beneficence and grace, as the author of *Tāj al-ʿArūs* asserts. However, the mention of these two verses in which this term appears gives a feeling of a consistent and necessary law which is fulfilled in a decisive way at special times.

The first verse which is in S. 14:15 clearly points to Moses who was ordered to remind his people of the destiny of the ancients, those who have won or lost as a fulfillment of the heavenly law. The reference here is to the past.

As for the second verse, S. 45:14, the reference in this verse is to the future, where those who have no hope and do not desire to see these days are described, in which the recompense for what their hands have brought forth shall be meted out.

As for the present, it is the moment of consideration in which men are asked to look back and to look forward until the present is reformed.

The principle of delimiting the days or special periods in which the influence of divine law appears in an obvious way does not contradict the Muslim principle in which the Qur'ān stipulates that God, ❴Each day He exercises power over matters❵, S. 55:29, and that ❴Those days We alternate among the people❵, S. 3:140. For as was previously mentioned, some of the periods are specialized in a particular manner as a result of particular attributes such as mercy or vanquishing, whereas kind, merciful treatment is applied to the righteous and to those of the straight path as guidance, preservation, support, and succor, as is wrath, destruction, and vanquishing meted out to those who are astray and cause others to err. All that is fulfilled according to a firm divine law.

It is no wonder that this term received careful treatment by Sufis, for it inspired them with a treasury of deep thought regarding the attributes and the divine names. They have written brilliant treatises about the activity of the names and attributes in whose exposition they varied. These include the writings of al-Ḥakīm al-Tirmidhī, Sahl al-Tustarī, Junayd, Dhū al-Nūn, Ibn al-ʿArabī, ʿAbd al-Karīm al-Jīlī, and al-Qāshānī. This led to the division of the learned men into sects based on their delving in the essence, the attributes, and the names of the days. Some came to be known as Scholars of the Essence (*ʿUlamāʾ Dhātiyyūn*), Scholars of the Attributes (*ʿUlamāʾ Ṣifāʾiyyūn*), and Scholars of the Days of God (*ʿUlamāʾ Ayyām Allāh*).

Due to the interpretation of divine influence in history—without causing indwelling or unity—and due to the necessity of divine law, it was possible for the Muslim philosophers of history at the end of the critical movement which followed Ṭabarī and those who came after him who attempted to satisfy curiosity on one hand and to direct the attention to the lessons of history, that Ibn Khaldūn called his book *al-ʿIbar*.

On the other hand, Ibn Khaldūn distinguishes two parts of history, the one of form (*shaklī*), which is external (*khārijī*) or descriptive (*ṣuwarī*) or by chain of authority (*isnād*) or reports (*akhbār*) or sayings (*aqwāl*) or events (*ḥawādith*), and the inner (*bāṭinī*) side which is in fact the meaning of all this. Ibn Khaldūn, however, always connects history with time and place. He also does not distinguish between sacred and secular history; rather, he sees a complete unity of progressive (*mutadarrij*) history in accordance with a fixed law. This is in spite of the fact that Islamic philosophers followed in the footsteps of Aristotle in not considering history as science. Aristotle's reason was that a science necessitates the existence of a general law which explicates the nature and cause of a collection of phenomena whereas history is concerned with individual events which occur in a particular place at a particular time.

It is possible that the researcher may pass over the point of lessons of history and its significance in the philosophy of history of Ibn Khaldūn and the necessity of tying it in the general religious plan, which results in the belief that when Ibn Khaldūn announced the relatedness of events to each other as a relation of cause and effect, he was focusing on secular history, separating it from its religious exigency. This is absolutely erroneous.

It is true that Ibn Khaldūn has a social interpretation of history which takes gradual progression into consideration; however, he never fails to warn us now and then of what is behind these positive laws which is the law of God and His will.

If the historian labors diligently in an attempt to recreate the past as it was, or close to what it was, through his analysis of documents, papers and ruins, externally and internally, with careful analysis, and to synthesize what is considered as true of these elements or those, in order to reconstruct it anew, that we may truly comprehend the past—if the historian does that, he must not ignore these decisive divine days and nights in the history of man and their role in determining history itself and in focusing its direction. We must not ignore the importance of individual experience in itself.

The Western historians have ruled out some of these experiences when they found that they are fundamental in relation to religions. The fact is that history in relation to religions is not merely an arena of social development by itself, to that must be added its being an arena of internal acquisitions and achievements.

Thus from religion itself man acquires an insight into the nature of history and through history we learn about the essence of religion and its deep internal influences. And if the lessons of history and its examples point to the existence of laws that have been revealed through religion, in history we find what binds the fundamental religious principles in the progression of events as the famous German saying points out, "The history of the world is world judgment."

Therefore: If we have seen that there are points of agreement among the religions concerning the unity of history in the light of the idea of creation and the existence of a divine goal and a higher wisdom and the veracity of God's care for His creation and the befriending (*wilāya*) of God to the faithful, etc., we have also found important points of disagreement which condition the view of history. The most obvious of these points is what is related to the Christian concept concerning God's entry into history through incarnation. Islam and Judaism disagree with this. Furthermore, Islam proclaims fulfillment of divine law through the revelation of the Qur'ān to the Prophet Muḥammad and the cessation of divine revelation special to prophets with the end of the Prophet Muḥammad's mission on earth. Both Christianity and Judaism disagree with this.

It has been said that such ideas, i.e., indwelling and cessation of revelation after the Prophet's joining the Friend above, present a problem to the philosophy of religion. However, we see that these problems have a relation to the philosophy of history also, thus we agree with the opinion that says that the historian, by the fact that he is a historian, has no convincing reason to announce the fallacy of any idea as long as it is considered to be true by those who hold to it, on condition that he has the necessary proofs from uncontested documents. All he can do is weigh the supporting and opposing evidence—if any exists—then he is to report this sincerely from a historical point of view. For if he finds evidence concerning the truth of an idea or its fallacy, he is to report that in all sincerity. He may be successful in uncovering the special circumstances which had caused a certain religious phenomenon to be reasonable.

From: *Fī al-Dīn al-Muqāran* (Alexandria, 1970) Selections

Appendix F
Factors That Influence History
by Rāshid al-Barrāwī

THOSE DAYS WE ROTATE among people❳ S. 3:140. This verse sums up in a few words the record of human history and of social progress since man appeared on the face of this planet to which we belong. Once man became capable of inventing the instruments and means of recording events that influence his life, we acquired awareness of the phases of the human saga, progress and what accompanies it of change that has affected the various aspects of human life whether economic, social, intellectual, or political. Societies developed due to human needs that soon became obsolete to be followed by other societies more able to survive and develop.

Great social systems came into being including slavery, feudalism, and bourgeois societies. Each of these systems represented a progressive stage from that which preceded, and prepared the way for that which followed. The movement from one order to another or from one civilization to another is a painful operation; it involves radical changes in the mode of living. Some of it comes about calmly and easily while the rest is actualized through revolution and violence.

These realities the Qur'ān expressed in a profound way in more than one place and through several methods. ❲And how many generations have We destroyed after Noah❳ S. 17:17. ❲How many populations have We destroyed because of their oppression and We established after them other peoples❳ S. 21:11. (See also S. 6:6; 25:36–38.)

These villages, generations, or nations whose people God has destroyed represent states, nations, societies, systems, and civilizations that have come into being and prospered. They became corrupt and deserved suffering and were therefore destined to destruction and annihilation. In explaining the reason for drowning the people of

Noah, God points to their error or sin ❨When they belied the prophets❩ S. 25:37. This cause we find referred to in verses which describe the destiny of the nations, e.g., ʿĀd, Thamūd, and ahl al-Rass. Here it becomes necessary to understand the factor of belying prophets in its wide scope. Prophets call their people to faith in the one omnipotent God, and in His decrees, orders,and guidelines for worship and behavior. These constitute the social and political aspects of life for humanity.

This succession of systems, civilizations, and nations reveals more than one meaning. In the first place, it means that each civilization comes into being to actualize the goals of a specific society in a specific time and within specific conditions and environmental factors. However, through the passage of time and the rise of new needs it becomes necessary that new civilizations of a higher order should replace it. It is through the succession of systems and civilizations from the lower to the higher that the development and progress of the social order takes place, i.e., the development and progress of humanity as a whole. The whole meaning is that there is not a civilization or a system that is made by man that can be considered eternal or good for all ages and all societies. We stress "made by man" because in this state it reflects the condition of lack and weakness in humanity.

There is a third meaning to the verse, ❨The people of Noah, when they belied the prophets, we drowned them❩ S. 35:37. This means that the people of Noah deserved annihilation because they belied the prophets on purpose. This is also true of the other nations about which the Qur'ān speaks. Thus society is responsible for the destiny that befalls it. In other words, we say that man fashions his own destiny with his own hands. God said, ❨For God will not alter the grace He has bestowed on a people until they alter what is in themselves❩ S. 13:11. The meaning is that God has made [His grace] contingent on human will and endeavor which points to the fact that He has endowed humans with capacity for such an endeavor, the responsibility for the condition they are in and the one they will achieve. The reason is that He has granted humanity intellect which is the organ of thought, discernment, and judgment concerning that which is right and that which is in error. Thus man is responsible for his action. He cannot place the responsibility for his error on outside agents.

Destruction does not occur suddenly. ❨Each nation has a term❩ S. 7:34. ❨Those settlements, We destroyed them when they oppressed;

and We set an appointed time for their destruction❳ S. 18:59. ❲No nation can hasten its appointed time nor can it delay it❳ S. 23:43. These verses encompass two essential truths that are affirmed by history. The first is the inevitability of the destiny of an oppressive nation. The second notes that this destiny is preceded and conditioned by precedents that are imposed through posited circumstances. This means that the civilizations that have disappeared did not collapse suddenly, but that the collapse was the final stage of a protracted operation through which the necessary conditions existed and interacted with one another. The civilizations that have succeeded one another in human history have never been the product of a passing whim that possessed a group of people. If that were true, these civilizations would have been the product of chance. Chance is never the factor in the march of history. This is attested to by other verses from the Qur'ān. S. 22:48; 29:53; 22:47

This means that oppression in its comprehensive social meaning inevitably leads to destruction, which is a long process. This does not contradict God's word that ❲It [the punishment] will come upon them suddenly❳ S. 29:53. This means that the occurrence of the historical event is the result of the accumulation and interaction of posited circumstances. The suddenness is channeled into the moment of the occurrence of the event; its connection is to the timing. During the period preceding the final stage, the situation deteriorates in successive stages which proves the Qur'anic verse quoted above ❲For God will not alter the grace He has bestowed on a people until they alter what is in themselves❳ S. 13:11. History bears witness to these truths. The Roman Empire did not collapse suddenly when attacked by the Barbarians who ransacked Rome; rather, the collapse was preceded by a protracted period of time during which decay permeated the Empire. The economic, social, and political foundations of the Roman Empire began to collapse slowly. These matters we learn from books such as *Qiyām wa-Inḥilāl wa-Suqūṭ al-Imbarāṭūriyya al-Rūmāniyya* (The Rise, Disintegration and Fall of the Roman Empire). Furthermore, it took the feudal system several centuries to disappear, during which time it witnessed many wars, as well as scientific, economic, and political revolutions. The same principles are applicable to the Western colonial system which followed the great geographical discoveries which led to the settlement of the new world in the Western hemisphere and the ability to reach South Asia via the sea route. This system soon came into conflict with national resistance. It was inevitable that two great events would take place to speed its [the colonial system's] end. These are the First World War and the Second World War.

What we have discussed about the destruction of nations, systems, and civilizations is equally applicable to their formation. In truth, these organizations begin small as a seed that proceeds to develop and grow. Then it succumbs to the factors of weakness and disintegrates. This process does not differ in matters concerning growth, development, and annihilation from that which humans, plants, and animals experience.

Those who were pioneers in following the prophets and messengers and appropriating their message were mostly from the lower classes of society, the poor, the slaves, and the servants. They had been deprived of their full social and political rights. They were oppressed, persecuted, and monopolized due to the existent social system.

The new messages called them to faith in God who is the Creator of the universe. He does not accept one group as superior by nature or that another group or groups are naturally inferior. The differences in human endeavor are contingent on good works. Thus it is natural that the weak of the earth flocked to the haven of the messages from heaven since they affirmed their humanity. They [the messages] do not distinguish in matters of punishment and recompense between them and the rulers. These messages promise salvation from suffering, from oppression, and from abuse. They assure the weak that they are the masters of the future since destruction is the destiny of their oppressive, despotic, and monopolistic enemies. Thus we have Moses promising his people that God will destroy their enemies and establish them in the earth as vicegerents. . . .

This leads to the evidence of a most important social truth, that those who are pioneers in following reformers and exponents of social change, and who eagerly join new systems come from those sectors of society that have been robbed of their legitimate rights and privileges.

History is the greatest witness to this, for we know that those of the Roman Empire who hastened to join Christianity were the slaves. Christianity promised them the heavenly kingdom and proclaimed that it was not exclusively for the masters. Rather, it informed them that the entrance of the rich into heaven is harder than that of a camel through the eye of a needle. It was also natural that many of Mecca's poor and its slaves hastened to believe in Muḥammad who used to say "God does not look at your image or your wealth; rather, He looks at your hearts and deeds." Furthermore, the greatest number of supporters of the French Revolution were the farmers (who sought liberation from economic and social bonds imposed on them by the feudal lords), the guild masters and their apprentices (who sought freedom from the power of the guilds), and the common people (who sought the right to participate in government which was exclusively restricted to kings, noblemen, and the upper ranks of the clergy). All this explains the slogan of that revolution which was "liberty, fraternity, and equality."

If wealth is not disgraceful as we have previously pointed out, excessive wealth which is beyond the limits is bound to push societies into the way of destruction since it leads to oppression (S. 96:6–7) and transgression ﴾If God were to increase the wealth of His servants, they would transgress in the world﴿ S. 42:27.

The rich are capable of monopolizing the political system and of utilizing it to serve their purposes and increase their wealth through various means, such as the legislation of laws and the establishment of systems that fulfill these goals. They also use their wealth to bribe those in authority to ignore their abuse of the masses (S. 2:188). History is full of the uncontested proof of what we have explained. The big landowners in England were able to produce legislation which allowed them to appropriate the common lands which provided some livelihood for the poor farmers. The latter were thus forced to move into the cities where the industrialists exploited them.

This is not the extent of this matter, for the classes that are excessively rich usurp political power in a direct or indirect way seeking additional profits. When these are not available in their own countries, they expand to those outside placing poor countries under their hegemony. They declare war and cause anarchy and division.

Excessive wealth encourages extravagance, deviation, sinfulness, and vanity, all of which are evils that destroy the structure of a society. God says ﴾If we decide to destroy a village, We order its rich people to transgress that it can be truly said "We destroyed it completely"﴿ S. 17:16. ﴾Likewise We have placed in every village its greatest criminals that they may deceive it; they deceive none but themselves﴿ S. 6:123. ﴾How many villages we have destroyed, their ways of living became vain. Their dwelling places will not be inhabited after them but for a while. We are the inheritors﴿ S. 28:58.

There is no doubt that corruption in the system of government is one of the most important factors that lead to the collapse of nations. One of the signs of this corruption is the injustice inflicted on the weak by the oppressors S. 28:4. Signs of corruption also include the covetousness of the rich for the little that the weak and the poor possess S. 38:21–24. Other signs are apparent in the lack of equality before the law and the preferential treatment of those in authority and power as they are not held accountable if they transgress. This is expressed by the Prophet as reported by Ā'isha, "Those before you were annihilated when those who are noble among them committed theft and were left free, while the weak who committed a theft were judged."

Among the most dangerous evils of the systems of government is the corruption of the clergy whose primary responsibility is expected to be the command of the good and the prohibition of evil. However, history presents us with examples that are contrary to this. God said, ﴾O ye who believe, many of the monks and the priests devour the wealth of people falsely and are an obstacle in the way of God﴿ S. 9:34. The history of the church in Europe presents us with more examples. The [church] has been able to make many give part of their property for charitable purposes. These possessions were administered by the church which received all the profits. Through various means, of attraction, threat, or outright war, the church was able to possess large areas of land until it was considered the largest and richest feudal prince in Europe. It was not satisfied with this; it devised the system of indulgences claiming that those who purchased them would be granted forgiveness from sin.

In many societies the clergy issued dispensations to please those in power. When the Church of Rome hesitated to grant King Henry VIII the right to divorce his wife, one of the [clergy] suggested to him the issuance of a decree making the king the highest official of the church in Britain. From this vantage point, he could fulfill his urges. It is not surprising to find that those who call for new sects and great revolutions, such as the French Revolution, take an adversary stance towards the clergy.

We have noticed that many of the verses [of the Qur'ān] place the responsibility of oppression, corruption, injustice, and vice on the leaders and the powerful. . . . Does the responsibility stop here, or in other words, are they solely responsible for the deterioration of a civilization or the destruction of a nation? The answer, with all certainty is in the negative. Those who stand by uninvolved hold part of the responsibility because they fail to fulfill their role in commanding the good and prohibiting evil, or at least in forbidding it through whatever they command of the means of conviction.

From: *Al-Tafsīr al-Qur'ānī li'l-Tārīkh* (Cairo, 1973) Selections

Appendix G
The Qur'anic Interpretation of History
by ʿImād al-Dīn Khalīl

IN THE QUR'ĀN, the interpretation [of history] proceeds from the vision of God which differs from a posited view in that it has a comprehensive knowledge of historical events in their three time elements: past, present, and future, and in their fourth dimension which often vanishes from human thought no matter how intelligent, incisive, and perceptive a person may be. This is the dimension that probes the depth of the human soul impinging on the nature of man, his intrinsic identity, and the dynamic movement of his inner being. It penetrates deeply into his intellectual, emotional, and psychic vibrations, and his antecedent will. . . . For it is the vision of the divine being which permeates all things with knowledge and has fashioned the historical event and placed it in its ordained place in the design of human and cosmic history.

Furthermore, the Qur'anic interpretation is never merely preordained givens which seek to fashion the preceding events of history in its arbitrary frame; rather it is a system which proceeds from an objective [position] (as it actually happened) not (as it should be) [or] in accordance with the determinist history of humanity. It is a crystallization of the main lines of the dynamics of history which the Qur'ān presents as general principles, or laws (*sunan*), and which are taken by the Muslim interpreters as a starting point. Not a falsification of history, these laws are for its interpretation and understanding and for the comprehension of its dynamic forces and the consequences of its occurrences and its complex and intricate courses. Thus it is a comprehensive and complete interpretation which provides the most accurate view of the laws that move this history. Since these laws are of His making and through His will, knowledge, and provision, this Qur'anic view of the interpretation and dynamics of history is perfect.

Theoretical methodologies look to the past in order to appropriate and select what buttresses their preconceived notions. The Qur'anic view envelops the past in order to consolidate it in rules and laws which are set before each researcher in history, attempting to comprehend and to formulate on the basis of this understanding the ways of his present and future life, since the times are one and the same laws govern all of life.

History in the Qur'ān becomes unified time. . . . The walls that separate the past, the present, and the future collapse and the three times commingle in a common destiny. Even the earth and the heaven, temporal time and divine time, the story of Creation and the Day of Judgment . . . always meet in the present moment in the Qur'ān. . . . This fast movement between past and future, between present and past, between future and present, clarifies the effort of the Qur'ān to remove the boundaries which separate time and show it as a contiguous living unity. The movement of history which encompasses creation becomes one movement beginning with the moment of God's creation of the heavens and the earth and moving towards the Day of Judgment.

Life in the world is a continuous historical event which is formed of the past and the present and is related to the future with the Day of Judgment, the final destiny of human activity in the world. Thus the Qur'ān provides us with a wonderful description which is characterized by the vitality and effusion of the flow of human history and the congruence of the past, the present, and the future. With this it moves us with dispatch and originality among the three times so that the partitions, impediments, and walls [that separate them] disappear.

The comprehensiveness of the Islamic method and its objectivity is evident in its total openness to all active forces in history—whether visible or hidden, intellectual or emotional, spiritual or material, natural or metaphysical—without fragmentation of the [Islamic] method or the dissociation of the world from its proper mooring in the universe and its complete relatedness to what surrounds it.

The Qur'ān posits for us initially the question of rules and laws that govern the movement of history according to the narrow path which does not err; from its ways there is no exit, for it proceeds from the essential human formation and its fixed given axis of instincts, character, thought, and emotions.

The judgment of the dynamics [of history] is totally logical because it is similar to recompense which is of the substance of action and of its nature. It is totally just because it recompenses the person, individually and in groups, in accordance with the nature of the roles they fulfilled in history. It is as though the Qur'ān wants to point our attention to the fact that we can foretell the almost inevitable results of a given aggregate of historical events because of its [the Qur'ān's] integral relation to the continuity and eternality of the historical laws, and by the evident and hidden relations, connections, and alliances in the world in which the person moves. These transcend in breadth and comprehensibility the geographical milieu and the economic condition in order [that one can be] open to the historical act itself, the act that is based on constant ethical values in the being of man and from which positive or negative responses are elicited.

Further, any delay or equivocation in the fulfillment of these laws would lead to the weakening of the dynamics of history and the absence of disciplinary recompense. Thus it would lead to a position which is contrary to truth and justice. The Qur'ān, in order to provide us with equanimity, reveals to us in more than one place the constancy of these laws and their fulfillment and the fact that they do not change or alter. They exist initially in the essence of the universal formation and in the heart of the relation between man and the world. . . . The Qur'ān has done nothing but uncover them and affirm their existence and weightiness in the movement of history. . . .

These rules and laws in the Qur'ān are not limited, nor are they arrested in details or temporary fragments. They expand in a flexible, open, and comprehensive [manner] to encompass the greatest number of occurrences and touch the greatest number of details and fragments, yet remain eternally the final summation, the concentrated symbols and the great proofs of the movement of history. They seek to tell us—in a short and poignant manner—that the movement of any human group in history is not haphazard. It is based on intellectual, spiritual, and volitional factors, contrary to what exists in the nonhuman world. It is completely responsible during its movement as it denies folly and indifference. Freedom moves from its hidden agitated form to a planned rational action in which man stands before God and the world to actualize construction, progress, and development according to what the prophets from time to time brought of teachings and plans which take humanity by the hand and guide it on this road. When the positive relationship between man, God, and the world is negated, when freedom is misused and responsibility is lost, when rational, sane planning is lacking and the ethical principles that proceed from the intellect, the spirit, and the will are diluted . . . the recompense that is corollary to deeds will come. It will lead humanity to deterioration, disintegration, and collapse.

The Qur'ān informs us through a great number of its verses that any historical event occurs as an expression of God's will which molds it through the will of man, or through direct action (*mubāshara*) in time and space. It is impossible to study the history of humanity but from this starting point. Divine action takes two forms in creating the event and forming it. The first is direct historical action. This direct action alternates between harmony with the laws of nature and reliance on implementation, and the transcendency of these measures and the rejection of their relativism—which is the miraculous. In each case, the direct divine act comes to remind people of their Creator and His word, which is being executed in the universe and the world, and His infinite power to act and make them present in facing their Lord, receptive to His [word], worshipping Him, and thankful for His beneficence which is ever productive, outpouring and creative. . . . God Who ﴾If He ordains a matter, He only commands it to be and it is﴿ S. 19:35.

God's direct act did not cease with the appearance of Adam and his progeny whom God endowed with mind, spirit, and will and taught all the names. He held them accountable for hearing, seeing, and the heart. This direct act continues. Meanwhile, indirect divine action functions through man himself. . . . Otherwise, would it have been possible for man with his limited capacities to depend on his own action to withstand the world? For Adam from the first moment of his descent was in dire need of God's action and guidance, lest he and his progeny be lost forever. . . . God almighty quickly responded through His absolute active and willful power which never ceases acting or creating . . . vis-à-vis man's impotence and his limited sensory endowments, his uncoordinated action, and his constant dependence on a will above his will and a vision more comprehensive than his own. S. 2:37

After that promise of guidance, God has chosen His prophets and apostles from the heart of the world through direct action, that they may fulfill their historical role which is relevant for the period in which they were sent. Then came the message of Muḥammad, the last link in this chain of apostleship, to grant the sons of Adam the straight path for their life in this world. This is the link that was fixed in a final manner, as it fulfilled all its purposes in God's Book and the Sunna of His Prophet, that it may remain on the Day of Resurrection a clear voice which guides the sons of Adam to the straight path. The Qur'ān itself announced this perfection during the last pilgrimage: ⟨Today I have completed for you your religion and fulfilled My grace to you and approved Islam as your religion⟩ S. 5:3. Thus all prophetic [missions] were direct divine acts personified through the choice of men to bear the trust. The prior preparation [of each prophet] was under the vision of God, [through] his mission as a prophet to his people or to all mankind and the continuous communication with him by revelation (*waḥī*) which comes in installments at intervals or through a direct meeting where a book is received which guides the human being on the way.

These prophecies were accompanied by a series of other direct actions which at times were in harmony with the laws of nature and at other times were outside them or contravened them. These were called miracles which came as a shock to move the person and to overcome or remove from his heart, his mind, and his feelings the walls which surrounded him and impeded him from the evident faith in God and the following of His prophets.

The direct act is in harmony with the laws of nature and utilizes them for the service of the believing community. It attacks the impediments that stand in the way of the fulfillment of its duty and punishes those who confront the way of God and deny His beneficence. . . . It occupies a large portion of the Qur'ān. We are able to discern it specifically in the verses connected with the movement of the *daʿwa* at the time of the Prophet and which the exegetes researched and reported [under the heading] of the causes of revelation (*asbāb al-nuzūl*).

In the emigration of the Prophet to Medina, in the battles of Badr, Khandaq, Ḥunayn, and others, the divine will transcended the material laws of nature and ordered the angels and the armies of God, which cannot be perceived by the armies of the world, to enter the battle and stand beside the believers and their Prophet as they struggled to implement God's rule on earth. (S. 8:5–14; 3:123–216; 9:26,40; 33:9)

Thus when we talk about direct divine action, the two universal powers that God utilizes to realize His word, [we refer to] the material power of nature which can be perceived and the power of the spirit which cannot be perceived. In the first case, we come across different samples of natural forces that confront human apostasy, arrogance, and vainglory. [These include] torrents, drought, hurricanes, clamor, eclipse, earthquake, tremor, drowning, lightening, flood, pests, plagues, communal death, disruption of society, fear, hunger, and total destruction.

In the second, we meet with the armies of God who cannot be seen, the armies of angels and spiritual powers that cannot be bounded, which in an instant can turn defeat into victory and grant the few strugglers an enormous capacity for resistance and steadfastness. The forces of the unknown which cannot be perceived or measured by our relative measurements are always the stronger and the speedier.

The Islamic interpretation [of history] is different from other interpretations because it provides great leeway for the unknown (*ghayb*) factor [functioning in the] past, present, and future, and makes the unknown one of the fundamental principles of the faith.

The history of civilization in the Qur'ān begins prior to Adam, for it includes every act in which God's will, spirit, and word intermingle (*tamtazij*) with matter, forming it into either a cosmic mass or into natural systems or creatures that carry the imprint of initial life, whether plant, animal, or human. Man comes as the vicegerent of God as the Qur'ān affirms in more than one place. [His role is] to build up the earth and he is brought down endowed for this mission, possessing the primary provisions to take on the world, to alter it, change it, and develop it. [This he does] by what God has imparted into his being of intellect, spirit, will, or physical characteristics including walking on two feet, the freeing of the hands, and the flexibility of the fingers, or by what God has prepared in the earth and what surrounds it of potentialities for vital interaction.

If we ponder our position in the universe for a while, we see that we are predestined, in truth, justice, and law, for we are part of God's creation whether we like it or not. We are predestined in vast areas of our lives. We are destined to be born and to die. We are destined to be resurrected and be judged for our deeds, to be taken to the Garden or to the Fire according to the just judgment meted out.

We are destined to belong to one region or to another, to a tribe or to a nation, to a race, to a color. We are forced to obey our biological and sensory needs and to fluctuate in our emotions between sadness and happiness, grief and joy, fear and security, fragmentation and unity. Besides all this we are destined to have our own personal identity, personal appearance, and personal fingerprints. Without these necessary obligations, life would be dissipated and would lose its unity, cohesiveness, and meaning. Without this predestination, humanity would be lost. Laws would become contradictory and the values of eternal truth and justice would disappear.

The arena left in which we can exercise our freedom is granted in order that we may be distinguished from the other creatures of God and be elevated above [the rest of] creation. This arena includes large areas such as the attitude we take towards the world, actions, goals, and our contributions to life. This freedom places man, nations, peoples, and civilizations at a bifurcation in the road. If our stance, deeds, and goals are in harmony with the laws of nature and the rules of life and coordinated with them, there will result a more abundant civilization, a more comprehensive human unity, a deeper personal happiness, and a destiny in the world and the hereafter more in tune with the purpose of the existence of humanity on the earth. This is what religions sought to realize in the world and it is what Islam seeks and will continue to seek in order to turn all humanity to Him. (S. 2:193; 8:39)

If the positions, actions, and purposes we take in exercising our freedom are contrary to the laws of the universe and the rules of life confronting it there will result a fragmented civilization, a total human disruption, deep suffering, and a bad end in this world and the next. This would be contrary to the natural role for which man was sent into the world. It would result in his disobedience, revolt, and refusal to execute his duty. This is what the posited theories seek to fulfill in the world and to which they seek to guide humanity.

In the Qur'ān there are hundreds of verses and references which urge man towards [understanding] the great meaning of civilization and inform him that his relationship with nature will not bear fruit unless there is toil, work, and activity. This is why Islam, the final message and the verification of the preceding messages, is a call to action on the restricted level as well as the larger scope of doctrine, religion, and method. [This means] the movement of man, nations, and peoples from ignorance and retardation to knowledge and civilization, from darkness into the light, from lazy, slothful reaction to nature and matter to one of perceptive activity. This movement which the Qur'ān requires is to be ever erupting, never tiring or ceasing. The [Qur'ān] asks that activity be not restricted to the level of the earth, teaching us that the homeland of humanity is not the earth but the whole creation. It also asks for a dynamic doctrine in all the universe.

Many verses in the Qur'ān clearly express the principle of the logic of the dynamic equilibrium (*al-tawāzun al-ḥarakī*) which refuses deviation and rest. It guarantees a wholesome growth for any civilization capable of preserving a point of balance between the experience of the spirit and that of matter, without veering towards either, ignoring the other, restricting it, or using means of suppressing it or eradicating it. This balance endows civilization with constant motion because the goals placed before it take on an ascending character and are not bound by any horizon nor impeded by any strong restrictions.

Faith, on which religion is structured, is always arrived at as a civilization factor (*'āmil ḥaḍārī*). It extends horizontally to cast the will of the believing community over the givens of time and space and to direct it in its correct paths and integrate it in its relations with the movement and laws of the universe and nature, increasing its potentialities, strength, positiveness, and integratedness. It also extends vertically into the depths of man to quicken in him the constant awareness of responsibility, of the alertness of conscience, and to direct him towards a race in time to utilize the opportunity before him in order to burst forth in potentialities and express his powers. [These powers] God has bestowed on him by means of the values in which he believes and the goals he strives to achieve, which in Islam constitute the total worship (*'ibāda*) by which man approaches God.

The struggle between Satan and man is wide, complicated, intertwined, and comprehensive. It is a confrontation between good and evil on the broadest fronts, an inevitable confrontation if human life is to transcend from laziness to energy, from calmness to agitation, from inertia to motion. It is an active tribulation without which human history would not take its positive form nor would it march to its ordained goals from the descent of Adam to the Day of Judgment. (S. 21:35; 6:53; 20:85; 29:3; 44:17; 38:24; 57:14; 85:10; 29:2; 8:28; 21:111; 22:53)

God's perpetual call to mankind—﴾O sons of Adam, do not be seduced by Satan﴿ S. 7:27—remains the pivot around which turns the struggle, the movement, and the progress or regression. For despite the fact that God has granted in man intellectual, spiritual, volitional, and active potentialities and taught him all names, He has not left him alone in his experience of struggle in the earth. Rather, he continues to supply him at intervals with the teachings of heaven, its just laws and its straight path that turns human activities in the world into a progressive movement, ever ascending in a balanced line with no retreat. (S. 20:123–24; 2:257; 21:18)

In its call to humanity to take advantage of the struggle and transform it into a progressive ascending movement, the Qur'ān rejects vehemently the tendency of some leaders and groups to lead to retreat and their reactionary stance which rejects any active cause since they seek the leadership positions. (S. 5:50, 104; 7:28, 70, 159; 26:74, 137; 2:170; 37:69–71; 43:22–24)

Free will and unrestricted choice of allegiance to one school or another which have been granted to humanity individually and collectively lead, by necessity, to the lack of unity of humanity and its being formed in one similar camp like numbers in a mathematical column. The value of life in this world and its constant "civilizational becoming" (*ṣayrūratuhu al-ḥaḍāriyya*) are latent in this struggle that exists between different conflicting collectivities of humanity. God's wisdom has willed that, even in the case of one camp, there should be division, difference, change, and struggle. This is the nature of human relations as long as men exercise their freedom of choice. This is the will of God in which human life was formed different from the lives of the other creatures, whether of higher or lower rank. (S. 42:8; 5:48; 10:19; 11:119; 16:93; 22:67; 10:99; 2:213,253; 23:70; 43:78; 8:65; 30:22–23; 22:40–41; 2:251)

That is the basic principle, conflict, and struggle innate in the sons of Adam [as they participate] in the movement of life towards that which is better. It transcends areas of inertness, silence, and corruption and gives power to the good forces in humanity that they may strive to enhance their ability to ascend in the face of the succeeding challenges that the struggle places before them. It strives to realize the believing community which executes the will of God in the world according to the full extent of the principles of faith (commanding the good and forbidding evil).

There are other verses which make evident to us how the struggle [takes place in] a living arena where the stances of the human community are revealed and where we become cognizant of the sincerity of the believers. For it is in the hell of battle and in its light that gold is distinguished from earth, the good from the bad. The experience becomes the great sieve which drops as it moves right and left all the weak, the hypocrites, the invalid, and the uncommitted as it proceeds towards its ordained destiny. (S. 47:31; 8:37; 9:16; 29:2–3; 47:4)

Life in the world from the Islamic point of view is similar to the water wheel. The courageous person is he who attempts to get on top in history one more time. Positions in life go in a circle and do not rest for anyone. [This is to insure] that humanity perceives the images of the application of the truth of the divine principles. This dynamic situation is similar to a man for whom it was written that he should dwell in a certain city. Then he is given the opportunity to leave it as long as his position and means make that possible. However, his destiny is always to return to his first city. The human being when he possesses a stronger will, a more resolute determination, a deeper faith, a better organized creativity and effort, will get a greater opportunity to travel to the farthest areas to discover more of the unknowns of nature and the world.

Each one of us is this man; in our collectivity and as a group, we belong to this ideology or that. We are always able to leave and take humanity with us to those far and beautiful horizons, if it is determined that we would return. For God's wisdom decrees that others be permitted to leave in their turn, because it is their right to travel after our will weakens and theirs becomes strong, our strength becomes faint while theirs becomes more resolute, our faith becomes shallow while theirs deepens, our creativity and endeavor disintegrate while theirs is coordinated. . . . If this happens, and it is bound to happen, if it is willed that universal justice should run its course, it is inevitable that according to the logic of rotation and the dynamics of what it holds of hope that we extend our efforts repeatedly to regain ascendancy, to arrive at a position of greater wealth, well-being, and comprehensiveness. This does not mean that the achievements of civilization are generally destroyed by a recurring decline. On the contrary, it generally persists in moving forward and backward, unless the strong nations practice the game of total destruction, which is not probable. . . . This is concerning material creation, that which we call civilization. . . . As for values, principles, moral doctrines for individuals, groups, and nations, ethical and spiritual practices and those that deal with the emotions, the intellect, and the conscience, i.e., in the realm of human relations, philosophy, art, modes of thinking, psychological, and social attitudes—these are susceptible to decline. They are not set aright unless there is a victory of the stronger doctrine which is more in line with the nature of the person and his role in the universe. This will not come about unless the total civilizational leadership is assumed by men of faith in God and in the Day of Judgment (who do not seek glory in this world nor evil) and until the Muslims assume their position (the middle one) in the heart of the world that they may be (a witness to humanity for them).

What distinguishes the Islamic position and separates it [from the others] is that it sets next to the question of the fall of nations, experience, and civilizations what could be called "optimistic determinism" (*al-ḥatmiyya al-tafā'uliyya*). . . . It establishes the inevitability of deterioration and fall; however, at the same time, it asserts the ability of any nation or group to return repeatedly to reestablish another nation, or to try a new experience, or to assume the leadership in civilization and doctrine, as long as it fulfills the necessary conditions. The first of these is the internal change whose positive nature was emphasized by the Qur'ān ﴾God will not alter what is in a people until they alter what is in themselves﴿, S. 13:11 and emphasized in the negative aspect ﴾God will not alter the grace he has bestowed on a people unless they alter what is in themselves﴿ S. 8:53. This change that extends to all areas of ethical and personal essences and all the relations of one person to the others enables the person as an individual and in the group to face the movement of history.

The Qur'ān sets the principle of personal change as a determinant in the fall and rotation [of civilization] and a means of recapturing [ascendancy], and thus we do not say [that it is by] persistence. It is not possible for any human group to persist in constancy, facing the confrontation, age after age, without weakening, distraction, or loss of persistence. It relegates its forward position to a group that is better prepared, more alive, and constant.

The Islamic affirmation of the principle of change in its positive and negative aspects gives human will its opportunity to fashion its destiny, by holding to it [destiny] or recapturing what has slipped through its hands. Then when this will is prepared to act in the arena of history, through the method of personal training and ethical preparedness, it may withstand the material and foreign challenges whatever their kind and no matter how strong. It molds and fashions it [destiny] anew for the welfare of man. Thus man returns—in Islam—to be victorious over determinisms and to recapture his eternal capacity for renewal, progress, and creativity. . . . This [position] is opposed by most posited theories, for they insist that if [a system or a civilization] is eliminated in the historical experience, there is no resurgence. Its destiny is determined in a world that does not acknowledge human freedom and choice, nor a capacity to withstand, to recapture, and to be victorious.

In the Christian interpretation, history is perceived as the upward progress of humanity towards the high ideals of Christianity regardless of the evil and the sins committed. Even though Christians may have colonized all the peoples of the earth, [abusing] women and massacring children, as long as Jesus saves on the cross, they are not responsible. They go forth in their destiny with no struggle and no resistance.

In the Islamic interpretation, individual responsibility expands to encompass the social aspect as we have mentioned earlier. No destiny of any group is determined except through its acts. Thus religious history is not governed by determinism that drives the believing nations ever upward in letters blazened with light; rather, these nations are susceptible to rise and fall, success and failure, ascent and collapse depending on their practices and institutions. Thus responsibility is an essential factor in the guidance of the destiny of the movement of history.

The warnings that God sends appear in the Christian interpretation of history as aimed at those who do not believe in sin and salvation. In Islam [these warnings] are seen as addressing each individual and each group that falter in following the straight path, ceasing to practice personal change and the resultant [responsibilities] of commanding the good and forbidding evil and appropriating the position of witness in the world. Further, vengeance may befall the Muslims themselves by mere deviation from the path and cessation from dynamic praxis and action, the cessation of which would find the Muslim group in the unenviable position of being in the rear. How many times it has found itself there!

Further, the Qur'ān affirms in more than one place that any nation, whether believing or unbelieving, assumes its own total responsibility towards itself before God and history. It will never carry the responsibility of another nation except according to what it dictates to itself of its own responsibility towards man and the world. (S. 2:134,141,286)

The question of the fall [of nations] takes several directions: political, administrative, economic, ethical, social, and ideological. We must remember that the Qur'ān does not provide details and explanations, nor does it touch on the passing or changing transient events of the day. Rather, it posits broad principles and comprehensive foundations in the different areas of life. It is up to us to assess the possible and total implications out of the details. For example, we can simply place our hands on the concentration of destructive negatives that may result from any political or administrative experiment in which its two poles meet, the oppressive leadership and the inert followers, or any social practice in which opulence and deprivation meet in a sad and fearful fashion, or any society that forgets its high ideals while low character abounds, or any historical activity which does not balance the spiritual and material values. These concentrations that may begin as parts and uncoordinated tiny daily segments, hard to perceive and apprehend, soon begin to gather and concentrate until they form dangerous currents that wash away all things in their way, impeding every effective effort, so that all achievement and creativity is given over to destruction and disintegration.

On the level of [political] leadership, the Qur'ān informs us that when the hour of the fall approaches, then a handful of evil, oppressive, and rich administrators, or some dictatorial criminals, assume and wield power in a manner that leads to disintegration and destruction of the group or the nation which has accepted them as leaders. . . . The Qur'ān pictures these oppressive [rulers] while at the peak of their greatness, wealth, and power as tools in the hand of God who uses them without their knowledge to bring down His just punishment to both parties responsible for the crime: the oppressive powerful [leaders] and the community that accepts their oppression. (S. 40:29; 17:16–17; 6:129,147; 33:67–68; 34:34–35; 16:34; 28:78.)

How can the believing community preserve its unity from disintegration, division, and collapse? The Qur'ān posits for us two necessary principles, not only for the assurance of the continuity of the unity, but also to help it grow and expand horizontally as well as vertically, to change it into a constant destiny towards the better and the more progressive in its practice and potentialities alike.

The first is the ethical commitment which seeks to form an ethics particular to the believing community which springs from the depth of the individual that it may color all social relationships. If prior to this effort we talked of the ethics of personal change, which is a constant personal volitional effort to preserve the values of the ethical society and its development, here we point to these same values which represent the vital areas of the civilization of nations and provide the push for its movement. . . . The more a society becomes committed to additional ethical values, the more it is able to preserve unity and extend its civilizational life and to push away the ghost of deterioration and fall. . . . Whenever a society abandons these commitments, ignores them and refrains from developing or deepening them by corporate praxis, it exposes its unity to disintegration and announces the imminence of the bad end of its civilizational efforts and potentialities.

The measurement of civilizational ascendancy is not in the size of production as much as it is in the ethical dimension of the civilized society and its striving to serve the total goals of humanity.

Jihād . . . is Islam's continuous activity in the world to bring down the errant "*Jāhilī*" leadership and to make freedom of belief possible for every person wherever he may be, regardless of time, space, race, color, tongue, education, or allegiance. In fact it is the justification of the existence of the Islamic community in every time and in every place, the key to its role in the world and its ideological goal. . . . Without this "*Jihād*" movement, the justification is eliminated and the key is lost. The Muslim community loses its capacity for unity, cooperation, and continuity.

The Qur'ān presents us with a formula for human endeavor on earth which is distinguished by balance, integration, and comprehensiveness between the values of the spirit and those of matter. This proceeds from our human constitution which is of the "breath of God" and a "handful of dirt." In its Suras and sections [the Qur'ān] talks about the Muslim experience, individual and corporate, as that which proceeds on its correct path of vicegerency on earth through the balance of spiritual and material needs. . . . Any alteration in this balance which the Qur'ān affirms and calls for as a necessary principle of vicegerency will inevitably lead to deterioration and disintegration of the individual and the group.

Islam forbids excesses whether their source is the body or the spirit. Meanwhile, there is no rejection, taboo, or disdain that is directed to the body because it is body, or to its nature or needs as detriments in the way of the spirit.

There are many verses that censure the followers of some of the previous deviant religions for their banning a great deal of the good things that God has sanctioned. There are also many verses that urge man to utilize the good things in moderation, without waste. Why else would God have created it and provided an abundance and variety of its benefits throughout the world? (S. 3:93; 6:105, 143–45; 10:59; 6:141, 148; 16:35)

Since the sources and powers of nature have been placed in principle in the service of man and in aiding him to progress in civilization and building the world, the relation between them is not by necessity one of fighting, struggle, conquest, and enmity. . . . Rather, it is a relation of harmony, mutuality, complimentarity, cooperation, integration, exploration, and research. It is the relation of the obedient servant to the capable lord.

The destiny of the individual and the collectivity which proceeds from choice forms here at first and then in heaven according to time progression. The difference between the two destinies may be in kind and quantity but not in essence. . . . Destiny occurs here and there. Those who are outside the way of God's guidance—whose decisive role the Qur'ān has proclaimed . . . following the fall of Adam—will find punishment awaiting them in the world before they arrive in heaven. It is suffering that comes to them through their hands and feet, shakes their being, removes their institutions, and covers their civilization with dust . . . , suffering that aims its whips sometimes at the soul and at other times at the body.

Destiny is the same according to the Qur'ān and its warnings. There is no division or duality, no separation or wall between heaven and earth, nor between the recompense of man here or there. Those who believe will find their happy destiny here at first, blessings that descend upon them from heaven, security, and assurance that penetrates their innermost [being]. (S. 7:96; 41:30–31; 2:38–39; 11:60; 16:30, 97,41,112; 20:23–24,52; 18:103–5; 7:96; 41:30–31,41.)

The Qur'ān presents us, in more than one place, with clear formulations about this relationship between the two destinies: faith in God in the light of the teachings of the prophets, generation after generation, which by necessity leads to total receptivity to Him and direction towards Him, and then to happiness in the two worlds, happiness in its more comprehensive and deeper meaning . . . or unbelief in God, which also leads by necessity to being receptive to oppressive leadership and directed towards it and being amalgamated into it. From that [will proceed] suffering in the two worlds, suffering in its more comprehensive and deeper meaning. In both cases the experience comes as a verification of what God promised Adam and his progeny, the day he descended to earth and became penitent. (S. 30:41; 2:38–39; 20:123–124; 11:52,60; 16:30,41,97,112; 17:72; 18:103–105; 3:148; 4:134; 5:65–66; 6:82; 7:35,152,156; 10:62–64; 11:3; 28:42; 39:25–26; 71:10–12)

Then comes the decisive verse in this domain: ﴿We give victory to our apostles and to those who believe in the life in this world and on the Day Witnessing is established﴾ S. 40:51. Here the question which constantly impinges on the believers, prior to the unbelievers, becomes irrelevant. How does it come to pass that we see that the nations who disbelieve in God are in the role of leadership and civilization? This question becomes irrelevant despite its importance and seriousness because the historical measurements do not relate to the momentary and transient in their judgment and decisions. Rather it comes as a basic concentration and stabilization of the movement of human history in its totality, its past and present, to which is added in the Qur'anic perception and in some posited theories a future dimension. Those who advocate man-made theories, in order to be objective and scientific, [attempt] to transcend the transient laws and the momentary theories [to arrive at] ones that are more comprehensive, general, and broader in scope. They themselves tell us, in much of what they write, about their present civilizations and the way they face inevitable destruction and disintegration within their own structures which move them steadily towards a bad end.

In order to be objective with ourselves and with our Qur'ān and with the movement of history itself, in order to ascertain the validity of the Qur'anic theory, we should include in our historical deduction the history of all humanity. We must extend our vision and our comparative deductions towards the future, for then and only then will we discern numerous truths. In the first place, the destiny of all messages from heaven is a decisive victory while the destiny of all oppressive leaderships is total destruction. Secondly, the believing communities even in their period of struggle and the confrontation with the forces of unbelief which exceed them in number and armaments, are happier and more deeply secure and certain, with a greater faith in the future and the destiny of the unbelievers even as they assume the leadership and control the resources of strength and wealth in the world. In the third place, happiness is not a partial or temporary matter, nor is it relative; rather it is a total experience that is intricately complicated. It extends its effectiveness into all areas of human endeavor and its expressions permeate all the potentialities of man—intellectual, physical, spiritual, emotional, instinctual, and those relating to conscience. It also extends to all collective human efforts, whether internal or external, and to the nature of one's attitude towards the world.

From: *Al-Tafsīr al-Islāmī li'al-Tarīkh* (Beirut, 1975) Selections

Notes

PROLOGUE

1. One could quote many leaders reflecting on this search including Anwar al-Sādāt in a speech on October 16, 1973 where he said, "I prefer world respect even without sympathy, to world sympathy if it is shorn of respect." Cited in Anthony McDermott, "Sadat Shakes Off the Past," *Middle East International* 31 (January, 1974), 15.

Examples of other reflections on this search include:

> "These people must realize that Muslims can easily abandon the principles of Islam or go astray from its path which has led them to great heights in history; but they will not be able to gain any authenticity or dignity of life outside of Islam. By appropriating Western culture we shall fall into emptiness. We will realize that no history will recognize us. Other nations will look down on us as upstarts who are kicked around by other cultures. We will have inferiority complexes." Muḥammad Saʿīd Ramaḍān al-Būṭī, *al-Islām wa-Mushkilat al-Shabāb* (Damascus, 1394 H.), p. 70. Unless otherwise specified, all translations are my own.

> "We thus embark on a new phase in the history of our revolution—the phase of building the modern state . . . and new society which we have chosen ourselves, the society of dignity, security, tranquility, and affluence." Anwar al-Sādāt in a speech reported in *al-Ṭalīʿa*, Cairo (October, 1971), pp. 165, 177.

2. "In another way, Muslims may find in many areas of their history their lost identity. Assurance will return to their souls which can constitute a factor in their progress. However, care must be exercised not to use excesses as some nations have done who have made history a school for lies and propaganda, and a means for the destruction of humanity and for wars." ʿAbd al-Munʿim Mājid, *Muqaddima li-Dirāsat al-Tārīkh al-Islāmī* (Cairo, 1964), p. 12.

> "History is the feeling of the nation and its memory. Each nation senses its being and forms its personality through its history. The unity of history produces closeness in feelings and attitudes and similarity in customs and traditions, in the memory of former glory, of hopes, of suffering, and in the similarity of a desire for a renaissance in the present, and hopes for the future. Historical memories bring the spirits of the members of society closer and constitute among them a kind of closeness of essence. History in all its contents of events, heroes, victories, and memories gives life to the spirits of the sons of the nation and creates in

them a buoyant spirit and urges them forward." ʿAlī Ḥusnī al-Kharbuṭlī, *al-Tārīkh al-Muwaḥḥad li-al-Umma al-ʿArabiyya* (Cairo, 1970), p. 3.

"History courses are the most important means of raising national consciousness and identity among students. Teaching history may not be the teaching of the past but the formation of a national feeling." Sāṭiʿ al-Ḥuṣrī, *Arāʾ wa-Aḥādīth fī al-Tārīkh wa-al-Ijtimāʿ* (Beirut, 1960), p. 30.

". . . I feel that I stand before a boundless world, a bottomless sea—and a trepidation restrains me from plunging into it since, from my point of vantage, I see no other shore to head for." Gamal Abdel-Nasser, *Egypt's Liberation: The Philosophy of the Revolution* (Washington, D. C., 1955), p. 17.

3. S. 24:55. All translations of Qur'anic verses cited throughout the text are my own.

PART ONE: INTRODUCTION

1. ʿIṣām al-ʿAṭṭār, "Al-Ghiyāb al-Islāmī al-Mudhhil," *Rasāʾil ilā al-Ṭalāʾiʿ al-Islāmiyya* 1 (Aachen, 1977), 1–2.

2. Nicholas Berdyaev, *The Meaning of History* (London, 1936), p. 39.

3. This is especially the case when considering Islam in Africa. Trimingham distinguishes between Muslim traditionalism and Neo-Islam, Humphrey Fisher between reforming and acclimatized Islam, and Darrell Reek between "Stranger Islam" and "Mende Islam," as cited in Darrell Reek, *Deep Mende* (Leiden, 1976), p. 77.

CHAPTER ONE: THE CHALLENGE OF ASCENDANCY AND DECLINE

1. Shakīb Arslān, *Li-mādhā Taʾakhkhara al-Muslimūn wa-Limādha Taqaddama Ghayruhum* (Beirut, 1965), p. 33.

2. The pilgrimage as a time when Muslims from all walks of life from various nationalities gather as equals before God to affirm their commitment to unity and His purpose was deemed an ideal time for such a conference since it would lead to collective action in all of *dār al-Islām*. See Rashīd Riḍā, *Tārīkh al-Ustādh al-Imām al-Shaykh Muḥammad ʿAbdu*, Vol. 2 (Cairo, 1931), 488–512, cf. 29, 254.

Mecca as an ideal background for such a conference was also seen by ʿAbd al-Raḥmān al-Kawākibī in *Umm al-Qurā* (full title: *Sijill Mudhakkirāt Jamʿiyyat al-Nahḍa al-Islāmiyya al-Munʿaqid fī Makka al-Mukarrama*) (Cairo, 1320H). For al-Kawākibī, the imaginary conference found causes of the decline in three areas: moral, political, and religious. These he outlined as: (1) Doctrines imposed on Islam, first among them the idea of *jabr*, (2) Ignorance, (3) The political change in Islamic countries from representative democracies to absolute monarchies, (4) Ignorance of Muslim princes, (5) Lack of freedom, (6) Neglect of religion which forbids man's worship of anything besides God, (7) The loosening of Islamic bonds since Islam insists that there should be no allegiance to non-Muslims, (8) Confusion about *dīn* and *dunyā*, (9) Decline of legal powers due to corruption and personal influence, (10) The Muslim ʿUlamā's concentration of their studies on religious matters and their neglect of mathematics and sciences, (11) The despair of Muslims concerning their ability to compete with the West, (12) The lack of national education aimed at raising the awareness and standard of the population to promote unity and fortitude in the face of the enemy, (13) Poverty, (14) The lack of organized groups such as political societies, etc., (15) The pride of the rulers and those *ʿUlamāʾ* who support them, (16) Religion in its present condition due to *taʾwīl, taḥrīf*, and incorporation of alien material. See Anwar al-Jundī, *al-Islām wa-Ḥarakat al-Tārīkh* (Cairo, 1968), pp. 841–42. Cf. Aḥmad ʿAbd al-Raḥīm Muṣṭafā, *Ḥarakat al-Tajdīd al-Islāmī fī al-ʿĀlam al-ʿArabī al-Ḥadīth* (Cairo, 1971), p. 74. Cf. Ḥusayn al-Jisr, *al-Ḥuṣūn al-Ḥamīdiyya* (Cairo, n.d.), pp. 2–3 where he sees the cause of decline in the ʿAbbāsid period due to translation from Greek to Arabic and in the modern period from Western languages into Arabic.

3. *al-Manār*, 10 (1907), 658, 680.

4. Mahmud Samra, "Some Ideas of Syrian Muslim Writers on Self-Criticism and Revivalism," *The Islamic Quarterly* 3–4 (July–December, 1975), 199.

5. Among causes of Muslim decline, Western authors have also singled out predestination where God is perceived as an arbitrary despot who does as He pleases. (Fatalism, modern Muslims have contended, was perpetrated by the Sufis and is not Islamic.) See W. St. Clair Tisdall, *The Religion of the Crescent* (London, 1895), pp. 54 ff.; The Earl of Cromer, *Modern Egypt*, 2 vols. (London, 1908); and Samuel Zwemer, *The Muslim World*, Vol. 4 (1914), 396–406. For the modern Islamic attack on saint worship as idolatry and as fatalism, see ʿAbd al-Qādir al-Maghribī, *al-Bayyināt*, Vol. 1 (Cairo, 1924), 181–86, 224–29; Vol. 2 (Cairo, 1925), 24–31, 124–29; *al-Manār*, 2 (1899), 33–39, 39–43, 51–56, 103–7; *al-Manār*, 4 (1903), pp. 12–20; Zaynab Fawwāz, *al-Durr al-Manthūr fī Ṭabaqāt Rabbāt al-Khudūr* (Cairo, 1894), pp. 47–54.

6. Aḥmad Muḥammad Jamāl, *Muftarayāt ʿalā al-Islām* (Cairo, 1975), p. 15.

7. Shakīb Arslān, *Limādha Taʾakhkhara*. He outlines what he perceives as errors in the Muslims' understanding and practice of their faith at the time he was writing. These include: (1) The Muslim's neglect of the Qurʾān. (2) The Muslim *ʿUlamāʾs* neglect of the study of science, (3) Satisfaction with religion in its apparent forms while neglecting its inner truth, (4) Despair in God's mercy and loss of self-confidence, (5) Muslim servitude to Europeans and the loss of Islamic confidence, (6) Muslims' conspiring with Europeans against other Muslims, (7) The loss of the spirit of self-sacrifice for the good of the *Umma*, something Europeans have utilized in achieving greatness, (8) Muslims' refraining from learning from Europeans in forming companies and societies, (9) Decline in the general morality especially among the rulers, (10) The corruption of the *ʿUlamāʾ* class who should be the guardians of the faith, (11) The superiority of the Europeans in their numbers as well as their steadfast desire to control Muslim countries, and their patience in following a designed plan, (12) The spread of ignorance in Muslim nations, (13) The lack of renewal in educational programs and the ossification of thought among the *fuqahāʾ*, (14) The excess absorption in thought about the hereafter while Islam is a religion of *dīn* and *dunyā*, (15) The imperialist-missionary propaganda. Cf. Anwar al-Jundī, *al-Islām wa-Ḥarakat al-Tārīkh*, p. 481.

8. Sāṭiʿ al-Ḥuṣrī, *Abḥāth Mukhtāra fī al-Qawmiyya al-ʿArabiyya* (Cairo, 1964), p. 344. Mūsā's ideas were given in a lecture on "Al-Tajdīd al-Iqtiṣādī Asās al-Tajdīd al-Ijtimāʿī" at AUC which was published in *al-Siyāsa al-Usbūʿiyya*, February 23, 1928.

9. Sāṭiʿ al-Ḥuṣrī, *Ārāʾ wa-Āḥādīth fī al-Waṭaniyya wa-al-Qawmiyya* (Beirut, 1944), p. 110.
10. Saṭiʿ al-Ḥuṣrī, *Difāʿ ʿan al-ʿUrūba* (Beirut, 1956), p. 67.
11. Ibid., p. 72.
12. Ḥusayn Mūʾnis, "Sharq wa-Gharb" in *al-Thaqāfa*, cited *ibid.*, p. 89.
13. Ibid., p. 74.
14. These would include among others Aḥmad Amīn, al-Afghānī, ʿAbdu, and Bayham. Muḥammad Jamīl Bayham, *Falsafat al-Tārīkh al-ʿUthmānī* (Beirut, 1925), p. 105, says that because the Ottomans did not treat the Arabs well, the light of learning and civilization was extinguished until the Ottomans found themselves lost in the darkness of ignorance. Ismāʿīl Maẓhar, *al-Islām lā al-Shuyūʿīyya* (Cairo, 1961), p. 39, holds the Arabs responsible for the Ottoman rule because they allowed the Turkish elements to rule Muslims with a non-Muslim government; cf. al-Afghānī, *al-ʿUrwa al-Wuthqā* (Cairo, 1927), p. 115.
15. See, for example, Muḥammad Jamāl al-Dīn Fanadī, *al-Kawn bayn al-ʿIlm wa-al-Dīn* (Cairo, 1972), p. 86. He says: "The enemies of Islam have striven from the period of its spread East and West to fight it by all means. Their weapons were to fabricate false traditions, to instigate insurrection, and to propagate immorality. [They did this through] the Crusades, through colonialism, and the control of thought." Cf. Maẓhar, *al-Islām*, p. 21. He says: "The Muslims have put a distance between themselves and the spirit of Islam. They have an attachment to the externals and have ignored the heart . . . I go beyond ʿAbdu and say that Muslims have hidden Islam with Islam (*ḥajabū al-Islām bi-al-Islām*)." ʿAbdu had said that "Islam is hidden by Muslims (*al-Islām maḥjūb bi-al-Muslimīn*)," *Ibid.*, p. 19.
16. Ismāʿīl Maẓhar, *al-Islām lā al-Shuyūʿiyya* (Cairo, 1961), p. 39.
17. Muḥammad Quṭb, *Hal Naḥnu Muslimūn?* (Cairo, n.d.), pp. 221–22.
18. See such authors as Fazlur Rahman, *Islamic Studies* 5 (December 1966), 322, 329; Muhammad Iqbāl, *The Reconstruction of Religious Thought in Islam* (Lahore, 1951), pp. 150–51; Ṭāha Ḥusayn, *Mirʾāt al-Islām* (Cairo, 1959), pp. 285–86; Aḥmad Amīn, *Yawm al-Islām* (Cairo, 1958), p. 137; Al-Kawakibī, *Umm al-Qurā*, pp. 58–61; ʿAbd al-Ḥamīd al-Zahrāwī, *al-Fiqh wa-al-Taṣawwuf* (Cairo, 1901).
19. Mazheruddin Siddiqi, "General Characteristics of Muslim Modernism," *Islamic Studies* 9 (March, 1970), 45–46.
20. ʿAbd al-Ḥamīd Mutawallī, *Azmat al-Fikr al-Siyāsī al-Islāmī fī al-ʿAṣr al-Ḥadīth* (Alexandria, 1975), p. 116.
21. Qusṭanṭīn Zurayq, *Maʿnā al-Nakba Mujaddadan* (Beirut, 1967), p. 24. It should be noted that Zurayq is a Christian and like other Westernized Christians opts for Western answers.
22. Ibid., p. 33.
23. Maẓhar, *al-Islām lā al-Shuyūʿiyya*, pp. 36–37.
24. ʿAbd al-Munʿim Mājid, *Tārīkh al-Haḍāra al-Islāmiyya fī al-ʿUṣūr al-Wusṭā* (Cairo, 1963), p. 289.
25. Some missionaries believed that by simply adopting Western technology, Arabs have taken a major step toward Westernization and thus by definition towards Christianization.
26. There are no studies that would show the percentages of Westernized

and semi-Westernized people in the Arab East. The percentages vary from country to country depending on the number of Western educational institutions, the kinds of governments that have been formed, the policies of these governments, the flow of emigrants from these countries (most of those emigrating from Arab countries following 1967 were Westernized—these include Egyptians from Nasserist Egypt, Syrians from the Baʿth regime as well as Iraqis, Lebanese and Palestinians).

27. A look at most women's magazines in the Arab world shows dependence on translations from Western sources. Parisian patterns for dresses have been published, as well as French dishes and Western beautification guidelines. Ads for shampoo have portrayed beautiful fair-haired Europeans. Ads for milk or baby food have carried pictures of blue-eyed, fair-haired European babies.

CHAPTER TWO: THE NATIONALIST AND SOCIALIST CHALLENGE

1. Abū al-Ḥasan al-Nadawī, *Ilā al-Islām min Jadīd* (Beirut, 1967), pp. 200–201. He writes: "This has become the religion of the educated elite who head the governments in most Muslim countries. . . . They are committed to the religion of materialism and Western philosophy of life which is based on atheism. . . ."

2. Gamal Abdel-Nasser, *Egypt's Liberation: The Philosophy of the Revolution* (Washington, D. C., 1955), p. 32. The anglicized form of Jamal ʿAbd al-Nāṣir' will be used throughout the book except when cited in transliteration. Further references to this work are cited in the body of the text.

3. Ibid., p. 34. In reflecting on this phase, Anwar al-Sādāt later wrote: "In every revolution there are two phases. First men lead the revolution; then the revolution leads the men." *Revolt on the Nile* (London, 1957), p. 26.

4. Later apologists for the revolution ascribed to it other motives which were, in fact, not conscious at the time of its inception. E.g., Jamāl al-ʿUṭayfī, *Ayyām Khālida fī Ḥayāt ʿAbd al-Nāṣir* (Cairo, 1971), p. 56. The 1952 revolution was concerned with ending imperialism, feudalism, and capitalist control of the government. It sought to establish social justice, a strong national army, and a sound democratic life ʿUṭayfī (p. 16). Cf. *Draft of the Charter* (Cairo, n.d.), pp. 6 ff. Aḥmad Amīn in *Yawm al-Islām* (Cairo, 1958), pp. 154–55, confesses his disenchantment with the leadership of al-Azhar and that of the nationalists at Cairo University. Since an Islamic unity would provide a powerful Islamic nation able to affirm its identity as one neither capitalist nor Marxist, he sees the leadership of the Muslim Brotherhood as providing the only alternative to decadence and impotence. Their program, based on the teachings of the Qur'ān, he outlines as follows: (1) Strengthening the moral fibre and resuscitating the feeling of dignity—freedom from weakness and hopelessness, (2) Warning against indulgence in sensual living, in materialism or imitation of the West—recollecting the glories of Islam, (3) Propagating education and knowledge, preservation of the Qur'ān by eliminating illiteracy through the construction of schools, the establishment of clubs, and through publications, (4) Establishing benevolent institutions for the nation, both economic and spiritual—factories, medical clinics, and the construction of mosques, (5) Treatment of social ills such as drugs, drunkenness, gambling, and

prostitution, (6) Promotion of good works, welfare, and aid to the poor, (7) Promotion of brotherhood among the Muslim nations, (8) Promotion of economic cooperation, (9) Defense of Islam and resistance to aggression, (10) Strengthening the supportive spirit.

5. The religious identity he discusses as the third circle which makes it the outermost, since he places Egypt in Africa as the second circle of identity. Abū al-Ḥasan al-Nadawī, "Kārithat al-ʿAlam al-ʿArabī wa-Asbābuha," *Majallat al-Baʿth al-Islāmī* 10 (1387h) (July, 1967), p. 7, quotes Nasser's saying that the establishment of a nation on the foundation of Islam is contrary to history.

6. ʿUṭayfī, *Ayyām*, p. 56.

7. They used Qur'ān quotes in their speeches stressing their commitment to Islam and its principles and seeking legitimation for their actions. See M. Colombe, "Egypt from the Fall of King Farouk to the February 1954 Crisis," *Middle East Affairs* 5 (1954), 188; cf. Daniel Crecelius, "Al-Azhar in the Revolution," *Middle East Journal* 20 (1960), 31–49.

8. The abolition of these courts came into effect on January 1, 1956, rendering a substantial number of religious functionaries civil servants dependent on government salaries for their livelihood. For details see Nadav Safran, "The Abolition of the Sharīʿah Courts in Egypt," *The Muslim World* 48 (1958), 20–28, 125–35.

9. Bayard Dodge, *al-Azhar* (Washington, D. C.: The Middle East Institute), pp. 157 ff.; cf. Safran, "Abolition of the Sharīʿa Courts in Egypt," *The Muslim World* 48 (1958), 27.

10. ʿAbd Allāh Muḥammad Māḍī et al., *al-Azhar fī Ithnay ʿAshara ʿĀman* (Cairo, 1964).

11. Crecelius, "al-Azhar," p. 36 ff.

12. Some scholars feel that it was due to Nasser's belief that the secessionist forces in Syria were led by the feudal and business classes that made him suspicious of the capitalists and the rich classes in Egypt. In October 1961 forty Wafdists were arrested and their property confiscated. In November of the same year, four hundred more were arrested and 8 banks and other commercial business and insurance institutions were nationalized. In December, 367 more companies were nationalized. Anthony Nutting, *Nasser* (New York, 1972), pp. 295 ff.

13. C. F. Jones, "The New Egyptian Constitution," *Middle East Journal* 10 (1956), 300.

14. *The Draft of the Charter*, (Cairo, n.d.), pp. 63 ff.

15. Ibid., p. 12.

16. Ibid., p. 77.

17. Ibid., p. 9 talks about the "unshakable faith in God, His Prophet and His sacred messages which He passed on to man as guide to justice and righteousness."

18. ʿUtayfī, p. 109; *The Draft of the Charter*, pp. 31–33, 44.

19. Crecelius, "al-Azhar," p. 43.

20. Aḥmad al-Sharabāṣī, *al-Dīn wa'l-Mīthāq* (Cairo, 1962).

21. S. 13:18–25 talks about God's covenant (*mīthāq*).

22. Sharabāṣī, *al-Dīn*, p. 77.

23. Ibid., p. 134.

24. These included Sayyid Quṭb, whose work will be discussed in the second part of this book.

25. Nasser referred to this war as "my Vietnam," where at one time up to 70,000 Egyptian soldiers were bogged down, even during the 1967 Israeli aggression. Anthony Nutting, *Nasser*, p. 338.

26. The word "pact" had acquired a derogatory connotation due to relentless anti-Baghdad Pact propaganda in the Egyptian press and media. It was aimed at foiling Dulles' efforts to form a pact among nations that bordered on the southern flank of Russia. Nasser, espousing nonalignment, did not want any of the Arab states to join in what to him was an American imperialist plan.

27. *The Islamic Pact* (Cairo, n.d.), p. 43, published by the Supreme Council of Islamic Affairs and distributed as a gift of *Minbar al-Islām*. The book also included several articles by various Muslim scholars condemning the pact: Shaykh ʿAbd al-Laṭīf Subkī compared it to Satan's temptation of Adam and Eve and prayed that God may "protect Islam from any plots made by such irresponsible people" (pp. 62–64). Shaykh Muḥammad Muḥammad al-Madanī compared it to the mosque of the hypocrites where the Prophet Muḥammad refused to pray (pp. 56 ff). While maintaining that true Islam was the policy followed in Egypt, "they are afraid of the Great Wall which is sponsored by the United Arab Republic, and which springs from the teachings of Islam and aims at helping the oppressed Muslims. . . . A sincere call for liberation and for maintaining Islamic dignity is now made from the land of al-Azhar" (p. 60).

28. *The Islamic Pact*, p. 32.

29. Ibid., p. 40.

30. Ibid., p. 44.

31. Ibid., pp. 46–49.

32. The conferees agreed that "the Islamic world forms one collectivity united by the Islamic doctrine . . . The political and intellectual attacks on the Muslim world necessitate that Muslims cooperate and aid one another in forming a world collectivity to provide pride and strength to defend and protect its doctrines and interests, and to participate in establishing world peace and the progress of human life towards a better condition. In order for this collectivity to be a reality, it is necessary that allegiance will be to the Islamic doctrine and the interests of the Muslim *Umma* in its totality above the allegiance to nationalism or other isms. It is also necessary for the Muslim countries to establish relations with one another in the different fields of politics, economics, and education." *Majallat Rābiṭat al-ʿĀlam al-Islāmī* (July 1965), year 13.

33. Fayṣal gave a speech in Iran, saying, "If we look at the Arab nation and the Iranian nation we do not find any discrepancy in goals or interests." Ṣalāḥ al-Dīn al-Munajjid, *al-Taḍāmun al-Marxī wa'l-Taḍāmun al-Islāmī* (Beirut, 1967), p. 124. This could justify Nasser's fears of Saudi cooperation with Israel since Iran was Israel's main supplier of oil.

34. al-Munajjid, *al-Taḍāmun*, pp. 128–79. Responding to a question on Tunisian television concerning the difference between the Arab League and the Muslim World League, Fayṣal said, "In truth the Arab League is a league that brings together nations that make one national identity. As for the Islamic

League, it is a league that is founded by Islamic countries and contains several nationalities. Arab nationalism will be one of them. . . . (Ibid., p. 208)"

35. Nasser, in a speech on February 22, 1966, said: "We are opposed to the Islamic Pact or the Islamic conference. We say that true Islamic cooperation is the cooperation of the struggling Islamic people against imperialism" (*al-Akhbār,* February 23, 1966, cited in al-Munajjid, *al-Taḍāmun,* p. 66). And in a speech in Suez on March 22, 1966, he said, "Reactionism was never of God's law. The law of God is always the law of justice and the law of justice, oh brothers, is socialism" (*al-Akhbār,* March 23, 1966, cited in al-Munajjid, *al-Taḍāmun,* p. 68). "This pact renders Islam inoperative in its highest principles and stabs it in its most forthright teachings" (Shaykh Zakariyyā al-Bardīsī, *Minbar al-Islām* [April 1966], p. 243, cited in al-Munajjid, *al-Taḍāmun,* p. 87).

36. See Morroe Berger, *Islam in Egypt Today* (Cambridge, 1970), p. 55.

37. *al-Mulḥaq al-Dīnī, al-Jumhūriyya* 30 (July 15, 1966) reports that "it has been decided to hold weekly meetings for the religious leaders and the imams of the mosques in the Office of Religious Affairs in the Headquarters of the Socialist Union."

38. Muḥammad Waṣfī, Director of Religious Affairs, announced that these meetings were part of "a complete revolutionary plan to prepare the leaders of al-Azhar to perform their positive role in the battle of construction and progress. . . . It will bring together imams of religion, the leaders of al-Azhar, the preachers and the Arab Socialist Union on the basis of total amalgamation with the progress of society and revolutionary interaction with the people" (*al-Mulḥaq al-Dīnī, al-Jumhūriyya* 28 [July 1, 1966]).

39. Muḥammad Waṣfī reported that the meetings were lively and precise. "You see each citizen carrying the book of God in one hand and the *Mīthāq,* the book of the revolution, in the other" (*al-Mulḥaq al-Dīnī, al-Jumhūriyya* 25 [June 10, 1966]).

40. Ibid., cited in Ṣalāḥ al-Dīn al-Munajjid, *Balshafat al-Islām* (Beirut, 1966), p. 70.

41. *Al-Mulḥaq al-Dīnī, al-Jumhūriyya* 26 (June 17, 1966) reported that instructions were given to the Imams to prepare their sermons in writing. They had to deal with contemporary issues and follow the guidelines of the ministry of *awqāf.*

42. Muḥammad Maẓhar Saʿīd, *Minbar al-Islām* (July, 1966), p. 68.

43. Kamāl al-Dīn Rifʿat, Secretary of the Daʿwa and Thought in the Socialist Union, said: "There is no contradiction at all between Islam and socialism; for Islam since its genesis had advocated socialism, and socialism is one of the principles of Islam" (*al-Mulḥaq al-Dīnī, al-Jumhūriyya* 28 [July 1, 1966]).

44. Ibid., cited in al-Munajjid, *Balshafat,* p. 75.

45. Muḥammad ʿAṭā in *al-Mulḥaq al-Dīnī, al Jumhūriyya* 27 (July 1, 1966), cited in al-Munajjid, *Balshafat,* p. 80.

46. Muḥammad Maḥmūd ʿAlwān in *Mulḥaq* 27 (June 24, 1966) is reported to have said, "All Sufism is socialism. The pioneer of socialism in Islam is Abū Dharr al-Ghifārī. The history of Sufism at different periods is nothing but the best image of socialism" (cited in al-Munajjid, *Balshafat,* p. 82).

47. Jamāl al-Dīn al-Ramādī (*Mulḥaq,* July 23, 1966). In the same issue ʿAbd al-Ḥalīm Dawakhlī wrote an article "Al-Islām thawra wa-quwwa"; Ḥasan Ḥabashi wrote "al-Islām Thawrah" in *Minbar al-Islam* 11, year 33, p. 152.

48. Muṣṭafā Bahjat Badawī, *Mulḥaq,* July 22, 1966, cited in al-Munajjid, *Balshafat,* p. 49.
49. Mūsā Sharaf in *Mulḥaq,* July 22, 1966, cited in al-Munajjid, *Balshafat,* p. 50.
50. Gamal ʿAbd al-Nāsir in a speech reported in *al-Ahrām,* July 23, 1966, cited in al-Munajjid, *Balshafat,* p. 52.

In a speech on June 25, 1962 Nasser said: "Socialism is sufficiency and justice; it is social justice . . . liberation from political, economic, and social exploitation. Socialism in this sense is the law of justice . . . the law of God. . . . Islam in its early days was the first socialist nation, the nation that Muḥammad established was the first socialist nation. He was the first to implement the policy of nationalization (*ta'mīm*)." ʿAbdallāh Imām, *al-Nāṣirīyya* (n.p., n.d.), pp. 366–67.

In a speech on April 25, 1964 in Sanʿā', Yemen before the religious leaders, Nasser said, "Islam was not only a religion. It was a religion that organized social justice in this world. It organized equality and provided equal opportunity. . . . All this we have expressed to you in one word—socialism." Ibid., p. 368.

In a speech before *Majlis al-Ummah* on November 12, 1964, Nasser said: "Our socialism is a scientific socialism based on science and knowledge. We have not said that it was a materialistic socialism. . . . We did not say that it was Marxist socialism. . . . We did not say that we have departed from religion . . . but we said that our religion is a socialist religion and that Islam in the Middle Ages fulfilled the first socialist experiment in the world." Ibid., p. 369.

51. Maḥmūd Shalabī, *Ishtirākiyyat Muḥammad* (Cairo, 1962).
52. Maḥmūd Shalabī takes Khadīja as a model of cooperative socialism because she hired men and shared the profit with them. He goes on to say: "Thus before the world knew socialism, the Arabs knew it and they implemented it as a healthy drop that emanated from the depth of the holy heart of an Arab woman" (cited by al-Munajjid, *al-Taḍlīl al-Ishtirākī* [Beirut, 1965], p. 67).
53. Maḥmūd Shalabī, *Ishtirākiyyat ʿUmar* (Cairo, 1964–65).
54. Maḥmūd Shalabī, *Ishtirākiyyat Abū Bakr* (Cairo, 1963).
55. *al-Islām Dīn al-Ishtirākiyya* (Cairo, n.d.), which includes the texts of radio and television speeches by the *ʿulamā'* on socialist topics including Shaykh Muḥammad al-Madanī, "Socialist Principles in Islam and Social Integration"; Shaykh Ghazālī, "Concerning Means of Acquiring Property and Limitations Placed Thereon"; Shaykh Aḥmad al-Sharabāṣī, "Money and Socialism in Islam," which talks about Muḥammad, ʿUmar I, and ʿUmar II as good socialists; Shaykh Muḥammad Abū Zahra, who says that the misuse of property was the cause of seizure in Islam.
56. Among these are *al-Mīthāq fī Ḍaw' al-Qur'ān,* which finds Qur'anic roots for the charter, and Muḥammad ʿAlī Māhir's *Muslim Yaqra' al-Mīthāq fī Ḍaw' al-Islām,* pp. 18–22, which is a similar attempt. The following verses are cited as examples: ⦃Unto us is the victory of the believers⦄ S. 30:47 meaning that the secret behind the success of the July 23 revolution is that it is in accordance with God's will; ⦃You are the best community brought forth to mankind⦄ S. 3:100 as meaning the Arab Circle; ⦃My righteous servants will

inherit the earth﴿ S. 21:105 as the necessity of revolution; ﴾The believers are a brotherhood﴿ S. 49:10 as against class structure; ﴾Oh ye who believe, fight . . .﴿ S. 9:123 against imperialists and feudalists; ﴾They who hoard gold . . .﴿ S. 9:346 as justification of nationalization. Cf. Aḥmad al-Sharabāṣī, *al-Dīn wa-al-Mīthāq* (Cairo, 1965); Muḥammadī al-Saʿīd, *al-Ishtirākiyya wa-al-Islām* (Cairo, 1964); *Maʿa al-Mīthāq* (Cairo, n.d.).

CHAPTER THREE: THE ZIONIST CHALLENGE

1. Muṣṭafā al-Rāfiʿī, *al-Islām wa-Mushkilāt al-ʿAṣr* (Beirut, 1972), p. 119. al-Rāfiʿī describes Zionism in these words: "It is a movement obsessed with destructive frenzy that utilizes all evil means against religions and nations. . . ." Zionists are "Those who breed corruption wherever they dwell. . . ."

2. See, for example, *Ḥawl Bayt al-Maqdis* published by the High Council for Muslim Affairs (Cairo, 1969). Cf. the proceedings of *The Fifth Conference of the Academy of Islamic Research* published by al-Azhar (Cairo, 1971) and Fuād Ḥasanayn Alī, *Filasṭīn al-Arabiyya* (Cairo, 1973), who writes "O Jerusalem, Land of Judgment and Resurrection, O eternal city, warring over thee continues. The wars of the Crusades did not cease on the 9th of December 1917 as General Allenby claimed with pride in front of the Jaffa gate prior to the takeover by International Zionism. It is as though Crusading Britain fought and Zionism reaped the victory. What befell your holy places at the hands of the Crusades is repeated today in an uglier form, within the sight and hearing of the world, at the hand of the Zionists," p. 165.

3. See, for example, Muḥammad M. al-Faḥḥām, "The Restoration of Jerusalem," *The Fifth Conference of the Academy of Islamic Research* (Cairo, 1971), where he writes about the Muslim conquest of Jerusalem: "He conquered it by the most honorable, refined, and immortal class of beings, human or angelic, ever known to this world. They met after the first time, under his leadership at the night of Ascension in the region" (p. 38). He goes on to say that there is no trace of the Temple of David or Solomon left since it was repeatedly demolished and the Temple of Jupiter was built in its place. Furthermore, "the Muslims have a greater right to David who was a Messenger of God. He preached Islam and like all other Prophets was a Muslim. David according to the Jews is merely a worldly king and has nothing sacred or prophetic about him. How can they ascribe or attach any religious sacredness to Him?" (p. 43). And "We need to go into the details of Jewish conspiracy and willful opposition against the personality of Jesus. It suffices here to state that conspiracy against him and his disciples continued throughout the centuries. The early Christians met with terror, torture, and extinction at the hands of the conspiring Jews. During the modern times we find several Jewish publishing houses in New York which are famous for their inclination toward Zionism. They publish material that is of the highest degree of indecency and offense to the person of Jesus" (p. 49).

4. Isḥāq Mūsā al-Ḥusaynī, "Makānat Bayt al-Maqdis fī al-Islām," in *Kitāb al-Muʾtamar al-Rābiʿ li-Majmaʿ al-Buḥūth al-Islāmiyya* (Cairo, 1968), p. 63.

5. Maḥmūd al-ʿĀbidī, *Qudsunā* (Beirut, 1972), pp. 156 ff.

6. Ibid., p. 156, reproduced a Zionist poster showing the Dome of the Rock with Hebrew slogans to the effect that "The Aqṣā Mosque in Jerusalem is built on the place of Solomon's Temple. This Mosque is our property."

7. The letter dated August 23, 1969, was written to Muḥammad Fawzī, Minister of War of the United Arab Republic. It is quoted in *Ḥawl Bayt al-Maqdis* (Cairo, 1969), pp. 3–6, published by the Supreme Council of Islamic Affairs of al-Azhar.

8. Al-ʿĀbidī, *Qudsuna*, p. 123, quotes the speeches of ʿAbd Allāh Sālim, foreign minister of Jordan at the United Nations in April 1971, where he said, "There is no peace without Jerusalem."

9. *The Fifth Conference of the Academy of Islamic Research* (Cairo, 1971), pp. 35–37.

10. "Never did the history of mankind reveal so outrageous a crime, and so glaringly an injustice, as the one that had been committed by a religious sect whose members had long been notorious for transgressing Divine commands, disobeying Prophets, and rebelling against every country they happened to settle in," according to Isḥāq Mūsā al-Ḥusaynī, "The Palestinian Question from the Islamic Viewpoint," *The Fifth Conference of the Academy of Islamic Research* (Cairo, 1971), p. 88.

11. The early writings of these reformers, especially those of Ṭāhā Ḥusayn and Aḥmad Amīn among others, extol the merits of Western humanism and morality and the fact that Westerners always keep their word.

12. Zafer Ishaq Ansari, "Contemporary Islam and Nationalism, A Case Study of Egypt," *Die Welt des Islam* 7 (1961), 11.

13. One of those who proposes an Islamic solution to the question of the ascendancy of Israel is ʿAbd al-Ḥalīm ʿUways, in his *Ṭarīqunā ilā al-Quds: Ruʾyā Islāmiyya* (Cairo, 1974). "To proceed from Islam . . . besides the assurance of help from God there is the affirmation of the road one reaches at the end. . . . It is the assurance of victory. Can God's will be overcome—His will which is all-powerful—could it be overcome by a missile launcher, an aircraft carrier, radiation or bombs . . . ?" (p. 28).

The basic principle of the new renaissance, says ʿUways, must be the rallying cry of Islam (*wā-Islāmāh*). This is especially crucial at this time because the world today is struggling among contradictory ideologies. Israel appears to get stronger with religious zeal and commitment to the Zionist ideology. The Arab world has for some time been in the middle of the cold war between capitalism and Marxism. The appropriation of Islam as a motivating ideology will insure the support of the masses and guarantee the utmost effort, zeal, and sacrifice.

This ideology must be bolstered by an historical awareness which is closely linked to it. It provides the theoretical principles that undergird the civilization, serving to ground the authentic heritage of the people and guarantee freedom from dependence on imported ideologies and doctrines. It thus offers the opportunity for leadership and eliminates "followership" and imitation of others.

Crucial to a renaissance and the liberation of occupied territory is the availability of arms, says ʿUways. These must be manufactured locally to insure constant supply and free the nation from dependency on others for survival. Destiny must be appropriated through constant struggle, *jihād*. ʿUways sees Islamic history as a successive effort at "defensive" *jihād* against enemies who seek to eliminate Islam. Thus constant vigilance and a "continuing revolution" are "the proper response to the conspiracies that are hatched day and night against our Arab Muslim *Umma*" (p. 73).

14. "In a few words, the political situation in the whole world is altered, for the victorious Arab has returned to the field on the 6th day of October. He has wrested the banner of victory and marched with it on the path. . . . The waves of despair began to disappear from the hearts of the Arabs and a new age dawned, the age of the authentic Arab, the brave warrior, the maker of history. . . ." Ḥusayn Mu'nis, "ʿAwdat al-ʿArabī ilā Makānihi fī al-Tārīkh" in *Wa Mādha baʿd Ḥarb October* (Cairo, 1974), p. 70.

15. Muḥammad ʿAbd al-Raḥmān Bayṣār, *al-Mu'tamar al-Khāmis li-Majmaʿ al-Buḥūth al-Islāmiyya* (Cairo, 1970), p. 13.

CHAPTER FOUR: THE CASE OF A QUR'ANIC EXEGETE

1. Muḥammad Aḥmad Khalaf Allāh, *al-Fann al-Qaṣaṣī fī al-Qur'ān al-Karīm* (Cairo, 1965), first published 1950–51. For a discussion of Khalaf Allāh's work see J. Jomier, "Quelques positions actuelles de l'exégèse coranique en Egypte," *MIDEO*, 1 (1954), 39–72; and Rotraud Wieland, *Offenbarung und Geschichte in Denken Moderner Muslime* (Wiesbaden, 1971), pp. 134–52.

2. Muḥammad Aḥmad Khalaf Allāh, "Ḥawl Jadal fī al-Jāmiʿa," *al-Risāla* 15 (September 19, 1947), 1067.

3. al-ʿAbbās, (single-name pseudonym) "Jadal fī al-Jāmiʿa," *al-Risāla,* 741 (September 15, 1947), 1017. The thesis was failed by Professors Aḥmad Amīn and al-Shāyib on the ground that it would cause unrest because it raised questions about religion. The same author reported in a later issue that Professor al-Shāyib failed Khalaf Allāh to get even with Professor al-Khawlī for failing one of his advisees. See al-ʿAbbās, "Khilāf bayn al-Asātidha," *al-Risāla* 744 (October 6, 1947), 1098.

4. Muḥammad Aḥmad Khalaf Allāh, "Ḥawl Jadal fī al-Jāmiʿa," *al-Risāla* 743 (September 13, 1947), 1067. For a refutation of this statement see ʿAbd al-Fattāḥ Badawī, "Ḥawl Jadal fī al-Jāmiʿa," *al-Risāla* 747 (October 27, 1947), 1182. Badawī contests Khalaf Allāh's claim that one cannot deduce from the Qur'ān. He cites the agreement of previous Muslim authorities that the Qur'ān is *kalām* and as such can serve in providing three logical evidences *al-dalālāt al-manṭiqiyya.* These include congruity (*muṭābaqiyya*), implicity (*taḍāmmuniyya*), and necessity (*iltizāmiyya*).

5. Khalaf Allāh, *al-Fann,* pp. 7–8.

6. See, for example, the Qur'anic descriptions of the sun setting in the spring or the Jews saying that they killed Jesus, son of Mary, the messenger of God.

7. Khalaf Allāh, *al-Fann,* p. 44.

8. Ibid., pp. 51–52.

9. E.g., did Lot know beforehand that the messengers were from God?

10. In S. 11 Abraham's wife receives the good news about having a son, whereas in S. 15 and 51 it is attributed to Abraham.

11. In S. 7 the spectators say that Pharaoh claimed to be a great magician while in S. 26 Pharaoh himself says it.

12. Khalaf Allāh, *al-Fann,* pp. 119–20. Khalaf Allāh points to the discrepancy between S. 28, S. 27, and S. 20 on the place where Moses was addressed by God.

13. Ibid., p. 124. See, for example, the Qur'anic stories of Lot. In S. 15 the angels inform him that they are messengers; suggesting that he offer his

daughters, they inform him of what is to befall the town. The conversation takes place between him and the people of the town after he realizes that his guests are messengers and will not be harmed. In S. 11 Lot is unaware of who the angels are and is disturbed at having to offer his daughters, after which the angels inform him that they are messengers and ask him to keep it a secret. The purpose of one narrative is to support the prophet, thus the emphasis is on Lot's emotional reaction, while the purpose of the other is to emphasize the punishment to befall the unbelievers.

14. E.g., S. 26:123–40.

15. See S. 2:49, S. 14:21–22 refers to what is yet to happen, yet discusses it as though it has already come to pass.

16. The Qur'ān gives three versions, for example, of the story of Moses casting down his rod. In one (S. 20:20) it becomes a snake, in another a serpent (S. 7:107) and in a third it wiggles as though like *jānn* (S. 27:10, 28:31). Khalaf Allāh cites al-Rāzī's attempt to reconcile these accounts. He concludes that what aided in this interpretation is the discrepancy in the story of the fall in the Old Testament and the Qur'ān since the latter talks about Iblīs as the cause of the fall while the former talks about the serpent. The two were integrated and it was decided that the *jānn* are a kind of serpent.

17. See S. 18:13–16, 83–98 about the *ahl al-kahf,* Dhū al-Qarnayn and the sun setting in a muddy spring.

18. See S. 39:67, 2:259–60. Khalaf Allāh, *al-Fann,* pp. 120, 171.

19. Ibid., p. 178. References to *asāṭīr* appear in S. 6:25; 8:31–32; 16:24, 38; 25:5–6; 46:17; 68:10–15.

20. Ibid., p. 182.

21. For example, see: al-ʿAbbās, "Jadal fī al-Jāmiʿa," *al-Risāla* 741 (September 15, 1947), 1017; Muḥammad Khalaf Allāh, "Ḥawl Jadal fī al-Jāmiʿa," *al-Risāla,* 743 (September 19, 1947), 1067; al-ʿAbbās, "Khilāf bayn al-Asātidha," *al-Risāla* 744 (October 6, 1947), 1098; al-Ṭanṭāwī, ʿAli, "Ilā Khalaf Allāh al-ʿĀmirī," *al-Risāla* 744 (October 6, 1947), 1107; M. A. Khalaf Allāh, "Ḥawl al-Fann al-Qaṣaṣī fī al-Qur'ān al-Karīm," *al-Risāla* 745 (October 13, 1947), 1121–23; Muḥammad Khalaf Allāh Aḥmad, "Khashyat al-Iltibās," *al-Risāla* 746 (October 20, 1947), 1164; ʿAbd al-Fattāḥ al-Badawī, "Ḥawl Jadal fī al-Jāmiʿa," *al-Risāla* 747 (October 27, 1947), 1182–84; 'Ulamā' al-Azhar, "al-Fann al-Qaṣaṣi fī al-Qur'ān," *al-Risāla* 747 (October 27, 1947), 1192; Muḥammad ʿAlam al-Dīn, "Ḥawl al-Fann al-Qaṣaṣī fī al-Qur'ān al-Karīm," *al-Risāla* 747 (October 27, 1947), 1194–95; M. A. Khalaf Allāh, "al-Usṭūra wa-al-'Iʿjāz al-Qur'ānī," *al-Risāla* 748 (November 3, 1947), 1205–8; ʿAlī al-Ṭanṭāwī, "al-Kalima al-Akhīra," *al-Risāla* 748 (November 3, 1947), 1121–22; ʿAbd al-Fattaḥ Badawī, "Ḥawl Jadal fī al-Jāmiʿa," *al-Risāla* 749 (November 10, 1947), 1234; M. A. Khalaf Allāh, "Ḥawl Jadal fī al-Jāmiʿa," *al-Risāla* 740 (November 17, 1947), 1268–70; Unsigned, "Ḥawl Risālat al-Qaṣaṣ al-Fannī fī al-Qur'ān," *al-Risāla* 750 (November 17, 1947), p. 1275; ʿAbd al-Mutaʿāl al-Ṣaʿīdī, "al-Fann al-Qaṣaṣī fī al-Qur'ān," *al-Risāla* 751 (November 24, 1947), 1294–95; ʿAbd al-Fattāḥ Badawī, "Ḥawl Jadal fī al-Jāmiʿa," *al–Risāla* 751 (November 24, 1947), 1289–92; Unsigned, "Min Khabar al-Jāmiʿa," *al-Risāla* 751 (November 24, 1947), 1307; Shaykh Sharbīnī et al., "Risālat al-Fann al-Qaṣaṣī fī al-Qur'ān," *al-Risāla* 752 (December 1, 1947), 1335; Unsigned, "al-Fann al-Qaṣaṣī fī al-Qur'ān," *al-Risāla* 754 (December 15, 1947), 1390.

22. "al-Fann al-Qaṣaṣī fī al-Qur'ān," *al-Risāla* 15 (October 27, 1947), 1192.

23. Ibid., cited on p. 1192.

24. ʿAbd al-Ḥāfiẓ ʿAbd Rabbih, *Buḥūth fī Qaṣaṣ al-Qur'ān* (Beirut, 1972), p. 222.

25. Ibid., p. 229. Cf. ʿAbd al-Fattāḥ Badawī, "Ḥawl Jadal fī al-Jāmiʿa," *al-Risāla* 749 (November 10, 1947), 1234.

26. Ibid., p. 1234. Cf. Muḥammad ʿAlam al-Dīn, "Ḥawl al-Fann al-Qaṣaṣī fī al-Qur'ān al-Karīm," *al-Risāla* 15 (October 27, 1947), 1194–95, who points to the error of using partial quotes by giving the example of someone citing part of S. 4:43 ﴾Do not approach prayer . . .﴿ without completing the verse.

27. Sharbīnī and other *ʿulamā'* of al-Azhar, "Risālat al-Fann al-Qaṣaṣī fī al-Qur'ān," *al-Risāla* 15 (December 1, 1947), 1335. The *Fatwā* read in part "We have concluded that the contents [of the thesis] are apostasy through which the author leaves the pale of Islam. When the writings are examined [it is clear] that the author is an unbeliever and that his supervisor is an unbeliever. No one should contact them to study the Qur'ān either at the university or outside. They should be punished according to Egyptian law because their work is a departure from Islam, the religion of the state." Cf. ʿAbd al-Mutaʿāl al-Ṣaʿīdī, "al-Fann al-Qaṣaṣī fī al-Qur'ān," *al-Risāla* 15 (November 24, 1947), 1294–95, who warned that by attacking Khalaf Allāh, the *ʿUlamā'* were making a hero out of him. He advised that Khalaf Allāh's work should be ignored since he is an unqualified novice who attempted to tackle a topic about which he had very limited knowledge.

28. ʿAbd Rabbih, *Buḥūth*, p. 240. Cf. al-Khaṭīb, ʿAbd al-Karīm, *al-Qaṣaṣ al-Qur'ānī fī Manṭūqihi wa-Mafhūmihi* (Cairo, 1965), p. 302.

29. W. St. Claire Tisdale, *The Original Sources of the Qur'ān* (London, 1905). Cf. ʿAlī al-Ṭanṭāwī, "Tadhkīr," *al-Risāla* 15 (November 17, 1947), 1277.

30. Muḥammad Aḥmad al-Ghumrāwī, "al-Fann al-Qaṣaṣī fi al-Qur'ān," in *al-Musājalāt wa-al-Maʿārik al-Adabiyya*, ed. Anwar al-Jundī (Cairo, 1972), p. 420. He asserts that Khalaf Allāh's work is full of mixing and error.

31. ʿAbd Rabbih, *Buḥūth*, p. 221. Cf. al-Khaṭīb, *al-Qaṣaṣ*, p. 296, where he says, "Sooner or later, events will make evident that it [the Qur'ān] is truth, all truth; and on that day history will stand humiliated before it." Cf. Badawī, "Ḥawl Jadal," p. 1183. Badawi writes that while the Qur'ān agrees with history books concerning certain events, its role is not to deduce the laws of history; rather it judges them. Furthermore, while both the Qur'ān and the historians place the narratives in order, the Qur'ān does it with more certitude.

32. al-Khaṭīb, *al-Qaṣaṣ*, p. 41, says: "The Qur'anic narratives are a survey of historical events that have occurred in time. They constitute the most authentic historical document available concerning the people and events they portray."

33. Muḥammad Farīd Wajdī, "al-Qaṣaṣ fī al-Qur'ān," *Majallat al-Azhar* 19 (1947), 12. There are Qur'anic verses and narratives that cannot be apprehended by the intellect due to our limitations. These will be made evident in the future as we progress in our knowledge. The atheists conspire to hide the scientific proof of the existence of the metaphysical world. (His reference is to spiritualists.)

34. al-Khaṭīb, *al-Qaṣaṣ*, pp. 42 ff.

35. al-Khaṭīb, *al-Qaṣaṣ*, p. 326.

36. S. 12:3. ⟨We do relate unto thee the most beautiful stories, in that we reveal to thee this (portion of) Qur'ān; before this those too were among those who knew not.⟩ S. 28:44 shows that Muḥammad was not present at the time the events took place and therefore had no knowledge of them; see also S. 3:44, 11:49. Sayyid Quṭb, *al-Taṣwīr al-Fannī fī al-Qur'ān* (Cairo, 1963), pp. 120–28.

37. S. 7 discusses the common experiences of different prophets. ʿAbd Rabbih, *Buḥūth*, p. 15.

38. See S. 11.

39. al-Khaṭīb, *al-Qaṣaṣ*, p. 49. Cf. ʿAbd Rabbih, *Buḥūth*, p. 14; Bakrī Shaykh Amīn, *al Taʿbīr al-Fannī fī al-Qur'ān* (Beirut, 1973), p. 215.

40. See S. 29:15 ff.

41. See S. 15:51. Amīn, *al-Taʿbīr*, p. 216.

CHAPTER FIVE: THE CASE OF THE FEMINIST MOVEMENT

1. Durriyya Shafīq, *al-Mar'a al-Miṣriyya* (Cairo, 1955), pp. 255–56.

2. *The National Charter* (n.p., n.d.), p. 74.

3. See Joseph P. O'Kane, "Islam in the New Egyptian Constitution: Some Discussions in *al-Ahrām*," *The Middle East Journal* 26 (Spring 1972), 139.

4. Among the several treatises on the subject, this study will make use of the writings of Saʿīd al-Afghānī, *al-Islām wa-al-Mar'a* (Damascus, 1964); Maḥmūd Shaltūt, *Min Tawjīhāt al-Islām* (Cairo, 1964); Maḥmūd Shaltūt, *al-Islām ʿAqīda wa-Sharīʿa* (Cairo, 1964); Maḥammad Nāṣir al-Dīn al-Albānī, *Ḥijāb al-Mar'a al-Muslima fī al-Kitāb wa-al-Sunna* (Cairo, 1965); Aḥmad al-Sharabāsī, *al-Dīn wa-Tanẓīm al-Usra* (Cạiro, 1965); Abū Raḍwān Zaghlūl ibn al-Sanūsī, *al-Mar'a bayn al-Hijāb wa-al-Sufur* (Beirut, 1967); Muḥammad ʿIzzat Darwaza, *al-Mar'a fī al-Qur'ān wa-al-Sunna* (Beirut, 1967); ʿUthmān Saʿīd al-Sharqāwī, *al-Islām wa-al-Ḥayāt al-Zawjiyya* (Cairo, 1967); al-Bahī al-Khūlī, *al-Islām wa Qaḍāyā al-Mar'a al-Muʿaṣira* (Kuwaiṭ, 1970); Muḥammad ʿAṭiyya al-Abrāshī, *Makānat al-Mar'a fī al-Islām* (Cairo, 1970); Muḥammad Ismāʿīl Ibrāhīm, *al-Zawāj* (Cairo, 1971); ʿAlī ʿAbd al-Wāḥid Wāfī, *al-Mar'a fī al-Islām* (Cairo, 1971); Miqdād Yālgin, *al-Bayt al-Islāmī* (Cairo, 1972); Muḥammad Abdul-Rauf, *Marriage in Islam* (New York, 1972); ʿAbd al-Nāṣir Tawfīq al-ʿĀṭṭār, *Taʿaddud al-Zawjāt* (Cairo, 1972); Muṣṭafā ʿAbd al-Wāḥid, *al-Usra fī al-Islām* (Cairo, 1972); Muḥammad al-Aḥmadī Abū al-Nūr, *Minhāj al-sunna fī al-Zawāj* (Cairo, 1972); Muṣṭafā ʿAbd al-Wāḥid, *al-Islām wa-al-Mushkila al-Jinsiyya* (Cairo, 1972); Muḥammad ibn Sālim al-Bayḥānī, *Ustadh al-Mar'a* (Cairo, 1973); Muḥammad Baltāji, *Dirāsāt fī Aḥkām al-Usra* (Cairo, 1974); Zakariyā Aḥmad al-Barrī, *al-Aḥkām al-Asāsīya li-l-Usra al-Islāmiyya* (Cairo, 1974); Muḥammad ʿAmāra, *al-Islām wa-al-Mar'a fī Ra'y al-Imām Muḥammad ʿAbdu* (Cairo, 1975). Current titles such as those listed below dealing with the Socialist and the modern role of women were consulted but not used in this survey of Islamic literature. See Samīḥ ʿAbd al-Fattāḥ Masʿūd, *Aḍwā' ʿAlā Mashākil al-Mar'a al-ʿĀmila* (Kuwait, 1972); Ṣalāḥ al-Dīn ʿAbd al-Ṣabbūr, *al-Nisā' Ḥīn Yataḥaṭamna* (Beirut, 1973); Khalīl Aḥmad Khalīl, *al-Mar'a al-ʿArabiyya wa-Qadāyā al-Taghyīr* (Beirut, 1970); ʿAbd al-Wāhid al-Bandārī, *al-Zawja al-ʿĀmila wa-al-Ḥuqūq al-Zawjiyya* (Cairo, 1969).

5. al-Abrāshī, *Makānat*, pp. 7–35; Abdul-Rauf, *Marriage*; al-Khūlī, *al-Islām*, pp. 10–27. The latter goes on to say that in Sparta women were allowed an

indefinite number of husbands, "a most repulsive custom!" Cf. Ibn al-Sanūsī, *al-Mar'a* pp. 13–16; cf. Darwaza, *al-Mar'a*, pp. 15 ff.

6. Al-Afghānī, *al-Islām*, p. 6.

7. Qāsim Amīn, *Taḥrīr al-Mar'a* (Cairo, 1900, rpt. 1970), p. 31.

8. See Shaltūt's works cited above in note 4 and *al-Qur'ān wa-al-Mar'a* (Cairo, 1959).

9. Ibid., pp. 9–23. This may also explain the nature of the literature since 1964.

10. "Marriage is the foundation of the family, the family is the foundation of society. . . . It is the highest form of safeguarding society. It is a door to happiness. It is loved and held dearly by those with a healthy nature." Abū al-Nūr, *Minhāj*, pp. 30, 34.

11. S. 51:49.

12. al-Khūlī, *al-Islām*, p. 44. On page 47 he reports that the Prophet said, "You who say so and so, by God, I fear for you from God . . . I fast and break my fast . . . I pray and I sleep . . . I marry women . . . That is my WAY, he who chooses another way than mine is not one of us."

13. Yālgin, *al-Bayt*, p. 17.

14. Abū al-Nūr, *Minhāj*, pp. 35 and 38, where he quotes S. 5:87 ⟨O ye who believe! Forbid not the good things which Allah hath made lawful for you, and transgress not. Lo! Allah loveth not transgressors.⟩

15. Sharqāwī, *al-Islām*, p. 19; cf. Darwazah, *al-Mar'a*, pp. 60–64.

16. Ibrāhīm, *al-Zawāj*, p. 208; ʿAbd al-Wāḥid, *al-Islām*, p. 188: "Nature necessitates that the path of each girl, whether educated or not, be the house and marriage . . ."

17. al-Abrāshī, *Makānat*, pp. 113–19.

18. At the turn of the century Qāsim Amīn called for equality for the sexes and for the liberation of women through education. That he had to appeal to men to allow women to learn led him to present education as a means of preparing a better wife and a more congenial companion for the husband. In *Taḥrīr al-Mar'a*, p. 58, he wrote:

> "Even in things that are her domain, things for which she is created, there is nothing in her that appeals to her husband. For most women have not made a habit of combing their hair every day, or taking more than one bath a week. They do not know how to use a toothbrush, nor do they take care of their clothing whose quality and cleanliness have a great impact on appealing to the man. They do not know how desire is generated in the man and how to maintain it and how to fulfill it. That is because the ignorant woman is unaware of the inner movements of the soul. She cannot comprehend the causes of attraction and repulsion. If she seeks to stimulate the man, she usually arouses the opposite reaction."

Contemporary writers are concerned that education is not preparing women for their role in the home:

> "What is the need of a girl for all the study of science and arts etc. . . . when she does not know how to take care of the house and family?" (ʿAbd al-Wāḥid, *al-Islām*, p. 188)

The official opinion of the Muslim Brotherhood was spelled out by Muḥammad al-Ghazzālī, *Min Hunā Naʿlam* (Cairo, n.d.), p. 204:

> "A woman's mission is to be a good wife and a compassionate mother . . . an ignorant rural woman is better for the nation than one thousand female lawyers or attorney generals."

And again:

> "Girls are to be educated in areas that belong to them and not to men. We do not want *at all* to educate women to be secretaries or managers of offices or a minister of government." (Ibid., p. 207.)

A contemporary author warns about the evils of educating women to be equal with men:

> "You who persist in educating women: strengthen yourselves before you begin your task, make religion her banner waving over her head, and her crown shining over her forehead . . . or you would lose her character . . . and would find her education, a path to evil and a way to corruption." (ʿAfīfī, *al-Marʾa*, p. 13.)

19. al-Bayḥānī, *Ustādh*, p. 75. The author affirms that between the two covers of his book is *all* that a woman needs to know. This includes details on such things as what to do when a woman gets in contact with a dog and the necessity of refraining from using a toothbruth (efficacy of using *siwāk*), etc. The only roles a woman could take outside the house would be those of gynecologist or midwife.

20. Margaret Mead's studies showing that male and female roles may be culturally conditioned are cited and condemned as false because they are based on the study of three tribes rather than the total experience of mankind. See Yālgin, *al-Bayt*, p. 71; cf. Wāfī, *al-Usra*, p. 117.

21. al-Abrāshī, *Makānat*, p. 17

22. al-Khūlī, *al-Islām*, p. 78.

23. Ibid., pp. 77–78; cf. Yālgin, *al-Bayt*, p. 84:

> "It should be known that a woman cannot be ideal in all her behavior and conduct, because her biological constitution makes her weak in initiative, will, and personality in a general way.
>
> This is what makes her deficient in her work, which she does not complete, and she does not fulfill her duties as she should. In this case, [the man] must bear with her as much as possible. Meanwhile she should not be left freedom of action for that would lead to further deviation and she would ignore her duties and not fulfil them to the utmost of her capacity."

See also ʿAbbās Maḥmūd al-ʿAqqād, *Hādhihi al-Shajara* (Cairo, n.d.), p. 23:

> "Women enjoy the pain of childbirth and childbearing, a feeling men do not share as they rebel against pain, whereas it is in the nature of women not to be able to distinguish between pleasure and pain (as they are the same thing to them)."

24. al-ʿAqqād, *Hādhihi,* pp. 10 and 13.
25. Yālgin, *al-Bayt,* pp. 63–66; on page 68, he says:

> "A look at the present and the past and at human history shows that the most famous were men. Science has developed on the shoulders of men. The most famous philosophers, physicians, mathematicians are men and not women, even until this day and even though women have had opportunities for learning for over a hundred years. . . ."

Cf. ʿAbbās Maḥmūd al-ʿAqqād, *al-Mar'a fī al-Qur'ān* (Cairo, 1959), p. 130, where he elaborates on the same theme:

> "The superiority of men over women is evident in professions in which women have had exclusive domain. . . . For the woman has busied herself with the preparation of food since humanity began, she has cooked food since prehistory. She learns it at home from her childhood. She loves food and craves for it and demands appetizers during her pregnancy, while seeking larger quantities of it during breast feeding. However, even after inheriting this profession for thousands of years, she does not reach the proficiency of a man who dedicates a few years for it, nor is she able to compete with him in the excellence of common meals, or in the creation of new tastes or the improvement of the old.
> She also is incapable of administering a kitchen where there are several workers whether male or female."

26. al-Abrāshī, *Makānat,* p. 17, says:

> "Man is responsible for the demands of life outside the home. The woman is responsible for things she can do with skill, e.g., raising children, sewing their clothing, feeding them and bathing them."

Cf. al-ʿAqqād, *Hādhihi,* p. 141:

> "A woman has every right that does not distract her from her primary duty, which is a duty in which she solely excels and which no one else can perform—i.e. her house and the new generation."

See also pp. 146–147 where he says, "Her role is that of mother, housewife and nurturer of the family. These are things that she can do that do not distort her mission, e.g., raising birds and chickens, making cheese and yogurt, growing fruits and flowers."

27. "It is despicable for the woman to wear men's clothes—such as pants which they wear now—for in this is an effort to draw attention to herself or to arouse . . . Islam goes also beyond that, for male and female are the creation of God according to the laws of the universe. We do not know why God created people as male and female; however, we know that it was in His wisdom. . . . For the man to imitate the woman and the woman to imitate the man is not only a transgression of a custom, rather, it is the trampling of law, and the invalidation of what God willed in His wisdom." al-Khūlī, *al-Islām,* p. 166. Cf. al-Albānī, *Ḥijāb,* pp. 66–67.

28. Yālgin, *al-Bayt,* p. 64. Cf. Wāfī, *al-Mar'a,* pp. 43–75, who isolates six distinctions between males and females—in religious duties, economic responsibilities, inheritance, witness at court, obedience, and responsibility for the family.

29. al-ʿAqqād, *al-Marʾa*, pp. 7–9; al Sharqāwī, *al-Islām*, p. 2. Cf. Wāfī, *al-Usra*, p. 116.

30. Shaltūt, *al-Qurʾān*, p. 60; cf. al-Khūlī, *al-Islām*, p. 73:

> "The authority in the house belongs to the man. The children belong to him and he spends on them. He is the owner of the house, he furnishes it and spends on it. Thus authority comes from responsibility, not because of a desire to detract from justice, equality, and the consent of the woman. It is his responsibility to pay for the home and to protect it."

31. Jane I. Smith and Yvonne Y. Haddad, "Women in the Aferlife: The Islamic View as Seen from Qurʾān and Tradition," *Journal of the American Academy of Religion* 53 (March, 1975), 39–50.

32. Yālgin, *al-Bayt*, p. 42.

33. Ibid., p. 77; al-Sharqāwī, *al-Islām*, p. 65; al-Bayḥānī, *Ustādh*, p. 23.

34. al-ʿAqqād, *Hādhihi*, p. 90; cf. Abū al-Nūr, *Minhāj*, p. 60:

> "God has established the relation between man and woman; if observed, one notes that the woman is weaker than the man. She comes to him and surrenders to him, knowing full well that he is capable of abusing her rights."

35. Yālgin, *al-Bayt*, p. 64. He goes on to say,

> "The woman should obey the husband because of what God created in him of superior capabilities and powers for administration and guidance of the affairs of life with wisdom, patience and vigor. She must also obey him for religious reasons, for such an obedience is a part of the application of Islam. If she disobeys, she will be punished on the day of judgment. However, this obedience is contingent on his refraining from asking her to commit the forbidden, such as drink wine, ignore prayer, dance with men, etc. . . ." p. 85.

36. al-Sharqāwī, *al-Islām*, p. 69.

37. Yālgin, *al-Bayt*, p. 77.

38. al-Bayḥānī, *Ustādh*, p. 23.

39. al-ʿAqqād, *Hādhihi*, p. 7.

40. al-ʿAqqād, *al-Marʾa*, p. 30.

41. The Prophet said, "The woman is created from a crooked bone. She will not be straightened for you. If you enjoy her, you enjoy her with her curvature (crookedness). If you attempt to straighten her, you will break her and what breaks her is divorce." Yālgin, *al-Bayt*, p. 84.

42. Yālgin, *al-Bayt*, p. 163.

43. al-Khūlī, *al-Islām*, p. 103.

44. Yālgin, *al-Bayt*, p. 163; Abrāshī, *Makānat*, pp. 35–36; Baltajī, *Dirāsāt*, p. 279; ʿAqqād, *al-Marʾa*, p. 131.

45. Shaltūt, *al-Islām*, p. 207.

46. Ibid., p. 201; cf. Baltājī, *Dirāsāt*, p. 517, who affirms that polygamy is in God's plan for man; otherwise, the Prophet and his followers would have been in error and in violation of the Qurʾān.

47. Ibid., p. 203.

48. al-Khūlī, *al-Islām*, pp. 90–93; Yālgin, *al-Bayt*, pp. 169–70; al-Abrāshī, *Makānat*, pp. 58–69.

49. Yālgin, *al-Bayt*, pp. 169–70.

50. al-Madanī, *Raʾy*, pp. 21–25.

51. Yālgin, *al-Bayt,* p. 42. He also reports that the Prophet said, "The best of your women is the child bearer, the compassionate who keeps the secret, the chaste, the dignified in her work, the submissive to her husband, the one who adorns herself in the presence of her husband, the inaccessible to anyone but her husband who listens to his words, obeys his commands and when they are alone offers him whatever he desires of her and does not display the vulgarity of men."

52. The Prophet is reported to have said, "You and your property are your fathers'. Your children are your best earnings. Eat of your children's earnings." He also said, "The best that you eat is of your earning. Your children are of your earning." Abū al-Nūr, *Minhāj,* p. 96.

53. al-Abrāshī, *Makānat,* pp. 39–40. The Prophet also said, "Heaven is under the feet of mothers," and a sign of the imminence of the eschaton is when "the woman will give birth to her master," i.e., a son who would treat her as a slave. ʿAbd al-Wāḥid, *al-Usra,* p. 84.

54. al-Khūlī, *al-Islām,* pp. 139–42.

55. al-Abrāshī, *Makānat,* pp. 44–45.

56. al-Sanūsī, *al-Marʾa,* p. 32. The Prophet is reported to have said, "Whenever a man meets with a woman alone, Satan is inevitably their third."

57. Yālgin, *al-Bayt,* p. 76.

58. al-Ghazzālī, *Min Hunā Naʿlam,* p. 200.

59. al-ʿAqqād, *Hādhihi,* p. 145.

60. Ibid., p. 22.

61. Amīn, *Taḥrīr,* p. 56.

PART TWO: INTRODUCTION

1. Fawzi Abdulrazak, *Arabic Historical Writings, 1973* (Cambridge, Massachusetts, 1974), lists 385 titles on history received by Harvard Library. His *Arabic Historical Writings, 1974* (Cambridge, Massachusetts, 1976) lists 965 titles, none on theory of history.

2. "Secular" historians such as Laroui (al-ʿUrwī), Ṣādiq al-ʿAẓm, Nadīm al-Bīṭār (a Christian), and Adūnīs, whose works have made a profound impact on contemporary intellectual circles, and "professional" historians including Ḥasan Ibrāhīm Ḥasan, Ḥasan Aḥmad Maḥmūd, Musṭafā Jawād, Muḥammad Jamāl al-Dīn Surūr, Saʿīd ʿAshūr, Ḥasanayn Rabīʿ, and Aḥmad ʿIzzat ʿAbd al-Karīm (president of the Egyptian Historical Society), whose impact is mainly on academic campuses, are outside the scope of this study.

3. ﴾Have they not traveled through the earth and seen the end of those who preceded them? They were stronger than those before. They built in the earth. God held them accountable for their transgressions and they had no defense against Him.﴿ S. 40:21

4. The theme of the hero as a leader is also evident in the writings of ʿAbbās Maḥmūd al-ʿAqqād. Among others, they include *ʿAbqariyyat Muḥammad, ʿAbqariyyat al-Ṣiddīq, ʿAbqariyyat ʿUmar,* and *ʿAbqariyyat al-Imām.*

CHAPTER SIX: THE APOLOGETIC RESPONSE

1. Maḥmūd al-Sharqāwī, *al-Tafsīr al-Dīnī li-al-Tārīkh* (Cairo, 1975), p. 4.

2. Ibid., p. 6. Maḥmūd al-Sharqāwī received his law degree from Cairo

University in 1953 and had a practice for three years. He became the editor of *Risālat Miṣr* and later *al-Majalla al-Islāmiyya* (1956–62). He has written over fifty books, among them: *al-Dīn wa-al-Dawla al-ʿAṣriyya, al-Anbiyāʾ fī al-Qurʾān al-Karīm, al-Madīna al-Munawwara, Makka al-Mukarrama, Ahl al-Bayt, Rābiʿa al-ʿAdawiyya, al-Qurʾān al-Majīd, al-Sayyida Zaynab, al-Mujtamaʿ al-ʿArabī, al-Dimūqrāṭiyya ʿInd al-ʿArab, al-ʿAdāla al-Ijtimāʿiyya ʿInd al-ʿArab, Janūb al-Jazīra al-ʿArabiyya, Ṭarīq al-Insān al-ʿArabī al-Jadīd, Batrūl al-ʿArab, Ṣuwar min al-Jazāʾir, Ruwwād al-Nahḍa al-ʿArabiyya, Maṣābīḥ ʿalā al-Ṭarīq, al-Mushkilāt al-ʿĀlamiyya al-Muʿāṣira.*

3. al-Sharqāwī, *al-Tafsīr al Dīni lʾil-Tārīkh*, p. 5.
4. Ibid., p. 5.
5. Sayyid Quṭb's ideas will be discussed in the following chapter.
6. Anwar al-Jundī, *Aḍwāʾ ʿalā Tārīkh al-Islām* (Cairo, 1957), p. 4. Among his other works: *Jurjī Zaydān, Jamāl ʿAbd al-Nāṣir wa-al-Thawra, Ruwwād al-Qawmiyya al-ʿArabiyya, Min Aʿlām al-Ḥurriyya fī al-ʿĀlam al-ʿArabī al-Ḥadīth, Aʿlām wa-Aṣḥāb Aqlām, Hādhā Huwa Jamāl, Min Aʿlām al-Islām, Tarājim al-Aʿlām al-Muʿāṣirīn fī al-ʿĀlam al-Islāmī al-Qawmiyya al-ʿArabiyya wa-al-Waḥda al-Kubrā, Naḥnu al-ʿArab, al-ʿĀlam al-Islāmī wa-al-Istiʿmār al-Siyāsī wa-al-Ijtimāʿī wa-al-Thāqāfī, al Fikr al-ʿArabī al-Muʿāṣir fī Maʿrakat al-Taghrīb, Inhiyār al-Ḥaḍāra al-Gharbiyya, al-Islām fī Ghazwa Jadīda li-al-Fikr al-Insānī, al-Islām wa-al-Thaqāfa al-ʿArabiyya, Uṣūl al-Thaqāfa al-ʿArabiyya, Dawrunā al-Jadīd fī al-Ḥaḍāra al-Insāniyya, Yaqẓat al-Fikr al-ʿArabī, Min Manābiʿ al-Fikr al-Islāmī, al-Qiyam al-Asāsiyya li-al-Fikr al-Islāmī wa-al-Thaqāfa al-ʿArabiyya, al-Shakhṣiyya al-ʿArabiyya fī al-Adab wa-al-Tārīkh.*
7. Anwar al-Jundī, *al-Islām wa-Ḥarakat al-Tārīkh* (Cairo, 1968), p. 16.
8. Ibid., p. 12.
9. Ibid., p. 496.
10. Ibid., pp. 14 ff.
11. Ibid., p. 489.
12. Ibid., pp. 437–45.
13. Ibid., p. 495.
14. Ibid., pp. 500–501.
15. Ibid., p. 502.
16. Ibid., p. 499. Cf. a translation of Sidney Hook, *The Hero in History* (Boston, 1943), available in Arabic as *al-Baṭal fī al-Tārīkh* (Cairo, n.d.).

CHAPTER SEVEN: THE TRADITIONAL RESPONSE

1. Sayyid Quṭb, *Fī al-Tarīkh: Fikra wa-Minhāj* (Jedda, 1967). Published posthumously in Saudi Arabia, this book appears to be a collection of articles by Sayyid Quṭb. An Egyptian reprint appeared after the death of Nasser and the liberalization of the laws of publication permitting the distribution of Muslim Brotherhood literature. For a biography of the author's life, see Muḥammad Tawfīq Barakāt, *Sayyid Quṭb* (Beirut, n.d.). Barakāt divides Quṭb's intellectual life into three phases. In the early part of his career, he came under the influence of ʿAbbās Maḥmūd al-ʿAqqād and became interested in Western thought. He published several volumes of poetry and stories including *Qiṣṣat Ashwāk* (which he renounced in later life as being contrary to Islam). Other books of his early career that he felt were errant from the truth included

Muhimmat al-Shāʿir fī al-Ḥayāt, al-Aṭyāf al-Arbaʿa, Ṭiflun min al-Qarya (Barakāt, pp. 3–4). Other books on nonreligious topics include *al-Naqd al-Adabī: Uṣūluh wa-Manāhijuh, al-Shāṭiʾ al-Majhūl, Kutub wa-Shakhṣiyyāt, Naqd Kitāb Mustaqbal al-Thaqāfa, al-Madīna al-Masḥūra*. Others announced but not published include *Ḥulm al-Fajr, Qāfilat al-Raqīq, Laḥaẓāt maʿ al-Khālidīn* and *Amerika allatī Raʾayt*. (According to Dr. Mujāhid Ṣawwāf of ʿAbd al-Azīz University in Mecca, this last manuscript is in the possession of his brother, Dr. Muḥammad Quṭb at that university). Announced but not published is *Naḥwa Mujtamaʿ Islāmī*. A book by that title was published posthumously in which the publishers compiled some of his articles. (Barakāt, p. 4).

Barakāt notes that Sayyid Quṭb appears to have become interested in Islamic topics around 1948. During this period he published *al-ʿAdāla al-Ijtimaʿiyya fī al-Islām, Maʿrakat al-Islām wa-al-Raʿsmāliyya, Dirāsāt Islāmiyya, al-Taṣwīr al-Fannī fī al-Qurʾān, Mashāhid al-Qiyāma fī al-Qurʾān*. The third period of his intellectual life, where he became completely committed to the Muslim Brotherhood cause and wrote strictly on Islamic topics, appears to have occurred during his first imprisonment. He revised the first thirteen volumes of *Fī Ẓilāl al-Qurʾān* and began to outline what he called the dynamic Islamic system (*al-Manhaj al-Ḥarakī al-Islāmī*). In volume 12, p. 9 of *Fī Ẓilāl al-Qurʾān,* he listed the books that he felt contained his message to modern Muslims. These include mostly those written between his first and second imprisonment. They are: *Maʿālim fī al-Ṭarīq, al-Mustaqbal li-Hādhā al-Dīn, Hādhā al-Dīn,* and *al-Islām wa Mushkilāt al-Ḥaḍāra*. He also sanctioned two books of the previous period, *al-ʿAdāla al-Ijtimāʿiyya fī al-Islām,* and *al-Salām al-ʿĀlamī wa-la-Islām*. This confirms what I was told by one of the officials of the Muslim Brotherhood, that *Fī al-Tārīkh: Fikra wa-Minhāj* is not considered among the books Sayyid Quṭb or the Muslim Brotherhood sanctioned as official literature of the Society.

2. Quṭb, *Tarīkh,* pp. 7–10.

3. Ibid., p. 16. In his *al-Salām al-ʿĀlamī waʾl-Islām* (Cairo, n.d.), Sayyid Quṭb develops the idea further and says: "The value of the doctrine for which we call is that it does not offer temporary solutions for temporary problems. Its strength is that it offers solutions and guarantees for its protection and realization [of the solution]" (p. 7). He further expounds on the comprehensiveness of the *ʿaqīda*: "The Islamic doctrine is the only example that humanity has witnessed in its history that is all-comprehensive to include every effort of man in all aspects of life. It does not restrict itself to one area or to a single trend. It does not give Caesar what is Caesar's and God what is God's. For what personally belongs to Caesar, according to the Islamic doctrine, belongs in its totality to God. Caesar has no right that others of his subjects do not have" (p. 9).

4. Quṭb, *Tarīkh,* p. 16.

5. Quṭb continues his analysis of American life by saying that their production, though plenteous, brings them nothing because it ignores the human element. This kind of life he characterizes finally as completely vacuous, despite the appearance of fullness. What appears to be laughter rings empty in the air; what appears to be joy is actually "the merriment of the beasts, not happiness or joy. For the boisterousness of drunkenness is not happiness, nor is animal-like merrymaking joy. It is the explosion of restricted energies under the pressure of exhausting work. It is a commotion such as that caused

by machines that are puffing [nothing but] vapor. . . ." Sayyid Quṭb, *Naḥwa Mujtamaʿ Islāmī* (Cairo, n.d.), p. 9.

6. Quṭb, *Naḥwa*, p. 8.

7. Ibid., pp. 23–24. In his *Fī Ẓilāl al-Qur'ān*, vol. 2, pp. 8–9, he expounds on the middle position, the ideal way for life and for the world. He sees Islam as the middle position for the following reasons: (1) In its location: it is the navel of the earth, in its center. (2) In time: it puts an end to infantile humanity that preceded it and safeguards the rational guidance of what followed it. It discards the mythologies of humanity and keeps it from distorting the rational; it integrates the spiritual heritage and the continuous growth of rational knowledge; it leads humanity on the straight path. (3) In doctrine: in Islam there is no excess of spirituality or undue emphasis on the material side of life. It follows the guidance of the natural (*fiṭra*), the spirit and the body, giving each its due. It works for the elevation of life. (4) In thought: it is not ossified in what it has inherited and does not close the windows to experience and enlightenment. It does not follow each claimant nor copy indiscriminately; it holds fast to its principles as it continues to investigate truth. (5) In organization: it does not leave life for either feelings and conscience or law. It guides and nurtures the conscience of humanity and guarantees order in life through the law. (6) In coordination: it does not eradicate the personality of the individual nor his resources, nor subsume it to either the group or the nation, although one is responsible to the group. Thus there is an integration between the needs of the individual and those of society.

8. Quṭb, *Naḥwa*, p. 32.

9. Quṭb admits, however, that he has no immediate practical suggestion on how to start humanity on its way to progress and development and the appropriation of the middle way (*Tarīkh*, p. 20). He would welcome suggestions, but the details must be worked out by experts other than he; they cannot be outlined in literature which is restricted to imagination and homiletics.

10. Ibid., p. 22.

11. Sayyid Quṭb, *Hādhā al-Dīn* (Cairo, n.d.), p. 7.

12. Ibid., p. 37.

13. Ibid., p. 38; in an Introduction to *Mādhā Khasira al-ʿAlām bi-Inḥiṭāṭ al-Muslimīn* (Cairo, 1961) by Abū al-Ḥasan ʿAlī al-Ḥusnī al-Nadawī, Quṭb writes: "[Islam] cannot function unless it has the leadership for in its essence, it is a doctrine (*ʿaqīda*) of eminence (*istiʿlā'*), and a way (*manhaj*) of leadership and a method of creativity (*ibtidāʿ*) not followership (*ittibāʿ*)." The degeneration of Muslims comes from their abandonment of the role of leadership that Islam imposes on them (p. 14).

14. Sayyid Quṭb, *Māʿrakat al-Tārīkh wa'l-Ra'smāliyya* (Cairo, 1952), p. 70.

15. Ibid., p. 79.

16. Quṭb, *Tārīkh*, p. 23.

17. Sayyid Quṭb, *al-Islām wa-Mushkilat al-Ḥaḍāra* (Cairo, 1968), pp. 181–82.

18. Quṭb, *Tārīkh*, p. 45.

19. Ibid., pp. 56–57.

20. Ibid., p. 60.

21. Ibid., pp. 52–54. Quṭb notes that a committee of Muslims was formed to rewrite Islamic history according to his proposed outline: "Introductions to

Islamic History," "Islam at the Time of the Prophet," "Islamic Expansion," "Arrest of Islamic Expansion," "The Islamic World Today," The committee was made up of the following: Shaykh Ṣādiq ʿArjūn, Dr. Muḥammad Yūsuf Mūsā, Dr. ʿAbd al-Ḥamīd Yūnis, Dr. Muḥammad Najjār, and Sayyid Quṭb.

22. Quṭb, *Naḥwa Mujtamaʿ Islāmī,* pp. 41–42.

23. Ibid., p. 64.

24. In *al-Islām wa-Mushkilāt al-Ḥaḍāra,* p. 187, Quṭb writes that *fiqh* is not separate from the *sharīʿa* or the *ʿaqīda.* Sayyid Quṭb's writings on *fiqh* were attacked by several Muslim authors. The most severe appears to be that of Dr. Wahba al-Zaḥīlī in "al-muʿtadūn ʿalā al-fiqh al-Islāmī," published in *Majallat al-Waʿy al-Islāmī* and republished by *Majallat al-Fikr al-Islāmī.* Barakāt reports that al-Zaḥīlī accused Quṭb of (1) "seeking the total destruction of *fiqh* by referring to it as paper jurisprudence *fiqh al-awrāq,* (2) of criticizing the division of *fiqh* into *ʿibādāt* and *muʿāmalāt,* and (3) calling for a transcending of *fiqh* and initiating *ijtihād* from point zero."

Quṭb's reflections on *fiqh* appear to have developed with the years. He believed that Islamic *fiqh* developed in the context of the Muslim society during its dynamic period as it faced the concrete situations day by day of Islamic life. Thus an Islamic society is essential for its growth. See *Fī Ẓilāl al-Qur'ān,* vol. 13, pp. 12, 20. On page 13 of *Fī Ẓilāl,* vol. 13, he distinguished between paper jurisprudence as essentially different from dynamic jurisprudence even though the latter is dependent on the former. Those who follow the literal prescriptions of the jurisprudence do not understand the difference between the two. They fail to take into account the context within which the ruling took its shape. Dynamic jurisprudence takes the situation of the development seriously as it meets each situation.

This necessity for distinction is clarified in *al-Islām wa-Mushkilāt al-Ḥaḍāra* where Quṭb admits that it would be ridiculous to establish Islamic *fiqh* in the social and economic situations in the United States and the Soviet Union since neither admits to the governance (*ḥākimiyya*) of Islam. It would be just as ridiculous to articulate these details, Quṭb feels, for "so-called" Muslim countries as long as they are not truly Muslim societies. Thus he dismisses efforts to rewrite *fiqh* for the Arab countries since the first premise for its effectiveness is the existence of an Islamic society totally committed to *tawḥīd,* the worship of the one God.

A discussion of the division of *fiqh* into *ʿibādāt* and *muʿāmalāt* can be found in *Khaṣā'iṣ al-Taṣawwur al-Islāmī,* p. 129. A discussion of the necessity of *ijtihād* can be seen in *al-Islām wa-Mushkilāt al-Ḥaḍāra,* pp. 186–87.

25. Quṭb, *Hādhā al-Dīn,* p. 7. Quṭb's thought is developed further in his book *Maʿālim fī al-Ṭarīq,* four chapters of which are reprinted in portions of his second edition of *Fī Ẓilāl al-Qur'ān.* This book is considered the most explicit about the Islamic movement. In it is a call to moral rearmament and to *jihād* to eradicate the anti-Godly forces in the world. There are only two possible systems of governance in the world, one Muslim where God is truly worshipped and His law is fully practiced, and the *Jāhilī* system, that of materialism, of the preoccupation with worldly concerns where governance is left to other human beings (p. 110).

Quṭb condemns all efforts to emulate the West, for "Islamic society is the civilized society" (p. 143). Since Islam developed civilization, it allows the

Muslim to acquire from non-Muslims learning (when capable Muslims are not available) in the areas of chemistry, biology, astronomy, medicine, industry, agriculture, and business administration (p. 175). However, it does not allow him to learn about his doctrines, the principles of the Islamic way, Qur'anic exegesis, *ḥadīth, sīra,* history, and the interpretation of its movement, nor about his society, government system, politics, art, and literature from a non-Muslim source, nor even from a Muslim whose commitment and piety he does not trust (p. 176).

When Islam is reestablished, it must be antinationalistic (a complete rejection of Nasser's efforts for Arab unity). "The *Umma* whose first contingency is made of Abū Bakr, the Arab, Bilāl, the Ethiopian, Ṣuhayb, the Byzantine, Salmān, the Persian and their noble brothers who continued this principle for generations." Unity must be based on the Islamic ideology. "The nation is *dār al-Islām*; the governor is God; the constitution is the Qur'ān" (p. 197).

Maʿālim fī al-Ṭarīq is considered Quṭb's finest work by several leaders of the Muslim Brotherhood. The Egyptian government condemned it as a seditious book since it called for the overthrow of the system. *Jarā'im ʿIṣābāt al-Ikhwān* (Cairo, n.d.), p. 44, alleges that copies of the book were found among ammunition caches during the crackdown on the Muslim Brotherhood.

26. ʿAbd al-Raḥmān ʿAlī al-Ḥajjī, *Naẓarāt fī Dirāsat al-Tārīkh al-Islāmī* (Damascus, 1975). The book is based on lectures delivered at Riyad University and at the Muslim World League Hall in Mecca in 1969. Dr. al-Ḥajjī is a professor at Baghdād University. He received his doctorate from Cambridge University. His dissertation and most of his publications deal with the history and culture of Muslim Spain.

27. Ibid., p. 13.

28. Ibid., pp. 14–15.

29. Ibid., p. 16.

30. Ibid., pp. 22–23.

31. Ibid., pp. 64, 67.

32. Ibid., p. 71.

33. Ibid., pp. 84–85.

34. Ibid., pp. 87–88.

35. Ibid., pp. 91–93.

36. Ibid., pp. 95–102. For a discussion of the rewriting of history in Egypt, see Jack Crabbs, Jr., "Politics, History, and Culture in Nasser's Egypt," *International Journal of Middle East Studies* 6 (October, 1975).

CHAPTER EIGHT: THE INTELLECTUALIST RESPONSE

1. Muḥammad Kamāl Ibrāhīm Jaʿfar, *Fī al-Dīn al-Muqāran* (Alexandria, 1970).

2. Ibid., p. 113.

3. Ibid., p. 112.

4. Ibid., p. 115.

5. Ibid., pp. 116–17.

6. Ibid., p. 116.

7. Ibid., p. 52.

8. In an interview with Professor Jaʿfar in the spring of 1976 I asked him to expound on these ideas. He admitted some interest in undertaking this as a longer-range project, but said that his research is now concentrated in other areas.

9. Muḥammad Jaʿfar, "Thaqāfat al-Muslim al-Muʿāṣir bayn al-Aṣāla wa'l-Tajdīd," *Majallat al-Waʿy al-Islāmī* 5 (January–March, 1976), 18.

10. Ibid., p. 18.

11. Ibid., p. 12.

12. Ibid., pp. 19–21.

13. Rāshid al-Barrāwī, *al-Tafsīr al-Qur'ānī li'l-Tārīkh* (Cairo, 1973). His other writings include: *Dirāsāt fī al-Sūdān wa-Iqtiṣādiyyāt al-Sharq al-Awsaṭ, Ḥarb al-Batrūl fī al-Sharq al-Awsat, al-Madhāhib al-Iqtiṣādiyya al-Kubrā, Majmūʿat al-Wathā'iq al-Siyāsiyya wa-al-Iqtiṣādiyya, al-Niẓām al-Ishtirākī min al-Nāḥiyatayn: al-Naẓariyya wa-al-ʿAmaliyya, al-Riqq al-Ḥadīth fı Ifrīqiya al-Burtughāliyya, al-Taṭawwur al-Iqtiṣādī al-Ḥadīth fī Ifrīqiya, Thawrat al-Batrūl fī Ifrīqiya, al-Madhāhib al-Ishtirākiyya al-Muʿ-āṣira, al-Niẓām al-Ishtirākī.*

14. al-Barrāwī, *al-Tafsīr al-Qurānī li'l-Tarīkh,* p. 9.

15. ⟨Those days We rotate among people.⟩ S. 3:140.

16. al-Barrāwī, *al-Tafsīr al-Qurānī li'-Tarīkh,* p. 199. al-Barrāwī's interpretation of the Qur'anic verses appears to be mostly dependent on Muḥammad ʿAli Darwaza, *al-Tafsīr al-Ḥadīth.*

17. ⟨For God will not alter the grace He has bestowed on a people until they change what is in themselves.⟩ S. 8:53.

18. al-Barrāwī, *al-Tafsīr al-Qurānī li'l-Tarīkh,* p. 200. Man's personal responsibility is supported by S. 10:44; 22:10; 75:14–15; 30:41.

19. ⟨To every nation there is an appointed time.⟩ S. 7:34.

20. al-Barrāwī, *al-Tafsīr al-Qurānī li'l-Tarīkh,* p. 202.

21. ⟨They ask thee for a hasty punishment; had it not been for an appointed time, the punishment would have come suddenly while they were unaware.⟩ S. 29:53.

22. al-Barrāwī, *al-Tafsīr al-Qurānī li'l-Tarīkh,* p. 203.

23. ⟨If God were to increase the wealth of His servants they would transgress in the world.⟩ S. 42:27.

24. al-Barrāwī, *al-Tafsīr al-Qurānī li'l-Tarīkh,* pp. 204–14.

25. Ibid., p. 216. S. 26:99; 33:67; 43:50; 40:47; 34:32. ⟨The weak will say to the arrogant, we followed you, will you take from us some of the fire?⟩ S. 40:47; and ⟨The arrogant said to the weak, did we hinder you from guidance after it had reached you? No, you were the transgressors⟩ S. 34:32.

al-Barrāwī also quotes the Prophet as saying, "God does not punish the common people according to the deeds of the elites until they witness among them that which is forbidden and they refrain from condemning it, then God will punish the common and the elite." Also: "God will punish the people who when treated unjustly refrain from altering [that treatment]." ʿUmar is reported to have said, "God does not punish the commoners for the sins of the elite unless they transgress in the open. Then all of them deserve the punishment." Ibid., p. 216.

26. Ibid., p. 218. S. 3:104

27. Khalīl is professor of Philosophy of History and Historical Methodology at Moṣul University. Besides this work, *al-Tafsīr al-Islāmī li'l-Tarīkh,* Khalīl has

written *Malāmiḥ al-Inqilāb al-Islāmī fī Khilāfat ʿUmar b. ʿAbd al-ʿAzīz, ʿImād al-Dīn al-Zankī, Khuṭuwāt fī al-Hijra wa-al-Ḥaraka, Luʿbat al-Yamīn wa-al-Yasār, Tahāfut al-ʿIlmāniyya, Dirāsāt fī al-Sīra*; he has also written a play, *al-Maʾsūrūn*, and on literary criticism, *Fī al-Naqd al-Islāmī al-Muʿāṣir* and *Mushkilat al-Qadar wa-al-Ḥurrīya fī al-Masraḥ al-Gharbī al-Muʿāṣir*. Quotes from several of these books appear at length in *al-Tafsīr al-Islāmī liʾl-Tārīkh*.

28. Khalīl, *al-Tafsīr al-Islāmī liʾl-Tārīkh*, p. 18. He refers to the translations into Arabic of Muhammad Iqbal's *The Reconstruction of Religious Thought in Islam* (Lahore, 1951) and Abdul Hameed Siddiqi's *A Philosophical Interpretation of History* (Lahore, 1969). He also refers to Rāshid al-Barrāwī's *al-Tafsīr al-Qurʾānī liʾl-Tārīkh*.

29. Reference is to translations and studies of works on Hegel's idealistic interpretation of history, Marx and Engels's materialistic interpretation, Spengler and Toynbee's civilizational interpretation, and Freud's sexual interpretation. *al-Tafsīr al-Islāmī liʾl-Tārīkh*, p. 18

30. Ibid., pp. 8–9.

31. Ibid., p. 11.

32. Ibid., p. 14.

33. Ibid., p. 97.

34. Ibid., p. 108.

35. Ibid., p. 109.

36. Ibid., p. 111.

37. S. 40:21–22, 82–83.

38. S. 47:13; 43:5–8; 50:36–37; 30:9. *al-Tafsīr al-Islāmī liʾl-Tarīkh*, p. 114.

39. Ibid., p. 116.

40. Ibid., p. 118. S. 19:35.

41. Ibid., p. 132.

42. Ibid., p. 133.

43. Ibid., p. 135.

44. Ibid., p. 136.

45. Ibid., p. 138.

46. Ibid., p. 141.

47. Ibid., p. 143.

48. Ibid., pp. 148–49.

49. Ibid., p. 153.

50. Ibid., p. 154.

51. Ibid., p. 155.

52. Ibid., p. 163.

53. Ibid., p. 183.

54. Ibid., pp. 185–87.

55. Ibid., p. 192.

56. Ibid., p. 194.

57. Ibid., pp. 195–96.

58. Ibid., p. 199.

59. Ibid., pp. 214–15.

60. Ibid., p. 220.

61. Ibid., p. 217.

62. Ibid., pp. 218, 282, 300–302.

63. Ibid., p. 223.

64. Ibid., p. 223. In his introduction to *al-Ma'sūrūn* (Beirut, 1970), Khalīl insists that Islam rejects the idea of a return to the past. It does not sever its relations to contemporary culture. It does not teach rejectionism but allows for choice, for the selection of that which is best, and which is consistent with the tenets of Islam. Ibid., pp. 12–13.
65. Khalīl, *al-Tafsīr al-Islāmī li'l-Tarīkh,* pp. 227, 300–302.
66. Ibid., pp. 233–34.
67. Ibid., p. 243.
68. Ibid., p. 247.
69. Ibid., pp. 247–49.
70. Ibid., p. 292.
71. Ibid., pp. 256–59.
72. Ibid., p. 258.
73. Ibid., pp. 266–73.
74. Ibid., p. 276.
75. Ibid., p. 272.
76. Ibid., pp. 313–15.
77. Ibid., p. 262.
78. Ibid., p. 260.
79. Ibid., pp. 319–23.

CHAPTER NINE: THE QUR'ANIC FOUNDATION

1. S. 2:30; Rāshid al-Barrāwī, *al-Tafsīr al-Qur'ānī li'l-Tarīkh,* (Cairo, 1973), p. 9.
2. Ibid., p. 10; S. 2:36, 30; 90:4.
3. Ibid., p. 10: S. 2:29; 14:32, 33; 2:164.
4. Ibid., p. 11; S. 5:1, 2, 4; 35:12; 16:5–8, 10, 66; 20:18, 54; 23:2; 36:71–73.
5. Ibid., p. 12; S. 40:79–80; 79:31, 33.
6. Ibid., p. 13. S. 6:38; 56:21; 16:68–69.
7. Ibid., p. 13. S. 22:23; 35:23; 76:12.
8. Ibid., p. 14. S. 20:53; 23:20; 36:80; 56:71–72; 2:61.
9. Ibid., pp. 14–15. al-Barrāwī notes that the Qur'ān makes reference to iron, gold, and silver but not to petroleum, coal, or other metals. This, he feels, is due to the fact that the other metals had not been known at the time of the revelation. S. 57:25; 34:12; 3:14; 9:34; 16:14; 55:22.
10. Ibid., p. 16. S. 11:37, 41; 54:13–14.
11. Ibid., p. 17. S. 18:96; 21:80; 34:10–13.
12. Ibid., p. 17. S. 3:49; 28:38; 27:44.
13. Ibid., p. 17. S. 16:81, 80; 88:16.
14. Ibid., p. 18. S. 22:23; 35:33; 76:12.
15. Ibid., p. 18. S. 76:15, 21; 18:31; 22:23.
16. Ibid., p. 18. S. 16:81, 80.
17. Ibid., p. 18. S. 76:13; 88:13.
18. Ibid., p. 18. S. 3:49.
19. Ibid., p. 19.
20. Ibid., p. 21. S. 8:53.
21. Ibid., p. 21. S. 36:19, 35.
22. Ibid., p. 20. S. 2:267.

23. Ibid., p. 25. These include land (S. 31:20; 15:19–20), water in the earth (S. 35:9; 32:27; 86:11–12). rain as a source of springs and wells (S. 39:21; 55:19–20; 35:12), pastures (S. 87:4–5; 79:30–31; 16:10), forests as a source of wood and fire (S. 56:71–73; 36:80, 71–73; 16:5–8).

24. Ibid., p. 28. S. 30:9.

25. Ibid., p. 28. S. 34:15, 18.

26. Ibid., p. 29. S. 13:4; 7:58; 6:99. The good earth provides an abundant yield. S. 41:10.

27. Ibid., p. 31.

28. Ibid., p. 32. S. 36:71–73; 40:79–80; 16:80; 36:80; 20:53, 54; 36:33–35; 35:9, 12. S. 2:71 provides an example since cows are used both for food and for farming.

29. Ibid., p. 36. S. 2:127; 36:33–35; 20:117; 34:11–13; 9:105.

30. Ibid., p. 37. S. 4:32; 7:189. al-Barrāwī expounds further that those who claim that S. 24:31 restricts women entering the labor force because they are to cover themselves do not understand that this verse refers to the wives of the Prophet as does S. 33:33. For his authority, he quotes Muḥammad ʿIzzat Darwaza, *al-Tafsīr al-Ḥadīth,* vol. 10, p. 45, where he says that the Qur'ān grants women the right to go unveiled to study, enter mosques, attend public meetings, and engage in commerce and other occupations.

31. Ibid., p. 43. To advocate cooperative farming, al-Barrāwī quotes S. 5:2 and 9:71 which say ⟨Cooperate in piety and good deeds⟩. He also quotes ʿUmar as saying, "If the foreigners come before God with [good] deeds and we come without, they are more worthy of Muḥammad on the Day of Resurrection."

32. Ibid., pp. 44–45. S. 7:42.

33. Ibid., pp. 47–48. S. 48:17.

34. Ibid., p. 65. S. 18:93–97; the story of Joseph provides an example of the efficient management necessary. S. 36:46–56.

35. Ibid., p. 95. S. 80:25–32.

36. Ibid., p. 97 ff. S. 106:1–2; 12:88; 62:9–11; 2:197; 25:20.

37. Ibid., p. 100. S. 11:84; 55:7–9; 6:152; 83:1–3.

38. Ibid., p. 105 ff.

39. Ibid., p. 117.

40. Ibid., pp. 119–154.

41. Ibid., pp. 172–173. S. 18:94; 59:7.

42. Ibid., p. 185. S. 49:13. The Prophet is reported to have said, "O ye people, your Lord, He is one. There is no ascendancy for an Arab over a Persian or a Persian over an Arab, a black over a red, or a red over a black except in piety."

43. Ibid., p. 191. S. 2:253; 17:55; 3:162–163; 20:75; 58:11; 46:19; 9:20.

44. Ibid., p. 197. ⟨Those days we rotate among the people.⟩ S. 17:17; 21:11; 6:6; 25:25, 26, 37–38.

45. Ibid., p. 199.

46. Ibid., p. 200. S. 8:52; 10:44; 22:10; 75:14–15; 109:1–3; 30:41.

47. Ibid., p. 201. S. 20:115–123.

48. al-Barrāwī shows extensive dependence on some modern *mufassirūn* including Muḥammad Darwaza, *al-Tafsīr al-Hadīth*; Muḥammad Fuād ʿAbd al-Bāqī, *al-Lūʾlūʾ wa-al-Murjān Fīmā Ittafaqa ʿAlayhī al-Shay-khān;* and Muḥammad Maḥmūd Ḥijāzī, *al-Tafsīr al-Wāḍiḥ.*

49. ʿAbd al-Raḥmān al-Ḥajjī, *Naẓarāt fī Dirāsat al-Tārīkh al-Islāmī* (Damascus, 1975), p. 107.
50. See Ibid., p. 18, where he describes Islam as a tree with branches (S. 14:24–26). On page 22 he talks about receiving history from those who are blind to its truth (S. 22:46).
51. Ibid., p. 16. S. 21:18.
52. Ibid., p. 117. S. 35:28; 67:15, 22.
53. Ibid., p. 110. S. 6:11 and 30:9. For this interpretation he acknowledges dependence on Sayyid Quṭb's *Fī Ẓilāl al-Qur'ān*, vol. 7, p. 142.
54. Muḥammad Kamāl Ibrāhīm Jaʿfar, *Fī al-Dīn al-Muqāran* (Alexandria, 1970), p. 114. S. 51:56.
55. Ibid., p. 114. S. 67:2.
56. Ibid., p. 115. S.11:102, 117; 17:16.
57. Ibid., p. 116. S. 14:5; 88:14.
58. al-Khalīl, *al-Tafsīr al-Qur'ānī li-al-Tārīkh*, pp. 99–100.
59. Ibid., pp. 100–103. al-Khalīl notes that some of the prophecies about the future were fulfilled during the lifetime of the Prophet; these include S. 30:1–7 which foretold the victory of the believers over the polytheists and S. 48:27 which refers to either Muḥammad's triumphant return to Mecca or the conquest of Khaybar. S. 3:12–13 shows that the *kuffār* were conquered as promised by God as He gave the victory. S. 48:28 and 40:77 were fulfilled as the Prophet witnessed the victory of Muslims before his death. Other prophecies that may have been fulfilled or are still to take place include S. 17:48; 21:96–97; 27:82, 93.
60. Ibid., p. 106. Al-Khalīl cites the following verses as proof of the unity of all religions. S. 2:136–138, 285; 3:3, 33–34, 50, 84; 4:47, 136, 150–52, 163–65; 5:14, 46, 48, 59; 6:83–87, 92; 29:46–47; 33:7; 42:13; 46:12, 30; 51:36; 53:36–54; 61:6–7. (al-Khalīl ignores S. 17:55 totally as it suggests that God may prefer some prophets over others.)
61. Ibid., p. 107. S. 3:62; 7:101, 176; 11:100, 120; 36:3, 111; 20:99, 133; 21:24; 7:7; 20:52; 2:14; 28:44–46.
62. Ibid., p. 109. S. 33:62; 35:43; 17:77; 18:55; 48:22–23.
63. Ibid., p. 111. S. 3:137–41; 6:34; 47:10; 30:42; 32:26; 37:136–38; 36:109; 16:36; 13:6; 15:13; 37:167–70.
64. Ibid., p. 112. S. 27:52; 25:40; 23:34; 29:34–35; 54:4–5; 69:11–12; 79:25–26; 22:45–46.
65. Ibid., p. 114. S. 40:21–22, 82–83; 47:13; 43:5–8; 50:36–37; 30:9.
66. Ibid., p. 274. S. 43:22–24; 56:41–55.
67. Ibid., p. 285. S. 4:97–98.
68. Ibid., p. 309. S. 7:96; 41:30–31; 30:41.
69. Ibid., p. 309. S. 2:38–39; 11:60; 16:30, 97; 20:23–24, 52; 16:41, 112; 18:103–5.

CHAPTER TEN: THE USE OF WESTERN SOURCES

1. Quṭb, *Tarīkh*, p. 39.
2. al-Ḥajjī, *Naẓarāt*, p. 12.
3. Ibid., p. 13. The quotes are from Muḥammad Asad, *al-Islām ʿalā Muftaraq al-Ṭuruq*, and Abū al-Ḥasan al-Nadawī, *al-Ṣiraʿ bayn al-Fikra al-Islāmiyya wa-al-Fikra al-Gharbiyya fī al-Aqṭār al-Islāmiyya*.

4. al-Ḥajjī, *Naẓarāt*, p. 14.
5. Ibid., pp. 22, 24.
6. Ibid., p. 25.
7. Ibid., p. 35. al-Hajjī quotes from an article by ʿIrfān ʿAbd al-Ḥamīd, "al-Mustashriqūn wa-al-Islām," *Majallat al-Waʿy al-Islāmī*, vol. 16, p. 35, where ʿAbd al-Ḥamīd says that "Orientalism as an intellectual discipline is the child of illegitimate parents: the missionary movement that designed it and colonialism that nurtured it. It continues to function in support of the goals for which it was brought into being, i.e., to destroy the foundations of the Islamic doctrine and to instill conceptions and visions that contradict this doctrine and to establish an intellectual network in the Muslim world that will operate within its orbit and propagate its ideas."
8. al-Ḥajjī, *Naẓarāt*, p. 55.
9. Ibid., p. 64; cf. Quṭb, *Tarīkh*, p. 37.
10. al-Ḥajjī, *Naẓarāt*, p. 65.
11. Ibid., p. 70. al-Ḥajjī quotes from Ṭabarī and Ibn Kathīr about the meeting between Heraclius and a prisoner who ran away from a Muslim prison camp. When asked what the Muslims were like, the prisoner said, "They are knights by day and monks by night."
12. K. M. Jaʿfar, "Thaqāfat al-Muslim," *Majallat al-Waʿy al-Islāmī* 5 (January–March, 1976), 12.
13. Jaʿfar, *Fī al-Dīn al Muqāran*, p. 94.
14. Ibid., p. 98.
15. Ibid., pp. 110–11.
16. Ibid., p. 112.
17. al-Khalīl, *al-Tafsīr al-Qurʾāni li-al-Tārīkh*, pp. 15–16.
18. Ibid., pp. 17–18.
19. Ibid., p. 23.
20. Ibid., p. 105.
21. Ibid., p. 166.
22. Ibid., p. 167.
23. Ibid., p. 168.
24. Ibid., p. 168. S. 17:13–14; 4:141. Individual responsibility is crucial. S. 17:84.
25. Ibid., p. 168.
26. Ibid., pp. 179–80.
27. Ibid., p. 207.
28. Ibid., pp. 231, 233.
29. Ibid., p. 244.
30. Ibid., p. 262.
31. Ibid., p. 263.
32. Ibid., pp. 302–3.

CONCLUSION: TOWARDS AN ISLAMIC UNDERSTANDING OF HISTORY

1. The term designates any order that is un-Islamic and is commonly used by those emphasizing the crucial necessity of maintaining an Islamic society. "*Jāhilīyya* is not a limited time in history; rather, it is a special spiritual and intellectual condition. This appears when the fundamental principles of hu-

man life as willed by God are abandoned, and when they are supplanted by fabricated principles based on transitory desires." Sayyid Quṭb, in an introduction to Abū al-Ḥasan ʿAlī al-Ḥusnī al-Nadawī, *Mādhā Khasira al-ʿĀlam bi-Inḥiṭāṭ al-Muslimīn* (Cairo, 1961), p. 15.

Bibliography

ʿAbd al-ʿĀṭī, Hammūda ʿAlī. "The Concept of Freedom in Muḥammad ʿAbdu." Master's thesis, McGill University, 1957.

ʿAbd Rabbih, ʿAbd al-Ḥāfiẓ. *Buḥūth fī Qaṣaṣ al-Qurʿān.* Beirut, 1972.

ʿAbd al-Raḥmān, ʿĀ'isha. *Al-Qur'ān wa-Qaḍāyā al-Islām.* Beirut, 1972.

Abdel-Nasser, Gamal. *Egypt's Liberation: The Philosophy of the Revolution.* Introduction by Dorothy Thompson. Washington, D. C.: Public Affairs Press, 1955.

Abdul-Rauf, Muhammad. *Marriage in Islam.* New York: Exposition Press, 1972.

Abdulrazak, Fawzi. *Arabic Historical Writings 1973.* Cambridge, Mass.: Harvard University Press, 1974.

———. *Arabic Historical Writings 1974.* Cambridge, Mass.: Harvard University Press, 1976.

ʿAbd al-Wāḥid, Muṣṭafā. *Al-Islām wa-al-Mushkila al-Jinsiyya.* Cairo, 1972.

———. *Minhāj al-Sunna fī al-Zawāj.* Cairo, 1972.

———. *Al-Usra fī al-Islām.* Cairo, 1972.

Al-ʿĀbidī, Maḥmūd. *Qudsuna.* Beirut, 1972.

Al-Abrāshī, Muḥammad ʿAṭiyya. *Makānat al-Mar'a fī al-Islām.* Cairo, 1970.

Abū al-Khashab, Ibrāhīm ʿAlī. *Al-Islām al-Maẓlūm.* N.p., n.d.

Abū al-Nūr, Muḥammad al-Aḥmadī. *Minhāj al-Sunna fī al-Zawāj.* Cairo, 1972.

Al-Afghānī, Jamāl al-Dīn. *Al-ʿUrwa al-Wuthqā.* Cairo, 1927.

Al-Afghānī, Saʿīd. *Al-Islām wa-al-Mar'a.* Damascus, 1964.

Al-Albānī, Muḥammad Nāṣir al-Dīn. *Ḥijāb al-Mar'a al-Muslima fī al-Kitāb wa-al-Sunna.* Cairo, 1965.

Alī, Fuād Ḥasanayn. *Filasṭīn al-ʿArabiyya.* Cairo, 1973.

ʿAlī, Kurd. *Al-Islām wa-al-Ḥaḍāra al-ʿArabiyya.* Cairo, 1968.

ʿAmāra, Muḥammad. *Al-Islām wa-al-Marʾa fī Raʾy al-lmām Muḥammad ʿAbdu.* Cairo, 1975.

Amīn, Aḥmad. *Yawm al-Islām.* Cairo, 1958.

Amīn, Bakrī Shaykh. *Al-Taʿbīr al-Fannī fī al-Qurʾān.* Beirut, 1973.

Amīn, Qāsim. *Taḥrīr al-Marʾa.* Cairo, 1900, Reprint., 1970.

Ansarī, Zafer Ishaq. "Contemporary Islam and Nationalism, A Case Study of Egypt." *Die Welt des Islam* 7 (1961), 3–38.

Anṣārī, Ẓafar Isḥāq. "An Inquiry into the Interrelationship between Islam and Nationalism in the Writings of Egyptians, 1945–56." Master's thesis, McGill University, 1956.

Al-ʿAqqād, ʿAbbās Maḥmūd. *Hādhihi al-Shajara.* Cairo, n.d.

———. *Al-Marʾa fī al-Qurʾān.* Cairo, 1959.

Al-ʿArabī, Aḥmad. "Al-Muslimūn bayn al-ʿAqīda wa-al-Idiyūlūjiyya." *Al-Fikr* 22 (November, 1976).

Arslān, Shakīb. *Limādhā Taʾakhkhara al-Muslimūn wa-Limādhā Taqaddama Ghayruhum.* Beirut, 1965.

ʿĀshūr, Maḥmūd. "Al-Islām wa-Ḥarakat al-Tārīkh." *Majallat al-Azhar* 47 (October, 1975).

Al-ʿAṭṭar, ʿAbd al-Nāṣir Tawfīq. *Taʿaddud al-Zawjāt.* Cairo, 1972.

Al-ʿAṭṭār, ʿIṣām. "Al-Ghiyāb al-Islamī al-Mudhhil." In *Rasāʾil ilā al-Ṭalāiʿ al-Islāmiyya.* Aachen, 1977.

Al-ʿAwaḍī, ʿAbd al-Laṭīf Muḥammad Ṣāliḥ. "Mafhūm al-Tārīkh ʿInd ʿUlamāʾ al-Muslimīn." *Al-Waʿy al-Islāmī,* Year 10, 119 (November, 1974), 30–35.

Al-ʿAẓm, Rafīq. *Tanbīh al-Afhām ilā Maṭālib al-Ḥayāt al-Ijtimāʿiyya fī al-Islām.* Cairo, 1900.

Baltajī, Muḥammad. *Dīrāsāt fī Aḥkām al-Usra.* Cairo, 1974.

Al-Barrāwī, Rāshid. *Min Ḥilf Baghdād ilā al-Ḥilf al-Islāmī.* Cairo, 1966.

———. *Al-Tafsīr al-Qurʾānī liʾl-Tārīkh.* Cairo, 1973.

Al-Barrī, Zakariyyā Aḥmad. *Al-Aḥkām al-Asāsīya li-lʾUsra al-Islāmiyya.* Cairo, 1974.

Bayham, Muḥammad Jamīl. *Falsafat al-Tārīkh al-ʿUthmānī.* Beirut, 1925.

Al-Bayḥānī, Muḥammad ibn Sālim. *Ustādh al-Marʾa.* Cairo, 1973.

Al-Bayṭār, Nadīm. "Al-Ḥaraka al-Thawriyya al-ʿArabiyya." *Mawāqif* 13–14 (December–April, 1971), pp. 91–98.

Berdyaev, Nicholas. *The Meaning of History.* London: Oxford University Press, 1936.

Berger, Morroe. *Islam in Egypt Today*. Cambridge, Mass.: Harvard University Press, 1970.

Ibn al-Sanūsī, Abū Raḍwān Zaghlūl. *Al-Mar'a Bayn al-Ḥijāb wa-al-Sufūr*. Beirut, 1967.

Al-Būṭī, Sa'īd Ramaḍān. *Al-Islām wa-Mushkilat al-Shabāb*. [Damascus], 1394H.

Chejne, Anwar G. "The Concept of History in the Modern Arab World." *Studies in Islam* 4 (January, 1967), 1–31.

———. "The Use of History by Modern Arab Writers." *The Middle East Journal* 14 (1960), 382–96.

Colombe, M. "Egypt from the Fall of King Farouk to the February 1954 Crisis." *Middle Eastern Affairs* 5 (1954), 185–92.

Crecelius, Daniel. "Al-Azhar in the Revolution." *The Middle East Journal* 20 (1960), 31–49.

Cromer, Evelyn Baring. *Modern Egypt*. 2 vols. London: Macmillan, 1908.

Dar, Bashir Ahmad. *Qur'ānic Ethics*. Lahore: Ashraf, 1960.

Darwaza, Muḥammad 'Izzat. *Al-Mar'a fī al-Qur'ān wa-al-Sunna*. Beirut, 1967.

———. *Al-Tafsīr al-Ḥadīth*. vol. 10. Cairo, 1962.

Dodge, Bayard. *Al-Azhar*. Washington, D. C.: Middle East Institute, 1961.

Draft of the Charter. Cairo, n.d.

Dūrī, 'Abd al-'Azīz. *Baḥth fī-Nash'at 'Ilm al-Tarīkh 'Ind al-'Arab*. Beirut, 1960.

Al-Faḥḥām, Muḥammad A. "The Restoration of Jerusalem." In *The Fifth Conference of the Academy of Islamic Research*. Cairo, 1971.

Faris, Nabih Amin. "The Arabs and Their History." *The Middle East Journal* 8 (Spring, 1954), 155–62.

———. "Development in Arab Historiography as Reflected in the Struggle Between 'Alī and Mu'āwiya." In *Historians of the Middle East*, edited by Bernard Lewis and P. M. Holt. London: Oxford University Press, 1962, 435–41.

Farrāj, Aḥmad. *Al-Islām Dīn al-Ishtirākiyya*. Cairo, n.d.

Fawwāz, Zaynab. *Al-Durr al-Manthūr fī Ṭabaqāt Rabbāt al-Khudūr*. Cairo, 1894.

Fū'ād, Ni'māt Aḥmad. *A'īdū Kitābat al-Tārīkh*. Beirut, 1975.

Fück, J. W. "Islam as an Historical Problem in European Historiography since 1800." In *Historians of the Middle East*, edited by Bernard Lewis and P. M. Holt. London: Oxford University Press, 1962, 303–15.

Gabrieli, Francesco. "The Arabic Historiography of the Crusades." In *Historians of the Middle East*, edited by Bernard Lewis and P. M. Holt. London: Oxford University Press, 1962, 98–108.

Gellner, E. "The Struggle for Morocco's Past." *The Middle East Journal* 15 (1961), 79–90.

Al-Ghazzālī, Muḥammad. *Min Hunā Naʿlam.* Cairo, n.d.

Gibb, Sir Hamilton. "Islamic Biographical Literature." In *Historians of the Middle East,* edited by Bernard Lewis and P. M. Holt. London: Oxford University Press, 1962, 54–59.

Al-Ḥajjī, ʿAbd al-Rahmān ʿAlī. *Naẓarāt fī Dirāsat al-Tārīkh al-Islāmī.* Damascus, 1975.

Ḥasan, Muḥammad ʿAbd al-Ghanī. *ʿIlm al-Tārīkh ʿInd al-ʿArab.* Cairo, n.d.

Haykal, Muḥammad Ḥusayn. *Ḥayāt Muḥammad.* Cairo, 1953.

Ḥitteh, Muḥammad Kāmil. *Al-Qiyam al-Dīniyya wa-al-Mujtamaʿ.* Cairo, 1974.

Hodgson, Marshall G. "The Unity of Later Islamic History." *Journal of World History* 5 (1960), 879–914.

Hook, Sidney. *The Hero in History.* New York: John Day Co., 1943.

Hourani, Albert H. "Introductory Remarks." In *Historians of the Middle East,* edited by Bernard Lewis and P. M. Holt. London: Oxford University Press, 1962, 451–56.

Ḥusayn, Muḥammad Kāmil. *Al-Taḥlīl al-Bayūlūjī li-al-Tārīkh.* Cairo, 1955.

Ḥusayn, Ṭāha. *Mirʿāt al-Islām.* Cairo, 1959.

Al-Ḥusaynī, Isḥāq Mūsā. "Makānat Bayt al-Maqdis fī al-Islām." In *Kitāb al-Mu'tamar al-Rābiʿ li-Majmaʿ al-Buḥūth al-Islāmīya.* Cairo, 1968.

Al-Ḥuṣrī, Sāṭiʿ. *Abḥāth Mukhtāra fī al-Qawmiyya al-ʿArabiyya.* Cairo, 1964.

———. *Arā' Wa-Aḥādīth fī al-Tārīkh wa-al-Ijtimāʿ.* Beirut, 1960.

———. *Difāʿ ʿAn al-ʿUrūba.* Beirut, 1956.

Ibrāhīm, Muḥammad Ismāʿīl. *Al-Zawāj.* Cairo, 1971.

Imām, ʿAbd Allāh. *Al-Nāṣiriyya.* N.p., n.d.

Inalcik, Halil. "Some Remarks on the Study of History in Islamic Countries." *The Middle East Journal* 7 (Autumn, 1953), 451–55.

Iqbal, Muhammad. *The Reconstruction of Religious Thought in Islam.* Lahore: Ashraf, 1951.

The Islamic Pact. Cairo, n.d.

Jaʿfar, Muḥammad K. I. *Fī al-Dīn al-Muqāran.* Alexandria, 1970.

———. "Thaqāfat al-Muslim al-Muʿāṣir bayn al-Aṣāla wa'l-Tajdīd." *Majallat al-Waʿy al-Islāmī* 5 (January–March, 1976), 18.

———. *Al-Taṣawwuf.* Cairo, 1970.

Jamāl, Aḥmad Muḥammad. *Muftarayāt ʿAlā al-Islām.* Cairo, 1975.

Jāwid, Nasīm Aḥmad. "Principles of Movement in Modern Islam: An Analysis of Some Ideas Developed in the 19th and 20th Centuries by Indo-

Pakistani Muslims in Justification of Change in Religious Thought and Structure." *Islamic Studies* 9 (December, 1970), 295–315.

Al-Jisr, Ḥusayn. *Al-Ḥuṣūn al-Ḥamīdiyya.* Cairo, n.d.

———. *Al-Risāla al-Ḥamīdiyya.* Beirut, 1887.

Jomier, J. "Quelques positions actuelles de l'exégèse coranique en Egypte." *MIDEO* 1 (1954), 39–72.

Jones, C. F. "The New Egyptian Constitution." *The Middle East Journal* 10 (1956), 300–307.

Al-Jundī, Anwar. *Aḍwā' ʿalā Tārīkh al-Islām.* Cairo, 1957.

———. *Al-Islām fī Maʿrakat al-Taghrīb.* Cairo, 1964.

———. *Al-Islām wa-Ḥarakat al-Tārīkh.* Cairo, 1968.

———. *al-Musājalāt wa-al-Maʿārik al-Adabiyya fī Majāl al-Fikr wa-al-Tārīkh wa-al-Ḥaḍāra.* Cairo, 1972.

Kāmil, ʿAbd al-ʿAzīz. *Al-Islām wa-al-Mustaqbal.* Cairo, 1975.

Kaplan, Morton. *On Historical and Political Knowing.* Chicago: University of Chicago Press, 1971.

Al-Kawākibī, ʿAbd al-Raḥmān. *Sijill Mudhakkirāt Jamʿiyyat Umm al-Qurā aw Mu'tamar al-Nahḍa al-Islāmiyya al-Munʿaqid fī Makka al-Mukarrama 1316 H.* Cairo, 1320.

Kenny, Lorne M. "The Khilāfah al-Rāshidah Period as Presented by Some Recent Egyptian Authors." Master's thesis, McGill University, 1960.

Khafājī, Muḥammad ʿAbd al-Munʿim. *Khulūd al-Islām.* Cairo, 1975.

Khalaf Allāh, Muḥammad Aḥmad. *Al-Qur'ān wa-Mushkilāt Ḥayātinā al-Muʿāṣira.* Cairo, 1967.

———. *Al-Fann al-Qaṣaṣī fī al-Qur'ān al-Karīm.* Cairo, 1965.

———. "Ḥawl Jadal fī al-Jāmiʿa." *Al-Risāla* 15 (September 19, 1947), 1067.

Khalīl, ʿImād al-Dīn. *Al-Ma'sūrūn.* Beirut, 1970.

———. *Al-Tafsīr al-Islāmī li'l-Tārīkh.* Beirut, 1975.

Al-Kharbūṭlī, ʿAlī Ḥusnī. *Al-Islām wa-al-Ḥaraka al-Muḍādda.* Cairo, 1973.

———. *Muḥammad wa al-Qawmīyya al-ʿArabiya.* Cairo, 1959.

———. *Al-Tārīkh al-Muwaḥḥad li-al-Umma al-ʿArabiyya.* Cairo, 1970.

al-Khaṭīb, ʿAbd al-Karīm. *Al-Qaṣaṣ al-Qur'ānī fī Manṭuqihi wa-Mafhūmihi.* Cairo, 1965.

Al-Khūlī, Amīn. *Al-Mujaddidūn fī al-Islām.* Cairo, 1384 H.

Al-Khūlī, al-Bahī. *Al-Islām wa-Qaḍāyā al-Mar'a al-Muʿāṣira.* Kuwait, 1970.

Kishk, M. Jalāl. *Al-Ghazū al-Fikrī.* Cairo, 1966.

Koning, Karen Lee. "The Crisis of the Intellectuals in the United Arab Republic, Especially as Reflected in Muḥammad Ḥasanayn Haykal's *Azmat al-Muthaqqafīn.*" Master's thesis, McGill University, 1971.

Lewis, Bernard, and Holt, P. M., eds. *Historians of the Middle East.* London: Oxford University Press, 1962.

Lewis, Bernard. *History: Remembered, Recovered, Invented.* Princeton: Princeton University Press, 1975.

———. "History-Writing and National Revival in Turkey." *Middle Eastern Affairs* 6–7 (June–July, 1953), 218–28.

———. *Islam in History: Ideas, Men and Events in the Middle East.* New York: Library Press, 1973.

———. "The Use by Muslim Historians of Non-Muslim Sources." In *Historians of the Middle East,* edited by Bernard Lewis and P. M. Holt. London: Oxford University Press, 1962, 180–91.

Lord, Laura Woolsey. "The Uses of History in Contemporary Indonesia." Master's thesis, Cornell University, 1959.

Maʿa al-Mithāq. Cairo, n.d.

Māḍī, ʿAbd Allāh Muḥammad et al. *Al-Azhar fī Ithnay ʿAshara ʿĀman.* Cairo, 1964.

Al-Maghribī, ʿAbd al-Qādir. *Al-Bayyināt.* 2 vols. Cairo, 1924, 1925.

Māhir, Muḥammad ʿAlī. *Muslim Yaqrāʾ al-Mīthāq fī Ḍawʾ al-Qurʾān.* Cairo, n.d.

Maḥmūd, Zakī Najīb. "Mīlād Jadīd." *Mawāqif* 1 (1968), 5–14.

———. *Tajdīd al-Fikr al-ʿArabī.* Beirut, 1971.

Mājid, ʿAbd al-Munʿim. *Muqaddima li-Dirāsat al-Tārīkh Al-Islāmī.* Cairo, 1964.

———. *Tārīkh al-Ḥaḍāra al-Islāmiyya fī al-ʿUṣūr al-Wusṭā.* Cairo, 1963.

Mawdūdī, Abū al-Aʿlā. *Al-Ḥaḍāra al-Islāmiyya: Ususuhā wa Mabādiʾuha.* Translated by Muḥammad ʿAṣīm al-Ḥaddād. Beirut, n.d.

———. *Naḥnu wa-al-Ḥaḍāra al-Gharbiyya.* Damascus, n.d.

Maẓhar, Ismāʿil. *Al-Islām lā al-Shuyūʿiyya.* Cairo, 1961.

McDermott, Anthony. "Sadat Shakes Off the Past." *Middle East International* 31 (January, 1974), 15–16.

Mubārak, Muḥammad. *Al-ʿAqīda fī al-Qurʾān al-Karīm.* Cairo, n.d.

———. *Dhātiyyat al-Islām amām al-Madhāhib wa-al-ʿAqāʾid.* Beirut, n.d.

Al-Mudawwar, Ṭāhā. *Bayn al-Diyānāt wa-al-Ḥaḍārāt.* Beirut, 1956.

Al-Munajjid, Ṣalāḥ al-Dīn. *Aʿmidat al-Nakba.* Beirut, 1968.

———. *Balshafat al-Islām.* Beirut, 1966.

———. *Al-Taḍāmun al-Marxī wa-al-Taḍāmun al-Islāmī.* Beirut, 1967.

———. *Al-Taḍlīl al-Ishtirākī.* Beirut, 1965.

Mu'nis, Ḥusayn. *ʿĀlam al-Islām.* Cairo, 1973.

Muṣṭafā, Aḥmad ʿAbd al-Raḥīm. *Ḥarakat al-Tajdīd al-Islāmī fī al-ʿĀlam al-ʿArabī al-Ḥadīth.* Cairo, 1971.

Mutawallī, ʿAbd al-Ḥamīd. *Azmat al-Fikr al-Siyāsī al-Islāmī fī al-ʿAṣr al-Ḥadīth.* Alexandria, 1975.

Al-Nadawī, Abul Hasan ʿAlī. *Islam and the World.* Translated by Muhammad Āṣaf Qidwāī. Lahore: Academy of Islamic Research and Publications, 1961.

———. "Kārithat al-ʿĀlam al-ʿArabī wa-Asbābuhā." *Majallat al-Baʿth al-Islāmī* 1 (July, 1967), 27–34.

———. *Mādhā Khasira al-ʿĀlam bi-Inḥiṭāṭ al-Muslimīn.* Cairo, 1961.

———. *Ilā al-Islām min Jadīd.* Beirut, 1967.

———. *Al-Ṣirāʿ Bayn al-Fikra al-Islāmiyya wa-al-Fikra al-Gharbiyya fī al-Aqṭār al-Islāmiyya.* Kuwait, 1965.

———. *Al-Ṣirāʿ Bayn al-Īmān wa-al-Māddiyya.* Kuwait, 1971.

Nasr, Seyyed Hossein. *Science and Civilization in Islam.* Cambridge, Mass.: Harvard University Press, 1968.

———. "The Western World and Its Challenges to Islam." *The Islamic Quarterly* 17 (June, 1973), 3–25.

The National Charter. N.p., n.d.

Nawfal, Sayyid, "Aʿdā' Allāh fī al-Qur'ān." *Al-Hilāl* 83 (November, 1975), 15–21.

Nimr, ʿAbd al-Munʿim. *Al-Musāwāt bayn al-Islām wa-al-Gharb.* Cairo, 1963.

Nutting, Anthony. *Nasser.* New York: E. P. Dutton and Co., 1972.

O'Kane, Joseph P. "Islam in the New Egyptian Constitution: Some Discussions in al-Ahram." *The Middle East Journal* 26 (Spring, 1972), 137–48.

Quṭb, Muḥammad. *Hal Naḥnu Muslimūn?* Cairo, n.d.

———. *Maʿrakat al-Taqālīd.* Cairo, n.d.

———. *Shubuhāt ḥawl al-Islām.* Karbalā', 1963.

Quṭb, Sayyid. *Fī al-Tārīkh: Fikra wa-Minhāj.* Beirut, 1974.

———. *Fī Ẓilāl al-Qur'ān.* 30 vols. Cairo, n.d.

———. *Hādhā al-Dīn.* Cairo, n.d.

———. *Al-Islām wa-Mushkilāt al-Ḥaḍāra.* 1968.

———. *Maʿrakat al-Islām wa-al-Ra'smāliyya.* Cairo, 1952.

———. *Naḥwa Mujtamaʿ Islāmī.* Cairo, n.d.

———. *Al-Salām al-ʿĀlamī wa-al-Islām.* Cairo, n.d.

———. *Al-Taṣwīr al-Fannī fī al-Qur'ān.* Cairo, 1963.

Al-Rāfi'ī, Muṣṭafā. *Al-Islām wa-Mushkilāt al-'Aṣr.* Beirut, 1972.

Ramaḍān, Sa'īd (al-Būṭī). *Al-Islām wa Mushkilat al-Shabāb.* [Damascus], 1394 H.

Reek, Darrell. *Deep Mende.* Leiden: Brill, 1976.

Riḍā, Muḥammad Rashīd. *Tārīkh al-Ustādh al-Imām al-Shaykh Muḥammad 'Abdu.* 2 vols. Cairo, 1931.

Ringgren, Helmer. *Studies in Arabian Fatalism.* Uppsala: n.p., 1955.

Rosenthal, Franz. "The Influence of the Biblical Tradition on Muslim Historiography." In *Historians of the Middle East,* edited by Bernard Lewis and P. M. Holt. London: Oxford University Press, 1962, pp. 35–45.

Sādāt, Anwar. *Asrār al-Thawra al-Miṣriyya.* Cairo, 1957.

———. *Qiṣṣat al-Waḥda al-'Arabiyya.* Cairo, 1957.

———. *Revolt on the Nile.* London: Wingate Publishing Co., 1957.

Safran, Nadav. "The Abolition of Sharī'a Courts in Egypt." *The Muslim World* 48 (1958), 20–28, 125–35.

———. *Egypt in Search of Political Community.* Cambridge, Mass.: Harvard University Press, 1961.

Al-Sa'īd, Muḥammad. *Al-Ishtirākiyya wa-al-Islām.* Cairo, 1964.

Sakhāwī, Muḥammad b. 'Abd al-Raḥmān. *Al-I'lān bī al-Tawbīkh.* Baghdad, 1963.

Salibi, K. S. "The Traditional Historiography of the Maronites." In *Historians of the Middle East,* edited by Bernard Lewis and P. M. Holt. London: Oxford University Press, 1962, 212–25.

Samra, Mahmud. "Some Ideas of Syrian Muslim Writers on Self-Criticism and Revivalism." *The Islamic Quarterly* 3–4 (July–December, 1975), 198–210.

Shafīq, Durriyya. *Al-Mar'a al-Miṣriyya.* Cairo, 1955.

Shalabī, Abū Zayd. *Tarīkh al-Ḥaḍāra al-Islāmiyya wa-al-Fikr al-Islāmī.* Baghdad, 1964.

Shalabī, Aḥmad. *Al-Mujtama' al-Islāmī.* 2d ed. Cairo, 1963.

Shalabī, Khayrī. *Muḥākamat Ṭāhā Ḥusayn.* Beirut, 1972.

Shaltūt, Maḥmūd. *Al-Islām 'Aqīda wa-Sharī'a.* Cairo, 1964.

———. *Min Tawjīhāt al-Islām.* Cairo, 1964.

———. *Al-Qur'ān wa-al-Mar'a.* Cairo, 1959.

Sharabāṣī, Aḥmad. *Al-Dīn wa'l-Mīthāq.* Cairo, n.d.

———. *Al-Dīn wa Tanẓīm al-Usrah.* Cairo, 1965.

Sharabāṣī, Rā'id al-Sa'īd al-Sharbīnī. *Mabādi' al-Ishtirākiyya fī al-Islām.* Cairo, n.d.

Sharaf, Mukhtār. *Ḥaqā'iq ʿan al-Tabshīr.* Cairo, 1975.

Al-Sharaqāwī, Maḥmūd. *Al-Dīn wa-al-Dawla al-ʿAṣriyya.* Cairo, n.d.

———. *Al-Tafsīr al-Dīnī li'l-Tārīkh.* Vol. 1. Cairo, 1975.

———. *Taqwīm al-Fikr al-Dīnī.* Cairo, 1960.

———. *Al-Islām wa-al-Ḥayā al-Zawjiyya.* Cairo, 1967.

Siddiqi, Abdul Hameed. *Prophethood in Islam.* Lahore: Idara Nashriyat-i-Islam, 1968.

Ṣiddīqī, ʿAbd al-Ḥamīd. *Tafsīr al-Tārīkh.* Translated by Kaẓim al-Jawādī. Kuwait, n.d.

Siddīqi, Mazheruddīn. "General Characteristics of Muslim Modernism." *Islamic Studies* 9 (March, 1970), 33–68.

———. "Intellectual Bases of Muslim Modernism." *Islamic Studies* 9 (June, 1970), 149–71.

Sinor, Denis, ed. *Orientalism and History.* Bloomington: Indiana University Press, 1970.

Smith, Houston. "Accents of the World's Religions." In *Comparative Religion,* edited by John Bowman. Leiden: Brill, 1972, pp. 1–18.

Smith, Jane I., and Haddad, Yvonne Y. "Women in the Afterlife: The Islamic View as Seen from Qur'ān and Tradition." *Journal of the American Academy of Religion* 53 (March, 1975), 39–50.

Smith, Wilfred Cantwell. "The Historical Development in Islam of the Concept of Islam as an Historical Development." In *Historians of the Middle East,* edited by Bernard Lewis and P. M. Holt. London: Oxford University Press, 1962, pp. 484–502.

———. *Modern Islam in India: A Social Analysis.* London: Victor Gollancz, 1946.

———. "Traditional Religions and Modern Culture." Address presented at the 11th Congress, International Association for the History of Religions, September 9, 1965, at Claremont, California.

Tisdall, W. St. Clair. *The Religion of the Crescent.* London: Society for Promoting Christian Knowledge, 1895.

———. *The Original Sources of the Qur'ān.* London: Society for Promoting Christian Knowledge, 1905.

Trimingham, J. Spencer. *Islam in West Africa.* Oxford: Clarendon Press, 1967.

Al-Tustārī, Abū Muḥammad Sahl b. ʿAbdallāh. *Tafsīr al-Qur'ān al-ʿAẓīm.* Cairo, n.d.

ʿUthmān, Ḥasan. *Manhaj al-Baḥth al-Tārīkhī.* Cairo, 1965.

Al-ʿUṭayfī, Jamāl. *Ayyām Khālida fī Ḥayāt ʿAbd al-Nāṣir.* Cairo, 1971.

ʿUways, ʿAbd al-Ḥalīm. *Al-Ṣafaḥāt al-Akhīra min Ḥaḍāratina.* Cairo, 1975.

———. *Ṭarīquna ilā al-Quds*. Cairo, 1974.

Wāfī, ʿAlī ʿAbd al-Wāḥid. *Al-Mar'a fī al-Islām*. Cairo, 1971.

Wahba, Tawfīq ʿAlī. *Al-Islām Sharīʿat al-Ḥayāt*. Cairo, 1975.

Wansbrough, John. *The Sectarian Milieu: Content and Composition of Islamic Salvation History*. London: Oxford University Press, 1978.

Al-Wardī, ʿAlī. *Mahzalat al-ʿAql al-Basharī*. Baghdad, 1955.

Wielandt, Rotraud. *Offenbarung und Geschichte in Denken Moderner Muslime*. Wiesbaden: Franz Steiner Verlag GMBH, 1971.

Yalgin, Miqdād. *Al-Bayt al-Islāmī*. Cairo, 1972.

Al-Zahrāwī, ʿAbd al-Ḥamīd. *Al-Fiqh wa al-Taṣawwuf*. Cairo, 1901.

Ziada, M. Moṣṭafa. "Modern Egyptian Historiography." *Middle Eastern Affairs* 8–9 (August–September, 1953), 266–71.

Zurayq, Qusṭanṭīn. *Maʿnā al-Nakba Mujaddadan*. Beirut, 1967.

———. *Naḥnu wa-al-Tārīkh*. Beirut, 1959.

ARABIC PERIODICALS

Al-Ahrām.

Al-Akhbār. February 23, 1966; March 23, 1966.

Majallat Rābiṭat al-ʿĀlam al-Islāmī.

Al-Manār.

Minbar al-Islām. April, 1966; July, 1966.

Al-Mulḥaq al-Dīnī, al-Jumhūriyyah. June 10, 1966–July 15, 1966.

The Muslim World.

Al-Risāla.

Al-Ṭalīʿa.

Index

Haddad, Yvonne Yazbeck

DATE DUE

CONTEMPORARY ISLAM AND THE CHALLENGE OF HISTORY

SEP 2 8 1982		OCT 3 1 1995	
OCT 1 2 1982			
OCT 2 6 1982		MAY 14 1997	JAN 1 9
APR. 9 1986			
MAY 1 1986		APR 2 7 2007	
OCT. 2 3 1987			
MAY 0 4 1992			
MAY 2 7 1992			

A WORTHY COMPANY

M. E. BRADFORD

Brief lives of the framers of the United States Constitution

PLYMOUTH ROCK FOUNDATION

The author wishes to acknowledge the assistance of the Kemper Educational and Charitable Fund in the preparation of the Introduction.

Published by the Plymouth Rock Foundation, Inc.
6 McKinley Circle, Marlborough, NH 03455

ISBN 0-942516-00-1

This book is dedicated
to

HON. JOHN P. EAST

United States Senator, North Carolina

Christian Statesman and Constitutionalist

TABLE OF CONTENTS

Introduction

The following biographical sketches are of the lives of the Framers of the United States Constitution who were present in Philadelphia during some part of the Great Convention. They are arranged in the sequence observed in the signing of the instrument which they produced there: from North to South, New Hampshire to Georgia.

(There were, of course, other Framers among the leading figures in the thirteen state ratification conventions who decided the fate of what had been proposed by these fifty-five. Their work had as much to do with the meaning of the entire process of making and adopting a Constitution as did that of the statesmen treated here, but they are best examined separately in the setting where they gave our fundamental law its force and authority.)

Insofar as available information has made it possible, the emphasis in each of the sketches printed here is upon the individual Framer's constitutional theory, on the variety of Union which he hoped to see created and his reasons for favoring or disapproving particular components of the draft under consideration. Yet I have also attempted to see each man against a backdrop of the community which he represented and to view his life in the round, working from a general evaluative statement to a description of his career prior to 1787 to a gloss upon his role in the Great Convention and then to final observations on his post-Convention experience. In this way I touch upon the professional, personal, economic, intellectual, and religious life of this "company of notables." An effort has been made to represent these men in their own language where important questions are at stake and to give the reader some indication of the special coloring or flavor of their distinctive personalities: in a limited way to follow the example of Plutarch, the favorite classical author of early Americans. The bibliographical notes attached at the end of each sketch are selective but should assist the reader in learning more about the life of the subject and especially about his politics in the late spring and summer of 1787.

The members of the Great Convention were men of the eighteenth century, but of the English and Scottish Enlightenment, not the French. They acted within corporate bonds, out of the momentum of a civilization already over one thousand years old when we achieved our national independence. It is easy for us to forget how homogeneous a nation we were in the beginning, apart from the slaves. Despite differences of region and religion, of wealth and class, we were even more united in culture than in blood. True enough, we continued to suffer from the great divisions which had riven English society since the 1640's and the period of the Commonwealth. By these we were brought eventually to fight a civil war. But Americans had not struggled through the Revolution to cut themselves off from their inherited cultural identity as a distinctive offshoot of English history, nor had they come to Philadelphia to drive such a wedge between their present and their past. Their task, rather, was one of preservation and of such innovations as were necessary if a known and cherished world was to be handed on intact to their posterity. They were not men who were speculative in their politics. With the possible exceptions of Madison, Hamilton, Wilson, and young Charles Pinckney, they were prescriptive Whigs who had made a revolution on the model of the Glorious Revolution of 1688—in order to continue as they were.

The majority of the Framers were for their time well-educated men. Their discourse was of history (British, Roman, American, Biblical, and to a lesser extent, European), of law, and of the recent unhappy experience of their countrymen under the Articles of Confederation. Their purpose in revising the government was not to invent the "best city" of the philosophers, but to raise a revenue, retire the public debt, establish a sound currency, remove trade barriers between the states, and provide for the common defense. As many as thirty-five of the fifty-five Framers were slaveholders. Most were either wealthy or comfortably situated, though many were weighed down by the damage done to their holdings by the war, by speculation, and an uncertain economy. Several had great plantations and most had considerable property. Nine or ten had large-scale commercial experience and others were successful merchants. Over half of them had had some experience in the legal profession, either as attorney or as judge; and although only five or six could be called aristocrats, most held a place in the gentry of their own states and were present in the Convention because their neighbors recognized that they were the kind of "natural aristocrats" who our forefathers agreed were most properly trusted with the responsibilities of government.

In addition, with no more than five exceptions (and perhaps no more than three), they were orthodox members of one of the established Christian communions: approximately twenty-nine Anglicans, sixteen to eighteen Calvinists, two Methodists, two Lutherans, two Roman Catholics, one lapsed Quaker and sometime-Anglican, and one open Deist—Dr. Franklin, who attended every kind of Christian worship, called for public prayer, and contributed to all denominations.

An internal transformation of American society in the direction of a secularized egalitarian state was the furthest thing from the minds of these men. The majority of them were committed to representative government, to the continued existence of the sovereign states, and to a dependence upon the virtue of the people acting as independent political, economic, and moral agents as the best security for the hope of a common future. But they also believed in the imperfection of human nature and had no patience with the notion that men were essentially good or that institutions were the culprit in the darker chapters of history. Those among the Framers who nodded conventionally toward the theory of natural rights belonging to some aboriginal presocial state would in most cases have agreed that such a hypothetical condition would have been a very unpleasant experience, "nasty, brutish, and short." They were closer to Hobbes than to Rousseau. Man, they recognized, was made to live in society and under government, out of providential necessity. In the place of a prince and an arbitrary Parliament which had denied them the rights of Englishmen, they worked to establish a Federal system of checks and balances under a sovereign law. Yet they were wise enough to realize that a government enforcing a law to cover every situation would eventually become a tyranny more dreadful than anything attempted by George III. Hence, they were careful to limit the fundamental scope of the law itself, leaving what they called "internal police" and many of the great questions concerning value and faith to the regulation of state and local government and to the operation of society itself. The world of eighteenth century America was a realm including many social, political, and religious establishments. The neutrality of the general government with respect to their interactions was not the neutrality of indifference that would permit the destruction of society.

We should remember that the Constitution and the Bill of Rights left Congregationalism in Connecticut and Massachusetts as the official religion of those commonwealths. When Madison thought briefly of interfering with these arrangements, he had to confront Caleb Strong and Roger Sherman and gave up the idea. Approximately thirty of the Philadelphia Framers were greatly involved with the growth and administration of their own particular denomination. A few were zealous proselytizers. Another twenty were conventional Christians, in most cases conforming to an inherited faith. Concerning John Rutledge and George Wythe and even Madison, there were rumors of Deism; but these were probably politically motivated calumnies, with all the evidence pointing to the contrary. Hugh Williamson was a very heterodox Presbyterian who speculated about "unfallen men" who lived on comets, and James Wilson was a nominal Anglican who was probably a freethinker in the privacy of his study. Others were "broad" churchmen who in the effort to practice tolerance adopted the kind of periphrasis in speaking of God which the Deists had made fashionable: they avoided the terms of reverence provided by Holy Scripture and spoke instead of the "Author of our being" or the "Great Architect." They were no more genuine skeptics than they were democrats, as was often made clear in their private correspondence.

With regard to the public experience of the members of the Great Convention in the course of their political careers, we can make some useful generalizations. For one thing, there was no anomaly in the selection of this particular group to serve as delegates in Philadelphia. Thirty-six of the fifty-five had been members of the Continental Congress. Most of them had been or were to be called upon repeatedly by their neighbors and peers to fill other offices of trust. Twenty were at one time governors of states; twenty were United States Senators. Eight were Federal judges and thirteen were members of the United States House of Representatives. Washington and Madison were President of the United States, and Elbridge Gerry Vice-President. Several served as diplomats in representing the Republic overseas. Others held cabinet posts. Their total political experience at the state and national level is so great as to suggest that as a company they are a dependable barometer of American attitudes and beliefs at the close of the eighteenth century: in the important things resembling most of their countrymen but more capable of making the necessary political discriminations that would "preserve, protect, and defend" the common good.

The differences of opinion which separated the Philadelphia Framers (and there were some) had to do with such questions as the proper method for counting the census and determining taxes and proportions of strength in the Congress, the possibilities of a tariff and a navigation act, the development of Western lands, regulations concerning impeachment and the executive veto, enforcing the sanctity of contracts and (as opposed to the future existence of slavery as an institution) the extension of the slave trade. With reference to most of these concerns, they *expected* to make compromises, working out of a good will for one another fostered in the common experience of winning our national independence. On the other hand, concerning the future of the several states as in some ways still sovereign entities, there was a hard fight. The extreme nationalists, represented by Madison, Hamilton, James Wilson, and (most of the time) Gouverneur Morris, wished to reduce the states as far as possible, to deny them equal representation in both houses of the Congress, and to give the general government a right to review and veto all state legislation. They were forestalled by the middle group in the Convention who acted in concert with a few Antifederalists who were not certain they wished to go beyond the revision of the Articles of Confederation, the official mandate which had brought them together. The little drama began with the initiative of the nationalists as embodied in a Virginia Plan. After some debate an adversary entered the lists in the person of the canny William Paterson and his "small state" or New Jersey Plan. Complication ensued, followed by stasis, hot weather, and some very hot tempers. At this point there was a recess for the Fourth of July and with the report from the Great Committee (made up of one member from each of the eleven states represented), the sensible center of the Convention took control: such men as Roger Sherman and Oliver Ellsworth, John Rutledge, William Richardson Davie, and William Samuel Johnson. From that time onward, the drama moved steadily toward resolution.

Once the Constitution had been signed, many members of the Convention continued to worry about the scope of the powers granted to the new Federal government and the way in which those powers might be expanded to benefit one part of the Union at the expense of another, one class of citizens in power at the cost of the liberty and property of their less organized countrymen. Finally, the Antifederalists emerged as two varieties of confirmed opponents of ratification of the proposed Constitution: old-fashioned Whigs who thought that the Revolution had been fought to preserve the autonomy of local communities from the designs of a remote and arbitrary power; and those who wanted fiat money, a moratorium on the payment of debt, and direct democracy. Both types of Antifederalists demanded that a Bill of Rights be included or added to the Constitution to replace the guarantees of liberty and property which they had enjoyed under English law.

In contrast there were at least four kinds of Federalists. One group was separated in politics from the Antifederalists only in that they saw in the Constitution, or in the Constitution *with* a Bill of Rights, none of the perils at which their more prescient antagonists took alarm. They were simply sanguine men who had, amidst the fires of revolution, developed a confidence in certain American leaders and their view of republicanism based on service rendered during that conflagration. They trusted George Washington and did not look beyond him. By 1798 many of them were ready for Thomas Jefferson.

A second species of commitment to the new enterprise of a "more perfect Union" I describe as the Federalism of fear. It had three branches or subspecies. The first can best be defined by reaction to Captain Shays' Rebellion in Massachusetts and to related but lesser upheavals in most of the other states. This Federalism issued from a horror of anarchy and the leveling mob. Confusion over property rights, laxness in law enforcement, resistance to tax policy, and violations of the minimum standards of civility drove many Americans (not all of them wealthy) who saw in New England the growing shadow of radicalism to look to a national power, an "energetic" government, for a negative on the forces of disruption. However, no national commitment to civil liberties or equal rights was a part of their concern, but instead a preservation of things as they were. Indeed, the same basically localist, status quo position was maintained by most of the frightened

Federalists, including the members of the two other subspecies: the numerous military Federalists who feared the incapacity of the states to resist external threats and the Federalists who were already concerned about the dangers of an American civil war should the chance of forging lasting bonds pass by forfeit.

The third group of Federalists I refer to as the "wealth and power" men. Robert Morris was often their spokesman, or Nathaniel Gorham of Massachusetts. Many were merchants and speculators. They saw in the Federal system a vehicle for what the English political philosopher Michael Oakeshott calls the "enterprise association" theory of the state—and saw also for themselves a good place in the business. In the ratifying conventions James Wilson of Pennsylvania put their case. With the glamour of wealth he began the great address, which is almost all we have from that state's proceedings, and from that theme he rarely strayed:

> For my own part, I have been often lost in astonishment at the vastness of the prospect before us. To open the navigation of a single river was lately thought, in Europe, an enterprise equal to imperial glory. But could the commercial scenes of the Scheldt be compared with those that, under a good government, will be exhibited on the Hudson, the Delaware, the Potomac, and the numerous other rivers, that water and are intended to enrich the dominions of the United States?

To the same effect Oliver Ellsworth of Connecticut described grants of authority and money to the central power as an "investment" whose value was to be calculated with a view to "returns." In the eyes of these Federalists the purpose of the state was commercial. Its job was to build canals, promote industry, and ensure the fulfillment of contracts—to assist in accumulating wealth.

The fourth group of Federalists as defined by circumstance are the "everlasting glory" men. Hamilton was the leader of these bolder spirits. His interest in the economic well-being of the country had its referent in the purpose he expected such prosperity to serve. These Federalists looked to the mark our new Republic would make in the pages of history. They were the would-be favorites of fortune, the servants of the *Zeitgeist*. Their preferred idiom was military and imperial and their patriotism Bonapartist. Though science or education, immigration, business, or agriculture might receive their encouragement, it was always with the larger "manifest destiny" of Americans as a unified force that these private enterprises were defined by them as worthwhile. Fortunately, this group of Federalists was small, though their errors dot the pages of our national history.

The fifty-five Americans who had a share in drafting the United States Constitution and who then communicated it to the people of the states for rejection or approval were aware of the momentous implications of their task.

The responsibilities of citizenship were, they recognized, part of the moral obligation of the Christian life. Even more serious were the duties of the ruler and magistrate, who would be held accountable to a higher Authority for the use which they made of their special powers. Yet on the whole they enjoyed the work and found there the kind of high adventure which belongs to the lawgiver as opposed to the warrior, the poet, and the saint. Out of the complex of motives for and against the Constitution which I have just described, we may construct a key to the subsequent course of American history. They regarded the Union as conditional—in George Washington's terms, an "experiment"—and knew that it would require work and minor revision if the fundamental law was to operate as they hoped—but not too much revision or too often. Nevertheless, they meant for their form of government to last and they were confident that it would, so long as it was not manipulated out of shape by ideology or human selfishness. They were not demigods and they did not "invent" their country. But assuredly the passage of time has earned for them the right to be called a worthy company, a term of praise which they would have clearly understood.

John Langdon

(June 26, 1741–September 18, 1819), merchant, soldier, and political leader of New Hampshire.

One of the two most important figures in his state at the time of the Constitutional Convention. A moderate commercial Federalist, with a genuine popular touch. Greatly loved by the people of his state, of whose values he was an epitome. A local-minded Federalist with no vision of the magical benefits of an energetic national government and no loyalty to the Union that did not derive from his loyalty to a state and a particular community. Son of John and Mary Hall Langdon, and great-grandson of Tobias Langdon of Portsmouth. Educated in the grammar schools of that community, on Yankee merchant ships, and as a clerk in one of the great mercantile houses in the West Indian trade. Soon in business on his own, a man of considerable property in his own right when the Revolution broke out. He was one of the first of the established members of his community to act against British authority and to put his own wealth in the balance in the struggle for American liberty.

John Langdon sat on the New Hampshire Committee of Correspondence and on another committee responsible for enforcing regulations against importation. In 1774, he led his neighbors in the seizure and confiscation of munitions from the British fort in their harbor. He was elected to the New Hampshire Assembly in 1775 and was made speaker of that body. The Provincial Convention in 1775 sent Langdon as a delegate to the Continental Congress. In 1776, he was elected colonel of the New Hampshire militia and in the following year served in the campaign against General John Burgoyne which resulted in the British surrender at Saratoga, New York. Because of his zeal in the Patriot cause, his investment of his person and his means in the struggle for independence, and because of his work in building ships for the new American Navy and as an agent for British prizes captured at sea, he became a very popular man in his state. From 1777 to 1781, he was speaker of the New Hampshire legislature. In 1783, he served another term in the

Continental Congress. In 1784, he was state senator, and in 1785, he became the President of his state. In 1786–1787, he was again chosen speaker of the legislature while New Hampshire's most famous soldier and patriot, General John Sullivan, had two terms as the state's chief executive. During General Sullivan's administration, while the legislature was in session at Exeter in September of 1786, New Hampshire experienced its version of Shays' Rebellion, a riot by a mob of disaffected men who surrounded the meeting of the General Court and Senate, demanded an "emission of paper money, an equal distribution of property, and release from debts." President Sullivan, with the militia at his back, dispersed these insurgents in an almost bloodless battle. But it was against the backdrop of their uprising that the New Hampshire legislature dispatched John Langdon and young Nicholas Gilman (a supporter of General Sullivan) to sit with the Constitutional Convention in Philadelphia, and to continue from there to the next session of the Continental Congress, bearing tidings in both assemblies that there was evidence in New Hampshire of "an infidel age" in which the "indolent, extravagant and wicked may divide the blessings of life with the industrious, the prudent and the virtuous." Or at least were likely to do so unless prevented.

Langdon and Gilman (traveling at Langdon's expense) did not take their seats in the Great Convention until late in July. But once there, they acted in concert and were steady in their support of the moderate Federalist position. They voted to give the new government adequate powers for the regulation of commerce, the support of a military establishment, and taxation. The merchants of New Hampshire were convinced that only a stronger central government could restore to them the trading opportunities which they had lost with the Revolution. John Langdon was a member of the committee that hammered out a compromise on the slave trade and supported the other important compromises which made the Constitution possible. He spoke at least twenty times during the debates and was a vigorous proponent of provisions restricting tariffs betwen the states. Langdon announced as his opinion that there should be no necessary hostility between state and national government. Because of his own experience with the parsimony of his neighbors in New Hampshire, he was opposed to having members of Congress compensated by the states, and also opposed to a Federal power to issue paper money. Altogether, his position during the Convention placed him somewhere near the center of the spectrum of opinions there represented. His only surprising act while in Philadelphia was to maintain that the national government might require (by a ⅔ vote) the authority to veto state laws hurtful to the general interest and harmony of the Union. And even here what he had in mind was the unruly democracy of the state legislatures with respect to debts, paper money, and egalitarian fancies. Within a decade he had changed his mind about giving such powers to the central government.

John Langdon was an active member of both of New Hampshire's ratifying conventions, the first in February and the second in June of 1788. With Nicholas Gilman he had assisted other advocates of the new Constitution in securing its referral to the several commonwealths by the Continental Congress. And he led the fight for ratification in New Hampshire, first arranging for the adjournment of the February convention, thus preventing an Anti-federalist victory, and then bringing in the committee report which persuaded the second convention to approve the document as written. His letter of June 21, 1788, to General Washington reporting these results gave to his state its cherished description as the "Key Stone in the Great Arch."

John Langdon was again elected President of New Hampshire in 1788, but resigned to enter the United States Senate with the organization of the new Congress. There he represented New Hampshire until 1801. He was for a time a leading Federalist and was the first President *pro tem* of the Upper House. A great holder of Continental securities, he supported Hamilton's funding system and the creation of the United States Bank. But he opposed the assumption of state debts and refused to support Jay's Treaty, reacting in the latter case to the interests of the West Indian trade. It is, however, unjust to attribute personal motives to every position Langdon assumed in the Continental Congress, the Constitutional Convention, or the Congress of the United States. By 1800, he had become disenchanted with the policies of the Federalist leadership, their plans for an all-powerful central government, and had aligned himself with the followers of Thomas Jefferson. On his return to New Hampshire, he served again in the state legislature, and was on two additional occasions elected speaker. In 1805, he became New Hampshire's first Democratic-Republican governor and was continued in that office until 1811, excepting one year's hiatus brought on by the Embargo. In 1812, he refused the Vice-Presidential nomination of his party, as he had earlier refused the post as Secretary of the Navy, and retired to private life, the comforts of his family, his church (Congregational), and his beloved Portsmouth. In his last decades John Langdon was a patriarchal presence in the public life of his state, almost an institution in himself, personifying both in office and out the will of the Granite State that every man should be left unhindered in the execution of his own business, and New Hampshire left free to be itself. (See Lawrence Shaw Mayo, *John Langdon of New Hampshire* [Port Washington, N.Y.: Kennikat Press, 1970]; Jere R. Daniell, *Experiment in Republicanism: New Hampshire Politics and the American Revolution, 1741-1794* [Cambridge: Harvard University Press, 1970]; Lynn W. Turner, *William Plumer of New Hampshire, 1759-1850* [Chapel Hill: University of North Carolina Press, 1962]; John Langdon-Elwyn, "Some Account of John Langdon," *Early State Papers of New Hampshire*, XX, ed. Albert S. Batchellor [Manchester, N.H., 1891], 850-880; William Plumer, "John Langdon," *Early State Papers of New Hampshire*, XXI, ed. Albert S. Batchellor [Manchester, N.H., 1892], 804-812; and Forrest McDonald, *E Pluribus Unum: The Formation of the American*

Republic, 1776–1790 [Indianapolis: Liberty Press, 1979], pp. 194–204, 348–350, *et passim*.

Nicholas Gilman

(August 3, 1755–May 2, 1814), merchant, soldier, and political leader of New Hampshire.

The proverbial silent New Englander, who through a long career in public life said little and followed the lead of more decisive men. Son of Nicholas and Ann Taylor Gilman of Exeter. Brother of John Taylor Gilman, several times governor of their state. Representative of the Essex Junto, one of the powerful political organizations of New Hampshire, in the Philadelphia Convention. Linked with his brother to General John Sullivan and the High Federalist faction in the state, but supportive of John Langdon (who was paying his expenses) once they reached the Convention. Educated in the public schools and employed early in helping to run his father's general store. Enlisted in the Continental Army upon the outbreak of the Revolution, and a captain in the regular service at the conclusion of the war. Employed again in the family business until his election to the Continental Congress for the period 1786–1788. A very handsome man. Described by a French diplomat as one of the proudest men in all America.

Nicholas Gilman was one of the first of the experienced soldiers to answer President Sullivan's call for militia to suppress the 1786 insurrection at Exeter. He was by this service and by a general reputation for sound opinions propelled into a place of confidence among the leaders of New Hampshire, and therefore elected one of the state's four delegates to the Great Convention. But as John Langdon had suspected, and as later events confirmed, he was not so obdurate a nationalist as to offend against the residual attachment to local things and local independence of his wealthy associate. Nicholas Gilman voted the moderate Federalist position throughout the Great Convention and, though inconspicuous there, the young man (he was 32 at the time) was very helpful to his older colleague in getting the Constitution transmitted to the states by the Continental Congress. Later, though not a member of the New Hampshire ratifying convention, he vigorously supported the new Constitution in his home state. He was elected by his neighbors to the first Congress convened under the new system, where he served in the House of Representatives until 1797.

At some point between 1797 and 1800, he began to have serious doubts about the Federalist commitment to big banks and to strong central government. Though in conflict with the politics of his more famous brother, he joined the Democratic-Republicans. In 1802, President Thomas Jefferson appointed him as bankruptcy commissioner and in 1804 he was elected by the New Hampshire legislature (where he often served even while holding national office) to the United States Senate. Gilman spent the rest of his life in that post. Though wealthy, he retained the confidence of the small farmers and plain people of the New Hampshire backcountry. He was a man well-liked and well-trusted in his corner of America. (See Forrest McDonald, *We the People: The Economic Origins of the Constitution* [Chicago: University of Chicago Press, 1958], pp. 39-41, and his *E Pluribus Unum: The Formation of the American Republic, 1776-1790* [Indianapolis: Liberty Press, 1979], pp. 194-204, 348-350, *et passim*; Jere R. Daniell, *Experiment in Republicanism: New Hampshire and the American Revolution, 1741-1794* [Cambridge: Harvard University Press, 1970]; Lawrence Shaw Mayo, *John Langdon of New Hampshire* [Port Washington, N.Y.: Kennikat Press, 1970]; Robert G. Ferris, ed., *Signers of the Constitution* [Washington, D.C.: U.S. Dept. of the Interior, 1976], pp. 169-170; William Plumer, "Nicholas Gilman," *Early State Papers of New Hampshire*, XXI, ed. Albert S. Batchellor [Manchester, N.H., 1892], 802-804; Lynn Warren Turner, *The Ninth State: New Hampshire's Formative Years* [Chapel Hill: University of North Carolina, 1985].)

Elbridge Gerry

(July 17, 1744–November 23, 1814), statesman, Signer of the Declaration of Independence and of the Articles of Confederation, leader of the Revolution in Massachusetts, merchant, and Vice-President of the United States.

Antifederalist. The Framer of the Constitution who was most frequently opposed to its general tenor and to many of its particulars. With George Mason, the formal adversary in the debates of the Convention. Decidedly an Old Republican and a protector of the Massachusetts *lares* and *penates*. But no democrat. Drawn to participate in the Great Convention by the shock of Shays' Rebellion and the economic insecurity of the government under the Articles of Confederation. Born and raised at Marblehead, Massachusetts. The third of twelve children of Thomas and Elizabeth Greenleaf Gerry. Father from Devonshire in England but, before 1735, one of the leading merchants in Massachusetts' second-largest town and a sober Puritan, who through foreign trade became a part of Marblehead's unusual "codfish aristocracy." Educated by the local clergy and at Harvard College, from which he was graduated in 1762. Then joined with his father and older brothers in the family business of shipping dried fish to Europe and the West Indies. Entered public life in May of 1772, when he was elected a representative from his rocky native peninsula to the General Court of Massachusetts. Propelled into the political arena by his alarm at innovations in the colonial policy of the British government.

From the time of the Sugar Act and the Stamp Act in 1764–1765, the Gerry family had led the way in Marblehead in organizing popular resistance to close and energetic regulation by the English of the political and economic life of their North American colonies. Marblehead, as a seafaring community, was particularly affected by these policies. In 1770 Gerry and his brother Thomas, Jr., were elected members of a local committee to enforce a boycott on tea. Numerous public meetings, some of them chaired by Elbridge's father, prepared the way for stronger measures. Furthermore, once in the legislature, young Gerry fell under the influence of Samuel Adams. In May of 1773, Elbridge Gerry was re-elected to the General Court; and when local self-government was interrupted in Massachusetts in 1774-1775, he was elected to the first Provincial Congress, which the citizens of the state assembled in defiance of the new royal military governor, General Thomas Gage. He was by that body appointed to the Executive Committee of Safety and reappointed upon his re-election to the Provincial Congress in 1775. As a member of Marblehead's Committee of Correspondence and of the equivalent committee of the state legislature, Gerry came to know the leading men throughout Massachusetts. With Adams and Hancock, he was responsible for the military preparations which led to the fighting at Lexington and Concord, and faced great danger in the months before hostilities broke out. He also made use of his pen in drafting the Essex Resolves and in the preparation of an atrocity narrative of the beginning of the war designed to stimulate American recruitment and patriotic fervor. In the months when Massachusetts fought almost alone, Gerry was also chairman of the state's Committee of Supply, some of the business of which was handled directly by the family firm in Marblehead.

In January of 1776, Elbridge Gerry was elected representative from Massachusetts to the Second Continental Congress. Once seated there, he was quick to urge separation from the "prostituted government of Great Britain." He was a member of the Congress' Committee on the Commissary and was much concerned in the administration of American military forces. Uneasy about alliance with France, he supported the recall of Benjamin Franklin. He continued to do government business through his brothers and the family firm in Marblehead, but frowned on profiteering and helped to arrange a convention among the New England states fixing the prices of many important items in exchange. He exhibited a keen interest in the soundness of the currency, in naval affairs, and in privateering—an activity in which he had been profitably involved since late in 1775. Gerry was a very influential and effective member of the Continental Congress; but in late 1779 and early 1780 he took great offense at criticism of his conduct in the press and the refusal by his colleagues to reduce Massachusetts' quota of supplies. He insisted that prices be measured according to the schedule agreed on in New Haven in 1778 and, when refused, withdrew to Boston to seek vindication before the state legislature there. For three years he remained nominally a member of Congress, though absent in protest at its misconduct. While back in Massachusetts, he served in the lower house of the legislature and prospered in trade and privateering. Shortly after his return to Congress and the conclusion of the Revolutionary War, Gerry was quite active in schemes for the development of the Northwest Territory, in the effort to reduce the standing army, and in the movement to abolish the Society of the Cincinnati. But as a member of the merchant class, he was also most concerned with the credit and financial responsibility of the United States. He asserted that the nation's commerce required that all outstanding obligations of the national government be retired. He left Congress in November of 1785 and in the following year was re-elected to the Massachusetts legislature. In 1786 he purchased a fine house in Cambridge, a confiscated Tory property; retired from business with a comfortable fortune in real estate and securities; and married a wealthy young woman from New York.

Elbridge Gerry brought to the Constitutional Convention in Philadelphia precisely those qualities which had drawn him into the American Revolution and then made it difficult for him to cooperate with his fellow countrymen in that endeavor. As he made clear in 119 speeches and in many other motions and secondings of motions, he had not come to Philadelphia to vote Massachusetts out of existence, or to compromise its political and cultural integrity. A revision of the Articles of Confederation that would provide for the commercial needs of the member commonwealths, raise a revenue, retire the debt (a good share of which he held), and discourage the raucous spirit of democracy abroad in the land would be quite enough. Some kind of viable Federal government was necessary if Massachusetts was to have its share of Western lands and if commercial treaties with foreign nations were to be negotiated and enforced. Furthermore, a special court to hear legal disputes between the states or between the citizens of different states might prove useful. A machinery was necessary for dealing with certain maritime claims and for raising an army out of a militia, but nothing that smacked precisely of the kind of power over local government and local concerns against which the Revolution had been fought, nor any measure that might bring into being on these shores the kind of artificial aristocracy or ministerial party of placemen living off the special favors of a sovereign government that had so plagued the United Kingdom since Sir Robert Walpole's administration. Gerry did not withdraw from the Great Convention when it moved against his kind of particularistic republicanism. He was successful in his attempts to modify many provisions of the original Virginia Plan, and his objections to other provisions finally retained helped to establish the universe of discourse within which the ratification debates in the states occurred.

The theory of American politics entertained by Elbridge Gerry is among the most difficult and complicated of the many positions brought into the Great Convention by the various Framers. Its mainsprings, fear of remote tyrannical authority and the "danger of the levelling spirit" in local populations, were, as Admiral Samuel Eliot Morison has observed, in conflict with one another. And the efforts of Gerry's more recent biographers to reduce his political practice and announced beliefs to a unified system have not been altogether successful. Gerry's reactions to energetic government from Whitehall, to the occupation of Boston, and to the Coercive Acts were in keeping with conventional Old Whig sentiment: the English had violated the

Constitution and had therefore forfeited their authority. But the inherited rights guaranteed under that prescriptive law to the people of Marblehead and to five hundred or so other communities were to be preserved, first through armed resistance and finally through revolution. The trouble was, however, that the lower orders, whose interests were as well served by this position as were the interests of their natural leaders, the local gentry, became excited by certain features of Whig rhetoric and were reluctant to be "dissuaded from acting too much on their own judgment." Gerry reported to one of his friends that "... the people feel rather too much their own importance; it requires great skill in gradually checking them to such subordination as is necessary to good government." The necessities of war and of economic life moved Elbridge Gerry to sound like a Federalist at certain points in his career and to espouse martial law and a regular army. He came to the Constitutional Convention declaring, "The evils we experience flow from the excess of democracy." His first concerns were social stability at the local level and the security of property. But these were only intervals, and their argument *was* necessity. During the "smallpox war" in Marblehead in 1773–1774, mobs of angry fisher folk had threatened to injure the property and persons of members of the Gerry family because of their involvement in the erection of a pest house on Cat Island and their promotion of inoculation. All "sense of order and distinction" went out of the people, and the town proprietors (with Gerry's assent) appealed to the hated Governor Hutchinson for the King's protection. The episode provides a model for the kind of "brushfire Federalism" that punctuates Gerry's entire career. But the basic impetus of his thought went the other way. Legitimate government, he believed, should be expressive of the "genius" of the people and depend upon their virtue. No constitutional arrangement could supply the lack of a public spirit. However, the rigid division of power among national, state, and local authorities would best encourage the survival of the requisite public character of the nation, which Gerry believed God had called out to set an example to the world. (And Massachusetts, of course, was to set the example for the nation). Hence Gerry opposed a strong executive, opposed an extensive system of Federal courts, and violently opposed any authority for the government of the United States to veto state legislation or to interpose its military authority in the domestic affairs of a state. Gerry did not support the demand of the small state representatives in the Great Convention for the equality of the states in the national legislature. But that is unimportant when we remember how little power he was willing to grant to Congress. Gerry was a "small republic" man. No one in that Philadelphia meeting spoke more forcefully for the Bill of Rights than did Gerry. And its utility, once included, he made very clear, would be in restraining the Federal authority. National control over the militia, over state elections, or Federal elections in the states, he cried out against. And, though he accepted the new Constitution, after an unsuccessful attempt to prevent its ratification in Massachusetts, he continued in the remainder of his career to express the same opinion: that limited government was good government, at least at the national level—or, as Professor George A. Billias has expressed it, the people should govern themselves "... as long as they agreed with him [Gerry] and other local authorities."

After the establishment of the new government under the Constitution, which Gerry had refused to sign, he experienced great hostility from the Federalist leaders of Massachusetts society. His letter to the state legislature accounting for his conduct as a delegate to the Constitutional Convention had drawn down upon him attacks of a very personal nature which questioned not only his judgment, but also his motives in recommending that the Constitution be approved "only with amendments." But since probably a majority of the people of Massachusetts shared Gerry's reservations about the Constitution, he retained a great political following, and was elected to the First Congress of the United States in February of 1789. He served in the House of Representatives until 1793, voted sometimes with the Federalists (for instance, on the Bank of the United States and the funding of the debt), sometimes with their opponents (in support of an extremely full Bill of Rights and for a separate treasury commission beyond Alexander Hamilton's jurisdiction). Once Gerry had left the Congress, he was again under attack for contradictory behavior, to which he replied that he was of no party, and feared a "nobility of opinion," of ideological orthodoxy, even more than an aristocracy of blood or a faction bent upon its own economic advantage. As a Presidential elector in 1797, he supported his friend John Adams, but drew further and further away from the Federalists as a party. And when President Adams appointed him, with Charles Cotesworth Pinckney and John Marshall, as part of a diplomatic commission to a hostile France, he became their outright enemy because of his role in the XYZ Affair in his disputes with his associates in the American delegation, his secret dealings with Talleyrand, and his apparently pro-French attachments. Gerry did not return to America with Marshall and Pinckney, supposedly because he hoped to prevent war on his own. He expressed a deep fear of French military prowess, and was for a time persuaded that only his presence in France could keep the peace. Finally, John Adams called him home in disgrace. He was ostracized in Boston by men of his own class. But as a Democatic-Republican, his popularity revived once more. Gerry was the Jeffersonian candidate for governor of Massachusetts every year from 1800-1803. He was one of Jefferson's electors in 1804. And in 1810, at the age of sixty-five, he was elected governor of his state. He did little to offend during this first term, but after re-election in April of 1811, he made a harsh attack upon the "treasons" of the Federalists, along with an attack upon the Federalist clergy, and presided over a redistricting of the state designed to give his party a majority in the Massachusetts senate. The manipulation was so outrageous as to attach his name forever to all such proceedings—the gerrymander. Gerry was denied a third term as governor in April of 1812 by Caleb Strong. But in the following months he was chosen by the caucus of his party to be Vice-President under Madison. In March of 1813 he was sworn in; and he continued in that post the remaining nineteen months of his life. Few Americans of his generation had so much to do with the nation's history, performed on so large a stage, and yet retained so intense an identity with their provincial origins as did Elbridge Gerry. (See Samuel Eliot Morison, "Elbridge Gerry, Gentleman-Democrat," *By Land and by Sea* [New York: Alfred A. Knopf, 1953], pp. 181-199; George A. Billias, *Elbridge Gerry: Founding Father and Republican Statesman* [New York: McGraw-Hill Co. 1976]; Clifford K. Shipton, "Elbridge Gerry," *Biographical Sketches of Those Who Attended Harvard College, 1690-1771*, XV [Boston: Massachusetts Historical Society, 1970], pp. 239-259; Eugene F. Kramer, "The Public Career of Elbridge Gerry," Ph.D. dissertation, Ohio State University, 1955; James T. Austin, *The Life of Elbridge Gerry, with Contemporary Letters*, 2. vols. [Boston: Wells and Lilly, 1827-1828]; Albert H. Bowman, *Struggle for Neutrality* [Knoxville: University of Tennessee Press, 1974]; and C. Harvey Gardiner, ed., *A Study in Dissent: The Warren-Gerry Correspondence, 1776-1792* [Carbondale: Southern Illinois University Press, 1968].)

Rufus King

(March 24, 1755-April 29, 1827), lawyer, diplomat, and conservative statesman.

Political leader in two Northern states. High Federalist, yet in essence a sectional figure. Throughout his career an unremitting enemy of the South and West. Inclined to value a strong central government both as a stimulant to trade and commerce and as a check on "the madness of Democracy." Marked in his childhood with the abuse of his family by envious and destructive mobs. Son of the unfortunate Captain Richard King, a wealthy merchant and landowner, and Isabella Bragdon King. Born at Scarboro, Maine, on the outskirts of the Covenant. Educated by the famous schoolmaster Samuel Moody, at Dummer Academy, at Harvard (graduated in 1777), and in the offices of the learned Newburyport, Massachusetts attorney Theophilus Parsons. Bereft of the support of his family by the collapse of Richard King's business under the stigma of Loyalism, and by his early death in 1775. Admitted to the practice of the law in 1780, after a few weeks' military experience during General John Sullivan's brief and unsuccessful expedition to Rhode Island in August of 1778. Acknowledged as a master of his profession within only a few years. Elected by Newburyport to represent that prosperous community in the sessions of the General Court for 1783, 1784 and 1785. Sent by the Massachusetts legislature as a delegate to the Continental Congress for 1784–1787. Served on a commission to adjust the boundary between Massachusetts and New York. Completed his term of service to the Bay State as one of its delegates to the Great Convention. Relocated in New York after marriage to the heiress Mary Alsop, only daughter of Joseph Alsop, president of the New York Chamber of Commerce. In the midst of this transition from Massachusetts to New York while sitting in the Philadelphia Convention.

Rufus King, at 32, was one of the youngest of the Framers. Yet he was outspoken in his participation in the Constitutional Convention, eloquent but sometimes (according to William Pierce) forceful to the point of "rudeness." Shays' Rebellion had its effect on this young attorney. Prior to that upheaval he had been suspicious of any system that might turn the future of New England over to a haughty agrarian aristocracy, indifferent to the necessities of trade and maritime commerce: reluctant to contemplate the creation of a more "national" government than was provided for by the Articles. Indeed, he was more attracted by the idea of a Yankee "subconfederation" than by the notion of a stronger union of all the former English colonies joined by the Confederation. But as a member of the Continental Congress for Massachusetts, he had already displayed many of the attitudes which he later brought into the Great Convention. One of these was a firm attachment to the mercantile interest—a connection made all the stronger by his new situation as son-in-law of John Alsop and friend of the leading political and legal lights of Gotham. Another was an absolute horror of political abstractions. By 1786 he had put away entirely any earlier faith he might have had in the "common man"; "the great body of the people are without virtue, and not governed by any Restraints of Conscience." "Equality," in his view, was the "unnatural Genius" of his age, "the arch Enemy of the moral world" whose disposition is to degrade what is worthy, not to raise what is low. To argue to the contrary was to advocate "principles that do not exist." After independence was achieved, King was quick to assure English friends that "there was no likelihood of our becoming zealous in the Propagation of Liberty and the Rights of Man." At least not if Rufus King had anything to do with the shaping of American policy. With his friend and colleague Gouverneur Morris, he does more to contradict the sanguine radical stereotype of early American political leader or "Father of the Republic" than any other member of the Constitutional Convention.

The merit of the new United States Constitution produced in Philadelphia, according to Rufus King, was that it did not rest on "romantic speculation," or run to "utopian lengths" in hankering after an experiment in "wild and mischievous doctrines." In the opinion of the delegate from

Massachusetts, the Framers had worked wisely and respectfully with the given materials of an already functioning American regime, acknowledging in the process the wisdom which teaches that the true statesman does not argue from definition and "may not apply unqualified metaphysical principles to [his craft]." In King's doctrine, this prudence was admirable because "experience, not abstraction ought to be our guide in practice and conduct." When the French Revolution came, King hated it as violently as did any American of note in his generation. He declaimed against the "detestable principles" of France and foresaw the spread of "Barbarism," fathered by "Philosophy." And, two years before, in Philadelphia, during the summer of 1787, his mind worked in the same way, on precisely the same assumptions.

In the Great Convention, Rufus King was helpful in striking the compromise on the importation of slaves and on the prohibition against a tax on exports. He persuaded his colleagues to include a provision guaranteeing the sanctity of contracts, fought to produce a strong, independent President with a power of absolute veto over legislation by Congress, and defended the separation of powers. But he foresaw the development of the country in the Southwest, and expressed his fear that Southerners might augment their voting strength by the simple expedient of importing slaves. Although he had introduced and supported legislation in the Continental Congress to exclude the "peculiar institution" from the territories, he was actually more interested in preventing or discouraging westward settlement of any kind than in an issue which "should be considered in a political light only." King was himself the son of a slaveowner, and did not free his last Negro until 1812. But as was evident in the remainder of his career, he was prepared to argue in almost any way to defend the power of the Northeastern states against the threat of a Southern hegemony. And the issue of slavery, as King admitted to his son in later years, was for him always "a question of *political power* between Northern and Southern interests."

After the conclusion of the Constitutional Convention, Rufus King made one final gesture in the politics of Massachusetts by standing for election to the state ratification convention in Boston. He was one of the leaders of the Federalists in that assembly, and played an important role in devising a strategy for his faction in their largely successful attempt to direct and channel the proceedings toward a decision for approval. As he had in Philadelphia, so in Boston did King warn the Children of Light against the "phantom of state sovereignty." Massachusetts could not prosper on its own, Union was the way to a monopoly of Southern trade and a market for fish in Spain—acquired at the "trifling" cost of navigation rights on the Mississippi: a cost which only the South and West would be asked to pay. If amendments to the Constitution were in order, let them be subjoined as "changes recommended," not as conditions of ratification. Since the fundamental "law of the land" was now to act upon individuals, there would no longer be a danger of too much of a tax burden upon Massachusetts. And in any case, if the business went wrong, there was always the corrective of secession—an alternative to national unity which King threatened at various times throughout his life, expected the West to exercise, and once overtly recommended to the Virginian, John Taylor of Caroline. But short of such extremity, New England should be content with the three-fifths formula for counting slaves for both taxes and representation since "it was the language of America." An accommodation with Spain, a commercial arrangement with England, and cautious dealings with the French. Such had been King's program for making use of national unity under the Articles, as, for instance, in the Jay/Gardoqui negotiations and in plans for a subconfederation that could force into existence a nationwide policy on imports, exports, and shipping. There was some danger that the South and West might get New England into a war. But not if the new government refused to authorize any big armies for attacks on hostile Indians or their foreign "sponsors": left the frontier to protect itself, and thus slowed its spread into the unoccupied lands.

With the Constitution adopted, Rufus King was elected as one of the original United States Senators from New York. In the Congress, he was the leading spokesman for the Washington administration in the Upper Chamber. King argued the case for Hamilton in many crucial circumstances surrounding his financial system. In 1791 he was elected one of the directors of the Bank of the United States. In 1794–1795, he was the principal defender of Jay's Treaty, in support of which he wrote some fine essays under the signature "Camillus." In January of 1795, he was re-elected to his place in the Senate by the New York legislature. But, now fatigued with the life of the legislator, King seized on the opportunity to become United States Minister to Great Britain (replacing Thomas Pinckney) when the post was offered to him late in 1795. As emissary to Great Britain, he was a great success and proved to be acceptable to most of the English leadership, including King George III. He continued to enjoy that role until he was removed at his own request in 1803. King prevented constant tensions between his nation and Whitehall from exploding into war, concluded two conventions with the British government and won from them many *ex officio* concessions—favors granted at least in part because Rufus King was such an open Anglophile, especially with reference to England's wars with the French Republic and, thereafter, with the empire of Napoleon. However, with the same attitudes King made many enemies in the United States, particularly with his effort to prevent the exile of Irish radicals to our shores, men full of French ideas "so false and so utterly inconsistent with any practicable or settled form of government."

On his return to New York in 1804, and again in 1808, Rufus King was the Federalist candidate for Vice-President of the United States on the ticket headed by his fellow Framer, Charles Cotesworth Pinckney. He purchased an estate on Long Island, played the gentleman farmer, and made good investments. Moreover, he continued to function (especially after Hamilton's death in 1804) as one of the respected leaders of a dying political party. But if Federalism was on its way to oblivion, the political career of Rufus King was not. Or rather in Rufus King the political theory of Federalism experienced a metamorphosis, a sea change which has to this day preserved its influence in the discourse of the Republic. For in 1813, when, in a backlash against a new war with England, King once again won a seat as Senator from New York, he was on his way toward a new political language foreign to the Federalism of his youth and middle years. All of this despite the fact that in 1816 he was the last Federalist candidate for the Presidency.

Though he avoided the separatism of his old comrades in the Hartford Convention of 1814, and though he collaborated in the war effort once the British began to endanger American coastal settlements, the Rufus King who returned to the Senate was tired of being ruled by Southerners and (in the words of his most recent biographer) "hoped for a new sectional alignment of parties." He got his chance to accomplish this purpose in 1819–1820 when the Territory of Missouri presented itself to the Congress as a candidate for full membership in the Union of the States. For Missouri wished to come in as a slave state. King found in this circumstance the engine which he required to "stir up a storm in the North." As Professor Robert Ernst has observed, "Although deeply critical of slavery itself, the Senator from New York was primarily and most deeply aroused over the political balance of power.... His interest in slavery was primarily political." Or, in Jefferson's opinion, "He [King] was ready to risk the Union for any chance of restoring his party to power." His instrument was the rhetoric of moral advantage, of freedom *vs.* slavery, the argument from definition designed to link North and West—one which foreshadowed Seward and Lincoln in attacking Southern influence as something to be isolated as evil. "I hold," said King, "that all laws or compacts imposing any such condition [as involuntary servitude] upon any human being are absolutely void because contrary to the law of nature, which is the law of God." At this explosion in violation of the "Compromise of 1787" and King's own announced devotion to the sanctity of contracts and abhorrence of French abstractions or metaphysical politics, James Madison declared himself to be "truly astonished," adding that if King's position on what the Constitution allowed had enjoyed any support in the Philadelphia Convention, it would have prevented its ratification. Other critics were less generous, called King a "moral hypocrite," and accused him of dishonesty in his account of what had been agreed in the Great Convention—particularly on the subject of a Federal power to exclude slavery from a territory that wanted it. King's crusade was popular in New York. He was re-elected to the Senate for another term and served there until 1825. Yet he was ahead of his time in this effort, even though the seed sown in 1820 reached maturity in decades to come.

After his retirement from Congress, Rufus King performed one final public service in attempting a second term as Minister to Great Britain. But his health broke, forcing in 1826 his return to New York, where at the age of 72, in the following year, he died. King was a great orator, a fine diplomat, and a close student of commerce and maritime law. His notes on the Constitutional Convention are very valuable; and he had a useful role in the writing of the New York State Constitution of 1821. He was a widely read man and a devout Episcopalian—having eschewed Congregationalism while in college. And he authored some useful legislation while in the United States Senate. Nonetheless, he was essentially a parochial spirit, a predictable product of his New England upbringing. When in the Continental Congress in 1785, he proposed the distribution of the New England pattern of township settlement with a corporate life, no large holdings, and a government provision for the churches, in the open lands of the West. We should remember that he was doubtful about the Constitutional Convention until convinced it would not endanger established New England modes and orders. He was a xenophobe and disliked immigration of most varieties. To say nothing of exposure to strange places and strange ways. Only when he could equate the nation with his portion of it was his patriotism at ease. In his role in the Missouri controversy, King is, moreover, a forerunner of all of those Americans since his time who have been willing to be disingenuous in their reading of the Constitution when they saw political advantage in revolution by construction. (See Robert Ernst, *Rufus King, American Federalist* [Chapel Hill: University of North Carolina Press, 1968]; Charles R. King, *The Life and Correspondence of Rufus King*, 6 vols. [New York: C. P. Putnam's Sons, 1894–1900]; Edward H. Brush, *Rufus King and His Times* [New York: Little, Brown, 1926]; James G. King, "Rufus King, Young Statesman of Massachusetts, 1755–1789," Ph.D. dissertation, Harvard University, 1966; David H. Fischer, *The Revolution of American Conservatism: The Federalist Party in the Era of Jeffersonian Democracy* [New York: Harper and Row, 1965]; Joseph L. Arbena, "Politics or Principle? Rufus King and the Opposition to Slavery, 1785–1825," *Essex Institute Historical Collections*, 101 (1965), 56–77; Dixon Ryan Fox, *The Decline of Aristocracy in the Politics of New York, 1801–1840* [New York: Columbia University Press, 1919].)

Caleb Strong

(January 9, 1745–November 7, 1819), lawyer and political leader of western Massachusetts.

Old school puritan and co-author of the article on religion in the 1780

Bay State Constitution: the article which preserved in Zion the hegemony of the established Congregational church. The kind of Federalist who thought of government as a means to an end—"discipline" and "virtue." Yet moderate in his attitude toward the uses of power, which is "of an encroaching nature." A firm supporter of the Constitution who, from its inception, doubted that the Union which it expressed and institutionalized could long survive: who declared "the territory of the United States is so extensive as to forbid us to indulge in the expectation that we shall remain many years united." A sedate and solid citizen, well liked by the plain people of his state. But not so much a favorite with the gentry of the coastal towns who, in the words of a contemporary, were uneasy with a leader "who calls hasty pudding luxury" and "whose wife wears blue stockings." His good sense a staple of the Great Convention. Behind John Adams, eventually the principal figure in the Massachusetts branch of his party. Of such personal authority that, in the ratification convention which opened in Boston on January 9, 1788, his testimony concerning the plain language, character, and good intentions of the Framers was of determinative influence in securing the majority needed for adoption.

Caleb Strong was born in Northampton, Massachusetts, the son of Caleb Strong, tanner, and of Phebe Lyman Strong. He was in direct descent from John Strong, who had emigrated to that section of the state after arriving in Massachusetts in 1630. After study with a local clergyman, Caleb entered Harvard College, from which he was graduated with highest honors in 1764. Following some experience in humble occupations and trouble with his health, Strong read law with Joseph Hawley and was admitted to the bar in 1772. He was chosen selectman of Northampton in 1774 and served throughout the Revolution on its Committee of Safety. In 1776 he was elected to the General Court and named county attorney, an office which he held for twenty-four years. In 1780 he was honored with a seat on the Massachusetts Council, but refused appointment to the Continental Congress, as he later refused an appointment to the supreme court of his state, for financial reasons. Caleb Strong in these years was not a rich man, and of no great distinction in his profession. Yet he grew in grace and favor in the eyes of his neighbors throughout these busy times—in part, *because of* his modesty. He served as a state senator from 1780 until 1789. And, as was mentioned above, Strong helped to draft the Massachusetts Constitution of 1780. When chosen as a delegate to the Philadelphia Convention, he had accumulated a great experience of American politics. But it was experience of politics at the local level, a fact which explains some features of his perspective upon the business of the Great Convention.

Caleb Strong did not speak frequently that summer of 1787. Much of the time he voted with Elbridge Gerry, later to be his adversary. He had a "narrow" view of the proper functions of a Federal judiciary, holding that "the power of making ought to be kept distinct from that of expounding the laws." He supported the Great Compromise on equality of state representation in the United States Senate and favored leaving to the states part of the responsibility for paying the salaries of Congress. He preferred annual elections for the House of Representatives but was, in the face of Southern objections concerning distance and expense, reasonable on this subject, as on all others. He liked the idea of the House having exclusive power to originate money bills, leaving to the Senate the power of amendment. But he voted against the selection of the President by an Electoral College. Caleb Strong left the Convention before its work was done, sometime late in August, because of sickness in his family. But he created no doubt concerning his support for the document produced there, once it was distributed to the people.

Strong, despite his stature among the delegates to the Massachusetts ratifying convention, also said very little in the course of its debates. For the most part, he answered questions and provided explanations. He defended compromises, saying "the Southern States have their inconveniences." But his role in the politics of his state was already so secure that he had nothing to prove in supporting the new Constitution, and there was no surprise in his being elected by the Massachusetts legislature as one of his state's original United States Senators. In Congress Strong was a vigorous supporter of Washington's policies, had a hand in drafting the Judiciary Act, and presented Hamilton's plan for the Bank of the United States. He was reelected to the Senate in 1793 and served there until his resignation in 1796. For a few years thereafter he was in the private practice of law. But in 1800, when faced by a Democratic-Republican tide and the candidacy of Thomas Jefferson, the leaders of Massachusetts Federalism called on Caleb Strong to be their candidate for governor. He was elected and for eleven of the following sixteen years continued in that office (1800–1807; 1812–1816), "so good and unexceptionable a man," according to John Adams, that he ran usually ahead of the ticket and was, in the Connecticut River Valley, almost unbeatable. Generally, a governor who left to his people the management of their own affairs—who observed that "inequality . . . arises from the nature of things, and not from any defect in the form of administration of government. All that the best government can do is prevent that inequality which fraud, oppression or violence would produce."

At the end of Caleb Strong's career came its most dramatic moments when, as a Yankee "nullifier," he withheld the forces of Massachusetts from full participation in the War of 1812 and moved his state toward secession or a new constitutional convention. And most immediately to the Hartford Convention of 1814. According to Strong and his associates among the senior New England Federalists, such measures were clearly within the scope of the United States Constitution. Only a rapid end of this war with England preserved the Union from a general withdrawal by the old Puritan commonwealths, all of which felt themselves to be "deserted" and dispossessed by the Virginia dynasty, or else out of place in a conflict with "the nation from which we are descended... the bulwark of the religion we profess." Strong's popularity was not injured by these adventures in sectionalism, in which he followed a well thought out Federalist doctrine of state sovereignty. He was again elected governor in 1815. However, he chose to retire at the end of this term, returning to Northampton, where he died some three years later, in the midst of his "rebellious" friends. (See James M. Banner, Jr., *To the Hartford Convention: The Federalists and the Origins of Party Politics in Massachusetts, 1789–1815* [New York: Alfred A. Knopf, 1970]; *Patriotism and Piety, The Speeches of His Excellency Caleb Strong, Esq... from 1800 to 1807* [Newburyport, Mass.: M. Blunt, 1808]; Henry Cabot Lodge, *A Memoir of Caleb Strong, United States Senator and Governor of Massachusetts, 1745–1818* [Cambridge, Mass.: J. Wilson & Son, 1879]; Anson E. Morse, *The Federalist Party in Massachusetts to the Year 1800* [Princeton: Princeton University Press, 1909]; William N. Chambers, *Political Parties in a New Nation: The American Experience, 1776–1809* [New York: Oxford University Press, 1963]; Richard E. Welch, Jr., *Theodore Sedgwick, Federalist: A Political Portrait* [Middleton, Conn.: Wesleyan University Press, 1964]; Paul Goodman, *The Democratic-Republicans of Massachusetts: Politics in a Young Republic* [Cambridge, Mass.: Harvard University Press, 1964]; and Clifford K. Shipton, "Caleb Strong," pp. 94-110, *Biographical Sketches of Those Who Attended Harvard College in 1764–1767* [Boston: Massachusetts Historical Society, 1972]; David H. Fischer, *The Revolution of American Conservatism: The Federalist Party in the Era of Jeffersonian Democracy* [New York: Harper & Row, 1965].)

Nathaniel Gorham

(May 16, 1738–June 11, 1796), merchant, financier, and land speculator.

Political leader of Massachusetts during and after the American Revolution. Commercial Federalist *par excellence*. A vigorous, active participant in the debates of the Great Convention; of a "lusty... agreeable and pleasing manner," according to William Pierce. In favor of a strong central government—even though he did not expect the Union to survive: "Can it be supposed that this vast country including the Western territory will 150 years hence remain one nation?" One of a large number of Northern Framers whose lives were damaged or destroyed by their economic and business "adventures" in the years following 1787. Son of Nathaniel Gorham and Mary Soley Gorham. Descended from John Gorham, who emigrated to the

Massachusetts Bay Colony in 1643. Of old Puritan stock but of limited means. Congregationalist. Born at Charlestown and, after only a minimum of education, apprenticed to Nathaniel Coffin, a merchant of New London, Connecticut, with whom he labored until 1759. On his return to Charlestown, successful in his own business while still a young man. Entered politics as the Bay State moved toward war.

Nathaniel Gorham prospered so greatly in trade that by 1780 he had become one of the leading men in his state. After election to the Massachusetts General Court (1771–1775), Gorham was chosen as delegate to the Provincial Congress (1774–1775), as member of the Commonwealth's Board of War (1778–1781), and as delegate to the state constitutional convention of 1779–1780. Under the new constitution, he served in the lower house (1781–1787) and in the upper chamber (1780) of the Massachusetts legislature. Of the former assembly he was speaker in 1781, 1782, and 1785. Even though much of his wealth was lost in the early stages of the Revolution, Gorham rebuilt his fortune with privateering and speculation, in property both movable and real, in the midst of that struggle. Though not a lawyer, from 1785–1796 he sat as judge of the Middlesex County Court of Common Pleas and in 1788–1789 on the Governor's Council. From 1782–1783 and from 1785–1787 he represented Massachusetts in the Continental Congress and was President of that body from June 1786 to January 1787. With the dignity of these offices and this public service at his back, Gorham took his place in the Constitutional Convention. He was chairman of the Committee of the Whole and sat on the Committee of Detail. Much of the time he voted with Rufus King and against Elbridge Gerry and Caleb Strong—thus dividing and cancelling the voice of his state when the roll was called. But he himself was heard on over forty occasions—heard *and* understood.

It was the theme of Nathaniel Gorham's performance in the deliberations of the Framers that "the business of America is Business." Or at least that it should be, so far as New England was concerned. At one point Gorham declared that "he desired it to be understood that the Eastern States had no motive to Union but a commercial one. They were able to protect themselves. They were not afraid of external danger and did not need the Southern States." Disunion, he warned the South, would leave it vulnerable to foreign attack *and* internal disruptions—as the Revolution had proved. But in return for a navigation act, a tariff and the "carrying trade" of the benighted hinterlands, New England might be moved to protect its Southern countrymen from their inherent weaknesses. *Quid pro quo* was his motif in several short speeches. Gorham also insisted that all of the states be given an interest in Western lands, suggested that the larger states be broken up into smaller units (so as to strengthen the general government), and continued to exhibit the interest in a sound currency and regular tax revenues that he had shown as a leader of the Continental Congress: first of all, in the plan of the

New England states to hold on their own a 1783 convention on revenue, once the Congress proved to be unable to agree on a monetary policy; and, later, when he was an emissary from the Congress to New Jersey when that state threatened to withhold its part of the Requisition of September 1785. When Southerners made fair to prohibit the passage of navigation acts in the text of the United States Constitution, Gorham asked, "If the Government is to be so fettered as to be unable to relieve [i.e., enrich] the Eastern States, what motive can they have to join it, and thereby tie their hands from measures which they could otherwise take for themselves?" Yet it was Gorham who voted to extend the slave trade from 1800 to 1808 in return for John Rutledge's support of Massachusetts' views on commerce. In Gorham's Federalism there is no ideological passion, no commitment to the grand abstractions of natural rights theory. Questions of interest and practicality stand in their place.

Nathaniel Gorham played no important role in American politics after his service in the Constitutional Convention. Though he did sit in defense of the new Constitution in the 1788 ratification convention of his state, for the most part his attention in the last nine years of his life was devoted to the development of a vast tract of land in New York, ceded to Massachusetts as part of a boundary dispute, and later sold to Gorham and Oliver Phelps of Windsor, Connecticut. Probably these two men represented a syndicate in the acquisition of six million acres. The purchase price was one million dollars, to be paid in three installments and in Massachusetts scrip. The speculators quickly cleared title to 2,600,000 acres in the eastern section of the grant, and sold it to settlers. But the Massachusetts paper rose suddenly in value, increasing the true size of the still pending debt. The result for Gorham and Phelps was insolvency, ruin, and disgrace. In 1796 Gorham died of apoplexy and remorse, a man once great, but fallen almost utterly from view, betrayed by the very spirit which he had displayed as one of the Framers of the Constitution. (See Orasmus Turner, *History of the Pioneer Settlement of Phelps and Gorham's Purchase and Morris' Reserve* [Rochester, New York: W. Alling, 1852]; Timothy Thompson Sawyer, *Old Charlestown: Historical, Biographical and Reminiscent* [Boston: J. H. West Co., 1902]; H. James Henderson, *Party Politics in the Continental Congress* [New York: McGraw-Hill, 1974]; Van Beck Hall, *Politics Without Parties: Massachusetts, 1780–1791* [Pittsburgh: University of Pittsburgh Press, 1972]; Stephen E. Patterson, *Political Parties in Revolutionary Massachusetts* [Madison: University of Wisconsin Press, 1973]; Joseph L. Davis, *Sectionalism in American Politics, 1774–1787* [Madison: University of Wisconsin Press, 1977]; Robert G. Ferris, ed., *Signers of the Constitution* [Washington, D. C.: U. S. Department of the Interior, 1976], pp. 170–172; Forrest McDonald, *We the People: The Economic Origins of the Constitution* [Chicago: University of Chicago Press, 1958], pp. 43–44.)

Roger Sherman

(April 19, 1721 o. s.–July 23, 1793), shoemaker, surveyor, lawyer, jurist, lay theologian, and statesman.

Next to Benjamin Franklin, the oldest man in the Great Convention. Mild Federalist, where commerce was concerned, but otherwise distrustful of any great increase in the Federal powers: "no state should be affected in its internal police," because "it is in the interest of each and of the whole [Union] that they should be separate within their proper limits." Hence, almost an Antifederalist in many of his opinions. In Philadelphia to create a "more effective government," but not a "national" government. In some respects a figure left over from the New England of the previous century, yet withal the most experienced legislator in the entire company. Described by John Adams (with some understandable exaggeration) as "an old Puritan, as honest as an angel and as firm in the cause of American independence as Mount Atlas." Yet according to Connecticut's Jeremiah Wadsworth, who knew Sherman well, "as cunning as the Devil." Despite his rustic, plain appearance and country speech, rightly identified by a farmer of his acquaintance as "twistical"—as skilled a politician as ever came out of colonial Connecticut. While in the Constitutional Convention, determined to protect the regime which he had done so much to shape. Convinced that "each state like each individual had its peculiar habits, usages and manners, which constituted its happiness." Able to accept the fact that any viable union of the states would have to rest upon a large variety of disparate versions of the corporate life. Yet eager to see a government that could promote American commerce, collect taxes, retire the debt, establish a sound currency, make treaties, raise and supply an army, and preclude the robbery of one state by another by means of duties. Instrumental in the adoption of the Connecticut Compromise, which provided for a bicameral legislature with the states represented equally in one house and according to population in the other; and in the ratification of the Constitution by Connecticut. An orthodox Congregationalist. And, though mayor of New Haven, a man of limited means. A genuine, trusted representative of all levels in the society of Connecticut.

Roger Sherman was born in Newton, Massachusetts, a descendant of Captain John Sherman of Dedham, Essex County, England, who had settled in Massachusetts *ca.* 1636. Roger was the son of William Sherman, farmer, cordwainer, and frontiersman, and of Mehetabel Wellington Sherman. In 1723 William Sherman moved to Stoughton, Massachusetts, where Roger received some education in the common schools and came under the influence of the local minister, the Rev. Samuel Dunbar, who inspired him to read widely in theology, history, law, and politics. The youthful Sherman also farmed and learned the cobbler's trade. After his father's death in 1741, Roger gathered up his tools and in 1743 moved to New Milford, Connecticut, where his elder brother William was already established. In 1745 he was appointed surveyor for New Haven County and continued in that office when Litchfield County was organized, serving until 1758. In this position Roger Sherman acquired considerable property and began to take an active part in the public life of the township, serving as town clerk, selectman, deacon of the local Congregationalist church, juryman, school committeeman, and town agent before the Assembly. He sat as Litchfield County Justice of the Peace from 1755 to 1761. In 1756 he became sole owner of New Milford's first store, which he had earlier operated with his brother. Between 1750 and 1761 he published a series of almanacs, which suggest something of the scope of his reading. And he also brought out a pamphlet against the circulation of unsound currency. He read law with William Samuel Johnson and in 1754 became a member of the Litchfield bar. When sent up by New Milford to the General Assembly in May of 1755, he had, at 34, achieved a remarkable alteration in his circumstances from the time of his arrival in Connecticut.

In the years preceding the American Revolution, Roger Sherman continued to represent New Milford in the Assembly (1755–56, 1758–61), and had some important experience with questions of military finance during the French and Indian War. In 1759 he was appointed Commissary for Connecticut troops operating out of Albany, New York. Shortly thereafter, he gave up his law practice and his situation as Justice of the County Court in Litchfield and moved to New Haven, where he set up a large general store close to the Yale campus. From 1764 to 1766 he was the deputy for New Haven in the General Assembly. In May of 1766 he was elected to the Governor's Council as Assistant, in which office he continued nineteen years. In 1765 he became a member of the County Court and Justice of the Peace in New Haven. In May of 1766 he began a 23–year tenure as Judge of the Connecticut Superior Court. Sherman also operated a store in Wallingford, Connecticut, and was a well–known figure throughout the state. He was close to the head of the ticket in most elections. When disturbances over the Stamp Act spilled over into social disorders and threats to person and property,

Sherman broke with his erstwhile friends, the Sons of Liberty, because he believed that "their proceedings tend to weaken the authority of the government." Despite his plain origins and popular touch, Sherman despised mob rule throughout his career, and once issued a warrant against Benedict Arnold as a check upon lawless radicalism. There was to be no scapegoating of Loyalists in New Haven while he was in charge—and no "unofficial" beatings of enemies of the kind for which Arnold was fined. Yet Sherman was early in his commitment to non-importation agreements as a peaceful response to hated British legislation, was the head of the New Haven Committee of Correspondence and even went so far as to organize pressure on New York merchants who had continued to do business with the mother country and had not signed the Association. During these years Sherman was also a benefactor of Yale College and served as their treasurer from 1765 to 1776. In 1768 the school awarded him an honorary master of arts degree.

For Roger Sherman, as for so many other Americans of his generation, the watershed experiences in his decision to practice armed resistance to British power came with the occupation of Massachusetts by the King's troops, the Intolerable Acts, and the closing of the port of Boston. Prior to 1773, he had been content to respond to offensive policies initiated by the ministers of George III with protest, commercial retaliation, and a few special worries concerning the prospects for appointed bishops and greedy placemen. In the late 1760's, as the almanacs demonstrate, he had been a Whig Loyalist, devoted to the principles of 1688, delighted by victory over France and the "gracious protection of his sovereign lord." The disputes over the Susquehannah lands in Pennsylvania concerned Connecticut more than fears of British invasion and open war. Furthermore, the leading men of the state did not wish to see the people provoked into "divisions and animosities among themselves," drained of their "public virtue." But though cautious about "rebellion" and determined that Connecticut should live by its Charter and the version of English constitutional theory that vindicated its authority, Sherman had for years entertained a very advanced view of the relation of Parliament to the English colonies in North America, maintaining that "the reverse of the Declaratory Act was true, namely that the Parliament of Great Britain had authority to make laws for America in no case whatsoever." Lexington and Concord, for Sherman, closed out the issue of King George III's authority under the Connecticut Charter. Yet after attending the original Continental Congress and signing the Articles of Association in 1774, Sherman made no serious objection to the 1775 Olive Branch Petition and was one of its signers. The mainspring of his politics, both at this time and at subsequent stages in his public life, was devotion to the established, well-tested, and long self-governing regime of Connecticut. To protect it, he became a party to the Declaration of Independence, serving with Jefferson, John Adams, Franklin, and Robert Livingston of New York on the committee called upon to formalize that secession with a proper document. Sherman acted in order to protect an *existing* Connecticut, not to defend some abstract principle.

Roger Sherman was a delegate to the Continental Congress from 1774–1781 and then again, briefly, from 1783–1784. While there, he was perhaps the most energetic, thorough, and regular member of that body. Eventually he became "Father Sherman" to the House, though hated by many "high-toned nationalists," who were made restive by his parsimony even while they feared and respected his power. Sherman was a signatory to the Articles of Confederation and also part of the committee which brought these proposals to a vote. He was active in support of Connecticut's claims to lands in Pennsylvania, and later had a part in the negotiations which surrendered the Wyoming River Valley lands for a firmer hold on the Western Reserve in Ohio. He was particularly concerned with the Commissariat for the Continental Army. Two of Sherman's sons served as paymasters, while a third, Isaac, did fighting service under Washington and rose to lieutenant colonel before the end of the war. For a time Sherman doubted the wisdom of appointing a Virginia aristocrat to command New England troops, and he took special pleasure from the victories of Northern generals. "This is the Lord's doing, and marvellous in our eyes!" he declared on hearing of Saratoga, using here the idiom of the Good Old Cause. But ultimately he accepted everything in the military arrangements except long enlistments and the prospect of a standing army. He turned his attention to the problems of financing and sustaining American forces in the field.

In the New England conventions called to consider the best policy for controlling prices and supporting the currency of the Confederation, Roger Sherman exerted a considerable influence. He was at the Springfield meeting in 1777, in New Haven in 1778, and at the Philadelphia session in 1780. But he was a realist about the prospects of a currency supported by so small and so irregular a national income. On the question of state emissions of paper money, Sherman was consistently negative. Instead, he called for taxes, retirement of debt, and frugality—cutting back on diplomatic operations, depending on militia rather than on regiments of the Continental Line, paying government purchasing agents by salary instead of with percentage commissions. For a time it appeared that Connecticut merchants, angry with low profits, had deprived Sherman of his seat in the Congress. But soon thereafter, he was reappointed and back in Philadelphia—supporting statehood for Vermont, warning against spending money not yet in hand, insisting on careful accounts. And in the Annapolis session, he was there to promote the common enterprise, scorning such local diversions as "plays, Balls, Concerts, routs, hops, Fandangoes and fox hunting." Cavalier nonsense was not to the taste of this sober statesman. Yet no member of the Congress was more mindful of his responsibility to his electorate.

In the years immediately preceding the Constitutional Convention, Roger Sherman concentrated on politics at the state and local level. In 1784 he was elected the first mayor of New Haven and continued to enjoy that honor until his death. Also in 1784, at the request of the legislature, he joined with Richard Law to codify and reconcile the statutes of Connecticut, a work finally published as *Acts and Laws of the State of Connecticut.* (Sherman had done essentially the same job in 1768.) He built a good house, continued with his judicial duties and presided over the complex and sometimes distressing activities of a large family. In these years his position in New Haven was "almost autocratic." At the age of 66 in 1787, it was reasonable to assume that Sherman was through with the national arena, even though he continued to follow politics with close attention. Yet once Connecticut finally, and with grave reservations, decided to send a delegation to the Great Convention, it was altogether natural that Roger Sherman—the summary representative of the decentralist sentiments of the state's ordinary citizens—be chosen after the younger and even more Antifederalist Erastus Wolcott had refused the appointment.

In the Constitutional Convention Roger Sherman spoke at least 138 times and was consistently present except for a brief period (July 20–August 6), just before an adjournment to wait on the reports of committees. Many of the rigid Federalists among the Framers feared that the senior member from Connecticut would agree to no more than a "patching" of the system of government under the Articles. They misjudged him. Yet they were correct in expecting that he would give them problems. Sherman had a clear view of the purposes which a new Constitution should serve: "The great end of the federal government is to protect the several states in the enjoyment of [such] rights [as concern local interests and customs] against foreign invasion, and to preserve peace and a beneficial intercourse among themselves; and to regulate and protect our commerce with foreign nations." On June 6 he had announced these objectives. Never did he agree that there were others of any major importance. Yet it was also his view that "the people immediately should have as little to do as may be about the Government. They want information and are constantly liable to be misled." Add to this his warning that "the Constitution should lay as few temptations as is possible in the way of those in power," and there emerges a very minimal sort of Federal government, neither energetic nor democratic, with the legislative branch having the greatest share of authority, limited as it might be. "Diversity," he maintained, was itself a "security against the abuse of power." He fostered the Connecticut Plan not only to protect the small states, but also to protect the states *per se.* Arguing against the theoretical egalitarianism of James Wilson, he came down sharply against a simplistic view of law in society: "the question is not what rights naturally belong to men, but how [the rights that men enjoy] can be... effectually guarded in society." Hence, it would "not comport with their interests if the Federal government were to interfere with the government of particular states."

Sherman had what was for an Antifederalist an unusual objection to the inclusion of a Bill of Rights in the Constitution. According to his most recent biographer, Christopher Collier, "opposition to anything like a Bill of Rights was a function of his states' rights position." For the Federal authority to define and guarantee human rights would result in a power of oversight concerning questions related to the internal order of the states. And on the "rights of man," the states were in no way agreed. Or rather, on the "rights of man" *in society*. The dour sage from Connecticut insisted, "State Declarations of Rights are not Repealed by this Constitution and, being in force, are sufficient." A Federal Bill of Rights might be either too radical or too conservative. But that was not the important distinction. What signified was rather that in either case the language involved would allow the general government to act upon the relations of individuals within the states on the basis of normative distinctions, not procedural rules, and thus would release that government to do whatever it conceived to be "good." Connecticut did not want Pennsylvania and Virginia voting to abolish the "New England Way." Nor would South Carolina agree that Massachusetts should have power to judge concerning slavery in Charleston. In Sherman's judgment, *any* reference to the "peculiar institution" would be a mistake—excepting perhaps a fugitive slave clause. The result of any official mention would be to extend jurisdiction into areas where it had not existed and would require eventually either approval or disapprobation of an established pattern. On the other hand, if nothing was said, either way, slavery could be left where it stood and the necessity to "part with" the deep South, for whom it was a *sine qua non*, avoided.

Sherman's other objections to a Bill of Rights were even more penetrating: if *any* restraints upon the Federal authority to regulate the lives of citizens were to be included, then all conceivable restraints that were intended would have to be added to them, lest silence be converted into license. It was better that the Constitution spell out what the government might do and then reiterate that its "objects were limited." Sherman's reasoning on these questions was as sophisticated as any that appears in the records of the Great Convention. It is understandable that he should have the reputation of being "one of the most sensible men in the world."

On the question of the relative importance of the three branches of the proposed Federal government, Roger Sherman came down decisively on the side of legislative supremacy. He wished to see the Chief Executive chosen by the Congress or the state legislatures. Moreover, he thought that the President should serve at the "pleasure" of the Congress. He wanted the national legislature to be involved in the writing of treaties and he disliked the idea of the Presidential veto. Federal judges, he believed, should be limited in power, appointed by the United States Senate, and subject to removal by the President upon recommendation of both Houses of the Congress. He was ready to question the propriety of allowing the Chief Executive to remove his own executive appointments, or to grant pardons. Sherman feared the political consequences of a standing army and declared, "We can't be too careful of military encroachments." He was directly responsible for the limitations on Federal authority over militia in the states. Furthermore, he hoped to keep at that level the process by which conditions for suffrage and office-holding were to be decided. He wanted no canal-making power and no national college, and doubted that the Congress should have authority to grant commercial charters. Only within a very restricted economic sphere was he any kind of Federalist. Yet he would accept what was "expedient," at least up to a point—so long as the future influence of the states was protected by their equal voice in one house of a bicameral legislature. Sherman wanted the general government to be representative of the *states,* not the people. He joined with the Southerners (with whom he may have made an arrangement in regard to slavery and navigation laws) in blocking the attempt to authorize a tax on exports. He was quick to point out Gouverneur Morris' omission of important commas from the sentence containing a reference to the "general welfare." Throughout the Convention, Sherman seemed to be involved in almost every important discussion. When a draft had been prepared for submission to the states, he was well satisfied and praised the document as one that "could not have been made on mere speculation."

Roger Sherman was extremely influential in the struggle over ratification in Connecticut, where there was probably a popular majority against the Constitution, and wrote a series of essays in the local papers urging adoption and assuring the ordinary citizens that "there are few powers vested in the new government but what the present Congress have power to do or request to be done." In the Connecticut ratification convention, he allowed the younger Oliver Ellsworth, his disciple, to carry much of the burden of debate. Yet Sherman's support was the determining factor in the overwhelming Federalist margin of victory, with many local-minded men brought over finally by Sherman's example. In 1789 he was elected one of Connecticut's original Congressmen and was one of the most outspoken members of the First Congress. A hard-money man, he wanted the debt retired in full, supported the main ingredients of Alexander Hamilton's financial "system" and was a figure in the compromise which authorized Federal assumption of state debts in return for the location of the permanent capital on the Potomac. He opposed the Bill of Rights, as he had promised to do, but then accepted it as prudent—given the temper of the people.

At the age of 70, in 1791 Roger Sherman was elected United States Senator from Connecticut and concluded his long career of public service in that office. All of his politics rested finally on the experience in self-government of "the Godly people of Connecticut," under their old colonial Charter. To the time of his death in New Haven in 1793, he labored for his people as a New England equivalent of Patrick Henry to leave a "negative" over hurtful innovation in their possession. In the Constitutional Convention, he had been Connecticut's member on the Great Committee, which had been appointed shortly after he had made the house aware that unless accommodation was attempted, their business was at "full stop" and that fruitless dissolution was likely. He had also helped to prevent the inclusion of a Federal veto power over state laws. Though an Old Light Congregationalist who believed to the end that the "threatenings of divine law against impenitent sinners... are [as important] as the promises of the gospel," he had a strong faith in the ability of his neighbors to conduct their own business with probity and justice. His Connecticut was in essence a closed society, a corporate regime of which he approved. He even went so far as to raise some doubt about the admission of "persons of different education, manners and customs" whose immigration might "tend to disturb... tranquility." But despite all of his craft, he was a statesman who recognized that debt was a moral question, a provincial who seconded Franklin's belated motion for prayers to be said over the Framers prior to the opening of their sessions, and a Senator who could openly advise his countrymen in a published sermon, "Let us live no more to ourselves, but to him who loved us and gave himself to die for us." Sherman's understanding of what was accomplished in Philadelphia differed drastically from that of James Madison and James Wilson, whose designs for a government he in many respects forestalled. The record of his participation in these events should serve as a correction of simplistic Federalist theories concerning their significance. For it was as much Sherman's Constitution as Madison's or Wilson's. Otherwise, Connecticut would have voted a resounding "no." (See Christopher Collier, *Roger Sherman's Connecticut: Yankee Politics and the American Revolution* [Middleton, Conn.: Wesleyan University Press, 1971]; Roger Sherman Boardman, *Roger Sherman: Signer and Statesman* [New York: Da Capo Press, 1971]; Lewis Henry Boutell, *The Life of Roger Sherman* [Chicago: A. C. McClurg and Co., 1896]; Oscar Zeichner, *Connecticut's Years of Controversy, 1750–1776* [Chapel Hill: University of North Carolina Press, 1949]; Roger Waln, Jr., pp. 199–306 of Vol. III, *Biography of the Signers to the Declaration of Independence* [Philadelphia: R. W. Pomeroy, 1823], ed. by J. Sanderson; Julian P. Boyd, "Roger Sherman: Portrait of a Cordwainer Statesman," *New England Quarterly*, V [April, 1932], 221–236; Richard J. Purcell, *Connecticut in Transition, 1775–1818*, 2nd ed. [Middleton, Conn.: Wesleyan University Press, 1963]; H. James Henderson, *Party Politics in the Continental Congress* [New York: McGraw-Hill, 1974]; Bernard C. Steiner, "Connecticut's Ratification of the Federal Constitution," *Proceedings* of the American Antiquarian Society, XXV, n.s. [April, 1915], 70–127; Larry Gerlach, "Toward a More Perfect Union: Connecticut, the Continental Congress and the Constitutional Convention," *Bulletin of the Connecticut Historical Society,* XXXIV [July, 1969], 65–78; Philip Harding Jordan, Jr., "Connecticut During the Revolution and Confederation, 1776–1789," Ph.D. dissertation, Yale University, 1962; Forrest McDonald, *E Pluribus Unum: The Formation of the American Republic, 1776–1790* [Indianapolis: Liberty Press, 1979], esp. pp. 291–294; and John G. Rommel, *Connecticut's Yankee Patriot: Roger Sherman* [Hartford: The American Revolution Bicentennial Commission of Connecticut, 1979].)

William Samuel Johnson

(October 7, 1727–November 14, 1819), lawyer, educator, religious leader, and statesman.

A figure of great distinction, both in Connecticut and in all the Confederation, *before* his election to a seat in the Constitutional Convention. A force for moderation, in Philadelphia and throughout his long career in public life. Decidedly a man of the law, of the great Anglo-American legal prescription, and no democrat. A man who declared in a moment of self-revelation, "I must live in peace or I cannot live at all." A neutral (with Loyalist leanings) during the Revolution, who nevertheless retained the regard of his neighbors even when they favored separation from the mother country. In 1787 perhaps the first citizen of his state. An Old Whig *cum* Federalist who had honored the English Constitution as sovereign before 1776 and who wanted another sovereign law to replace it once independence had been achieved. Son of the Rev. Dr. Samuel Johnson (1696–1777), Connecticut's first native-born Anglican minister, first president of King's College, and a philosopher of note, and of Charity Floyd Johnson, originally of Brookhaven on Long Island. Great-great-grandson of Robert Johnson of Yorkshire, England, who in 1638 had come over the ocean to assist in founding a "godly commonwealth" at New Haven. Born at Stratford, Connecticut, where his father had a flourishing parish. Educated at home and at Yale, where he was graduated in 1744 and took an M.A. in 1747. Also awarded an honorary M.A. from Harvard and M.A. and LL.D. from Oxford. Trained for the church, but, to Samuel Johnson's great disappointment, turned to the law. Read thoroughly in that discipline under the direction of William Smith, Jr., of New York. Admitted to the Connecticut bar in 1749. Rose swiftly to the head of his profession, with a practice among New York merchants and in his own state. Though a devout Anglican throughout his days, chosen for public responsibilities in Stratford as early as 1753 (military). Selectman of his town in 1760. Represented Stratford in the House of Representatives in 1761 and

1765–1766. From 1766 to 1776 (except when in England), member of the Council or upper house of the Connecticut legislature. Colonial agent of his state in London from 1767–1771. Reluctantly caught up in the quarrel between the Colonies and the British government.

William Samuel Johnson was one of Connecticut's delegates to the Stamp Act Congress of 1765 and signed the petitions produced by that body. He openly disapproved of every English attempt to raise a revenue out of North Americans who had no representation in Parliament. After a brief delay, while he doubted the utility of resistance, this American Dr. Johnson became a strong supporter of the colonial embargo on trade with Great Britain—at least until distasteful laws such as the Sugar Act, the Stamp Act, and the Townshend Duties were repealed; and the extension of vice-admiralty jurisdiction to a new court in Halifax where Americans might be tried without a jury of their peers, revoked. While acting as agent for the Connecticut government (and despite his connections in the hierarchy of the Church of England and his 1766 Oxford doctorate in law), he acquired a reputation in the mother country as a spokesman for the "popular party" and a vigorous defender of the right of all Englishmen, everywhere, to the protection of their Constitution. But he argued this case on the grounds of legal, historic, and inherited rights—not upon a philosophical doctrine of natural rights. Indeed, he had a horror of dialectical politics, so much so that he once declared, "Certain political questions, like some intricate points in Divinity, had better never be meddled with. The discussion of them can hardly do any good and will certainly produce much mischief. While they serve to whet the wits of men, they more surely sharpen their tempers toward each other." He called for prudence among his countrymen in their responses to "despotic" English policies, and for an avoidance of noisy abstractions, realizing all the while that a revolution against British authority conducted in the name of abstract rights or precisian legal claims would produce a weak, divided, almost ungovernable nation in the colonies, once they acquired their independence. Moreover, such changes would mean the end of the order of things in Connecticut which he well loved. As the fires of revolution spread among his countrymen, Johnson asked, "When shall we come to a right understanding of these great or at least curious questions of right... [and see] that it is dangerous or at least unnecessary to define precisely these deep and difficult objects?" Until 1787 he got no answer.

After returning to New England following his tenure as London agent for Connecticut, William Samuel Johnson did all that he could to further "moderate men or moderate measures." "With no others" would he "be concerned." Because of what he had seen in England, he doubted that there was a conscious plot against the liberties of Americans on the part of the ministers of King George III: "The truth perhaps is that neither side is so bad or have so mischievous designs as the other imagines... and [yet] we are in danger of falling together by the ears in the dark." He knew, as early as 1766, that revolution was likely. But he was determined to resist the trend. For the thought and the language of the new American leaders, those who would most likely inherit authority once the conflict began, disturbed him deeply. In Massachusetts there was an outcry for the Rights of Man. But for Johnson, the "principles and spirit of the [English] Constitution" were sufficient. He continued as a member of the Governor's Council, the first Episcopalian to be so elevated in Connecticut. He was appointed Judge of the Superior Court and colonel of the militia. And he received the official "thanks of the Assembly" for his labors in England. In 1774 he was elected delegate for Connecticut to the Continental Congress. The last of these honors he refused, and the other posts he resigned. Dr. Johnson delayed announcing his disapproval of the Declaration of Independence as long as he could, nor was he about to leave Stratford, or bear arms against its citizens. About his American identity, there was never any doubt. But in 1777 when a law required that officers of the Connecticut courts swear an Oath of Fidelity to the new, independent government of the state, Johnson declined. He returned, for what he thought would be the duration of the conflict with England, to private life.

The circumstance of the Revolution, however, drew William Samuel Johnson back from the fringes of his society sometime before the war was concluded. In the summer of 1779, after a number of British raids on the exposed coast of Connecticut, Johnson's neighbors asked him to negotiate an immunity for Stratford with the threatening British authorities in New York. Reluctantly, the cautious conservative attorney agreed to intercede, on condition that the townspeople sign a pledge to support and exonerate him should any blame attend the enterprise. On learning of these events, Connecticut authorities were horrified and Johnson was arrested. Gov. Jonathan Trumbull and the members of the Council found no fault in Johnson's part in this business. But in order to clear away the confusion he felt himself compelled to swear allegiance to the new regime. Soon thereafter his entire situation began to improve, and he resumed the practice of law. He was called upon by the officers of the state government to plead the case of Connecticut in a special court set up to hear the dispute over the Susquehanna lands in Pennsylvania. And in 1784 he was chosen as a delegate to the Continental Congress for the following year. In that capacity Johnson won for Connecticut a concession of considerable proportions in the new Northwest Territory. All at once he was again a very respected figure, mentioned as a probable governor, recognized as the leader of the Connecticut bar, and thought of in terms of a college presidency, either at King's College [now Columbia] or at the College of Philadelphia. Johnson was still a Connecticut delegate to Congress when nominated for a seat in the Constitutional Convention. His was the first name chosen by the Connecticut Assembly.

William Samuel Johnson when he first heard of the prospects of an attempt to revise the Articles of Confederation had been opposed. He feared that his countrymen were in a mood to make a bad government worse. Yet, once in Philadelphia, he was pleased by the quality of the various delegations and gave himself to the work at hand. Since 1783 he had been of the opinion that the absence of commercial regulations and the failure to raise a revenue had left the Congress without the power necessary to conduct any kind of government. And, like most colonial leaders, he had been alarmed by Captain Shays' Rebellion, which had spilled over the Connecticut border at Sharon. Perhaps, with these eruptions as a backdrop, the "timidity and obstinacy" of the states could be overcome without endangering their existence or taking away too much of their power. After June 2, when he arrived at the Great Convention, until its work was finally done, William Samuel Johnson was constant in his attendance of each day's sessions. He joined with his Connecticut colleagues, Roger Sherman and Oliver Ellsworth, in arguing for equal representation for the states in the national legislature—or at least in one of its chambers. Said Johnson, since state governments were not to be destroyed and the new Federal authority was "not for the people of America but for the political societies called states which compose the Union. . . , they [the states] must, therefore, have a voice in the second branch, if it was meant to preserve their existence, the people composing already the first." Johnson was very effective in making his case for the United States Senate, with an equal vote for each state. As one of the senior members of the Convention, he was eloquent for preserving "some portion of sovereignty" in the states. Ours would be a Union of the States, both federal and national in its design, or no Union at all.

Both Sherman and Ellsworth spoke more frequently than William Samuel Johnson. Due to their efforts Connecticut got most of what it wanted. Yet combinations with the delegations of other states were necessary to the success of a cautious policy—usually combinations with the men of the South. Johnson was quick to help, to defend the compromise on representation, and even to suggest that the planters be allowed to vote all of their Negroes when some of his fellow Northerners sought to make a point about slavery. Such "considerations" of "morality," the Connecticut delegates insisted, belonged only "to the states." His friend Jeremiah Wadsworth reported, "The Southern delegates are vastly fond of him." His manners and sweetness of temper were proverbial. He was no Puritan, and had a long record of public service. Charming and gracious to all, he was a gentleman, and had a few slaves of his own. But, most importantly, he set himself against any trend that would lead his country toward a commitment to ideological politics. He continued to be unwilling to argue from definition. With regret he had come away from the protection of a sovereign law, and to that kind of protection he now hoped to repair. To law and equity based on experience and the English form of jurisprudence—all of it that could be preserved in the new order of things.

Law and equity, but not disembodied principle, which is easily corrupted into a license for despotism.

William Samuel Johnson went from Philadelphia back to Connecticut, where, after a brief trip to New York and acceptance of the presidency of Columbia College, he led the discussion and made the defense of the new Constitution in his native state's ratification convention. Despite his new assignment in the Empire State, Johnson was chosen as one of Connecticut's original United States Senators, in which office he served until 1791, when the government removed to Philadelphia. In the Senate he supported Hamilton's financial system and was an influence in securing the adoption of the Judiciary Act of 1789, expressing always his eagerness to preserve a continuity with English antecedents. His tenure as the first president of Columbia and successor to his father continued until 1800. In that office he distinguished himself greatly, recruiting a good faculty and establishing the school on a firm foundation for its future development. Unlike many college presidents of his day, he kept the spirit of the French Revolution (which he deplored) off the campus of his school. Age and poor health forced his retirement. However, once back at Stratford he revived and lived to the great age of 92, making him the longest-lived of the Framers. In his last years he was instrumental in organizing the Protestant Episcopal Church in America, thus fulfilling his father's dream, was a guide and counselor to the young attorneys and public men of his state and a beloved patriarchal figure. (See Elizabeth P. McCaughey, *From Loyalist to Founding Father: The Political Odyssey of William Samuel Johnson* [New York: Columbia University Press, 1980]; William Allen Benton, *Whig-Loyalism: An Aspect of Political Ideology in the American Revolutionary Era* [Rutherford, N. J.: Fairleigh Dickinson University Press, 1969]; George C. Groce, Jr., *William Samuel Johnson, A Maker of the Constitution* [New York: Columbia University Press, 1937]; E. Edwards Beardsley, *The Life and Times of William Samuel Johnson, LL.D.* [New York: Hurd and Houghton, 1876]; Larry Gerlach, "Toward a More Perfect Union: Connecticut, the Continental Congress and the Constitutional Convention," *Bulletin of the Connecticut Historical Society*, XXXIV [July, 1969], 65–78; Evarts Boutell Greene, "William Samuel Johnson and the American Revolution," *Columbia University Quarterly*, XXII [June, 1930], 152–178; David C. Humphrey, *From King's College to Columbia, 1746–1800* [New York: Columbia University Press, 1976].)

Oliver Ellsworth

(April 29, 1745–November 26, 1807), lawyer, jurist, and American statesman.

Mild Federalist, but only on the condition that the small states keep their equality of representation in one house of the national legislature. The least idealistic of Puritans. Vigorous defender of states' rights within the Federal Union. Warm advocate of the compromise between the sections on the counting of slaves for the purpose of allotting Congressional seats. Enemy of the teleocratic or normative approach to the relation of the Federal power and the internal operations of the member commonwealths: "Let every state import what it pleases. The morality or wisdom of slavery are considerations belonging to the states themselves. What enriches a part, enriches the whole, and the states are the best judges of their particular interest. . . . Let us not intermeddle." A great inducement to moderation and confidence in their future within the Union for the Southern Framers present in the Great Convention. A man of the letter of the law from his early youth. After 1789 utterly alarmed at the influence of the French Revolution on some of his countrymen. An Anglophile, where American interests were not threatened by English power. As a judge, precisely the kind of person that he was as a Framer, convinced that "it is of more importance, for a judicial determination, to ascertain what the law is, than to speculate what it ought to be." An active member of the Constitutional Convention, where he spoke 84 times. A father of the great tradition of the moderate or "cotton" Whigs—the party of Daniel Webster, Rufus Choate, and Robert Winthrop.

Oliver Ellsworth was born at Windsor, Connecticut, the son of Captain David Ellsworth and Jemima Leavitt Ellsworth. His great-grandfather, Josiah Ellsworth, had come from Yorkshire, England, to Windsor *ca.* 1650. Oliver's father intended him for the Congregationalist ministry and had him prepared to enter Yale by the Rev. Joseph Bellamy of Bethlehem, Connecticut. Young Oliver went up to New Haven in 1762, but was not happy among the sons of Eli, and at the end of his sophomore year transferred to the College of New Jersey, from which he was graduated in 1766. Upon returning home, he took up the study of theology but did not long continue in that labor and turned instead to reading in the law, as had many of his friends at Princeton. To support himself in this endeavor, he cut and sold timber and farmed land belonging to his father. In 1771 he was admitted to the bar. However, he did not prosper rapidly in the law. But Oliver Ellsworth was a man of firm convictions. Slowly he developed a reputation for competence and rectitude. In 1773 his neighbors in Windsor named him their deputy to the General Assembly. Within a few years he was the most famous attorney in Connecticut, with land and houses, money to lend, and interests in many enterprises. His style in speaking and writing turned magisterial, and his appearance became "scrupulously elegant." In 1775 he moved to Hartford and was never far from the center of Connecticut's political life in the remainder of his career.

During the American Revolution Oliver Ellsworth committed himself to the Patriot cause almost from the beginning. From 1775 he was a member of the Connecticut Committee of the Pay Table, which supervised the state's military expenditures. Two years later he became the State's Attorney for Hartford County, in which office he continued until 1785. In 1777 he was chosen as one of Connecticut's delegates to the Continental Congress, where he sat until 1783. And in 1779, while serving as deputy from Hartford, he was made a member of the Connecticut Council of Safety, the chief governing body of the state for purposes of self-defense. From 1780–1785, Ellsworth had a place on the Governor's Council. In Congress, Ellsworth was much involved with American maritime concerns. He was appointed to a committee to hear appeals from state courts and admiralty and in that capacity sought to uphold the authority of the general government. He was also vigorous in collecting supplies for Washington's army, scrupulous in his management of funds while on the Board of Treasury, interested in treaties and trade, and eager to bring peace with England, assuming that the restoration of friendly relations with the mother country, once independence had been achieved, would best serve the development of England's former colonies. In the Continental Congress Ellsworth often voted with members of a New England "bloc" and often gave priority to the special concerns of his own state. After the conclusion of the war, though he was a confirmed cultural pluralist from his first appearance on the national scene and though he was unwilling to surrender Connecticut's control over its own identity, Oliver Ellsworth served gladly with James Madison and Alexander Hamilton on a special committee of the Congress called upon to create a comprehensive system of administration. In 1784 Ellsworth was appointed a member of Connecticut's Supreme Court of Errors, and shortly thereafter was named a judge of the Connecticut Superior Court. Meanwhile, behind the scenes he moved cautiously toward nationalism, writing to Governor Jonathan Trumbull, "There *must,* Sir, be a revenue somehow established that can be relied on, and applied for national purposes as the exigencies arise, independent of the will or views of a single state, or it will be impossible to support national faith or national existence. The power of the Congress must be adequate to the purposes of their constitution. It is possible, there may be abuses and misapplication, still it is better to hazard *something*, than to hazard all." In such a cautious spirit and though still a "local-minded" man, Ellsworth went toward the Constitutional Convention, hopeful, as he said in Philadelphia, of "building on the states"—out of their integrity, not at its expense—"our general government."

In the Great Convention the motto of Oliver Ellsworth, in dealing with High Federalists who were likely to spoil the business completely, was in keeping with his politics at other important times in his life: "Let not too much be attempted." As his biographer, William Garrott Brown, has observed, Ellsworth did not "conceive of the people of the whole country either as the true constituency of the Convention, or as the source of authority for the new government." The sovereignty of the general government, in its restricted sphere, would have to be derived from the states. He would have nothing to do with a theory like James Wilson's—that the Declaration of Independence created one nation, not thirteen. Ellsworth wanted a Union "partly federal and partly national." It fell to him to make the final motion that every state be represented equally in the second branch of the Congress of the United States (June 29), even as they had been under the Articles of Confederation. He carried much of the burden of debate for the small state men opposed to the Virginia Plan for Union. The United States Senate would be like the House of Lords in the English system—a check on foolish popular majorities. It could not dominate, but it might restrain. "We know," Ellsworth said in Philadelphia, that "the people of the states are strongly attached to their own constitutions. If you hold up a system of government destructive of their constitutional rights, they will oppose it. The only chance we have to support a general government is to graft it on the state governments," so that "the United States are sovereign on their side of the line dividing jurisdictions—the states on the other"—with both having "power to defend their respective sovereignties."

Ellsworth was opposed to including a Federal power of veto over state legislation. Furthermore, he hoped to minimize Federal authority over state militias and to preclude by law uninvited Federal invasions of states experiencing internal disorders. If the President was not to be chosen by the state legislatures, he recommended that members of the Electoral College be selected there. And he favored provision for the salaries of members of the proposed Congress through legislation in the states. To the centralizers among the Framers, he issued a warning which looked toward the political difficulty of ratification: "If we are so exceedingly jealous of the state legislatures, will they not have reason to be jealous of us?" Concerning the regulation of suffrage, he spoke to the same effect: "The states are the best judges of the circumstances and temper of their own people." Ellsworth's part in the discussion of slavery should be interpreted in the context of these related misgivings about attempting too much. Indirectly he reproached George Mason for being moralistic about the slave trade, while continuing one of America's major slaveholders. He observed with irony that if slavery "was to be considered in a moral light, we ought to go farther and free those already in the country," knowing that the Virginians, who could raise all the slaves that they needed and sell the surplus at a greater profit if the trade were discontinued, would agree to nothing of the kind. Ellsworth was a realist who saw the danger of division, probably at the Delaware River, with states ready to "fly into a variety of shapes and directions" if the Framers were doctrinaire. As Connecticut was protective of its own peculiarities, so he expected other states to be of theirs. Throughout his lifetime he opposed disestablishment of the churches in Connecticut. Moreover, in the Continental

Congress he had supported a proclamation against "evil amusements," such as "play going, gaming, and horse races." But such Godly sentiments were only *advisory*. Ellsworth was unusual among his New England "brethren" in recognizing that all Americans did not and would not share in one system of values. If a Constitution were to be produced, every portion of the Union could be asked to agree upon procedures and to surrender whatever authority or practice that was not essential to its well-being—just as Connecticut was willing to give up its preference for an annually elected national legislature, once Abraham Baldwin had explained the inconvenience such an arrangement would impose on Georgia and South Carolina. Slavery, as the Connecticut men understood, was not negotiable if Union was to be achieved. Ellsworth, who was the only Connecticut delegate who neither owned slaves nor had slaveholders in his family, had little patience with self-serving declarations. Toward the end of the Convention he admonished his colleagues that time was running short. On or about the 25th of August, with most of the discussion complete, he left Philadelphia—knowing that Sherman and Johnson could represent his views while he saw to his judicial duties in Connecticut.

In the struggle over ratification of the Constitution in Connecticut, Oliver Ellsworth played a central role. In the state convention of January, 1788 called upon to judge of that document, Ellsworth made the principal address, in which he argued that under the terms of the Federal compact "this is a government of strictly defined powers," in which the "particular states retain their sovereignty" where it is not clearly surrendered. He compared Connecticut, surrounded by states which under the Articles were free to tax its commerce if shipped through their ports, to "Issachar of old, a strong ass crouching down between two burdens" [Genesis 49:14]. Ellsworth's exposition of the Constitution was accepted by an overwhelming majority of the Connecticut ratifying convention. He also wrote many essays in the press, under the name "Landholder," which urged approval of what had been achieved in Philadelphia. Some of these were in reply to Elbridge Gerry and Luther Martin. They were widely circulated in several states.

From 1789 to 1796, Ellsworth was United States Senator from Connecticut, in which office he was one of the firmest pillars in the Washington administration. He was the author of the Judiciary Act and responsible for the adoption of most of Alexander Hamilton's financial "system." He wrote the act accepting North Carolina's cession of her Western lands and another act which provided government for the unorganized territory south of the Ohio River. His embargo on Rhode Island compelled that troublesome commonwealth to ratify the Constitution and join the Union. In return for location of the nation's permanent capital on the Potomac, he persuaded Southerners to agree to a Federal assumption of state debts. During his years in the Senate, he was perhaps its most influential member and is to be remembered for his role in creating the instruments and agencies of a new government under the Constitution. He believed in judicial review as a means of preserving the Constitutional balance of powers between the individual states and the United States. In 1796, President Washington appointed Oliver Ellsworth Chief Justice of the United States Supreme Court, in which office he continued until 1800. On the Federal Bench, Justice Ellsworth was involved in only a few important cases and showed little disposition to expand the scope of the High Court's authority. In *Wiscart vs. Dauchy*, his ruling (based on his own authority as author of the Judiciary Act of 1789) restricted the review power in cases of equity and is in contradiction with the judicial logic of his successor, John Marshall. Ellsworth also affirmed the authority of the English common law in the courts of the United States. In one instance, he went so far as to enforce it against the British consul in Charleston, S. C. Perhaps his most unusual decision, in *United States vs. Isaac Williams*, maintained that United States citizens had no right of expatriation. Justice Ellsworth found the life of the Federal judge to be extremely wearisome and tedious, particularly the long journeys on the circuit.

In 1799, President John Adams named Oliver Ellsworth, William Richardson Davie of North Carolina, and William Vans Murray of Maryland to serve as Commissioners to the French Republic to negotiate an accord that would adjust differences which had brought the two countries to the brink of war. The French had been seizing and harassing American vessels under the decree declaring all trade with England to be contraband. The American emissaries had been dispatched in the expectation that they would deal with Talleyrand and the Directory—the government which had recently insulted a mission made up of Charles Cotesworth Pinckney, Elbridge Gerry, and John Marshall. Instead, they were confronted with the recently elevated First Consul, Napoleon Bonaparte. The new French government would not agree to reparations indemnifying Americans for losses, but the French did accept a redefinition of contraband which restricted the term to mean military supplies and agreed to follow more responsible and regular policies in their treatment of captured American property. The issue of this negotiation was the Convention of Montefontaine in October of 1800. Neither Federalists nor Democratic-Republicans were satisfied with this treaty, though the Congress ratified it in February, 1801. Oliver Ellsworth's health had collapsed during the long voyage to Europe, and he was ill during much of the negotiation. In the attempt to regain his strength, he tarried a while in France and visited briefly in England. The European experience confirmed his opinion of the French Revolution as one which "ignored the selfish nature of man" and he was further convinced of the importance of English heritage to Americans. Upon his return to the United States, Ellsworth retired from national politics, though he served again from 1802 until his death in 1807 on the Connecticut Governor's Council. In these last years his health continued to decline, but he remained cheerful and active in agriculture (on his farm near Windsor) and in the affairs of his state. Throughout his life he was an orthodox Congregationalist and disapproved of the Deism of such advanced spirits as the new President, Thomas Jefferson. Yet he never encouraged any of the secessionist tendencies that were so widespread among the New England Federalists following Jefferson's election: indeed, refused to do so even though he had in 1794 recommended to John Taylor of Caroline the legality of peaceful secession as an option open to the South. At the time of his death, Oliver Ellsworth was Connecticut's leading citizen, one of the "river gods" of the Connecticut River Valley who had directed their state in a temperate course during the difficult period of transition which saw the birth of the Republic. (See William Garrott Brown, *The Life of Oliver Ellsworth* [New York: Da Capo Press, 1970]; Richard J. Purcell, *Connecticut in Transition, 1775–1818*, 2nd ed. [Middleton, Conn.: Wesleyan University Press, 1963]; Christopher Collier, *Roger Sherman's Connecticut: Yankee Politics and the American Revolution* [Middleton, Conn.: Wesleyan University Press, 1971]; Larry Gerlach, "Toward a More Perfect Union: Connecticut, the Continental Congress and the Constitutional Convention," *Bulletin of the Connecticut Historical Society*, XXXIV [July, 1969], 65–78; Bernard C. Steiner, "Connecticut's Ratification of the Federal Constitution," *Proceedings* of the American Antiquarian Society, XXV, n. s. [April, 1915], 70–127; Philip Harding Jordan, Jr., "Connecticut During the Revolution and Confederation, 1776–1789," Ph.D. dissertation, Yale University, 1962; Michael Kraus, "Oliver Ellsworth," pp. 223–235 of Vol. 1 of *The Justices of the United States Supreme Court, 1789–1969: Their Lives and Major Opinions* [New York: R. R. Bowker/Chelsea House, 1969], ed. by Leon Friedman and Fred L. Israel; H. James Henderson, *Party Politics in the Continental Congress* [New York: McGraw-Hill, 1974]; William C. Dennis, II, "A Federalist Persuasion: The American Ideal of the Connecticut Federalists," Ph.D. dissertation, Yale University, 1971; and Ronald John Lettieri, *Connecticut's Young Man of the Revolution: Oliver Ellsworth* [Hartford: The American Revolution Bicentennial Commission of Connecticut, 1978].)

Alexander Hamilton

(Jan. 11, 1757–July 12, 1804), soldier, lawyer, statesman, economist, and political philosopher.

Founder of the Federalist Party, and its leader, both in New York and throughout the nation. Though one of the Fathers of the Republic, important in the Constitutional Convention primarily as a foil to milder nationalists, who could appear to be reasonable in comparison with his attitude toward the concentration of power. The most extreme of High Federalists. With James Wilson and two or three other delegates, ready to abolish the several states as distinct political entities. Yet skilled in state and local politics, and primarily responsible for securing New York's ratification of the document produced in Philadelphia. As one of the authors of *The Federalist* and as author of the doctrine of implied powers, a permanent influence on the interpretation of the United States Constitution. A man of extraordinary gifts, almost a prodigy, but possessed of a certain confidence, with a touch of swagger and hyperbole, that earned him enemies throughout his career. Born on the island of Nevis, one of the Leeward chain in the West Indies. Natural son of James Hamilton of Ayshire, Scotland, fourth son of Alexander Hamilton, the laird of Grange; and of Rachel Fawcett, the daugher of a French planter and physician. The union of his parents, perhaps sanctioned by some kind of ceremony, but illegal, and, by reason of certain irregularities, at best a common law marriage. Marked throughout his life by the stigma of his origins. Without a father from an early age and all but an orphan at eleven. Educated privately on St. Croix, in apprenticeship to the island firm of Nicholas Cruger; at Francis Barber's school in Elizabethtown, New Jersey; and at King's College [now Columbia] in New York, where he was enrolled in 1773. A superb and systematic student and at seventeen, with the growing dispute between the American colonies and the ministers of George III, a fledgling orator and political pamphleteer. Left school without a degree for military responsibilities in the American army in the spring of 1776.

Alexander Hamilton did commendable service as a captain of artillery during the retreat from New York, in the following campaign in New Jersey, and in Washington's winter raids on Trenton and Princeton. But, to his good fortune, either some of his writings or his conduct in the field had caught the attention of the Commander in Chief. Washington's function was so much more than that of general that he required a large staff to sift and organize the information coming into his hands and to execute his orders. Most particularly he needed a secretary with judgment and a skilled pen. As General Washington's aide-de-camp, Hamilton was promoted to the rank of lieutenant colonel, given some of the distinction which his spirit craved, and then thoroughly occupied for the next four years. He distinguished himself in this role and, in the process, established a reputation and a set of contacts which determined the direction of his future development as a public man. But after a small quarrel with General Washington late in the war, Hamilton asked for and received permission to return to duty in the Continental Line, where, at Yorktown, he won glory in a fierce assault on one of Lord Cornwallis' redoubts—a successful night attack which led to the English capitulation. Following the great victory, Hamilton retired from the army and was elected to the Continental Congress, where he sat from late in 1782 on into 1783.

Early study, reinforced by his military experience and the deep-set bias of his mind, disposed Alexander Hamilton to be the consistent "friend to vigorous government": energetic, "creative," yet potentially coercive central government, "national Sovereignty, transcendent and entire." From 1778 through 1787, with an ever-growing firmness, it was Hamilton's view of the American political situation that, once free of George III, we should find a sovereign to act in that sovereign's stead, and should then, with obedience, strengthen that power as best we could. In substitution for Crown in Parliament, some other ground of unity would be required—some American equivalent of the smooth working complexity of Britain's ancient, inherited regime. Only for a short time, as a politically precocious boy, did Hamilton stand in point of tangency with the radical Whigs and expand upon "the sacred rights of mankind... not to be rummaged for among old parchments or musty records [but] written, as with a sunbeam, in the whole volume of human nature by the hand of the divinity itself." Reading in David Hume and leadership experience in the struggles of the Revolution corrected these opinions. By 1778 Hamilton spoke chiefly of the right of "self-preservation" if he spoke of natural rights at all. And in any case, even as a youthful enthusiast of independence, the young philosopher never ceased to approve of the English Constitution as the "best in the world." The Coercive Acts of 1774, the Prohibitory Acts of the next year, and George III's "Proclamation for Suppressing Rebellion and Sedition" had forced Americans to give up their hope of an English "league" of states under a common crown and to consider the Parliament at Westminster as an enemy. Separation from the mother country was, by British policy, made inevitable. But even as independence approached, a guarantee of that liberty for which "he should be as willing a martyr . . . as any man whatever," he took pause and shared with his friend John Jay his anxiety that "the same state of the passions which fits the multitude . . . for opposition to tyranny and oppression . . . naturally leads them to a contempt . . . of all authority."

During the year following Washington's triumph in Virginia, Hamilton read law, wrote his own manual for legal studies, and in April of 1782 was admitted to membership in the New York bar—doing all of this while he served as a delegate to the Continental Congress. But the Alexander Hamilton who in 1783 returned from his political service to open an office on Wall Street and begin most successfully to practice his profession had been cured of any regard for democracy that he might once have entertained and driven beyond any patience he might once have had with the sovereignties of the states. In the Congress he had worked hard to make government in the Confederation functional: to collect the impost, to use army pressure in supporting the funding system of Robert Morris, and to pass a diluted revenue plan. And, as he had done even while still a soldier, he urged behind the scenes that the government be completely redesigned and set upon a proper financial basis. To that end, in 1786 he secured his own election as a New York representative to the convention in Annapolis, Maryland, which was to consider the regulation of interstate commerce and other national problems. There, with James Madison and John Dickinson, he persuaded his colleagues to agree in an address to the states calling for a more general and ambitious assemblage to gather in Philadelphia the following May, there to devise such changes in the bonds of their lawful connection "as shall appear to them necessary to render the constitution of the Federal government adequate to the exigencies of the Union." Hamilton (now an elected member of the incoming New York legislature) was responsible for his state's participation in the Annapolis Convention of 1786, and later took the lead in persuading it to send representatives to the Great Convention of 1787. To bestir the great magnates of his state, he wrote and spoke of the spread of principles of the "leveling kind" and of the security against despotism which only a new government could provide. With the help of Captain Shays, he made Federalists out of narrowly local men.

What Alexander Hamilton hoped to produce through the law-proposing deliberations in Pennsylvania was not so much a government structured in a particular fashion, with a particular set of institutions, but rather a power. As Forrest McDonald writes, "What was important was to organize one [a government] and to endow it with as much power in relation to the powers of the states as possible." Hamilton accepted the necessity for popular support, for affection and attachment and habit in the operations of an effective republican authority. And he also accepted the need for at least one chamber in the national legislature to be chosen by the people at large. But his final objective, even in these concessions, was to engineer in the United States, *on* a republican *basis* (since we *must* have it so), a perfection of the English political system against which we had just finished making war. His differences with the other Framers resolved themselves into disputes over *which* English political tradition we should foster on these shores, the heritage of Sir Robert Walpole and the "system" of the commercial Whigs or that of the "Oppositionists," the champions of distributed power, both Tory and Country Whig. The notion of attempting something completely original and unrelated to the Anglo-American past had really very little support among the authors of the Constitution. Except insofar as some of Hamilton's adversaries insisted that the states would not be one unless they were secure in being many: insisted that the fact of our national origins in established and independent multiplicity be made the basis of our Union. Part of Hamilton's reaction to this insistence bespeaks familiar varieties of military and commercial Federalism. Part of it comes from the fact that he was more or less an immigrant, who never learned to understand or to work with an American political heritage already in place before the Revolution commenced. But the most important ingredient in the position which he assumed in the Great Convention and persisted in as Washington's "first minister" and as head of a national party was his dream of an American Empire, of national happiness and prosperity, power and glory fostered and encouraged through the instrument and agency of government—and particularly with financial policy.

Hamilton did not speak frequently while in Philadelphia. During much of the Convention he was in New York, handling pressing personal business and settling a quarrel between friends. Since the two other delegates from his state in most instances negatived his vote and then, on July 10, cancelled it outright by leaving Independence Hall in disgust with the centralist tendencies of the compact being made there, Hamilton found it difficult to attach any importance to what he might say or do in answering the obstructionism of John Lansing and Robert Yates. Hamilton first left the Convention on June 29, rejoined it briefly in mid-August, and then early in September resumed his seat and was constant in his attendance until the Constitution was finished and signed. But he was present long enough and often enough to get his view of the business on the record and to assist some of the less "high-toned" Federalists in defining the alternatives before the house and in resolving consequent disputes. On June 18, after listening quietly as the Convention divided into two more or less distinctive camps, represented by Randolph and Paterson, Hamilton rose to deliver a speech of five hours' duration. The entire address, which shocked many of his colleagues, concerned the necessity for granting sufficient force to the general government.

Since men "are rather reasoning than reasonable animals," Hamilton argued, and will not honor any authority merely for reason's sake, they must be acted upon directly by the national power, so that interest, necessity, opinion, habit, respect, and ambition make of them better citizens. Free government was superior to absolute monarchy because it could "interest the passions of the community in its favor" and thus beget "public spirit and public confidence." The security of a government lies thus in attachment and custom, not in devotion to abstract principle or philosophical conviction. But the voice of the people is not the voice of God. And the immediate necessity for the American statesman is to "cure the people of their fondness for democracies." To that end, he recommended that the chief executive of the Republic be elected to serve for a life term; and that the members of the Senate, acting in the place of a House of Lords, be provided with an equivalent security in office. For thus the great merits of the English Constitution might be replicated here, innovation checked, property made secure, and a modicum of honor and disinterested virtue in office guaranteed. At least if balanced by a House of Representatives chosen on as "broad" a popular basis as was reasonable.

What Hamilton advocated in this address was of course no tyranny, but rather a regime of the kind Americans, as colonials, had insisted upon *before* the Revolution. He was as attached to Liberty in 1787 as in 1775—Liberty as he understood it. But he would have no part in fostering either a threat to property by legislative confiscation or a threat of general exploitation and unearned advantage by an aristocratic cabal. Better to leave the permanent interests or divisions of society balanced in an institutionalized tension, with the President to preside over their interplay. "Real liberty," Hamilton declared, "neither is found in despotism or the extremes of democracy, but in moderate governments—if we incline too much to democracy, we shall soon shoot into a monarchy."

Hamilton's objective in advancing his plan was to put his fellow Framers in mind of the importance of "stability and permanency" in government and of the respect of foreign powers that our country would have to earn if it expected to survive. That his model for administration winked at monarchy, he admitted freely. Most probably, the alternative to something close to monarchy *was* (from the appearance of things in the United States of 1787) democratic excess, followed by a "man on horseback." Especially once the country had been developed, open lands filled, and widespread inequalities aggravated. His fondest hope was that the Convention would make a fundamental law which Americans would come to love and respect: the kind of law that would diminish the odds in favor of future disorders. But he did not expect most of the other delegates to agree with much of what he proposed. To lift the debates toward consideration of a realistic theory of government would be enough. As he foreknew, his colleagues were not about to abolish the states, to reduce them to the status of mere administrative districts, or to allow the "Governour" [President] to appoint their chief executives. Neither would they give to the national government a veto over legislation in the states. Or the power to create state courts. Such arrangements had already occasioned one revolution. And, for this generation, one was enough. William Samuel Johnson, the wise old man of Connecticut, summarized the Convention's reaction to Col. Hamilton's performance when he declared that "the gentleman from New York [is]. . . praised by every body. . . [but] supported by none."

In his other participations in the debates of the Great Convention, Alexander Hamilton made few broad generalizations or sweeping proposals, and in most cases spoke briefly and to the question at hand. At one point he expressed his distrust of republics, and on another indicated that we might come to monarchy in the end. He identified the great division among the states as being between North and South, commerce and agriculture—not between small and large. He called the states "artificial," in indifference to their various histories. He objected to the election of the President by any formula not involving the people. And he warned the Convention that they would have to produce something, since there would be no second chance to write a Constitution. When the document on which they had agreed left Philadelphia for presentation to the Continental Congress and transmission to the states, it was represented as the approved handiwork of ten delegations "and Mr. Hamilton." Even though he had, on the last day of their gathering, reminded his fellow Framers that "no man's ideas were more remote from the plan than his were known to be" and continued to speak of it thereafter as a "frail and worthless fabric." A fabric which would need young Mr. Hamilton for a "prop."

Yet, to speak fairly, no other American did more to secure the adoption of the new Constitution by the states he so despised than did Alexander Hamilton. In person he organized and conducted the campaign for ratification in New York. And, against great odds, arguing and maneuvering in person, he (with the help of John Jay and Chancellor Robert Livingston) overcame Governor George Clinton and the political leadership of the Empire State. In the moment of crisis during the ratification convention in Poughkeepsie, the advocates of the new Constitution made good use of the approvals voted by other states, with arguments of the benefits that would accrue to New York if it voted yes, and finally of a threat to divide the state—a threat of secession by New York City, which would then join the Union on its own. Hamilton promised that the states would survive the change. The Antifederalists conceded that a new frame of government was needed, that New York could not go its own way, and that prior amendments might make a new instrument palatable. Then they gave way.

On the national scene, as author of most of the material in *The Federalist*,

Hamilton exercised an even greater influence. Of the entire collection of eighty-five essays, Hamilton wrote fifty-two, John Jay five, and James Madison the rest. All of this done in the midst of intense political activity in his own area. It was a remarkable tour de force. Hamilton's part in creating the composite Federalist of Publius foreshadowed the view of the nature and purpose of the revised Federal Union he was to represent in the remainder of his public career. And the same might be said of Madison's contribution. Though in 1788 they appear as Publius in collaboration, what they wrote in that capacity contained the inference of quarrels between them soon to come. Madison in his essays emphasized the division and limitation of powers within the Federal system, Hamilton the good results those powers might produce. Both Madison and Hamilton wrote on subjects which were suggestive of their particular perspectives on what the new government would mean. Hamilton discussed economic concerns, the administrative and judicial functions of the new national authority. Madison wrote in contrast on political theory and history, and on what the government could not do. Both men agreed on the dangers of democracy and the mischief-making propensity of human nature. But Hamilton worked toward employing the passions of that "great beast," the people, to good ends, toward building a practical and progressive politics on a foundation of human weakness, while Madison worried about restraining the impact of these shortcomings with a careful set of counterpoints and negations. Hamilton did not concern himself with making the government "control itself." He thought instead of the limitless potential of sovereignty "as to all those objects entrusted to its management." The two men only appeared to approve of the same Constitution. Or rather, they favored it for very different reasons, with consequences that divided the Union within less than a century.

Alexander Hamilton was appointed, as he had expected to be, the nation's original Secretary of the Treasury in President Washington's cabinet, and exercised probably his greatest influence on the subsequent history of his country while in that office. His financial system for funding the national and state debts, for converting those liabilities into a basis for credit and commercial activity, and for organizing the Bank of the United States have been remembered since his time simply as "Hamiltonianism." These policies when, in 1791, combined with his Report on Manufactures and his written opinion for Washington regarding the constitutionality of the Bank, made of Hamilton the target around which Madison and Jefferson were finally able to gather an opposition party. And thus they were able to construct a lever to redirect the country away from the ambitious designs of the Secretary of the Treasury. The centerpiece of Hamilton's financial magic was, to be sure, nothing but a modification of another British institution, the Bank of England, with tariffs added in support. It made many of his Federalist friends rich men, sometimes at the expense of simple folk who did not understand assumption of discounted paper. Hamilton was, in fact, as Broadus Mitchell has observed, a "holdover from the mercantilist age, utilizing government as an indispensable engine of national improvement." But for his own profit he sought only the fame that belongs to the lawgiver and founder of cities. At the famous dinner party of April 11, 1791, he declared to Jefferson and the other members of Washington's cabinet that Caesar was a greater man than Bacon, Newton, or Locke. Hamilton enacted his role in public life for the sake of glory such as Caesar knew.

Hamilton left the Treasury in 1795, after Washington had rejected much of his plan for commercial development; after he had helped to subdue the Whiskey Rebellion, and after he had reached the point of open conflict with Jefferson. When the Democratic-Republicans established a party newspaper, with Philip Freneau as editor, Hamilton was ubiquitous in reply and was, in Jefferson's words, a "colossus" and "without numbers. . . an host within himself." Hamilton made the most of Jeffersonian involvement with Citizen Genet and the American enthusiasm for the French Revolution. He participated in discussions of foreign affairs within the Washington administration—once injuring his reputation for probity by communicating his impression of American policy to an English friend, Major George Beckwith. And he fought the spread of Jacobinism on these shores with all of his energy. Particularly with his pen did he thunder that "democracy" and "Christian civilization" were incompatible. Outside of the cabinet, he continued to support a pro-British rather than a pro-French connection, emphasizing our continuing commercial connections with the mother country. Moreover, though he approved of Washington's position of noninvolvement in European conflicts, he did not lose sight of the advantages of war as an instrument for internal transformation of the nation. His conduct in the Treasury, and his support of Jay's Treaty, had offended the South. By 1798, he was a politically damaged man—even in New York. Differences with John Adams (not his kind of Federalist) made his problems worse. But despite Adams' succession, Hamilton still had friends in the cabinet, a following, and some genuine power. He continued to retain the regard of the former President, who had been (in Hamilton's words) an "Aegis very necessary" to his own role in the affairs of the Republic. Along with the aging Washington, Hamilton was called back into military service; and in 1798 he was commissioned a major general. However, American diplomats arranged a settlement with France in the Convention of Montefontaine and averted the danger of war. Washington died. The quarrel with Adams grew worse. The Jeffersonians decided they could win the election of 1800 without going through with their plans for secession. John Jay would not take his friend's advice about changing the process for selecting electors in New York. And Hamilton's season on center stage in the drama of American politics was at an end.

Or rather, almost at an end. For Alexander Hamilton played a role in the election of his enemy Thomas Jefferson to be the nation's third President—a role which was instrumental in bringing about Hamilton's death. When Jefferson and Aaron Burr received an equal number of electoral votes for the Presidency, and the resolution of this impasse fell to the House of Representatives, Hamilton advised his fellow Federalists to support Thomas Jefferson, a mistaken man of principle, over the opportunist, Aaron Burr. Yet much of Hamilton's time in his years out of office was taken up not by his obligations as party leader but with the responsibilities of a growing family and an active, distinguished, and profitable practice of law. With his wife, Elizabeth, the daughter of General Philip Schuyler, he built a country place, the Grange—named after the home of his childhood, and the Hamiltons' ancestral seat in Scotland. He continued to worry about the quality of the nation's leadership—despite the fact that Jefferson was "behaving better" than he had expected. To counter the impact of the organized network of the Democratic-Republicans, he drew up a plan for an organization of his own, the Christian Constitutional Society. At about the same time he began to think more and more about religion. He had learned from disappointment and from the death of his son Philip in a duel that his notion of the will was not enough.

When Hamilton for the second time placed a check on the boundless ambitions of Aaron Burr, a check administered by Hamilton during a New York gubernatorial contest, Burr challenged him to a duel. The Federalist leader accepted Burr's challenge, but refused to fire upon his adversary. On the heights of Weehawken, Burr was less scrupulous, and gave to Hamilton a wound which, on July 12, 1804, at two o'clock in the afternoon, proved mortal. (Though Presbyterian by upbringing, Hamilton was an Episcopalian and a few hours before his death received the last rites from New York Bishop Benjamin Moore.) There was a nationwide interval of shock when these events were reported. A revulsion set in against Burr which, ironically, made of Hamilton's death his final public service.

It was characteristic of Alexander Hamilton, both as Framer and as servant and leader of the early Republic, to be a curious combination of self-confidence and deep desire to demonstrate his own worth. He had perhaps too much faith in "heroes" and "great men," and too little in the democratic arrangements which are the essence of a civil society. We should take very seriously his admonition to Jay that "it will not do to be overscrupulous. *It is easy to sacrifice the substantial interests of society by a strict adherence of ordinary rules.*" In economics as in politics he was anachronistically impressed by the honor that could be achieved by managing people and distressed to think that "America if she attains greatness must creep to it." He liked the great game, and he played it for all the ordinary reasons, but also for "heads." Yet his service in designing, selling, organizing, and financing a viable government cannot be contested. Indubitably, he is the author of one of the accepted views of the American regime. And his insight into the dangers to the nation posed by European ideologies has something to teach us even now. For it was Hamilton who declared of the egalitarians of his day that they were "courting the strongest and most active passion of the human heart, *vanity.*" The example of that Hamilton, schooled by Blackstone, Hume, and Swift, will not soon be out of date. (See Forrest McDonald, *Alexander Hamilton: A Biography* [New York: W. W. Norton & Co., 1979]; Gerald Stourgh, *Alexander Hamilton and the Idea of Republican Government* [Stanford: Stanford University Press, 1970]; Broadus Mitchell, *Alexander Hamilton,* 2 vols. [New York: Macmillan, 1957, 1962]; John Chester Miller, *Alexander Hamilton, Portrait in Paradox* [New York: Harper, 1959]; Louis M. Hacker, *Alexander Hamilton in the American Tradition* [New York: McGraw-Hill, 1957]; Nathan Schachner, *Alexander Hamilton* [New York: A. S. Barnes, 1961]; Douglas Adair [with Marvin Harvey], "Was Alexander Hamilton a Christian Statesman?" pp. 141–159 of Adair's *Fame and the Founding Fathers* [New York: W. W. Norton & Co., 1974], ed. by Trevor Colbourn; Linda Grant De Pauw, *The Eleventh Pillar: New York State and the Federal Constitution* [Ithaca: Cornell University Press, 1966]; Harold C. Syrett, ed., *The Papers of Alexander Hamilton,* 26 vols. [New York: Columbia University Press, 1961–1967]; and *William and Mary Quarterly,* 3rd ser., XII, No. 2 [April, 1955], Alexander Hamilton Bicentenial Number.)

John Lansing

(January 30, 1754–December 12, 1829) lawyer, statesman, and jurist.

Antifederalist, both by principle and by connection. Not frightened by Captain Shays, nor by signs of economic instability. More apprehensive of "the loss of civil liberty" through "coercion" than of "dissolution of the Union," and thus immune to the central strategy of Federalist rhetoric. In all of New York the wealthiest member of his party. And, despite the link with Governor George Clinton and the Yates brothers, one of the most disinterested. A Hudson River patrician, with a great estate at Lansingborough and 40,000 acres in the Blenheim Patent (Schoharie County, New York), who had his doubts about "energetic" or "consolidated" government of every kind. Son of Gerrit Jacob Lansing and Jannetje Waters Lansing. In religion, Dutch Reformed. A descendant of Gerrit Lansing, who had emigrated from the Netherlands in the 1640's to settle on the Manor of Rensselaerwyck. Born in Albany, where he was educated. Read law with Robert Yates. Continued that legal training with the gifted and very conservative James Duane of New York City. After admission to the bar in 1775, served as military secretary to General Philip Schuyler. Elected six times to the New York Assembly, from 1780–1784 and in 1786 and 1788. In the last two of these terms chosen as Speaker of the Assembly. Selected as one of New York's delegates to the Continental Congress in 1784 and 1785. Mayor of Albany, 1786–1790. New York commissioner in 1786 boundary dispute with Massachusetts and in a later negotiation with Vermont. A slaveholder.

Though still a young man, John Lansing was an experienced political figure when selected with his erstwhile mentor, Judge Robert Yates, to represent the dominant antinationalist sentiment of his state in the Great Convention. Alexander Hamilton was included as a third member of their delegation as an empty concession to the defeated centralizers of New York City. Lansing and Yates (their families were joined by marriage) went to Philadelphia as men well *instructed*, whether or not the "Country Party" leaders had given them overt directions. They were authorized to consider a revision of the Articles of Confederation—that much, but no more. Once certain that their associates would attempt something more ambitious, the two New York Antifederalists, on July 10, went home, explaining their reasons for withdrawal in a long epistle in apology to Governor George Clinton. While in the Convention they were quiet, took notes, and generally supported the position of William Paterson of New Jersey, the spokesman for the small states. But their natural allies were not Paterson, Dickinson, and Read, all of whom accepted the Constitution once an equal voice for each of the states in the United States Senate had been included; but rather, Mercer and Martin of Maryland, Mason of Virginia, and Gerry of Massachusetts, all of whom doubted the wisdom of attempting a completely new frame of government—a government national in its nature and remote from the particularistic "genius" of the local community. Lansing made only one major speech in Philadelphia, an attack on "consolidation" delivered on June 16. His point was that the distinct sovereignties of the states should be preserved; and that "all reasoning on systems unaided by experience has generally been productive of false inferences." He accused the centralizers of being "theoretic" and of desiring "a perfection which never existed." Lansing's notes on the sessions which he attended, though not published until 1939, are sometimes useful as a correction of other records, particularly as a supplement to Madison's somewhat selective memory of these events. His second speech, on June 20, was essentially a gloss upon his earlier presentation, though there he elaborated on his argument against "inequality of representation" with an appeal to the conservative spirit of the American people and the related argument concerning the limited authority of the Convention.

During the June 1788 debates of the New York ratification convention in Poughkeepsie, John Lansing shared with Melancton Smith the major responsibility for carrying the Antifederalist side of the debate against such Federalist worthies as Hamilton, Jay, and Chancellor Robert R. Livingston. He had a violent exchange with Hamilton concerning whether or not that artful Scot at one point in Philadelphia had actually called for the abolition of the states. Moreover, Lansing made many of the motions for amendment and conditional ratification on which the struggle over the Constitution was finally to turn. His share in these deliberations was distinguished—argued always from history, experience, and a reverence for an already existing political regime. Against a consolidation of the states Lansing invoked the analogy of King Henry IV of France and his "mad scheme" of a united Europe. He called upon the spectre of despotism once "sword and purse" were under one control. He insisted on the attachment of a "bill of rights." He argued against a broad jurisdiction for the United States Supreme Court and for an amendment allowing for the recall of United States Senators. But, most importantly, he sought to include as a condition of New York's ratification the understanding that if the Constitution were not properly amended in a new Great Convention, his state would reserve the right to withdraw from the compact. This motion (and many others) failed because it came too late—and because the Federalists agreed to attach numerous "recommendations" to the act of ratification. Yet Lansing fought to the end, and on the best of grounds.

In 1790 John Lansing was appointed to a seat on the New York Supreme Court, where he served for eleven years and was Chief Justice from 1798 onward. In 1801 he became Chancellor of his state, an office in which he served until 1814. In his final years he was an acknowledged leader of the New York bar. A measure of his reputation for rectitude came in 1804, when the legislative caucus in Albany nominated him as the Democratic-Republican candidate for the governorship. Hamilton advised the Federalists to support Lansing in order to avoid the alternative of Aaron Burr. With such backing in addition to his own merit, John Lansing had reason to be confident of election. However, when George Clinton attempted to bargain with Lansing for the appointment of his nephew, DeWitt Clinton, as Chancellor as the price of his support, Lansing withdrew from the race. Later Lansing made public his reason for standing aside. He was a consistent figure throughout his public life. Though, according to Pierce, troubled by a small stutter, he was a fine figure of a man, genial, and well-spoken, with some degree of learning. For a time he was a regent of the University of the State of New York and took also an interest in the development of Columbia College. One evening in December of 1829, while in New York City on business, John Lansing left his hotel to post a letter—and forever disappeared under circumstances never explained. (See C. G. Munsell, *The Lansing Family* [New York: Private Printing, 1916]; De Alva Stanwood Alexander, *A Political History of the State of New York*, 2 vols., [New York; Henry Holt and Co., 1906]; Joseph Reese Strayer, ed., *The Delegate from New York; or, Proceedings of the Federal Convention of 1787, from the Notes of John Lansing, Jr.* [Princeton: Princeton University Press, 1939]; Linda Grant De Pauw, *The Eleventh Pillar: New York State and the Federal Constitution* [Ithaca: Cornell University Press, 1966], pp. 56–64 *et passim;* E. Wilder Spaulding, *New York in the Critical Period, 1783–1789*

[New York: Columbia University Press, 1932]; Robert Allen Rutland, *The Ordeal of the Constitution: The Antifederalists and the Ratification Struggle of 1787–1788* [Norman: University of Oklahoma Press, 1966], pp. 259–261 *et seq.*; and Alfred Fabian Young, *The Democratic-Republicans of New York: The Origins, 1788–1797* [Chapel Hill: University of North Carolina Press, 1967].)

Robert Yates

(January 27, 1738–September 9, 1801), lawyer, jurist, and leader of the Revolution in New York.

A decided Antifederalist, who in 1788 declared, "There is not a step towards this business that I ever agreed to; nor is there a sentence in it that I will ever agree to . . . ." Called by Allan Nevins "the Pym . . . of the Revolution in New York." Yet in no sense a champion of popular government, despite his early commitment to American independence. Though of middling origins, comfortable with the hegemony of the Hudson River patroons, having himself married a Van Ness. Unwilling that the General Welfare Clause of the Constitution should authorize ostensibly benevolent interference with "the most trifling concerns of every state." Son of Joseph Yates and Maria Dunbar Yates. Of the Dutch Reformed faith. Born in Albany, the city to which his great-grandfather had emigrated *ca.* 1700. Given opportunities by his family. Read law with William Livingston after receiving a solid classical education in New York City. Admitted to the bar May 9, 1760, in Albany, where he was to reside for the rest of his life. An alderman of that city from 1771 to 1775. A member of the Committee of Safety in 1775. Elected to four consecutive terms in the Provincial Congress, 1775–1777. Chairman of the New York State Committee on Military Operations, 1776–1777. Member of the Commitee of Thirteen which drafted his state's first constitution. A slaveholder.

In 1777 Robert Yates was appointed Justice of the New York State Supreme Court, where he continued until 1798. From 1790 until his retirement at the age of sixty, he was the chief justice of that court. In 1789 he was the Federalist candidate for governor, and in 1795 the Antifederalist candidate for the same office. Robert Yates was the floor leader of the Antifederalists during New York's ratification convention which began at Poughkeepsie June 19, 1788. But he spoke there only once—to give the lie to what Hamilton claimed he [Hamilton] had said about abolishing the states in the Convention at Philadelphia—and, in view of what he knew of the determination of the Federalists, did not play his part well. Yet he was one of the most popular men in New York, had by the legislature been unanimously elected as delegate to the Great Convention, was the nephew of the leading Antifederalist propagandist, Abraham Yates, and was himself the co-author of a letter to Governor George Clinton in which he and his erstwhile pupil John Lansing explained why they had withdrawn from the Constitutional Convention and had advised their fellow New Yorkers not to approve its results. It was Robert Yates and John Lansing who defined the Antifederalist position in their state, maintaining that the Framers had exceeded their authority, that their document would be "destructive of the political happiness of the citizens of the United States," and that state sovereignty was a better security for civil liberty than consolidated government. In other words, after this letter was published in December, 1788, Yates was the natural choice as Antifederalist leader, with his contacts with other Antifederalists all over the country and his knowledge of Federalist arguments of every kind. Especially so with George Clinton restrained by his role as governor.

In view of his party's large majority among the delegates elected to the New York ratifying convention, Robert Yates was over-confident of victory. And among the Antifederalists he was not alone. Though he had a full set of notes on what had been said in Philadelphia before his departure on July 10, 1787 (notes first published in 1821), Yates had great difficulty in preparing the "previous amendments" which were supposed to be attached as preconditions of a ratification, and thus revise or prevent the creation of a consolidated government. Yet, after Virginia had ratified it might have accomplished nothing if Yates, Melancton Smith, and Lansing had been better organized. Robert Yates voted against ratification of the Constitution, knowing that with the threat of New York City's secession from the state the document would win approval. Yet, once ratification was complete and amendments recommended subsequently, he called for acceptance of the new government. Despite his support among all levels of the population of the Empire State and despite his two almost successful attempts to win election as governor, the remainder of Richard Yates' career was a slow decline toward obscurity. As an old man, he practiced a little law and served as commissioner in land disputes. He died in greatly reduced circumstances. (See U.S. Senate Document 728, 60th Congress, 2nd Session [1909], p. 205; Alfred Fabian Young, *The Democratic-Republicans of New York: The Origins, 1788–1797* [Chapel Hill: University of North Carolina Press, 1967]; Jonathan Pearson, *Contributions for the Genealogies of the First Settlers of the Ancient County of Albany* [Albany, N. Y.: J. Munsell, 1872]; Stephen E. Sale, "Colonial Albany: Outpost of Empire," Ph.D. dissertation, University of Southern California, 1973; Linda Grant De Pauw, *The Eleventh Pillar: New York State and the Federal Constitution* [Ithaca: Cornell University Press, 1966], pp. 62–63, 86–87, *et passim;* E. Wilder Spaulding, *New York in the Critical Period, 1783–1789* [New York: Columbia University Press, 1932], pp. 237–238, *et passim;* Carol Spiegelberg, "Abraham Yates," M.A. thesis,

Columbia University, 1960; Robert Yates, *Secret Proceedings and Debates of the Convention Assembled in Philadelphia in the Year 1787 . . . From the Notes Taken by the Late Robert Yates, Esquire, Chief Justice of New York, and Copied by John Lansing, Jr., Esquire, Late Chancellor, etc.* [Albany, N. Y.: Webster's and Skinner's, 1821]; and James H. Huston, "Robert Yates' Notes on the Constitutional Convention of 1787: Citizen Genêt's Edition," *Quarterly Journal of the Library of Congress*, 35 [July, 1978], 173-182.)

William Paterson

(December 24, 1745–September 9, 1806), lawyer, statesman, and jurist.

The smallest of the Framers, and spokesman in their company for the special interests of the smaller states. Pre-eminently a "man of law" and defender of the Anglo-American tradition of inherited legal rights. Born in County Antrim or County Donegan, Ireland, to Richard and Mary Paterson, Ulster Presbyterians who emigrated to North America in 1747. Grew up in Princeton, New Jersey, where his father, a peddler and tinsmith, settled in 1750, after some years of wandering. There the elder Paterson opened a store and smithy; the family prospered and young William, following preparation in local private schools, entered the College of New Jersey. On graduation in 1763, he began to read law in the office of Richard Stockton, the Signer, worked in the family business, and took an active part in the cultural and intellectual life surrounding the college. In 1766 he took the M. A., and two years later passed his examination for the bar. In 1769 Paterson attempted to establish a rural practice of his profession near New Bromley, but in 1772 returned to Princeton. Shortly thereafter he moved again to South Branch, but did not settle finally in New Brunswick until 1779.

When the Revolution reached New Jersey, William Paterson was an obscure young attorney with a few influential friends. But the mildly republican stand which he took during that conflict propelled him rapidly into a place among the acknowledged leaders of his state. In 1775, Paterson was elected member for Somerset County in the Provincial Congress. In 1776 he was chosen secretary of that assembly and called upon to assist in drafting the new state constitution. In the latter enterprise he struggled, under pressure, to preserve what was best in the English legal tradition for the new American order of things his neighbors were attempting to create. Also in that cause he served from 1776–1777 as a member of the Legislative Council and from 1776 until 1783 as the Attorney General of New Jersey. Keeping his charge, he was diligent in the prosecution of traitors, Loyalists, and temporizers—and yet careful to restrain his fellow Patriots from partisan extremities and lawless acts. During these years he was, in effect, the civic sense of his society on horseback, working at a frenetic pace and becoming in the process the personification of the continuity of law linking colonial past to independent present. From his performance in this role he acquired a great reputation and a confiscated estate, Raritan Plantation, including a fine house for his family and slaves.

William Paterson returned to private life and a large, lucrative practice in 1783. But it was inevitable that he would be chosen as one of the representatives from New Jersey, once his state had decided in 1787 to participate in the Constitutional Convention. Paterson did not attend the sessions in Philadelphia after the end of July except to return briefly late in September for the signing of the Constitution. Yet while Paterson was present in these debates, he functioned, formally speaking, as the antagonist in the drama of group composition. The initiative seized with Gov. Edmund Randolph's presentation of what came to be known as the Virginia Plan for a new frame of government was blurred when Paterson introduced and won support for an alternative model. The ideas of Randolph, Madison, and the other Virginians had a majority of the delegates behind them. But that majority was not large or firm enough to survive a challenge. The process of writing and ratifying a Constitution would, if it were to prevail in the states, require near unanimity among the members of the Convention. And it became clear that Paterson's objections to some provisions of the plan preferred by the larger states would have to be accommodated if the meeting were to produce any meaningful results.

The Paterson Plan differed from the proposal of the Virginians in its insistence that the states have an equal vote in a unicameral legislature. It was the position of the New Jersey delegation that it had no authority from its instructions to agree to a government that negated the equal powers of the several states in the nation's legislature: the equality provided by the Articles of Confederation. The rest of Paterson's proposals seemed to create fewer problems: a plural executive, elected by the legislatures; a national judiciary, with specific powers; an authority over trade, taxes, and tariffs; a machinery for adding states, citizens, etc. Yet, as has been remarked by Forrest McDonald, the New Jersey Plan was in one respect, apart from the question of representation, more centralist than that of Virginia. For it declared that the component parts of the Republic would be "bound" by the "decisions" of the Congress, subject to compulsion by force to ensure their obedience, "anything in the respective laws of the Individual States to the contrary notwithstanding." This grant of power, making it possible that the Congress might do with the states what it wished, alarmed many of the delegates present in the Convention and was carefully removed from the final version of the Constitution. In its place stands language concerning "the supreme law of the land"—a very different matter.

Yet there was no genuine contradiction in Paterson's plan, once we understand its purpose. For he was never an ardent Antifederalist like Martin, Lansing, and Yates. Or even a conditional Antifederalist like Mason and Gerry. Under the Articles of Confederation, the people of New Jersey had been caught in a painful situation between the trade and tariff regulations of New York and Pennsylvania. Their currency was unsound, and their state did not appear to be viable as an independent economic unit. If other states were to retain their identities, New Jersey would need the protection for its interests that an equal strength in the national legislature would ensure. But Paterson had no objection to the abolition of the states, throwing all Americans into "Hotchpot." And he desperately wanted a change in government to regulate commercial barriers between the states. A Federal government dominated by the power of a few of its largest member states is what he could not abide. However, he was a reasonable man, and agreed without complaint to a revision calling for a House of Representatives apportioned according to population and a Senate securing the equal representation of the states. Once New Jersey received the concessions on which it insisted, its delegates in the Convention said very little. And William Paterson, seemingly satisfied, went home. But until that time he was a very active force in the discussions, and among those who kept careful notes on the sessions he attended. In New Jersey he supported with vigor the instrument which he had signed, and had, through his statewide acquaintance and numerous contacts, a real influence on the ratification voted in Trenton in December of 1787. But the decision there was never in doubt—once the Virginians and Pennsylvanians surrendered the principle of equal representation.

William Paterson was elected United States Senator for New Jersey in the First Congress. While there, he was co-author of the Judiciary Act of 1789 and included it it a provision for judicial review. He resigned that post upon his selection in 1790 to be governor and chancellor of his state. The city of Paterson was established during these years, under the charter of Hamilton's Society for the Establishment of Useful Manufactures granted at the recommendation of Gov. William Paterson. In 1793 he was, by President Washington, appointed Associate Justice of the United States Supreme Court. In that office he continued until his death, with much of his time in these years spent in travel to preside over distant trials. He participated, as a severe Federalist, in cases concerned with the Whiskey Rebellion, violations of the Sedition Law, and infringements upon the nation's neutrality. Writing the decision in the important case of *Van Horne's Lessee vs. Dorrance*, he invalidated a Pennsylvania statute as contrary to the Constitution. While riding the circuit, it was his habit to give lectures from the bench on the dangers of conflating justice with abstract "natural rights," on the toxins of metaphysical egalitarianism, and on the real possibility that democratic excesses might produce in the population of America "a set of drones or of idle extravagant wretches [who] live upon the earnings of others" by voting themselves their money. The great scholarly achievement of his career was the *Laws of the State of New Jersey* (1800)—a work which he prepared at the behest of the New Jersey legislature. In it he determined the force still preserved by the prescription of English law in the courts of his state, its limits and the alterations made in it by acts of the New Jersey legislature since its first establishment in 1702. It was a labor that defined his life. (See Julian P. Boyd, "William Paterson, 1745–1806: Forerunner of John Marshall," pp. 1–23 of *Lives of Eighteen from Princeton* [Princeton: Princeton University Press, 1949], edited by Willard Thorp; Gertrude S. Wood, *William Paterson of New Jersey, 1745–1806* [Fair Lawn, N. J.: Fair Lawn Press, 1933]; Rudolph J. and Margaret C. Pasler, *The New Jersey Federalists* [Rutherford, N. J.: Fairleigh Dickinson University Press, 1975]; Richard P. McCormick, *Experiment in Independence: New Jersey in the Critical Period, 1781–1789* [New Brunswick: Rutgers University Press, 1950]; Leonard B. Rosenberg, "The Political Thought of William Paterson," Unpublished Ph.D. dissertation, New School for Social Research, 1967; Richard McCormick, "The Political Essays of William Paterson," *Journal of the Rutgers University Library*, XVIII [June, 1955], 38–49; Michael Kraus, "William Paterson," on pp. 163–174 of Vol. I, *The Justices of the United States Supreme Court, 1789–1969: Their Lives and Major Opinions* [New York: R. R. Bowker/Chelsea House, 1969], ed. by Leon Friedman and Fred L. Israel; Leonard B. Rosenberg, "William Paterson: New Jersey's Nation-Maker," *New Jersey History*, LXXXV (Spring, 1967), 7–40; R. C. Haskett, "William Paterson, Counsellor-at-Law," Ph.D. dissertation, Princeton University, 1952; and John E. O'Connor, *William Paterson, Lawyer and Statesman, 1745–1806* [New Brunswick: Rutgers University Press, 1979].)

William Livingston

(November, 1723–July 25, 1790), lawyer, statesman, first elected governor of New Jersey.

In the Constitutional Convention, New Jersey's elder statesman and one of the oldest, most prestigious, and respected members when the sessions were convened. Son of Philip and Catharine Van Brugh Livingston. Grandson of the illustrious Robert Livingston, first lord of the manor, and brother of Philip and Peter Van Brugh Livingston. Born at Albany, New York, and raised by his grandmother, Sarah Van Brugh. As a youth lived on the frontier with missionaries among the Mohawks. Educated at Yale and in the law offices of James Alexander, a vigorous Whig. Associated early with such distinguished attorneys as John Morin Scott, William Peartree Smith, and William Smith, Jr. (with whom he prepared a digest of the provincial laws). A very successful attorney and a leader in the popular cause. A Calvinist in religion, and as a Presbyterian constantly in opposition to the more conservative and Anglican DeLancey faction. A member of the New York Assembly from 1759–1761, and one of the dominant figures in New York politics until 1769, when his party broke up over the question of British taxation. A gifted poet and essayist and author of some of the best of early American satire, Livingston then withdrew in disgust from law and politics and moved to Elizabethtown, New Jersey, to enjoy a literary retirement as a gentleman farmer.

The outbreak of the Revolution drew William Livingston away from the rural peace of Liberty Hall and into the midst of the great events of his time. He was a member for Essex County Committee of Correspondence, and then a delegate to the First and Second Continental Congresses. In June of 1776, he left that post to command the New Jersey militia as brigadier general, but later in that year was called from the field to become the chief magistrate of his state.

Throughout the next fourteen years, until his death in 1790, William Livingston was governor of New Jersey. As much as any man, he may be credited with having created the government and institutions of a sovereign state. While the Revolution continued, New Jersey was frequently a battleground of competing armies, and there was a considerable division of loyalties among its population. Yet, with moderation and careful stewardship, Governor Livingston pulled it together and guaranteed its respectable contribution to the struggle for American liberty. In his later years, the people of his state would not let him retire, seeing in his patient and patriarchal presence a summary of what they had fought to achieve. Yet he continued to enjoy whenever possible the pleasures of agriculture and the life of the mind. Though sometimes a slaveholder, he also gave moderate encouragement to the initial efforts toward the abolition of slavery in his state, cautioning always against coercive schemes to that end.

Governor Livingston said little during the Constitutional Convention, but his name and reputation gave weight to the New Jersey delegation. He performed when present as a moderate Federalist, one of those greatly disturbed by the outcry for paper money and equality in the 1786 riots in New England. He did not arrive in Philadelphia until June 5 and missed many of the debates in July, but he played a major role as chairman of the committee which drew up a compromise on slavery. Returning home, he exercised his potent influence in behalf of ratification and was responsible for the speed and unanimity of New Jersey's response. He is a figure of reference when we think of the great role played by aristocratic Whig gentlemen in the formation of the Republic. (See Rudolph J. Pasler and Margaret C. Pasler, *The New Jersey Federalists* [Rutherford: Fairleigh Dickinson University Press, 1975]; Richard

P. McCormick, *Experiment in Independence: New Jersey in the Critical Period, 1781-1789* [New Brunswick: Rutgers University Press, 1950], pp. 256–258, *et passim*; Theodore Sedgwick, Jr., *A Memoir of the Life of William Livingston* [New York: J. and J. Harper, 1833]; John Stevens, "William Livingston, Governor of New Jersey," *Magazine of American History*, II [August, 1878], 484–488; Margaret B. Macmillan, *The War Governors in the American Revolution* [New York: Columbia University Press, 1943]; Dorothy R. Dillon, *The New York Triumvirate: A Study of the Legal and Political Careers of William Livingston, John Morin Scott, William J. Smith, Jr.* [New York: Columbia University Press, 1949]; Harold W. Thatcher, "Comments on American Government and on the Constitution by a New Jersey Member of the Federal Convention," *Proceedings of the New Jersey Historical Society*, LVI [October, 1938], 285–303, and "The Political Ideas of New Jersey's First Governor," *Proceedings of the New Jersey Historical Society*, LX [July, 1942], 184–199; Philip Davidson, *Political Propaganda in the American Revolution* [Chapel Hill: University of North Carolina Press, 1941]; Milton M. Klein, "The American Whig: William Livingston of New York," Ph.D. dissertation, Columbia University, 1954; Michael Lewis Levine, "The Transformation of a Radical Whig under Republican Government: William Livingston, Governor of New Jersey, 1776-1790," Ph.D. dissertation, Rutgers University, 1975; and Carl E. Prince *et al.*, *The Papers of William Livingston* [Trenton: New Jersey Historical Society, 1979—], 3 vols. to date.)

Jonathan Dayton

(October 16, 1760-October 9, 1824), soldier, lawyer, and land speculator.

A leader of the Federalist Party in New Jersey for a quarter of a century. Son of General Elias Dayton of Elizabethtown, New Jersey, who was chieftain of a powerful faction among the New Jersey Whigs. The youngest of the Framers. Elected to sit in the Great Convention in his father's place. Educated at the College of New Jersey, where he took the B. A. Episcopalian. A soldier in the Continental Army, rising to the rank of captain at the age of nineteen. Served under his father and the Marquis de Lafayette. Captured, but exchanged, and returned to service in time for the Battle of Yorktown. A leader in the Society of the Cincinnati throughout the remainder of his life. Studied law after the war and began (often in association with Elias Boudinot) a lifetime of speculation in Western lands—lands to which no one in New Jersey had clear right or title.

Jonathan Dayton, perhaps in consequence of his youth, said very little during the Constitutional Convention, but faithfully followed the leadership of William Paterson and Governor William Livingston, the acknowledged spokesmen for his state. He did, however, speak on a few occasions and was one of the Framers who announced that he would sign the Constitution while objecting to some of its provisions. Dayton did not arrive in Philadelphia until June 21, but stayed the course once he took his seat. He was hostile to the 3/5 compromise on the representation of slaves, maintained that a simple majority was enough to ratify a treaty, and suggested that Rhode Island in its disorders was a justification for invasion of that state by Federal troops. He sat in the Continental Congress in 1788 and was elected to represent New Jersey in the House of Representatives in the first Congress under the new Constitution. He did not, however, attend that opening session, as he preferred a seat in the New Jersey Council, and in the following year, a term as speaker in the state assembly. He was again elected to the House of Representatives for the 2nd, 3rd, 4th, and 5th Congresses. During the last two of these terms, he was chosen Speaker of the House. A High Federalist, he supported all the programs of his party.

From 1799–1805, the New Jersey legislature sent Jonathan Dayton to serve in the United States Senate. There he opposed the repeal of the Judiciary Act of 1801, but differed with many other Federalists in his support of the Louisiana Purchase (1803). In keeping with New Jersey's position from the original organization under the Articles—a position implicit in their enthusiasm for the new Federal Constitution—he was always eager to see new lands opened for settlement in the West. And by that enthusiasm he was politically and morally tainted. Only a fortuitous illness prevented Dayton from accompanying Aaron Burr in his 1806 expedition to carve out a new empire from Spanish and American lands in the Southwest. His complicity in that grand design was, however, well known. Therefore, he was indicted for treason, and though not finally prosecuted, politically ruined. Nonetheless, he remained popular in New Jersey, continuing to hold local office and sitting in the Assembly in 1814–1815.

Jonathan Dayton is an example of those Federalists who saw in the new national government a means to general and personal prosperity and to American power and glory. Of New Jersey Federalists, he was among the most controversial—intensely ambitious, abrasive, and often engaged in questionable schemes. But his last years were peaceful and included a final visit with his old commander, Lafayette. His monument is that section of Ohio between the Big and Little Miami Rivers in which he developed 250,000 acres and which includes the city of Dayton, named after him. (See Rudolph J. Pasler and Margaret C. Pasler, *The New Jersey Federalists* [Rutherford: Fairleigh Dickinson University Press, 1975]; George A. Boyd, *Elias Boudinot: Patriot and Statesman, 1740–1821* [Princeton: Princeton University Press,

1952]; Anonymous, "Jonathan Dayton, 1760–1824, Patriot and Statesman and Founder of Dayton, Ohio," *New Jersey Genesis*, VI (October, 1956), 113–116; Theodore Thayer, *As We Were: The Story of Old Elizabethtown* [Newark: New Jersey Historical Society, 1964]; Robert G. Ferris, ed., *Signers of the Constitution* [Washington, D. C.: U.S. Dept. of the Interior, 1976], pp. 156–157; Thomas P. Abernethy, *The Burr Conspiracy* [New York: Oxford University Press, 1954]; Richard P. McCormick, *Experiment in Independence: New Jersey in the Critical Period, 1781–1789* [New Brunswick: Rutgers University Press, 1950]; and Forrest McDonald, *We the People: The Economic Origins of the Constitution* [Chicago: University of Chicago Press, 1958].)

David Brearly

(June 11, 1745–August 16, 1790), lawyer, soldier, statesman, and jurist.

Able assistant of William Paterson in the preparation of the New Jersey Plan, and a father of the doctrine of judicial review in American law. A descendant of John B. Brearly of Yorkshire, England, who, in 1680, emigrated to the area around Trenton in New Jersey. Son of David and Mary Clark Brearly of Spring Grove. Educated at the College of New Jersey, but took no degree. Early in being identified with the colonial cause in the conflict with the government of George III. Entered the practice of law before 1770, probably at Allentown. Colonel of New Jersey infantry regiments from 1776 through 1779. Member of the New Jersey constitutional convention of 1776. Elected chief justice of his state's supreme court in June of 1779. Served with distinction in that office for ten years. In 1780 author of a decision in the case of *Holmes vs. Walton*, in which he overturned a state law allowing for decisions in jury trials where only six jurors were in the box. Ruled the law invalid by reason of its conflict with the organic law, Anglo-Saxon justice understood historically, of which the courts were proper guardian.

David Brearly was, of the New Jersey delegates, the most regular in his attendance of the Philadelphia Convention. He served on a committee called upon to distribute seats in the original House of Representatives; and on another committee, formed late in August, whose duty it was to clear up a variety of smaller problems, postponed matters that were yet unresolved when the Constitution was almost complete. For this latter committee, Brearly, acting as chairman, made the official report. His only important speech in almost four months argued in favor of William Paterson's position that the small states would be "destroyed" unless an equal vote was preserved to each of them as a security for their sovereign existence. He also spoke briefly of the advantage of electing the President by a majority of both Houses of Congress. Yet he was prepared to see the states abolished completely or made equal in size. Brearly took notes during the Convention, some of which survive. Certain sections of Paterson's plan of government were probably given to him by his judicial colleague.

Though well respected, both in New Jersey and in the Great Convention, Judge Brearly was not a wealthy man. Most of his career was public service. According to newspaper reports, he was eloquent in his support of the Constitution during New Jersey's ratification convention of December, 1787, carrying all objections to the document before him in those debates at Trenton. In 1789, President Washington named David Brearly judge of the United States District Court of New Jersey, where he served for the final months of his life. In his last years he was also Grand Master of the New Jersey Masonic Lodge, and vice-president of the Society of the Cincinnati in that state. He was a devoted member of the Protestant Episcopal Church. (See Richard P. McCormick, *Experiment in Independence: New Jersey in the Critical Period, 1781–1789* [New Brunswick: Rutgers University Press, 1950]; Austin Scott, "Holmes v. Walton: The New Jersey Precedent," *American Historical Review*, IV [Spring, 1899], 3–19; *New Jersey Archives, First Series*, XXXVI [New York: AMS Press, 1974], p. 29; Robert E. Ferris, editor, *Signers of the Constitution* [Washington, D. C.: United States Dept. of the Interior, 1976], pp. 148–149.)

William Churchill Houston

(Circa 1746–August 12, 1788), educator, lawyer, and political leader of New Jersey.

A Framer who attended the Convention for less than two weeks and who, while there, contributed nothing. Mortally ill with tuberculosis when he got to Philadelphia. Significant as a barometer of political sentiment in the state which he hoped to represent. Born in South Carolina. Son of Archibald and Margaret Houston, later of Cabarrus County, North Carolina. Trained in the Poplar Tent Academy and by the local Presbyterian clergy. Dispatched at the age of eighteen to the College of New Jersey, where he took the B. A. in 1768, was made master of the grammar school and then tutor. Appointed Professor of Mathematics and Natural Philosophy at the College of New Jersey in 1771 and held that position until 1783. Treasurer of the College, 1779–1783. Deputy Secretary of the Continental Congress 1777–1778. After studying with William Paterson, admitted to the bar in 1781. Resigned from the College in 1783. Briefly a soldier in the New Jersey militia, 1776. In the state legislature,

1777–1779, and member of the New Jersey Council of Safety in 1778. Elected to the Continental Congress four times, 1779–1781, 1784 and 1785.

William Churchill Houston emerged as a popular attorney in the Trenton area after his resignation from teaching. He was, at various times, clerk of the New Jersey Supreme Court (1781–1788), receiver of Continental taxes (1782–1785), clerk of the state assembly, commissioner to settle salary claims by the New Jersey troops, commissioner in disputes between Connecticut and Pennsylvania over the Wyoming Valley claims, and attorney for the East Jersey proprietors in the Dividing-Line controversy. He served as a delegate to the Annapolis Convention. In 1787 he was a highly respected citizen of his state and a leading Presbyterian. But it was expected, even before his withdrawal, that he would not be able to sit through the Philadelphia Convention. Even so, he was named a delegate and given the opportunity to serve, his health permitting. Though absent from most of the Convention, he did live to sign the report of the New Jersey delegates to their state legislature. (See Thomas Allen Glenn, *William Churchill Houston* [Norristown, Pa.: privately printed, 1903]; Thomas Jefferson Wertenbaker, *Princeton, 1746–1896* [Princeton: Princeton University Press, 1946]; Varnum L. Collins, *President Witherspoon, A Biography*, 2 vols. [Princeton: Princeton University Press, 1925]; Richard P. McCormick, *Experiment in Independence: New Jersey in the Critical Period, 1781–1789* [New Brunswick: Rutgers University Press, 1950]; and H. James Henderson, *Party Politics in the Continental Congress* [New York: McGraw-Hill, 1974].)

Benjamin Franklin

(January 17, 1706–April 17, 1790), printer, man of letters, diplomat, scientist, and American statesman.

At eighty-one, the eldest of the Framers. In the world at large, the most famous American of his generation—though, in 1787, not quite the figure among his fellow Americans that General Washington was. The benign patriarch of the Great Convention, lending seriousness, order, good humor, and dignity to its proceedings. A Deist and a secularized Puritan. Bent on good works, looking for practical solutions to particular problems. A mild Federalist after the Albany Congress of 1754, where he had drawn up a plan for a general American government. Yet of most importantce as an aegis for the process of compromise and composition in which he played only a secondary role. Nonetheless, an influence over the negotiations which produced the most difficult accommodation of the entire Convention as leader of the committee that proposed an equal vote for each state in the United States Senate and a division of strength in the House of Representatives according to population. With John Dickinson, his old adversary in Pennsylvania politics, suggested that arrangement not long after the Virginia delegation had presented its plan of government and New Jersey had made an answer. Enforced his point with a characteristic homely metaphor: "When a broad table is to be made, and the edges of the planks do not fit, the artist takes a little from both, and makes a good joint." In that small homily is condensed a lifetime of experience in business, politics, diplomacy, and pragmatism which he brought to bear upon the ideological rigors of the youthful would-be lawgivers and men of system. Not particularly pleased by the final form of the Constitution, but firm in his support of it, urging each member of the Convention still present at its September conclusion to "doubt a little of his own infallibility" and to join in the necessary experiment of strengthening the general government by signing the document. With Washington, a powerful inducement to ratification by the states due to the widespread respect for their opinions among the rank and file of all Americans.

Benjamin Franklin was born in Boston, Massachusetts, the son of Josiah Franklin, who in 1682 had come to the "Godly Commonwealth" from Northamptonshire, England, and Abiah Folger Franklin, the pious Josiah's second wife. Benjamin was his father's tenth and last son (hence the given name), and the youngest son of the youngest son for five generations. He had some basic tutoring and almost a year at the Boston Grammar School. But his father, Josiah, a soap and candle maker, lacked the means to provide him with further formal schooling and therefore the dream of a career in the ministry for the gifted child of his old age had to be put aside. Benjamin was for a year or two apprenticed to his father, but did not like the work, and at the age of twelve went to learn the printer's trade with his half-brother, James Franklin. He continued in James' employ until 1723; read widely on his own (especially the English Augustans); wrote under the pseudonym of "Silence Dogood" for his brother's newspaper, the *New England Courant*; and learned his business—publishing the paper himself when James was locked away in jail for offending the authorities.

But finally Benjamin grew restive, determined that James took advantage of him, and ran away, at the age of seventeen, to Philadelphia, where, according to Franklin's own recollections, he arrived in a disheveled condition, with almost no money, yet little doubt concerning his future prospects. He obtained employment as a printer almost as soon as he arrived in Pennsylvania. But, after misleading encouragement from Governor William Keith, Franklin planned to set up a shop of his own and voyaged to London to purchase the necessary equipment—with money that Sir William was supposed to advance on credit. When no word or letters of credit came from his erstwhile patron, in 1724 Benjamin found employment in London printing-houses, learned more about his trade, and saw a bit of the world. In 1726 he had accumulated the reserves necessary to pay for his return to North America, but in the process of preparing for the journey he acquired a new mentor, the Quaker merchant, Thomas Denham, who took Benjamin into his Philadelphia firm, taught the boy the mysteries of selling and keeping accounts and then died in 1728, leaving a portion of his estate to the protégé. For a few months following Denham's decease, Franklin went back into the service of a senior printer of Philadelphia for whom he had worked before. But before long he gave up training other men's apprentices and with his friend Hugh Meredith set up on his own.

In 1730 Franklin bought out Meredith, took Deborah Reed as his common-law wife, began to publish the *Pennsylvania Gazette* (commenced by another man in 1728), and started his rapid rise to financial independence, political influence, and wide reputation. Out of their shop, the Franklins traded in stationery, books, salves and ointments, news, houses, land, and Negroes. Soon Franklin had the contract for all Pennsylvania government printing. He published broadsides, some books, his newspaper, and an assortment of small jobs. But in 1732 he brought out the first in a series of publications by means of which he reached into households throughout the British colonies in North America. And along the way he became a byword and a mythic figure in expressing the prudent, practical spirit of a new society. Between 1732 and 1758, *Poor Richard's Almanac* came to be second only to the Bible in its popularity in America. Eventually its fame reached even to Europe, where, along with Franklin's fame as a scientist, it awaited the sage when he arrived in England in 1757.

But first came Franklin's public career as Philadelphia's leading citizen. From 1736–1751 he was clerk of the Pennsylvania Assembly and from 1751–1764 he was a leading member of that body. From 1737–1753 he was the postmaster of Philadelphia. After asking for the post, he received appointment (with William Hunter of Virginia) as Deputy Postmaster General for all the colonies, a position which he held from 1753–1774, during which time he greatly reformed that service. In 1755–1756 he played the major role in organizing the defense of the Pennsylvania frontier against Indian depredations and was elected, at the age of 51, colonel of the Pennsylvania militia. In 1748 he took David Hall as a partner and divided with him the income of the very successful firm he had established almost twenty years before. Finally, as he had read systematically both to learn and to polish his style while still a boy, as he had founded the Junto for discussion of interesting and instructive topics among his young friends in Philadelphia while still far from established in his profession, in 1743 he proposed by circular letter to correspondents all along the length of settlements on this side of the ocean the creation of an American Philosophical Society—of which he offered, for a time, to serve as secretary.

Franklin's philanthropies and good works were legion. He organized private fire brigades and non-sectarian churches in Philadelphia. With local physicians, he sponsored the building of Pennsylvania Hospital, and he played the central role in founding a preparatory school and college (which became the College of Philadelphia and then the University of Pennsylvania) in his city. Franklin reformed the "watch" (police) of Philadelphia, initiated a project for lighting the local streets, and fostered the first circulating library in America. He joined the Masons and became the Grand Master of his lodge. Hardly any project of importance in Pennsylvania got under way without Ben Franklin being somehow involved in its promotion. The city was proud to have him as its citizen. And when publication of his researches in electricity brought him membership in the Royal Society in 1756, Franklin's neighbors took almost as much pleasure from the honor as did the recipient.

In science or "natural philosophy," Franklin's range of interests ran the gamut from medicine to geology to firsthand observations of whirlwinds. Of course, he invented and promoted his famous stove. He made observations on weather and the Gulf Stream, while on a voyage. He invented the lightning rod, and many other practical devices. But it was the study of electrical phenomena and his kite that earned him such fame as to inspire the philosopher Immanuel Kant to describe him as "the new Prometheus who had stolen fire from heaven." As a scientist, Franklin enjoyed correspondence with gifted persons throughout the world. But he was chiefly concerned with knowledge that could be applied to the control of nature. His natural philosophy was like his plan in the sphere of ethics, to compose an "Art of Virtue." He looked to results.

In Pennsylvania politics Benjamin Franklin emerged, in company with the cautious Joseph Galloway, as a leader of the Antiproprietary Party and opponent of the Penn family and their governors. Because the Penns often prevented necessary legislation, because they were niggardly and selfish in their attitude toward taxes necessary for the common defense, because they left the frontier of the old Quaker colony open to attack during the French and Indian War, Franklin and his associates favored the revocation of their Charter and the creation of a new royal government to replace the structures created under the Proprietors. Franklin went to London as agent for the Pennsylvania Assembly from 1757–1762 to request of the Privy Council that the Penns' repeated vetoes of money bills for defense be set aside. After being successful in this lesser enterprise, he was in 1764 returned to England to lobby in behalf of the creation of a Crown Colony of Pennsylvania. In both of these ventures Franklin's objective was one that he had announced as early as 1754 following the Albany Congress in three letters to Governor William Shirley of Massachusetts: arbitrary government "must seem hard measure to Englishmen who cannot conceive that, by hazarding their lives and fortunes in subduing and settling new countries, extending the dominion and increasing the commerce of the mother nation, they have forfeited the native rights of Britons." Proprietary government that left a people helpless went against the English Constitution. And so did the Stamp Act (1765) and later revenue bills passed by a Parliament which contained no American members. Franklin as agent for Pennsylvania (as he was later to be for Georgia, New Jersey, and Massachusetts) opposed such innovations as imprudent as well as improper, but was not so outraged by the bills as were his countrymen back in Pennsylvania. As a temperamental diplomat who despised mobs, crimes against property, and seditious printing—and as an advocate of the great advantages of royal government—Franklin did not at first think of associations, boycotts, tar and feathers. He even went so far as to recommend that some of his friends be named as stamp distributors and sent over some stamped papers to be sold in his shop, adding in comment, "We might as well have hindered the sun's setting." For a time his American popularity was at a low ebb. There was even talk of burning his house. But in the famous "examination" of Franklin by the House of Commons, a preliminary to repeal of the

Stamp Act, he comported himself so well and with such lucid eloquence that, once the interview was published, suspicion of his motives disappeared and his reputation was even larger than before.

In these long years as agent, Benjamin Franklin openly valued the status of the North American colonies *within* the British Empire and the flow of English constitutional history more than did many of his fellow Americans. An Anglophile, he was clearly a reluctant revolutionary. But never did he doubt that, in some sense, America was one country and England another. True enough, he wished to preserve the English character of the colonies: since "the number of purely white people in the world is proportionately very small," and since "the English [with the Saxons of Germany] make the principal body of white people on the face of the earth,... why should the Palatine boors be suffered to swarm into our settlements... why increase the sons of Africa by planting them in America, where we have a fair opportunity, by excluding all blacks and tawnys... ?" Franklin was a conventional xenophobe, made all the stronger in his cultural identity by the pleasure he took from life in England and from a large circle of English friends. Soon he became the American member of the British intellectual establishment—"Dr." Franklin, thanks to a 1759 honorary doctor of laws degree from St. Andrews University. For many years the agent from Pennsylvania had promoted the conception of an internally independent, almost self-governing America within a British Empire—bound together by loyalty to a king and a common history, and by statutory limitation and division of powers. Yet at some point late in the 1760's, Franklin began to doubt that either reason or a common heritage and blood would in the end solve the political problems of British America. To the attention of his countrymen he offered an old Italian proverb: "Make yourselves sheep and the wolves will eat you."

Yet to the time of his return to Pennsylvania in 1775, Franklin struggled to prevent a war between England and its colonies, continued to work for peace even after he had begun to doubt the motives and the judgment of his sovereign lord, King George III. As to the King's ministers, Franklin had never had much confidence in them: the Earls of Dartmouth and Hillsborough, George Grenville, Charles Townshend, Lord North. Franklin's friends among the men of power included William Pitt, the Earl of Chatham, Edmund Burke, and Burke's patron, the Marquis of Rockingham. And they were rarely in office. In fact, as Franklin's fame grew, and as his position obliged him to bring to Whitehall unpleasant appeals and bad news from beyond the Atlantic, many of the Tory aristocrats grew to fear and resent him. In his turn, Franklin came to believe that the leaders of Parliament "wished to provoke the North Americans into an open rebellion which might justify a military execution and thereby gratify a grounded malice which I conceived to exist here against the Whigs and dissenters of that country." The task of unofficial American ambassador proved to be a thankless one—particularly when Franklin was roundly abused before the Privy Council by Solicitor General Wedderburn when he had come before them to present a Massachusetts petition calling for the removal of a royal governor.

The letters of Thomas Hutchinson had through the offices of other men come into Franklin's hands, and he had sent them back to America to confirm that placemen were giving the English government terrible and disruptive advice, which in folly had been accepted. Recurring briefly to the Calvinism of his childhood, Franklin observed, "Divine Providence first infatuates the power it designs to ruin." He admitted his role in relaying to Whig leaders in America the purloined letters of Governor Thomas Hutchinson and Lieutenant-Governor Andrew Oliver addressed to officials in London. For his trouble in protecting innocent persons, in the Cockpit on January 29, 1774, Franklin was excoriated as an adventurer of "no honour" who had made the term "man of letters" into a "libel"; a miscreant, deserving the "mark and brand," having "forfeited the respect of societies and of men." Immediately Franklin's appointment as postmaster was revoked, and there was a public relish of his humiliation among "the King's friends"—those stalwarts who could with enough money always be persuaded to "vote according to their consciences."

Yet despite such invective and after the call for a Continental Congress in America, Franklin tried once more to warn of the long, pointless war that was to come. Two of his publications, parodies of the British logic that was driving America toward an appeal to arms, *Rules by Which a Great Empire May Be Reduced to a Small One* and *An Edict by the King of Prussia*, were widely distributed and often remarked. And there were hasty consultations with allies such as Pitt and Burke. However, as he by this time foresaw, Franklin was not heard, even by his political lieutenant, Galloway, or by his illegitimate son, William Franklin, the last British governor of New Jersey. But when forced into revolution, Franklin went toward the break with firm resolve, though sore of heart. Later, after American freedom had been accomplished and his work for the Republic as diplomat in France was concluded, he wrote with some sense of satisfaction to a friend in England on the question of who had been loyal in 1776, ". . . it was [for Americans] a resistance in favour of a British constitution, which every Englishman might share in enjoying, who should come to live among them; it was resisting arbitrary impositions, that were contrary to common right and to their fundamental constitutions, and to constant ancient usage. It was indeed a resistance in favour of the liberties of England, which might have been endangered by success in the attempt against ours. . . . " The Franklin who reached Philadelphia just in time to serve in the Second Continental Congress and to be the eldest Signer of the Declaration of Independence was no magically transformed figure, but rather a man of the prudent English Enlightenment, the friend of David Hume and champion of history as a "moral study"—the same person who had gone to England in 1764 to make a Crown Colony of Pennsylvania.

Benjamin Franklin was not long re-established as an American-in-residence until he was once again called upon to resume his role as American-abroad, a role for which he provided the original definition. But first he had almost eighteen months at the administrative center of the American Revolution. Franklin was elected to the Congress within days of his arrival on these shores. For a few weeks he was quiet, digesting the scene. Fighting had already occurred at Lexington and Concord. An army was in the making. To satisfy the moderates in Congress, he agreed to one last petition to the Crown. But he expected to accomplish nothing, despite the "olive branch" temperance of its appeal. And in July he proposed his own "Articles of Confederation and Perpetual Union." They were rejected as premature, but they served as a basis for the Articles prepared later by John Dickinson. From the beginning of official American diplomacy with the formation of a Congressional committee to deal with the possibility of outside support for the Revolution, Franklin had a hand in the business. Indeed, "unofficial" suggestions from a French envoy that aid would follow upon a Declaration of Independence made Franklin a vigorous advocate of that measure. He served with Thomas Jefferson (as his editor) on the committee called upon to prepare the document. With John Adams and Edward Rutledge, Franklin was commissioned to meet with his old friend, Lord Howe, on Staten Island, there to inform him that all future peace negotiations would have to accept the independence of the colonies as a predicate for the settlement of all difficulties. Franklin presided over the Pennsylvania Constitutional Convention of 1776, which reflected some of his favorite constitutional theories. He established the United States Postal Service. He wrote instructions for the first American emissaries. And he want on a winter journey to Canada to stir the flames of revolution in Canada. However, when the French urged serious consideration of a treaty of friendship, Benjamin Franklin, because of his international stature, previous visits to and wide acquaintance in France, was asked, even though he was soon to reach the age of seventy, to sail one last time across the seas and represent his country. His service as American "commissioner" or minister to France, from 1776–1785, was the triumph of his career, revenge upon the English and directly instrumental in the achievement of American independence.

While in France, Franklin acted out the details of a favorite myth of the French intellectuals—the legend of a bygone Golden Age, where before they had been confused and corrupted by the impedimenta of a complex social identity, men lived in a simple *polis*, according to the leadings of nature and the dictates of reason. In France Franklin could adopt the identity of a citizen of the Republic of Letters, even though he could not be a Frenchman. Therefore he could represent America as a citizen of the world—as the proper habitat of such beings: and manifest an interest in America's survival, which Frenchmen, as the most enlightened of nations, could share with him. The canny townsman of Philadelphia, in his fur hat, was thus a new Solon or Lycurgus—a symbol for French hopes for a better future of their own. No wonder he secured for Washington the loans and gifts, fleets and armies which drove even the stubborn, angry George III to accept the loss of colonies as a *fait accompli*.

In France Franklin was the hero as *litterateur* or *savant*. The French were socially fascinated by the old man in plain dress who came, instead of the trivial aristocrats to which they were accustomed, to represent an infant republic. He visited Voltaire and joined a lodge of Freemasons, flattered French ladies, set up his own press at Passy, attended meetings of the Academy of Sciences (of which he was a member), and persuaded the foreign minister of Louis XVI, the Comte de Vergennes, that the interest of his master was to ensure American independence, lest the Anglo-Saxons make a premature peace with one another and release England's power to concentrate on its natural enemy. Finally he became a cult, not a diplomat: a figure whose image could be found in most French households and recognized at all levels of French society. As an unofficial overseas "secretary of state," Franklin encouraged privateering, bought supplies, dispatched assistants to other countries; issued passports, treated with "unofficial" English representatives, and, in the end, in 1783, negotiated a general peace in the Treaty of Paris. Some envious younger American diplomats complained of Franklin's method in conducting the business of the Republic in France. The Congress ignored them, and refused Franklin's offer to resign. Indeed, they kept him in France long beyond the time when he wished to retire. But because of France's attitude toward the aging sage, they had little choice. In Philadelphia, the French *chargé* had informed them that no other ambassador would do. Finally, with the arrival of Thomas Jefferson, Franklin was free to go home to die. He had talked the French into deep and dangerous involvement in a war which brought them only revenge and moral self-satisfaction. And he had then persuaded the English to accept American ownership of the West, as far as the Mississippi. Franklin played his cards as they came, and enjoyed the game. Approaching eighty, he still believed that the advantage of being a "reasonable creature" was that "it enables one to find or make a reason for everything one has a mind to do." No other American, however zealous, could have done the job he did at Versailles.

When Benjamin Franklin reached Philadelphia in September of 1785, he was 79 years old. Almost immediately he was elected President of the Supreme Executive Council of Pennsylvania, in which office he served for three terms, until 1787. Even though tired and frail, there was to be little time for work on the *Autobiography*, a book which he had begun a decade earlier while still in England. Or for corrrespondence with friends or his favorite types of natural observation. The public business of Pennsylvania used up most of the energy that remained—along with his new Society for Political Enquiries. At first Franklin was not selected to be a delegate from his state to the Great Convention. Though he had urged a revision of the Articles of Confederation from a time even earlier than that of his final return to America, it was thought that he would be physically unable to attend the meeting called to that purpose. Therefore, when his health improved, he became in late March by unanimous vote of the legislature, a late addition to the company of the Framers. In France, according to John Adams, "Franklin's reputation was more universal than that of Leibnitz or Newton, Frederick or Voltaire." In Philadelphia he was simply the wise old grandfather of the Republic, the philosopher as tradesman. In that capacity at the end of his days, he served in the Great Convention, attending almost every session.

Benjamin Franklin's contributions to the drafting of the United States Constitution were in his support of a provision which allowed for easy naturalization of foreign immigrants, in his opposition to property limitations on the suffrage, and in his regular appeals for moderation, in one case calling for a minister to pray over his fierce and determined younger colleagues. "How has it happened, Sir," he asked General Washington, "that we have not hitherto once thought of humbly applying to the Father of lights to illuminate our understanding?... I believe that without His concurring aid we shall succeed in this political building no better than the builders of Babel." Franklin opposed giving absolute veto power over the proposed Congress to the executive, and did not approve of allowing a President to seek a second term. He feared the development of an order of American "placemen," and therefore contended that a chief executive (which he would have preferred to replace with a council) and his aides should receive no salary. Money bills, he believed, should originate in the lower house of the Congress, where the "public spirit of our common people" would be represented, and should not be rewritten in the United States Senate. Such procedures were part of the package for which he had made the motion when the Great Committee of one man from each state was called upon in July to revive the Convention. He seconded Mason's motion for a council to advise the President, moved to include a Federal power for building canals, and opposed a financial test for holders of Federal office. Finally, he called for a careful definition of treason and for rules relating to the examination of such charges, as well as for explicit procedures for impeachment and trial of a chief magistrate. Peace and order required great clarification in these areas, so that tyranny and political harassment might be avoided.

At times Franklin jested. At other times he chided the enthusiasts of the Convention with small analogies and humorous tales. Some of his speeches were prepared in writing, and read for him by James Wilson. In good spirits, meaning as he had at 25 to "keep his friends in countenance," he accepted the role to which circumstances assigned him in the four months of deliberation. But he had been serious in what he said about the Hand of Providence and in recommending prayer. He had a genuine confidence in the future of the then ramshackle combination of "little republics"—especially once it became a bona fide Union, and not just a loose confederation: as much of a national government as they could abide. And though not entirely satisfied with the Constitution produced by his associates, he was moved by its completion to prepare a peroration for the entire Convention and to make his famous remark concerning the "rising sun" and the emblem on the back of Washington's chair.

Benjamin Franklin died thirteen months after the adjournment of the Constitutional Convention. Twenty thousand people attended his funeral, and his death was remarked throughout the civilized world. Clearly, he summarized one side of the American character. As Carl Becker has written, Franklin was satisfied with "the best possible rather than the best conceivable worlds." And he made it—and himself—up as he went along. As we learn from his masterpiece, the *Autobiography* (1781, 1818), he was by practice an "amiable chameleon," an eminently practical man who could write for his Quaker friends an antislavery petition to a Congress which, as he well knew, could not accept it; and at the same time, keep a slave (belonging to his son-in-law) in his own house. It made no sense to trouble his old age with contradictions. And, besides, he could free Bob in his will. Certainly the Franklin who balanced "freedom of the press" with the "liberty of the cudgel," a freedom to assault obnoxious and trouble-making journalists with legal impunity, was not the conventional champion of human rights. The "rights of man," for him, meant self-government, and perhaps a gradual movement toward constitutional monarchy in a country such as France. But it did *not* mean, for instance, that the state, in defending itself and the liberty of its citizens in a free country, was unable to call upon a man for all the property that he possessed.

Despite his devotion to the nation's future prospects as a free people, Franklin thought at times that he might leave America and live among his gifted friends in England or France. But only as an American living abroad. To one of his countrymen he observed, "We are the sons of the earth and seas and, like Antaeus, if in wrestling with Hercules we now and then receive a fall, the touch of our parents will communicate to us fresh strength and ability to renew the contest. Be quiet and thankful." Benjamin Franklin's entire career is a comment on what he meant by such advice. (See Carl Van Doren, *Benjamin Franklin* [New York: Viking Press, 1952]; David F. Hawke, *Franklin* [New York: Harper & Row, 1976]; Leonard Labaree *et al.*, editors, *The Papers of Benjamin Franklin* [New Haven: Yale University Press,

1959—], 21 vols. to date; Gerald Stourzh, *Benjamin Franklin and American Foreign Policy* [Chicago: University of Chicago Press, 1969]; William S. Hanna, *Benjamin Franklin and Pennsylvania Politics* [Stanford: Stanford University Press, 1964]; Benjamin H. Newcomb, *Franklin & Galloway: A Political Partnership* [New Haven: Yale University Press, 1972]; Carl Becker, *Benjamin Franklin* [Ithaca: Cornell University Press, 1946]; J. A. Leo Lemay, ed., *The Oldest Revolutionary: Essays on Benjamin Franklin* [Philadelphia: University of Pennsylvania Press, 1976]; Robert F. Sayre, *The Examined Self: Benjamin Franklin, Henry Adams, Henry James* [Princeton: Princeton University Press, 1964]; M. E. Bradford, "Franklin and Jefferson: The Making and Binding of Self," pp. 137–152 of *A Better Guide Than Reason: Studies in the American Revolution* [La Salle, Ill.: Sherwood Sugden and Company, 1979]; Bruce I. Granger, *Benjamin Franklin: An American Man of Letters* [Ithaca: Cornell University Press, 1964]; D. H. Lawrence, *Studies in Classic American Literature* [New York: Doubleday-Anchor, 1955]; Edward S. Corwin, "Franklin and the Constitution," *Proceedings of the American Philosophical Society*, CXI [Fall, 1956], 283–288; Paul W. Conner, *Poor Richard's Politics: Benjamin Franklin and His New American Order* [New York: Oxford University Press, 1965]; Verner W. Crane, *Benjamin Franklin and a Rising People* [Boston: Little, Brown, 1954]; J. A. Leo Lemay, "Benjamin Franklin," pp. 205–243 in *Major Writers of Early American Literature* [Madison: University of Wisconsin Press, 1972], ed. by Everett Emerson; and Mary E. Rucker, "Benjamin Franklin," pp. 105–125 of *American Literature, 1764–1789: The Revolutionary Years* [Madison: University of Wisconsin Press, 1977], ed. by Everett Emerson.)

Robert Morris

(January 31, 1734–May 8, 1806), "merchant prince" of Philadelphia, financier of the American Revolution, and banker.

Called "the Great Man," with a mixture of irony and respect. At the time of the Constitutional Convention perhaps the wealthiest man in North America. The Commercial Federalist *par excellence*. With Roger Sherman, a Signer of all three of the nation's basic documents: the Declaration of Independence, Articles of Confederation, and the United States Constitution. Yet a conservative in almost every sense of the term. The most influential member of the Pennsylvania Delegation to the Great Convention. A large, confident, and jovial figure; one who could write to a friend, "I have never failed to get the better of my Enemies on the day of Trial." Not a learned man, but ingenious, described by a political contemporary as one who in argument "bears down all before him." By 1787, greatly hated by those who believed he had profited improperly from his services to the Patriot cause.

Born in or near Liverpool, England. Brought to Maryland at the age of thirteen by his father, Robert Morris, a tobacco merchant. Orphaned shortly thereafter (1750), and left with little schooling and an inheritance of about $7,000. Apprenticed at this early age in the countinghouse of Charles Willing, which became the firm of Willing, Morris and Company when Robert came into his majority. Later, under a succession of names this trading and banking house prospered greatly and survived to act an important part in supplying weapons and ammunition to an infant Continental Army. And Robert Morris, as a very young man, became one of the leading citizens of the extremely commercial city of Philadelphia.

In 1765 Morris signed the non-importation agreement to protest the Stamp Act. In October of that year he was part of a local committee that forced the collector of the stamp tax to close his office. Yet he was no rebel—just one of a host of American merchants who had learned to despise English mercantilist economic policy as it affected American business. And he never regarded the idea of independence from the mother country as anything more than a desperate last resort. However, for "the Principles of the British Constitution... [he was] content to run all hazards." On St. George's Day, April 23, 1775, when news of the Battle of Lexington reached Philadelphia's leading citizens in the midst of their annual celebration of their English inheritance, Robert Morris realized that a mortal struggle was in the offing, and decided to stand with his adopted city. In close sequence, Morris became a member of the Philadelphia Committee of Correspondence (1775–1776), of the local Council of Safety (1775–1776), and of the Pennsylvania Provincial Assembly (1775–1776). From 1775–1778 he sat in the Continental Congress, where he quickly became important in organizing his countrymen for the purposes of defense. The Congress bought through his firm, arranged for transport and credit, and borrowed from it. Morris helped to plan coastal fortifications, to sponsor privateers, to build an American Navy, and to instruct American diplomats sent abroad. He made money out of his patriotism, but he gave good value for his services. With John Dickinson, he voted against the Declaration of Independence; yet, unlike Dickinson, he signed it once it had been approved in August of 1776: put his hand to the instrument of revolution even though he continued to hope for an eventual restoration of some kind of tie with England. From 1776 to 1779, 1780 to 1781, and from 1785 to 1786, he occupied a seat in the Pennsylvania legislature under the 1776 Constitution of that state—a system of government of which he completely disapproved. And during a period of three crucial years, 1781–1784, he held the office of Superintendent of Finance under the Articles—the highest civilian position created by the Confederation.

Morris' long struggle to bring solvency to the Congress and support to

American armies in the field went through several stages before he was given sole authority over that enterprise. First of all, he purchasd tobacco in the name of the government for trade with France, Holland, and the West Indies. In 1778 he served as chairman of the Committee on Finance. And, once the authority of that body expired and Morris withdrew to the Pennsylvania legislature, he often, in the name of George Washington, applied directly to states for supplies and money. And he continued to borrow money for the government on his own credit, when nothing else was available and emergency action was required. For he had faith that the future of America was one of "Power, Consequence and Grandeur." Moreover, he was perhaps unique among the Framers in understanding how the transformation of the country would come about. From his position at the center of the nation's commercial life, he could foresee where present trends might lead.

On assuming dictatorial authority over the confused and disordered state of the new nation's finances, Morris made use of all his remarkable skills. And he pledged to the Congress, "The United States may command everything I have except my integrity, and the loss of that would effectually disable me from serving them more." As Superintendent, Morris eliminated many previously authorized army posts, offices, and agencies; had expenses reported directly to his offices; instituted a system of purchase contracts; secured new French and Dutch loans; and raised some money from the imposts he persuaded the Congress to levy. With his own reputation and about $5 million, he instituted regularity where chaos had been. He gave government securities to creditors and paid interest on them. He established plans for a sinking fund to reduce outstanding notes, as retirement became convenient. Yet he disavowed responsibility for direct payment on demand for past debts, leaving such for subsequent settlement by Congress. When Washington needed to pay the army under his command in order to march it south to Virginia, Morris, in person, rushed coin to motivate the uneasy Northern regiments into cheerful assent to a long campaign far away from home. Despite his hopes, Morris was unable to convert the business of his office as Superintendent into a basis for a stronger union of the states, or to assume all outstanding war debts under the Confederation. But he moved the government some distance in that direction, toward agreement to the idea that federal taxes should be used to pay the war debt. The prospect of such arrangements made uneasy the decentralists in Congress and the state governments who knew that Morris would use his authority to increase the importance of the general government in order to bring about constitutional change. Therefore, the policy which Morris advocated was never seriously implemented—indeed, was contrary to the letter of the Articles. But, in any case, Morris had done an amazing job, having paid all of the debts he had contracted in it and leaving a small surplus in the Treasury.

Another expedient for changing the administration of the nation's business from a "rope of sand" into a lasting bond between the several states was the 1781 chartering, under Morris' supervision, of the Bank of North America, which opened its doors in January, 1782, with about $500,000 capital. The financier mingled the affairs of the Confederation with those of the Bank, and both with enterprises of his own. He prospered from this network of connections. But that possibility, and the means to it, had been accepted by the Continental Congress when they had first asked Morris to control the nation's purse strings. Even so, envy and abuse, charges and accusations, compelled him to give over the task of "preaching to the dead" and wait for a more auspicious moment to reform the country into what he believe would be economically viable, with a coercive power to raise a revenue. What he feared was that the states would pay off their debt to the Confederation by honoring the claims of creditors within their own boundaries and would then subtract that sum from what he expected them to send to the Treasury. In one sense, Morris' plan for a powerful national government was a victim of American military success. That unity and economic cooperation would be as important in peace time as in war was difficult to argue *after* a war fought for liberty, against a remote sovereign insisting on its power to tax.

Out of office, Morris acquired the contact with the Farmers-General of France for a monopoly of the tobacco trade with that country. He revived his old dream of developing Orange Grove plantation on the Mississippi (in Louisiana) with hundreds of slaves and every improvement. He had bought a great country house outside Philadelphia, rebuilt his home in that city, and made plans for an even grander "palace." He dabbled again in state politics, working to revise the Pennsylvania Constitution of 1776 and to protect his bank. He sent ships to Iberia and the Orient, to the West Indies and the Southern states. And when the Annapolis Convention was called, Robert Morris made certain that he was a delegate to that meeting. When his state answered the call from Annapolis for a larger convention to be held in Philadelphia in May of 1787, Morris led the ticket in the legislature's selection of Pennsylvania's delegates.

Once in the Great Convention, Robert Morris was surprisingly silent for a man of such self-confidence and obvious influence over the proceedings. But Morris knew his limitations. Moreover, Gouverneur Morris and James Wilson were both present to speak for him, except when Wilson sounded too "democratic." And General Washington was in the chair. To these particulars, Morris had addressed himself. Prior to the formal opening of the Convention, he had unsuccessfully argued that the vote of the states should be weighted according to their population and their property. Morris seconded a motion that United States Senators be appointed to serve "on good behavior"—for life. Otherwise he kept silent and worked behind the scenes as host for much of the social activity of the gathering. Moreover, once the

Constitution was signed, Morris put the great resources of his influence to work in supporting ratification, especially among public creditors—security holders who, as a group, had an interest in the establishment of the proposed Federal government.

In 1789 Robert Morris was elected one of Pennsylvania's original United States Senators, and served in that office until 1795. Senator Morris voted the Federalist line. He played a major role in the maneuvering that brought the nation's capital to Washington, D. C., where he had property. And, once the new government was in operation, Morris began to speculate heavily in frontier lands. His energies continued to be great and his self-confidence unshakable. Inflation in the purchase of securities, along with an international depression, collapsed his empire. In 1797 came bankruptcy, and in 1798, arrest and confinement for failure to pay debts. "Morris' Folly," designed by L'Enfant, was left incomplete, a comment on the theory of Richard Henry Lee, announced with reference to the financier, that "the spirit of commerce is the spirit of avarice." Yet despite his ruin, his arrogance, and his debt of $3 million, Robert Morris was a generous man and a patriot. Though untouched by democratic dogma or the abstractions of his sometimes-enemy/sometimes-employee, Thomas Paine, Morris was full of public spirit, brave, and farsighted. He was a member and supporter of the Episcopal Church, of which his brother-in-law, William White, was the Pennsylvania bishop, and of many public causes. When released from the Prune Street debtors' prison in 1801, Robert Morris was a broken man. His protégé, Gouverneur Morris, had secured an annuity to Mrs. Robert Morris, on the returns from which the family lived modestly. In a little house not far from the scenes of his fame, death came to Robert Morris in his 73rd year. Of all the commercially-minded Framers to be ruined in the years following their service in the Great Convention, Morris' fall was the greatest, and most instructive. (See Eleanor Young, *Forgotten Patriot, Robert Morris* [New York: Macmillan, 1950]; Clarence L. Ver Steeg, *Robert Morris, Revolutionary Financier* [New York: Octagon Books, 1976]; Ellen Paxson Oberholtzer, *Robert Morris, Patriot and Financier* [New York: Burt Franklin, 1969]; John Bach McMaster and Frederick D. Stone, *Pennsylvania and the Federal Constitution, 1787–1788* [New York: Da Capo Press, 1970], pp. 703–704, *et passim;* E. James Ferguson, *The Power of the Purse: A History of American Public Finances, 1776–1790* [Chapel Hill: University of North Carolina Press, 1961]; E. James Ferguson *et al.*, eds., *The Papers of Robert Morris, 1781–1784* [Pittsburgh: University of Pittsburgh Press, 1973—]; H. James Henderson, *Party Politics in the Continental Congress* [New York: McGraw-Hill, 1974]; Frederick S. Rolater, "The Continental Congress: A Study in the Origin of Our Public Administration, 1774–1781," Ph.D. dissertation, University of Southern California, 1970; Robert Waln, Jr., pp. 191–374 of Vol. V of *Biography of the Signers to the Declaration of Independence* [Philadelphia: R. W. Pomeroy, 1824], ed.

by John Sanderson; Henry Simpson, *The Lives of Eminent Philadelphians* [Philadelphia: William Brotherhead, 1859], pp. 702-722; Forrest McDonald, *We the People: The Economic Origins of the Constitution* [Chicago: University of Chicago Press, 1958], pp. 54-57; and his *E Pluribus Unum: The Formation of the American Republic, 1776-1790* [Indianapolis: Liberty Press, 1979], pp. 50-57.)

James Wilson

(September 14, 1742–August 21, 1798), lawyer, jurist, political philosopher, "projector," land speculator, and statesman.

Signer of the Declaration of Independence and of the Constitution. The man principally responsible for Pennsylvania's approval of the proposed U.S. Constitution. Architect of the Pennsylvania State Constitution of 1790. A theoretical democrat *and* a High Federalist who in much of his career lived in conflict with the spokesmen for the popular cause, both in Pennsylvania and elsewhere in the country. A metaphysical progressive who thought of the state as an instrument for the pursuit of perfection, believing at the same time that government had "the right of acquiring everything without which its perfection cannot be promoted or obtained." A *philosophe* of democracy who first attacked the peculiar institution and then bought slaves. A dialectician who could "bewilder truth in all the mazes of sophistry, and render the plainest proposition problematical." Able, through "the power of moral abstraction," to recommend that we love men far away, "so unknown, or so distant as to elude the operation of our benevolence," yet unable to act the part of kinsman to members of his own family left behind him in his native Scotland, or to pay his debts to the relatives and friends who launched him on his American career, even when they needed the money and he did not. A man of noisy sentiment and moral intuition, but apparently a humbug—particularly in his expansive expressions of faith in the common man and in the future of America. Never so interested in the will of the people as in the sponsorship of the "better sort," with the hope of making a dollar. Capable, without hesitation, of putting his own opinions in place of the preferences of his constituents because he knew how they would have felt "if possessed of equal information." Among the Framers, second only to Gouverneur Morris in the frequency of his speeches (168) in the Philadelphia Convention. Perhaps a precursor of American political thought in the years to come, but in 1787 not a representative of the frame of mind that finally produced the United States Constitution.

James Wilson (nicknamed "James de Caledonia") was born in Fifeshire, near the university town of St. Andrews in Scotland. He was the eldest son of William Wilson, yeoman farmer and elder of the Kirk, and of Alison Landale Wilson, a strong-willed woman of deep religious faith. After early schooling in the Cupar Grammar School, young James proceeded to St. Andrews, where in 1757 he was granted a scholarship. He commenced a course of studies that was expected to lead into a career in the ministry of the Church of Scotland. However, when young James' father died in 1762, the young man withdrew from St. Mary's, the theological college of the University to which he had transferred upon the completion of his B. A. in the previous year, and took a job as a tutor in a gentleman's house. This occupation did not satisfy the ambitious young Wilson, who believed himself to be destined for a higher station in life. Friends and relatives were happy in North America. In 1765 he asked for an equivalent opportunity and was given it by the little village of his boyhood—by the Annans, Balfours, Landales, and Wilsons. With a stake and a brief taste of the merchant's life in Edinburgh, James set sail for the New World.

Upon his arrival in Pennsylvania in 1766, armed with letters of reference, Wilson received almost immediate appointment as tutor in Latin at the College of Philadelphia. He was given an honorary M. A. by the small American school, and soon was recognized as a man of learning and ability. Shortly thereafter (again with aid from a kinsman), he arranged to read law in the office of the distinguished John Dickinson. In 1767 Wilson was admitted to the Philadelphia bar. The following year he set up practice in Reading, Pennsylvania. Two years later, he moved westward to Carlisle, married into a family of importance and began to prosper among his litigious Scotch-Irish neighbors. Soon he had half the legal business in the county and cases throughout the state, as well as in New Jersey and New York. He gave literary lectures at the College of Philadelphia. He traded in land, bought Negroes and a big house. In 1774, he was chosen as chairman of the Carlisle Committee of Correspondence and was elected to the Provincial Assembly. He finished a manuscript that he had first drafted in 1768, entitled *Considerations on the Nature and Extent of the Legislative Authority of the British Parliament* (1774). In this work he maintains that since "all men are, by nature, equal and free," Parliament could have no authority over Englishmen in America, who were connected to the mother country only through obligations to a common King—provided that King did not "withdraw his protection" from them. The skill displayed in this performance helped to propel James Wilson into the forefront of leadership in a Pennsylvania moving steadily toward independence. And from that rank he did not retire in the remainder of his life.

In 1775 James Wilson was sent by Pennsylvania to be one of its delegates in the Second Continental Congress. Once there, he combined his influence with the conservative leaders of the "old regime" in Pennsylvania politics, the spokesman for the "Proprietary Party" and balanced government under the

Charter of the Penns. With his old mentor, John Dickinson, and Robert Morris, Wilson approached with hesitation the fateful prospect of outright revolution and permanent separation from Great Britain. Wilson's theme in his *Considerations* had been the desirability of something like the English Commonwealth of Nations that emerged in the later history of the Empire. In February of 1776, he prepared a reaffirmation of that doctrine, though (according to Wilson's own interpretation of the event) he carefully coupled it with conditions designed "to lead the public mind into the idea of Independence." This strategy was too abstruse for the Congress, which refused to publish the document. As the pressures of war gathered upon Philadelphia, Wilson put aside his reservations and voted—almost reluctantly—for the Declaration of Independence. By this time he had already lost much of his following among Pennsylvania radicals. Yet he persisted in representing his state with the best of his energy and judgment. Wilson called the democratic Pennsylvania Constitution of 1776 "the most detestable that ever was formed." Even so, his enemies continued him in the Continental Congress until September of 1777. There he served on committees urging relinquishment of frontier lands by the states (he wanted the general government to confirm his titles in the West); calling for a national power to collect taxes and raise a revenue; and negotiating a treaty of friendship with the Indian tribes of the Northwest. In keeping with his position in the Great Convention, he also called for representation in the Congress according to the concentration of free white population, and an end to voting by states.

After leaving Congress, Wilson delayed briefly in Maryland, and then moved his home from Reading to Philadelphia, where he became counsel for many wealthy Loyalists, *avocat general* for the French maritime and commercial courts in the United States, the political leader of the merchant aristocracy, an investor in privateering, and an advocate for land-jobbing corporations and banks. He argued a case before the legislature for the Bank of North America—a bank of which he was a director—in which he maintained that ". . . the United States have general rights, general powers, and general obligations, not derived from any particular states, nor from all the particular states, taken separately; but resulting from the union of the whole. . . . " In this language there is clear evidence that, well before the Constitutional Convention, James Wilson was already the friend of implied authority and concentrated power, the enemy of state sovereignty, and the supporter of a notion of natural rights which conceived of them as applying more to the conflict of "the weak against the strong" than to the quarrel of "the citizen against the state." Abandoning the faith of his youth, Wilson became an Anglican—though, in truth, he was more a Deist than a Christian of any sort. He moved in the highest circles—and perfected the stiff, haughty manner which made of him perhaps the most hated figure in his state: so hated that, in the fall of 1779, the people of Philadelphia formed themselves into a militia on its way to being a mob and besieged Wilson's house, as if it "had been the local headquarters of the British Grenadiers." Wilson's conservative political associates, hearing rumors of the attack, fortified "Fort Wilson," fired on the multitude when it arrived, suffered and gave many casualties (both dead and wounded), and, once troops arrived to restore peace, dispatched the Caledonian to refuge in the country. This support in a moment of crisis did not signify that Wilson actually enjoyed the life-and-death personal loyalty of many friends. Contemporary records indicate that he was a cold man, with no gift for fellowship. But in 1782, he did retain the respect of the conservatives (called Republicans) in Pennsylvania politics. For in that year, as they recovered control of the legislature, they returned Wilson to his old seat in the Continental Congress—a seat which he also occupied in 1785–1787. They were unable to save the Bank of North America, but with the selection of James Wilson, they did lay the groundwork for the Constitutional Convention.

During the Great Convention James Wilson was almost unique among the Framers in reasoning from a systematic philosophical position, resting on a general metaphysic, in recommending that particular provisions be included in the proposed United States Constitution. Wilson came to the deliberations of the Convention with a set of assumptions concerning American politics and the meaning of the Articles of Confederation not shared by many of his colleagues. First of all, Wilson never accepted the historic and well established; multiplicity of cultural identities reflected in the thirteen state governments as a given of any viable plan for a stronger union. Indeed, Wilson denied, in the face of all evidence and opinion, that the states were sovereign in their connection through the Articles of Confederation. His argument (supported by only a few American thinkers before the ante-bellum debates concerning slavery and secession) was that the states were dissolved, along with the tie to England, by the Declaration of Independence; and that the Continental Congress represented "the people of the United States," taken collectively, who are the "We" of the Declaration. He called the states "imaginary beings" and asked his fellow Framers "to proceed by abstracting as much as possible from state governments. Elsewhere he added that, as to the purposes of Union, the states "should be considered as having no existence."

Perhaps the explanation of Wilson's animus against the states is, as some scholars have argued, that, like some of the other recent immigrants among the Framers, he could not recognize the importance of the old colonial divisions as a locus of political emotion and personal loyalty, even in the process of creating a Federal Union. Although he was later to be the proponent of a theory of dual sovereignty which was used to pacify the Antifederalists (and, by a curious inversion, to augment the authority of the general government and the Federal bench), one *and* many was a doctrine he could not comprehend. Or it may have been that the reality of American politics present in the Constitutional Convention offended his uniformitarianism, his love for the ecumenic dream of King Henry IV of France, or his Scottish "common sense" philosophy. But another plausible explanation of his conduct was the unwillingness (or inability) of the Continental Congress to grant him those rich appointments and valuable Western lands which he so earnestly desired. In the records of the Great Convention there is much support for the theory of Pennsylvania Antifederalists that Wilson had in mind an appointment as Chief Justice of the United States as soon as he was given a place in that assembly.

James Wilson opposed the Great Compromise on representation of the states in the United States Senate with more vehemence and determination than was displayed by any of the other champions of the proportional Virginia Plan. His charge against the formula finally adopted was that it violated "the inherent, indisputable and unalienable rights of men." And, with absolutely no effect on his fellow Framers, he made the same complaint against Madison's plan to attach a property qualification to the franchise; against schemes such as the Electoral College for an indirect selection of Presidents; against requiring a two-thirds vote for the ratification of treaties; and related provisions. Yet, despite his official obeisance to the unadulterated "will of the people," he taught another doctrine on the assignment of powers to the United States Supreme Court. These he wished to see both extensive and detailed—including a power to review (with the Chief Executive, whom he also exalted) the actions of Congress even before they faced any challenge at law. Wilson was an overt champion of judicial activism, of "legislation" by the courts; and of the "imperial Presidency," in a company to whom all such notions seemed completely foreign. Wilson was "inelastic, doctrinaire and full of bombast"—going so far as to suggest that the highest purpose of union was the "reformation" of the American mind. Though he served on the Committee of Detail, whose members composed the first draft of the Constitution, the theory that he was a major influence on the final form of the document is unsupported, a myth of those scholars who prefer his teaching to that of the Framers of genuine importance. Wilson is perhaps most useful in directing our attention to what the authors of the Constitution did not intend for it to mean.

Though often disappointed in the Great Convention, James Wilson was the dominant figure in the Pennsylvania ratifying convention of 1787. There he placated Antifederalists with promises that "all rights not specifically given to the general government" were "reserved to the states"—and that therefore no Bill of Rights was needed to complete the Constitution, since such definitions were properly the business of the "sovereign" states, who could make and enforce their own versions of "universal truth." For days he held the floor, answering all objections to the Federal compact—often with arguments he had not used in the Great Convention. Here his oratory was at its best—so brilliant that his friend Benjamin Rush spoke of the performance as "a blaze of light." And, in his major address to this gathering of delegates from throughout his state, he held out a vision of America's future, a dream of power and glory moving westward, filling those who owned a share in it with "awe and apprehension"—of a land so vast, with such infinite potential, that it was rich beyond the wildest dreams of avarice. In these remarks, and in his earlier October 6, 1787, speech in the State House Yard, following soon after the adjournment of the Constitutional Convention, Wilson carried the case for the proposed Federal Constitution in Pennsylvania. And, through his sanguine "astonishment" at the thought of what might be, he foreshadowed the painful and ironic conclusion of his public career in the decade to come.

With the installation of President George Washington and the formation of the government under the new Constitution, James Wilson did not receive the highest judicial honor within its gift. Though he directly solicited the post of Chief Justice of the Supreme Court, and though the most important Federalist in Pennsylvania, Robert Morris, had lobbied to win him the job, Washington recognized the problems that might issue from Wilson's passion for speculation, from the rumor of his debts, and from riots like the one in Carlisle, Pennsylvania, in January of 1788—where the capstone was a burning of Wilson in effigy in a town which had once been his home. Therefore, Washington wisely turned away from the proud, learned Scot, called by his enemies "Lieutenant-General of the Myrmidons of power," and appointed John Jay of New York. Wilson was, however, offered the position of Associate Justice, which he accepted. Soon after his elevation to the High Court, he was asked to give a course of lectures in the law at the College of Philadelphia, of which he was a trustee. The results of this labor, published mostly after his death, were the first studies of their kind to be produced in North America—an attempt to create an American jurisprudence based on consent instead of authority. Wilson had a central and positive role in writing the balanced Pennsylvania Constitution of 1790. He began, at the behest of the state legislature, a complete digest of the laws of Pennsylvania. Finally, it appeared that his efforts in so many fields of endeavor, his great energies, were beginning to bear fruit. It was rumored that James Wilson had become one of the richest men in the country. America was "the home of limitless progess," said James Wilson. And "it is the glorious destiny of man to be always progressive." But what some authorities have referred to as the "compulsive and irrational" dimension of his commitment to progress of a personal kind was beginning to catch up with him, even as he contributed to the growth of the Republic.

Between 1792 and his death in 1798, James Wilson plunged more and more deeply into land speculation. He was a large investor in the Illinois-Wabash Company. He bought an interest in one of the infamous Yazoo companies, as well as other lands in Pennsylvania and New York. He bought on option, and then tried to hold on, while at the same time adventuring in other commercial and manufacturing schemes. Depression and war in Europe—a war that cut off immigration—dried up investment funds and lowered the value of all frontier properties. Still, Wilson came up with larger and larger designs, asking Dutch investors to buy 500,000 acres through him and to ship over their own immigrants to purchase the land. In intervals between these frantic efforts to shore up his financial empire, Wilson did a little business as Federal judge, rode the circuit, and wrote an important opinion in *Chisholm vs. Georgia*, in which he argued, from his familiar definition of the Union as representing the whole people of the United States and not a bond between the people of the states, that the citizen of one state could sue the government of another state—in this case, a state where Wilson had lands. His object was to "develop" the intention of the Framers. The 11th Amendment to the Constitution cancelled this ruling—and reproached the Federalists on the Court for reaching after unwarranted authority. Wilson's opinion was called a "rhapsody," and contemporaries spoke of his willingness to "twist any text" to strengthen the power of the general government. Perhaps he, and not Marshall, was the father of judicial review based on implied powers. But he went about the task with the same lack of scruple that he displayed in his land dealings and therefore provided no aegis for his successors in imaginative construction of the fundamental law. Finally, his colleagues on the Court reminded him that it was "of more importance to ascertain what the law is, than to speculate what it ought to be." But the distinction that they were making was not of the kind that Wilson understood. In the end, creditors began to call in his notes. The United States Congress still refused to shore up his claims. Hundreds of thousands of dollars were due. Wilson, though a justice of the United States Supreme Court, fled, "hunted," in his own words, "like a wild beast." Twice he was arrested. As he had deceived others, now it became clear that he had also deceived himself. Ironically, he found final shelter in the South, with his friend Justice James Iredell at Edenton, North Carolina. There, of a "nervous fever," crying out in remorse, he died in shame—one of the most curious, brilliant, gifted, and distressing figures in the political history of his country. (See C. Page Smith, *James Wilson, Founding Father, 1742–1798* [Chapel Hill: University of North Carolina Press, 1956]; Arnaud B. Leavelle, "James Wilson and the Relation of Scottish Metaphysics to American Political Thought," *Political Science Quarterly*, LVII (Fall, 1942), 394–410; Geoffrey Seed, *James Wilson: Scottish Intellectual and American Statesman* [Millwood, N. Y.: KTO Press, 1978]; W. E. Obering, *The Philosophy of Law of James Wilson: A Study in Comparative Jurisprudence* [Washington, D. C.: Catholic University Press, 1938]; Robert G. McCloskey, "James Wilson," pp. 79-96 of Vol. I of *The Justices of the United States Supreme Court, 1789–1969: Their Lives and Major Opinions* [New York: R. R. Bowker/Chelsea House, 1969], ed. by Leon Friedman and Fred L. Israel; Robert Waln, Jr., pp. 111-175 of Vol. VI of *Biography of the Signers to the Declaration of Independence* [Philadelphia: R. W. Pomeroy, 1825), ed. by John Sanderson; R. L. Brunhouse, *The Counter-Revolution in Pennsylania, 1776-1790* [Harrisburg: Pennsylvania Historical Commission, 1942]; Robert G. McCloskey, ed., *The Works of James Wilson*, 2 vols. [Cambridge: Harvard University Press, 1967]; John Bach McMaster and Frederick D. Stone, *Pennsylvania and the Federal Constitution, 1787-1788* [New York: Da Capo Press, 1970]; and H. James Henderson, *Party Politics in the Continental Congress* [New York: McGraw-Hill, 1974].)

Gouverneur Morris

(January 31, 1752-November 6, 1816), statesman, diplomat, lawyer, planter, and financier.

Though a representative of Pennsylvania in the Constitutional Convention, by way of an appointment which he did not seek, more properly identified with landed magnates of New York's Whig aristocracy. The least sanguine of the Framers, but one of the most brilliant. Grandson of Lewis Morris I, and youngest son of Lewis Morris II, lords of the manor and justices of the King's Bench. Born at Morrisania, the famly seat in Westchester County, to his father's second wife, Sarah Gouverneur Morris. Of distinguished Dutch, Huguenot, Welsh, and English ancestry. Educated in a French school at New Rochelle, in the Academy of Philadelphia, at King's College, and in the law offices of that great Tory, William Smith. Destined by birth, training, and ability for a life of public service and political importance.

Gouverneur Morris' portion from his father was £2500, the "best education that's to be had," and a network of connections, by blood and marriage, with the great families of two states. Of this, as with everything else that came his way, he made the most. He was admitted to the bar at the age of nineteen. And, by the time the American Revolution had directed his talents into another channel, had given earnest of what might have been a distinguished career as an attorney. But like his father and grandfather, both of them great defenders of colonial rights under the English Constitution, he was, even while away from his original profession, devoted to the concept of liberty as achieved through law. And he gave to this commitment his unqualified support at important points throughout his career. Therefore, he was uneasy about the possibility of radical egalitarian consequences *within* the English colonies in North America, coming as a side effect of their struggle to win some kind of independence, and was slow to align himself with the warmer spirits among the Sons of Liberty. Until 1775 he continued to hope for a peaceful reconciliation with the mother country: an accommodation guaranteeing to British America an internal autonomy and right of self-determination. When that hope dimmed following the publication of the Intolerable Acts and the appearance of a British fleet off Sandy Hook, he threw himself wholeheartedly into the effort to create on this side of the Atlantic a completely separate, strong, and united republic: one which could restrain the spirit of that great reptile, "the Mob." As did half of his family, including his eldest brother, Lewis Morris, third lord of the manor, who had signed the Declaration of Independence, he became a rebel in order to control a revolution—so that New York might not become a democracy in the process of becoming free.

Morris' participation in the American Revolution began with his election as a delegate from a meeting of Westchester freeholders to the new authority, the Provincial Congress meeting in New York City in May of 1775. There young Morris immediately distinguished himself with his ideas on currency, his moderation, and his freedom from cant. With other young aristocrats, he offered himself as a soldier in February of 1776, but was returned to his seat in the Provincial Congress when the Continental Congress refused to organize the battalion planned by the gentry of New York. In the Provincial Congress he was among the first to call for a final break with Great Britain, though he preferred it should be done quietly, lest the people be excited into "rashness and presumption." He was among the authors of New York's new constitution of 1777—a document which required that he compromise with Robert R. Livingston on behalf of slavery, and with John Jay in the cause of religious intolerance. After Sir William Howe had occupied the city of New York, Morris served on a committee charged with coordination of the defense of the Hudson River counties and the northern borders of the state. He observed the campaign which ended in victory at Saratoga, reported on the fall of Ticonderoga, and was a severe inquisitor into the activities of Loyalists, even of those who had been his friends. As a part of the inner Council of Safety, he helped to run the state from its little capital at Kingston.

New York sent Gouverneur Morris to a seat in the Continental Congress in 1777. There he displayed a great concern for military operations, became a friend of Lafayette, and gave constant support to the leadership of General Washington, whom he had met and admired the year before. For the Congress he spent part of the winter of 1778 at Valley Forge. Later he authored legislation for military reforms, supervised much of American diplomacy, wrote pamphlets to negate the blandishments of British offers of amnesty, planned invasions of Canada and raids on the coast of England. He wrote the instructions which Franklin carried to France, and the plan for a final peace with England. Furthermore, he joined with Robert Morris in the labor of funding the Revolution, trying to sustain the Continental Army in the field. He drew plans for a treasury board which anticipated Hamilton's grand design of a decade later. And when in May of 1779 he lost his place as a member for New York (thanks to his "neglect" of that state's desire to prevent the independence of Vermont), he immediately moved to Philadelphia, set up in the practice of law, and in 1781 joined Robert Morris as Assistant Superintendent of Finance—a post which he held until 1785.

Robert Morris was himself responsible for the election of his friend, lieutenant, and business partner to a place in the Pennsylvania delegation to the Philadelphia Convention. Gouverneur did not particularly wish to take part in these deliberations, since family business following upon the death of his mother greatly occupied him in New York. He had bought out the interest of his brothers in Morrisania and had become, in effect, the lord of the manor there. But, apart from the absence of a few weeks, he did attend the Convention with regularity and spoke more frequently (173 times) than any other member of that body. He brought to it wit, good humor, great oratorical gifts, and a completely formed political philosophy. His unsentimental evaluation of human nature often shocked his opponents in these debates. The depravity of men was his axiom. And for advanced views of a metaphysical human equality, he had only cheerful contempt: "He who wishes to enjoy natural Rights must establish himself where natural Rights are admitted. He must live alone." This doctrine is more Hobbes than Locke. And to moderate it, Morris would add only that the natural law of life is that men "live in society" and "do what that condition requires." The foundation of his doctrine was commitment to the sanctity of property as the basis of civilization. Financial and commercial confusion under the Articles was, however, only a part of his politics in 1787. The rest he argued from definition and the record of human history.

According to Gouverneur Morris, the form of government which the Framers made ready to attempt should "depend upon the established institutions and the political maturity of the people." And in this teaching he seemed moderate indeed. He expected to preserve the states, and even voted to deny Congress the veto over their legislation. Yet he could be as ruthless for the new sovereign that he had in mind as he had been against the old. Where deliberation failed, other means of effecting change would have to be considered. Even before the Convention officially opened, it appears that he suggested to the members already in Philadelphia that the equal representation allowed to the small states in the Continental Congress might be, on this occasion, denied them by fiat if they would not agree to such an arrangement. And he made the same threat concerning Delaware's role under the new government when Gunning Bedford spoke of foreign alliances for that tiny commonwealth. Small, unreasonable states might be abolished with the sword. Yet there was no contradiction in his argument. For he also maintained that the choices before the house were so severe, between a strong government and a despotism following civil war, that republican scrupulosity about consensus was a luxury he and his associates could ill afford.

Gouverneur Morris was, among the Framers, almost the definition of a High Federalist. What he wanted from Philadelphia was a government strongly national in character. He called for a President elected for life or, failing that, eligible for re-election. He preferred a Federal property qualification for freeholder suffrage; and an appointed Senate, chosen by the President, serving without pay and for life. Unlike most of the Framers, he expected the United States Supreme Court to have broad review powers. His model for a new United States was clearly undemocratic. "Give the votes to the people who have no property," he said, "and they will sell them to the rich." Or else vote themselves the possessions of those more prosperous. Morris' proposals were anathema to most of the Southern delegates. Though he himself had recently inherited slaves, and, in the view of many, had a flavor of sectional prejudice, he made the only serious attacks on the peculiar institution itself (as opposed to the slave trade) offered during the Convention. He advocated a power to tax exports, an end to the slave trade, and a suspension of the three-fifths compromise on the political representation of slaves, probably because it allowed the slaveholders to augment their power with a simple act of purchase. He was also negative about the admission of new states from the West: "The Back members are almost always averse to the best measures." He announced a fear that the South and the West would get "the maritime states" into wars. Yet he pretended to speak for "America" and the "rights of mankind." However, he accepted the important compromises, once they were achieved, and was so respected for his gifts of style and language by friends and adversaries alike that the task of preparing the final draft of the Constitution was placed in his hands.

After the adoption of the new Constitution by the states, Gouverneur Morris went to Europe to pursue his business interests, traded in commodities and debt, promoted speculations in land, and in 1790, acting for President Washington, opened unofficial negotiations with the British concerning trade, frontier forts, reparations for stolen slaves, and the exchange of diplomatic representatives. He grew very rich, but accepted an appointment early in 1792 as United States Minister to France. During the dark days of the Terror, he was the only foreign minister who kept to his post in Paris. He had tried, while still a private citizen, to save the government and the life of Louis XVI. Morris was, in fact, entrusted with the King's private funds not long before his execution. And, as American minister, his house became a refuge to a great many who had, in his presence, flirted with advanced ideas which Morris had warned against. Morris was, as his valuable diary indicates, appalled by the fanatical ideology of the Jacobin republic. The French recognized this, and, in consequence, requested his recall after Washington had expelled "Citizen" Genêt. His time in France made the gentleman from New York if anything more conservative than he had been before, and more appreciative of the stability of the new government arranged for in Philadelphia. But he remained overseas for another four years, active in trade, in travel, and in his various "adventures," before returning home. Once back he rebuilt the mansion on his estate. He was elected United States Senator for New York in 1800 to fill out another man's term. In that capacity he supported the Louisiana Purchase, even though it might mean the addition of new Southern states, and urged that the United States take a hand in suppressing the slave uprising in St. Dominique. The French Revolution, he thundered, had released a poisonous doctrine upon the world. Any measure calculated to restrain the ideologically disguised imperial ambitions of France deserved the approbation of those responsible for the future of this Republic.

A Jeffersonian majority in the New York legislature prevented the re-election of Morris in 1802. Undeterred, he retired to Morrisania and private life. In the years remaining he continued to prosper in trade. He married and had a son. He was generous with his friends, his church (Protestant Episcopal), and with worthwhile public causes. The tall figure with the wooden leg (he had lost the leg in an accident at the age of 28) was a familiar sight on Wall Street and at great public occasions, such as those when he delivered the eulogies for Hamilton and George Clinton. In 1810 he was appointed by the legislature as chairman of a board of commissioners called upon to build the Erie Canal. His only other significant involvement with things political came in 1812, when, outraged by our tacit alliance with Napoleonic France in a war with England and against the best interests of "Christian civilization," he called for the secession of New York and New England from the Union. Morris' pamphlet, "Address to the People of the State of New York," led to the Hartford Convention of 1814. It argued the legality of secession on the evidence of his experience in the Constitutional Convention of 1787 and from a High Federalist point of view. It is too little known by our constitutional historians. Morris lived to see his plan of secession fail through Yankee timidity, but enjoyed as a consolation the restoration of the Bourbon dynasty in France.

Gouverneur Morris was an eminently civilized American and a great patriot. An Old Whig, loyal to the values represented for him by his distinguished ancestors and the mentors of his youth, his was essentially a politics of experience, scornful of the regnant abstractions of Enlightenment radicalism. He is a correction of our conventional view of the Framers as speculative men of "big ideas." Yet he was an advocate of the abolition of slavery, by moderate and gradual means, in his own state, even though he had no faith in the "rights of man" which we ordinarily associate with such a position. His part in the Great Convention and in early American politics indicates something of its complexity. And his influence on the document is greater than we are often led to believe. (See Max M. Mintz, *Gouverneur Morris and the American Revolution* [Norman: University of Oklahoma Press, 1970]; Howard Swiggett, *The Extraordinary Mr. Morris* [Garden City, N. J.: Doubleday and Co., 1952]; Theodore Roosevelt, *Gouverneur Morris*

[Boston and New York: Houghton Mifflin Co., 1888]; Beatrix C. Davenport, editor, *A Diary of the French Revolution by Gouverneur Morris,* 3 vols. [Boston: Houghton Mifflin Co., 1939]; Daniel Walther, *Governeur Morris: Witness of Two Revolutions* [New York: Funk and Wagnalls Co., 1934]; and Jared Sparks, *The Life of Gouverneur Morris, with Selections from His Correspondence and Miscellaneous Papers,* 3 vols. [Boston: Gray & Bowen, 1832].)

Thomas Mifflin

(January 10, 1744–January 20, 1800), merchant, Revolutionary leader, soldier, and Pennsylvania politician.

Perhaps the most popular political figure in his state at the time of the Constitutional Convention, but of no influence on its deliberations. A mild commercial Federalist, and a man of considerable wealth, but of no consistent political philosophy. Made important in Pennsylvania by his conspicuous role in bringing the state to a full commitment to the struggle for American independence. Born in Philadelphia, of distinguished Quaker origin. Son of John and Elizabeth Bagnell Mifflin. Educated in a Quaker school, at the College of Philadelphia, and in the countinghouse of William Coleman, a Philadelphia merchant often associated with John Mifflin's enterprises. At twenty, Thomas Mifflin visited Europe, and upon his return to Philadelphia, entered a trading partnership with his brother George. In business, entirely successful, but drawn to politics by his concern for colonial rights. Outspoken in his opposition to the Stamp Act and instrumental in the adoption of non-importation agreements. With Charles Thomson, Benjamin Rush, and George Clymer, a leader in the popular movement to establish Committees of Correspondence. Four times elected to the Provincial Assembly (1772-1776) and sent by that body to represent Pennsylvania in the First and Second Continental Congresses, where he was one of the youngest and most radical members. Famed for his oratory and for inspiring the citizens of his state to exertion and sacrifice in the Patriot cause.

Soon after the opening of hostilities at Lexington and Concord, Thomas Mifflin was elected a major in one of the first regiments raised in Pennsylvania, and on June 23, 1775 was appointed General George Washington's aide-de-camp. He took part in the siege of Boston, but in August of 1775, was persuaded to accept the post of Quartermaster General of the entire Continental Army, a position which he held (except for a brief interval during the 1776 campaign in New York) until March, 1778. In the beginning he was an efficient quartermaster, though he longed for martial glory and on a few occasions distinguished himself under fire. In December of 1775, he was commissioned colonel and in May of the following year promoted to the rank of brigadier general. However, much of his reputation was due to his status as a soldier-politician, with the backing of a sizable faction within the Continental Congress. For a time Washington made good use of Mifflin's influence in Philadelphia and often employed him as liaison with congressional and state authorities. Mifflin was present at the battles of Trenton and Princeton, was appointed major-general in February of 1777, and was assigned the duty of preparing the defenses of Philadelphia. On several occasions his speeches persuaded soldiers to stay with the Army even in the dark days after the retreat from New York and through New Jersey. Moreover, he brought fresh troops from Pennsylvania to participate in Washington's reconquest of most of New Jersey. But he grew to overvalue his own military importance, became jealous of Washington's other officers, tired of his duties as quartermaster, and gradually withdrew from direct involvement in the war effort "for reasons of health." Once Philadelphia had fallen to Sir William Howe, Mifflin pressed upon Congress his request dated October 8, 1777 that he be allowed to resign as major and Quartermaster General.

However, Thomas Mifflin was not officially relieved of his responsibilities as a soldier until February of 1779, or of his responsibility for Washington's commissary until March of 1778. And during this period when he was neither in nor out of the Army, he became a willing tool of American political leaders dissatisfied with General Washington's leadership and determined to replace or restrain the Virginian in his role as Commander in Chief. Mifflin's assistants made a complete failure of their duty to provide for the encampment at Valley Forge during the dreadful winter of 1777–1778. The affairs of Mifflin's department degenerated into a terrible confusion and he was called upon to face a court-martial once his records had been presented and not approved. The charges included idleness, duplicity, and criminal partiality—putting the interests of a faction and a state ahead of the needs of the country. Meanwhile, General Thomas Conway and General Horatio Gates were put forward by some of the most radical spirits in the Congress and the Army as better suited to the military purposes of a "revolutionary people" than the cautious and socially conservative Washington. Mifflin and Gates were appointed to a Congressional Board of War to oversee the activities of forces in the field, and Thomas Conway was appointed Inspector-General. Evidence of collusion linking these officers and their patrons in the Congress with a design to force Washington's resignation came to light. And they, instead of Washington, were injured. General Gates, with great difficulty, was able to extricate himself from the collapse of the "Conway Cabal." General Conway himself was forced out of the army, and Thomas Mifflin's often-repeated request that he be allowed to resign finally honored. However, though discredit for involvement in the maneuvering against Washington and for mismanagement of his office as Quartermaster General attached to Thomas Mifflin's name and denied him any role of importance in national politics once the Constitution was approved, he retained the affection and support of the people of Pennsylvania throughout his time of troubles and for the rest of his life. For them he was a physical embodiment of the spirit of the Revolution.

After his withdrawal from the Army, Mifflin rose quickly in Pennsylvania politics, in which he had never ceased to be involved even while a soldier. He was re-elected to the state assembly in 1778 and to the Continental Congress from 1782 to 1784. Ironically, he was the President of that body when General Washington returned to it his commission as American Commander in Chief. On the state level, Mifflin opposed the radical Democrats who called for cheap money and price controls, fought to revise or cancel the radical Pennsylvania Constitution of 1776, and at the same time successfully continued to represent himself as the champion of the ordinary citizen and enemy of the "wicked Tories." After three more years in the legislature, he was elected to the Supreme Executive Council of Pennsylvania in 1788 and succeeded Benjamin Franklin as its President. In 1789–1790 he was also chairman of the state constitutional convention which cancelled the legal effects of Pennsylvania's liberal and revolutionary Constitution of 1776. Mifflin was elected Pennsylvania's first governor under this new instrument in 1790 and was continued in that office for nine years: the three terms allowed by statutory limit. He was, generally speaking, a good governor. After leaving that office, he served a final year in the state legislature.

The paradox of Thomas Mifflin's public life is summarized by the distance between the form of his political appeal and the substance behind it. According to his erstwhile friend Benjamin Rush, Mifflin's popularity was "acquired by the basest acts of familiarity with the meanest of the people. He avoided the society of gentlemen, and cherished that of mechannicks." Yet on most days, Mifflin rode from his estate in the suburbs to his office dressed in the full uniform of a general, riding a fine horse and followed by a retinue of Negro servants in livery. He ended his career as a Jeffersonian and a Lutheran. But apart from a few pleasantries with the French ambassador and a reluctance to quash the Whiskey Rebellion, nothing in his policy or conduct greatly offended the conservative disposition of the social and economic leaders of Philadelphia, especially the Quaker merchant princes, whose political support Mifflin retained long after he had forfeited his membership in their religious community. Though he died in financial straits and was buried at the public expense, though he had run through a great fortune and was notorious for his fondness for the bottle, though his political career was more a matter of eloquence and a pleasing exterior than of fixed and well-considered beliefs, Thomas Mifflin was a hero to the people of his state. And he remains a useful measure of their political development during the Revolution, under the Articles, and in the early years of the Republic. (See

Kenneth R. Rossman, *Thomas Mifflin and the Politics of the American Revolution* [Chapel Hill: University of North Carolina Press, 1952]; Forrest McDonald, *We the People: The Economic Origins of the Constitution* [Chicago: University of Chicago Press, 1958], pp. 61–63; J. Edwin Hendricks, *Charles Thomson and the Making of a New Nation, 1729–1824* [Rutherford: Fairleigh Dickinson University Press, 1979]; David F. Hawke, *In the Midst of a Revolution* [Philadelphia: University of Pennsylvania Press, 1961]; Harry Martin Tinkcom, *The Republicans and Federalists of Pennsylvania, 1790–1801: A Study of National Stimulus and Local Response* [Harrisburg: Pennsylvania Historical and Museum Commission, 1950]; Robert L. Brunhouse, *The Counter-Revolution in Pennsylvania, 1776–1790* [Harrisburg: Pennsylvania Historical Commission, 1942]; William Nisbet Chambers, *Political Parties in the New Nation: The American Experience, 1776–1809* [New York: Oxford University Press, 1973]; Ronald M. Baumann, "The Democractic Republicans of Philadelphia: The Origins, 1776–1797," Ph.D. dissertation, Pennsylvania State University, 1970; Richard A. Ryerson, "Leadership in Crisis. The Radical Committees of Philadelphia and the Coming of Revolution in Pennsylvania, 1765–1776: A Study in the Revolutionary Process," Ph.D. dissertation, Johns Hopkins University, 1973.)

George Clymer

(March 16, 1739–January 24, 1813), merchant, banker, Signer of the Declaration of Independence and leader of the movement toward the Revolution in Pennsylvania.

A commercial Federalist, but also affected by Pennsylvania's experience with mob rule and "the excesses of democracy." A quiet, thoughtful, modest man. Of little influence on the debates of the Framers, but respected by all of his colleagues for his services to the infant Republic and for his strength of character. Throughout his life, an admirer of the satires of Jonathan Swift. More of a strict republican than most of those present in the Great Convention. Best known for his work in financing the American war effort and for his role as a leader of the Continental Congress after the independence of the Colonies had been declared. A man of great wealth, but possessed of a genuine popular touch. Religious, and probably Quaker by origin, but a member of the Episcopal church during his maturity. A generous contributor to the cultural life of his city, where he became a well-beloved figure and ornament of public occasions. A peacemaker, but with courage.

George Clymer was born in Philadelphia, the son of Christopher Clymer and Deborah Fitzwater Clymer and grandson of Richard Clymer, who had emigrated to that city from Bristol, England. George was orphaned in his infancy and grew up under the guardianship of his uncle, William Coleman, a substantial figure in the commercial life of the Quaker Commonwealth. After some schooling at home and a course of reading in Coleman's considerable library, Clymer became a clerk in the countinghouse of Robert Ritchie, and, later, an associate of Reese Meredith and his son, also merchants of note. Eventually Clymer became a partner in this firm, which he combined with his uncle's business after Coleman's decease. His rise was marked by membership in the Philadelphia Common Council, 1767–1770. He also married into the Meredith family and in 1773 was, with the intensification of America's quarrel with the mother country, a man of mark in the business life of Pennsylvania.

George Clymer was strongly opposed to the mercantilist economics of the British Navigation Acts. In his view, they restricted the development of firms like his own in a fashion that was unfair to colonials—making of them something less than freeborn Englishmen. In 1773 he headed an *ad hoc* committee that compelled officials of the Crown charged with enforcing the Tea Act to resign from their posts as consignees and withdraw from the service of George III. He was one of the first in Philadelphia to call for complete independence. And he underwrote the ensuing conflict by exchanging all of his own specie for Continental currency. Clymer was a member of the Pennsylvania Council of Safety and one of the first two treasurers of the new system of government established by the Continental Congress. In 1776 he was elected a delegate from his state to that assembly and took his seat in time to sign the Declaration of Independence, after its adoption. In Congress Clymer soon became a man of all work, active in promoting the general loan (money borrowed from American citizens to finance the Congress), building links between the various states, inspecting the army in the field at Ticonderoga, and directing the defense of his city when the general government, under threat of British invasion, removed to Baltimore. Clymer actually worked to the point of physical collapse. British troops vandalized his home in Chester County. And the war almost destroyed his fortune. Yet he persisted, returning to Congress for two additional terms (1777; 1780–1782), where he continued to assume a great variety of considerable responsibilities. Clymer also served in the Pennsylvania legislature from 1780–1782 and from 1784–1788, where he opposed the ill effects of the radically democratic Pennsylvania Constitution of 1776 and advocated a return to something like the traditional structure of state government under the Proprietors, with a clear division and limitation of powers and no threat of mob rule. Once, with the expectation of educating his children, Clymer retired to Princeton, New Jersey, assuming that independence had been achieved. (Earlier, he had attempted to withdraw from public life while still resident in Pennsylvania.) But duty drew him back to Philadelphia, where, in the midst of the city's worst experience of radical demagogy and pseudo-democratic frenzy, he participated in the defense of the home of his colleague James Wilson ("Fort Wilson") against the attack of an armed mob. Yet, despite his horror at such outrages, Clymer continued to have much confidence in his ordinary neighbors, and they to have confidence in him. Or at least confidence in their deliberate sense as reflected by republican institutions.

In the Great Convention George Clymer (who had liked the old government under the Articles) opposed a tax on exports, warned against rapid expansion in the West, and objected to restrictions on Pennsylvania's taxing power over commerce passing through its territory. He opposed the provision of an authority to give binding instructions to members of Congress. But in general he was silent, ever present and supportive of whatever his friend George Washington seemed to approve. In the Pennsylvania legislature it was Clymer who made the motion for a state ratification convention. And he labored successfully in organizing Federalist forces to win the battle there. Upon the adoption of the United States Constitution, Clymer was elected to a seat in the House of Representatives of the First Congress (1789–1791) and then appointed a collector of the excise taxes on spirits brewed in Pennsylvania (1791–1794). Retiring to private life, he encouraged various worthwhile civic causes, including the Pennsylvania Academy of the Fine Arts, and the Philadelphia Society for Promoting Agriculture. He continued a career in banking fostered by his original association with the Bank of North America and later served as the first president of the Bank of Philadelphia. Unlike his former associate Robert Morris, he prospered as part of the system he had helped to create. Clymer disliked the French Revolution once it became an "armed doctrine," but did not approve of efforts to crush out republicanism in France. As he grew older, his identification with Federalism declined. Never did he doubt the legality of secession, or believe that the Union would automatically survive. A careful man, he illustrates the pattern of American leaders who were "radicals" for the Revolution, but did not expect independence to disturb the internal order of their society. In his old age, he was one of Philadelphia's most honored citizens, respected by all ranks of society. (See Robert L. Brunhouse, *The Counter-Revolution in Pennsylvania, 1776–1790* [Harrisburg: The Pennsylvania Historical Commission, 1942]; Page Smith, *James Wilson* [Chapel Hill: University of North Carolina Press, 1956]; H. James Henderson, *Party Politics in the Continental Congress* [New York: McGraw-Hill, 1974]; Robert Waln, Jr., "George Clymer," Vol. V of *Biography of the Signers to the Declaration of Independence* [Philadelphia: R. W. Pomeroy, 1823], pp. 173–246; Henry Simpson, *The Lives of Eminent Philadelphians* [Philadelphia: William Brotherhead, 1859], p. 211; John Bach McMaster and Frederick D. Stone, *Pennsylvania and the Federal Constitution, 1787–1788* [New York: Da Capo Press, 1970], pp. 704–706; Robert G. Ferris, ed., *Signers of the Constitution* [Washington, D. C.: U. S. Department of the Interior, 1976], pp. 154–156; Charles H. Lincoln, *The Revolutionary*

Movement in Pennsylvania, 1760–1776 [Philadelphia: University of Pennsylvania Press, 1901]; Richard A. Ryerson, "Leadership in Crisis. The Radical Committees of Philadelphia and the Coming of Revolution in Pennsylvania, 1765–1776: A Study in the Revolutionary Process," Ph.D. dissertation, Johns Hopkins University, 1973; Henry Martin Tinkcom, *The Republicans and Federalists of Pennsylvania, 1790–1801: A Study of National Stimulus and Local Response* [Harrisburg: Pennsylvania Historical and Museum Commission, 1950]; Walter H. Mohr, "George Clymer," *Pennsylvania History,* V [Oct., 1938], 282–285; Jerry Grundfest, *George Clymer: Philadelphia Revolutionary, 1739–1812* [New York: Arno Press, 1982].)

Thomas FitzSimons

(1741–August 26, 1811), leader of the Revolution in Pennsylvania, vigorous nationalist, militia officer, and one of Philadelphia's "merchant princes."

Commercial Federalist, *par excellence.* Yet also led to advocate a stronger national government by threats of disorder in Pennsylvania. Described by his contemporaries as "an aristocrat" and, unlike his friend George Clymer, not restrained in his politics by questions concerning the aboriginal "rights of man." Pious Roman Catholic, one of only two in the Great Convention. Born in Ireland, but emigrated to Philadelphia in his youth, where he quickly went into trade. Married (in 1761) Catherine Meade, the daughter of the powerful and wealthy Robert Meade. With his brother-in-law formed a partnership under the name of George Meade and Company, which prospered greatly in the West India trade.

With the outbreak of the American Revolution, FitzSimons—first cautiously and then enthusiastically—endorsed the Patriot cause. During the war he commanded a company of militia which he had raised himself (1776–1777), was a member of the Philadelphia Committee of Correspondence, of the Council of Safety, and the Navy Board. His firm provided fire ships for the protection of the city, gathered supplies for military use, and in the last years of the conflict, donated five thousand pounds to the Continental Army. In 1782 FitzSimons was elected to a seat in the Continental Congress, where he urged payment of the government's debt to its soldiers and the retirement of other debts owed by the Confederation. Though an opponent of the ultra-democratic Pennsylvania Constitution of 1776, he was elected a member of the unusual Pennsylvania Board of Censors, and from 1786–1789 was a powerful member of the state legislature. A founder of the Bank of North America, he was one of its directors from 1781–1803.

In the Great Convention FitzSimons was regular in his attendance, but said little to distinguish himself in the debates of the Framers. He favored a constitutional restriction on the rights of suffrage, a provision allowing states to continue to charge duties on commerce originating outside their borders, the reservation of high national office to men of means, and the right of Congress to tax both imports and exports. However, he believed that both the Senate and House of Representatives should have a hand in drafting treaties with foreign powers, and that Congress should have the authority to improve navigation or port facilities. The right of secession, in his opinion, would be retained by all approving states. Generally, he voted with the High Federalists, following the lead of Robert Morris. In their company, he helped to persuade the Pennsylvania legislature to call for a ratification convention soon after work on the Constitution had been completed.

Once the new government was established, Thomas FitzSimons served in the House of Representatives for three terms (1789–1795). In Congress he was an energetic advocate of the program of Alexander Hamilton. He called for a high tariff, retirement of the national debt, and internal improvements. Then, after defeat by a Democratic-Republican, he returned to Philadelphia. There he became president of the Philadelphia Chamber of Commerce and Director of the Insurance Company of North America. But he held no further offices, except for a place in a commission to liquidate British claims advanced under the terms of Jay's Treaty. Even so, in his final years he continued to enjoy some political influence, opposing Jefferson's Embargo of 1807–1809, and recommending that the First United States Bank be rechartered. FitzSimons suffered great losses as a consequence of the collapse of the empire of Robert Morris; and, like so many of the Framers from a commercial background, he went into financial ruin and bankruptcy. Thereafter his fortunes and his reputation improved, but were never completely restored. FitzSimons was a great contributor to his church and for many years a trustee of the University of Pennsylvania. A dignified man and a great friend to the Irish citizens of his city, he was a generous person throughout his life. (See Robert L. Brunhouse, *The Counter-Revolution in Pennsylvania, 1776–1790* [Harrisburg: Pennsylvania Historical Commission, 1942]; Henry Simpson, *The Lives of Eminent Philadelphians* [Philadelphia: William Brotherhead, 1859], pp. 372–373; Robert G. Ferris, ed., *Signers of the Constitution* [Washington, D. C.: U.S. Department of the Interior, 1976], pp. 163–164; John Bach McMaster and Frederick D. Stone, *Pennsylvania and the Federal Constitution, 1787–1788* [New York: Da Capo Press, 1970], pp. 706–707; Charles H. Lincoln, *The Revolutionary Movement in Pennsylvania, 1760–1776* [Philadelphia: University of Pennsylvania Press, 1901]; Richard A. Ryerson, "Leadership in Crisis. The Radical Committees of Philadelphia and the Coming of Revolution in Pennsylvania, 1765–1776: A Study in the Revolutionary Process," Ph.D. dissertation, Johns Hopkins University, 1973; and J. A. Farrell, "Thomas FitzSimons," *Records of the American Catholic Historical Society of Philadelphia*, XXXIX [Sept., 1928], 175–224.)

Jared Ingersoll, Jr.

(October 27, 1749–October 31, 1822), lawyer and political leader of post-Revolutionary Pennsylvania.

In the Great Convention, the tame Antifederalist from Philadelphia, chosen by the great commercial Federalists who controlled the legislature of his state as a meaningless concession to its liberal minority. Actually convinced before 1787 that a stronger central government was necessary to the future of the United States. Never really a democrat, though concerned about state sovereignty *and* the financial needs of a general government. Spoke only once in the entire Constitutional Convention, to specify that he "did not consider the signing, either as a mere attestation of the fact, or as pledging the signers to support the Constitution at all events," but as the best thing to do at the time. Born in New Haven, Connecticut. Son of Jared Ingersoll, Sr., one of the leading Tories in America, and of Hannah Whiting Ingersoll. Father a representative of the Colony of Connecticut in England, and later Stamp-Master General of all New England under the notorious Stamp Act. Rendered unpopular by his acceptance of this appointment. Moved by Whitehall to Philadelphia, where the Crown had made him a Vice-Admiralty Court Judge for Pennsylvania. The younger Jared Ingersoll was educated in the best schools of Connecticut, at Yale (from which he was graduated with a B. A. in 1766); by reading in the law (primarily with Joseph Reed in Philadelphia, after his family's relocation there in 1771); and at the Middle Temple (1774–1776). Admitted to the Pennsylvania bar in 1773. Advised by family to be absent from the country as the Revolution approached. No longer a Loyalist when, after a two-year tour of Europe and some association with Benjamin Franklin in France, he returned to Philadelphia late in 1778. Shortly thereafter, a Patriot, even though his father had been driven into retirement and exile in Connecticut for refusing to approve of American independence. Perhaps made a supporter of the Revolution by what he had seen and heard in Great Britain and on the Continent. Attorney for President Joseph Reed of the Supreme Executive Council of Pennsylvania and for the powerful merchant Col. Charles Pettit, an Antifederalist into whose family Ingersoll had married. Later attorney for the even wealthier Stephen Girard. Linked to the Constitutionalists, who supported the democratic Pennsylvania Constitution of 1776 and local autonomy for the states, by personal associations. Understandably, a very cautious person. A devout Presbyterian and an old-fashioned "man of the law," with perhaps the finest practice in a community of distinguished attorneys. Member of the Continental Congress for Pennsylvania, 1780–1781. Probably silent in the Constitutional Convention because of the anomaly of his situation within the Pennsylvania delegation.

After the establishment of a government under the new Federal Constitution, Jared Ingersoll, Jr., served on the Philadelphia Common Council in 1789 and as Attorney General of Pennsylvania from 1790–1799 and from 1811–1817. From 1800 to 1801 he was United States District Attorney for Pennsylvania. Displeased by the conduct of Jefferson's first administration, he was identified as a mild Federalist for the remainder of his life. He was the choice of Pennsylvania Federalists for the Vice-Presidency in 1812. But, essentially, he was not a political man. In 1791, Ingersoll was admitted to practice before the United States Supreme Court. And in that arena he participated in some of the most famous of the early cases to be tried there, including *Chisholm v. Georgia* (1792) and *Hylton vs. United States* (1796). In these actions, Ingersoll contended generally for a strict construction of the Constitution and against the doctrine of "implied powers." He was attorney for Senator William Blount of Tennessee when his old colleague and fellow Framer was threatened with impeachment for his role in a Western plan to get Britain to conquer Louisiana and Spanish Florida. In 1820–21, at the end of his career, Jared Ingersoll, Jr., was briefly presiding Judge of the District Court for the City and County of Philadelphia. At the time of his death at the age of 73, his son, Charles Jared Ingersoll, was already established as a leader of the American bar, though in his legal philosophy he was the antithesis of his traditionalist father and grandfather. (See Charles Jared Ingersoll, "Jared Ingersoll," pp. 594–596 of *The Lives of Eminent Philadelphians* [Philadelphia: William Brotherhead, 1859], ed. by Henry Simpson; Robert G. Ferris, ed., *Signers of the Constitution* [Washington, D. C.: U.S. Department of the Interior, 1976], pp. 175–176; Franklin Bowditch Dexter, *Biographical Sketches of Graduates of Yale College, with Annals of the College History*, Vol. III [New York: Henry Holt, 1903], pp. 184–187; Horace Binney, *Leaders of the Old Bar of Philadelphia* [Philadelphia: Sherman and Sons, 1859]; L. H. Gipson, *Jared Ingersoll: A Study of American Loyalism in Relation to British Colonial Government* [New Haven: Yale University Press, 1920]; John Bach McMaster and Frederick D. Stone, *Pennsylvania and the Federal Constitution, 1787–1788* [New York: Da Capo Press, 1970], pp. 707–709; H. James Henderson, *Party Politics in the Continental Congress* [New York: McGraw-Hill, 1974]; Henry Martin Tinkcom, *The Republicans and Federalists of Pennsylvania, 1790–1801: A Study of National Stimulus and Local Response* [Harrisburg: Pennsylvania Historical and Museum Commission, 1950]; and W. M. Meigs, *The Life of Charles Jared Ingersoll* [New York: Da Capo Press, 1970], pp. 18–25.)

John Dickinson

(Nov. 8, 1732–Feb. 14, 1808), lawyer, planter, statesman, and political philosopher.

One of the most prominent members of the Convention, and a leading citizen of both Pennsylvania and Delaware for over twenty years prior to that meeting. The most learned of the Framers; also undoubtedly the most undervalued and misunderstood member of their notable company. The only one of the Fathers of the Republic to play a role in every significant moment in its history from the Stamp Act Congress of Nov., 1765, through the 1787 deliberations in Philadelphia. Best remembered as "the Penman of the Revolution."

Born in Talbot County, Maryland, John Dickinson was the son of Judge Samuel Dickinson and Mary Cadwalader Dickinson, both Quakers. With his older brother, Philemon, he grew up in Delaware in Kent County, in a fine house that still stands southeast of Dover. As an heir to a substantial property (six square miles), he was first educated privately and then in the offices of John Moland, a leader of the Philadelphia bar. Young John finished this preliminary training in 1753 and was then dispatched to London and the Middle Temple for four years of the best of English legal preparation. On his return he established himself quickly in his profession, becoming eventually one of the most respected of American attorneys. In 1760 Dickinson was elected to the assembly of Delaware, where he served as speaker. In 1762 he won a seat as a Philadelphia member of the Pennsylvania legislature. There he became a champion of the proprietary government, opposed to all plans to cancel the Charter of the Penns and substitute in its place direct supervision by officers of the Crown. He cherished the old constitution of Pennsylvania, even though, as he admitted, it was subject to abuse. For it embodied a pious respect for the political rights of colonials, particularly in regard to self-government, and a new constitution granted by King-in-Parliament might not. Even at this stage in his career, Dickinson was more concerned with preserving established liberties than with reaching after new ones. He put his trust in law, not men, and never feared to be made unpopular by opposing some momentarily popular idea.

John Dickinson, after a struggle with the faction led by Benjamin Franklin, was not re-elected to the Pennsylvania legislature in 1764. However, he remained a political power by exercising his abilities as a pamphleteer. In 1765 he produced *The Late Regulations Respecting the British Colonies... Considered*. He was the author of resolutions agreed to in the Stamp Act Congress. And in 1767–1768 he issued, first in the newspapers and then as a book, his *Letters From a Farmer in Pennsylvania*, a work which made of him, in the space of a few months, the recognized spokesman for the North American colonies in their disputes with the new and aggressive policy of the ministers of George III. Sustained by this surge of American acceptance and international acclaim, he was, in 1770, returned to his seat in the Pennsylvania legislature, where he played a dominant role in the sequence of events which issued finally in the independence of the United States. In that year he married Mary Norris, daughter of the wealthy Isaac Norris, long a leader of the Philadelphia commercial establishment, and thus reinforced his already considerable position in the local aristocracy. The Dickinsons' home near Philadelphia, Fairhill, became, for a time, the center of the public life in their state. In December of 1776 it was burned in retaliation by British troops—thus identifying John Dickinson as one of those most directly responsible for what the British saw as a "rebellion."

In 1771 John Dickinson, speaking for the Pennsylvania legislature, drafted a "Petition to the King" seeking redress of grievances. He became, in 1774, the chairman of the Philadelphia Committee of Correspondence and later in that year was appointed a member for Pennsylvania in the Continental Congress. For his colleagues in Congress he wrote the *Declaration and Resolves of the First Continental Congress* (1774) and the *Declaration of the Causes of Taking Up Arms* (1775). He was also the author of the anthem of the Revolution, the famous "Song of the Farmer." And of much else besides. In all of these roles Dickinson labored to define the quarrel of the colonies with the imperial government in England in terms of their common political heritage in the English Constitution and the prescriptive rights of Englishmen. If there had to be a revolution, and he knew that it was likely that there would be, he was determined that it should be accomplished on the proper grounds. For he feared an internal transformation of American society in a radically democratic direction, as prophesied by some excited voices in New England, as much as he feared the armies of George III: feared the one as a product of the other. The protection of known and proven modes and orders was the purpose of every public gesture of his life. Though in moments of extremity he could agree to prudent change, when no other method for conserving could be found.

In such a spirit of realism, after long resistance and a try at every alternative, Dickinson accepted the Declaration of Independence, though he did not vote for it, made the best speech of his life against it, and left his post in Congress to assume the duties of brigadier general of the Pennsylvania militia rather than grace with his presence the moment of its adoption. Dickinson's objections to a final break with England in July of 1776 included disapproval of the timing of the measure (before a union of the states had been achieved, a new "house" prepared to replace the old) and disapproval of Jefferson's vehement language. But the core of his anxiety was not circumstantial. It had to do instead with his unwillingness to agree to a definition of his America as an entity now completely "outside" the stream of British history: as a reflection of fashionable ideas in contrast to the legal and customary continuity he had been trained to defend. And even after American independence had been achieved, he continued to resist such an abstract definition of its significance.

John Dickinson composed the first draft of our original instrument of government, the Articles of Confederation; and, following the clamor caused by his principled stubbornness in July of 1776 and a brief retreat to home ground in Delaware, he was returned by his old neighbors to serve in the Continental Congress for 1779. In their name in that session of Congress he signed the Articles he had helped to write. Dickinson served as a private soldier in the Battle of Brandywine, and aided his entire region in defense planning and preparation in the face of invasion. In 1781 he became President of Delaware's Supreme Executive Council. From 1782–1785, in a vindication that followed the electoral defeat of the extreme democrats in the Quaker State, he was the President of Pennsylvania. With these overlapping terms as chief executive of two states, Dickinson's experience in elected office came to an end. Yet after retiring to Delaware and the Dickinson estate, he was called upon again to attend (and chair) the Annapolis Convention of 1786; and in 1787 to lead the Delaware delegation to the Constitutional Convention. In support of the end product of that gathering, Dickinson wrote a series of essays entitled *The Letters of Fabius*, a set which bears an interesting comparison to *The Federalist Papers*. And in the two decades of life which remained to him, he continued to give effective political support to the very cautious, decentralized conception of the Federal Union outlined in that final work of advocacy—most of the time as a Jeffersonian Democrat: championed the view of a balanced regime of divided powers which he had bespoken in the Great Convention itself.

John Dickinson's role in the Philadelphia debates was less than his stature would have led his contemporaries to expect, and more than subsequent scholarship has been willing to allow. One explanation of his intermittent performance is that he missed some of the discussion because of illness. Another is his uneasiness with the idea of concentrated power, a new and stronger national government and what it might mean to the nation's future. But Dickinson did have an important share in the shaping of our Constitution, despite sickness and temperamental fear of change. And that portion of his public life played out within the Convention was in keeping with, and drew its authority from, all that he had said and done before in his country's service.

Throughout the Constitutional Convention, from the time of his initial remarks, John Dickinson championed both the necessity for a new instrument of government, able to raise money, provide for defense, conduct foreign affairs, and establish a currency, and also the need to preserve and protect the "agency" of the sovereign states within the new system. He was the first delegate to suggest that the states have equal representation in the U. S. Senate. He voiced a concern with the possibility of intrusion by the Supreme Court into matters not properly under their jurisdiction—such as the domestic institutions of the states. And he warned repeatedly against proposed innovations which had to recommend them nothing but speculation and theory: innovations which violated what was already ineluctably "given" in the pattern of American life. An instance of Dickinson's protective concern for institutions rooted in place and history, *grown* but not *made*, is his constant reference to the advantage of giving influence in the Congress and in other features of the fundamental law to the thirteen state legislatures. For these assemblies, operating from the colonial beginnings and through the Revolution, were in his opinion the particular repositories of our already existing liberty as a people and the proper source for local charters of liberty. Let there be a Bill of Rights in Virginia, for Virginians, to be interpreted by them. In Delaware, let there be another, different Bill of Rights, read by different men. And in the Constitution, careful delimitation, not subject to subsequent construction by the Federal courts, of the distinctive spheres and responsibilities of state and national governments. In these arguments Dickinson reasoned from experience and the record, from authority and analogy—particularly to republican Rome and England. But never from definition. Among the Framers he is the chief spokesman for the Old Whig tradition so important to subsequent American political thought. And for one of the most influential interpretations of the American Revolution.

John Dickinson was in agreement with the more decided Federalists in the Convention that there was a danger of fostering democratic excesses with the creation of a new government; with many of his associates he foresaw the ominous prospect of a greedy proletariat in America's future, a propertyless mass ready to vote itself the properties of other and better men. But he also agreed with the decided Antifederalists that concentrated national authority might readily be converted into an instrument for creating an artificial aristocracy of "placemen," friends of the administration in power made wealthy by economic privilege and sponsorship. To avoid both of these doleful alternatives and to secure the nation's political temperance, a careful distribution of powers was absolutely required. Hence Dickinson's many references to the example of the English Constitution. Though, from our own history, we could not reproduce English institutions, we should, with the materials at hand, attempt to produce their effect. And thus should erect only such a government as would allow the virtue of our people to express itself through forms suited to their "genius," reflective of their "deliberate sense" of themselves.

For Dickinson, despite the peculiarity of his Quaker origins, was an American Burke, the faithful steward of an old regime. Like his Irish counterpart, he had the passion of a convert for an acquired religion: a devotion to an American variant of English constitutionalism, rooted in Saxon antiquity and enthroned as sovereign in 1688. Neither wealth nor enlightenment were, in his view, primary reasons for strengthening the Union, but instead the human products of an inherited way of life and the liberty needed to practice it—the kind of liberty for the sake of which the Revolution had been fought. Finally, his view of the new U. S. Constitution was of a document that any reasonable Antifederalist could accept. The jealous vanities of the several states could not be allowed to stifle the general government, as they had the Continental Congress. Otherwise they were the objects of his special care in Philadelphia. For they were identified as the sources of our attachment to the political bond, replacing here the stability produced in the mother country the ancient patterns of English life and law. Nor did Dickinson, at the end of his political career, struggle in vain. None of his important arguments was effectively challenged in the Convention. And it was his kind of Constitution, as represented by his speeches in the Convention and in *The Letters of Fabius*, that won ratification in the states. His, more than Madison's or Hamilton's or even Washington's. He is, with Charles Cotesworth Pinckney of South Carolina, definitive of the moderate Federalist position of 1787–1788 and a key to the meaning of what was achieved with their particular assistance.

In his last two decades John Dickinson lived as a private citizen in Delaware, kept a fine house in Wilmington, farmed his acres in Kent County, collected an edition of his essays, advocated a moderate approach to the abolition of slavery in his state, and counseled his neighbors against rash and imprudent conduct of every kind. In religion he was, by turns, both Quaker and Episcopalian. He broke with the Federalists because they had violated the fundamental law hammered out in Philadelphia. (See Charles J. Stillé, *The Life and Times of John Dickinson, 1732–1808* [New York: Burt Franklin, 1969]; John H. Powell, "John Dickinson, Penman of the American Revolution," Ph.D. dissertation, University of Iowa, 1938; James M. Tunnell, Jr., "John Dickinson and the Federal Constitution," *Delaware History*, VI [Fall, 1955], 288–293; M. E. Bradford, "A Better Guide Than Reason: The Politics of John Dickinson," pp. 79–96 of *A Better Guide Than Reason: Studies in the American Revolution* [La Salle, Ill.: Sherwood Sugden & Co., 1979]; John Dickinson, "The Political Thought of John Dickinson," *Dickinson Law Review*, XXXIX [Oct., 1934], 1–14; H. Trevor Colbourn, *The*

Lamp of Experience: Whig History and the Intellectual Origins of the American Revolution [Chapel Hill: University of North Carolina Press, 1965], pp. 107-119; and Robert L. Brunhouse, *The Counter-Revolution in Pennsylvania, 1776-1790* [Harrisburg: Pennsylvania Historical Commission, 1942]; James H. Hutson, "John Dickinson and the Federal Constitutional Convention," *William and Mary Quarterly*, 40 [April, 1983], 256-282; Milton E. Flower, *John Dickinson: Conservative Revolutionary* [Charlottesville: University of Virginia Press, 1983; Stanley K. Johannsen, "Constitution and Empire in the Life and Thought of John Dickinson," Ph.D. dissertation, University of Missouri, 1973.)

George Read

(September 18, 1733–September 21, 1798), Signer of the Declaration of Independence (though he opposed it), lawyer, jurist, and political leader of Delaware.

A very High Federalist, though careful of the interests of the smaller states. With John Dickinson, the leader of the Delaware delegation. Author of the instructions which forced them to hold out for an equal voice in Congress for each of the states. Son of John Read of Dublin, Ireland, and of Mary Howell Read. Born in Cecil County, Maryland, into a family of considerable means. Episcopalian. Educated at Alison's Academy at New London, Pennsylvania, and in the offices of John Moland, a distinguished Philadelphia attorney. Admitted to the Philadelphia bar in 1753, but soon relocated to New Castle, Delaware, where his family then resided. A punctilious lawyer of profound learning and large practice while still a young man. Appointed Attorney General for the Three Lower Counties by the Crown in 1763, a post which he held until late in 1774. Opposed to the Stamp Act and an advocate of non-importation. Elected to the legislature of his colony in 1765. Like his dear friend John Dickinson, a very reluctant revolutionary, and no democrat. Sent by Delaware to the First Continental Congress in 1774. A member of the Second Continental Congress, which in July 1776 declared for American independence. The only member of that body to vote against the resolution of independence and still sign the Declaration. The presiding officer and dominant member of the Delaware state Constitutional Convention of 1776. Guaranteed in that labor that revolution against external British authority would not bring about radical change within his society. Member of the Delaware Legislative Council from 1776-1779. Became Acting President of Delaware in September, 1777, after the capture of President John McKinley. Unremitting in his efforts in that office in the task of civil and military preparation.

Relieved as President of Delaware in March of 1778 and, by reason of ill-health, of his post on the Council in the following year. Assented only with great reluctance to the Articles of Confederation because they did not guarantee Delaware's access to Western lands or set proper limits on interstate tariffs and taxation. Appointed Judge of Appeals in Admiralty by the Continental Congress in 1782. Returned to the Delaware Legislative Council from 1782–1788.

George Read was one of Delaware's delegates to the 1786 Annapolis Convention, and in the next year was dispatched to Philadelphia. In the Constitutional Convention he spoke strongly of the advantage of doing away with the states as separate political entities and, failing that unlikely political expedient, of the necessity for giving Congress the power to repeal state laws. However, these arguments were clearly part of a rhetorical strategy designed to protect the people of his state from political impotence and to secure for them as much influence as could be acquired. He was among those Federalists made uneasy by talk of holding goods in common and the cancellation of debts. He attended almost every session of the Convention and spoke on numerous occasions, usually in brief but to the point. He wished United States Senators to hold office "during good behavior," or at least for a nine-year term; and for the President to have the largest possible appointive powers. Though uncertain of the authority of the Philadelphia Convention, he feared the combination of the great states might reduce Delaware to a "cipher," and in the face of their designs, once threatened to lead a walkout. Yet he was eventually satisfied with the new government, that it was not "putting new cloth on an old garment," and on his return to Delaware was instrumental in securing early ratification.

George Read was United States Senator from Delaware under the new Constitution from 1789 until 1793. While in Congress, he voted consistently for the Federalist program. On September 18, 1793, he resigned from the Senate to become the chief justice of his state, a position he held until his death. Never a man of great wealth, Read enjoyed his estate on the Delaware, his gardens, his servants, and his repose. Socially, he was one of the most conservative of the Framers, and the greatest single influence over the politics of his state. Quiet and composed, a lawyer's lawyer and a man of the prescription, he was a force for order in his world, a moralist of the "public virtue" in the early life of the Republic. (See William T. Read, *The Life and Correspondence of George Read, Signer of the Declaration of Independence* [Philadelphia: J. B. Lippincott and Co., 1870]; John A. Munroe, *Federalist Delaware, 1775–1815* [New Brunswick: Rutgers University Press, 1954]; George H. Ryden, *Delaware—The First State in the Union* [Wilmington: Delaware Tercentenary Commission, 1938]; and Robert G. Ferris, ed., *Signers of the Constitution* [Washington, D. C.: U.S. Department of the Interior, 1976], pp. 206–208.)

Richard Bassett

(April 2, 1745–Sept. 15, 1815), planter, lawyer, jurist, and political leader of Delaware.

Though a man of great wealth and influence in his own region, one of the silent, inconspicuous figures in the Constitutional Convention. Son of a tavernkeeper, Michael Bassett, who deserted his wife, Judith. Richard Bassett was born in Cecil County, Maryland, and raised by his kinsman, Peter Lawson, from whom he inherited the 6,000–acre estate of Bohemia Manor, near the Delaware line. In his youth Bassett read law, first at home and then in Philadelphia. In 1770 he received a license to practice in Dover, Delaware, where he kept a town house. He had another home in Wilmington. And it was to his adopted state that his public life belonged.

During the Revolution Bassett was a captain in the Delaware militia and served on the Delaware Council of Safety. He was a member of the Delaware constitutional convention and sat in both houses of the state legislature. In 1786 his associates in that body sent him as one of their representatives to the Annapolis Convention, and in the following year dispatched him as part of the Delaware delegation to Philadelphia. There he followed closely the leadership of John Dickinson. He was also a member of the Delaware ratifying convention,which on Dec. 7, 1787, gave its unanimous support to the new Federal Constitution.

In the remainder of his political career, Richard Bassett had a considerable part in the political affairs of Delaware and in the government of the Republic. From 1789 to 1793 he was a United States Senator. From 1793 to 1799 he was Chief Justice of the Court of Common Pleas in his state, and from 1799 to 1801 he was governor of Delaware. In that year John Adams named Bassett, a loyal Federalist, as one of the notorious "midnight judges." He was confirmed in this appointment. But the Democratic–Republicans abolished his seat on the U.S. Circuit Court, and he spent the remainder of his life in retirement.

Richard Bassett was one of the most devout of the Framers. He was converted to Methodism during the Revolution and became a close personal friend of Bishop Francis Asbury, who held meetings on his plantation. Bassett freed his slaves and then employed them as hired labor. But he was no egalitarian or champion of radical change. Rather, he should be remembered as one of the pillars of the old order in Delaware, an aristocratic order which preserved its authority through the Revolution and into the early years under the new Constitution. When in the U.S. Senate, he voted usually with the Southern Federalists, and opposed Alexander Hamilton's financial system.

He was a mild Federalist even during the Constitutional Convention, where he opposed giving the Congress a veto over legislation in the states. He is best remembered for his contributions to the life of his chosen church, his generosity toward what he saw as the work of God. (See Robert E. Pattison, "The Life and Character of Richard Bassett," *Papers of the Historical Society of Delaware*, XXIX (1900), 3-19; Robert G. Ferris, editor, *Signers of the Constitution* [Washington, D. C.: United States Dept. of the Interior, 1976], pp. 142-143; Henry C. Conrad, *History of the State of Delaware* [Wilmington, 1908]; John A. Munroe, *Federalist Delaware: 1775-1815* [New Brunswick: Rutgers University Press, 1954]; and George H. Ryden, *Delaware—The First State in the Union* [Wilmington: Delaware Tercentenary Commission, 1938].)

Gunning Bedford

(1747-March 30, 1812), lawyer, jurist, and political leader of Delaware.

The stormy petrel of the Constitutional Convention, and an influence upon its deliberations by way of his fierce devotion to the interests of his adopted state. Born in Philadelphia, educated at the College of New Jersey (later Princeton), where he was Madison's roommate, and in the law offices of that cautious and reluctant rebel, Joseph Reed. He was admitted to the Pennsylvania bar, and then moved southward, first to Dover and later to Wilmington, where he began to practice his profession. A devout Presbyterian. Ostensibly Bedford did some military service during the Revolution; but he is not to be confused with his soldier cousin of the same name, a politically prominent Delaware contemporary. To distinguish himself from his kinsman, who was Col. Bedford and then Governor Bedford of their state, Bedford the Framer styled himself Gunning Bedford, Jr. Throughout their careers, the two men often worked to the same ends, as, for instance, in Delaware's ratifying convention of December, 1787, where the new Constitution was first approved by a state.

Gunning Bedford was, by turns, an elected member of the Delaware legislature, of the state council, of the Continental Congress, and of the Federal Convention of 1787. He was chosen as a member of the Delaware delegation to the Annapolis Convention, but did not attend. From 1784 to 1789 he was the attorney general of his state. In 1789 President Washington appointed him the first Federal District Judge for Delaware, in which office he performed until his death.

Most of Gunning Bedford's adult life was spent in public service. Yet he was a man of modest means. In person he was large and convivial, corpulent and direct. His powers as an orator were considerable; William Pierce describes him as a "bold and nervous speaker" with "a very commanding and striking manner." In theory, and later as a judge, he was a very moderate Federalist. Yet he was nonetheless prepared to threaten the Philadelphia Convention with the possibility that the small states might make foreign alliances of their own if a Constitution protecting their influence and integrity were not agreed to by the delegations of Massachusetts, Virginia, and Pennsylvania—the great powers represented on that floor. "Do your worst," he challenged. His firmness at a crucial point helped to force the compromise on equal representation in one chamber of the national legislature—a concession which Delaware had set as a condition for its agreement to a stronger bond of union. He thereby strengthened the hand of Mason, Dickinson, Gerry, and other moderates in restraining the more ardent centralizers present in that assembly.

Gunning Bedford was originally suspicious of the motives of certain leading figures in the Great Convention. But he had, by stages, come to favor replacement of the Articles of Confederation with an instrument able to protect his neighbors from foreign enemies *and* the high tariffs of Maryland and Pennsylvania. Moreover, he hoped to see Delaware acquire an interest in the public lands to the west. He was opposed, however, to giving the Congress a power of veto over legislation in the states and reluctant to assign great authority to the President or the U. S. Supreme Court. He was regular in his attendance of the Convention, spoke frequently, and was a member of several committees. He gave his support to the important compromises which resulted in a final agreement. After ratification, his role in Delaware politics was as a trusted advisor to the Delaware establishment. He was a mild abolitionist, but considered slavery to be a concern of the sovereign commonwealths. Twice he was a Presidential elector, and for years championed the cause of education in his city. He illustrates the paradox of Delaware Federalism: an enthusiasm for a stronger government rooted in essentially provincial concerns, made necessary by the size of their state; but nothing like the Federalism of Wilson, Hamilton, or Gouverneur Morris. (See John A. Munroe, *Federalist Delaware, 1775–1815* [New Brunswick: Rutgers University Press, 1954], pp. 105–109, *et passim*; Robert G. Ferris, editor, *Signers of the Constitution* [Washington, D. C.: United States Dept. of the Interior, 1976], pp. 143–144; George H. Ryden, *Delaware—The First State in the Union* [Wilmington: Delaware Tercentenary Commission, 1938].)

Jacob Broom

(1752–April 25, 1810), surveyor, farmer, merchant, entrepreneur, banker, and civic leader of Wilmington, Delaware.

A quiet man of moderate views, and one of the least of the Framers. Son of James Broom, blacksmith, and of Mary Willis Broom, a Quaker of Chester, Pennsylvania. In religion a member of the Swedish Lutheran community. Jacob Broom took little part in the American Revolution. But he was, from his early years, a man of mark in Delaware, active in the development of his state, repeatedly burgess and chief burgess of his native town Wilmington, and a member of the state legislature from 1784–1788. In 1786 he was appointed delegate from that assembly to the Annapolis Convention and, in the following year, was named again to be one of the representatives of Delaware, this time in the larger meeting at Philadelphia. There he voted consistently as a commercial Federalist. During the debates he made only one significant speech—against premature adjournment without agreement upon a draft to send on to the states. He was, in great measure, responsible for Delaware's early approval of the document produced. And he continued in the Federalist faith throughout the remainder of his days.

Contrary to the usual report, Jacob Broom was no "plain man" out of place in a gathering of notables. He built the first cotton mill in Delaware, served as the first U. S. Postmaster of Wilmington, was a developer of lands, scientific farmer, and Justice of the Peace. Almost every significant commercial venture initiated in his proximity enjoyed his support, as did other educational and religious enterprises. When the Du Pont family first arrived in the United States, they settled on lands purchased from Jacob Broom. He was first director and then chairman of the board of directors for the Delaware Bank. In the years following the Constitutional Convention, Broom prospered greatly. He became clearly one of the leaders of the Federalist oligarchy in his state. His son, James M. Broom, served a term as a Federalist member of the House of Representatives. A grandson was National American Party ("Know Nothing") candidate for President in 1852. (See William W. Campbell, "Life and Character of Jacob Broom," *Papers of the Delaware Historical Society*, LI [1909], 1–37; John A. Munroe, *Federalist Delaware, 1775–1815* [New Brunswick: Rutgers University Press, 1954]; Robert G. Ferris, ed., *Signers of the Constitution* [Washington, D. C.: United States Dept. of the Interior, 1976], pp. 150–151 and 233–234; and George H. Ryden, *Delaware—The First State in the Union* [Wilmington: Delaware Tercentenary Commission, 1938].)

Luther Martin

(Ca. February 20, 1748–July 10, 1826), lawyer, soldier, jurist, and American statesman.

The "Maryland bulldog." Antifederalist. The tireless champion of the sovereignty of the states. Most vigorously engaged in the Constitutional Convention when he heard it argued that Maryland was not sovereign prior to the adoption of the Articles of Confederation, but a mere "political subdivision" of a nation created with the Declaration. Most himself when declaring, "I consider it an incontrovertible truth, that whatever by the constitution government may do, if it relates to the abuse of power by acts tyrannical and oppressive, it some time or another will do." Of the opinion that only "total ignorance of human nature" or hypocrisy could justify a great concentration of powers in the general government. A serious classical republican, yet convinced that loose talk about "equality of liberty and rights" would result in "mobocracy . . . scorching, feverish, convulsive." Even less a democrat than most of the Federalists in the Great Convention. Committed to the proposition that the political rights of Americans had their proper repositories in the several member commonwealths of the Union, and not in some state of nature. A cheerful pessimist, though devoted from childhood to "the sacred truths of the Christian Religion." An Episcopalian, an Old Whig and a legalist. Probably, with William Paterson, his old friend from college days, a co-author of the New Jersey or "Small State" Plan. Certain that the aim of the Federalists was "to leave the states at the *mercy* of the *general government*, since they could not succeed in their *immediate* and *entire* abolition." In fifty-three speeches, fought them all the way. Left the Convention early in order to avoid being present at the signing. Continued throughout the remainder of his life, even when identified by party as a Federalist, in the position which he represented in Philadelphia. In his generation one of the most eminent lawyers in America, and a great original.

Luther Martin was born near New Brunswick, New Jersey. He was the son of Benjamin and Hannah Martin, pious evangelical Protestants of English stock whose ancestors had come to New Jersey and Massachusetts in the middle of the seventeenth century. Though Luther's father was a farmer, he managed to send the boy, with the help of a legacy from his father, to the College of New Jersey, from which he was graduated with honors in 1766, after two years' preparation in the grammar school and four years in the college. Upon receipt of his diploma, Luther Martin went immediately to Maryland, where he obtained a teaching position in Queen Anne's County on the Eastern Shore. At that time he swore the required Oaths of Abjuration and Test and promised to conform to the Church of England. For the remainder of his career, he was a member and supporter of the Maryland social and political establishment—perhaps the most conservative of all the old colonial regimes, which changed little after independence and was suspicious of even that small degree of external authority over its affairs represented by the Articles of Confederation. After three years' teaching at the academy in Queenstown, Martin began to read in the law, first with Solomon Wright, the father of one of his students, and then with Samuel Wilson, Esq., of Back Creek, Maryland. In 1770, with debts mounting up, Martin took another school at Onancock in Accomack County on the Eastern Shore of Virginia. But in September of 1771, the pedagogical period of his life ended when he presented himself at Williamsburg to be examined for admission to the Virginia bar by George Wythe, the future Chancellor, and John Randolph, the King's Attorney-General. After succeeding in this examination and qualifying for practice in Accomack County, Martin looked away from the tidewater to the newer settlements along the frontier where lawyers were not so plentiful. And in 1772 he took a tour of the West, all the way to Fort Pitt, meeting while on his journey some of the principal men in those parts, including Captain Michael Cresap, his future father-in-law. When he returned to the Eastern Shore, however, he found that a situation had opened for him in the local courts and was shortly thereafter licensed in Maryland, as he had been in the Old Dominion. Within two years his income was "at or near £1000 per year."

In 1774 with the outbreak of revolutionary sentiment in most of the American colonies, even conservative Maryland was caught up in the times. Luther Martin had learned the Whig version of British history while at the College of New Jersey. In the company of the squires, he was elected to the Committee of Observation in Somerset County. In December of that year he was a delegate to the Provincial Congress at Annapolis. He was active in restraining the Tories in his portion of the state. As a patriotic gesture, he became engaged in the manufacture of salt, and had some practice in the new Maryland and Virginia courts established by the independent state governments. In these years Martin's close friendship with Samuel Chase, Maryland political leader and future Justice of the United States Supreme Court, was established. He was drawn further and further into the politics of transition. And when Sir William Howe published a broadside designed to foster Tory sentiment in Pennsylvania, Delaware, and the Eastern Shore of Maryland, Luther Martin wrote a "humble address" in reply. It caught the eye of his influential neighbors and in February of 1778, he was appointed Attorney General of the state of Maryland, a post which he held for the next twenty-eight years, the longest incumbency in such an office in the history of the Republic to this date.

As Attorney General Luther Martin became something like an institution in the life of his state. The post left him free to continue in a practice of his own and gave him a kind of security in both a financial and a political sense. Moreover, it taught him the meaning and importance of a "state *independent* and *sovereign*," of the effect of the Revolution on Maryland, as nothing else could have done. During the Revolution Martin was a fervent prosecutor of active Tories, of whom there were a number in Maryland, and sent several of them to the gallows. For a few months he served with the Baltimore Light Dragoons, an elite cavalry unit, when it was dispatched to Virginia to face Col. Banastre Tarleton in the campaigns that led up to Yorktown. In the course of his legal responsibilities he traveled to every corner of his state and became familiar with the people, their occupations, attitudes, religions, and the various ways of life to be found within its boundaries. To supplement this considerable social and political experience, Luther Martin made use of the scholarly resources available to him as Attorney General and undertook a careful and profound study of the law. He purchased confiscated property in Baltimore, married Maria Cresap, and concentrated on becoming not only the leading attorney in Maryland, but also the best. His figure in old-fashioned dress became a familiar sight on the streets of that thriving port city. Bemused in thought or buried in a book—so preoccupied and near-sighted that, according to legend, on one occasion when he accidentally bumped into a cow that had wandered onto Baltimore Street, he tipped his hat, apologized, and continued on his way. Martin's arguments in the courts even at this early date became famous for their orotundity, antiquarian scholarship, otiose circumambient development, and irresistible conclusion.

In 1784 Luther Martin was elected to the Continental Congress, but because of official obligations could not attend. However, when in 1786 the Maryland legislature decided to send delegates to the Constitutional Convention and when many of the state's other leading men refused to serve because of their fear that in their absence a "paper money bill" might be proposed in the legislature, Luther Martin felt himself obliged to accept appointment. He arrived in Philadelphia in time to take his seat on June 9, 1787, and continued to act his part as Framer until September 4, when he and his fellow Anti-federalist, John Francis Mercer, left the meeting in disgust to return to Maryland to organize opposition to the document they knew would be presented there for approval. Some scholars argue that Martin rejected the Constitution simply because of its hostility to state monetary and debtor-relief experiments—because he was a supporter of Samuel Chase. But this view does Martin an injustice and is belied by the comprehensive political doctrine with which he confronted the proposals of the Federalists. In Luther Martin's opinion, the general government existed to support and protect the political integrity of the states to whom the people had surrendered their sovereign political rights by long usage and continuous participation. A Federal government should prevent foreign invasion and the abuse of one state by another. When it fails to do so, "the time may come when it shall be the duty of a State, in order to preserve itself from the oppression of the general government, to have recourse to the sword." Martin did not defer to the ingenuity of James Madison, the dialectics of James Wilson, or the personal authority of General George Washington. On June 27th and 28th of the Convention, he gave his reasons for voting against them all: If the "General Government was meant merely to preserve the State Governments," then what the Federalists proposed would not suffice. Optimistic talk about all the wonders which a revised Union might bring impressed him not in the least. For throughout his life he was of the persuasion that "the man who pretends to expect by universally republicanising the world, to effect the perfectibility of human nature, the perfectibility of human reason, and the perfectibility of human happiness, or to introduce a millennium on the earth," should be treated as "an enthusiastic visionary. . . or a crafty villainous impostor."

Contrary to the popular misunderstanding of his role in the Great Convention, Luther Martin did not come to Philadelphia to act the role of spoiler or mere obstructionist. He was ready to see a revision of the Articles. As noted above, he had a hand in devising a new plan of government of which he approved. And some of his specific proposals, such as the Electoral College for choosing the President, were finally adopted by the Convention. He served amicably on the committee that produced the compromise on representation in the United States Senate. Moreover, on July 14, he moved the adoption of the committee's report, "to make a trial of the plan, rather than do nothing." Even though he owned slaves, Martin opposed on normative grounds any authorization allowing the continuation of the slave trade. In addition, he foresaw the possibility that some states might increase their political power simply by purchasing Negroes. He disapproved of including Federal judges in a Council of Revision or of neglecting to specify the scope of their authority. He wanted no Federal power of veto over legislation in the states. But he also disliked leaving with the states the power to prevent creation of new commonwealths out of their frontier holdings and chided James Wilson for his selective indifference to the reality of political bodies.

In his view, United States Senators should be compensated by the communities they were to represent, and the states left to subdue their own internal rebellions, to govern their own militia. He voted against allowing re-election of Presidents, and feared the creation of a "royal party" out of the power of appointment. He disliked the "elastic clause" (Article I, section 8), which permitted whatever legislation seemed necessary to the exercise of powers granted, and opposed the authorization of a direct tax, unless the states first failed to meet their quotas. He supported freedom of religion, but saw no harm in a mild religious test to keep "pagans and atheists" out of offices of trust. With George Mason, he said a word in behalf of leaving an option for relief of debtors and emission of paper money—to protect poor men when specie became too scarce. Martin objected to the secrecy of the proceedings of the Constitutional Convention. He doubted that the people of the states would approve of the results, but suggested that the Constitution be sent to the state legislatures and then, after amendments had been recommended from every quarter, reconsidered in a second, and perhaps a third, Great Convention. Hasty approvals, he observed, would only strengthen suspicion that the entire business was a plot by monarchists and advocates of special power for large states. Yet he also moved that acts and treaties adopted by the United States Government "shall be the supreme law." He wanted a new Constitution, but only if produced under the proper conditions, containing the necessary provisions. Those Framers who could tolerate only their own plan of government, he accused of "pride," as with "master-builders." Founding was not to his taste, but rather preserving. On all of these points he told the other Maryland delegates how he stood when they met in private session. And in a private conversation with George Washington, he was equally candid. Hence he went back to Annapolis eager to expose the centralists "whose object and wish it was to abolish and annihilate all state governments, and to bring forward one general government over this extensive continent. . . ." Better two or more confederacies than a unity of the wrong kind.

In 1788, after presenting it as an address to the Maryland legislature, Luther Martin published *The Genuine Information, Delivered to the Legislature of the State of Maryland, Relative to the Proceedings of the General Convention, Lately Held at Philadelphia.* Sections of this pamphlet and other essays opposing the Constitution Martin placed in newspapers, both in Maryland and in other states. He was a delegate to the Maryland ratification convention held in Annapolis in April of 1788, but he was literally unable to speak because of laryngitis. He did, however, change his attitude toward the Constitution following the adoption of the Bill of Rights, particularly in view of the 9th and 10th Amendments. Once Thomas Jefferson, whom he had never admired, became the head of the opposition party, Martin came to identify himself with at least part of the position of his old adversaries, the Federalists. In the following years his law practice continued to expand and provided him with more business than he could manage. His income was over $10,000 a year. Frequently he had cases before the new

Federal courts. Changes in the Maryland judicial system moved Martin to retire as Attorney General of that state in 1805. From 1813 to 1816 he was Chief Justice of the Baltimore Court of Oyer and Terminer, where he lectured juries on democratic "wickedness" and "licentiousness." From 1818–1822 he was once again, briefly, Attorney General. However, during most of this late period of service to his state, he was unable to perform the duties of his office in consequence of a paralytic stroke which he suffered in 1819. Martin wrote frequently for the political press. He prepared a careful reply to Jefferson's abuse of his father-in-law, Col. Cresap, in *Notes on the State of Virginia.* Often his energies were dispersed in too many directions. And, throughout his career, he had a reputation for drinking a good deal more than was seemly. Justice Joseph Story described the famous and successful advocate as "... poor and needy; generous and humane, ... negligent and profuse." But in the courts, in legal brief and argument, the pieces of his life came together, and Luther Martin was most himself.

The cases which earned for Luther Martin a lasting reputation as trial attorney took place at the local, state, and Federal level. He defended the shoemakers of Baltimore in their right to organize and strike against low wages—proof that in 1809 he was still an unusual Federalist, moved by the same concerns that had made him a friend to paper money twenty years before. When a large number of free Negroes began to concentrate around Baltimore, Martin defended the local constables and jailer, who had adopted a policy of confining all Negroes who appeared to be runaways or who lacked proper identification. Such a practice, Martin contended, was "necessary to public safety." Yet he also defended slaves and free persons of color who had been hastily charged with crimes, and he enforced contracts for manumission on condition of service performed. In his last term as Attorney General, when confronted with the invasion of his state by sanctimonious abolitionist agitators from Pennsylvania, in 1818 Luther Martin brought them to indictment and trial on a charge of inciting slaves to be discontented with their lot. Though the youthful Roger B. Taney got his abolitionist preacher client off with a warning, Martin took satisfaction at having discouraged future "visits" of the same kind. His most famous cases, however, were before the United States Supreme Court. There he frequently used his authority as a member of the Constitutional Convention to embarrass those justices like John Marshall who hoped to use their office to enlarge the Federal power. Before Marshall, sitting at the district level, Martin successfully handled the defense of Aaron Burr in a trial held in Richmond in 1807. And in the process he revealed President Thomas Jefferson to be as indifferent to the civil liberties of American citizens who were obstructing his will as John Adams or any other Federalist had ever been in their most highhanded moments. In *Fletcher vs. Peck* (1810), Martin maintained the continuing authority of British law in determining Georgia's legal right to the unsettled lands beyond her western boundaries prior to and during the Revolution. When the thirteen colonies had seceded from the British family of nations, Martin argued, they had carried with them the title to only such lands as were actually within their jurisdiction in 1776. His view was thus that the Yazoo lands in question had never been legally sold to Yankee speculators by the Georgia legislature and that therefore his client Fletcher had indeed been cheated when he made a purchase from the speculators. Martin's most important case before the High Court was *McCulloch vs. Maryland* (1819). In some respects it was the capstone of his career. In it he drove the Federalist justices to the wall, and left them with nothing but an *ipse dixit* to sustain their defense of the Federal powers. Of the reasoning of Daniel Webster and other attorneys for the government who were defending the United States Bank against the right of the state of Maryland to tax, Martin observed, with reference to their use of the doctrine of implied powers:

> . . . it was maintained, by the enemies of the constitution, that it contained a vast variety of powers, lurking under the generality of its phraseology, which would prove highly dangerous to the liberties of the people, and the rights of the States, unless controlled by some declaratory amendment, which should negative their existence.
>
> This apprehension was treated as a dream of distempered jealousy. The danger was denied to exist; but to provide an assurance against the possibility of its occurrence, the 10th Amendment was added to the Constitution. . . .
>
> We are now called upon to apply that theory of interpretation which was then rejected by the friends of the new Constitution, and we are asked to engraft upon it powers of vast extent, which were disclaimed by them, and which, if they had been fairly avowed at the time, would have prevented its adoption.

In peroration, Luther Martin read aloud to the Court the youthful John Marshall's own promise given during the 1788 Virginia ratification convention that the Federalists understood that all powers not "expressly delegated" to the government of the United States are reserved to the states. Martin lost part of his case, but he surely won the day.

Within less than a year Luther Martin had suffered the paralytic stroke which deprived him of the power of speech. In the care of his friends he survived until 1826. In respect for the magnitude of his achievements, the Maryland legislature passed a nonpareil act in February of 1822 which collected a license fee of five dollars from each member of the Maryland bar for the support of Luther Martin. The act was repealed in 1823, and Martin spent his final years in New York in the home of Aaron Burr. Luther Martin's career greatly complicates the simplistic view that all the Antifederalists were great democrats and prospective Jeffersonians. (See Paul S. Clarkson and R. Samuel Jett, *Luther Martin of Maryland* [Baltimore: Johns Hopkins University Press, 1970]; L. Marx Renzulli, Jr., *Maryland: The Federalist Years* [Rutherford: Fairleigh Dickinson University Press, 1972]; Henry P. Goddard, *Luther Martin: The Federal Bulldog* [Baltimore: J. Murphy and Company, 1887]; Norman K. Risjord, *Chesapeake Politics, 1781–1800* [New York: Columbia University Press, 1978]; Philip A. Crowl, *Maryland During and After the Revolution: A Political and Economic Study* [Baltimore: Johns Hopkins University Press, 1943] and his "Antifederalism in Maryland, 1787–1788," *William and Mary Quarterly,* 3rd Series, IV [October, 1947], 446-469; Forrest McDonald, *E Pluribus Unum: The Formation of the American Republic, 1776–1790* [Indianapolis: Liberty Press, 1979], pp. 295-301; pp. 172-232 of Vol. III of Max Farrand's edition of *The Records of the Federal Convention of 1787* [New Haven: Yale University Press, 1966], for a printing of Martin's 1788 pamphlet *The Genuine Information;* and Everett D. Obrecht, "The Influence of Luther Martin in the Making of the Constitution of the United States," *Maryland Historical Magazine, XXVII, No. 3 [Sept., 1932],* 173-190, and *No. 4 [Dec., 1932],* 280-296.)

Daniel Carroll

(July 22, 1730–May 7, 1796), planter and member of the aristocratic political establishment of Maryland.

According to his colleague William Pierce, "a man of large fortune and influence." Member of the collateral line of the great tidewater clan of Carroll. A "law and order" Federalist, disgusted by the feverish popular spirit abroad in the America of 1787. Interested in a sound currency and in preserving the value of property. Convinced that stability induced by a stronger central government might put an end to the disruptions of the times, arguing that most objections to the new Constitution were "chiefly propagated in Maryland by men whose interests would be deeply affected by any change in government, especially for the better, and those to whose embarrassed circumstances regularity and order would be extremely inconvenient." Clearly the voice of authority within the Maryland delegation to the Great Convention. Born at Carroll Manor in Prince George's County. Son of Daniel Carroll (1696–1751) of Upper Marlborough, Maryland, and of Eleanor Darnall Carroll (1704–1796). Brother of John Carroll, Archbishop of Baltimore (1735–1815). One of two Roman Catholic Framers. Like his Howard County and Annapolis cousins, ostensibly descended from Florence O'Carroll, King of Ely *ca.* 1205. A man of quiet importance and "plain good sense."

Daniel Carroll was, between 1742 and 1748, educated in Flanders by the Jesuits of St. Omers, and then by a "grand tour" of Europe. Returning from his travels, he married a cousin from the other side of the Carroll family, and settled down to manage his inheritance, direct his slaves, and grow tobacco. Like many of his class in the Maryland of the 1770's, he was no violent proponent of the Revolution. Yet he served as a member of the state Council of Safety from 1777–1781, as a Maryland senator from 1781–1790, and as a delegate to the Continental Congress for 1781–1783, where he signed the Articles of Confederation in the name of his friends in Annapolis. For a time he was the elected president of the Maryland senate. And during the war he played a part in gathering supplies for the American forces. Yet he was chosen as a delegate to the Constitutional Convention because other Maryland leaders refused to accept appointment.

Daniel Carroll the Framer was essentially a private person; a shareholder (with George Washington) in the Patowmack Company, a project to extend the river with canals; a speculator in frontier lands; a Mason; and a generous supporter of his church. He was not ill at ease with his associates in the Constitutional Convention. Many of them he knew socially, particularly the important Virginians. Yet unlike a number of the Framers, he did not appear in Philadelphia in search of a role to play before the gallery of history. A mature and wealthy man, one of the senior members of the Convention, he was a median figure in its debates, standing something like halfway between the extremes of opinion present on that floor. After his arrival on July 9, he was in almost constant attendance, and spoke on perhaps twenty different occasions. Carroll wanted a new Constitution, not a revision of the Articles. And he wanted the new government to have the power to tax the people directly. Yet he wished to deny to the new Congress the power to tax exports, to act without a large majority from most states as a quorum, or to create a powerful federal court. He wished the general government to pay the salaries of the members of the new Congress, lest the states bind it too closely. But, once the Constitution was in force, he opposed the doctrine of implied powers, favored the adoption of the 10th Amendment as check upon Federal usurpations, and rejected the Bank of the United States as a wicked Yankee plot. On the issue of equal representation in the United States Senate, he supported the position of Delaware, New Jersey, and Connecticut. And, though leaning a little in the direction of the nationalists in his political theory, he did not lean very far. Carroll hoped to see the Framers and the communities which they represented work toward a civil agreement, a unanimity through concessions, remembering always that "experience overrules all other calculations."

Daniel Carroll was eloquent in his support of the instrument of government produced in Philadelphia. He defended the document before the Maryland legislature; wrote, as "A Friend of the Constitution," a reply to the Antifederalist Samuel Chase in the *Maryland Journal;* and conducted an energetic campaign through correspondence for ratification by his state. After the government was formed, he served from 1789–1791 as a Maryland member of the House of Representatives, where he supported the Bill of Rights, assumption of state debts, and the location of the national capital in his part of Maryland, on the banks of the Potomac. His friend President Washington then named him as one of the three commissioners to survey and define the District of Columbia, where he and his family owned land. He served in this office until the year before his death. Never a serious politician or a man hungry for major office, he died at his home at Rock Creek, Maryland, at the age of sixty-six. (See Sister Mary V. Geiger, *Daniel Carroll, A Framer of the Constitution* [Washington, D.C.: Catholic University of America, 1943]; Richard J. Purcell, "Daniel Carroll, Framer of the Constitution," *American Catholic Historical Society Records of Philadelphia*, LII [June, 1941], 65–87 and [September, 1941], 137–160; Philip A. Crowl, *Maryland During and After the Revolution* [Baltimore: Johns Hopkins University Press, 1943], L. Marx Renzulli, Jr., *Maryland: The Federalist Years* [Rutherford: Fairleigh Dickinson University Press, 1972]; Annabelle M. Melville, *John Carroll of Baltimore* [New York: Charles Scribner's Sons, 1955]; and Charles Albro Barker, *The Background of the Revolution in Maryland* [New Haven: Yale University Press, 1940].)

John Francis Mercer

(May 17, 1759–August 30, 1821), soldier, lawyer, and political leader in both Virginia and Maryland. Violent Antifederalist.

Fearful of granting power to a general government throughout his career. Connected with the Chase faction in Maryland following his service as member of the Continental Congress for Virginia. Inclined to regard even the Articles of Confederation as perhaps a threat to the sovereignty of the states. Outraged by an eleven days' attendance at the Great Convention (August 6–August 17, 1787). Returned home convinced that the entire proceedings were an "aristocratic" or monarchist plot against the liberties of the people. Yet reluctant to allow the citizens of his state to vote on anything directly, or without a great restriction of the suffrage. Son of the illustrious Col. John Mercer of Marlborough in Stafford County, Virginia, and of Ann Roy Mercer, the Colonel's second wife. Episcopalian. One of nineteen brothers and sisters, some of whom played important roles in the history of their state. First educated at home, later at William and Mary. Enlisted as lieutenant in the 3rd Virginia Regiment early in 1776. Promoted to captain the following year. Aide-de-camp to Gen. Charles Lee. Resigned from the service in 1779, after his commander was court-martialed following misconduct in the Battle of Monmouth. Returned to uniform in the fall of 1780 as lieutenant colonel of infantry under General Lawson. Served for a time in command of a unit of mounted dragoons with Lafayette. Commander of a corps of militia grenadiers in the Yorktown campaign.

While still under arms, John Francis Mercer read law at Williamsburg with Governor Thomas Jefferson. He practiced briefly at Fredericksburg. But for the remainder of his life he was chiefly occupied with politics and planting. He served in the Virginia House of Delegates in 1782, and again in 1785–1786. From 1783–1785 he sat in the Continental Congress. Early in 1785 he married an heiress, Sophia Sprigg of Cedar Park in Anne Arundel County, Maryland, and took up residence on her ancestral estate. After the habit of his family, Mercer was involved in speculation in Western lands, and thus linked to the "paper money" forces in his adopted state. Yet in 1787 a very wealthy young man. Selected as a Maryland delegate to the Great Convention because many of the state's most eminent political figures refused to serve. But very active and outspoken during his short stay in Philadelphia.

In 1783, while in the Continental Congress, John Francis Mercer had declared, when an impost was proposed, that "if the Federal compact is such as has been represented [i.e., allowing for a power to collect customs tax], I will immediately withdraw from Congress and do everything in my power to destroy its existence." In precisely such a spirit did he appear briefly in the Constitutional Convention. His first share in the proceedings there was a blunt statement that the plan under consideration was "objectionable," followed by a statement that "it never could succeed." He mocked the solemn deliberations of his associates and sneered, "It is a great mistake to suppose that the paper we propose will govern the United States." The themes of his twenty or so speeches were *force* and *influence:* by one or by the other were men to be governed. If the tyranny of monarchy or of "high-toned government" by way of an aristocratic faction in Congress (artistocracy here meaning men of privilege) were to be avoided, the executive would need the authority to hand out a few offices and thus create its own party in the national legislature. Otherwise the best men would never come away from the appointments which they held in the states to serve the central government. Mercer said also a few words against a proposed tax on exports, and about rivalry between the sections. He attacked the idea of allowing the U. S. Supreme Court to review decisions of lower courts by way of constitutional construction. Mercer was negative and contentious on all counts. But it was to the theme of appointments that he returned on several occasions. Clearly the topic interested him. Perhaps Jefferson was correct in observing of Mercer, "Vanity and ambition seem to be the ruling passion of this young man and as his objects are impure, so are his means. Intrigue is a principal one on particular occasions as party attachment in the general."

After withdrawing from the Great Convention, John Francis Mercer returned to Maryland and fought the adoption of the new Constitution. He was a delegate to his state's ratification convention, spoke there against adoption, and was sent by Antifederalists to Maryland's House of Delegates from 1788–1789 and from 1791–1792. In 1791 he took a seat in the U. S. House of Representatives, where, as a violent opponent of Hamilton, he continued until 1794. As a Democratic-Republican Mercer returned to the Maryland legislature in 1800 and, after a somewhat embarrassing flight from a duel, was elected governor of the state in 1801. He was re-elected in 1802 and later served three additional years in the House of Delegates. Like John Randolph of Roanoke, Mercer broke with his party on the question of war with England, disapproved of the French Revolution and the Emperor Napoleon. In his last years he lived quietly at Cedar Park. (See H. E. Buchholz, *Governors of Maryland from the Revolution to the Year 1908* [Baltimore: Williams and Wilkins Co., 1908]; L. Marx Renzulli, Jr., *Maryland: The Federalist Years* [Rutherford: Fairleigh Dickinson University, 1972]; Jackson Turner Main, *Political Party Before the Constitution* [Chapel Hill: University of North Carolina Press, 1973]; Robert E. and B. Katherine Brown, *Virginia, 1705–1786: Democracy or Aristocracy?* [East Lansing: Michigan State University Press, 1964); Dorothy Brown, "Party Battles and Beginnings in Maryland," Ph.D. dissertation, Georgetown University, 1962; Philip A. Crowl, *Maryland During and After the Revolution* [Baltimore: Johns Hopkins University Press, 1943], p. 112; Norman K. Risjord, *Chesapeake Politics, 1781–1800* [New York: Columbia University Press, 1978]; James Mercer Garnett, "John Francis Mercer," *Maryland Historical Magazine*, II [September, 1907], 191–213; and H. James Henderson, *Party Politics in the Continental Congress* [New York: McGraw-Hill, 1974]; Vol. 5, pp. 5–73 and 101–106 of *The Complete Anti Federalist*, edited, with commentary, by Herbert J. Storing [Chicago: University of Chicago Press, 1981].)

James McHenry

(November 16, 1753–May 3, 1816), physician, soldier, statesman, and leader of Maryland Federalists.

General Washington's secretary in the last years of the Revolution, and still his faithful retainer during the Constitutional Convention. A man of inherited wealth who did not practice his profession or follow any other calling apart from politics after independence was achieved. Son of Daniel and Agnes McHenry, he was born in Ballymena, County Antrim, Ireland. Educated in Dublin and, after his family's emigration to Baltimore in 1772, at the Newark Academy in Delaware. A student of medicine in Philadelphia under the redoubtable Dr. Benjamin Rush. A very refined gentleman and a member of an already prosperous family established in the importing business when the War for Independence broke out. Like all Ulster Presbyterians, inclined to resent British authority even before he found a good excuse to do so. James McHenry volunteered for military service at Cambridge, Massachusetts, in 1775. After a time on the staff of the military hospital for the forces surrounding Boston, he was named surgeon for the 5th Pennsylvania Battalion. He was captured in 1776 with the fall of Fort Washington in New York, paroled in January of 1777, and exchanged the following year. His probity and manners soon called him to the attention of the Commanding General, whose right hand he was from the spring months in Valley Forge until 1780, when he was detached to the staff of the Marquis de Lafayette. There he held the rank of major. He left service in 1781 when he was elected to the Maryland senate, where he sat for five years. From 1783–1786, he was a Maryland representative to the Continental Congress and was elected to represent the commercial community of Baltimore in the Great Convention.

James McHenry was in Philadelphia for only a few days before he was called back to Baltimore by illness of his brother. He returned to share in the deliberations of the Framers on August 6, kept notes on what he observed and heard, both within and without the Convention, and said little. However, his presence in Philadelphia put Maryland back in the Federalist column by cancelling the Antifederalism of James Francis Mercer or Luther Martin. In the Convention, McHenry took his lead from Madison, Randolph, and George Washington, except for a little support given to George Mason against Yankee schemes for the control of commerce. He was the delegate to the Convention who argued the case for the proposed Constitution before the Maryland legislature. His efforts were instrumental in gathering a pro-Constitutional majority in Maryland's ratifying convention, where he also served. Subsequently he acted as a spokesman for the Federalist cause in many of the struggles in Maryland during the early years of the Republic. He was a member of the state assembly from 1789 to 1791, and once again a state senator from 1791–1796.

James McHenry was one of those Federalists driven to support the idea of a stronger Union and a government capable of using force to protect property and preserve the sanctity of contract as a result of popular unrest, mob spirit, and talk of "levelling" in his own city and state. He deplored the French Revolution and its American admirers. The Charles County debtors' riot of June, 1786, and associated agitation among the lower orders in other sections of the state, persuaded the merchants and great planters of Maryland to give up their characteristic suspicion of any plan for general government. Once committed to Federalism, McHenry stuck with it, reinforced in his conviction by events like the formation of the Democratic Societies in Baltimore and the riots of June 22, 1812. Therefore, McHenry accepted the post of Secretary of

War in President Washington's Cabinet in January of 1796 and continued in that office until May, 1800, when President Adams called for his resignation. The charge against McHenry made by the Democratic-Republicans concerned his construction of a "standing army" prepared to negate the results of the next general election. The complaint of the Adams Federalists was disloyalty and collusion with Alexander Hamilton in the attempt to deny President Adams the nomination of his party for a second term. There was some truth in both accusations.

In the last years of his life, James McHenry was a private man, the ultraconservative patriarch of a dying party, who devoted his energies to the life of his church, his family, and to a little writing. He was opposed to the War of 1812, but not politically active except as a counselor to younger men. Many of his disciples and their descendants helped to form the Whig Party in Maryland. (See Bernard C. Steiner, *The Life and Correspondence of James McHenry* [Cleveland: Burrows Brothers Co., 1907]; Manning J. Dauer, *The Adams Federalists* [Baltimore: Johns Hopkins University Press, 1953]; Philip A. Crowl, *Maryland During and After the Revolution* [Baltimore: Johns Hopkins University Press, 1943]; L. Marx Renzulli, Jr., *Maryland: The Federalist Years* [Rutherford: Fairleigh Dickinson University Press, 1972]; and Dorothy Brown, "Party Battles and Beginnings in Maryland," Ph.D. dissertation, Georgetown University, 1962.)

Daniel of St. Thomas Jenifer

(1723–Nov. 16, 1790), politician, leader of the Revolution in Maryland, and perennial officeholder.

Named so curiously to distinguish him from other Daniel Jenifers. Always a friend to those in authority, at least until their power began to wane. Usually a High Federalist, taking his lead in the Convention from General Washington, Madison, and other Virginia nationalists. A convivial man, with an eye to the main chance. An unscrupulous, charming opportunist, a great host and giver of parties, but devious nonetheless. A person of genuine social skill and aplomb, called upon throughout his life to perform in offices of trust. Son of Daniel Jenifer of Charles County and of Elizabeth Hairson Jenifer. Born at Coates Retirement (Ellerslie), near Port Tobacco. Of English and Swedish descent. Episcopalian. An educated man, particularly skilled in matters of finance. Wealthy, both by birth and by acquisition. Representative of Maryland's old aristocracy, of tobacco, slaves, and great plantations.

Daniel of St. Thomas Jenifer began his career in public service early in his life and was, by turns or simultaneously, Justice of the Peace, Proprietor's

Agent and Receiver-General in charge of proprietary revenues, justice of Maryland's Western Circuit, member of the provincial court (1766), and, from 1773 until the end of the British rule, member of the Royal Governor's Council. He enjoyed the special favor of the last two Proprietors of Maryland and sat on a boundary commission which settled disputes with Pennsylvania and Delaware. And he established a network of friendships and associations which made him one of the principal men in the colony.

For reasons made obvious in the just concluded summary of his good fortune as servant of the King, Daniel of St. Thomas Jenifer was slow to embrace the banner of American Independence. With other leaders of the "popular [i.e., aristocratically republican] party" in Maryland such as Samuel Chase, William Paca, Charles Carroll of Carrollton, and Charles Carroll, barrister, he was cautious in renouncing all connection with the mother country, and hoped for some sort of reconciliation that would leave the state in their hands but under the nominal authority of the Crown. However, when the English moved toward the enforcement of their policy with the sword and declared the American colonies to be beyond the protection of the law, in rebellion, the Maryland gentry—and Jenifer with them—joined a shadow government and prepared to defend their community. From 1775–1777, Daniel of St. Thomas Jenifer was the elected president of the Maryland Council of Safety. As an authority on this period of Maryland history has remarked, "Jenifer made the transition from courtier to rebel quite easily." But independence brought great disorder in Maryland, disobedience to all authority, threats to property, indifference to debt, and an effusion of paper money. The times forced the Maryland aristocracy to many expedients which, with Jenifer included, they very much disliked; and made Federalists of them, when the opportunity to be a Federalist arrived.

From 1777 to 1780, Daniel of St. Thomas Jenifer served as president of the Maryland state senate. From 1778 to 1782, he had a seat in the Continental Congress, where he continued the interest in supplies for the army and in Western lands which he had shown in the politics of his own state. He speculated in confiscated Tory properties, became a close friend of General Washington, made his peace with former Loyalists who had avoided exile, engrossed new and profitable offices, particularly as Intendent of State Revenue and financial manager of Maryland (1782–1785), and improved his estate at Stepney, near Annapolis. He was a Maryland delegate to the Mount Vernon Conference of 1785 and was by the time of the Philadelphia Convention, in view of his long experience in the political life of his state, an obvious choice as delegate from Maryland. During the Convention his presence was constant, his position constant, and his voice almost unheard. At 64, he was one of the oldest of the men there. He was not so positive about the Constitution in his report to the Maryland legislature. Within three years of his departure from Philadelphia he died at Annapolis, in quiet retirement. (See Ronald

Hoffman, *A Spirit of Dissension: Economics, Politics, and the Revolution in Maryland* [Baltimore: Johns Hopkins University Press, 1973]; Robert G. Ferris, ed., *Signers of the Constitution* [Washington, D.C.: U. S. Department of the Interior, 1976], pp. 177–178; Philip A. Crowl, *Maryland During and After the Revolution* [Baltimore: Johns Hopkins University Press, 1943], pp. 28–29 *et passim;* Charles Albro Barker, *The Background of the Revolution in Maryland* [New Haven: Yale University Press, 1940].)

George Washington

(February 22, 1732–December 14, 1799), planter, soldier, statesman, and first President of the United States.

The moving force behind the Constitutional Convention, whose "presence propelled the meeting forward as his agreement to be there had insured that it would be held." In the struggle for ratification in the states, the one man whose support for the new Constitution made possible its approval. For Americans of his generation, the summary figure, the man on the white horse who came in his own person to embody their sense of nationality. And for that portion of American history concluded with the War Between the States, the political icon against which the conduct of all public men might be measured. As early as 1775, recognized as the "pattern" for other Americans "to form themselves by." Persuaded by Madison, Randolph, and other friends to lend his personal prestige won in the Revolution to the labor of revising the Articles of Confederation, lest the honor he had achieved in arms be compromised by the political incapacity of the nation which his military victories had produced. Of the opinion in 1786 and early 1787 that the Republic was "fast verging to anarchy and confusion" and that "without some alteration in our political creed, the superstructure we had been seven years raising at the expense of so much blood and treasure must fall." The definitive military Federalist and full of doubts concerning democracy. Yet too much the soldier according to the Roman myth, the Cato Uticensis or Cincinnatus, to abandon the people in the chaos of popular tumult after he had led them to freedom in war. Acting out a role throughout his adult life in keeping with a concept of public virtue not now readily understood and an essentially religious conviction that God would hold him accountable for the ultimate meaning of American Independence as revealed in our history.

George Washington was born at Wakefield Plantation in Westmoreland County, Virginia, the son of Augustine Washington and his second wife, Mary Ball Washington. He was descended from Lawrence Washington of

Sulgrave, Northampton, England, and from many generations of solid yeomen and rustic gentry who produced finally the Rev. Lawrence Washington of Purleigh, Essex, whose son John emigrated to Virginia in 1657 or 1658 after his father had been deprived of his living by Puritans on charges of drunkenness and Anglicanism. Augustine Washington was the grandson of John Washington and the son of Lawrence Washington of Bridges Creek, Westmoreland County. He lived in Westmoreland until 1735, when he moved to other plantations on the Potomac and Rappanhannock Rivers. Augustine Washington was a man of monumental proportions, a figure of great energy, and an established member of the Virginia gentry. But his death in 1743 left his son George and the five younger children unfinished in their education and in a position of financial ambiguity. George Washington's elder half-brother, Lawrence, was his teacher and role model during his adolescent years. There may have been some training in a local plantation school, and the boy did learn a good deal of mathematics, including geometry, trigonometry, and surveying. We know from his correspondence as a mature man that he was familiar with much military history, that he read in biography, agricultural science, and in the standard classics of British letters known to a young gentleman of his era. And he had a special passion for the theater. Yet most of his formation came from a life out-of-doors, from hunting, farming, and travel, and from the social life of his region. The youthful Washington was a close friend of George William Fairfax, the son of William Fairfax, cousin and representative of the proprietary magnate, Thomas, Lord Fairfax, of Northern Virginia, a land baron on a grand scale. George's half-brother Lawrence was married to William Fairfax's daughter Anne. The two boys were sent to the Shenandoah Valley with Lord Fairfax's surveyor to examine some of his undeveloped lands being prepared for settlement. Young George learned the rudiments of surveying during that 1748 adventure and in the following year was appointed in his own right county surveyor for Culpeper County, Virginia. He also undertook for commission (approximately £1500 in a two-year period) many surveys in what is now Virginia and West Virginia. While a surveyor, he learned how to survive on the frontier and how to manage on his own. For the remainder of his life he continued to be greatly concerned with the development of the West, and he was directly familiar with conditions there to a degree not duplicated in the lives of the other Framers.

Lawrence Washington fell ill with tuberculosis in 1751–52 and George accompanied him in his journey to the island of Barbados in the West Indies—George's only sea voyage and travel beyond the boundaries of what was to be the United States. But Lawrence's health did not improve in consequence of his stay in the tropics. He died in July of 1752, leaving to George a reversionary interest in Mount Vernon. With Lawrence's death, George Washington's hope of the English education such as his two older brothers had received was at an end. And, for the time at least, he gave up his dream of a British regular commission, such as Lawrence had held. But he did receive in his half-brother's place an appointment as military Adjutant for the Southern District of Virginia, and soon thereafter a similar appointment for his own region, the Northern Neck and Eastern Shore. Thanks to William Fairfax's suggestion, young Major Washington was chosen as emissary to the French posts on the Ohio frontier by Governor Dinwiddie, who had been ordered by George II to confront such encroachments. At twenty-one, George Washington was given the difficult assignment of delivering to the French an ultimatum ordering them to leave English territory. The Governor had attached an attendant mission of negotiation with the Six Nations—the Indian tribes in the area. Leaving in late November of 1753 with a small party, Washington encountered terrible weather and French evasion. But he delivered Virginia's ultimatum all the way to the shores of Lake Erie. After treating with the Indians, he returned through trackless wilderness, swimming almost frozen rivers, and displaying a hardihood that was to sustain him in later times of trial. His narrative of this adventure was printed by Governor Dinwiddie and was widely read in both England and America.

In 1754 Washington rose to the rank of lieutenant colonel and then colonel of the Virginia militia. On the Governor's orders, he led a small force which sought to challenge French control of the Ohio River Valley; but he met defeat at Fort Necessity in a battle which was a major cause of the French and Indian War. Confusion in questions of rank and authority brought on by Governor Dinwiddie and the pending arrival of British regulars compelled the youthful Colonel to resign his commission late in 1754. But in 1755 he was back in service as colonel and aide to General Edward Braddock. For his bravery and exemplary conduct at the Battle of Monongahela he earned international fame and the restoration of his authority over Virginia's forces charged with defending that colony's frontier. But there followed more disputes concerning precedence and embarrassing experiences in the struggle for command authority with officers holding the King's commission. Moreover, Washington's efforts were not backed up by the authorities in Williamsburg. After traveling all the way to Boston in 1756 to see Governor Shirley of Massachusetts (George II's Commander in Chief in North America) in order to determine the scope of his responsibility as commander of Virginia's troops, he was not given the status he desired. In 1757 he had an equally unsatisfactory encounter with Governor Shirley's successor, John Campbell, the Earl of Loudoun. He was denied not only the necessary support for his campaign in the West, but also the King's commission, which he so clearly had earned. Not surprisingly, therefore, late in 1758 Washington resigned his rank and retired to Mount Vernon, full of anger and disgust with colonial officials. On the occasion of this retreat from public responsibilities, the young Colonel's officers praised him as mentor, the only man able to support "the military character of Virginia," a chieftain who could by example "inculcate those genuine sentiments of true honor and passion for glory from which the greatest military achievements have been derived." This address to their former commander seems prophetic. For at twenty-six Washington seemed already much older than his years and had established an international reputation. After Fort Necessity he had written his brother Jack, "I heard the bullets whistle, and, believe me, there is something charming in the sound." During General Braddock's retreat Washington had three horses shot from under him and bullets had pierced almost every item of his clothing. Yet he came from that "inferno" with no mark on him. And his action that day had astonished the old soldiers present, who agreed with the young Colonel when he acknowledged "the miraculous care of Providence that protected me beyond all human expectation." On that field of battle, the "myth" of George Washington as an American Achilles was established—a myth that survived the quiet years that followed.

In January of 1759, George Washington married Martha Dandridge Custis, the wealthy widow of Daniel Parke Custis, and shortly thereafter Washington took his seat in the House of Burgesses for Frederick County. He received the thanks of the Virginia legislature for his military service to his neighbors and then settled in to a place on the back benches. He was also a Justice of the Peace and a member of the vestry for the local Anglican parish. He enlarged his house at Mount Vernon and improved his lands. During these domestic years the Washingtons traveled to Williamsburg, Annapolis, Alexandria, and other familiar places of resort, amusement, and social gathering within the confines of the closed world that had grown up around Chesapeake Bay. He had time for hunting, his favorite pastime, and for long political conversations with his learned and thoughtful neighbor, George Mason. He had power of attorney and authority to act as agent for the members of the Virginia regiment who had served under him in the effort to secure for them bounty lands in the West allotted in reward for their part in the French and Indian War. In that cause he made a canoe trip down the Ohio from Fort Pitt, far into the West, up the Great Kanawha in an attempt to locate the lands in question. The neglectful or indifferent attitude of the British government toward this obligation, the questionable practices of his English factors, the business that came before his court in Alexandria, and the memory of indignities suffered during his military campaigns built up in Washington a hostility toward the English colonial system which exploded into overt antagonism with the passage of the Stamp Act. George Washington was a proponent of the non-importation agreements (as were most Virginians), which prohibited trade with the mother country until the hateful revenue bills had been repealed by Parliament—whose members, according to the Virginia planter, had "no more right to put their hands into my pocket, without my consent, that I have to put my hands into yours for money."

After 1770 and the renewed resistance to encroachments by Parliament upon the inherited liberties of Englishmen in America, George Washington was not in the forefront of those who advocated violent resistance and entertained the possibility of independence. Before he could go as far as Patrick Henry, he would have to find evidence in British policy that America was being subjected to "a regular plan at the expense of law and justice to overthrow our rights and liberties." Yet by 1774 he recognized the tendency of the times to force the colonials into independence, once subjection had been identified as the only alternative to that "dernier resort." Washington presided at Alexandria on July 18, 1774, in a meeting where the freeholders of his county adopted George Mason's "Fairfax Resolutions." It was Washington's opinion of the prospective struggle that "more blood will be spilt on this occasion, if the ministry are determined to push matters to the extremity, than history has yet furnished in the annals of North America." He had hoped to see a rational division between the authority of the Crown and Parliament and the liberty of the subject. But he was not prepared to have that question settled by force, because for Washington liberty meant the self-determination of peoples. And Americans were no longer Englishmen in the same sense as those electors who governed themselves in selecting a House of Commons. He disliked the Boston Tea Party and disliked the idea of withholding payment of debt. But the passage of the Intolerable Acts and British occupation of Boston moved him to join other Virginia patriots at the first provincial convention or "revolutionary" legislature in the late summer of 1774 after the Royal Governor had dissolved the Virginia Assembly. A provisional government of Virginia was the result of these proceedings. And by that government Washington was sent as one of Virginia's seven delegates to the First Continental Congress. In the Congress he grew impatient with petitions to George III, which he called "whining." "Something should be done," he ventured, "to avert the stroke and maintain the liberty which we have derived from our ancestors." When returned to the Second Continental Congress in May of 1775, he appeared in Philadelphia in the buff and blue uniform of a colonel of the Virginia militia. For by that time he had become convinced that British policy "exhibited an unexampled testimony of the most despotic system of tyranny that was ever practiced in a free government." Its conduct was "subversive of the laws and Constitution of Great Britain itself." What was in question was the inherited legal rights of Englishmen residing in the North American colonies.

After Lexington and Concord, with an ill-organized and unruly army of New England militia besieging the British forces in Boston, and the willingness of Massachusetts' sister colonies to come to her aid still in doubt, it occurred to John and Samuel Adams that it might be wise for the old Puritan Commonwealth to turn its hosts over to the Continental Congress and then ask for a Southern general to command them. It is not certain that George

Washington anticipated being given this assignment. Indeed, he announced himself to be unworthy of it. Yet when the call of duty came, it could not have been a complete surprise, for there had been much talk in Philadelphia of such a possibility. Certainly Washington looked the part of Commander in Chief—almost six feet, four inches tall, and over two hundred pounds, athletic, and with the eye and bearing of a general. At the time of his appointment George Washington was the only member of the Continental Army. Yet, according to his most recent biographer, James Thomas Flexner, "from the first moment of his command Washington was more than a military leader; he was the eagle, the standard, the flag, the living symbol of the cause."

Almost immediately following his receipt of command, Washington moved to organize and train the forces surrounding Boston, to gather and coordinate other American units placed under his authority, to dispatch officers for the command of independent operations, and to write Congress and the governors of the states, urging that they create what became the Continental Line—a corps of long-enlistment, regular regiments, a "standing army" which would not have to be replaced every few months. In the spring of 1776, Boston was liberated by guns brought overland from Fort Ticonderoga. But after that "victory" and the attendant British retreat to Halifax, Nova Scotia, Washington faced larger and larger invading armies, not mere garrisons. Until French reinforcements reached North America and French fleets operated along our coasts following recognition and a treaty of alliance with France in 1778, American strategy had to be defensive, with hope of an occasional victory brought about by English overconfidence or carelessness in a war with such ill-equipped, amateur adversaries. Such a victory came with the first British attack on Charleston. And later, when Washington defeated the Hessians at Trenton and Gates isolated Sir John Burgoyne at Saratoga. The pattern for these unexpected triumphs had of course been set at Bunker Hill. But, as the British grew more respectful and more methodical, for the most part all that the Americans could achieve against Lord Cornwallis, Sir Henry Clinton, and the Brothers Howe was survival as a force in being. First, Washington was driven out of New York. Then, he was obliged to retire from New Jersey. After recovering a portion of the latter state in a brilliant campaign that turned on the frozen field of Princeton, he was compelled to retire on Pennsylvania and defend the seat of the government in Philadelphia. The capital city slipped out of his hands at Brandywine Creek (September 11, 1777) and could not be recovered in the fog and mist of Germantown (October 3–4, 1777).

The turning point came during the following terrible winter at Valley Forge. The "conspiracy" of General Thomas Conway and of a few members of the Congress came to nothing. Though the fortunes of Washington's army had reached their nadir, confidence in its Commander continued as before.

And thanks to Baron von Steuben's drill and other invisible evolutions of character, the force that emerged from that ordeal was ready to fight a long war and to give battle to any English army in their path. Supply procedures had been reorganized. French and Dutch money brought weapons and ammunition. Sir William Howe was relieved by Clinton, who retired toward New York. At Monmouth Court House, Washington fell upon him and fought there an engagement which persuaded the British that conquest of the Northern and Middle states would require a great increase in their expeditionary forces. Soon there was a French garrison in New England under the Count de Rochambeau and a French fleet at anchor in Boston harbor. The scene of the war shifted to the South, where Whitehall believed there was a chance of preserving at least some of the colonies. Washington watched anxiously and sent troops and officers to forestall the disaster that seemed to be in prospect, particularly following the fall of Charleston in 1780. But his old lieutenant, General Nathaniel Greene, ably supported by partisans and the long rifles of the Southern frontier, proved to be equal to the task. Fighting for survival in the concluding stages of what was supposed to have been a final attempt at subjugation—having been depleted at King's Mountain and at Cowpens—Lord Cornwallis risked a desperate engagement with Greene at Guilford Court House, North Carolina, and then withdrew to the protection of British sea power in a fortified camp at Yorktown in lower Chesapeake Bay. The sea power did not appear. But Washington did. After a feint at New York, French and American forces under Rochambeau and Washington marched swiftly overland to the headwaters of the Chesapeake Bay and were then transported by boat to the Virginia tidewater, where they invested Cornwallis' position. For all intents and purposes, the 1781 surrender of Lord Cornwallis' army, following a brief siege, marked the end of the Revolutionary War. For another year, Washington kept a force in the field, and smaller units under arms until the Treaty of Paris was signed in 1783. Then, in keeping with his own notion of public virtue, the American Cincinnatus returned his commission to the Congress and retired to Mount Vernon to farm. In a letter to the Marquis de Lafayette, eschewing fame, power, and favor, in self-conscious fulfillment of his role, Washington declares: "I am become a private citizen on the banks of the Potomac, and under the shadow of my own vine and my own fig tree. . . . I am not only retired from all public employments, but I am retiring within myself, and shall be able to view the solitary walk and tread the paths of private life with heartfelt satisfaction. Envious of none, I am determined to be pleased with all, and this, my dear friend, being the order for my march, I will move gently down the stream of life until I sleep with my fathers." Had the citizen/soldier not understood the part he was playing in such traditional terms, he might well have converted his army into a source of political power. At Newburgh, New York, in February of 1783, the conditions had been ripe for a coup d'etat. Washington's final service to the Republic as Commander in Chief during the War for Independence was to quiet this unrest and give the Congress another chance to govern the country, now at peace, under the Articles of Confederation.

It was not, however, very long after his return to private life before Washington began to talk and write among his friends concerning his dissatisfaction with the incapacity of the government under the Articles. Once out of uniform, he was free to speak his mind. Always from the example of his military experience, he called for a stronger central government, one that could defend itself and deserve the respect of nations. He despised the petty vanities of state officials who had been too jealous of their authority to let him defend the country and he was ever mindful of the fact that the consistent pattern with revolutions throughout the history of the world was that they ended in tyranny. What Americans needed was a Constitution to replace the one they had lived under as Englishmen: a "liberal and energetic constitution, well guarded and closely watched to prevent encroachment [which] might restore us to respectability and consequence" and "establish the dominion of law over licentiousness." Of the latter there was a good deal in the states—riot, a clamor for paper money, and a cry of equality, particularly in New England, which, according to the General, had gone too far toward "the levelling principles." In 1785 Washington hosted the Mount Vernon Conference, which settled disputes between Maryland and Virginia. That meeting led to the Annapolis Convention of 1786, which in turn called for the Great Convention, instead of contenting itself with drawing up commercial accords between the states. Washington was pleased by all of this activity, for he was alarmed by the reports of popular unrest in New England. He feared "some awful crisis" was in the offing, and wrote of "combustibles in every state" waiting for the torch. He was not surprised that he was chosen at the head of the ticket in the selection of a Virginia delegation to Philadelphia. Yet for a time, he was reluctant to commit himself to attend for fear of being caught up in an angry debate. But his young friends prevailed upon him by telling him that the meeting would fail if he were not present.

When the Great Convention officially convened on May 25, 1787, on a motion of Robert Morris, seconded by John Rutledge, George Washington was elected unanimously to be its presiding officer. Though he spoke only once in the entire Convention, to recommend that each member of the House of Representatives be chosen from a district of 30,000 voters instead of 40,000, it is difficult to overestimate Washington's influence on these proceedings. Most of the Framers either desired his good opinion or were restrained by the thought of his disapprobation. Moreover, he apparently did much to direct the proceedings through post-adjournment persuasion in the social context of The City Tavern and various private homes. For Washington the entire Convention was part of an educational process, creating that community of interests to which it hoped to give law. Washington helped to draw up the Virginia Plan. Later he had to check James Madison and some of its other ardent advocates when they were about to destroy the Convention rather than modify the model they had in mind. In all disputes, Washington's response was like that of Benjamin Franklin—sage and temperate. In some cases, a mere disapproving look from the chair may have been enough to turn the course of history. Furthermore, as Pierce Butler later reported, Washington "shaped" many delegates' "ideas of the powers to be given to a President" as "members cast their eyes toward General Washington" and consulted "their opinions of his virtue." That most Americans knew George Washington would be the first President of the United States was of central importance in securing their approval of the Constitution in the state ratification conventions, even as his support of the document agreed upon in Philadelphia had been so strong a motive for many of the Framers who placed their signatures upon it on September 17, 1787.

Because of the delicacy of his situation as President of the Constitutional Convention and probable candidate for the Presidency of the United States, George Washington did little but urge forward his friends in the Federalists' campaign to win ratification. But after the process was complete and the Electoral College was called upon to select a Chief Magistrate, Washington acquired some ironic distance from burdens still to come and wrote to a friend, "My movements to the chair of government will be accompanied by feelings not unlike those of a culprit, who is going to the place of execution." In 1788 he was elected unanimously to fill, and in a sense to create, the office which he dreaded. Despite the overwhelming support and admiration of the American people, the task was as difficult as he had expected it to be. Washington served two terms as President, from 1789 to 1797. During his first term he had to form a government on the basis of a very general outline given in the Constitution. His second term was taken up by troubles with England and France and by the emergence of partisan politics, which he deplored. The great divisions of sentiment and principle, reflected in the Constitutional Convention itself, had by 1796 resulted in a contested election between Thomas Jefferson and John Adams over the right to be his successor. In office Washington was a very mild nationalist who did not think of the Presidency as a source of innovations in policy. He envisaged the government to be little more than a referee and expected American society, if "protected from disorder and attack, to prosper on its own." Hence, he favored the plan for a national bank and other elements of the financial system of his Secretary of the Treasury, Alexander Hamilton, yet disapproved of Hamilton's plan for internal improvements. Finally, he was a jealous guardian of the dignity and legitimate power of his limited central government, both in his own conduct and in his response to popular upheavals, such as the Whiskey Rebellion. When the time came for him to pass on his responsibilities to President John Adams, he did so with a sense of relief, leaving the country in his

"Farewell Address" a final statement of his political philosophy.

In what scholars have called the Age of Democractic Revolution, George Washington was an anachronism. There survives a famous story told concerning a liberty which Gouverneur Morris took with General Washington as part of a youthful wager and of the icy stare that Morris got for his trouble. Washington was no "man of the people" to be clapped on the shoulder. In moments of seriousness his formality was severe and aristocratic—the product of a code developed under the old regime in Virginia. Yet he was a republican, in the classical sense, and altogether in character when he declared, "The approbation and affection of a free people [are] the greatest of earthly rewards." There is no explaining his life without reference to an ancient concept of honor. As Donald Davidson has written, "Washington in his national aspect [as hero] represents the difficult Federal conception at a time when it was really Federal, not 'consolidated.' " In his old age Washington warned against the example of the French radicals, "the poison of their principles." And for American "Jacobins," he had even less patience. In 1798 President Adams called him back into uniform to face the possibility of a French invasion. Should Citizen Bonaparte bring his armies to Louisiana and threaten our frontiers, Washington did not doubt the issue because, as he had observed some years before, "a sense of dedication to freedom . . . is natural to the American air." Fearing not so much what external enemies might accomplish as what internal divisions and their bitter fruit might bring, still wondering if "mankind when left to themselves are unfit for their own government," yet hopeful that a few virtuous leaders might continue to set all right and give the people good counsel, the old soldier spent his final days in the labor that he loved best, calling back to his standard the younger men who had served him so well. In his 67th year while seeing after his estate, he caught a chill and died soon thereafter of respiratory complications. In his will, though he had condemned abolitionist agitation as "inducing more evils than it could cure," and though he was a conventional Virginia planter in buying and selling such Negroes as were required in order "to live up to his rank," Washington freed those slaves at Mount Vernon who were not part of the inheritance of his wife's grandchildren. Underneath the stoic reserve and great self-discipline, there was sentiment and a warm heart. It was no marble figure who after the Revolution in the farewell to his officers in New York could barely speak and who embraced them all, one by one. The standing of George Washington's reputation as transformed by American myth is, on examination, in no way undeserved. (See J. C. Fitzgerald, ed., *The Writings of George Washington*, 39 vols. [Washington, D.C.: Government Printing Office, 1931–1944]; James T. Flexner, *George Washington*, 4 vols. [Boston: Little, Brown and Company, 1965–1972]; Douglas Southall Freeman, *George Washington*, 7 vols. [New York: Scribner's, 1948–1957], vol. 7 by John A. Carroll and Mary W. Ashworth; Bernard Mayo, *Myths and Men: Patrick*

Henry, George Washington, Thomas Jefferson [Athens: University of Georgia Press, 1959], pp. 25–48; Marcus Cunliffe, *George Washington, Man and Monument* [Boston: Houghton Mifflin, 1958]; Forrest McDonald, *The Presidency of George Washington* [Lawrence: Regents Press of Kansas, 1973]; Duncan J. MacLeod, *Slavery, Race and the American Revolution* [London: Cambridge University Press, 1974], pp. 130–138; John C. Miller, *The Federalist Era, 1789–1801* [New York: Harper & Row, 1960]; John Marshall, *Life of George Washington*, 5 vols. [Philadelphia: C. P. Wayne, 1804–1807]; Donald Davidson, *Attack on Leviathan: Regionalism and Nationalism in the United States* [Chapel Hill: University of North Carolina Press, 1938], pp. 212–227; Samuel Eliot Morison, *By Land and Sea: Essays and Addresses* [New York: Alfred A. Knopf, 1953], pp. 161–180; and Washington Irving, *The Life of George Washington*, 5 vols. [New York: C. P. Putnam's Sons, 1857].)

James Madison

(March 16, 1751–June 28, 1836), political philosopher, planter, Virginia statesman, and fourth President of the United States.

Though "little and ordinary" in his person (5′6″) and soft in speech, the master spirit of the Great Convention, able (through a surrogate) to make of his ideas the business of the house. Yet not precisely a measure of the kind of majority reflected in the Constitution. A protean figure, formed layer by layer out of the raw materials of temperament, reading, and experience. Yet, in retrospect, almost impossible to reconstruct. Described by a colleague in the Continental Congress as "a studious man . . . and [the] master of every public question that can arise, or he will spare no pains to become so." Quite properly denominated by Patrick Henry, who had watched him closely, as a "theroretic statesman"—best suited, by his own account, to "the intellectual pleasures of the closet." Yet on occasion capable of absolute political pragmatism, of legislative "management" and after-the-fact rationalization of a tampering with the record of events in which he had played an important role. Described by the Spanish Ambassador as ". . . full of subterfuges, evasions and subtleties . . . devoid of that good faith which he always puts on display when speaking and writing, and which squares so little with his political conduct"; or, in the more colorful idiom of a frequent adversary, as a "cunning devil" driven by "deep and mischievous designs." Certain that the members of the Constitutional Convention were acting their parts "for the ages," on the great stage of universal human history. Present in Philadelphia to earn for himself the everlasting fame of the lawgiver. Confirmed to the end of his days in the ". . . inexhaustible faith . . . that a well founded commonwealth may . . . be immortal." And thus give to its creator a similar status. Better prepared than any other Framer for this meeting. A great source of information on history and "political science," having composed detailed memoranda, "Vices of the Political System of the United States" and "Notes of Ancient and Modern Confederacies." Floor leader for the Federalists. Spoke 161 times, on almost every subject of importance to be discussed in the debates. Supported much of his attack on critics of plans for a stronger government with the rhetoric of the false dilemma: either what I recommend or chaos and disorder, "dissolution of the Union." Irritated and eventually depressed when the Convention did not go along with what he proposed. Fearful of an eventual fulfillment of his own well-calculated prophecies of separation into three confederacies. During the last three months of the Convention periodically stubborn and petulant—even to the point of putting the entire process of lawmaking at risk. Of necessity, restrained by older and steadier hands. But, lacking support for the Constitution he had hoped to secure, later possessed of such good sense as to prefer another, less ambitious instrument of fundamental law, once it had been adopted. Never so much a nationalist or centralizer as Gouverneur Morris, Hamilton, or James Wilson. A conscientious republican, yet alarmed by "symptoms of a levelling spirit" which "give notice of future danger." The last surviving Framer, and their first historian by way of the detailed records of the Great Convention which he preserved for publication after his death. Not precisely the "Father of the Constitution," but in his twenty-eight contributions to *The Federalist* one of its most important expositors. In his long public career able to test and modify his political theories many times. Always ready to follow "experience," which, according to his political preceptor David Hume (and also according to Hume's pious adversaries in the Scottish School of Common Sense), was a better guide than doctrinaire slogans. Therefore, frequently oversimplified by his modern admirers.

James Madison was born at Port Conway, Virginia, at the home of his maternal grandfather, Francis Conway, and was the oldest child of James Madison, a respected squire, and of Nelly Conway Madison. The Madisons had first come to Virginia *ca*. 1652, and had risen to a modest but substantial condition by moving westward with the frontier. At his father's plantation, Montpelier, James grew up in the open-air, gregarious and hearty Piedmont society of Orange County, which was to be his emotional and moral *locus*, his base of power and point of reference for the next eighty-five years. Young James was taught to read and write by his paternal grandmother, Frances Taylor Madison, whose father had held original title to a 13,500-acre estate situated at the foot of the Blue Ridge. After some local tutoring, James Madison, in the company of other planters' sons such as John Tyler and John Taylor of Caroline, was sent at the age of eleven to the boarding school of the Rev. Donald Robertson, trained at Aberdeen and Edinburgh. There he studied for five years. For another three years he read with the Rev. Thomas Martin, the rector of his parish church, brother to the future Framer, Gov. Alexander Martin of North Carolina, and tutor to the younger Madison children. Martin was a recent graduate of the College of New Jersey and urged Col. Madison to send his son there—and thus avoid the unhealthy climate of Williamsburg, the seat of William and Mary. When James went north to Princeton in 1769, the Virginia boy was unusually well prepared for higher education, especially in the classics.

Madison was extremely industrious while in residence at the College of New Jersey, completing the undergraduate curriculum in two years and then staying over for another year of graduate studies—in Hebrew, ethics, and theology—with President John Witherspoon. Upon his return to Virginia in 1772, he continued to prepare for a career in the ministry, but despaired of his health and fell into a long and serious depression during which he showed little interest in the things of this world which "are useless in possessing after one has exchanged time for eternity." Eventually the youthful scholar, with the help of a loving family, overcame his melancholy, and gave up the idea of life in the church. Madison had been so happy at Princeton that he was perhaps dispirited simply by removal from a congenial atmosphere. The life of the professor would have suited him very well. But in any case the thoroughness of his education, particularly in history and political philosophy, would give him an advantage throughout the remainder of his public life, and mark him as one of the most thoughtful of the early American statesmen. Moreover, Madison left Princeton a Whig. And a Whig he remained in the troubled times to come.

As the Revolution loomed on the horizon James Madison the younger was elected to the Orange County Committee of Safety in 1775. In the following year Col. Madison, the leading citizen of that community, got his son elected to a seat in the Virginia Convention which drafted a new state constitution and to the first legislature convened under its authority. Madison's only important contribution during these years of apprenticeship was some refinement upon the language concerning religious freedom in George Mason's draft of the Virginia Declaration of Rights. (Madison had already, in the years of inactivity, proved himself to be a friend of toleration by defending the Baptists in his area against acts of petty persecution.) However, in 1777 the political career of this somewhat proud, prim, and distant young man almost came to an end. Despite their regard for James Madison the elder, the freeholders of Orange County refused to return his bookish and uncommunicative son to a place for which he made no suit. In retrospect Madison understood that his neighbors saw in his "extreme distaste" for "personal solicitation" only "a mean parsimony or proud disrespect." Usage required conviviality, a good portion of strong drink, easy circulation, and the direct appeal. In failing of election Madison learned the lesson that the political habits of Virginia were not to be despised by men who aspired to the public favor of the citizens of that state. Of that truism he had to be reminded from time to time—especially when the nascent schoolmaster and seminarian seized temporary control of his disposition. But he never forgot that there were limits on his independence of judgment and his political style if he wished to accomplish anything at all. Though cool and reticent by nature, Madison eventually learned most of the social arts that are a necessary part of the science of politics in a republic.

In 1777, once again after some intervention by his devoted father, James Madison was given a seat on the Virginia Council of State, where, under the direction of Governors Patrick Henry and Thomas Jefferson, he was responsible for the preparation of many state papers, thereby acquiring useful experience in the day-to-day operations of government. Madison served on the Council until he was elected to represent Virginia in the Continental Congress for 1780. During his three years as a member of that body, he rapidly matured in his political thinking and developed a national point of view on many important questions. As a member of Congress he distinguished himself in connection with such issues as trade, defense policy, war debt, foreign relations, the administration of Western lands, and (especially) finance. No member of that assembly was a stronger supporter of the proposed impost or for plans to increase the powers of the Confederation to raise a revenue. In the view of the young delegate from the Piedmont, "imbecility" was threatening to "blast the glory of the Revolution." Virginia often refused to pay his salary, members from other states neglected to attend, and the Continental Army was on the verge of collecting its pay with the sword. Madison was able to arrange for Virginia's cession of her Western lands on terms agreeable to the state leadership in Richmond. In determining the proportion between population and taxation for the Southern states, he persuaded his associates to accept the ratio of three-fifths in counting slaves, which later became the formula for representation under the new Constitution. Much of the Congress came to notice the anomaly of so much thoroughness and application in a colleague so young and frail. It was their report that "sense, reading, address, and integrity" made the young legislator remarkably persuasive. Yet this was the time of near-paralysis and failure for government under the Articles. Knowing what should be done and how to do it did not reconcile Madison to the frustrations of his situation as Congressional leader. Gladly he served on a committee to "prepare to invest congress... with full and explicit powers for effectually carrying into execution in the several states all acts or resolutions passed. . . . " With some of his friends he speculated about the "implied right of coercion" and of the need to "compel obedience." But the times were not yet right for the implementation of such advanced doctrines. More economic confusion and a few riots and uprisings like the one Captain Shays would soon provide were a precondition for convincing the mutually suspicious leaders of the various states that a stronger government, one "not too democratic," would be required if the Union and the societies which it protected were to survive. While awaiting the appearance of such "instructive" conditions, Madison returned home to Virginia and resumed his study of the "public" law, at which he had made some beginning as early as 1773.

Yet once restored to the comfortable ambiance of Montpelier and his loving family, Madison did not completely eschew all politics. In 1784 he was once again elected to the Virginia House of Delegates. There, though a conventional Anglican throughout his life and no closet Deist like his friend Jefferson, he was instrumental in bringing about a complete separation of church and state. Also he did yeoman service in strengthening the basis of state finances. And most importantly, at the state level he continued to urge that action be taken to shore up the general government. He was a guiding force behind the Mount Vernon Conference (1785) and the subsequent Annapolis Convention (1786), where with other "choice spirits" he planned out the set of maneuvers which led finally to the Great Convention in Philadelphia the following May. In these years Madison established working relationships with General Washington and the brilliant Colonel Hamilton of New York. In 1786 Madison was re-elected to the Continental Congress, where he took further steps in behalf of the Constitutional Convention.

Perhaps the best way to explain what James Madison hoped would be accomplished through a new constitution is to begin by describing the conditions which he expected the improved government to correct. The most important problems of the Confederation were as follows: failure of the states to comply with requisitions; encroachments by the states on the authority of the general government, as in the case of Georgia's treaties with Indians; violations of the law of nations and of treaties authorized by state legislatures, as in the refusal of some Virginia planters to honor their debts in London and Glasgow; trespasses by the states upon the rights of their sister commonwealths, as in state duties on goods shipped through their ports but destined for merchants beyond their boundaries; "want of concert in matters of common interest," such as international trade, naturalization, and grants of incorporation for national purposes. But Madison's most serious concerns were with the democratic excesses of the state legislatures in issuing paper money, and the contempt for the country created overseas by the powerless condition of the Continental Congress. "The idea of erecting our national independence on the ruins of public faith and national honor must be," he insisted, "horrid to every mind which [has] retained either honesty or pride." These vices were "democratic" and resulted from the control of state governments by a "majority faction." A general government both "federal and national in its principle"—a government with a power to veto legislation in the states—might readily correct these vices without sliding into despotism. In aiming at his version of political justice, Madison spoke at times of individual and religious rights, and also of the right of citizens to vote." The Federal veto power over state laws would, he believed, work to secure such rights. What is noteworthy in this connection is that the Constitution as finally adopted included no such power of veto or "oversight." Neither did it transfer out of the hands of states the power to define the scope and number of "civil rights" belonging to their citizens. The exception to this generalization is a prohibition on theft by legislation with respect to paper money and the violation of contracts. Along with religious freedom and the suffrage, they indicate most of what Madison had in mind when he talked about the "rights of men." *Inability* to secure the states against internal disorders, *inability* to check injustices spawned by multiplicity and uncertainty of the state law, and *inability* to restrain the interest groups (agricultural, commercial, manufacturing, etc.) in their competition for influence over the entire political system were the glaring weaknesses of government by the Confederation. Much of what Madison proposed for inclusion in the Constitution follows directly from his critique in "Vices of the Political System of the United States." He would have been amazed to see his ideas used to justify government activity aimed directly at changing the economic and social conditions of men, both within and without the social bond. He did not trust society in its relation to the state—at least where the small polis was concerned. But he never imagined that the latter would be asked to absorb the former at some future moment in our nation's history.

It was because of his reservations concerning the "unreasonable" relationship of society to the homogenous republic that Madison developed his theories of the "extended republic" and the "multiplicity of factions." But even though in 1787 in Philadelphia he did emphasize the unwholesome and centrifugal influence of the sovereign states on the development of an American political identity, Madison was always an advocate of specifically *divided and balanced powers within the proposed Federal structure.* As he summarized the problem, "In framing a government which is to be administered by men over men,—the great difficulty lies in this: you must first enable the government to control the governed; and, in the next place, oblige it to control itself." Trust in the power or watchfulness of the people would not be enough. "Auxiliary precautions" would be necessary. And the parts of the Federal structure itself would restrain one another. They would pit the ambitions of one man against the ambitions of another, and of group against group. Domination would be impossible in a "large and various republic." Stability would result, allowing for the development of a "third force," a group "disinterested" in its approach to most national questions, devoted to the laws, and inclined to reverence them as they grew older and better established.

Madison looked with anxiety toward the subsequent history of the Republic.

And though such parts of the Constitution as were finally settled on by the majority of the Framers and also approved by James Madison were the most uncontroversial components of his original political "model," Madison understood their long-range implications better than did most of his colleagues. "In framing a system which we wish to last for ages," observed the Virginia lawgiver, "we should not lose sight of the changes which ages will produce. An increase of population will of necessity increase the proportion of those who will labour under all the handicaps of life & secretly sigh for a more equal distribution of its blessings. These may in time outnumber those who are placed above the feelings of indigence. According to equal laws of suffrage, the power will slide into the hands of the former." Hence Madison wanted authority transferred from the states, who were subject to the politics of envy and resentment, into the hands of a not-too-consolidated government in which the powers were clearly distributed, "few and defined." Because contemporary experience connects enforced egalitarianism with the activities of the central authority and the sovereignty of the states with resistance to such measures, it is easy for us to overlook Madison's purpose in devising a Federalism of his own. In his day it was the agency of the states which appeared to threaten property and the social order. In that context it was reasonable to advocate a stronger government to control the levellers, to intimidate mobs, not encourage them, to protect the institution of slavery and other property, not to undermine it, etc. Prof. Adrienne Koch has contended that Madison, in designing a constitution, did not try to guarantee "too much" in the way of "rights." Out of prudence he said nothing about women or Negroes or suffrage. The proper interpretation is, however, that he did not wish to establish too much of what modern civil libertarians describe as rights. Our problem with much scholarship on this question is that it reads Madison's long-term objectives out of the idiom, the vehicle of his rhetoric, and thus overburdens what was, for the Framers, a convention of address. Madison hated sameness and uniformity in a way that made equality not merely unlikely but finally impossible. At the state level, where he knew it belonged, he accepted the conventional Virginia view, that the right to vote belonged to freeholders and later in his life revised that formula by adding "housekeepers and heads of families." Furthermore, he made a part of his appeal for the Virginia Plan that it would offer security to the special interests of the Southern states, *i.e.*, protect them from the loss of their slaves.

Madison was on the floor, speaking quietly and reasonably in behalf of *his* version of the United States Constitution on most of the days when the Great Convention was in session. Moreover, he served on the Committee of Style and the Committee on Postponed Matters. Whenever some point of importance fell into dispute, he "took the lead," using what Pierce called "the most correct knowledge [of] . . . the affairs of the United States" to be found among the political leaders of his generation. First of all, he fought that proposal which gave representation to the states by making them equals in the United States Senate. No one contended longer for proportional representation. He wanted the President to serve during good behavior, or, failing that, for a very long term; and then he fought allowing the states to elect the President. At every turn, he urged that Congress be given a veto over state laws. All of these battles he lost. Furthermore, though he urged his proposals upon his fellow Southerners as a protection of their regional interests (which he acknowledged at every opportunity), they would not agree with him concerning a tax on exports, a navigation law, or Federal control of the militia. Even on regulations concerning executive authority to veto Federal legislation, the number of votes in the Senate necessary to appoint judges, and the power for said judges in a council of revision designed to assist the President, Madison broke with most of his fellow Southerners, while simultaneously announcing a firm devotion to their cause.

In Philadelphia Madison actually did all that he could to persuade the rest of the Framers to take power from the states. To that end he reviewed for the house his study of earlier confederations and conjured up specters of tyranny to frighten his associates into concurrence with the Virginia Plan. Once he was through, however, not even all of the delegates from Virginia agreed that there was "less danger of encroachment from General Government than from State Governments." By Madison's own admission, the states were represented in the process settled upon for election of the United States Senate, in the selection of the President, and in the machinery for adopting, rejecting, and revising the Constitution. Yet much of the Constitution as finally approved suited Madison very well: it rested on the people of the states, represented in their conventions, and it was not a "treaty" between legislatures. Moreover, through the Federal Chief Executive, it acted upon the people. Yet none of the components of the new system would be too strong. Judges would at least require Senatorial approval, and the President could be impeached or overridden. Even the "impetuous vortex" of "legislative supremacy" had been avoided by specific grants of power to the executive and judiciary branches of government, by the reservation of powers to the states, and by the "defined and limited objects" of all Federal authority as specified by the instrument itself.

Though momentarily perplexed and angry, declaring on one occasion that "it was vain to purchase concord in the Convention on terms that would perpetuate discord," Madison finally accepted the inevitable and began to adjust his long-range planning to the advantages of the Constitution as it was going to read, once completed. The basic maxim of his statecraft, that "all men having power ought to be distrusted," had been observed. According to Madison's viewpoint, such caution was important in establishing the new government, and would be even more crucial in the years to come. Though

Senators would not serve nine years, they would at least serve six. The government would have an aristocratic element and the President would be no mere cipher. Taxes would finally be collected and a defense maintained.

A national university to train leaders in a "national spirit" might have filled out the design further in the direction of adequacy, but the other Framers were unpersuaded of the advantages of a "national" education, as they had been with the other more ambitious elements in Madison's original plan. The basis for the lawgiver's hope would therefore have to continue to be people like his yeoman neighbors in Orange County: "Viewing the subject in its merits alone, the freeholders of the Country would be the safest depositories of Republican liberty. In future times a great majority of the people will not only be without land, but any other sort of property. These will either combine under the influence of their common situation; in which case, the rights of property and the public liberty will not be secure in their hands: or which is more probable, they will become the tools of opulence and ambition." There were clouds on the pastoral horizon—clouds which commerce and industry would not disperse. Establishing a government which for the people would seem habitual and which would command pious respect would therefore have to be done quickly and done well. On leaving Philadelphia, Madison hoped for the best, polished up his amazing if sometimes self-serving *Notes*, and prepared to plead the case for a Constitution very different from the one he had expected to support before the Continental Congress in New York and at home in Virginia.

In the Great Convention James Madison had insisted at one point that "the states never possessed the essential rights of sovereignty" and he had elsewhere added "the people would not be less free as members of one great Republic than as members of thirteen small ones." By the time he collaborated with Hamilton and John Jay in producing *The Federalist*, his emphasis had already begun to change. And once the Constitution had been adopted by all of the states, it changed again—in the direction of his old adversaries, the Antifederalists. But what is most interesting is the interval between Madison's emergence (*ca.* 1791) as party leader of the Democratic-Republicans and his advocacy in Philadelphia of the Virginia Plan: the period when he was a mild Federalist on at least partially Antifederalist grounds.

In his contributions to *The Federalist*, for the benefit of a New York audience Madison made a few conventional noises about "energy" and "stability" in government. Moreoever, he repeated his familiar objections to the "imbecility" of the Confederation and refuted the theoretical assumption left over from such authorities as Montesquieu that only small republics could avoid being transformed into despotisms. But, as for instance in No. 39, he added constructions of the operations of the new authority whose case he argued that were not part of his discourse in Philadelphia. The "jurisdiction" of the new government, he insisted, "extends to certain enumerated objects only, and leaves to the several States a residuary and inviolable sovereignty over all other objects." The Constitution provides for a regime "neither wholly federal, nor wholly national." The states in their capacity to approve or reject it are "distinct and independent." As Forrest McDonald has insisted, Madison's performance as Publius emphasizes the restraints built into the new system, what it cannot do, rather than its potential for good works and creativity. The differences between his essays and Alexander Hamilton's contributions to the same set foreshadow their conflicts in the next fifteen years. Looking horizontally over the spread and disposition of the parts of the authority they were attempting to recommend, adverting to history and "political science," Madison emphasized its conformity to republican principles. Looking vertically up and down the Federal "chain of command," speaking of economic concerns and of the administrative and judicial capacities of the new Federal "engine," Hamilton viewed each grant of power as an opportunity. Before the series had been completed, Madison was forced to hurry home to Virginia and stand for a seat in the Virginia ratification convention of June 1788.

In Richmond, Madison carried much of the Federalist burden in the struggle against George Mason and Patrick Henry. Assisted by his "convert," Governor Edmund Randolph, he went almost so far as to tell the Antifederalists that the Constitution was just what they had in mind: "The powers of the general government relate to external objects, and are but few." All of their fears of centralized government were such as he himself would feel were the Constitution not so mild in its dealings with the liberties of citizens and the rights of the states. Stronger national authority was necessary to collect a tax, pay our debts, and defend our frontiers. Currency had to be stabilized and popular cries for paper money restrained. The alternatives were defeat and internal chaos. Moreover, the South, if war came, would "need" the Union—particularly if its institutions were to survive the threat of "servile insurrection." Furthermore, there was the Fugitive Slave Clause, a guarantee never before available. No need to worry about the implied power hidden behind language concerning the "general welfare" and "necessary and proper."

Madison complained of appeals to "apparent danger." The burden of proof for such contentions, he maintained, fell on his opponents, who were unjustly out to frighten Virginia into obduracy. As to the possible emancipation of slaves by Federal action, there was "no power to warrant it." Concerning the Federal judiciary he was equally encouraging: "the jurisdiction of these courts is very small . . . all controversies directly between citizen and citizen will remain with the local courts." The government was not "consolidated." Nor should it be. The "watchfulness of the states"—their "extensive means of influence"—would protect its purity. Even the taxing power was finite: "I may say, with truth, that there never was a more economical government in any age or country, nor which will require fewer hands or give less influence." Subsequent amendments to specify a few more limitations on the general government would do nicely. James Madison promised to support them. But previous amendments, such as Henry and Mason wished to make as a condition of ratification, would destroy the Union, and forfeit forever all the advantages the new Constitution should bring.

The Federalists won this fight. Madison fell ill during the debates, and had to leave parts of the battle to other Federalists, such as Edmund Randolph and Col. Henry Lee. But in some cases this change was fortunate for the Federalist cause. Madison was not a powerful speaker and impressed only those already on his side or interested in close analysis. Even so, this was his most impressive public performance, under great pressure and in danger of being overwhelmed as a traitor to his own people. Clearly, George Washington's commitment to the same view of the questions Madison examined with such grace and quiet care did more to carry the day than dialectics and rhetorical concession. Yet Madison won great respect for his efforts in the ratification convention, and he was later to declare that what was said there and in other such assemblies was the authoritative gloss on the fundamental law of the land. Thus the Constitution as Madison presented it in Richmond in June of 1788 has by his own announcement more authority than what he argued in Philadelphia and in *The Federalist*.

Patrick Henry denied the cunning Mr. Madison the seat in the original United States Senate which Madison so much desired, and attempted to deny him also the opportunity of being elected to the House of Representatives. Yet despite a gerrymander and the formidable opposition of James Monroe, Madison won a House seat and was there in New York when the members of the new government assembled. From 1789 through 1797 Madison was the leader of a Southern bloc in the Congress. Moreoever, he was instrumental in filling out the skeletal framework provided by the Constitution in the establishment of the component parts of the government. Fulfilling his promise to the Virginia ratifying convention, Madison introduced and passed through the First Congress twelve amendments to the Constitution, ten of which became the Bill of Rights. Though they were not precisely what the Antifederalists had prescribed, they did much to pacify the friends of liberty who had originally opposed so drastic a change from the Articles of Confederation. For a time Madison continued to be of help to President Washington. But with his close friend, the Secretary of State Thomas Jefferson, he began to doubt the merit of certain measures undertaken by the old hero at the suggestion of Mr. Hamilton, his Secretary of the Treasury. After declaring, "We are in the wilderness, without a single footstep to guide us," Madison settled on his choice of persona, as defender of the strict construction of the Constitution, and attacked Hamilton's plan for internal improvements, the Jay Treaty, and the effect of debt assumption on the economy of the Southern states. Concerning Yankee speculation in currency and land, he cried out and declared of the entire Federalist program that had Virginia Federalists foreseen its adoption, they would never have supported the Constitution for ratification.

In four years out of office, Madison assisted his aging father in the operation of Montpelier and learned his role as husband to Dolley Payne Todd, whom he had married in September of 1794. Yet these were also years of intense and partisan political activity and of more of the kind of writing that he had done while party leader in the Congress. Madison was the author of the Virginia Resolutions of 1798, which called for state resistance to the unconstitutional acts of the Adams' administration and was unquestionably a party to plans for a more violent resistance had the Federalists moved to corrupt the political process by way of using the excuse of war or military necessity. In later years both Madison and his admirers would deny the obvious reading of these events as a precedent for nullification or secession. Their explanation was disingenuous. Even in the Great Convention Madison had maintained, "The use of force against a state would probably be considered by the party attacked as a dissolution of all previous compacts by which it might be bound." Shooting, however, was unnecessary, as Antifederalist rhetoric won for Jefferson the election of 1800.

If James Madison had been a good populist and disciple of Patrick Henry while out of power, he tended back toward Federalism once restored to authority as Secretary of State under President Thomas Jefferson. Madison was the principal advisor of our third President. In his official capacity he engineered the Louisiana Purchase of 1803 and helped to win approval in Washington for this unconstitutional bargain. He also counseled his friend Jefferson on party matters and arranged for the seizure of West Florida. In handling diplomacy with France, Spain, and England, Madison displayed great skill, but more craft than republican simplicity. However, he was unable to reconcile New England to the Embargo instituted in response to English offenses against American ships, and unable to purchase Florida. On Jefferson's retirement in 1809, Madison ascended as heir presumptive to the Presidency.

The central event of James Madison's two terms as Chief Executive was the War of 1812. His conduct as wartime President was not above criticism, for he propelled the nation into mortal conflict without having made the necessary preparations. Hence it was no surprise that the first two years of the war did not go well for the United States. Moreover, many in this country and in England believed that in joining the Emperor Napoleon as the enemy of England, we had made common cause with tyranny and given offense to all Christian civilization. Madison, in contrast, believed the war to be a necessary coda to the American Revolution, securing for us our unquestioned place among the nations. With Bonaparte defeated, England turned in anger to administer a proper punishment on her "upstart relations." A British expedition burned Washington and another crossed into New York. Maine was under pressure and New England prepared for secession. Then came a chain of American victories which no one could have expected. The English were driven back into Canada, defeated on the Great Lakes, and deprived of their control over the territories north of the Ohio. More importantly, General Andrew Jackson crushed their Indian allies in Alabama and drove back the flower of their army from the precincts of New Orleans. The young men in Washington had laughed at the indecisive "little commander-in-chief with his little round hat and huge cockade," as he visited the military departments attempting to restore morale. But with the Treaty of Ghent, which restored the status quo antebellum and finally gained the freedom of the seas, Madison had achieved his purposes and preserved his reputation for leadership and sagacity.

Other acts of Madison's Presidency went against the announced principles of the party he had helped to create: the rechartering of the United States Bank; the creation of a military and naval establishment; and the Tariff Act of 1816. Yet in February of 1817, in his final act as President, Madison vetoed legislation providing for public works and internal improvements. The apparent violations of Democratic-Republican dogma were by implication justified by the experience of the war. Absolutely inactive government could not defend the country. American commerce and manufacturing had to be encouraged. But a teleocratic state was still foreign to Madison's political philosophy.

Upon leaving office in March of 1817, James Madison retired to Montpelier, where the former President enjoyed entertaining visitors, polishing his *Notes of Debates in the Federal Convention of 1787* (which he had always planned for publication after his death), collecting his correspondence, and writing occasional comments on the political events of the day. In 1819 Madison became a member of the Board of Visitors for the University of Virginia, where from 1826 to 1834 he served as Rector, following Jefferson. During the Missouri controversy of 1819–1820, Southerners employed Madison to refute the "higher law" theories of Rufus King and the claim that the Fathers had meant to exclude slavery from all new states organized in the West. Later, during the nullification controversy, nationalists had called upon Madison to deny the Constitutional theories of John C. Calhoun. Madison consistently attacked abolitionists as unpatriotic and treated talk of peaceful secession or state resistance to "unjust" laws as illegal. The "right of revolution" was another matter, but could be invoked only after great provocation. There were over one hundred slaves at Montpelier, none of whom Madison freed. He disliked the "peculiar institution," was a gentle, loved master, but could not imagine the free Negro as citizen. No one recognized the frailty of the Union better than did its last surviving architect. And since his reputation as Founder and Lawgiver would depend on its survival, he edited the history of his own previous activities just as he had edited his *Notes*—to shore it up a bit. In 1829, Madison was a delegate to the Virginia Constitutional Convention, where he acted the role of peacemaker and voted to sustain the great influence of the older slaveholding counties of his state. He died in his 86th year after remarking to the inquiry of his niece as to the change in his condition, "Nothing more than a change of mind, my dear."

Of all the original generation of American statesmen and of all the Framers, James Madison is the most difficult to explain. Because his career was so long and so full of change, because he spoke with so many voices, he defies interpretation. Yet his republicanism was consistent and sincere, as was acknowledged by all those who knew him well. (See Irving Brant, *James Madison*, 6 vols. [Indianapolis: Bobbs-Merrill, 1941–1961]; Douglas Adair, "James Madison," pp. 124–141 of *Fame and the Founding Fathers* [New York: W.W. Norton & Co., 1974], ed. by H. Trevor Colbourn; Ralph Ketcham, *James Madison: A Biography* [New York: The Macmillan Company, 1971]; Alexander R. Landi, "The Politics of James Madison," Ph.D. dissertation, University of Dallas, 1973; Edward McNall Burns, *James Madison, Philosopher of the Constitution* [New York: Octagon Books, 1973]; Norman K. Risjord, *Chesapeake Politics, 1781–1800* [New York: Columbia University Press, 1978]; George Carey, "Majority Tyranny and the Extended Republic Theory of James Madison," *Modern Age*, XX [Winter, 1976], 40–53; H. James Henderson, *Party Politics in the Continental Congress* [New York: McGraw-Hill, 1974]; Adrienne Koch, *Jefferson and Madison: The Great Collaboration* [New York: Alfred A. Knopf, 1950]; Neal Riemer, *James Madison* [New York: Washington Square, 1968]; Adrienne Koch, *Madison's "Advice to My Country"* [Princeton: Princeton University Press, 1966]; Paul Eidelberg, *The Philosophy of the American Constitution: A Reinterpretation of the Intentions of the Founding Fathers* [New York: The Free Press, 1968]; Virginia Moore, *The Madisons: A Biography* [New York: McGraw-Hill, 1979]; Adrienne Koch, *Power, Morals and the Founding Fathers: Essays in the Interpretation of the American Enlightenment* [Ithaca: Cornell University Press, 1961]; Douglas Adair, "That Politics May be Reduced to a Science: David Hume, James Madison and the Tenth Federalist," pp. 93–106 of *Fame and the Founding Fathers* [New York: W.W. Norton & Co., 1974], ed. H. Trevor Colburn; Gaillard Hunt, ed., *The Writings of James Madison*, 9 vols. [New York: G.P. Putnam's Sons, 1900]; Roy Branson, "James Madison and the Scottish Enlightenment," *Journal of the History of Ideas*, 40 [April/June, 1979], 235–250; Henry Adams, *History of the United States during the Administrations of Jefferson and Madison*, 9 vols. (New York: Charles Scribner's Sons, 1889]; William T. Hutchinson *et al.*, eds., *The Papers of James Madison*, 20 vols. [Chicago: University of Chicago Press, 1962–1977];

Robert A. Rutland *et al.*, eds., *The Papers of James Madison*, vols. 11, 12, and 13 [Charlottesville: University Press of Virginia, 1977, 1979, 1980]; James H. Smylie, "Madison and Witherspoon: Theological Roots of American Political Thought," *The Princeton University Library Chronicle*, XII, No. 3 [Spring, 1961], 118–132; Richard Buel, Jr., *Securing the Revolution: Ideology in American Politics, 1789–1815* [Ithaca: Cornell University Press, 1972].)

George Mason

(December 11, 1725–October 7, 1792), planter, political philosopher, and statesman.

One of the noblest and most disinterested of the many impressive figures who emerged from Virginia's original experiment in self-government and later were responsible for its dominant role in the formation of the Union which joined the newly independent states. At the age of 61 when he attended the Great Convention, for the first time beyond the boundaries of the old Chesapeake world which had produced him. When he arrived in Philadelphia, in some degree committed to the basic features of the Virginia Plan, which was later presented by Governor Edmund Randolph for the delegation from his state. But before the Convention was over, the sternest opponent in the company of the document produced by its deliberations: so outraged about what had been done that he declared, "I would have lost this hand before it should have marked my name to the new government." A staunch classical republican with "a temperament . . . like the younger Cato, constitutionally stern, firm and honest . . . a most decided enemy to all *constructive* and *implied* powers." Fearful that the new Constitution would deliver the Southern states "bound hand and foot to the Eastern [Northern] states and enable them to exclaim, in the words of Cromwell . . . 'The Lord hath delivered them into our hands.' " Spoke 136 times and present in every session. Angry with the course taken by the debates before they were over, insisting to his son, "I would not, upon pecuniary Motives, serve in this Convention for a thousand pounds a day." Yet stirred to a new-found zeal for battle against the adoption of the Constitution when he returned to Virginia. In his Antifederalism a cause for the greatest concern among the proponents of the new system of government because of the magnitude of his reputation among American leaders both in Virginia and throughout the country. More than any of the other Framers responsible for the proposal of a Bill of Rights by the First Congress of the United States.

George Mason of Gunston Hall was the fourth of his name and line to occupy a position of importance in the Northern Neck of Virginia. He was a direct descendant of Colonel George Mason of Worcestershire, England, a substantial yeoman with aristocratic connections in the Vale of Evesham, who in 1651 migrated to the Potomac River Valley in Virginia after service at Worcester in the ill-fated army of King Charles II. The Masons prospered in Virginia and by the time of the birth of the fourth George Mason held some 5000 acres at Dogue's Neck below Alexandria, plus sundry other plantations, both in Maryland and Virginia. George Mason IV was the son of George Mason III and Ann Thomson Mason. He was connected by marriage, business, political association, and friendship with the Mercers, the Lees, the Brents, the Fitzhughs, and other significant families. With his father's death in 1735 (by drowning during a storm), the George Mason who was to become a Framer fell under the guardianship of his mother, a most capable woman, and his uncle by marriage, John Mercer of Marlborough, a distinguished attorney, whose considerable library was to become young George's private college. But before the period of this tutelage, George Mason had some training in the local grammar schools and from private instruction. However, his most important teacher was his mother, from whom he learned the art of being the master of a great plantation and the necessity for personal management, planning, and careful accounts. Yet throughout his life, study was Mason's principal delight, so much so that he became one of Virginia's most learned men—particularly in constitutional questions. Indeed, his intellectual abilities were so considerable that one of the most distinguished historians of the period of the American Revolution has maintained that Mason had a "talent that far outweighed Madison's."

In 1749 George Mason became a justice of the Fairfax County Court. In the same year he was elected vestryman of Truro Parish, an office with considerable civic responsibilities. Also in 1749 he became a partner in the Ohio Company, and in April of 1750 he married Anne Eilbeck of Mattowoman—a neighbor from directly across the Potomac who brought him connections with the most important families of Charles County, Maryland. In 1755 Mason began work on the house that was to be symbolic of their lives, Gunston Hall, which was completed in 1758. Also in that year George Mason was first elected by the freeholders of Fairfax County to the House of Burgesses, where he served until 1761. Yet even at that early age he found the ordinary moil and seethe of political life in the larger arena not to his taste—something to be endured only when the duty of a gentleman, his public virtue, required it of him.

The 1760's and the first four years of the following decade were for George Mason a private time. Using the valetudinarian plea of chronic gout, the squire of Gunston Hall refused further service in the House of Burgesses, though he retained his Fairfax County offices. Nevertheless, this was a busy period for George Mason, and not without its political implications. The business of the Ohio Company did not prosper, since Indian policy issuing from Great Britain discouraged further white settlement beyond the mountains following the conclusion of the Seven Years War. Yet under an earlier grant Mason claimed fifty to sixty thousand acres in western Virginia and Kentucky and composed a long and learned annotation, "Extracts from the Virginia Charters, with Some Remarks upon Them" (1773), in defense of such claims. With the passage of the Stamp Act, Col. Mason (who had acquired that rank for service as quartermaster in the war against the French) favored and observed the terms of the Association, which forestalled trade with the mother country. He even went so far as to publish an open letter under the signature "A Virginia Planter" in the *London Public Ledger* in the spring of 1766: a letter which encouraged English merchants to correct the mistaken attitude of their government toward the colonies in North America. He grew irritated with the arrogance and the blunders of the King's ministers and after the adoption of the Townshend Duties hoped to see the revival of a policy of non-importation. Or, better still, non-exportation. But he was not yet very far toward revolution, and scorned the idea of American independence. Much of his time in these years went toward the building of churches and to the development of the social and economic institutions of his region. This was also a period of close association with his neighbor Col. George Washington, with whom he shared much of his thinking on political questions.

George Mason's political position as a conditionally loyal but profoundly uneasy subject of King George III places him firmly in the camp of those apologists of American resistance who argued more from legal theory and precedent than from a definition of human nature. In his public letter "To the Committee of Merchants in London" he writes, "We claim Nothing but the Liberty and Privileges of Englishmen, in the same degree, as if we had still continued among our brethren in Great Britain." To this he added the appeal of the common blood: "Let our fellow Subjects in Great Britain reflect that we are descended from the same Stock with themselves, nurtured in the same Principles of Freedom. . . . We are the same people with them in every respect, only not yet debauched by Wealth, Luxury, Venality and Corruption." In the same vein he advised his neighbors, "We must maintain the liberty which we have derived from our ancestors." To claim that British Americans would forfeit this heritage lightly was a lie of "ministerial" propaganda: "the wildest Chimera that ever disturbed a Madman's brain has not less Truth than this Opinion." Even so, "such another experiment as the Stamp-Act," he informs the merchants, "would produce a general Revolt in America." The Townshend Duties were not quite so offensive as the Stamp Act, yet George Mason responded to them as he had to the earlier provocation by drafting bills designed to muffle or circumvent their effect—bills presented to the House of Burgesses by Col. George Washington or some other member from the Northern Neck. And he urged his neighbors to become serious about enforcing the restrictions on trade to which they had agreed. He wrote essays in the American press, then finally came to the opinion that there was a "premeditated design" and system "to introduce arbitrary government in America," to corrupt the relationship of the King and his British American subjects and to "dissolve the original Compacts by which our Ancestors bound themselves and their Posterity to be dependent on the British Crown." At this point strictly constitutional arguments ceased to be of any avail. Reduced to "desperation," Americans had the right to act upon the principle of self-preservation and to appeal to the sword—the god of battles. In the Fairfax Resolves (July 18, 1774), George Mason brought together these developments in his thought to produce one of the most significant political statements of the period preceding the American Revolution. It was not casually that he had observed of the ancient poets that "they have made a kind of Being of Necessity and tell us that the Gods themselves are inclined to yield to her."

The circumstances surrounding the twenty-four Fairfax Resolves, which were adopted by the freeholders of that county in a meeting presided over by George Washington, and which became the mandate for the local Committee of Safety and an admonitory message to the new government of Virginia and proposed Continental Congress, were developments in New England, the Intolerable Acts, the threat to the integrity of the other colonies posed by the British response to the Boston Tea Party, and attendant outrages. Mason wrote these resolutions knowing that war was almost inevitable. Yet he included in them expressions of thanks to the friends of America in the mother country. British history in the tradition of documents like the one in which he speaks continues to be part of his consciousness. But there is also something new—an insistence that Americans should act in concert, a tribute to Massachusetts for "acting in the Common Cause of all British America." The forms of remonstrance and petition are carefully observed, but the breath of life is not in them. Instead, at the heart of his matter is the refusal to be treated like a conquered people and the suggestion of provision for military preparation. In this document Mason crossed over into the company of those Americans who were ready for independence if they could be free in no other way. Thus necessity and nature combined.

From 1775 to 1776, George Mason was the representative from Fairfax County to the Virginia Convention—the *ad hoc* government of the state. He was forced to accept this assignment by the election of George Washington to the Continental Congress and by the consensus of his neighbors. Almost immediately he became a member of the Committee of Safety, which took over the executive powers of the departed royal governor, Lord Dunmore. In 1776 Mason was the leading member of the special convention which drew up a new constitution for the independent state of Virginia, and from 1776 through 1781 he sat in the Virginia legislature for Fairfax County. These were the most active political years in his career. Mason was himself the principal author of the Virginia Declaration of Rights, which laid a predicate for the Declaration of Independence adopted within the next three months. There were many competing versions of the original Virginia constitution; but, according to the participants, "that proposed by George Mason swallowed up all the rest." In the view of authorities on Mason's thought, the distinguishing characteristic of this document is its almost complete similarity to the old colonial government of Virginia under the British Crown, with a limited executive, an appointed council, and stringent property qualifications for seats in both houses of the legislature. Mason's constitution is no democratic document, but it is republican in the classical sense. Its object was to restrict and distribute power, not to enforce an *a priori* ideological plan on Virginia society. Members of the council and governors could not serve consecutive terms. Governors and members of the council of state were chosen by the legislature, and senators by a college of electors. Mason wanted no permanent class of politicians *or* military officers. Gentlemen and freeholders should rule and defend the state, considering their time of service in various offices and ranks as the price of liberty, a duty—not an opportunity for advancement. As he had learned from Roman history, power is most safely entrusted to those who have something better to do and who prefer a private station.

Those who read the Virginia Declaration of Rights out of context are often misled by the statement of its first paragraph that "all men are by nature equally free and independent, and have certain inherent rights, of which, when they enter into a state of society, they cannot, by any compact, deprive or divest their posterity; namely, the enjoyment of life and liberty, with the means of acquiring and possessing property, and pursuing and obtaining happiness and safety." The record of the debates surrounding the adoption of this language indicates both how much and how little was intended by it. For one thing, slaves were specifically excluded from the protection of its sweeping generalization by the reference to a "state of society." The advocates of the Virginia Declaration, according to Edmund Randolph, included this phrase to reassure conservatives that they meant to foster no "civil convulsion" in the relation of the races. Indeed, George Mason, though he deplored the slave trade as harmful to Virginia, and was of the opinion that "every master of slaves is a petty tyrant," was always an opponent to every threat to the "peculiar institution" and later sponsored legislation which made it difficult for his neighbors to free their slaves. His antislavery sentiments were not to any important degree pro-Negro, but instead followed from the basic tenets of his republican theory: that to discourage an increase in the number of slaves should make way for additional white immigration into the Southern states. The Roman Republic had been undermined by excessive dependence upon slaves. Yeomen were what a virtuous

Virginia required. Mason was certainly no egalitarian. In drafting "The Fairfax County Military Association," he wrote of "gentleman and freeholder." They were not the same, but together they made up a society. They were its "constituent members." The Marquis de Chastellux advised his fellow countrymen, following a 1780 visit to Virginia, to take American statements about the "rights of men" in this way and not as had the "half-philosophers . . . who have invariably mistaken the word *people* for mankind in general." For the Virginia documents refer to planters and farmers who are freemen, participate in government, and own slaves—both "citizens and masters" who "perfectly resemble the bulk of individuals who formed what were called *the people* in the ancient republics."

In 1777 George Mason was named a member of the commission called upon to revise the laws of Virginia. In that company he urged the necessity of preserving the force of the English common law in Virginia's courts—just as he had insisted upon the necessity for the Bill of Rights to replace the English Declaration of Rights of 1689. Mason was active in promoting a sound currency and retirement of debt. He encouraged domestic manufacturing and trade with France. He took responsibility for organizing systems of supply for the Continental Army, supported recruitment of troops, and drew up a realistic tax plan. With Patrick Henry, whom he valued as "the first man upon this continent, as well in abilities as public virtue," he secured the authorization for the 1779 expedition of George Rogers Clark to subdue British outposts in the West along the Ohio. And he labored continuously to develop a consistent and defensible policy for the settlement of Virginia's frontier. Then he began to weary of the unpatriotic and trivial spirit so often present in the ordinary deliberations of the legislature. He was provoked by talk of repudiating legitimate debts to British merchants and with the mistreatment of former Loyalists who had done nothing to prevent American independence. Though no longer in the legislature, he once again exerted his influence behind the scenes. Despite his Anglican orthodoxy he joined James Madison in opposing a bill for state support of "Teachers of the Christian religion" and called for legal disestablishment and separation of church and state—a process left incomplete in the reforms of 1776, which went only so far as toleration. Furthermore, he continued to watch over the interests of the Ohio Company and developments in land policy. Slowly he came to see the necessity for strengthening the general government into a power that could raise taxes and wage war. In 1785 he attended the Mount Vernon Conference, which settled disputes between Maryland and Virginia concerning the Potomac and Chesapeake Bay. In 1786 he agreed to return to the legislature and oppose proposals to issue paper money. He was proud of what had been achieved in the Revolution and wrote to his son, "Taking a retrospective view of what has passed, we seem to have been treading upon enchanted ground." To defend and to secure the miracle of liberty, he agreed to attend the

Great Convention as one of the delegates from Virginia. He was prepared for a change, if the change was not too great.

George Mason went northward toward Philadelphia and the Constitutional Convention filled with a kind of enthusiasm for his task as Framer and once there was pleased to see that America had sent "her first characters" to serve in the labor of designing a new government. In the early weeks of the Convention he exhibited none of the "heterodoxy" against Federalist principles which Madison had predicted, based on an earlier conversation with him concerning the business at hand. But as the weeks drew out into months and after he had listened to the political theories of such nationalists as Hamilton, Wilson, and Gouverneur Morris, Mason took pause and began to raise questions about the intentions of his fellow Framers and the probable impact of their collusion on the liberties of his countrymen. He was not troubled by the necessity for compromise in giving equal representation to the states in the Senate. He stood by his agreement to the central features of the Virginia Plan. All that he required in addition were a few modifications in the direction of moderation. Though he feared that the New Englanders might overreact to popular upheavals such as Shays' Rebellion, he concurred with them that "we have been too democratic." He opposed the direct election of Presidents and recommended a large property qualification for United States Senators, but he could not tolerate the idea of creating a plutocracy through the instrument of law. He was too democratic for that.

Mason was also uneasy when he heard talk about abolishing the states: "The State Legislatures also ought to have some means of defending themselves aganst encroachments of the National Government." The state legislatures should elect Senators. They should determine for themselves laws governing the suffrage within their boundaries. They should be left free to declare a moratorium on payment of debts in times of economic unheaval. They should be protected from harassment by the Federal courts and from over-regulation of their militia. In July Mason grew to be more and more testy and negative in his reaction to what the majority of the Framers seemed willing to accept. The Presidency was too strong. A triple executive was more to his liking, with one member from the South, one from the Middle Colonies, and one from New England. Or failing that, a kind of Privy Council of six (two from each section) to surround and protect the chief executive. It was not proper that the President should be re-elected, that he should appoint Federal judges, or that the law should require a three-fourths vote to override his veto. The idea of a power to tax the exports of the states filled him with alarm, as did the idea of a standing army. The amending process was too cumbersome and would lead to oppression. And most importantly, it was not safe for the South to agree to navigation acts passed by a mere majority. Or for the states and the people at large to do without a Bill of Rights restricting the power of the "Sovereign."

As the discussion moved toward consensus, Mason grew impatient and acerbic, and in his role as *vir bonus*—the plain blunt man—rumbled about the hunger for power that hides behind "pretty speeches Replete with Patriotism and moral cant." It was "a privilege of age" to "speak without reserve." On August 31, he announced that he expected to oppose this Constitution. He did not like the compromise between the Deep South and New England on the slave trade and navigation acts. He did not like the omission of sumptuary laws needed to improve the "manners" of the people. He had had some experience in writing constitutions, had composed a Bill of Rights copied in many of the states, and knew better than to surrender the public liberty. There would have to be a second Convention. Stockjobbers and placemen were not to be given the substance of his state. Mason was present to the end and almost immediately after the signing wrote up his "Objections to This Constitution of Government," which was published in newspapers throughout the country and distributed as a handbill. Washington was furious, and Madison appalled. But many in the Old Dominion clearly agreed with what Richard Henry Lee had written to Mason from New York after receiving a report on the Constitution from his old friend: ". . . if it should be established, either a tyranny will result from it, or it will be prevented by a Civil war."

In his "Objections," Mason had sounded the tocsin for the battle to come. No Declaration of Rights, no guarantee of the common law, an imbalance among the branches of government, and a judicial system "so constructed and extended as to absorb and destroy the judiciaries of the several states." Mason had wanted a new Constitution, but not this Constitution. He expected the general government to protect self-contained and self-sustaining local communities. But he had learned from a lifetime of study and experience that others might well prefer Leviathan: "When we reflect upon the insidious art of wicked and designing men, the various and plausible pretenses for continuing and increasing the inordinate lust of power in the few, we shall no longer be surprised that freeborn man hath been enslaved, and that those very means which were contrived for his preservation have been perverted to his ruin."

In the Virginia ratification convention of June 1788, George Mason and Patrick Henry were the leaders of the Antifederalists. Mason, dressed in somber black, moved that the agenda provide for the consideration of the Constitution *seriatim*—section by section. Henry, on the other hand, ranged freely from fissure to fissure, flaw to flaw, weaving together a broad indictment of the whole. The two old-fashioned republicans had settled on this strategic division of responsibilities before they entered the hall, arm in arm. The Virginia convention was an adversary proceeding, not a process of deliberation like the Constitutional Convention in Philadelphia. Despite their age and the absence of some of their more capable supporters, this format gave a certain advantage to the two formidable orators and defenders of the regional things. They had come to Richmond for a kind of vindication; for they had been subject to villainous abuse. Mason was called a "poor old man" who by reason of age had lost his wits. This argument was suggested in Mason's presence at the time of his election to the convention, and he replied to his inconsequential opponent: "Sir, when yours fail, nobody will ever discover it." Of Henry it was said that he wished to destroy the Union. His reply, foreshadowing arguments made by other Southerners seventy years later, was that Union was to be valued only on certain terms. In the end, Henry and Mason were defeated, though a shift of only four votes would have given them the victory. But in another sense, they won the day. For the issue in the convention came down finally to a choice between previous or subsequent amendments to the Constitution and to specifications concerning the proper understanding of the language of the document as it stood. Thanks to George Mason and Patrick Henry, Virginia spoke with a united voice in these regards.

George Mason attacked the handiwork of the Great Convention, still hoping to see "the beneficial parts of it retained." "Is it to be supposed," he asked, "that one national government will suit so extensive a country, embracing so many climates, and containing inhabitants so very different in manners, habits, and customs?" Of the new government he maintained, "Its power is calculated to annihilate totally the state governments." If the "Sovereignty, Freedom and Independence" of each state are not guaranteed explicitly, no "inspiration" will be needed to predict what the taxing power, the appointive power, the judicial power, and a standing army can achieve. The Federalists did not trust their fellow citizens, even with the civil liberty guaranteed under the English Bill of Rights. Talk of disunionist objectives was a bugbear: "I have never in my whole life heard one single man deny the necessity and propriety of the union." The slave trade is an evil, but even worse is the absence from the Constitution of a guarantee "that will prevent the northern and eastern states from meddling with our whole property of that kind." Revision would require "a clause in the Constitution to secure us that property. . . . " The "necessary and proper" clause and the reference to "general welfare" were equally offensive. "Will powers remain to the states which are not expressly guarded and reserved?" Mason asked. "Artful sophistry and evasions" did not satisfy him. The Federalists were good at these, while they left the financial interests of their fellow Virginians open to "stockjobbers" and Northern speculation. As to the judicial power, "There is no limitation. It goes to everything." It was an engine to bring on "one great national consolidated government" by slow and imperceptible stages. Hence, he preferred prior amendments or conditional ratification.

James Madison heard what was said, had a gastric attack, and denied that there was any "power. . . given to the general government to interpose with respect to property in slaves now held by the states." Edmund Randolph said the same. And young John Marshall on the subject of the judicial power declared, "I hope no gentleman will think that a state will be called at the bar of the federal court. . . . It is not rational that the sovereign power shall be dragged before a court." Other Federalists rose to deny Mason's reading of the Constitution. Their assurances were sufficient to hold a few wavering votes in line, but not without subsequent amendments responsive to Mason's anxieties. George Wythe, Edmund Pendleton, and other moderate men had listened when Mason (borrowing from St. Paul) had summarized, "They have done what they ought not to have done, and have left undone what they ought to have done." Amendments were drawn up and a conditional note was included in the instrument of ratification. Madison, having learned his lesson, presented them to the Congress of the United States in 1789. Mason was not entirely satisfied with Madison's version of Virginia's suggestions, but he acknowledged the improvement. With the additions of a stronger restraint on the judiciary, a clearer regulation of elections, a change in the size of the majority needed to pass navigation acts, and a Presidential council which would exercise those "executive powers now vested in the Senate," he could at such a time "cheerfully put his hand and heart to the new government." These changes he was unable to secure, with consequences that became apparent even to Madison in the early years of the Republic.

One scholar has described George Mason in all of his rectitude as the "veritable superego of Virginia politics"—the "conscience" of the Old Dominion. That he did not trust human nature so far as to give ambitious men great and unspecified powers is true. The proper conclusion of a revolution made against the abuse of authority was not to provide for a repetition of that abuse. Mason, like Patrick Henry, believed that the "genius" of a free society was best expressed through limited and time-tested institutions, working its way upward out of local communities represented by private and "independent" men. George Washington's charge against him, that he lacked the "manly candor" that would have permitted him to admit to "an error in his opinions," comes to nothing when we regard the whole pattern of Mason's life. In his last years he refused a Senate seat, but visited with leading political figures on a regular basis as they passed through Alexandria and stopped at Gunston Hall. Amidst his three hundred slaves, his children, and his grandchildren, he presided like the patriarchs of old. He did not live to see the fulfillment of many of his darker prophecies, but he could write to his son, in some satisfaction, that his "conduct as a public man . . . has been such as will administer comfort to me when I shall most want it, and smooth the bed of death." Retirement and a private station were his preference in any case. His political influence on his own period in American history has for the most part been either distorted or grudgingly acknowledged, and his importance to the subsequent course of American politics has been generally overlooked.

Yet General Fitzhugh Lee was correct in writing of him in the 1890's that George Mason was in large measure responsible for those features of the Constitution "which embrace the sovereignty of the states" and the intellectual forebear, the aegis and preceptor, of other Southerners who withdrew from the Union in 1861. (See Robert A. Rutland, *George Mason, Reluctant Statesman* [Charlottesville: University Press of Virginia, 1963]; Helen Hill Miller, *George Mason, Gentleman Revolutionary* [Chapel Hill: University of North Carolina Press, 1975]; Pamela C. Copeland and Richard K. MacMaster, *The Five George Masons: Patriots and Planters of Virginia and Maryland* [Charlottesville: University Press of Virginia, 1975]; Duncan J. MacLeod, *Slavery, Race and the American Revolution* [London: Cambridge University Press, 1974], pp. 38–39, 72–73, *et passim*; Edmund Randolph, *History of Virginia* [Charlottesville: University Press of Virginia, 1970]; Willi Paul Adams, *The First American Constitutions: Republican Ideology and the Making of the State Constitutions in the Revolutionary Era* [Chapel Hill: University of North Carolina Press, 1979]; Norman K. Risjord, *Chesapeake Politics, 1781–1800* [New York: Columbia University Press, 1978]; Kate Mason Rowland, *The Life of George Mason, 1725–1792*, 2 vols. [New York: G. P. Putnam's Sons, 1892]; Robert A. Rutland, ed., *The Papers of George Mason*, 3 vols. [Chapel Hill: University of North Carolina Press, 1970]; Paul Eidelberg, *The Philosophy of the American Constitution* [New York: The Free Press, 1968], pp. 53–56, *et passim*; Jack P. Greene, "Character, Persona and Authority: A Study of Alternative Styles of Political Leadership in Revolutionary Virginia," pp. 3–42 of *The Revolutionary War in the South: Power, Conflict and Leadership* [Durham: Duke University Press, 1979], ed. by Robert Higgins.)

Edmund Jennings Randolph

(August 10, 1753–September 12, 1813), lawyer, political leader of Virginia, and American statesman.

By turns, both Federalist *and* Antifederalist—the former by reason of temperamental caution and/or circumstance, the latter by conviction. In the context of the Constitutional Convention, perhaps most properly described as an enthusiastic advocate of a *very limited* Federal Union: an instrument of government stronger than the Articles of Confederation but much milder than what the Convention produced. According to his most recent biographer, John J. Reardon, animated by "the idea of a national government neither dependent on nor destructive of the authority of the state governments." Yet shocking to other High Federalists when he "strongly implied that he considered the preservation of the ultimate power of the states more important than the Union itself." In the Great Convention, a troubled figure. In even greater difficulty during the Virginia ratification convention of June, 1788. Driven to support the proposed Constitution by fear of the alternative to adoption (as he understood that dark prospect)—or by his desire for the good opinion of the leaders of his state. Called a "trimmer" by many, and described as "the Benedict Arnold of Virginia" by his old ally, George Mason. The Framer whose early introduction of a revised plan of government determined the shape of the entire Constitutional Convention, whose motion (much revised) produced the resulting United States Constitution, who then scrupled to sign it, and who later was responsible for defending it in Richmond when it was considered by representatives of the people of his state. A Federalist *per se* only for a Constitution never written, but a supporter of the document produced in Philadelphia because the other horn of the dilemma (riot, disunion, "democratic licentiousness") looked even more dangerous to the good of the country. A vigorous advocate for a Bill of Rights containing explicit limits on the power of the Federal courts and of the other branches of the general government, especially with regard to the states. The uncertain and ambiguous heir to one of Virginia's most honored names, an aristocratic republican who hoped to preserve the kind of society in which the Randolphs had played so great a role. Brought up in an atmosphere of privilege balanced with great responsibility to do public service and practice law. Finally, in a new and partisan political arena, the victim of his own habitual search for a "middle way" and for the grounds of consensus.

Edmund Jennings Randolph was born at Tazewell Hall, near Williamsburg. He was the son of John Randolph, Clerk of the House of Burgesses and the Crown's Attorney General, and of Arianna Jennings Randolph, daughter of the Attorney General of Maryland. Randolph's uncle (and role model) was the vast and jovial Peyton Randolph, perhaps the most prominent public figure in the Virginia of his day and (at various times) Attorney General and Speaker of the House of Burgesses. Edmund's grandfather was Sir John Randolph, the first native Virginian to be knighted—a man of great distinction who held most of the offices that in due course came to his sons and grandson. Sir John's grandfather, the founder of the dynasty, was the fabled William Randolph of "Turkey Island." In a deferential society, where names had a negotiable value, Edmund Randolph started life with a genuine advantage. Though by the times prevented from following the family pattern with a period in the Middle Temple, young Edmund was educated at William and Mary and in the law offices of his father. However, the onset of the American Revolution greatly complicated the established way of life for Edmund Randolph beyond that point. For when prospects pointed toward armed conflict with Great Britain, John Randolph would not lift his hand against his rightful sovereign. Therefore, with the disestablishment of Virginia's colonial government, he removed to England, selling all of his property, and refusing to act for either side. Peyton Randolph, who had made Edmund his heir, was cautious and measured in his reactions to offensive conduct by Crown and Parliament. But in the end he sided with his neighbors—and his nephew Edmund with him. However, Peyton Randolph died in 1775, while acting as President for the Continental Congress. At that time, Edmund Randolph, who was serving as aide-de-camp to General George Washington, was forced to return to Virginia, and without the comforting auspicies of family, organize a life of his own. No wonder that he could say, "I am a child of the Revolution." Yet he remained at the same time a Randolph, a man of the old prescription in some very important respects.

Upon his return to Williamsburg, at the age of twenty-three Edmund Randolph was elected by his neighbors the youngest member of the Virginia Constitutional Convention of 1776. At this time he became engaged to Elizabeth Nicholas, the daughter of the pious Robert Carter Nicholas, also a member of the Convention. Randolph sat on a great many committees. Because he had earlier spent some months as judge on a Court of Admiralty, he was called upon for information regarding the handling of Tory property. Edmund Pendleton, who was presiding, also assigned him to a Grand Committee, which prepared a Declaration of Rights and a general plan of state government. Another committee acting in this same convention sent instructions for independence to Virginia delegates at the Continental Congress meeting in Philadelphia.

In the Virginia Convention, young Edmund Randolph behaved in keeping with his upbringing and connections. Both he and his future father-in-law were made uneasy by talk of "equality" in a slaveholding state, though George Mason assured the house that only citizens were covered by such language. There was a general fear that they had acted with "too great an indifference to futurity." Randolph did nothing to assert himself or to presume upon the "old lions" who had enjoyed power in the time of his father and uncle and who were accustomed to ruling the state. Equal or no, no reapportionment for the frontier counties was attempted. And, according to Randolph, it was agreed "that every body and individual came into the Revolution with their rights and was to continue to enjoy them as they existed under the former government." Change when necessary, but held to a minimum. Young Randolph learned his lessons well. Under the new state government, he was appointed (in the orderly line of Randolph succession) Attorney General of Virginia—a post which he held for ten years.

In 1779 and again in 1781–82, he was elected to the Continental Congress, where he supported the import duty of 5% and doubted the power of Congress to charter the Bank of North America. There he also became a friend of James Madison, the young delegate from Orange County, Virginia, who had served with him in the Virginia Constitutional Convention. His first term in

Congress was uneventful and he returned quickly to Virginia. For a time he was mayor of Williamsburg and Clerk of the House of Delegates. Moreover, he practiced a little law on his own, because the business of Attorney General did not occupy all of his time—or fill his purse. But when he went back to Philadelphia, British armies were moving in and out of Virginia and he was convinced of the priority of national concerns. He also recognized the opportunity for service in the formation of national policy. In these months in Congress, Randolph's awareness of the necessity for a stronger general government, with real powers, grew rapidly. With Madison he served on a committee asked to draw up a plan for strengthening the government. He appealed to the states, in the name of the Congress, to send in their overdue payments to the treasury for military supplies. And he became familiar with land speculators and the problems of diplomacy. After 1782, Randolph was a moderate nationalist—though with no desire to see the states reduced to insignificance.

Back in Virginia during the years following his service in the Continental Congress, Randolph played his part in a concerted effort to bring about a strengthening of the Union. But, at the same time, he came to believe, after watching post-war Virginia, that a well-ordered state government could, in most respects, take care of its own. In 1786, at the age of 33, he was elected governor of Virginia. And from that position of authority he assisted in arranging the September, 1786 Annapolis Convention, for which, as a member, he wrote the first draft of an appeal to the states—an appeal which led to the Constitutional Convention of the following May. Randolph had the major role in selecting the Virginia delegates to the Philadelphia meeting, was personally responsible for persuading his old commander in chief, General Washington, to attend, and was present himself to speak "officially" for the Old Dominion. The strategy followed by the Virginia delegation as a whole was well considered. It was decided during their private deliberations that the best course was to have Governor Randolph, well-spoken and a fine figure of a man, move the consideration of a plan of government essentially the handiwork of James Madison. For Madison held no great office, was not a powerful speaker, or, at this point in his career, a person of presence. Those "associated republics" (what Randolph called them) who were met in this Convention would need a little goading. It would be good to have a state governor remind them of their present need for "sufficient checks against the democracy"—debtors, mobs, and Captain Shays. A Constitution could be a law to restrain feckless majorities, to forbid the making of "wanton laws," and a power to overawe the anarchic, silence the perverse. Therefore, on May 29, once the Great Convention had been properly organized, Edmund Randolph rose and proposed a formula for a completely new government, not a revision of the Articles. More or less, what he proposed concerning the purpose and structure of the Federal power was in the end adopted by the Convention. But, ironically, not with the concurrence of Edmund Randolph.

For some of the circumstantial detail he required to ensure that no later metamorphosis of this government could occur was not added to his outline. And other, ominous detail was included in its place.

After giving the Convention a definition of its "business," Governor Randolph sat quiet for some time, speaking only to answer emphatically every charge that he intended to threaten the integrity of the states. The purpose of Union would be to protect the states, both from popular tumult within and from foreign enemies without. Then he began to get restless. He did not like the Great Compromise on representation in the United States Senate. He wanted a plural executive to secure the interests of the sections. He insisted on a two-thirds vote of both Houses of the proposed Congress for laws regulating commerce. He was irritated by Yankee unwillingness to count three-fifths of the Negro slaves as a security for the "peculiar institution." Moreover, apportionment should be attached to a required census in the fundamental law. Otherwise the Congress might feel free to perpetuate itself. And he insisted on a clear specification of all Federal powers, with a statement attached saying that only those stated had been granted by the sovereign states. Finally, limitations on the authority of the Federal judiciary should be written into the Constitution itself. On September 10, 1787, Edmund Randolph announced that without these and other changes in the document as proposed, and without provision for a second convention, following recommendations for amendment from the states, he would not be a party to the business now almost complete. With Elbridge Gerry of Massachusetts and George Mason of his own state, Randolph attended the entire Constitutional Convention and still refused to sign the proposed instrument of government. According to his apology, he could not endorse a plan that would "end in Tyranny."

But this resolve on Randolph's part to stand against the majority of the most distinguished political company assembled in America to that date did not survive his return to Virginia. And from the moment of his first vacillation back toward Federalism, the road for his career spiraled slowly downward toward ignominy. First, once back in Virginia, Randolph saw that early reception for the Constitution was mixed, that states were ratifying, and that more debate over what it should include would not produce a larger consensus. He saw also that the Union might divide into smaller confederacies, and that it would be "expedient" to ratify first and then revise. Therefore, Randolph began to rumor that his failure to sign did not necessarily mean opposition to ratification. He was uncertain as to how he might vote on the question, but he did not let the Antifederalists know how he was leaning. After all, he had written a pamphlet criticizing the Constitution. He had been elected by the people who did not care for it. Randolph delayed important communications between the states—particularly with New York, whose governor was against ratification. This strategy prevented the attachment of the prior amendments he supposedly favored. Then, in Richmond, he surprised all Virginia by coming out in support of unconditional ratification. No wonder that Patrick Henry reflected on Randolph's character in the ratification debates. No wonder that George Washington made Randolph the first Attorney General of the United States. No wonder that Randolph prospered greatly. And no surprise that Thomas Jefferson called him "the poorest cameleon I ever saw, having no colour of his own, and reflecting that nearest him."

But Edmund Randolph was still unable to settle into one consistent position after leading the Federalists in the debates of the ratification convention. For there were elements in his view of the Union that would never satisfy certain members of that party. First of all, he defined the Federal power in reference to its limitations, not its scope: that it contained no authority over the "existing state of slavery," no sanction for sponsorship of "internal improvements," or for a Bank of the United States. Indeed, no Virginian present in the Great Convention had *"the smallest suspicion of the abolition of slavery"* by any Federal action, or of any other innovation not based on "powers expressly given." As for the General Welfare, the "sweeping clause," it could refer to nothing more than the reasons for a power to tax—not to every kind of legislation or court decision that might seem useful. Even when the Bill of Rights passed the Congress of the United States and came to be considered by the Virginia legislature, Randolph continued to complain that the powers reserved to the states by the 9th and 10th Amendments were not named *seriatim*, and the powers given the Federal government likewise made specific. Randolph could not accept that he was defending the position of the "other side." A world divided into permanent political parties, where politicians made lasting commitments, was not to his taste. Nor could he comprehend why his political habits angered the leaders of the early Republic. Yet even when he followed influence or bowed to a drift in popular sentiment, Edmund Randolph persisted in searching for a "middle way."

As the first Attorney General of the United States, Randolph tried not to take a position in the quarrel between Thomas Jefferson and Alexander Hamilton. His ostensible objective was to serve George Washington—to be above faction. Yet he opposed the plan for a Bank of the United States as unconstitutional, opposed other parts of the Hamiltonian system, and wrote essays in the press defending Jefferson's foreign policy. And when Jefferson resigned, the Sage of Monticello persuaded President Washington to make Edmund Randolph his successor as Secretary of State. From January 1, 1794–August 19, 1795, Randolph occupied a position of genuine power. In meetings of the Cabinet, he continued to dispute with the High Federalists led by Hamilton. Randolph was for the most part a successful Secretary of State. He was able to arrange the recall of the obnoxious Citizen Genêt as minister for the French Republic. He moved Spain toward the Treaty of San Lorenzo, which opened New Orleans and the Mississippi to the commerce of the West. And he gave good direction to John Jay, former Chief Justice of the United States, who had been sent to England to negotiate a treaty arranging for commercial relations and resolving certain questions not settled by the conclusion of the Revolution. But Hamilton was conducting a foreign policy of his own. Jay's Treaty, drawn to Hamilton's specifications, created a general cry of outrage throughout the United States. The Federalists were angry with Randolph for agreeing with critics of the handiwork of the proud Mr. Jay. And their malevolence found an instrument to serve their purpose in dispatches from Genêt's replacement in North America, Joseph Fauchet, captured by the British and turned over to the friends of England in the United States in order to injure Edmund Randolph. These dispatches contained reports of the French diplomat's conversations with Secretary Randolph—reports which suggested that the Secretary had been improperly confidential and had asked Fauchet for loans of money for certain American merchants who favored close ties with France. The enemies of Randolph used these dispatches to persuade President Washington to doubt Randolph's honesty and loyalty and to conduct an interrogation of the Secretary of State. In anger, Randolph resigned. And, at the age of forty-two, his public career was at an end. Randolph prepared and published in his own defense, *A Vindication of Mr. Randolph's Resignation* (1795). But it fell on deaf ears. On the whole, James Madison's judgment of the episode stands up rather well: "His greatest enemies will not easily persuade themselves that he [Randolph] was under a corrupt influence of France and his best friend can't save him from the self-condemnation of his political career as explained by himself."

Edmund Randolph returned to Richmond, and in the remaining eighteen years of his life enjoyed a successful practice of law. He had little to do with politics in his retirement, though the hatred of the Federalists pursued him in trumping up a great charge of $49,154.89 shortage in the accounts for diplomatic and consular funds for the Department of State. Eventually the claim was paid off, though Treasury Department Federalists later added to it over $60,000 of compound interest. Sixty-five years after Randolph's death, these attacks on his probity were refuted and withdrawn. Randolph approved of the Virginia and Kentucky Resolutions of 1798. He spoke of secession as a Constitutional last resort. A conventional Episcopalian, he warned against the seductive example of Jefferson's Deism. He denied that the Declaration of Independence had the status of law or did anything but signify a separation from England. For the instruction of the young men, he sometimes reminisced on his days in the Great Convention. But the most important work of his old age was a history of Virginia through the Revolution—a work not published until 1970. The theme of this labor of love was the character of Virginia public leadership produced through negotiated consensus, a species of leadership made possible by English gentlemen who joined no party and who put the good of the *patria* above their own careers. (See John J. Reardon, *Edmund Randolph: A Biography* [New York: Macmillan Publishing Company, 1975]; M. D. Conway, *Omitted Chapters of History Disclosed in the Life and Papers of Edmund Randolph* [New York: G. P. Putnam's Sons, 1888]; Forrest McDonald, *E Pluribus Unum: The Formation of the American Republic, 1776–1790* [Indianapolis: Liberty Press, 1979], pp. 339–340, *et passim*; Norman K. Risjord, *Chesapeake Politics, 1781–1800* [New York: Columbia University Press, 1978]; Edmund Randolph, *History of Virginia* [Charlottesville: University Press of Virginia, 1970], edited, with an Introduction by Arthur H. Shaffer; Charles F. Hobson, "The Early Career of Edmund Randolph, 1753–1789," Ph. D. dissertation, Emory University, 1971; Keith B. Berwick, "Moderates in Crisis: The Trials of Leadership in Revolutionary Virginia," Ph. D. dissertation, University of Chicago, 1959; H. J. Eckenrode, *The Randolphs: The Story of a Virginia Family* [Indianapolis: Bobbs-Merrill Company, 1946].)

John Blair, Jr.

(1732–August 31, 1800), lawyer, jurist, and political leader of the Revolution in Virginia.

A Federalist by way of prudence. From the early days of the Revolution in search for some authority to replace the Crown. Uncertain in his approach to independence from Great Britain, holding on to the hope of some continuing formal connection as long as he could. Also uncertain in his approach to the creation of a new and stronger Federal government. Chosen as a delegate to the Great Convention to represent the Virginia establishment, as one of the old "ruling class," and for his learning in the law. But not always willing to vote with Washington, Madison, and McClurg, nor to support every particular in the "Virginia Plan" as presented by Governor Edmund Randolph. A highly respected figure, though he never spoke in any of the sessions of the Convention.

John Blair, Jr., was born at Williamsburg, the son of John Blair, Sr., and Mary Monro Blair, the daughter of the Rev. John and Christian Munro. He was the grandson of Archibald Blair, an Edinburgh-trained physician, and great-nephew of James "Commissary" Blair, Virginia Deputy of the Bishop of London, founder of the College of William and Mary, and the leading citizen of the colony in his time. John Blair, Sr., was Acting Governor of Virginia (in 1758 and again in 1768), Deputy Auditor General (1728–1732), Auditor General (1732–1771), member of the House of Burgesses (1734–1741), Clerk of the Council (1741–1743), and a member of that body until 1770, when forced to resign by the infirmities of great age. Governor Blair was a man of wealth but a patriot withal. From 1763 he was a member of the Virginia Committee of Correspondence and a Whig legalist who doubted the power of Parliament to place an internal tax upon Virginians.

John Blair, Jr., grew up in an atmosphere of privilege and intense political concern—a very conservative atmosphere. He was educated at the College of William and Mary and in the Middle Temple (1755–1756), where he was a protégé of his father's old friend, Governor Robert Dinwiddie.

Upon his return to Virginia, young Blair established a successful practice of law in Williamsburg and appeared before the General Court, "where he enjoyed a respectable share of the business before that tribunal." From 1766–1770 he sat in the House of Burgesses as the representative of the College of William and Mary, in which role he acquired a reputation for conservatism, gentleness, and gravity. Moreover, even in these years he exhibited "that strict attention to his dress which was characteristic of the colonial regime;... [a quality which] he preserved to the last." He was opposed to Patrick Henry's Stamp Act Resolves of 1765; served as Clerk of the Council from 1770–1775; was a member of the Privy Council from 1776–1778; and was a member of Virginia's Constitutional Convention of 1776, where he served on the committee called upon to draft a plan of government. In October of 1777 Blair was elected by a joint vote of the two houses of the Virginia legislature as a judge of the General Court, of which body he was chosen Chief Justice in 1779. During the period of the Revolution, Judge Blair signed the Virginia Association of June 22, 1770, which called for a boycott on the importation of British goods until the Townshend Duties were repealed. He underwrote the Association of May, 1774, calling for a meeting of the colonies in a Continental Congress. Yet he continued to maintain that peaceful means of protesting the policies of the British government should be explored in all detail before harsher measures were applied.

John Blair, Jr., attended faithfully almost every session of the Great Convention, even though he kept silent outside the Virginia caucus. Blair opposed control of money bills by the House of Representatives, and, along with his fellow Virginians, reacted with alarm at the idea of an export tax. He agreed with George Mason that the election of the President should be in the charge of the state legislatures. And for a time he favored a plural executive. He had doubts about the document finally produced; yet he voted for the Constitution since he was convinced that further indecision would bring chaos and ruin. Blair was also a Federalist delegate to the 1788 Virginia ratification convention, where he was once again quiet but supported the motion for approval.

He was a planter and slaveholder as well as judge. But his real life was in the courts, and there he was not reluctant to speak his mind. In 1780 he became a Chancellor of the Virginia High Court of Chancery and a member of the Court of Appeals. In 1782 he took part in the celebrated case of *The Commonwealth of Virginia vs. Caton et al.*, in which he and George Wythe declared the power of their court to rule an act of the Virginia legislature unconstitutional. In 1787 he participated in the case of *Commonwealth vs. Posey*, in which the applicability of English law and precedent to American court decisions was upheld. In keeping with the Judiciary Act of 1789, President George Washington appointed John Blair, Jr., an Associate Justice of the United States Supreme Court, a post in which Blair served until his resignation in 1796. As a member of the High Court, Blair continued to be a strong Federalist; and in *Chisholm vs. Georgia* (1793), he maintained that there was a Federal jurisdiction in disputes between citizens living in one state and governments of other member states. (The definition of state sovereignty embodied in this ruling was explicitly rebuked in the adoption of the Eleventh Amendment to the Constitution.) However, unlike some of his associates in this decision, Blair did not fall back on "implied" powers or deny the sovereignty of the states in many questions.

The burden of riding the circuit disposed John Blair, Jr., to retire from the Supreme Court. He spent his last four years at home in Williamsburg, where he is buried in the graveyard of Bruton Parish Church, near to the place where he had worshipped since the days of his youth. (See J. Elliott Drinard, "John Blair, Jr., 1732–1800," *Reports of the Virginia State Bar Association*, XXXIX [1927], 436–449; Fred L. Israel, "John Blair, Jr.," pp. 109–115 of Vol. I, *The Justices of the United States Supreme Court, 1789–1969: Their Lives and Major Opinions* [New York: R. R. Bowker/Chelsea House, 1969], ed. by Israel and Leon Friedman; Robert G. Ferris, ed., *Signers of the Constitution* [Washington, D. C.: U. S. Department of the Interior, 1976], pp. 145–146; Frederick Horner, *History of the Blair, Banister and Braxton Families* [Philadelphia: J. B. Lippincott Co., 1898]; and Forrest McDonald, *We the People: The Economic Origins of the Constitution* [Chicago: University of Chicago Press, 1975], pp. 74–76.)

James McClurg

(1746–July 9, 1823), physician, banker, speculator, and minor Virginia politician.

As much out of his element in the Great Convention as any delegate to that assembly. Yet a man of fixed and decisive political opinions. A very High Federalist, concerned with the security of large investments and fearful of social instability. Present in the Constitutional Convention because Washington and Madison (who arranged for his appointment when Patrick Henry and Richard Henry Lee refused to attend) could count on his support should Mason, Blair, and Randolph pull in another direction. A man of means, a great holder of securities, and an influential member of the medical profession.

James McClurg was born near Hampton in Elizabeth City County, Virginia, where his father, Dr. Walter McClurg, was superintendent of Hampton Small Pox Hospital and a very successful physician. After careful preparation in an atmosphere of privilege, young James attended William and Mary College, from which he was graduated in 1762, having made a fine record. He then continued his studies in medicine at the University of Edinburgh, from which he received the M.D. in 1770. His thesis, "De Calore," was well respected; and in 1772 he published a monograph, *Experiments upon the Human Bile and Reflections on the Biliary Secretions,* which was translated into many languages. At that time Edinburgh was perhaps the finest medical school in the world, and McClurg did additional post-graduate research in Paris and London.

In 1773 James McClurg returned to Virginia, but was not politically active prior to the Revolution. However, once the war broke out, he served as surgeon of the Virginia militia, as physician-general and director of hospitals for the state. In 1779 he was appointed Professor of Anatomy and Medicine at William and Mary, but there is no clear record that he ever assumed the post. McClurg moved to Richmond when the capital of Virginia was relocated there. Eventually he was recognized as one of the finest physicians in his state and was elected president of the Virginia Medical Society in 1820 and 1821. Volume I of *The Philadelphia Journal of Medical and Physical Sciences* was dedicated to "The Elegant Scholar and Accomplished Physician, Dr. McClurg." He served one term as a member of the Virginia Council of State, and was in that office when selected to play a larger role in Philadelphia.

James McClurg attended the Great Convention until the last week in July. He may have left when the Convention adjourned to let the Committee of Detail prepare a draft reflecting the agreements reached during that month. Madison wrote McClurg urging him to return, and their correspondence continued throughout the following weeks. While serving as a delegate, the Virginia physician urged that the proposed Federal Congress be given a veto over legislation in the states. Perhaps at Madison's request, he made one other significant motion. On July 17, he recommended that the President of the United States be elected to serve "on good behavior"—for life, unless his impeachment seemed necessary. In effect, this resolution would have produced "an elective monarchy." The suggestion was not well received, since in the matter of executive authority, as in much else, McClurg was too much the "high-toned" Federalist for his colleagues. Indeed, he went so far as to raise the question of the President's need for a military force—militia or a standing army—to enforce his will. No more explosive issue came before the Convention.

On McClurg's return to Virginia, he reported to Madison that the new Constitution would be supported in the "towns" and by "the friends of Order." He referred to Pennsylvania accounts of a "tendency to Insurrection" in Virginia, and grumbled of "continued depravations of manners" and threats to suspend payment of debts. He deplored the popular leaders of his state. His view of the proposed Federal authority maintained that it was necessary to prevent "anarchy and civil convulsions."

Under Washington's administration, James McClurg became one of the original directors of the Bank of the United States. There is some evidence that he was proposed as a successor to Thomas Jefferson as Secretary of State. Yet he was put aside as he had been when Madison had mentioned him for an equivalent assignment under the Articles—"because he was subject to a charge of speculation"—and the post went to his friend Edmund Randolph. For a time he continued on the Council of State, and he was three times mayor of Richmond (1797, 1800, 1803). It was agreed by all who were of his acquaintance that no more loyal Federalist was to be found in Richmond. In the history of Southern politics, he is to be remembered as an evidence of Madison's skill in political tactics and as a great anomaly. (See Robert M. Slaughter, "James McClurg," pp. 731–732 of *American Medical Biographies* [Baltimore: The Norman, Remington Company, 1920], ed. by Howard A. Kelly and W. L. Burrage; W. B. Blanton, *Medicine in Virginia in the Eighteenth Century* [Richmond: The William Byrd Press, 1931], pp. 328–335; Forrest McDonald, *We the People: The Economic Origins of the Constitution* [Chicago: University of Chicago Press, 1975], pp. 73, 88–89; and Vol. 10 of *The Papers of James Madison* [Chicago: University of Chicago Press, 1977], ed. by Robert A. Rutland *et al.*, pp. 120, 134–135, 154, 155, 157, 161, 162, 165, 166, 233, and 234.)

George Wythe

(1726–June 8, 1806), lawyer, jurist, professor, Virginia statesman, and Signer of the Declaration of Independence.

One of the most distinguished men elected to be a delegate to the Constitutional Convention. Would most likely have exerted a considerable influence on the drafting of the United States Constitution had he not been called away from Philadelphia by illness in his family. Present in the Great Convention for only a few days, but present in spirit through his effect on two generations of political thought in Virginia. The unquestioned leader of the bar in his state. A man of spotless reputation, called by many "the American Aristides." Mild Federalist, but closer in his basic attitudes to George Mason than to Madison, James Wilson, or Gouverneur Morris. Devoted to the position that "not men but laws should be sovereign." An embodiment of the nomocratic, customary, and prescriptive tradition in English legal theory as it survived on these shores. Following the decision to seek independence, directly responsible for the preservation of the common law in Virginia as the leader of a committee (including Mason, Thomas Ludwell Lee, Edmund Pendleton, and his own former student Thomas Jefferson) called upon to revise the Old Dominion's legal code. Co-author of the instrument of ratification adopted by the Virginia convention which met to consider and judge the proposed United States Constitution in June of 1788.

George Wythe was the second son of Thomas Wythe and Margaret Walker Wythe. His father was a member of the House of Burgesses, a man of property, and a great-grandson of Thomas Wythe, gentleman, who had emigrated to Virginia *circa* 1680. For three generations George Wythe's progenitors had been, variously, justices of the Elizabeth City County courts, sheriffs and/or members of the local vestry. His mother was the daughter of a wealthy Quaker and was the descendant of the learned and well-known Rev. George Keith. George Wythe was born at his father's plantation, Chesterville, on the Back River, Elizabeth City County, Virginia—a property which George inherited after the untimely death of his elder brother, Thomas. He was educated at home, chiefly by his accomplished mother, and at the College of William and Mary. Later he read law with his uncle by marriage, Stephen Dewey, and in 1746 was admitted to the Virginia bar in Prince George County. But most of the vast erudition for which in later years he was rightfully celebrated was a consequence of a lifetime's habit of disciplined private study.

George Wythe established a legal practice in Spotsylvania County, where he married the sister of his partner, John Lewis. But he made no name for himself until 1754, when he served briefly as attorney general of the colony, and 1755, when he was elected to the House of Burgesses for Williamsburg—where he had moved and where he thereafter made his home, at least until the capital of Virginia was moved to Richmond. In Williamsburg and in York and Elizabeth City Counties, Wythe slowly (starting about 1748) established a reputation of his own. He was admitted to practice before the General Court and, with the arrival of Governor Francis Fauquier (who became his fast friend), grew rapidly into the polished figure of his mature years. William Small (Professor of Mathematics and Natural Philosophy at William and Mary) and the youthful Thomas Jefferson (then a student at the college) completed with Wythe and Governor Fauquier a small and select circle of wits. From 1758–1761 Wythe represented the college in the

House of Burgesses and from 1761–1768, Elizabeth City County. From 1769 to 1775 he was clerk of the House and a master of the office. In 1768 he was mayor of Williamsburg. In 1769 he became a member of the William and Mary Board of Visitors and was called upon to regularize and publish an edition of Virginia's colonial laws. He handled correspondence with Virginia's agent in London and in 1774 was elected member of the Virginia Committee of Safety, the rulers of his state for almost two years. Finally, in 1775 he was chosen by his fellow Virginians to be one of their delegates to the Continental Congress.

During the years of conflict with British authority which preceded the outbreak of the Revolution, George Wythe rose to be one of the two or three most respected members of the Virginia bar and a leader of the state legislature. Apart from the practice of his profession, Wythe found time to devote to learning sought for its own sake, and for the training of young men such as Jefferson in the mysteries of the English legal tradition "from doomsday down." The father of his second wife, planter and architect Richard Taliaferro, built for him a fine house on Palace Green in the little capital city, a place which became a center of political conversation and planning. In the House of Burgesses it was Wythe who was called upon to speak for his colleagues in drafting a petition to the Crown against the adoption of the Stamp Act. Wythe's argument concerning the claims of colonials upon their inherited rights as Englishmen was so forceful and provocative that his fellow legislators tempered his language. He was perhaps the first of the English colonials in North America to call for the political independence of the colonies from the authority of Parliament, but within an English Commonwealth of Nations. Wythe was also early to recognize the necessity for a complete separation from Great Britain and for a regular army to give substance to the language of revolution.

George Wythe during his brief term in the Continental Congress was a vigorous supporter of the position of Richard Henry Lee and of the party that had grown impatient with further efforts to compromise with England. After signing the Declaration, he returned to Virginia to work on the revision of the legal code, to serve as speaker of the House of Delegates (1777) and to design the Virginia State Seal—the belligerent symbol of republican intransigence with the appropriate motto: *Sic Semper Tyrannis*, "thus ever with tyrants." In 1778 Wythe became one of the three original judges of the Virginia High Court of Chancery and in 1779 Professor of Law and Police at William and Mary, the first American to hold such a position and the second or third in the English-speaking world. As professor, Wythe literally created an academic discipline, initiating such procedures as moot courts and mock legislatures which supplemented his more conventional lectures and tutorials. Wythe trained the first formally educated lawyers in our history—among them John Marshall, James Monroe, and Henry Clay—and gave to the entire

Southern bar a lasting impetus and direction. He continued in his professorship until his duties as judge required his relocation in Richmond in 1791. As Chancellor (alone in this distinction for thirteen years, after the Court of Chancery was left with only one judge) and ex-officio member of the State Superior Court, he served until his death in 1806.

Chancellor Wythe came to Philadelphia for the Constitutional Convention on May 15 and departed, because of the mortal illness of his wife, on June 4. His only significant function during the Great Convention was in drawing up the rules which governed its operations. But he had a larger role to play in Virginia's pivotal ratification convention. Much of the time during these deliberations Wythe was called upon to chair a committee of the whole. But on June 24, Wythe stepped aside from that post of honor and moved for the adoption of the proposed Constitution, with recommended amendments attached. Wythe on his own part submitted a list of corrective alterations, an act which led the distinguished legal historian Charles Warren to describe him as "the father of the Bill of Rights." Wythe's personal authority with many in the Antifederalist camp allowed him to bring the business to a head in a way that warmer advocates of the new government could not. And most particularly because of the Antifederalist context within which he urged ratification, he could appear to speak for Virginia and not some distant abstraction. Wythe's plea for the Constitution of 1787 was in keeping with his authority as master of the ancient law. Liberty, he argued, cannot exist outside of society. Theories concerning the aboriginal "rights of man" were not to his taste: "Experience . . . is the best guide." He admitted the imperfections of the document under discussion. Yet, the experience of Americans during and after the Revolution (a course which he rehearsed) had demonstrated that a stronger government was necessary for the preservation of the various societies joined by the Union. That it was Wythe who called for the question was assuredly no accident. Of the Federalists, only he was safe against *ad hominem* attack. Concerning the disinterestedness of his motives not a word could be said.

In his last years George Wythe continued to occupy a post of honor in the Virginia courts, to practice the faith (Episcopalian) in which he had grown to manhood, to run his own law school in Richmond, and to personify the public virtue of his state. A man of small physical stature, he seemed to shrink with the lengthening of years. Yet he kept his intellectual vigor and his curiosity. At seventy, he mastered the Hebrew language. He taught a special course in literature, ancient and modern, for the young people of his city. And he even learned to write with his left hand when the other was broken.

Wythe deplored the efforts of the French to export their Revolution to America. He disapproved of Jay's Treaty and of Hamilton's view of "implied powers." He presided over public meetings called to consider these developments. But he was most himself on the bench: "[If the whole legislature] should attempt to overstep the bounds prescribed to them, . . . I, in administrating the public justice of the country, will meet the united power at my seat in the tribunal; and pointing to the Constitution will say to them, 'Here is the limit of your authority; and hither shall you go, but no further.' " Such were his words in the case of *Commonwealth vs. Caton.* Law should be sovereign, not men. To the end, at eighty, he was jealous of the public liberty: always the man who had written (speaking for all of his neighbors), in limiting the scope of Virginia's approval of the Constitution, "[We] declare and make known that the powers granted under the Constitution being derived from the people of the United States, may be resumed by them whenever the same shall be perverted to their injury or oppression and that every power not granted remains with them, and at their will." Wythe's mark on the life of the mind in the South was indelible. He was a source of continuity with the strict school of common law jurisprudence. And his Federalism was of a kind that would not preclude a Southern secession in the decades yet to come, particularly if the fundamental rule of law seemed to be in doubt. (See Burke Davis, *A Williamsburg Galaxy* [Williamsburg, Va.: Colonial Williamsburg, 1968], pp. 149–157; Imogene Brown, *American Aristides: A Biography of George Wythe* [Madison, N.J.: Fairleigh Dickinson University Press, 1980]; John Sanderson, *Biography of the Signers to the Declaration of Independence* [Philadelphia: R. W. Pomeroy, 1823], Vol. II, pp. 158–180; W. Edwin Hemphill, "George Wythe, the Colonial Briton," Ph.D. dissertation, University of Virginia, 1937; Robert G. Ferris, editor, *Signers of the Declaration* [Washington, D.C.: Department of the Interior, 1976], pp. 154–156; David John Mays, *Edmund Pendleton, 1721–1803: A Biography,* 2 vols. [Cambridge: Harvard University Press, 1952]; Hugh Blair Grigsby, *The History of the Virginia Convention of 1788* [New York: Da Capo Press, 1969]; Allan Dudley Jones, "The Character and Service of George Wythe," *Reports of the Virginia State Bar Association,* XLIV [1932], 325–329; Oscar L. Shewmake, *George Wythe: Teacher, Lawyer, Jurist, Statesman,* [Richmond: n.p., 1950]; and Edwin Lee Shepard, "George Wythe," pp. 90–95 of *The Virginia Law Reports Before 1880* [Charlottesville: University of Virginia Press, 1977], ed. by W. H. Bryson.)

William Richardson Davie

(June 20, 1756–November 29, 1820), lawyer, planter, statesman, military hero of the Revolution.

With Charles Cotesworth Pinckney, one of the mildest of Southern Federalists, though ever faithful to that creed. Forced to see the necessity for an effective central government by his service as Commissary General for North Carolina and the armies of General Nathanael Greene. Son of Archibald and Mary Richardson Davie. Born at Whitehaven in Egremont Parish, County Cumberland in England. Of distinguished Scottish ancestry in both the paternal and maternal lines. Presbyterian. Migrated with his family to the Waxhaw settlement in South Carolina. Educated at Queen's Museum, Charlotte, North Carolina, and at the College of New Jersey, where he took the B.A. with the class of 1776. Began the study of law under Judge Spruce Macay at Salisbury, North Carolina, but interrupted his studies to enlist in the Patriot cause in 1777. Served under General Allen Jones of the Halifax District Militia, later his father-in-law. Was successively lieutenant, captain, and major of cavalry. Wounded while leading a charge at Stono, near Charleston, in 1779. After recovery, commander of a legion of Carolina irregulars, which he raised with his own funds. Following Camden, as colonel of his partisans, one of the major obstacles to British conquest of the South, especially distinguished by his check of Cornwallis at Charlotte Court House in September of 1780. For the remainder of the war, as Commissary General for Greene, part of the inner council of staff officers who planned the defeat of the British armies in the South. At the end of the war, one of the most popular men in the Carolinas. Tall and of a commanding presence, gifted in speech, and connected by marriage with the most powerful men in his state. Admitted to the North Carolina bar in 1779 and active in his profession during the following two decades.

In the Great Convention, William Richardson Davie spoke infrequently but very much to the point. He favored a Union "partly federal, partly national," in which local prejudices and interests "could not be denied to exist" and had a right to representation. He spoke bluntly of Northern unwillingness to allow the South political representation for its slaves and declared, "if the Eastern states meant therefore to exclude them . . . the business was at an end." Originally he had preferred that the Senate be weighted to represent wealth and property. But he changed his position, after listening to the arguments of the delegates from the smaller states, and swung the members from North Carolina behind the Great Compromise of equality for the states in the Upper House of the new Congress. Davie left the Constitutional Convention late in August, convinced that most of the great questions had been decided. And with James Iredell he led the fight for ratification in North Carolina. During the first ratification convention at Hillsboro, General Davie carried the debate for the Federalist cause, and though defeated, laid a groundwork for final approval in a second convention held at Fayetteville on November 16–23, 1789. His publication of the debates of the first convention of July, 1788, plus his efforts in the composition of pamphlet literature and in the organization of a pro-Constitution political machine, were recognized by all as having been instrumental in bringing North Carolina into the Union.

From 1786 to 1798, William Richardson Davie sat continuously in the lower house of the North Carolina legislature, the House of Commons. He was active in behalf of the establishment and early administration of the University of North Carolina, selected its faculty and drew up its curriculum. He was responsible for ordering the revision and codification of the laws of his state, arranged for cession of Tennessee to the Union, was chairman of North Carolina's boundary commission, and commander of the state's militia. In 1798, he was elected governor of North Carolina by a legislature dominated by a large majority of Jeffersonians—a measure of his great popularity. President Adams appointed Davie as brigadier general in the regular army during the mobilization against France and in 1799 sent him as part of a peace commission to Paris, where he was instrumental in negotiating the Convention of Montefontaine in October, 1800.

General Davie returned from his diplomatic adventure to a North Carolina with a changing political atmosphere. The Democratic-Republicans had achieved as part of the "Revolution of 1800" an internal transformation of the state; and for the rest of his life, William Richardson Davie, by reason of the firmness of his convictions, was a private citizen of little political influence. He failed in 1803 in his effort to win a seat in the United States House of Representatives and in disgust with politics retired two years later to his plantation at Tivoli, in Lancaster County, South Carolina, to his books and to his passion for scientific farming. General Davie hated Jacobins and electoral condescension. In reaction to the French Revolution, he recommended for the Federal service only officers "untainted in any manner by French politics or principles." He was opposed to the War of 1812 because he thought it motivated by domestic politics and because he regarded England in her struggle with Napoleon as the defender of the "civilized community of man." Indeed, he looked forward to the extermination of the French Emperor and his revolutionary armies, adding, "These mad men possess nothing upon which you can certainly calculate, no moral principle, no fixed political data: they seem to have no system but anarchy, no plan but plunder." Davie refused all appointment under the Democratic-Republicans. Yet he recommended against support for Aaron Burr as an alternative to Jefferson. Though consistent in his Federalism, he was always a Federalist of the Southern variety. When New England threatened secession in 1812, he maintained that that option had been left to the states in the Philadelphia Convention. And he rejoiced in the triumph of American arms at New Orleans. Furthermore, when his friend Justice James Iredell dissented from the decision of a Northern Federalist majority of the High Court in the case of *Chisholm vs. Georgia,* General Davie concurred vehemently, observing that Justice James Wilson's argument from the "spirit of the Constitution" and the implied powers read like a "rhapsody" or a radical poem, but not like law. Iredell in his dissent had held that the states were "sovereign as to all powers not expressly delegated to the Federal Government by the Constitution." Davie concluded, in support of his old companion, that there could be no limit to a government free to set aside the law whenever it found *"moral"* excuse for such innovations. William Richardson Davie had never been a supporter of that teleocratic kind of Federalism. Instead, he was one of those aristocratic Old Whigs who gave to our nation its original political configuration and impetus, a man of such impressive rectitude that even the passage of two centuries cannot obscure his stature. (See Blackwell P. Robinson, *William R. Davie* [Chapel Hill: University of North Carolina Press, 1957]; Jackson Turner Main, *Political Parties Before the Constitution* [Chapel Hill: University of North Carolina Press, 1973], pp. 311–317; Lisle A. Rose, *Prologue to Democracy: The Federalists in the South, 1789–1800* [Lexington: University of Kentucky Press, 1968]; James H. Broussard, *The Southern Federalists, 1800–1816* [Baton Rouge: Louisiana State University Press, 1978]; Louise Irby Trenholme, *The Ratification of the Federal Constitution in North Carolina* [New York: AMS Press, Inc., 1967]; J. G. de Roulhac Hamilton, ed., *William Richardson Davie: A Memoir, Followed by His Letters,* with Notes by Kemp P. Battle [Chapel Hill: University of North Carolina Press, 1907].)

Hugh Williamson

(December 5, 1735–May 22, 1819), preacher, physician, land speculator, scientist, and North Carolina politician.

A very mild, very reasonable Federalist, looking toward a system that would "secure the existence of state governments" in a union of "equally sovereign" states. Unwilling to surrender to the Federal power the authority to "restrain the states from Regulating their internal police." With the oath required of state officers to support the new Constitution, suggested "a reciprocal oath [to be] required from the National officers, to support the Governments of the States." Moved to enthusiasm for a strengthening of the central government by his large holdings in Western lands, his commercial experience, and his service in positions of responsibility which he occupied during the Revolution. In the company of the Framers, a curious figure, a "projector," as Swift uses that term. Like a character in a whimsical English novel in the number of his identities and careers. During the period of the Great Convention, a Southern Yankee, but a resident of Pennsylvania and New York for most of his life. Nonetheless, a faithful and effective representative of his Tarheel constituency during that fateful summer in Philadelphia.

Hugh Williamson was born at West Nottingham, Pennsylvania, into a Scotch-Irish family. His father, John W. Williamson, came from Dublin to the Quaker colony in 1730 and, sometime during the following year, married Marie Davison, whose family had migrated in 1718 from County Derry, Ireland, bringing their infant daughter with them. Hugh was the eldest child of this union. Educated in local and Delaware preparatory schools and in the College of Philadelphia, from which he was graduated in 1757. Hugh had been destined by his pious parents for a career in the ministry; but after two years' delay in settling his father's estate and following theological training in Connecticut, Williamson gave up on the idea of a life in the service of the church and returned to his alma mater as a professor of mathematics. He was, however, licensed to preach by the Presbyterians, and held some services at the behest of his mentor, Dr. Samuel Finley, and the Presbytery of Philadelphia. In 1764, Williamson turned away from teaching and mathematics as he had from divinity, and began the study of medicine in Edinburgh, London, and Utrecht, where he submitted a thesis and took an M.D. degree in 1766. For some years thereafter, he practiced this profession in Philadelphia. But he found it a strain on his composure and slowly withdrew in search of a fourth vocation. Business came next, and he persisted in it rather well. Even, so, abstruse researches and the pleasures of science continued to occupy much of his time. In 1768 Williamson was made a member of the American Philosophical Society. In 1769 he served on a commission appointed to observe the transits of Venus and Mercury. He read a paper on the subject of climate in North America—an essay which finally resulted in his famous *Observations on the Climate in Different Parts of America* (1811), and in an honorary LL.D. from the University of Leyden. His astronomical observations also bore fruit in an original theory concerning the life of superior beings beyond this earth which appears in "An Essay on Comets," printed in the first volume of *The Transactions of the American Philosophical Society.* In the company of the Framers, he was clearly the virtuoso.

With the onset of the American Revolution Hugh Williamson began to pay attention to the world of politics. In 1772 trade carried him to the West Indies on a journey also designed to raise funds for an academy at Newark, Delaware. And the latter purpose also carried him to England, where he became a close friend of Benjamin Franklin and participated in some of his electrical experiments. Williamson read a paper of his own, on eels, before the Royal Society—a paper which appears in its *Transactions* for 1775. As a philosopher, he moved with ease in the highest circles, and received a contribution from King George III himself. He wrote a public letter to Lord Mansfield, *The Plea of the Colonies*, which appeared as a pamphlet: a letter in which he insisted that Americans wanted only "a reconciliation . . . on constitutional principles," not (as Mansfield had maintained) "absolute independence." Finally, Hugh Williamson played his first direct role in the history of American politics during this English visit. First, he advised certain members of the Privy Council (in February of 1774) that there would be civil war if they did not change their policies. Then, on a visit to an office where colonial papers were stored, he pretended to be an official and made away with letters to the ministry from two prominent Tories, Governor Hutchinson and Lieutenant-Governor Oliver of Massachusetts—letters which he turned over to Dr. Franklin, who dispatched them to America. Their arrival in New England inflamed the situation to a point that the regular governments of those colonies could not continue to function and only force could rule.

In 1776 Williamson was in Holland, and after hearing of the Declaration of Independence he sailed for home, carrying American dispatches. When the British captured his ship, he actually escaped by rowing a small boat to shore near the Delaware Capes. Soon thereafter Williamson relocated in Charleston, South Carolina, where he practiced medicine and carried on some trading in association with a younger brother. Then he shifted his base of operations to Edenton, North Carolina, where he continued in the same occupations. At this time, his business was with the French West Indies, business which the British blockade made impossible to conduct from Philadelphia or Baltimore. Thus, in effect, General Howe made Hugh Williamson a North Carolinian. For over twenty years he kept that identity and made of it a source of great influence over our national destiny.

Once established in the South, Hugh Williamson, on the basis of his good reputation as a physician, was soon appointed Surgeon General of North Carolina. He served at the Battle of Camden, South Carolina, and did distinguished work on both sides of the line, among both British and American forces. He went freely back and forth and had real success, both with the wounded and in promoting smallpox inoculation. With a North

Carolina garrison facing the British in Southern Virginia, Williamson so carefully arranged for the housing, dress, diet, and drainage of its camp that it had an exceptional record for good health under circumstances that ordinarily produced great losses. Soon he was so popular as to be elected to the state House of Commons for Edenton in 1782. In the same year he was elected by the North Carolina legislature as one of their delegates in the Continental Congress. He served there for three years, and then returned to the local House of Commons. He was once more elected to the Continental Congress in 1787 and was given a seat in the Constitutional Convention by a general consensus concerning his merits as a statesman and legislator. Williamson as North Carolina politician was clearly a representative for commercial and speculative interests. He was a mercantilist, an enemy of paper money, an active merchant, and the holder of over 70,000 acres of frontier land. In 1783 he had voted to exclude slavery from the territories because "slaves are an encumbrance to society." Yet he had no passion on this subject. And in 1784 he was ready for another Southern, slaveholding state to come into the Confederation when Vermont won admission—in order to "preserve the Balance." Indeed, by 1787 Williamson had absorbed much of the spirit of North Carolina particularism into his political thought and was assuredly no Philadelphia Federalist in disguise during the deliberations of the Great Convention.

In the conversations and debates of the Framers, Hugh Williamson was quite outspoken. He was the most articulate of the members from North Carolina—at times almost too articulate. He often repeated earlier motions, and suggested numerous minor revisions in the proposals of other delegates, particularly where the definition of the Presidency was concerned. Williamson's most important decision during the entire Convention was to support equality in the voting strength of the states in the United States Senate. He opposed a Federal veto power over state legislation, opposed a power to tax exports or an authority to pass navigation acts with less than a majority of two-thirds. He did not want the Constitution to prohibit the importation of slaves since it was "more in favor of humanity from a view of all circumstances" to let the Deep South continue the trade and join the Union. In general he was "less afraid of too few than of too many laws."

Williamson warned the Convention against the danger to "the Southern interest" that could come from giving to the North a majority in the new Congress with the means of perpetuating that advantage. He wanted members of the Electoral College paid out of national funds, members of Congress paid by their states, and no internal tariffs between the states. When tempers flared, he counseled moderation; and when debate on the size and make-up of the proposed United States Senate had exhausted its purpose, he insisted, in the name of realism, that "[unless] we concede on both sides, our business must be at an end." Williamson did not wish the Chief Executive of the new government to be given too much authority. His own preference was for a triple executive, with one member from New England, one from the Middle States, and one from the South. Failing to secure that arrangement, he preferred that the President be elected by the state legislatures. Williamson, according to his first biographer, was not thought to be very "democratic," though he had humor and could be very spirited and magnetic. He often appeared to be haughty, and some of his oratory seemed overblown and florid to the Framers and those who had heard him in the Continental Congress. But, all pedantry aside, he was clear about one thing—he wished to get for North Carolina all the seats in the new Congress that he could persuade his colleagues to give them.

Though he worried about its future consequences (he expected that the nation would eventually drift into monarchy), Hugh Williamson was a vigorous supporter of the United States Constitution once it had been delivered to North Carolina. Following the Great Convention, Williamson went directly to the Continental Congress in New York, where he continued to sit until government under the Articles officially expired. Then he served as the unofficial ambassador to the government that eleven states agreed to in 1788 when they accepted the Constitution. But he did get back to Edenton and to his political base in the South in time to sit as a delegate in his state's second ratification convention, held in Fayetteville in November, 1788—and to make the motion there that finally brought the state under the Constitution. He reassured his neighbors that the Federal Courts would not intrude in state matters. He presented the document as no threat to the integrity of the states or the liberty of their citizens. Indeed, he praised it highly as a marvel of political sagacity.

Once North Carolina became a member of the Union, it immediately picked Hugh Williamson as one of its members in the House of Representatives. He completed his political service to his adopted state with two terms in Congress, 1789-1793. He disliked the attitude of the Northeast toward the navigation of the Western states on the Mississippi and its importance to their commerce. He voted for an excise (because he was a prohibitionist) but opposed the bill for a Bank of the United States. And when Congress considered subsidies and special considerations for New England enterprises, Williamson sounded a warning: "I wish the Union may be perpetual [but] the remedy is plain" for the South should the power of government be used to rob it by "unequal taxes." In other words, he considered secession as a legitimate possibility if the South did not enjoy those protections in the Union that it had been led to expect.

In 1793 Hugh Williamson settled permanently in New York, where he had married into an old Tory family. By this time, he had become a man of means, and was respected as a savant. As he had been a trustee of the University of North Carolina, he became a trustee of the University of the State of

New York and of the College of Physicians and Surgeons. He was a founder of the Literary and Philosophical Society of New York and he was a prominent member of the New York Historical Society. He continued with his scientific work and publications, including a history of North Carolina. At the age of 83, he died in New York City, and was buried at Trinity Church. (See David Hosack, *A Biographical Memoir of Hugh Williamson* [New York: C. S. Van Winkle, 1920]; Louise Irby Trenholme, *The Ratification of the Federal Constitution in North Carolina* [New York: AMS Press, 1967], pp. 74–77, 79–80, *et passim*; Fletcher M. Green, *The Role of the Yankee in the Old South* [Athens: University of Georgia Press, 1972], pp. 9–10; Delbert H. Gilpatrick, "Contemporary Opinion of Hugh Williamson," *North Carolina Historical Review*, XVII [January, 1940], 26–36; John Washington Neal, "Life and Public Service of Hugh Williamson," *Historical Papers Published by the Trinity College Historical Society*, Series 13 [1919], pp. 63–115; Helen Jenkins, "The Versatile Dr. Hugh Williamson, 1735–1789," M. A. thesis, University of North Carolina, 1950; and Forrest McDonald, *We the People: The Economic Origins of the Constitution* [Chicago: University of Chicago Press, 1975], pp. 75–76.)

William Blount

(March 26, 1749–March 21, 1800), planter, merchant, land speculator, and political leader of North Carolina and Tennessee.

A reluctant Framer who, though in favor of a stronger national government, feared the political repercussions of being involved in creating one, and doubted that North Carolina would approve of any large-scale revision of the Articles of Confederation. Great-grandson of Sir Thomas Blount, who had settled on Pamlico Sound in North Carolina *ca.* 1662. Son of Jacob Blount, grandson of Thomas, and Barbara Grey Blount. Born on his grandfather's plantation at Rosefield, in Bertie County. Of very distinguished lineage, Anglo-Norman and Scottish, with quarterings reaching as far back as the Conquest, and connected by kinship to important families in both Virginia and his own state. Educated at home, and in the business of his father, which was principally politics and trading in land. Presbyterian.

William Blount, along with the other "Tar River" Blounts, took the Patriot side in the American Revolution. In 1776 he was enlisted as paymaster in the North Carolina forces, and from that time onward his life was spent in public service. From 1780–1784 he was a member of the lower house of the North Carolina legislature, where he served as speaker. And, from 1788–1790 he sat in the upper house of the same assembly. He was twice appointed member for his state in the Continental Congress, first from 1782–1783 and again from 1786–1787. He was serving in the Congress when, at the age of 38, he was asked by North Carolina to represent it in the Philadelphia Convention.

William Blount said almost nothing in the debates over the Constitution, was late arriving to the sessions and was then absent from them for almost a month on business in the Congress. Before the call had gone out for a Great Convention, Blount had expressed the opinion that the Union might break up into two or three lesser confederations. He did not have a "long view" of the proceedings he so neglected. Furthermore, he was among those aristocratic republicans who had been alarmed by a rising popular spirit in the western counties of North Carolina and the other states. But his reaction to these developments differed from those of similar men who shared in his concern. His family had been one of those to learn a salutary lesson from the 1770–1771 Regulator movement in the Carolinas. To preserve cohesion and the authority of its leaders, a deferential society required that concessions work both ways, both up and down. Moreover, the Blounts of Blount Hall had always been interested in the development of the West. Their fortune was, even after one hundred and twenty years, still to be made there, if anywhere. For, as he recognized, the movement of power and wealth tended in that direction. A strong Federal authority would increase the value of Blount holdings in what was soon to be Tennessee. Yet William Blount, if he hoped to make his way there, could not afford to make Gov. Tryon's mistakes and offend the backcountry. Therefore, he signed the Constitution only "to attest the fact that it was a unanimous act of the states," not to express his "approval" of the document.

William Blount was not at all surprised by North Carolina's original refusal to ratify. He was, moreover, very careful about the kind of support which he gave to the Federalist cause, and waited until the new instrument of government had been ratified in all the other states, except Rhode Island, before he took any public stand. His term as state senator produced a Caswell-Blount resolution calling for a second convention, which easily passed both houses of the legislature. And he sat as a delegate from Tennessee County—in the transmontane West—during the Fayetteville deliberations which finally brough North Carolina into the already functioning Federal Union. But Blount was denied the reward for Federalist loyalty which he most desired, a seat in the new United States Senate, which went to Benjamin Hawkins.

Therefore, after helping to arrange for the cession of North Carolina's Western lands to the United States, Blount himself in 1790 moved to Tennessee, settling first at Rocky Mount and then in Knoxville. Once there, he sought and received from the national government appointment as Governor for the Territory South of the River Ohio, an office which he performed with tact and skill in dealing with both Indians and frontiersmen until Tennessee became a state in 1796. He presided over the constitutional convention for the new state, and was elected one of its original senators. Blount as territorial governor and United States Senator continued in his land speculations and at one time held title to or options on over one million acres. But by this time he had left the Federalist camp and joined with the Jeffersonians, chiefly because of their promise not to neglect the West. Then the paper empire collapsed. Notes were called in, and the Federalists took advantage of Blount's foolish involvement in a plan to give Spanish Florida and Louisiana to England to expel him from the Senate, and thus embarrass his party. Efforts to impeach or punish further failed; and upon Blount's return to Tennessee, he found that his popularity there was undiminished, as is proved by his election, in 1798, to the state senate, and his elevation by that body to its speakership. Though disgusted by "Jacobins" and the leveling doctrines of the French, he had the kind of popular touch that was to be a characteristic of Southern leaders in the generations to come. Certainly his political career would have continued had it not been cut short by his untimely death at the age of fifty. (See William H. Masterson, *William Blount* [Baton Rouge: Louisiana State University Press, 1954]; Thomas Perkins Abernethy, *From Frontier to Plantation in Tennessee* [Chapel Hill: University of North Carolina Press, 1932]; Louise Irby Trenholme, *The Ratification of the Federal Constitution in North Carolina* [New York: AMS Press, 1967].)

Alexander Martin

(1740–Nov. 2, 1807), merchant, lawyer, planter, soldier, and political leader of North Carolina during the Revolution, under the Articles, and after the adoption of the new United States Constitution.

The voice of the Carolina Piedmont in the Great Convention. A moderate in the context of the politics of his state, with some reputation as a "trimmer." In Philadelphia, a man of no settled convictions, but "suspicious of the ultranationalism of the Convention." Less a Federalist than any other member of the North Carolina delegation. Left Philadelphia in late August doubting the value of the Constitution that was emerging, but changed in his opinion within a few months of his return to the Salisbury/Guilford County region of North Carolina which was his base of power. Not a man to lead when others were loath to follow.

Alexander Martin was Scotch-Irish, born in Hunterdon County, New Jersey, the son of the Rev. Hugh Martin, originally of County Tyrone, Ireland, and of Jane Martin. The Martins were Presbyterians. They had five sons, four of whom emigrated to North Carolina, while the fifth settled in Virginia. Alexander Martin, the eldest, was educated at the College of New Jersey, from which he was graduated in 1756, at the age of sixteen, and from which he received an M. A. three years later. Young Martin then moved to Virginia and thereafter to the village of Salisbury, North Carolina, where he set up as a merchant. Became a Justice of the Peace in 1764, King's Deputy Attorney in 1766, and Judge of the King's Bench for the Rowan County Court of Oyer and Terminer for 1774–1775. Martin's legal practice was small, but at times dangerous. In 1770–1771 as Commissioner of Salisbury and officer of the court at Hillsboro, he was confronted by Regulators, forced to sign an agreement concerning his fees, and beaten by the mob. Yet he urged conciliation of his angry neighbors in writing the haughty Governor Tryon, who rebuked him for this interference.

Under the Royal Governor, Martin served in the North Carolina House of Commons (1773–1774) for Guilford County, where he had moved after the unpleasantness at Salisbury. And in the second and third Provincial Congresses (1775), which had been assembled *ex officio* to administer the business of the colony as it moved toward independence. Like many of his origin, Alexander Martin came from a family already impatient with the policies of the English government before their arrival in the New World. He took the side of the protesting Americans or Patriots from the first and was appointed lieutenant colonel of the Second North Carolina Continental Regiment in September of 1775. He served in the "Snow Campaign" against the South Carolina Loyalists ("Scovellites"), was at Moore's Creek Bridge in February of 1776 and at the defense of Charleston the following June. After being promoted to colonel of his regiment, he marched it northward to join Washington's army, where he saw action at Chad's Ford and elsewhere. On October 4, 1777, he participated in the Battle of Germantown. Here, however, Washington's efforts to surprise and overwhelm the English army only recently settled in Philadelphia were frustrated by weather, disobedience, and poor communications. Martin meandered during this engagement, wandering sometimes in the fog. He was charged with cowardice, subjected to a court-martial, found "not guilty," but not so completely exonerated as to be of further use to the service. He resigned his commission on November 22, 1777, returned to North Carolina, and was almost immediately elected to represent Guilford County in the state senate.

Alexander Martin was a member of the upper house of the North Carolina Assembly from 1778–1782, and during 1787–1788. He was the Speaker of the senate during all of these years except for the term of 1778–1779. In 1781 he became acting governor when Governor Thomas Burke was captured by local Loyalists. For a time in the early months of 1782, Burke was restored to his office, but Martin succeeded him and continued as governor from 1782–1785. Martin was so successful in securing support among the citizens of Western North Carolina that he left office only because the law restricted his tenure to three out of any six years. In some respects, he was a weak governor, magnifying the powers of the Assembly over those of his own office. Yet, as a state senator, he exercised almost as much authority as he had as chief executive, serving in 1780 with John Penn and Oroondates Davis on a Board of War, and in 1781 on an equivalent Council Extraordinary with Governor Richard Caswell and Allen Jones. These special boards attempted to transact the important military business of the state during the period of its greatest danger. Martin led them in this effort—as he later attempted to lead the Assembly while chief executive. He proposed a plural religious establishment, a moderate and conciliatory policy toward Loyalists, better treatment for Indians and for the frontier, and a careful approach to the cession of North Carolina's lands beyond the mountains to the authority of the Continental Congress. Though he did not push, he did advise. There was, we may thus infer, some consistency in his view of the proper order of government in North Carolina, and some willingness to see power applied when nothing but the application of power would suffice. But in general Alexander Martin was clearly a champion of limited government, a man who pledged on his first election as Governor of North Carolina that "the sole object of my administration shall be to maintain and defend the Sovereign Independent power of this state. . . ." It was thus difficult for him to play the Federalist, though he sometimes tried.

Governor Martin made no speeches or motions in the Constitutional Convention. He seconded only three proposals, one of which sought merely to add another seat for North Carolina in the original House of Representatives. He supported the effort to give equal voice to each of the states in the United States Senate. Hugh Williamson spoke of this near-silence as the conduct of a man who had "exhausted his fund" of leadership. The trouble was that Martin had come North to see "thirteen Independent Sovereignties" made a Nation, while at the same time "preserving the particular interests of the Individual states." Such was not the business he found in Philadelphia. But he had recognized the need for a united policy on trade and military matters and for a national revenue even while serving as the jealously Antifederalist leader of North Carolina. Moreover, he was a member of the Society of the Cincinnati, which was almost synonymous with Federalism. Therefore he decided to give the proposed reform in government a chance, offered to go as a Federalist for the North Carolina ratification convention to be held in Hillsboro in July of 1788—offered and was defeated by his old friend Dr. David Caldwell. Yet in the same year Martin was elected again to the state senate. And in the following year he was elected as North Carolina's first governor under the new Constitution—which had finally been adopted by a second ratifying convention in November of 1789. He served three additional terms in the office, making him the most re-elected governor in the history of his state. The Federalists helped to put Martin back in power. But the policies of Alexander Hamilton had him by 1790 once more in the other camp. He complained of Federal "interference" and "intrusion," of "extravagance" and "mindless folly." He wrote, asking a member of Congress, "Will not the Central Government quickly bear down the state government?" Of the High Federalists he observed, "They should establish a new government on the affections of the people and not exercise powers that appear to be doubtful." He took alarm at talk of "implied powers." And, when elected by the Antifederalists as United States Senator at the end of a long tenure as governor, he renewed his old pledge: "to preserve inviolate . . . the individuality and internal sovereignty of the state."

As Senator from North Carolina he kept this pledge until the end of his term, supporting economy, opposing Jay's Treaty (for its failure to recover stolen slaves), opposing expansion of the military establishment, new Federal courts, and a growing civil list. Yet after the French insult to the delegation of Pinckney, Gerry, and Marshall, Alexander Martin anticipated a shift in the sentiment of his state. As a Christian (Episcopalian), Martin already deplored the French Revolution. And how could he be expected to tolerate the Jacobins, their heirs in the Directory, or their American friends after what the Regulators had done to him? Hence, Martin made a political mistake and voted for the Alien and Sedition Acts. After a halfhearted effort to win re-election, it was time to return to his new home at Danbury, to his comfort, his books, and his family—his mother, brothers, and their numerous children. There had been too much wild talk, too many noisy radicals. Now there was time for poetry (Martin wrote conventional eighteenth century verse), for promotion of the University of North Carolina (of which he had been a trustee since 1790), and for a final appearance in the Assembly (1804–1805, including another turn as Speaker of the senate). In a long poem about Columbus, he looked forward to the future of the country, symbolized by the new national capital being built in Washington City:

> Thy worth a grateful nation there shall own,
> In fair Columbia's plain thy name revise
> Long dormant—where another Rome shall rise
> With her broad Capital near Tyber's stream.

At the time of his death in 1807, Alexander Martin had spent over thirty-five years in the service of his state. A bachelor, he owned 10,000 acres and at least seventy slaves. In 1793 Princeton awarded him an LL.D. He seems, when compared to the decisive men who joined him in Philadelphia during those momentous months of 1787, an uncertain figure: standing out in some relief against the backdrop of his fellow Framers. Yet he is more of a forecast of American politics to come than were the would-be lawgivers and votaries of Fame who were so absolutely certain about the Union they would make. (See Richard Walser, "Alexander Martin, Poet," *Early American Literature*,

VI [Spring, 1971], 55-61; Robert M. Douglas, "Alexander Martin," pp. 274-280 of Vol. III, *Biographical History of North Carolina: From Colonial Times to the Present* [Greensboro: Charles L. Van Noppen, 1905]; Louise Irby Trenholme, *The Ratification of the Federal Constitution in North Carolina* [New York: AMS Press, 1967]; Norman K. Risjord, *Chesapeake Politics, 1781-1800* [New York: Columbia University Press, 1978]; Francis Nash, *Presentation of Portrait of Governor Alexander Martin to the State of North Carolina . . . November 16, 1908, by the North Carolina Society of the Sons of the Revolution* [Raleigh, N. C., n.p., 1909]; and Elizabeth Winston Yates, "The Public Career of Alexander Martin," M. A. thesis, University of North Carolina, 1943.)

Richard Dobbs Spaight

(March 25, 1758-Sept. 6, 1802), soldier, planter, statesman, and political leader of North Carolina.

In 1787 moved to favor a stronger legal Union by experience in arms and state government and by service in the Continental Congress. In the company of the Framers a strong Federalist, but soon after the adoption of the new United States Constitution greatly changed in his opinion of the value of consolidated Federal authority. Before the Great Convention, made impatient with the states by their failure to support the Revolution and their subsequent unwillingness to support national functions under the Articles. After the new government was in place, soon angry with the Northern Federalists because of their economic exploitation of the South and their tendency to make of authority an end in itself. Devoted to the idea of a "union of sovereign states preserving their civil liberties and connected together by such ties as to preserve permanent and effective government," though he doubted the possibility of such balance. Of the opinion that those gathered with him in Philadelphia had assembled to produce "a system not described, . . . that has not occurred in the history of man." Though moderate in his politics, a Hotspur, and quick to take offense at all things personal. Confident of his own abilities and of the propriety of his employment in posts of responsibility.

Richard Dobbs Spaight was born in New Bern, North Carolina, the son of Richard Spaight, an Irish gentleman, and Elizabeth Wilson Spaight. His father was a retainer of his kinsman the Royal Governor Arthur Dobbs, was a member of the colonial council, Secretary of the Colony, and paymaster of the local forces during the French and Indian War. Richard Dobbs Spaight was orphaned at the age of eight and educated in Ireland, among relatives, and at the University of Glasgow, in accordance with the arrangements of his guardian and great-great uncle, Governor Dobbs. In 1778, upon completion of that schooling, he returned to North Carolina and quickly accepted a commission in the local militia. In 1780 Spaight fought at the Battle of Camden as an aide to Major General Richard Caswell. He was later promoted to Lieutenant Colonel Commandant of Artillery, but left active duty in 1781 upon his election to the North Carolina House of Commons for New Bern and Craven County. Spaight served two years (1781–1783) in his first appearance in the legislature, then a two-year tour in the Continental Congress (1783–1785), and thereafter returned to the North Carolina House of Commons, of which he was the elected speaker in 1785. In the Continental Congress the youthful Spaight served on a committee to organize a government for the territories in the West. He was one of the Southerners opposed to prohibitions against the spread of slavery along the frontier, and was quick to show anger at the shortcomings of his "tightfisted and unpatriotic" Yankee colleagues, sometimes offering to prove up his point on the field of honor. Returning to the state legislature by his own choice, from 1785–1787 Spaight exercised a remarkable influence for a person of his years. In state politics, in an investigation of state judges, he proved to be a strict constructionist, very hostile to judicial activism and usurpation by review. In 1787, the North Carolina General Assembly elected him as one of their representatives in the forthcoming Constitutional Convention scheduled to meet in Philadelphia.

In the Great Convention Richard Dobbs Spaight attended every session and was more of a nationalist than the rest of the delegation from his state. He did not approve of equal representation for the states in the United States Senate. In his report to the North Carolina legislature, he rejoiced in the Northern agreement to a strong Fugitive Slave Clause, and had no fear of navigation acts passed by a simple majority, since the "Northern Brethren" needed some inducement to cooperation. At one point he even favored a suffrage based on the number of "white inhabitants." Yet he leaned toward the thinking of the Antifederalists in supporting the election of United States Senators by the state legislatures and a two-thirds vote for the ratification of treaties. He favored seven-year terms for Senators and for the President of the United States, and had some doubt about the value of electors chosen by the various state legislatures. Yet, in his view, the advantage of having Senators elected in that fashion was in the check to "consolidation" they would thus provide.

In the July, 1788 North Carolina ratification convention held at Hillsboro, Richard Dobbs Spaight was one of the strongest and most frequently heard voices speaking in behalf of the new instrument of government. His construction of the document produced in Philadelphia allowed him to assure his neighbors that it would not destroy the states or put them under the power of a hostile Northern majority. He assured his fellow Carolinians that Federal courts, under the Constitution, would not have jurisdiction over state concerns, or attempt to apply the Constitution to state and local (or personal) activities beyond its scope. He agreed with William Richardson Davie that North Carolina's fear of consolidation was a "bugbear," but was, with the other Federalists present in this assembly, unable to persuade the majority to vote for approval. Spaight did not attend the later convention held in Fayetteville in November, 1789, which finally ratified the new Constitution.

From 1787 through the following four years, Richard Dobbs Spaight was often in poor health, and for a time left the United States to recuperate in the West Indies. In 1787, when his name was proposed for chief executive of his state, he received only moderate support. And in 1789 he withdrew his name as a candidate for one of North Carolina's original seats in the United States Senate. But, after his return from the Indies, he became (in 1792) North Carolina's first native-born governor, in which office he served three one-year terms. In 1798 he was chosen to be a member of the House of Representatives from North Carolina, where, after re-election, he sat until 1801. In Congress he joined the Democratic-Republicans (with whom he had been affiliated since 1789), advocated repeal of the Alien and Sedition Acts and opposed the impeachment of his colleague in the Great Convention, Senator William Blount of Tennessee. In the disputed Presidential election of 1800, Spaight voted consistently for Thomas Jefferson. Upon his return to North Carolina, he was elected to the lower house of the legislature in 1801 and, in the following year, to the upper chamber. This election of 1802 was hotly contested by young John Stanly, a Federalist, who so thoroughly offended Spaight that the former governor described his rival as "a liar and a scoundrel" and offered him "satisfaction." The result of these sharp words was a duel. On the fourth exchange between these now bitter adversaries, Spaight fell mortally wounded. Ordinarily one fire would have been enough for honor. But Stanly had called Spaight a "dodger," an insult which the older man could not endure. Spaight, dead at the aged of forty-four, was buried at his estate, Clermont, near New Bern.

Spaight's change from Federalist to Jeffersonian may have cost him his life, but it was symptomatic of what was happening among the political leaders of the South who did not long remain within Washington's party once the General had retired from office. In his private life Spaight was typical of his class, quiet and responsible. He was a devout Episcopalian and a vigorous supporter of education, having served as one of the original trustees of the University of North Carolina and as a member of the governing board of the local academy. Though a man of great wealth (over one hundred slaves and many plantations), Spaight for the most part left his private business in other hands, and devoted his life to the public service for which he had been prepared since childhood. His son, Richard Dobbs Spaight, Jr., was, in his footsteps, elected governor of North Carolina in 1834. (See Alexander B. Andrews, "Richard Dobbs Spaight," *North Carolina Historical Review,* I

[April, 1924], 97–120; John H. Wheeler, *Sketch of the Life of Richard Dobbs Spaight of North Carolina* [Baltimore: William K. Boyle, 1880]; Robert G. Ferris, ed., *Signers of the Constitution* [Washington, D. C.: U. S. Department of the Interior, 1976], pp. 212–213; H. James Henderson, *Party Politics in the Continental Congress* [New York: McGraw-Hill, 1974]; Louise Irby Trenholme, *The Ratification of the Federal Constitution in North Carolina* [New York: AMS Press, Inc., 1967]; and an unpublished entry on Richard Dobbs Spaight by Gertrude S. Carraway which will appear in the University of North Carolina Press' *Dictionary of North Carolina Biography*, ed. by William S. Powell.)

John Rutledge

(September, 1739–July 18, 1800), lawyer, jurist, and patriarchal chieftain of the people of South Carolina during the American Revolution.

After the conclusion of the war, called by them (with affection) "Dictator John," in memory of the two years (February 3, 1780–January 29, 1782) when he held absolute sway over the lives and fortunes of a people who had given him something like the old Roman office. For fifteen years following the achievement of independence the most respected man in his state. The Southern Framer most instrumental in bringing about amity between the sections during the Great Convention. An Old Whig, a man of the ancient prescription, and as far removed from allegiance to the abstractions of natural rights as any of the Fathers of the Republic. A "nabob," with the habit of command and no patience with effrontery, of either the intellectual or the personal variety. Yet a man of tact and judgment. One of the men who would have to approve of the Constitution if a firmer Union was to be accomplished in Philadelphia. A Federalist only if the established regime of South Carolina could find a source of strength and security in that camp. A man of great property, but in 1787, like most Carolina planters, short of funds. An exotic experience for New England delegates to the Constitutional Convention. A figure of reference in any history of Southern political thought. And, according to one analysis, the Father of the Constitution.

John Rutledge was born in Charles Town, the son of Dr. John Rutledge, a physician, and Sara Hext Rutledge, the only daughter of the very wealthy Colonel Hugh Hext. John Rutledge's uncle (and eventually his role model) was Andrew Rutledge, Speaker of the Commons House of Assembly and the leader of the South Carolina bar. Both the father and uncle were graduates of Trinity College, Dublin, Ireland, the sons of a French and Scotch-Irish farmer of County Tyrone. Though always at the center of a large family (he had six brothers and sisters), John Rutledge lost both his father (1750) and his uncle (1755) while still a child. He was educated by his father, by the

Episcopal minister of Christ Church Parish, and by Dr. David Rhind, a respected tutor. Later he read law with James Parsons, also speaker of the house. In 1757 he journeyed to Great Britain, where, according to the pattern with South Carolinians of his class, he studied in the Middle Temple, and was called to the English bar in 1760, trying and winning two cases in London courts before his return home. Within two years of his first appearance in the courts of South Carolina, Rutledge had become one of the three most successful attorneys in the province. In 1761 he was elected to the Commons House from Christ Church Parish and continued to carry out that assignment until, during the Revolution, he rose to be the president and governor of an independent and sovereign nation and state.

As an attorney, John Rutledge earned an average of perhaps £9,000 a year between 1762–1774. While still a very young man, he was the acknowledged measure of propriety in his world, the spokesman of a closed, conservative order which set a high premium on eloquence, skill in debate, knowledge of the inherited law, and personal honor. Rutledge was involved in all manner of commercial business for the great merchants of his very commercial city. Yet his political activity was also constant. In 1764 he was Royal Attorney General for the colony. In 1765 he was a South Carolina delegate to the Stamp Act Congress in New York, where he chaired a committee which petitioned the House of Lords for redress. He also drew up a remonstrance for the local legislature against abuses of office by the Royal Governor Thomas Boone. And in 1774 he was the first man selected to speak for South Carolina in the Continental Congress.

John Rutledge approached a final division between the North American colonies and their mother country with great hesitancy and many reservations. In the First and Second Continental Congresses Rutledge insisted that Americans not press their case with appeals to theories concerning the rights of man, but draw their arguments instead from the English Constitution and their "inherited rights." He opposed all moves toward independence so long as there seemed to be any hope of reconciliation. In March of 1776, Rutledge became the first President of the Republic of South Carolina, under a constitution he himself had helped to draft when government under a Committee of Public Safety no longer seemed sufficient. Yet on taking office, he described the authority with which he would rule as only temporary, operative until "an accommodation of the unhappy differences between Great Britain and America can be obtained." John Rutledge concurred with his brother Edward (who signed the Declaration of Independence) that the identity of South Carolina would be in more danger if subject to the government of New England than it was from the fleets and armies of King George III: "I dread their low cunning and . . . leveling Principles." Yet after Charleston was attacked in June of 1776, the Rutledge brothers accepted the necessity of formal independence for the organization and protection of a war effort, since outright submission was the only alternative. Later, when developments under the Articles required that the Republic of South Carolina be converted into a state and joined to other free states, Rutledge vetoed the proposed Constitution of 1778 and resigned his office because it was too much like the New England instruments of government—and because it would make accommodation with Great Britain impossible. In other words, though the leader of a rebellion, he continued to look backward toward a still English, self-governing America. The British conquest of Charleston and the Low Country in 1780 finally turned the thinking of John Rutledge in a new direction, toward a recognition of South Carolina's vulnerability and of its future role as part of an American nation. Yet as he fled Charleston, governor again but now of an almost vanquished people, he was still a defender of the old regime, *not a democrat* and *not a revolutionary* by disposition or local practice. Where he was, in his saddle, was now "the seat of government," and he, in effect, *the state of South Carolina*—the entire state, which now signified the Upcountry as much as it did Charleston and its environs. On the men of the Piedmont, the frontier, and the remote sections of the state Rutledge was forced to depend. They assisted him in restoring self-government to South Carolina. And "Dictator John" did not forget, once the fighting was done. War fostered unity in South Carolina of a kind never known in colonial times. Or at least unity among various kinds of Patriots. After 1782 the back-country was never again without influence in South Carolina politics.

To rescue South Carolina, after organizing the militia, John Rutledge rushed north for assistance. The devastation of British rule had once and for all cured him of Anglophilia. In North Carolina he got men and a base of operation. From Congress he got (after an interruption called Horatio Gates) General Nathanael Greene. Rutledge was tireless and omnipresent in prosecuting the war. The South Carolina partisans harassed Lord Cornwallis' outposts, interrupted his communications, and, at King's Mountain, joined other militia to destroy his Tory allies. The British surged out of their stronghold and, after a defeat at Cowpens and a drawn battle at Guilford Court House, ran into a corner at Yorktown. Behind Cornwallis, South Carolina was slowly cleared of enemy forces and on October 14, 1782, the Charleston garrison under General Alexander Leslie marched down to its boats and embarked. Meanwhile, in the months before final victory, John Rutledge had called an election and assembled a new legislature at Jacksonborough. It passed statutes providing for confiscation, banishment, and amercement of Loyalist properties. But the outgoing governor had already pardoned repentant Loyalists, punished some of the worst offenders, and pacified the most troubled areas of the state. And the new laws probably prevented even harsher measures. Moreover, they were soon modified. Payment of debts was suspended, indigo made negotiable currency. Then, with satisfaction and general congratulations, John Rutledge gave up the staff of office and retired to the House as a member for St. Andrew Parish. His most difficult trial as leader of South Carolina was now a thing of the past. But he had a major role yet to play in the larger arena of national politics.

In 1782 and 1783, John Rutledge returned to the Continental Congress as a representative of his state. But he declined a position on the national court set up under the Articles, and declined to serve as minister to the Netherlands. Instead, the remainder of his career was to concentrate on judicial duties in South Carolina. In 1784 Rutledge was appointed chief judge of a new state court of chancery. From 1784 through 1790 Rutledge also held a seat in the legislature. When the Constitutional Convention was called for Philadelphia in May of 1787, it was inevitable that John Rutledge lead the delegation sent to it from his state. He, Charles Cotesworth Pinckney, Charles Pinckney III, and Pierce Butler preconsulted concerning what position they would assume during the debates and (apart from some deviations by young Pinckney) managed to act in concert most of the time—according to a design drawn up for them by John Rutledge.

During the Constitutional Convention John Rutledge behaved like a man who was conscious of the power in his hands. He spoke often, briefly, and to the point. And he chaired the committee which drafted the original version of the Constitution drawn up once the major differences that divided the house had been adjusted: the Committee of Detail. It was Rutledge who introduced into the document language; which describes it as "the supreme law of the land"—a cautionary expression, designed to restrain the lawless, but not the High Federalism some imagine it to be. Like his brother Edward, John recognized the peril carried in an authority for "destroying Provincial Distinctions and of making every thing of the minute kind bend to what they [Puritans and centralizers] call the good of the whole." Therefore he insisted that James Wilson's detailed description of the judicial powers be reduced to a simple jurisdiction over cases relating to the few concerns which were truly Federal in their implications; opposed giving the new Congress a veto over state legislation; and opposed a provision for lower Federal courts, under the Supreme Court. Just the opposite of judicial activism is what John Rutledge expected to foster with his "supremacy clause." As he saw matters, the problem in 1787 was that the Supreme Court and the Constitution might be allowed no authority whatsoever if such authority were not claimed in explicit terms. Besides, he was a man of law and wanted a "government of laws," particularly as a check on "democratic power," which "however unexceptional [it] may at first appear, . . . in its efects [continues to be] arbitrary, severe and destructive."

John Rutledge had absolutely no patience with antislavery rhetoric applied to the advantage of Northern political and economic power. "Religion and humanity," said he, "had nothing to do with this question. Interest alone is the governing principle with nations." Refusing to be humbugged, he threw down the challenge: "The true question at present is whether the Southern States shall or shall not be parties to the Union." On almost every important issue to divide the Convention, John Rutledge insisted that discussions should begin with a recognition of political reality already in force, that they should be "guided . . . by long experience." The small states would have an equal voice in the United States Senate, or they would have it under the Articles. The South would either hold slaves on the present basis, or under the new Constitution. No nation was being invented, since a nation was already in existence. Only "fools" would give up the slave trade as South Carolina was being asked to do, or neglect to insist on counting their slaves for purposes of representation. Only hypocrites would pretend to be excited about a "moral issue" when actually in the midst of a power play—for their own profit attempting to decrease the voting strength of a partner in a matter of mutual concern. "Property was certainly the principal object of society," and, instead of numbers, should be the basis of representation. Let seats in the House of Representatives be distributed according to the contribution paid into the national treasury by each state. Let seats in the House of Representatives be elected by the state legislatures and United States Senators serve without pay. By these means property could be protected, and the stability of government ensured. South Carolina knew about these things. It did not elect a legislature on the basis of population alone, since that procedure would not reflect "the sense of the whole community." Rutledge capped his argument with ease: "If this Convention had been chosen by the people in districts it is not supposed that such proper characters would have been preferred."

John Rutledge expressed himself briefly on many points disputed or explored during the Great Convention. He recommended good salaries for Federal judges and the election of the President by the United States Congress. He held that the historic rights of Englishmen had, as a result of the Revolution, their repositories in the states, and that they did not require Federal reaffirmation, by a remote authority, since that arrangement had caused all the trouble in the first place. He favored wealth as a condition of service for United States Representatives, Senators, and the President. He hoped to see the powers of Congress specified, rejected any tax on exports, criticized the notion that elected officials might hold appointed posts, urged the quiet members of the Convention to speak up, and finally, complained that the proceedings had grown tedious and overly particular. After taking the measure of his associates, he decided to bring the question to a head, and, through an agreement with the members from Connecticut, closed out the conversation concerning slavery, the slave trade, and political representation—thereby opening the way to a resolution of many other divisions in the house. What Roger Sherman and Oliver Ellsworth desired was a security for Connecticut's claims in the Western Reserve of Ohio, either in the United States Senate or in the Supreme Court. What Rutledge needed was an increase in the number of slaves sufficient to develop the open lands of the Southwest and to replace Negroes stolen by the British during their occupation. Out of this accommodation of finite needs rose a larger spirit of accommodation—one that was not fully destroyed until 1860.

After bringing in the August 6 report of the Committee of Detail—a draft of the Constitution shaped by the skill of his hand—most of the work of John Rutledge as Framer was complete. On his return to South Carolina, he informed the Low Country that the Yankees had behaved well and that, on balance, his neighbors should approve the Constitution. He had, at least with reference to his own state, been quite correct in recommending that no elaborate apologia be attached to the proposed Constitution when it was transmitted for approval. In 1784, when a tavern keeper had insulted one of the Rutledge household slaves, the South Carolina legislature had defined it to be a crime, punishable by exile, to thus offend John Rutledge. And Carolinians told with affection and amusement the story of Chancellor Rutledge coming late to the bench, at 10:45, and declaring, "When this court sits is ten o'clock, and no other hour." In such a context, how could Rutledge be refused ratification, especially since most of the gentry agreed with him in this case. Though most of South Carolina disapproved of the United States Constitution, with regard to its merits, many of the its citizens voted for it as a gesture of confidence in the men who had led the state in mortal strife—with particular confidence in John Rutledge.

Once the new government was organized, President Washington called John Rutledge from his post as Chancellor of the Southern District of South Carolina to be Associate Justice of the United States Supreme Court. Rutledge accepted the assignment, met with the High Court in 1790 and rode with certain of his colleagues on the Southern Circuit. Yet no cases were argued before the Court in 1790 through August, 1791; and Rutledge resigned to become Chief Justice of the South Carolina Court of Common Pleas, where he made a great reputation for both justice and severity. As he had done as King's Attorney, he protected the rights of slaves and held it a crime to lie about a man's color. In 1795, when Chief Justice John Jay resigned from the Supreme Court, Rutledge was openly eager to be appointed in his place, and was given it by his old friend. He presided over one term of the High Court, but his temporary appointment was not confirmed by the Federalist United States Senate—in part because of exaggerated rumors concerning the instability of his mind, but chiefly because he had led an attack on Jay's Treaty in a South Carolina public meeting: an attack which warned the South against servile acquiescence to violations of the Compromise of 1787. In a state of depression at this rebuff, Rutledge withdrew from public life. Yet respect for this undervalued Father of the Republic remained unchanged in his own city. In 1798 and 1799, he served final terms in the Assembly. His disposition improved. He practiced a little law, and visited his friends. At the age of sixty he died at the home of his son-in-law, the Episcopal Bishop of South Carolina, the Rev. Dr. Robert Smith, in the shelter of the church of his childhood, which Rutledge had labored to protect from disestablishment during the Revolution—as with so much else from the old order. He was buried in St. Michael's churchyard, under the most modest of inscriptions. There is much evidence to support a theory that John Rutledge has been, in the history of his reputation, among the most neglected of the Framers. Like John Dickinson of Delaware, he has received little emphasis in the scholarship because his career gives little support to the now accepted theories of the origins of the American regime. (See Richard Barry, *Mr. Rutledge of South Carolina* [New York: Books for Libraries Press, 1971]; Forrest McDonald, *E Pluribus Unum: The Formation of the American Republic, 1776–1790* [Indianapolis: Liberty Press, 1979], pp. 289–290 *et passim;* Leon Friedman, "John Rutledge," pp. 33–49 of Vol. I of *The Justices of the United States Supreme Court, 1789–1969: Their Lives and Major Opinions* [New York: R. R. Bowker/Chelsea House, 1969], ed. by Friedman and Fred L. Israel; Charles Gregg Singer, *South Carolina in the Confederation* [Philadelphia: Porcupine Press, 1976]; Margaret B. MacMillan, *The War Governors in the American Revolution* [New York: Columbia University Press, 1943]; Ernest M. Lander, Jr., "The South Carolinians at the Philadelphia Convention, 1787," *The South Carolina Historical Magazine,* LVII (June, 1956), 134–155; George C. Rogers, *Evolution of a Federalist: William Loughton Smith of Charleston, 1758–1812* [Columbia: University of South Carolina Press, 1962], pp. 112–188 *et passim;* Allan Nevins, *The American States During and After the Revolution* [New York: Macmillan Company, 1924]; John Drayton, *Memoirs of the American Revolution, From Its Commencement to the Year 1776, Inclusive; As Relating to the State of South Carolina . . .,* 2 vols. [Charleston: A. E. Miller, 1821]; Lisle A. Rose, *Prologue to Democracy: The Federalists in the South, 1789–1800* [Lexington: University of Kentucky Press, 1968]; Jerome Nadelhaft, "The Revolutionary Era in South Carolina," Ph.D. dissertation, University of Wisconsin, 1965; Raymond G. Starr, "The Conservative Revolution: South Carolina's Public Affairs, 1775–1790," Ph.D. dissertation, University of Texas, 1964; S. Sidney Ulmer, "The South Carolina Delegates to the Constitutional Convention of 1787: An Analytical Study," Ph.D. dissertation, Duke University, 1966; Edward McCrady, *The History of South Carolina in the Revolution,* 2 vols. [New York: Macmillan Company, 1901 and 1902]; Robert W. Barnwell, "Rutledge, 'The Dictator,' " *Journal of Southern History,* VII [May, 1941], 215–224; and Hoyt Paul Canady, Jr., "Gentlemen of the Bar: Lawyers in Colonial South Carolina," Ph.D. dissertation, University of Tennessee, 1979.)

Charles Cotesworth Pinckney

(Feb. 25, 1746–Aug. 16, 1825), solidier, statesman, lawyer, and planter.

Federalist candidate for the Presidency in 1804 and 1808; and for the

Vice-Presidency as running mate for John Adams in 1800; member for South Carolina in the Constitutional Convention of 1787, and one of its leading spirits; indubitably an aristocrat, a Carolina "nabob" who, with John Rutledge and John Dickinson, bespoke an American flowering of the Old Whig tradition of liberty through inherited, ancient law. Already the first or second man of his state when the Convention assembled, what he said during its debates was received by his associates as the considered opinion of the Lower South, and was weighed by them accordingly. Brought up in a milieu that connected property, education, and public service, he practiced a quiet virtue which required that he efface himself and represent the corporate things.

Charles Cotesworth Pinckney was the son of Charles Pinckney, Esquire (1699–1758), chief justice of South Carolina, and of Eliza Lucas Pinckney (1722–1793), the most gifted woman to live in the colony during its development as an English possession. His grandfather was Thomas Pinckney (1666–1705), the founder of the line. And his elder cousin/preceptor was Charles Pinckney II, a legal and political force in pre-Revolutionary South Carolina. The boy grew to manhood in an atmosphere where privilege was balanced by duty, in the expectation that he would fulfill an inherited role. Charles Cotesworth Pinckney was educated at Westminster School, at Oxford (where he studied with Sir William Blackstone) and in the Middle Temple. In France he was instructed in botany, chemistry, and military science to complete his preparation. Thanks to his mother's skill as a planter, he returned to his homeland as a man of great property, personally acquainted with the leaders of British and French society. And as a qualified member of the English bar, after one round on the circuit. Nonetheless, he was from his earliest youth modest and gentle in manner, full of all grace in every circumstance and condition. Throughout his life, he attempted to perform a part assigned to him in his father's will: "to prove . . . of service and advantage to his country, [and] an honour to his stock and kindred." From his first appearance in the South Carolina Commons House of Assembly in 1769, his was, in the words of his biographer, the politics of "experience" and prescription, not of private fancy or speculation. Said another way, he was never a man to surprise his friends.

Charles Cotesworth Pinckney brought to the Constitutional Convention no draft of a new compact, as did his youthful cousin Charles Pinckney III, but only his conviction shaped in the crucible of the Revolution, that the United States should not fight another war without the concentrated strength necessary to defend itself, and the related conviction that a national policy concerning foreign trade, currency, and finance was needed to relieve the burden of debt that weighed upon South Carolina and the other states. He was, in other words, a moderate military Federalist, a soldier politician, in whom the lawyer had been submerged by the exigencies of war. In Philadelphia he spoke plainly and displayed for effect none of his considerable erudition. Neither did he claim any special authority from the distinction of his name. Instead he went to the heart of whatever question was before the house and in the debates continued in an effort begun when, in 1775, he sat in the provisional Provincial Congress and put on a uniform to assist in organizing the defenses of the Southern coast. For, as he had written a friend during the Revolution, "the freedom and independence of my country are the gods of my idolatry."

A Pinckney (Picquigny) had been among the barons who forced King John to sign the Great Charter. And, in South Carolina, a Pinckney had, for three generations, stood ready to protect "the inherited rights of Englishmen." The defense of the patrimony had always presupposed the possibility of a final recourse to arbitration by the sword, and did so especially when Americans were threatened by Parliament's determination to bind them "in all cases whatsoever." In 1787 no new objectives animated the Pinckneys and the other Carolina gentry attending the Convention, even though the times called for extraordinary measures, a revision of the Articles, and the application of talents rarely employed on the field of arms. Out of the resources of their common identity, a set of political reflexes tried and proven, they would do their work on the spot. And Charles Cotesworth Pinckney would articulate the predominant pragmatism of their approach.

General Pinckney, as a junior officer, saw service in the first attack on Charles Town, in the first attempt to recover Georgia from British occupation; in the Florida campaign of 1778; and, as an aide on the staff of General Washington, during the battles of Brandywine and Germantown. He was captured with his city in 1780 and exchanged, after resisting considerable British pressure to defect. He rejoined the army in 1783 and was commissioned a brigadier general before his discharge from active duty. Later, at George Washington's behest, President John Adams promoted him to major general, during the 1798 preparations for war with France. In all of these martial adventures, young Pinckney answered to his personal sense of honor, expressed the outrage of his family at the Crown's replacement of Carolina worthies (like his father) by mere "placemen," and made use of the military training he had received at the royal military academy at Caen. But most importantly, he learned from his life as a soldier that South Carolina would not be secure on its own, in isolation, outside a union of the former colonies and a close cooperation among them. And he brought this lesson back to the politics of his state, even before he put off the uniform of the Continental Line.

After the Revolution Charles Cotesworth Pinckney was very active in the rebuilding of the Lower South, had a secure and almost constant place in the South Carolina legislature and a successful practice at law. Some years he made above £5000 in his profession. Most new legislation and a new state constitution passed under his shaping hand. And in many respects his word *was the* authority in the Low Country—his, and that of the Rutledge brothers, to whom he was connected by marriage. After the establishment of the new national government, Pinckney stayed at home in Carolina, becoming eventually the most famous citizen of the state. From 1790–1796, he sat in the state senate, saw to his crops, and gave constant and devoted support to the Episcopal church. He was a large and genial man, a social being and the acknowledged head of a large family of kin and connection. At his plantation, Belmont, he entertained important visitors to his region and the local aristocracy. But a few important parts of his adult life had to be played out a long way from Charleston, if Charleston was to be well served.

The political rule of thumb observed by Charles Cotesworth Pinckney in the Great Convention is one that he stated succinctly in a letter to his old friend General Andrew Pickens: "The great art of government is not to govern too much." Like his brother-in-law, Gov. Edward Rutledge, he was uneasy about the probable effects of political combination with New England and its "leveling principles." At the beginning of the debates he announced his uncertainty about how much revision of the Articles could be attempted under the mandate which most of the delegates had received from their several states. He was consistent in maintaining that they could only "recommend" to the states, not conclude. But he developed a confidence in his colleagues as the days of deliberation ran into weeks and months. He was favorably impressed by the generous spirit of some of his Yankee counterparts—as he had been during the war. He accepted the 3/5 rule on representation of slaves, the twenty-year extension of the slave trade, the prohibition of taxes on exports, and the unanimous agreement of all present that the new Constitution provided no authority to touch slavery in the states that chose to have it—not even at some remote future date. This government, he believed, would be limited enough to reflect what Americans, by way of the Revolution, had become. And to protect the special interests of the South. For parts of this network of compromise he made the necessary motions himself. Indeed, he liked the new Constitution so well when it reached its final form that, during the Convention's last days, he pledged publicly to fight for its approval in South Carolina. And he kept that pledge, acting as the leading supporter of ratification during the debates in the legislature of his state and in the special convention of January, 1788, called to pass judgment on the new law. Without Charles Cotesworth Pinckney, no Constitution could have been agreed upon in Philadelphia or approved in the Lower South.

General Pinckney was offered many posts of responsibility under the new government he had helped to create—a seat on the United States Supreme Court, and a variety of offices in Washington's cabinet. But he refused these honors without hesitation. Only in the case of a special diplomatic posting as emissary to France in 1796 did Pinckney accept a non-military assignment from the national government formed in 1788. Because the French did not perceive him to be a friend of their revolutionary movement, he was not recognized by the Directory as Minister James Monroe's successor; and, after threats, was forced to flee to Holland. In 1797 President John Adams named him, with John Marshall and Elbridge Gerry, as a member of a new mission to Paris, in the hope of reducing tensions betwen the two republics. The results of this embassy were not favorable. French demands for a loan and a bribe brought from Pinckney an outraged "No! No! Not a sixpence!" And brought him home a hero, to enjoy his moment of national acclaim.

In the South the Federalist Party declined into insignificance after the election of 1800. Charles Cotesworth Pinckney was loyal to it. But he did not much complain at the conduct of Jefferson and his Virginia successors, except perhaps for their foreign policy toward France. For this Pinckney was never in agreement with the "commercial" Federalists and their energetic government, was opposed to the Alien and Sedition Laws, and was turned against the French Revolution only after the Terror began and the Jacobins came to power. He did not care for the intemperance of Jeffersonian politics. And he hoped the United States would avoid the examples of ideological excess he had seen in France. Yet there is no Framer who kept further away from the upper reaches of democratic thought, not one who avoided with more consistency the taint of egalitarian hypocrisy, the humbug of which he complained when Virginia slaveholders attacked the trade so as to increase the value of their property. Indeed, during the South Carolina ratification debates Pinckney warned his fellow Southerners against any clamor for a Federal Bill of Rights because it might contain some language about the natural equality of men. On this subject he was never confused. He wanted U.S. Senators to serve without pay, and Congressmen to be elected by the various state legislatures. There is no evidence that he ever feared his Negroes. Yet neither was his conscience troubled by his possession of them.

Pinckney enjoyed his later years. He was, in 1805, elected President General of the Society of the Cincinnati. And to the end of his life he functioned as patriarchal leader of the bar and oracle in his city and state, universally trusted and admired. He embodied the best qualities of a very special civilization, and left to Carolina as his legacy the example of a prudent and ample spirit, a civility rare in any time and place. (See Marvin R. Zahniser, *Charles Cotesworth Pinckney, Founding Father* [Chapel Hill: University of North Carolina Press, 1967]; Frances Leigh Williams, *A Founding Family: The Pinckneys of South Carolina* [New York: Harcourt Brace Jovanovich, 1978]; Ernest M. Lander, Jr., "The South Carolinians at the Philadelphia Convention, 1787," *South Carolina Historical Magazine*, LVII (June, 1956), 134–155; George C. Rogers, Jr., "South Carolina Ratifies the Federal Constitution," *South Carolina Historical Association Proceedings* [1961], pp. 41–61 and *Charleston in the Age of the Pinckneys* [Norman: University of

Oklahoma Press, 1969]; Charles Gregg Singer, *South Carolina in the Confederation* [Philadelphia: Porcupine Press, 1976]; James H. Broussard, *The Southern Federalists, 1800–1816* [Baton Rouge: Louisiana State University Press, 1978]; Lisle A. Rose, *Prologue to Democracy: The Federalists in the South, 1789–1800* [Lexington: University of Kentucky Press, 1968]; and Hoyt Paul Canady, Jr., "Gentlemen of the Bar: Lawyers in Colonial South Carolina," Ph.D. dissertation, University of Tennessee, 1979.)

Pierce Butler

(July 11, 1744–February 15, 1822), soldier, statesman, and political leader of South Carolina.

An aristocrat, a "man of family," by either the English or the American definition. Very wealthy, and of considerable influence in his adopted state. Yet, like so many Carolina and other Southern public men who came after him, a gentleman with a genuine popular flair, with a considerable following among plain men "up the country" at every stage in his career. A minimal Federalist, and never a regular member of the party which came to bear that name. But, because of the South's military and economic experience during and after the Revolution, ready to support a strengthening of the general government even before he was elected to a seat in the Great Convention. Not, however, prepared to accept any proposal which might threaten the future integrity or continued existence of the regime he had been chosen to represent in Philadelphia. Even though he "considered the interests" of the Eastern and Southern states "to be as different as the interests of Russia and Turkey," determined to serve both his region *and* the Republic, if he could. Born in County Carlow, Ireland, as the second son of Sir Richard Butler, fifth baronet Cloughgrenan, and of Lady Henrietta Percy Butler, daughter of Sir Henry Percy of Seskin, County Wicklow. Descended on one side from the Duke of Ormonde. Father in Parliament 1729–1761. After the fashion of younger sons, Pierce Butler sought his fortune in a military vocation. Following some training in the law, entered commissioned service in 1765 in His Majesty's Twenty-Ninth Regiment of Foot. Posted to Canada, where he rose to the rank of major. Resigned from British service in 1773, after marrying Mary Middleton, an heiress and daughter of the late Colonel Thomas Middleton, planter and commander of the South Carolina militia. Immediately identified with the ruling gentry of the Low Country. A supporter of South Carolina's struggle to resist British authority from the moment of his settling there.

Pierce Butler was appointed Adjutant General of his state in February of 1779, having been elected to a seat in the legislature in the previous year. Into the cause of the Revolution he poured money and goods as well as his personal security. His opinion in military matters was consulted with great respect. He was active in the 1780 defense of Charleston but, with the fall of the city, fled the state with his family to avoid capture by British troops. After some time in North Carolina and in Philadelphia, Butler returned home to resume his political career and to restore his plantation in Prince William's Parish. He served in the legislature throughout the following years and took part in the leadership of the democratic forces from the western counties of the state. Financed by a large personal loan negotiated in Amsterdam, he recovered his fortune, pushed for reform in the pattern of representation in the South Carolina legislature and for relocation of the state capital to Columbia. Somewhat hypersensitive in dealings with men of his own class, Butler was often at odds with important figures among the ruling gentry. Throughout his life he was a man of independent views. Yet, from planting and some trade, hard work and shrewd speculation, he came to be worth over $1,000,000, and to own many plantations and hundreds of slaves. In 1787 he was a natural choice for a place in the South Carolina delegation to the Continental Congress and the Constitutional Convention.

In the Great Convention Pierce Butler (always addressed as "the Major") spoke on at least fifty occasions. And the mode of his discourse there was usually impressive—cautious, prudent, and full of the information provided by a cosmopolitan experience. Agreeing to a firmer connection to the Northern states was difficult for this Carolina nabob. For from his first coming to the New World as a soldier of King George III, Butler had acquired a distaste for New England manners and New England ideas. Nor did most of the Middle Colonies suit him any better. As early as 1782 he had concluded, from observing sectional tensions in the Continental Congress, that the Northern politicians meant to control the Union and to acquire influence and authority over the future development and internal life of the Southern states. To this arrangement, or to a tax on exports—either in 1787 or at some subsequent date—he would never agree. Nor to any power, or *prospect of power*, over Negro slavery in the states. From early in the Convention it was Butler who, against "innovation" and "running into an extreme," invoked the authority of Plutarch's Solon: that the delegates should give to the people of the states "not the best Government [they] could devise; but the best [that their countrymen] would receive." No root-and-branch "founding" would be allowed, only a building upon orders and institutions already in place and worthy of preservation.

Of the Framers, none was so suspicious of the dangers to liberty in an elaborate system of Federal courts, empowered with a vague authority over questions of constitutional interpretation as was Pierce Butler, or more determined that the new national legislature represent and protect property instead of some general notion of individual rights. Butler wanted members of the Congress tied to the states by the manner of their election—in the various legislatures—and, particularly in the case of senators, by the source of their salaries. He spoke openly of the possibility of future revolts following "encroachments" upon the states; opposed giving Congress veto power over laws made in the states; and called for sharp, enumerated restrictions upon the scope and authority of the proposed United States Senate and House of Representatives. Philosophically, Butler held moderate views on the justification of slavery. Usually he defended the institution with only the argument from circumstance. But with his insistence that the South be made, by the Constitution, forever secure against any possibility of a future outside attack upon the "peculiar institution," he was absolutely firm and definitive: "the security that the Southern states want is that their negroes *may not* be taken from them." Butler was also the author of the Fugitive Slave Clause in Article IV of the Constitution and of a proposal that slaves be counted equally with freemen in the census.

In the Great Convention Pierce Butler exhibited apprehension that too energetic a government was being made: a government with too many judicial powers, too many legislative powers, and with an executive branch that might spawn a "Cromwell or a Catiline." Yet for the sake of economic stability and national defense, he signed the document on which most of his associates were finally agreed. The nation was growing to the south and west. There was a balance of powers which recalled the English Constitution. In South Carolina, when the legislature debated the proposed instrument of government, Butler advised his neighbors to approve it and hope for the best. But the remainder of his public life was a long and steady withdrawal from this position. Though he supported the various components of Hamilton's financial plan in the same spirit that he had exhibited in opposing effusions of unsupported paper money at home. As one of South Carolina's original United States Senators (1789–1796), Pierce Butler spent most of his time in opposition to the government. In his view the Judiciary Act went too far, the Tariff Bill of 1789 was a threat to Southern prosperity, and Jay's Treaty an abomination. More and more he outraged the Charleston Federalists. And, with Charles Pinckney III, he was instrumental in Jefferson's victory over them in the Presidential contest for South Carolina's electors in 1800. As a Democratic-Republican Butler returned briefly to public life by replacing in the Senate, from 1803 to 1804, John E. Calhoun, who had died in office. But, like John Randolph of Roanoke and the strict Republicans of the *Tertium Quid*, he found Jefferson once in office too much like a Federalist in disguise. And, in disgust, he eschewed all further involvement in politics, confining his irritation with a government he now regretted having helped to create to the boundaries of private correspondence with such friends as James Monroe. But while still in office, Butler had specified what he intended in his original approval of the Constitution, had done so by denouncing John Marshall's decision in *Marbury vs. Madison*:

> The right of the Court to give opinions on laws or Acts of the Legislative body extends no further than to explain the true Construction, intent and meaning of the Laws as they may affect the concerns between Man and Man. . . . If Courts had authority to say what power shall be law, their power would be greater than the sovereignty of the Country and no Legislature would be needed . . . an absurdity too great to be Admitted.

He assailed the French Revolution as a possible influence on this country and made constant reiterations that "the powers of the General Government are [in the fundamental law] so defined as not to destroy the Sovereignty of the Individual States." In his old age Pierce Butler presided in great splendor at Hampton Point on St. Simon's Island, and in his home in Philadelphia. For a time he was a director of the Second Bank of the United States. And, even though it put his property in peril, he was a warm advocate of war with Great Britain in 1812. He died in Pennsylvania at the age of 77. It is impossible to mistake in him one of the forefathers of the principal political tradition of the South. In many ways he is a mirror of Southern motives in the adoption of the United States Constitution. (See Lewright B. Sikes, *The Public Life of Pierce Butler, South Carolina Statesman* [Washington, D. C.: University Press of America, 1979]; Sidney Ulmer, "The Role of Pierce Butler in the Constitutional Convention," *Review of Politics*, XXII [July, 1960], 361–374; George C. Rogers, *Evolution of a Federalist: William Loughton Smith of Charleston, 1758–1812* [Columbia: University of South Carolina Press, 1962]; John H. Wolfe, *Jeffersonian Democracy in South Carolina* [Chapel Hill: University of North Carolina Press, 1940]; Raymond G. Starr, "The Conservative Revolution: South Carolina Public Affairs: 1775–1790," Ph.D. dissertation, University of Texas, 1964; Ernest M. Lander, Jr., "The South Carolinians at the Philadelphia Convention, 1787," *South Carolina Historical Magazine*, LVII [June, 1956], 134–155; and James H. Hutson, "Pierce Butler's Records of the Federal Constitutional Convention," *Quarterly Journal of the Library of Congress*, XXXVII [April, 1980], 64–73.)

Charles Pinckney III

(Oct. 26, 1757–Oct. 29, 1824), planter, lawyer, soldier, and statesman.

One of the youngest of the Framers, and the liveliest member of a sober tribe. His grandfather was William Pinckney (1704–1766), Commissary General of South Carolina and one of three sons born to the founder of the dynasty, Thomas Pinckney of County Durham. And his father was Charles Pinckney II (1731–1782), who was counted among the leading citizens of

Carolina in the years preceding and during the Revolution. This Pinckney was a pillar of the bar, a member of His Majesty's Council and president of the state senate after independence. However, with the fall of his city to Sir Henry Clinton in 1780, he experienced a failure of the nerve, thought on his houses, servants, and lands, and sought the King's protection. His son, as an officer in the militia, was at this time a prisoner of the British, but remained obdurate in his rebellion, as did his cousins Thomas Pinckney and Charles Cotesworth Pinckney, officers in the regular Continental forces. They (with the rest of the family) were humiliated by the apostasy of their kinsman and the leader of the Pinckney "connection." But particularly Charles Pinckney III. Once the British were defeated, the South Carolina legislature amerced the estates of notorious turncoats—including Charles Pinckney II. He died unforgiven by his son, who spent the remainder of his life being more visibly loyal to South Carolina, the nation, and the values of his class than anyone could rightfully expect him to be: did so in order to live down the shame of his father's public disgrace.

In his time, Charles Pinckney III held most of the offices of trust in the gift of his society. Educated at home, and early in the public life, he was by turns a member of the South Carolina legislature, a governor of his state, representative to the Continental Congress, United States Senator and United States Representative under the new Constitution. He was often mentioned as a potential President of the Republic and served a term as its ambassador to Spain. Within a few years of the Philadelphia deliberations, he had, like most of the Southerners originally involved in writing and ratifying a Federal instrument, left the party of central authority and energetic government. In 1800, working against his distinguished second-cousins, he delivered South Carolina to Mr. Jefferson. Soon he was the acknowledged leader of the Democratic-Republicans in the lower South. In that role he became a favorite of the Carolina Up Country, and built a fine home just outside Columbia, which became a center of political activity. In his remaining years, his was a part that he enjoyed playing, in that he always sought the center of the stage and habitually saw his own function as heroic, even when partisan enthusiasms for his side of the political drama sometimes injured his reputation as a gentleman. To his Federalist contemporaries, he was "Blackguard Charlie," though their language was, on the whole, too severe.

From the time of his election to the Continental Congress, Charles Pinckney III was an enthusiastic advocate of a stronger and more binding replacement for the Articles of Confederation. In 1787 he arrived in Philadelphia with a draft version for a new compact between the states. Some of his proposals were embodied in the final version of the Constitution as adopted in 1788. But the draft itself died in committee. Congressman Pinckney's idea for a new government is somewhat difficult to reassemble from the arguments and votes that he contributed to the proceedings in Independence

Hall. For he supported both a Federal veto over legislation by states, and a restriction upon the legislative powers of Congress to change state laws and institutions. He spoke of equality as a "leading feature of the United States" and of slavery as a positive good that required no moral apology. His draft of a Bill of Rights contained no philosophical preamble. He praised the Constitution of Great Britain as the "best . . . in existence." And his proposals for a large property qualification for holders of high national office belied his occasional democratic posturings.

A wealthy man who owned hundreds of slaves, Charles Pinckney III was basically an aristocrat who was willing to trust his less fortunate neighbors so long as they did not seem to threaten the world he and they had fought to preserve. It was to secure the fruits of the Revolution that Pinckney sought a new and more democratic constitution for his state, opposed the Jay Treaty because it neglected the West, called for the opening of the Mississippi Territory to slavery, and acted as a mild centralist in the Great Convention: a military Federalist who had been impressed by the incapacity, during the British conquest of the state, of South Carolina *on its own* and of the Continental Congress to offer it effectual support. In February 1820, Pinckney made a definitive comment on his personal performance as Framer and short-term Federalist. The setting for these remarks was the debate over the admission of Missouri as a state. In them he specified in unmistakable terms that a government capable of doing more in the domestic sphere than raising taxes and maintaining a military establishment, a government empowered to reform the moral shortcomings of its component parts on the basis of abstract normative propositions or a general theory of human nature, was not what he had in mind. Argued Pinckney, had there been any "intention . . . to touch slavery, no Constitution would have been achieved." Hence, according to the compact, the right to own slaves ought to be "sacredly preserved." For ". . . if you say there shall be no slavery, may you not say there shall be no marriage?" Charles Pinckney III was indeed a nationalist, but only in a very limited sense. (See Frances Leigh Williams, *A Founding Family: The Pinckneys of South Carolina* [New York: Harcourt Brace Jovanovich, 1978]; Andrew J. Bethea, *The Contribution of Charles Pinckney to the Formation of the American Union* [Richmond: Garrett & Massie, 1937]; W. S. Elliot, "Founders of the American Union: Charles Pinckney of South Carolina," *De Bow's Review*, I, N. S. [April, 1866], 372–378; Charles C. Nott, *The Mystery of the Pinckney Draft* [New York: The Century Company, 1908]; S. Sidney Ulmer, "The South Carolina Delegates to the Constitutional Convention of 1787: An Analytical Study," Ph.D. dissertation, Duke University, 1966; and Ernest M. Lander, Jr., "The South Carolinians at the Philadelphia Convention, 1787," *South Carolina Historical Magazine*, LVII [June, 1956], 134–155; Mark D. Kaplanoff, "Charles Pinckney and the American Republican Tradition," *Intellectual Life in Antebellum Charleston*, eds., Michael O'Brien and David Moltke-Hansen [Knoxville: University of Tennessee Press, 1986], 85–122.)

Abraham Baldwin

(November 22, 1754–March 4, 1807), lawyer, statesman, educator, and clergyman.

The archetypal Southern Yankee. A great force for reconciliation between the sections in the Constitutional Convention. Instrumental in effecting the compromises on slavery and on equality of representation in the Senate which made possible a final agreement among most of the delegates present. A very moderate Federalist, brought by the experience of the Revolution and the situation of Georgia after its conclusion to recognize the need for a stronger central government. But after 1789 never a Federalist, *per se*, of any of the recognized varieties. Son of Michael and Lucy Dudley Baldwin. born in North Guilford, Connecticut. Father a blacksmith who moved to New Haven in order to improve the opportunities of his children. Graduated from Yale College in 1772. After further study, licensed to preach by the established church in 1775. Congregationalist. For four years tutor on the faculty of his *alma mater*. Renowned for his piety, learning, and skill with his students. Resigned in June of 1779 to devote himself to his duties as a chaplain in the American army. Called to the professorship of divinity at Yale in 1781 upon the death of Napthali Daggett, but declined. After his military service was at an end, entered the study of law. Made a member of the Connecticut bar in April of 1783.

Abraham Baldwin did not, however, make his career in his home state. Instead, he joined a large company of New England's ambitious young men who, after independence was achieved, sought their fortunes in the developing regions of the South, particularly in Georgia, where these fugitives from Zion rose to positions of great importance. In January of 1784, The General Assembly of this southernmost member of the Union granted Baldwin's petition to practice in its courts. In the next year he was given lands in Wilkes County, and elected to represent it in the House of Assembly. From that point he climbed quickly. Because of his energy, prudence, and application, he was called upon to perform tasks not of interest to other less literate men.

Baldwin was sent to represent Georgia in the Continental Congress from 1785 to 1789. Meanwhile, on the local scene he played a great part in the planning and foundation of a university for his adopted state. Baldwin drew up a bill which provided for the entire educational system of Georgia. He arranged for its funding, and in particular for that of a college. He was one of the college's original trustees and was responsible for its being modeled after Yale, though with less emphasis on theology. For a time Abraham Baldwin was titular president of Franklin College, which became the University of Georgia. He served on its board until his death.

But despite his continued interest in the educational example of Yale and his service to members of his family back in Connecticut, once a Georgian, Abraham Baldwin was a complete convert to the Southern view of most social and political questions and a dependable spokesman for Southern attitudes and interests in any office which he held. In Philadalphia the most important of his eight speeches before the Great Convention concerned Negro slavery. In it he described the right to own and acquire slaves as one of Georgia's "favorite prerogatives." He insisted that the question was of a local nature, mocked the theory of human equality with reference to Hindu superstition, and concluded that his new neighbors were "decided on this point." He was a "divided sovereignty" man, like Gen. William Richardson Davie of North Carolina and John Langdon of New Hampshire, convinced that the government could be strengthened, with the authority of the states in their own spheres left intact. And in that expectation he made common cause with the men of his birthplace, the members of the Connecticut delegation. Indeed, he even sat with Connecticut during much of the Convention, and gave a report on the whole proceedings to his old friend, President Ezra Stiles of Yale. The view of the place of slavery in the Republic entertained by Sherman, Ellsworth, and Johnson was moderated by the Puritan from Georgia, as was his view of the importance to the small states that they retain their equality with the other commonwealths in the United States Senate. For originally Baldwin had favored a division of the Senate based on property. His Northern friends persuaded him to change his vote. The result of this anomalous association of delegations was Union.

After the Great Convention, Baldwin returned to the Continental Congress. Once the Constitution had been ratified, he was elected by Middle Georgia to sit ten years in the House of Representatives, and thereafter to serve eight more as one of Georgia's United States Senators. For a time in the 7th Congress (1801–1802) he was president *pro tem* of the Upper House. His life as a Southerner was spent almost entirely in public duties. Yet he was never a wealthy man. Indeed, he scorned the schemes which made rich men of many a Federalist officeholder. He opposed Hamilton's plan for funding the assumption of state debts, Jay's Treaty, and the Alien and Sedition Laws. He fought to repeal the Judiciary Act of 1801 and voted to convict Justice

Chase on three articles of his impeachment. With regularity he assailed all attempts to present to Congress petitions against slavery and the slave trade. He disliked the tariff, disliked big spending, and supported the candidacy of Thomas Jefferson, since he felt the Virginian would be the kind of President who would reflect a restricted conception of the Federal power. In his last years Abraham Baldwin (with his colleague from Georgia, General James Jackson) became one of the South's most trusted figures—wise, moderate, accommodating, but firm. In 1802, it was he who, as the leader of a commission, resolved to general satisfaction the dispute over Georgia's Western lands. It was he who avoided war along the Southern frontier; and he who cried out, even in the last of life, the theme of his long stewardship—caution and restraint: "Hold the wagon back." All of this from a onetime Congregationalist parson. From such wonders have we grown. (See Henry C. White, *Abraham Baldwin, One of the Founders of the Republic and Father of the University of Georgia* [Athens, Ga.: McGregor Press, 1926]; Charles C. Jones, Jr., *Biographical Sketches of the Delegates from Georgia to the Continental Congress* [Boston: Houghton Mifflin and Co., 1891]; Franklin Bowditch Dexter, *Biographical Sketches of Graduates of Yale College, with Annals of the College History,* Vol. III [New York: Henry Holt, 1903], pp. 432-434; Albert B. Saye, *New Viewpoints in Georgia History* [Athens: University of Georgia Press, 1943]; Fletcher M. Green, *The Role of the Yankee in the Old South* [Athens: University of Georgia Press, 1972], pp. 11–12; Kenneth Coleman, *The American Revolution in Georgia, 1763–1789* [Athens: University of Georgia Press, 1958], pp. 267–282; and Franklin Bowditch Dexter, ed., *The Literary Diary of Ezra Stiles* [New York: Charles Scribner's Sons, 1901], Vol. III, pp. 293–295.)

William Leigh Pierce

(1740–December 10, 1789), soldier, merchant, and political figure in Georgia in the years immediately following the Revolution.

Remembered today for his incisive sketches of colleagues in the Great Convention. One of the "military Federalists," convinced by the experiences of war (and by the complicated vulnerabilities of his adopted state) of the need for a stronger central government, one capable of defending the nation's frontiers. Identity of parents and place of birth unknown. Probably born in Virginia. Obviously well educated. Served throughout the Revolution as an officer in the Continental Army. Aide-de-camp to General John Sullivan and then to General Nathanael Greene. Received the thanks of Congress and a sword for his valor under fire at the Battle of Eutaw Springs, September 8,

1781. Left service as a brevet major, and in 1783 went into trade in Savannah, becoming eventually the head of the house of William Pierce and Company. Married into a distinguished South Carolina family. Elected member of the Georgia House of Assembly in 1786. Chosen by that body as a delegate to the Continental Congress for 1786–1787. One of six Georgians appointed as representatives of their state in the Constitutional Convention, and one of four who actually attended.

William Pierce was a bit late in his arrival in Philadelphia; and he left the Convention sometime in July to join William Few in the Continental Congress, where they appealed for aid in dealing with the frontier and Indian problems of Georgia. But he was present in the company of the Framers long enough to give us an assessment of it by way of his prose-portraits, the best we have of its members at that moment in their lives. During the deliberations of the Convention, Pierce spoke four times. Members of the lower house of the proposed Congress, he argued, should be elected by the people, and those of the upper house by the states. With this distinction he hoped to see the wealth and property in society protected from democratic excess and the people secured against abuses of authority. He wished to see the states surrender some, but not all, of their authority. He also advocated a three-year term for the proposed United States Senate.

In September of 1787, William Pierce and William Few cast the vote of Georgia in the Continental Congress to convey the new Constitution to the states for ratification. It was William Pierce who carried a copy of the instrument back to Savannah in the following week and arranged for its publication there. His support was influential in securing its approval in Georgia. Yet his life turned swiftly. While in Philadelphia, he could congratulate himself and write with pleasure, "I possess ambition [and] the flattering opinion . . . of my friends." But he did not long survive the conclusion of his brief service on the great stage of national politics—in what he called "the wisest Council in the world." In 1789 he was honored by his comrades-in-arms by his election as vice-president of The Society of the Cincinnati in Georgia. But his business failed, and his health was frail. At his untimely death he left among his effects a manuscript since described as "Pierce's Reliques," including certain notes on the Convention and his famous sketches, which were first published almost forty years after their composition. (See Kenneth Coleman, *The American Revolution in Georgia, 1763–1789* [Athens: University of Georgia Press, 1943]; Charles C. Jones, Jr., *Biographical Sketches of the Delegates from Georgia to the Continental Congress* [Boston: Houghton Mifflin and Co., 1891], pp. 155–159; Albert B. Saye, "Georgia Delegates to the Federal Convention of 1787: Who They Were and What They Did," M. A. thesis, University of Georgia, 1935; and his *New Viewpoints in Georgia History* [Athens: University of Georgia Press, 1943].)

William Houstoun

(March, 1757–1812), lawyer, planter, and political representative of the aristocracy of Georgia.

A "nabob," and one of the great planters of the Convention. Rightly described by his colleague from Savannah, William Pierce, as "a gentleman of family." Wealthy, at least in property, thanks to estates purchased in his name *by* the family and *for* the family of Houstoun from among properties amerced or confiscated in Georgia from Houstouns who had been loyal to George III. In Philadelphia, though not outspoken, a confident figure. Yet, since 1787, almost lost from the record of history. Youngest of the five sons of Sir Patrick Houstoun, fifth baronet Houstoun of Renfrewshire, Scotland (1698–Feb. 5, 1762), who had come out to General Oglethorpe's fledgling colony as a young man, and of Lady Priscilla Dunbar Houstoun (Oct. 31, 1711–Feb. 26, 1775). Born at Rose Dhu, his father's plantation on the Ogeechee River. Educated at home, in local schools, and, between 1776 and 1781, at the Inns of Court. Attentive to his connections in Great Britain, and no warm advocate of the Revolution. Yet, upon his return to America, not tainted by the stigma of Loyalism. Therefore able to keep in the family the large holdings of his Tory brothers, Sir Patrick Houstoun (1742–1785), the sixth baronet, and Sir George Houstoun (Oct. 19, 1744–June 9, 1795), the seventh baronet Houstoun. Episcopalian.

William Houstoun was on August 3, 1782, admitted to the bar by the act of the General Assembly. He was elected in that year to represent Chatham County in the Georgia legislature. Soon after his first appearance in the House of Assembly (1783) he was chosen by it to be a delegate from his state to the Continental Congress. Because of a delay in receiving his credentials, he did not serve that year at the national level. But he was, even so, re-elected in 1784, and soon thereafter journeyed north to join William Gibbons in representing his state. Houstoun continued in this appointment until 1786 and acquired while in the Congress a reputation for capability and a fiery disposition.

The William Houstoun who sat from May 31 to July 26 of 1787 in the Great Convention is summarized in his letters home in which he refers to Georgia as "my country"; in his unreasoning fear that the other states might—in impatience with its failures in cooperation—decide to expel or abolish his own; and in the episode, reported by a contemporary, when Houstoun appeared in the Congress wearing his sword after a delegate from Rhode Island, James Manning, had, in Houstoun's opinion, "reflected upon" the Southern states. For, in the words of a witness to this event, Houstoun was "quick to avenge any insinuation" against Georgia or the region to which it belonged. Yet Houstoun's reputation in the Continental Congress was generally good. He was a member of the "Grand Committee" which first considered useful changes in the Articles of Confederation and, despite his sectional loyalties, always the advocate of a stronger government. Like most of the major figures in Georgia, he saw in the new Constitution a security for the integrity and future development of his state, the exposed southern frontier of the nation. In Philadelphia, Houstoun voted the Federalist line on most issues, with the exception of sectional questions like the slave trade. Indeed, he went so far as to recommend a strong Federal supervision over the drafting of state constitutions, lest there be disorders or disputes over the legitimate source of authority such as had plagued Georgia during the Revolution. During the Philadelphia sessions he spoke seven times, but apparently left when William Few returned from the Continental Congress in New York.

In 1788 he married the daughter of Nicholas Bayard III. In his remaining years William Houstoun was as much connected with the state of New York as with his birthplace. In 1790 he was admitted to practice before the United States Supreme Court. From time to time he returned to Georgia. But most of his very obscure, very private life found him in the city of New York, where he died at the age of fifty-five. (See Edith Duncan Johnston, *The Houstouns of Georgia* [Athens: University of Georgia Press, 1950], pp. 317–342; Charles C. Jones, Jr., *Biographical Sketches of Delegates from Georgia to the Continental Congress* [Boston: Houghton Mifflin and Co., 1891], pp. 118–119; Forrest McDonald, *We the People: The Economic Origins of the Constitution* [Chicago: University of Chicago Press, 1958], pp. 85–86; Albert B. Saye, "Georgia Delegates to the Federal Convention of 1787: Who They Were and What They Did," M. A. thesis, University of Georgia, 1935; W. Berrien Burroughs, "William Houstoun," *Men of Mark in Georgia*, Vol. I, ed. William J. Northern [Atlanta: A. B. Caldwell, 1907], pp. 173–174.)

William Few

(June 8, 1748–July 16, 1828), soldier, farmer, lawyer, banker, and political leader of Georgia during and after the American Revolution.

The only genuine frontiersman among the Framers. An exceedingly mild Federalist who supported the Constitution because Georgia, as an undeveloped state on the southern boundary of the nation, required external protection. A silent presence at the Great Convention, though frequent in his attendance and instrumental as a member of the Continental Congress in the transmission of the document produced there for examination in the several states. Son of William and Mary Wheeler Few. Devout Methodist. Born near Baltimore in Maryland, but raised, after father's failure as a tobacco planter, in the North Carolina "backcountry" near Hillsboro. Only two years of schooling, but much practical training in clearing land and farming on his own or with his father's "servants." Both father and uncle involved in the Regulator movement, protesting abuse by the colonial government which in 1771 resulted in the Battle of Alamance. Uncle James Few hanged as "outlaw" by Governor William Tryon, family farm destroyed, and father forced to flee in order to avoid prosecution. William was left behind to complete his father's business, settle suits, sell land, and move in 1776, to a new home near Wrightsboro, Georgia.

William Few climbed rapidly to a position of leadership in the upper counties of Georgia as the movement toward American independence spread into that state. As a young man in North Carolina, he had read voraciously from whatever books he could find, and had developed a particular interest in law and politics. Not only did he handle the complicated business affairs of his family, but he also attended other sessions of the court when he could. Once in Georgia, he won admittance to the bar and set up practice in Augusta. A vigorous Patriot, a frontier Whig in the Regulator tradition, he was chosen lieutenant colonel of the local militia regiment of dragoons and, along with his brother Benjamin, did some distinguished service against British troops, Tories, and Indians loyal to the Crown during the years when most of Georgia was under English control. Few was elected to the Georgia Provincial Congress in 1776. During the Revolution he served in the Assembly in 1777 and 1779, and was at those times a member of the state Executive Council. Later, Few represented his state in the Continental Congress (1780–1785), and at the same time continued to hold posts of importance at home, as Indian Commissioner, Surveyor General, and member of the legislature (1782–1784, 1786). By this time he had become the recognized spokesman of the Georgia frontier.

Few's votes in the Constitutional Convention reflected Georgia's interest in slavery, in debt retirement, and in the national defense. He missed five or six weeks of the debates because discussion of Indian depredations drew him to the Continental Congress; but while present in Philadelphia, he generally supported the views of his associates in the Georgia delegation, and was a signatory to the document which they all approved. After returning home from the Great Convention and the Congress in New York, Few served in the Georgia ratifying convention, in the state's constitutional convention, and, once the Federal Constitution was adopted, was sent by his state as one of its original United States Senators (1789–1793). At the end of his abbreviated term in the Senate, he resumed his life in Georgia, got involved in the dispute over the Yazoo fraud (against the speculators), sat again in the state legislature, and in 1796 was appointed Judge for the Second Judicial District of Georgia. Surprisingly, he resigned this post in 1799 and removed to New York, where he found the climate to be more salubrious and where he had made friends while representing Georgia under the Articles and as United States Senator. Inverting the life pattern of his friend Abraham Baldwin, Few prospered in the North, where he served four years in the New York State Assembly (1802–1805), became State Inspector of Prisons (1802–1810), Alderman of New York City (1813–1814), and United States Commissioner of Loans (1804–1816). From 1804–1814 he was director of the Manhattan Bank and ended his career in the presidency of the City Bank (1814–1816). He died a very wealthy man. In his later years Few retired from politics because of his distaste for the Federalist atmosphere of public life in his adopted state. He had lost his connection with that party not long after the approval of the new Constitution, and was indeed never an advocate of "energetic government"—as the High Federalists understood that doctrine. Few was a classic illustration of the myth of the self-made man, the American success story, though he brought a little of frontier Carolina with him as he rose to the summit. (See William W. Abbott, "The Structure of Politics in Georgia: 1782–1789," *William and Mary Quarterly*, XIV [January, 1957], 47–65; Charles C. Jones, Jr., *Biographical Sketches of the Delegates from Georgia to the Continental Congress* [Boston: Houghton Mifflin and Co., 1891], pp. 34–39; "Autobiography of Colonel William Few of Georgia," *Magazine of American History*, VII [November, 1881], 343–358; Albert B. Saye, *New Viewpoints in Georgia History* [Athens: University of Georgia Press, 1943]; Robert G. Ferris, ed., *Signers of the Constitution* [Washington, D. C.: U. S. Department of the Interior, 1976], pp. 161–162; and Kenneth Coleman, *The American Revolution in Georgia, 1763–1789* [Athens: University of Georgia Press, 1958].)

ABOUT THE AUTHOR

M. E. Bradford is Professor of English at the University of Dallas, where he has taught for the past 20 years.

Prior to his 1967 return to his native state of Texas, Prof. Bradford was on the faculty of the United States Naval Academy, Hardin-Simmons University, Northwestern States University of Louisiana, and Vanderbilt University (Teaching Fellow). He has been a visiting lecturer at Dartmouth College, Claremont College, Louisiana State University, the University of Texas at Austin, Vanderbilt University, the University of South Carolina, Hillsdale College, Georgetown University, Hampden-Sydney College, University of Southern Illinois, and the University of Colorado.

In 1970, he received a National Endowment for the Humanities summer grant, and in 1977 and 1983 he was an NEH Senior Research Fellow. In the summer of 1978 he did work under the grant from the Texas Educational Association and, in 1981, he received a summer research grant from the Kemper Educational and Charitable Fund.

American political rhetoric, the literature of the South, and the English origins of American political thought have been the special subjects of Professor Bradford's research. He has edited *Arator*, by John Taylor of Caroline, and *The Form Discovered: Essays on the Achievement of Andrew Lytle*. With George Core he co-edited Richard Weaver's *The Southern Tradition at Bay*. He is the author of *A Better Guide Than Reason: Studies in the American Revolution, The Generations of the Faithful Heart: On the Literature of the South*, and *Remembering Who We Are: Observations of a Southern Conservative*. With Dr. James McClellan he is co-editing a six-volume edition of Jonathan Elliot's *Debates of the Several State Conventions on the Adoption of the Federal Constitution* for the James River Press.

Professor Bradford was born in Fort Worth, Texas, May 8, 1934. He was educated in the public schools of that city, took his B.A. (1955) and M.A. (1956) at the University of Oklahoma, and his Ph.D. in English at Vanderbilt University (1968). From 1956 to 1959, Professor Bradford was on active duty as an officer in the United States Navy.

He is a member (and former president) of the Philadelphia Society, the Sons of the Confederate Veterans, Modern Language Association, the South Central Modern Language Association, and the American Studies Association. He is a regular contributor to *National Review*, an Associate Editor of *Modern Age*, and from 1982-1987 served as a member of the presidentially appointed Board of Foreign Scholarsips.

Professor Bradford is a Baptist. He and his wife have one son. They reside in Irving, Texas.

Concerning the

PLYMOUTH ROCK FOUNDATION

The Plymouth Rock Foundation, Inc., is an uncompromising advocate of Biblical principles of government and Christ's perfect Law of Liberty as the only true foundation for individual freedom and right civil governance. It works to honor The Lord God through a ministry of programs and publications that

- *advance Biblical principles of self and civil government, and*
- *proclaim the facts concerning the Christian heritage of the United States of America.*

Plymouth Rock is a non-denominational, non-proft, public foundation incorporated in the Commonwealth of Massachusetts (1970). Financial support for its ministry comes soley from those who are led by The Lord to share with it that which He has entrusted to them. Such contributions are deemed to be tax deductible by the U.S. Department of the Treasury.

For further information on Plymouth Rock, its programs and its publications, please contact the Foundation's general office in Marlborough, New Hampshire 03455.

JOHN G, TALCOTT, Jr.
President

RUS WALTON
Executive Director

TCRM Publishing
Ft. Lauderdale, FL